Women Helping Women

Elyse Fitzpatrick

Carol Cornish

General Editors

Harvest House Publishers

Eugene, OR 97402

Cover design by Koechel Peterson & Associates, Minneapolis, Minnesota

WOMEN HELPING WOMEN
Copyright © 1997 by Harvest House Publishers
Eugene, Oregon 97402
www.harvesthousepublishers.com

Library of Congress Cataloging-in-Publication Data

Fitzpatrick, Elyse, 1950–
    Women helping women / Elyse Fitzpatrick and Carol Cornish.
        p.   cm.
    Includes bibliographical references and index.
    ISBN-13: 978-1-56507-617-4
    ISBN-10: 1-56507-617-6
    1. Peer counseling in the church. 2. Women—Pastoral counseling of. 3. Women—Religious life. I. Cornish, Carol, 1945– . II. Title.
BV4409.F58   1997
253'.5'082—dc21   97-5437
                                                                                    CIP

06 07 08 / CH / 12 11 10

*To all the Titus 2 women who counsel and nurture
their sisters, and particularly to Rosemary, Thelma, and Jessica,
who counsel and nurture me.*

—Elyse

*To those dear sisters in the Lord who have allowed me
the great privilege of discipling them, and also to those who have
discipled me—especially my mother, Helen Daring Woodland,
whose love and prayers are a source of constant encouragement.*

—Carol

ACKNOWLEDGMENTS

If I have achieved any modicum of consistency in biblical thinking there is one person who can take credit for it: Dr. George Scipione of the Institute for Biblical Counseling & Discipleship. The Lord has used Skip to affect change in the lives of many people, including both students and counselees. He has modeled humility, godliness, diligence, patience, and wisdom, and has been God's gift to the body as a pastor, counselor, and friend. Skip, words can't say how thankful I am.

Thanks also to the faculty and staff of Westminster Theological Seminary in Escondido, California, especially John Sowell, Mark Futato, Iain Duguid, and Dennis Johnson; to the family at Evangelical Bible Book Store (my "personal library"); to Ed Bulkley at "Return to the Word" and Steve Miller at Harvest House for their ministry of encouragement; and to Pastor Dan Deaton. Thanks to the members and leadership at Crossroads Community Church, who prayed for me and patiently listened to my dreams and discouragements. Thanks to my mom, Rosemary, who cheerfully and diligently helped me edit every chapter. Yes, mom, I'll learn where to put commas. And thanks most of all to my family, especially my husband Phil, who prayed for me and encouraged me and never once complained.

—Elyse

One of the sweetest blessings I received in working on this project was the eager help of so many brothers and sisters in the Lord. Lorrie Skowronski, Penny Orr, and Diane Tyson have been faithful friends and colleagues whose wisdom, discernment, and love for God continues to challenge me to grow in Christlikeness.

At Cornerstone Christian Fellowship, my pastor, Warren Lynn Snyder, prayed for and with me and gave me valuable insights into ministering to hurting people; associate pastor Jim Rich evidenced keen interest and aided my research; Peggie Lanzone, Betty Jean Rothenberger, Cheryle Radcliff, Joyce Templeton, and Lynn Popp regularly prayed for and fostered my efforts. I owe much to Dr. Gary Shogren, professor of New Testament at Biblical Seminary, for his continual encouragement, wise feedback, and godly example of brotherly love.

My thanks also go to Dr. Robert Vannoy for graciously sharing with me his insights on 1 Samuel 25, Cindy Appel for her patience with my computer questions, Randy Grossman for help with Puritan resources, and Steve Miller at Harvest House for his unwavering enthusiasm.

Special thanks go to my husband, Rolly, and my son, Darren, whose love and gentle humor spurred me on.

—Carol

CONTENTS

Counsel that Leads to Abundant Living

For almost two thousand years, Christians have comforted and encouraged one another with the knowledge that Jesus is their Good Shepherd. In contrast with the thief who comes to steal, kill, and destroy, Jesus stated that He had come that His sheep might have life, and might have it abundantly (John 10:10). This was no idle whim of our Shepherd; He purchased this abundant life through His death.

In our day there seems to be a lot of confusion about what constitutes an abundant life. In fact, the phrase *abundant life* has come to mean almost anything. For instance, to some it means psychological health; to others it means material prosperity; and still others believe that it means freedom from suffering. In contrast, we believe that abundant life is found in the pursuit of God-honoring holiness. It is holiness—the humility of spirit, the mourning over sin, the hunger and thirsting for righteousness—that will produce in us that happy blessedness that Jesus spoke of in the Sermon on the Mount (Matthew 5–7). Abundant life is life that is freed from the power of sin and filled with the power of the Holy Spirit, focused on the pleasure of God and resting in His love. Our goal is to help you and the women you influence grow toward this kind of abundant living.

Sadly, what Christian women need to know to live an abundant life is not found in many of today's "Christian" self-help books. Instead of guidance in knowing and pleasing God, which is the way to finding abundant life, we are given man-centered philosophies on how to love ourselves more, how to get more out of life, how to assert ourselves. Our greatest need is being ignored. What we need most of all is to know God. We need to be intimately acquainted with Him because He has designed us to live for Him. He knows us completely, since He is the One who "looks from heaven; He sees all the sons of men . . . He who fashions the hearts of them all, He who understands all their works" (Psalm 33:13,15).

The first step we must take is to admit that we were created for His pleasure rather than our own. Our true happiness and abundant life springs
out of setting our eyes, our hopes, and our desires on Christ and keeping
them there. Once we determine to keep our focus on Christ, love for our
neighbor will grow. This love of God and love for our neighbor will energize us to reach out and offer God's love and freeing truth to others. It will
motivate us to study and live lives of godliness so that others will be blessed.

A godly, abundant life is a life that has found the practicality of theology.
Many Christians mistakenly think that theology is not practical. Nothing
could be further from the truth. But because Christians are not commonly
taught how to apply the Bible to their everyday lives, this misconception
persists. This book demonstrates the practical application of what the Bible
teaches about how to live and please God. It illustrates the application of
these truths in one-on-one relationships with other Christian women—it
is a book about women helping women to be freed, restored, and comforted in their faith in the Good Shepherd.

While this book does not cover every problem a Christian woman might
face, we have attempted to provide a basic, crucial starting point and guide
for right thinking in some of life's more prevalent problems. The authors'
greatest desire is that this book will encourage our Christian sisters to start
at the right place when seeking to give help in time of need. If it is your
heart's desire to live a faithful Christian life to God's glory, walking in
Christ's promised abundant life, you won't succeed in your goal if you start
with yourself as the center or focus of life or if you start with human
philosophies as your guide. You must begin at the right place, with God as
the source and meaning of all of life, with His glory and pleasure as paramount, and with His Word as the light upon your path and the only guide
for life.

Abundant life can be yours because you have a loving Shepherd who is
watching over you. He has provided a lush pastureland for your nourishment; He has given you living water; it is He who restores your soul. You
can find a rich, rewarding life with God now and for eternity and you can
share this life with your sisters. It is our prayer that women will help one
another walk in this abundant life for God's glory.

PART I

Starting in the Right Place

CHAPTER I

The Philosophy of Biblical Counseling

Elyse Fitzpatrick, M.A.

Biblical counseling isn't just some dry academic exercise in splitting hairs or arguing over insignificant practices. Biblical counseling is about *vision* and *faith* and *hope*. It is the *vision* of a church that embraces Jesus Christ and His Word as sufficient for counseling—a vision that glows brightly in anticipation of God's provision. It is a *faith* in the God who has given us everything we need for growth in godliness. And it is about *hope*. Hope isn't just wishful thinking, but rather a confident expectation that God will continue to use His Word to change His people into His image. The authors of this book all believe in the philosophy and methods of biblical counseling. What that means is that we believe the Bible is sufficient to answer every problem and meet every need that we, as God's children, have—more on that in a moment.

First, let me say that many people have gone before me and written at greater length and in greater depth than I can possibly cover in this chapter. Yet for the purpose of this book—which is to better equip women to counsel other women biblically—I believe it's possible to affirm within these few pages that the Bible really can serve as a foundation for the counsel we give in response to the problems women face today. Indeed, biblical counseling is the tool that God has given to help us help others to live lives that are biblically enlightened, spiritually fulfilled, eternally meaningful.

Biblical counseling has had a profound effect on my life. As I have, over the past few years, begun to counsel myself biblically, my life has changed radically. In the hope that I don't sound like a cultist who has embraced some "new thought," let me say that I believe I have finally discovered what Christianity is all about. *It's about loving and serving God.* I know that sounds elementary. But until recent years, even though I knew I was to serve God, I never had my priorities straight. I never understood that my problem was *me*—not my husband, job, kids, car, parents . . . you fill in the blanks. I was confused and the psychological philosophies that had crept into my thinking were making things worse. Didn't I need to learn to love myself? Didn't I need to get *my* needs met? Didn't I have a need for romance? For security? For significance? How could God expect me to pour my life out for others when I was so miserable myself? Didn't I need to fill my own "love cup" before I could fill others? And what if my circumstances never change?

These thoughts and many others like them clouded my thinking and crowded their way into my faith and filled me with despair. Around the same time that I was struggling with these questions, my husband and I went to a couples' retreat where a Christian psychologist was speaking. After the meeting, I waited in line to speak with him. When my turn came, I said, "My life isn't working out like I want it to. I know that my needs aren't being met," I cried. "I'm just so miserable all the time. What am I to do?" I'll never forget the doctor's response: "I'm afraid that you'll have to find some way to get your needs met or else things will just get worse and worse." How hopeless that left me—I had to wait for my circumstances to change before I could be a joyous servant of God!

Today, however, I look at my life differently. I am thankful that the Lord has set me free from the bondage of having to wait for others to change or for my perceived needs to be met before I can be joyous. I am thankful that I now understand that I've been called to serve and lay down my life. That is what biblical counseling has done in me. Looking at life in this way isn't any "new faith"; it is real Christianity. It is a reflection of what Jesus meant when He said,

> *If anyone wishes to come after Me, let him deny himself, and take up his cross daily, and follow Me. For whoever wishes to save his life will lose it, but whoever loses his life for My sake, he is the one who will save it (Luke 9:23-24).*

Much of what we hear from the psychological community seems opposed to these simple words. We hear that we possess an innate goodness. We hear that our problems are really the responsibility of our parents or environment.

We hear that we need to focus more on loving ourselves. We've heard these things so often that Jesus' words seem archaic and out of touch. For instance, how am I to lose my life and deny myself while I'm seeking to affirm and love myself? The fact that Luke 9:23-24 seems impractical or contradictory demonstrates how far down the road of worldly thinking we have come. It's only because of choosing to follow biblical thinking that I can unashamedly state, "My life has changed!"

I no longer question whether I'm supposed to lose my life, deny myself, or take up my cross. Now I understand that I'm not to be concerned with whether my perceived "needs" are being met. These "needs" are not issues for me any longer because I believe that God has given me everything I need for life and godliness (2 Peter 1:3). It's not that I'm perfect, I'm not. In fact, I'm far more aware of my sin now than ever before. It's just that life makes sense now and I'm confident that my loving Father is in control. He will give me everything that I truly need to please Him. All the while I'm growing in grace and learning more and more about what it means to be content. As Paul wrote,

> *I have learned to be content in whatever circumstances I am. I know how to get along with humble means, and I also know how to live in prosperity; in any and every circumstance I have learned the secret of being filled and going hungry, both of having abundance and suffering need. I can do all things through Him who strengthens me (Philippians 4:11-13).*

May I paraphrase these verses for you in today's jargon?

> *I have learned to be content whether or not I think I'm getting my "needs" met. I know how to get along when my husband (pastor, employer, child, or whoever) is on the ball and looking out for my every interest. I also know how to be joyous when things aren't working out according to my expectations. I have learned the secret of being content because I have the best husband (job, employer, child, house . . .). I have also learned the secret of contentment while watching everything fall apart, my husband ignores me, I get passed over for a job promotion, my child comes home with a note from the teacher, and my washing machine overflows. How is it that I have contentment through all of this? It is because I am confident that God is with me. He gives me the strength to persevere through every trial while at the same time working His character in my life, which is the most precious work there is.*

Do you see what I'm getting at? Biblical counseling is more than just a different methodology or way of doing counseling. We're concerned about something more than arguing over insignificant practices. It's an overriding philosophy that flows out of the knowledge of God's supremacy, love, and adequacy. God is now the center of my life. I put my trust in Him. In theological terms, this is called being "theocentric" or "God-centered." I think that for much of my Christian life I was "anthropocentric" or "man-centered." Although I would never have admitted it, I lived most of my Christian life as though God was my errand boy, sent to satisfy my wandering desires. Although I would have agreed that God was at the center of all of life, in reality I continued to live a life that demonstrated my independence. I sang songs about being redeemed (purchased) by Christ's sacrifice and then childishly demanded my own way.

The Focus of Biblical Counseling

The presuppositions or underlying beliefs that support the methods of biblical counseling start with God at the center. He is supreme. His will and glory take preeminence. He is sovereign. He will work all things according to His good plan. His ultimate goal is to glorify Himself and change us into the image of His Son so that we will glorify Him. Once I truly believed and took to heart these primary truths, everything else in my life fell into place. Now the fruit of the Spirit—love, joy, peace, longsuffering, goodness, kindness, meekness, faith, and self-control—can flow out of my life (though at times more slowly because I refuse to humble myself before the Lord!). These virtues are replacing the grumbling, bitterness, comparing, fear, anger, self-deception, self-indulgence, demandingness, lust, and self-pity that previously marked my life. Not only did those attitudes and tendencies formerly mark my life, they revealed a heart set on having it "my way"—they dishonored the Lord. These changes are what biblical thinking and living has done in my life.

As I learned to counsel myself biblically, my life was changed. You can change, too. God's Word and Spirit are available to all of His children when they are willing to trust and obey.

The Goal of Biblical Counseling

What is your goal as you speak with, counsel, or seek to comfort your sisters in the Lord? Do you have a goal? If you have no goal, you have probably found yourself mired in helping relationships that seem to be going nowhere. If you have wrong goals, such as merely alleviating the perception of pain or furnishing a shoulder to cry on, you may have found yourself fighting against God as He works in His children's lives. I believe that the biblical counselor should have one overriding goal: *to encourage and assist believers to grow in the likeness of Christ.* This growth manifests itself in faithful living in our homes, workplaces, schools, churches, and in the world. This is accomplished through the application of the Word of God in very specific ways and by the work of the Holy Spirit as believers respond in faith.

A Specific Goal for Women

As I think specifically about women and the way I perceive biblical counseling for them, I am drawn to the woman of Proverbs 31. This model woman has all the qualities that we should desire to see developed in the lives of those whom we counsel. The first description of her is that she is "excellent" (verse 10)—this word means she is mighty, strong, virtuous, and full of valor, power, ability. This is no wimp woman! Think about the antitheses to those adjectives: small, limited, fearful, and weak. Sadly, some Christian women have accepted the notion that being weak is somehow equivalent to being godly. Contrary to this Milquetoast quality, God describes a woman who is of great worth as being strong, powerful and able (Proverbs 31:10). Of course, I'm not saying that she should be sinfully assertive or demanding. She must be in subjection to fellow believers, her husband, and the leaders in her church congregation. It's just that her submission must flow out of a heart of strength and obedience rather than her self-focused needs. In fact, God stresses this point two more times in Proverbs 31: "She girds herself with strength, and makes her arms strong" (verse 17), and, "Strength and dignity are her clothing, and she smiles at the future" (verse 25). Proverbs 31 goes on to describe her as being trustworthy (verse 11), righteous (verse 12), industrious (verses 13-16, 19, 22, 24, 27), confident (verse 18), generous (verse 20), and secure (verses 21, 25). Overall, she is committed to her God and her relationships.

One of my favorite descriptions of this woman is that she "smiles at the future" (verse 25). Literally this means that she "laughs at the days to come," or "celebrates the years yet ahead." She isn't overly concerned with her outward appearance, knowing that outward charms may be a deceptive sham. Instead she is attentive to her inner self, which is characterized as "fearing the Lord."

This is the secret of her strength, dignity, and optimistic attitude. She fears the Lord. She understands that she must fear the Lord rather than people or their opinions of her. In this way she follows Sarah, who followed Abraham and did what was right "without being frightened by any fear" (1 Peter 3:6). Her reverence for the Lord and His commands outweigh every other consideration in her life. As A.W. Tozer wrote, "No one can know the true grace of God who has not first known the fear of God."[1] As a woman seeks to grow in her reverential awe of the Lord, she will become more and more Christlike.

As a counselor, you must ask, "How has this counselee's faithful service to her family, her church, her culture been diminished by her present difficulties?" Once you understand what changes need to be made, the next question is, "How are these changes to be brought about?" Will change be accomplished through mere talk? Through regression therapy? Through having her learn to love herself more? The answer to those questions will reveal the difference between counseling that is truly biblical and counseling that is based on clinical psychology.

Scripture and Biblical Counseling

Can God's Truth Transform Us?

During the last 50 years the American church has witnessed a battle. The battle was over the *inerrancy* of Scripture. The question that initiated this conflict was, "Is the Bible correct, completely accurate, and truthful, or are there errors that diminish the overall reliability of Scripture?" The church fought valiantly for truth. Now most conservative denominations and independents wholeheartedly embrace inerrancy. But now there is another battle looming on the horizon. Indeed, it is already upon us. This battle is over the *sufficiency* of Scripture. The question is this: "Are we who believe that the Bible is correct and truthful now going to acquiesce to the world by saying that although it is correct and truthful, it is partially irrelevant?" It is futile to argue for the reliability of Scripture if that Scripture is then to be relegated to the periphery of a believer's life. *What good is truth if that truth doesn't inform and transform?*

The Bible Is Sufficient

The biblical counselor is one who wholeheartedly believes that the Word of God is not only inerrant but is also sufficient. She believes that the Bible speaks in a general way to every area of life. Even though it isn't meant as a chemistry or physics textbook, it does teach the chemist that the universe is orderly because it reflects the character of God. There are chemical laws that can be relied upon because there is a God who can be relied upon in the work of overseeing His creation.

In addition to speaking generally, the Bible also speaks specifically. It speaks specifically to the issues of life, such as "Who is God?"; "How can I know and serve Him?"; and "How can I love my neighbor?" Biblical counselors believe that the Bible speaks comprehensively to every relational issue.

What exactly do we mean when we say that the Bible is sufficient? The word *sufficient* may be defined as "sufficing, adequate, especially in amount or number to the need, enough."[2] It is adequate, ample, and abundant. It meets the need. It fulfills God's purpose for it. It is not deficient or scanty. The biblical counselor believes that the Word of God is adequate for the task of counseling. In fact, she believes that it contains everything needed for a person to achieve God's goals of loving Him and others. To illustrate this point, let me direct you to a few pivotal passages.

2 Peter 1:3-4

. . . seeing that His divine power has granted to us everything pertaining to life and godliness, through the true knowledge of Him who called us by His own glory and excellence. For by these He has granted to us His precious and magnificent promises, in order that by them you might become partakers of the divine nature, having escaped the corruption that is in the world by lust.

Everything we need to become partakers of the divine nature has been provided for us in His precious and magnificent promises, the Word of God. Everything we need for sanctification (the changing of our heart and life from the old to the new) is available to us. Change is accomplished through God's Word as we interact with it in faith. Indeed, the Word is powerful, even to the point of disclosing the hidden motives of our hearts, as our next verse shows.

Hebrews 4:12

The word of God is living and active and sharper than any two-edged sword, and piercing as far as the division of soul and spirit, of both joints and marrow, and able to judge the thoughts and intentions of the heart.

Only the mirror of the Word has the power to enlighten blind eyes to motives and attitudes. Even the most sensitive and discerning of counselors cannot judge or absolutely know the heart. Nothing reveals hidden motives and intentions but the Word, which is sufficient for godly change engendered by candid self-evaluation.[3] Just listen to the way that the Bible describes itself. It is not some dead, lifeless manuscript; rather, it is *living, active,* and *powerful.* The Word of God is spiritually alive. The Holy Spirit uses God's Word to make us alive in Christ and sanctify us. It can bring to life your dead, stony heart. It can ignite that smoking wick of your soul. In every area of darkness, in your confusion and desolation, the Word of God brings clarity, wisdom, and life.

2 Timothy 3:16-17   The Apostle Paul also taught on the sufficiency of the Word:

> *All Scripture is inspired by God and profitable for teaching, for reproof, for correction, for training in righteousness; that the man of God may be adequate, equipped for every good work.*

Notice how the Bible describes its function: It causes those who are taught, reproved, corrected, and trained by it to become "adequate." Through the work of the Holy Spirit, the Word of God causes you to be sufficient to the task that God places before you. The Bible can equip you by giving you every tool you need for every "good work" God places before you. Do you desire to become what God wants you to be? If so, then the Bible is sufficient for equipping you. As Dr. Jay Adams says,

> *Every counselor is out to change his counselee in some way. Here is how God says that Christian counselors must do so. They must use the Scriptures in the way He has indicated. . . . "But, can't we bring other ideas into our counseling. . . ?" If your ministry of changing people is biblical, that is all that is necessary. The church didn't have to sit around for 1900+ years waiting for Freud and others to tell Christians how to change people. God has been in the business of doing this since the fall. No, if understood and used properly, the Bible will make you, as a "man of God" adequate.*[4]

Every counselor has some goal in mind when he or she begins counseling. The biblical counselor, however, recognizes that change can take place only when the Holy Spirit is given the opportunity to work in the counseling process. The Word of God is that instrument of change as a person responds to it in faith.

What About Scientific Knowledge?

A Right Perspective of Science

But what about scientific knowledge that's not covered in the Bible? For example, the Bible doesn't give instructions on how to repair a car or develop a vaccine for polio. Do biblical counselors believe that scientific information from outside of the Bible is insignificant? Of course not. Biblical counselors believe that the blessings of *true science* are part of God's common grace. For instance, biblical counselors will draw upon the knowledge gained in the medical sciences when they are searching for answers to perplexing behavior.

There is a vital difference, however, between God's *common grace* as demonstrated to the world in general and His *special revelation,* which is given to His people. The Bible wasn't written as a science textbook. It was written to give revelation of God and His works in the world. Part of the revelation of knowing who He is and how He works involves learning how to love Him and our neighbor. The Bible gives us both illustration of and instruction in right living. It warns about the ultimate consequences of unrighteous living. All of the Law and the Prophets are written around the commandment to love God and others. Isn't that what counseling is all about? Isn't counseling about helping Christians relate to and interact properly with God and others?

Indeed, Romans 15:4 teaches that everything written in the Old Testament was written "for our instruction, that through perseverance and the encouragement of the Scriptures we might have hope." The Holy Spirit carefully recorded historical events in the Old Testament—not just for information's sake, but so that we might know how to live in this present age.[5] All of Scripture was given to us so that we might grow. First Peter 2:2 tells us, "Like newborn babes, long for the pure milk of the word, that by it you may grow in respect to salvation."

Is Psychology True Science?

Earlier I stated that biblical counselors respect *true science.* It's important that we recognize that not all disciplines that go by the name "science" are true science. Some of these disciplines are really philosophies. Psychology is one of them. As John MacArthur states, "Modern psychologists use hundreds of counseling models and techniques based on a myriad of *conflicting theories,* so it is impossible to speak of psychotherapy as if it were a *unified and consistent science*"[6] (emphasis added).

Indeed, psychotherapy's categorical conclusions are no longer being accepted as scientific fact by many people. Ed Bulkley, writing in *Why Christians Can't Trust Psychology*, states,

> . . . *human thinking and behavior* cannot *be categorized scientifically because each human is unique and one's reaction to events, circumstances, and other stimuli cannot be predicted or tested using the scientific method. Most psychotherapeutic theories cannot be empirically tested and verified. It is impossible, for example, to scientifically examine the Freudian concepts of the id, ego, or superego. . . . It is misleading for psychologists to claim that they scientifically examine minds, emotions, beliefs, values, and behaviors.*[7]

The belief that psychology is scientific is problematic for Hilton Terrell as well. Terrell holds a doctorate in psychology as well as an M.D. He believes that the study of the soul, which is the definition of the term *psychology*, is scientifically impossible:

> *The nonmaterial aspect of us, however you wish to carve it up, cannot be known—other than by introspection, which the Bible itself tells us is not a trustworthy thing to lean upon, and by the elucidation of the Scripture itself . . . the mind is impervious to outside observation [and is by definition], beyond the pale of the natural sciences which require something to have material existence—to be measured and studied.*[8]

This bankruptcy of psychology was dramatized by a Stanford professor of psychology and law and a dozen friends who presented themselves at mental hospitals in 1973.

> *All repeated exactly the same opening words, "I feel empty," or "I feel hollow." Following this admission, they acted normally. They related to others as they would ordinarily. All were admitted. The length of stay in the hospitals was between seven and fifty-two days. Requests for release on the basis that they were normal were viewed as confirmatory signs of illness. Those who spent a portion of their hospital stay writing about their time were labeled as obsessive and compulsive. . . . When released, all retained the diagnosis "schizophrenic" with the added note, "in remission."*[9]

Even *Time* magazine questioned the scientific validity of Freud's analysis in a recent front-cover story entitled *Is Freud Dead?*[10] Examining those who have critiqued Freud's systems, writer Paul Gray cited certain developments that "raise doubts not only about Freud's methods, discoveries and proofs and the vast array of therapies derived from them, but also about the lasting importance of Freud's descriptions of the mind."[11] Frank Sulloway, a scholar of science history at M.I.T., is quoted as saying, "Psychoanalysis is built on quicksand."[12] Although many therapies are not Freudian *per se,* his influence on mental health practices is profound. "If Freud's theories are truly as oozy as his critics maintain," Gray asked, "then what is to keep all the therapies indebted to them from sinking into oblivion as well?" Gray continued, "What [Freud] bequeathed *was not* (despite his arguments to the contrary), *nor has yet proved itself to be, a science*"[13] (emphasis added).

Thomas Szasz, Professor of Psychiatry at the State University of New York Health Science Center, is a outspoken critic of psychotherapy and the entire philosophy of mental illness. He writes, "I am convinced that psychiatric explanations and interventions are fatally flawed and that, deep in their hearts, most people think so too."[14]

Those who support a psychological philosophy cannot even decipher the truth about psychology. As former psychologist Richard Ganz writes, "Clinical psychology comes to no consensus in its view of human beings—with one critical exception. It is unified in its belief that people are free from God."[15] At one time Freud was considered the ultimate source. Now most psychologists look upon Freud's theses as fallacious. Which of the many schools of psychology is right? Behavior Modification, Person-Centered Therapy, Rational-Emotive Therapy, Gestalt Therapy, Existential Psychotherapy, Transactional Analysis, Family Therapy, or Multimodal Therapy? These are all major systems of therapy that ebb and flow in popularity like the tides. This is affirmed by Raymond J. Corsini in *Current Psychotherapies,* which is a textbook for psychology students:

> . . . the field of psychotherapy is in constant ferment and change. "Minor" systems begin to become more popular. "Major" systems begin to fade. Some systems begin to change. Splitting occurs with contending groups heading rival viewpoints. New ideas, new concepts, new views which amount to complete new systems, arise. In illustration of this, there are currently at least 250 innovative systems of psychotherapy in existence.[16]

He continues,

> *It is important to note that what some authority considers to be psychotherapy may be completely different from how another person sees the process. There is no way to settle any differences; so even though A and B may be doing completely* different *and* contradictory *things, both are doing psychotherapy. We come to the same conclusion as Lewis Carroll in his* Through the Looking Glass *that a word means what you want it to mean (emphasis added).*

Isn't that astonishing? Corsini, a proponent of psychotherapy, acknowledges that there is *no absolute truth* in this so-called "science"! What kind of scientist writes disclaimers on his ability to distinguish absolute truth? Is it wise to wholeheartedly embrace a philosophy as though it were a science? Just because psychology has trained "experts" using therapeutic terminology and theories doesn't make it a science. It is, in fact, a philosophy. Norman Geisler and Paul Feinberg define the traditional view of philosophy in this way:

> *. . . we would learn that the word* philosophy *comes from two Greek words which mean "loving wisdom." This idea of wisdom was central in the thought of the ancients. In this view of philosophy, the primary role of philosophy was ethical education. That is, philosophy was to teach the good life.*[17]

Psychologists are seeking to teach people how to live "the good life." It is in this area that psychology is in competition with the Bible. It seeks to answer such questions as, Who is man? What are his problems? And, How should he live? Because psychology claims to answer these questions it is a philosophy, not a science.

True Life in Christ

Long ago Jesus made it clear that He had come to give abundant life to those who followed Him (John 10:10). Does the church that He shed His precious blood for need the ideologies of atheists? Must His followers now turn to Sigmund Freud, Alfred Adler, Carl Rogers, or B.F. Skinner for abundant life? Is there no longer any source of absolute truth for the believer? Who has the authority to claim absolute truth? Surely not these men who seemingly developed their systems as replacements for what they believed to be an obsolete and restricting religion— Christianity. Charles Sykes, the author of *A Nation of Victims*, wrote:

The prophets of the therapeutic seemed to agree, at least to the extent of rec-
ognizing religion as the greatest barrier and rival to their . . . movement.
The doctrines that were to evolve into a sort of universal tolerance for every
sort of peculiarity, deviance, abnormality, and even crime began with a vir-
ulent intolerance for traditional forms of faith[18] *(emphasis added).*

Is all truth relative? Can absolute truth be known? Do Christians believe that
words simply mean what you want them to mean? Wouldn't the majority
of Christians respond to these questions with an impassioned *no*? Most Christians
believe that there *is* a truth that can be known, and that truth comes from God.

Counsel That Never Changes

The Bible is clear. There is *one* truth that sanctifies (changes) mankind. Jesus
Christ identified it when He prayed, "Sanctify them in the truth; Thy word is
truth" (John 17:17). God's Word never changes. It isn't "in" today and passé
tomorrow. Indeed the Bible says of itself, "Forever, O LORD, Thy word is settled
in heaven" (Psalm 119:89). The wonderful confidence that a biblical counselor
can have is that the basis for the counsel he gives won't have to be updated
every other year. God's Word is timeless: "The sum of Thy word is truth, and
every one of Thy righteous ordinances is everlasting" (Psalm 119:160).
Inasmuch as the counsel that he gives is truly biblical, he may be assured that it
is also eternal and powerful. Consider this passage from Isaiah:

So shall My word be which goes forth from My mouth; it shall not return to
Me empty, without accomplishing what I desire, and without succeeding in
the matter for which I sent it (Isaiah 55:11).

After reading these wonderful passages about the power and timelessness of
the Word, don't you have to wonder with Isaiah, "Why do [I] spend money for
what is not bread, and [my] wages for what does not satisfy?" (Isaiah 55:2).
Solomon cautioned about putting trust in man's reason: "There is a way which
seems right to a man, but its end is the way of death" (Proverbs 14:12).

How to Discern Truth

How are we to judge truth? Are we to judge truth as Werner Erhard, founder of
"EST" states, " . . . something experienced is true; the same thing believed is a
lie"?[19] On several occasions I have had the opportunity to speak with women

who have had an experience "with God" that the Bible fails to identify as typical or appropriate. Since the Bible is the ground upon which all of our relating with God must be founded, in each case I tried to gently confront the veracity of their experiences. When I pointed out the fact that their experience was extra-biblical and should therefore not be sought after, their method of determining truth (or their "epistemology") immediately became evident. They usually said something like this: "I know that the Bible doesn't talk about this, but for me, it really worked. I know what I experienced. I know that God met me."

Following William James, most Americans tend to judge truth on the basis of pragmatism. This means that they believe that something is true *if it works*. "The error of pragmatism," states John MacArthur, "is that it regards methodologies that 'work' as more important and more viable than those that are biblical."[20] Truth, however, cannot be determined by our subjective experiences, nor by what "works." Truth cannot be determined by whether something appeals to our reason or not (Proverbs 3:5). Our reason must be informed by our faith. According to Augustine, faith is a prerequisite for the full understanding of God's revelation. Unless we truly believe, our understanding will be partial and distorted. As George Scipione states, "We must think biblically though all areas of life."[21] *We must learn to discern truth and error solely on the basis of Scripture.* The Word of God testifies about itself in this way:

> The law of the LORD is perfect, restoring the soul; the testimony of the LORD is sure, making wise the simple. The precepts of the LORD are right, rejoicing the heart; the commandment of the LORD is pure, enlightening the eyes. . . . the judgments of the LORD are true; they are righteous altogether (Psalm 19:7-9).

The Lord Himself describes His Word as perfect, sure, right, pure and true. It is the standard by which all other knowledge must be measured. We read in Psalm 119:128, "I esteem right all Thy precepts concerning everything." God's definitions and categories are the criterion that we must use to distinguish truth from error. Not our experience ("But I felt good!"), not our pragmatism ("But it worked!"), not our reason ("But I like my own way of thinking!"), but rather God's revelation.

In addition to learning to discern truth, we must also learn to discern the source of that truth. Psalm 1:1 tells us, "Blessed is the man who does not walk in the counsel of the wicked." Tozer warns about receiving counsel from the ungodly;[22] he wrote:

Listen to no man who fails to listen to God. . . . No man has any right to offer advice who has not first heard God speak. No man has any right to counsel others who is not ready to hear and follow the counsel of the Lord. True moral wisdom must always be an echo of God's voice. The only safe light for our path is the light which is reflected from Christ, the Light of the World.[23]

Even the Apostle Paul warned the Colossian church about worldly philosophies:

See to it that no one takes you captive through philosophy and empty deception, according to the tradition of men, according to the elementary principles of the world, rather than according to Christ (Colossians 2:8).

The Bible Is Relevant

Please understand, I'm not saying that I believe that Christian psychologists have *purposely* set out to undermine the church's confidence in Scripture. I believe that most of them have a sincere desire to help people in a meaningful way. Only God knows the heart. I am saying I believe that a lack of confidence in the relevance of Scripture is unfortunately some of the fruit of their labors. I believe that this has happened in part because the majority of psychologists have spent years and years in graduate school getting advanced degrees in psychology, while spending comparatively few hours receiving training in theology. They have immersed themselves in the work of the "Great Psychologists." Perhaps because of this imbalance in training the Bible just doesn't seem to address the deep problems of life. Perhaps they believe that psychology is "deeper" because some may have a superficial understanding of the depth, riches, and wisdom in the Word. David Powlison inquires probingly into our appreciation of the Word:

What do you see when you look at your Bible? Do you see a book crammed with relevance? Do you see a book out of which God bursts as He speaks to what matters in daily life? Is your Bible packed with application to the real problems of real people in the real world: inexhaustible, immediate, diverse, flexible? Or is the Bible relatively thin when it comes to addressing human struggles?[24]

He describes the lack of confidence some psychotherapists have in the Bible: "Christian psychotherapists generally believe that the Bible is insufficient when it comes to exploring and explaining the significant goings-on in the human psyche."[25] This lack of confidence stems from unbiblical beliefs about the uniqueness of man's problems—beliefs that would have been remedied had the psychologist spent more time studying sound theology.

First a Theologian: Knowing God in His Word

By contrast, the biblical counselor is first a theologian. Don't let that term frighten you. Theology is simply the study of God. Sadly, in these days, it is not uncommon to hear Christians berate the study of theology. I have often heard preachers make such foolish statements as, "We don't want any dry old theology. We want God!" I don't believe that they mean what they say. I hope that what they mean is that they don't want to just study books about God, but that they want to *know* Him. The problem with statements such as these is that they significantly muddy the water and discourage the diligent study of the Word. Once again, *theology is the study of God*. David Wells writes,

> ... *theology is the sustained effort to know the character, will, and acts of the triune God as he disclosed and interpreted these for his people in Scripture, to formulate these in a systematic way in order that* we might know him, learn to think our thoughts after him, live our lives in his world on his terms, and by thought and action project his truth into our own time and culture[26] *(emphasis added).*

How can we have a personal knowledge of God if we don't know about Him? How can we know how to have a relationship with Him if we haven't studied His precepts? How can we know how to live and please Him if we aren't aware of His commands? We must remember that doctrine (what we believe) and practice (how we live) go hand-in-hand. How will we distinguish truth from error if we don't have a systematic knowledge of the truth?

Lack of love for theology is the greatest reason the church is floundering in weakness and heresy today. "A church that is neither interested in theology nor has the capacity to think theologically is a church ... for whom Christian faith will rapidly lose its point."[27] If we do not have a systematic theology, we open ourselves up to the most blatant heresy. "When we believe in nothing, we open the doors to believing anything."[28] Given the sad state of theological perception in the church, it should not be surprising that we are living in a time when the most bizarre practices are hailed as revivals from God. The church's apathy about theological issues is borne out by the mercenary practices of some evangelical publishers. According to Wells, *only 12.2%* of the books published for Christians "deal with understanding the Christian faith. . . . The rest of what is published is devoted either to the issues raised by psychology and the need for inner wholeness and balance (59.9%) or to the issues raised by hedonism (pleasure-seeking) and narcissism (love of self) (27.9%)."[29]

Theology was once spoken of as the queen of all sciences. It is apparent that the queen has fallen on hard times. The American church needs a revival of the ardent love that our forefathers had for the study of the Word of God. They did not think that theology was meaningless and dry. They were willing to give their lives to uphold the truth and confront theological error. George Wishart, who was martyred in the year 1546, made this statement after having mounted the scaffold upon which he was burned *for his theology:* ". . . love the Word of God for your salvation, and suffer patiently and with a comfortable heart for the Word's sake, which is your everlasting comfort; but for the true Gospel, which was given me by the grace of God, I suffer this day with a glad heart."[30]

The biblical counselor has a high view of theology. He has immersed himself in the Word of God and is overwhelmed with the depth and relevance of the Scripture. He believes that the Bible is sufficient because he understands the commonalities in all men that the Bible speaks to. The biblical counselor believes that the Word of God is sufficient, efficacious, and eternal. As you learn to apply the Word to your everyday life, as demonstrated throughout the remainder of this volume, you will see that the Bible is undoubtedly sufficient.

Are Christianity and Psychology Compatible?

You may be wondering, "Aren't psychology and Christianity compatible? After all, 'All truth is God's truth.' " While it is true that all truth comes from God, we must be diligent to discern truth from error. We must be careful not to call error "truth" so that we might accommodate our philosophy. Let's just look at a few basic questions to decide whether psychology and Christianity are compatible.

The Foundational Issues

The Nature of Man   First, let's look at the question of the nature of man. Psychology teaches that man's nature is either neutral (a blank slate) or basically good. In contrast, the Bible teaches that man was created in the image of God but that image was marred by the fall. The Bible describes man's heart as being "deceitful . . . and is desperately sick" (Jeremiah 17:9). The Bible doesn't say that man's heart is neutral, much less good; it teaches quite plainly that the unregenerate man's heart is evil.

The Nature of Man's Problems   What about the source of man's problems? Psychology teaches that man has problems for one of a number of reasons. The Freudian psychotherapist teaches that man has problems because he was improperly socialized as a child. In fact, he has all kinds of pressures within his unconscious mind that cause him to behave in socially unacceptable ways. The behaviorist teaches that man's problems stem from his environment. Man has no mind, but is a machine. If he is given the right stimulus, the right actions will be forthcoming. Neither the Freudian psychotherapist nor the behaviorist believe that man is responsible before a holy God. On the other hand, the Rogerian person-centered therapist would say that man has problems because he hasn't learned to tap into and trust the wonderful power within. He just needs to love and accept himself as he is. Then he will be able to function properly in society. While the Rogerian psychologist might say that man is responsible to achieve self-actualization, he also would deny that man is responsible before God. Sykes defines this self-focused philosophy as he quotes Bernie Zilbergeld, author of *The Shrinking of America*:

> *In the therapeutic view, people are not regarded as vile or as having done anything they should feel guilty about, but there is certainly something wrong with them. Specifically, they are too guilty, too inhibited, not confident and assertive enough, not able to express and fulfill themselves properly, and without a doubt not as joyful and as free from stress as they ought to be.*[31]

For the psychologist, everything rests on subjective feelings. How a person *feels* about God, the self, life, relationships, and even truth is all that matters. The capacity to think and act volitionally is disdained. As Wells writes, "The psychologizing of the faith is destroying the Christian mind."[32]

What does the Bible teach? The Bible is clear: Sin is the problem. Each one of us experiences difficulties and problems in this life because of the influences of the world, the flesh, and the devil. We have trouble because of our own sins or other people's sins against us. We live in a sin-cursed world. God holds each man accountable for his own actions (Ezekiel 18:20; Romans 14:12). God commands that our entire heart, soul, mind, and strength be devoted to worship and serve only Him (Matthew 22:37). When we fail to do so, we experience problems. *This is as it should be.* The Bible refers to this process as "sowing and reaping" (Galatians 6:7-8). We have problems in our lives when we fail to recognize and worship God as King and instead worship our own ideas, expectations and desires—false gods. This is a common problem for us all; John Calvin taught that the heart of man was bent to manufacture idols. Our hearts are always worshiping and serving. The Christian has been given a new heart to worship and serve only the true God, a God that is not formed by the thought of man (Acts 17:29). Sadly, the rest of the world worships and serves other gods—gods of their own making.

As Christians we continually make choices about whether we will worship and serve God or our own thoughts and desires. We experience despair and futility when we endeavor to bring along our former deities, "the gods of Egypt," and incorporate them into our worship of Jehovah (Psalm 78:33). Oftentimes the Lord lovingly arranges specific troubles in our lives to free us from our false gods and to turn our hearts wholly toward Him (Psalm 78:34-35). When we as believers experience God's discipline, it is because He is calling us to wholehearted devotion (Hebrews 12:11). Thus we must question whether it is ethically right for a Christian to encourage an idolater in his idolatry by helping him develop better "coping mechanisms" while ignoring the source of his difficulty: idolatry.

The Nature of Change   What about the method of change? Can the methods of psychotherapy and Christianity be harmonized? The psychotherapist believes that free association is the appropriate process to use for uncovering unconscious motivations. Once the client gains personal awareness and understanding, he can change. He believes that the interpretation of dreams and the examination of relationships with parents will bring about change. Was he wounded as a child? Was his fragile psyche damaged? He must release built-up psychological pressure through venting and "working through" his pain. Does he think that he had good parents? All the more reason to believe that there is some terrible abuse hidden in his unconscious self. This terrible "truth" manifests its hidden presence in the form of anger, fears, addictions, and "dysfunctional" relationships. Unless this truth is uncovered, confronted, worked through, and experienced, troubles will persist. On the other hand, the behaviorist believes that changing the environment in which his client lives will bring about change. If rewards and punishments can be structured into his client's life, then his client will eventually change. Does his client eat too much? Put a rubber band on his wrist and tell him to snap himself whenever he overeats. He'll eventually change his eating habits. The person-centered therapist has a different approach; he thinks that all his client needs is to be affirmed. He doesn't need any advice from outside—no, he just needs to get in touch with his own inner goodness and wisdom. There really aren't any good or bad behaviors—just ineffective, self-defeating ones. The person-centered therapist sings along with Whitney Houston that the greatest love of all is learning to love yourself.

The Bible, however, teaches that change comes about through confession, repentance, and obedience. There is no need for hours and hours of free association, venting, and dream analysis; no need to structure contrived rewards or punishments; no need to sit in front of the mirror every morning reciting your "Twenty Affirmations." The process of change (what the Bible calls sanctification) is accomplished by following these simple steps: First, you must recognize your action as sinful (not merely ineffective or self-defeating) (Ecclesiastes 7:20; Romans 3:23) and confess it to God, to whom you owe worship and obedience (John 1:9; Revelation 3:19). Second, you need to ask for His forgiveness. Third, you must repent. Repentance involves putting off your former manner of life, seeking to renew your mind, and putting on the new habits that God commands (Ephesians 4:22-24). Finally, you must habitually practice each of these steps in faith (Philippians 4:9). As you seek to do these things, you'll be empowered by the Holy Spirit (2 Thessalonians 2:13) and enlightened by the Word (Psalm 119:130). Remember, too, that the power that sin once held over you has been broken (Romans 6:14). You are now able to walk in "newness of life" (2 Corinthians 5:17). Please don't misunderstand; this is no man-centered "pull yourself up by your own bootstraps" regime. This is the very plan of God for transforming lives! As you seek to comply with God's design for your life you can be changed! Listen to Paul's encouragement to the Corinthians:

> *Do you not know that the unrighteous shall not inherit the kingdom of God? Do not be deceived; neither fornicators, nor idolaters, nor adulterers, nor effeminate, nor homosexuals, nor thieves, nor the covetous, nor drunkards, nor revilers, nor swindlers, shall inherit the kingdom of God.* And such were some of you; *but you were washed, but you were sanctified, but you were justified in the name of the Lord Jesus Christ, and in the Spirit of our God* (1 Corinthians 6:9-11, emphasis added).

Are we in any worse condition than the Corinthians were? Look again at that list of sins. These weren't pure little Sunday School children; these were rank pagans! And yet God changed them. Look again at what Paul says: "And such *were* some of you ... " (emphasis added). How were these fornicators, homosexuals, thieves, drunkards, and swindlers changed? Through therapy? Of course not. They were changed by being washed, sanctified, and justified by the Lord Jesus and the Spirit of God. Are the resources of God sufficient? Of course they are. They always have been. The heart of man is the same now as it was in the early church. And God's resources are just as powerful today as they were in the days of the Corinthians.

Two Competing Systems

Are psychotherapy and Christianity just two different ways of doing the same thing? Are they just different paths to the same truth? No, psychology and Christianity are two utterly different and competing systems. They have differing presuppositions, or underlying beliefs. They use differing methods. They seek to accomplish different goals. Unfortunately, many Christians have tried to integrate these two opposing beliefs. As Ed Payne, physician and publisher of the *Biblical Reflections on Modern Medicine* told *World* magazine,

> Integration implies a merging of things that can be merged. Take a field such as psychology, which is not only formed without biblical principles in mind, but is in its majority, anti-God and anti-Christian. It doesn't make sense— not even common sense—that you can merge what is God's with what is rebellion against God.[33]

David Wells concurs; he observes that "the psychologizing of life cuts the nerve of evangelical identity because the common assumption beneath the self movement is the perfectibility of human nature, and this assumption is anathema to the Christian gospel."[34] When people try to merge the two systems, the pure, life-giving water of Christianity is so polluted that it becomes impotent.

Ask yourself these questions: How would the apostle Paul have responded to the kind of self-serving, man-centered counseling that seems so common today? How would he have responded to teaching that encourages self-love and self-aggrandizement? How would he have responded to psychotherapy's focus on man-made schemes of perfection? He said, "Are you so foolish? Having begun by the Spirit, are you now being perfected by the flesh?"

(Galatians 3:3). What do you think? It was Paul who fought against this false doctrine when he warned Timothy of the apostasy to come:

> *Realize this, that in the last days difficult times will come. For men will be* lovers of self, *lovers of money, boastful, arrogant, revilers, disobedient to parents, ungrateful, unholy,* unloving, *irreconcilable, malicious gossips, without self-control, brutal, haters of good, treacherous, reckless, conceited,* lovers of pleasure rather than lovers of God *(2 Timothy 3:1-4, emphasis added).*

What do you think the apostle would say to the Christian psychotherapist who states that self-love is imperative to the development of love for God and others? He would say that *self-love itself is the impediment to loving God and others as he should.*[35] It isn't surprising that this heresy is widespread; it always has been. What *is* surprising is that it has been so freely adopted by the church for whom Christ shed His blood. The Word of God irrelevant? Insufficient? Hardly. If you wonder whether the Word has lost its power or is somehow insufficient in these last days, let me encourage you to meditate on Revelation 19:11-13:

> *I saw heaven opened; and behold, a white horse, and He who sat upon it is called Faithful and True; and in righteousness He judges and wages war. And His eyes are a flame of fire, and upon His head are many diadems; and He has a name written upon Him which no one knows except Himself. And He is clothed with a robe dipped in blood;* and His name is called The Word of God *(emphasis added).*

Biblical counseling is a comprehensive philosophy grounded firmly upon the belief that the Word of God is powerful enough to change the people of God by the Spirit of God into the image of Jesus Christ. This philosophy may seem simplistic and naive. It may seem like the "rantings of small-minded know-nothings who glory in their ignorance." But when we speak of the Bible's sufficiency we mean "something living and active, inexhaustibly rich, comprehensive and relevant, is sufficient for a very complex job."[36]

Why the Church Has Embraced Psychology

I can't imagine a modern person-centered therapist's doctrine finding a hearing with Luther or Calvin. What is at foot in the Christian community that we are so willing to embrace another gospel? Why can't Christians see through this deception? I believe that there are two answers to this question.

Many Christians Have Embraced Religious Humanism   We hear a lot of talk about secular humanism, but it seems to me that many Christians embrace religious humanism without even knowing it. Humanism is "a doctrine, attitude, or way of life centered on human interests or values; especially a philosophy that asserts the dignity and worth of man and his capacity for self-realization through reason and that often rejects supernaturalism."[37] Most American Christians now live as if the chief end of man is to discover and fulfill himself and live happily ever after. Indeed, the entire Christian experience has simply become another way to get one's personal "needs met." As David Wells writes, God's "providence in the world diminishes to whatever is necessary to ensure one's having a good day. . . . "[38] Jesus is seen as the "Need-Meeter" rather than the Son of God to whom we owe allegiance, obedience, devotion, and worship.

At the same time that the Reformers held to a belief in the dignity of regenerate man—in his God-given ability to know and communicate with God because he has been re-created in His image—they held just as strongly to a belief in the depravity of man. Along with them we must remember that first and foremost Jesus was sent to save sinners—to appease a holy God's wrath at our rebellion and to show the riches of the mercy of God. We have forgotten this truth and instead have come to view the unregenerate as wounded victims. Consider this illustration:

> . . . suppose a man escapes from prison. Certainly he will have grief. He is going to be in pain after bumping logs and stones and fences as he crawls and hides away in the dark. He is going to be hungry and cold and weary. His beard will grow long and he will be tired and cramped and cold—all of these will happen, but they are incidental to the fact that he is a fugitive from justice and a rebel against law.[39]

Certainly the sinner is heartbroken and "wounded." The Bible speaks to these things, but we must understand that they are incidental to the fact that he is in this condition because he has rebelled against God and he is a fugitive from the Lord. It is this historical belief in the depravity of man and his utter dependence on God that our culture has rejected. "Sure," we say, "we'll *accept* God, just as long as doing so increases our personal awareness and well-being." This is a salvation that costs us little in the way of sacrifice and dying to self. In this light it is not surprising that Christians have been beguiled by psychology. *Psychology is simply the seductive daughter of humanism.* We must understand that she has sway over us because we live in her father's house. We've been eating his bread and drinking his wine for almost 100 years now and his thoughts permeate our minds. From time to time when we awaken from our stupor and wonder if we aren't headed in the wrong direction, psychology comes over and fills our cup again. She tells us that the problem is that we haven't gone far enough in loving and fulfilling ourselves. "The problem," she whispers, "isn't sin or self-absorption. No, the problem is that you don't really believe that you deserve good. You must learn to love and accept yourself." Or as one popular pastor teaches, "Sin is not what shatters our relationship to God; the true culprit is the jaundiced eye that we turned on ourselves."[40]

To the Christian who is seeking to love and fulfill himself, the Bible will seem thin and irrelevant. "Where are the strategies for self-actualization?" the modern Christian wonders. We must resolutely embrace the fact that the Bible wasn't written to undergird humanism's vain philosophies. Man's cry for independence and happiness is not encouraged in Scripture. When modern man goes to the Bible to find self-fulfillment he is seeking the dead among the living. Because he's lost the understanding that a person's main purpose in life is to know and glorify God, he's thirsty for the wrong thing. He thinks he needs one thing while Jesus is offering something else, something infinitely better. Like the woman at the well, he wants water, but Jesus wants to free him from spending his life seeking to satisfy his natural thirst. He wants to give him life. In this sense, those who critique biblical counseling are right. The Bible isn't a psychological textbook. No, its much better than that. It is utterly different from that. *The goal of psychology is the self-fulfillment and gratification of man and the Bible refutes this kind of ambition as futile.* Christians must seek to put off their humanistic thinking and begin to seek the mind of Christ. This brings me to the second part of our answer.

Many Christians Have No Confessional Belief   Many Christians are infatuated with humanism and psychology because they have never fully embraced the true gospel nor have they taken the time to plumb the depths of Scripture for themselves. They hear certain "catch phrases" and accept them without trying them against the standard of the Word. Even though 46 percent of Americans describe themselves as born-again, evangelist Billy Graham states that "most have not accepted true Christianity . . . they believe the Bible, but they don't read it or obey it." Pollster George Gallup, Jr. states that this is "a nation of biblical illiterates. . . . The stark fact is, most Americans don't know what they believe or why."[41] In a culture that lacks defined confessional beliefs, belief does not disappear—it multiplies. In fact, it is now possible for a person to believe almost anything and still maintain his or her standing as a "Christian."

If we as Christians want to see true change take place in lives, we must return to diligently studying our Bibles. That may seem like a ridiculous statement, but it is so vital. We must once again embrace coming to know God through His Word. How many Christians do you know who have read through the entire Bible? How much time do we ourselves spend trying to understand it? In addition, we must seek out churches that do not entertain but rather inform, nurture, and correct us. We must pray that God will open our hearts to the light of His Word and that we will seek to walk in it. We must repent of our self-serving ways and seek instead to lay down our lives for Christ and others. It is only as we do these things that we will be able once again to discern good and evil, as Hebrews 5:13-14 states:

> *Everyone who partakes only of milk is not accustomed to the word of righteousness, for he is a babe. But solid food is for the mature, who because of practice have their senses trained to discern good and evil.*

Can you discern between good and evil? Do you know the difference between truth and error? Are you prey for every new wind of doctrine? Do you have a passion for truth? It is only as you seek to grow in a systematic knowledge of God through His Word that you will be able to discern truth and understand His will for your life.

Why has psychology found a home in the church? Because we have not been good Bereans. Luke, the author of the book of Acts, extolled the people from Berea because they were more "noble-minded than those in Thessalonica, *for they received the word with great eagerness, examining the Scriptures daily, to see whether these things were so*" (Acts 17:11, emphasis added). Do you receive the Word with great eagerness? Do you meditate on it? When you hear teaching, do you examine the Scriptures to see if what you are hearing is true? Do you judge truth by how it makes you feel or by the Word of God? The problem of false doctrine in the church is more than just a blip on our theological computer screen. Humanism and the practical outworking of it, psychology, is a virus that has infected our entire operating system.

Becoming a Student of the Word

In the chapters that follow, we will be looking at the biblical directives for some of the problems Christian women face today. We hope that you will not implement this counsel as merely another "technique" to add to a bag of man-centered methods. In addition, we caution you not to believe anything that we have written unless Scripture plainly teaches it. You must go to the Scriptures for yourself and seek out the truth. Test what we say. Pray that God will give you wisdom so that you will be able to think, counsel, and disciple other women in this day.

By the way, we should add that if you take a stand for God's truth and confront humanism and man's philosophies, you may be persecuted. But you can rejoice! In every area where you are truly standing for God's Word and His righteousness, you will be blessed. Remember the words of our Lord:

> *Blessed are those who have been persecuted for the sake of righteousness, for theirs is the kingdom of heaven. Blessed are you when men cast insults at you, and persecute you, and say all kinds of evil against you falsely, on account of Me. Rejoice, and be glad, for your reward in heaven is great, for so they persecuted the prophets who were before you (Matthew 5:10-12).*

We know that we don't have all the answers; nor do we think that all of our answers are faultless. The Bible teaches us not to trust our own understanding. But we do believe that the answers we have offered are a good place to start and are biblically sound. We encourage you to be a good student of the Word—a student who receives it with eagerness as she disciples other women to the glory of God.

CHAPTER 2

The Methods
of
Biblical Counseling

Elyse Fitzpatrick, M.A.

Entire books have been written on the methods of biblical counseling, and the space limitations of this chapter make it impossible for us to consider the entire scope of the subject. Instead, let me present a very brief outline of the process of biblical counseling, and then refer you to books and training sites that can help provide you with more extensive instruction.

Jay Adams, in his ground breaking book *Competent to Counsel*, defines biblical counseling as counseling that is motivated by love and deep concern, in which clients are counseled and corrected by verbal means for their good, ultimately, of course, that God may be glorified."[1]

Notice that Adams states that biblical counseling is motivated by love and deep concern. He is talking about the same kind of love that Jesus illustrated in the parable of the lost sheep (Matthew 18:11-14). We live in an age when people are confused about how love functions. Many people believe that love doesn't challenge, correct, or pursue. Happily, our God's great love is not weak "unconditional acceptance."[2] Our God's strong love caused Him to reach out to us with His truth and make a way for us to know and serve Him. It caused Him to commit Himself to our change.

In biblical counseling, we are motivated by our love for God and for our brothers and sisters in Christ. We reach out to them and come alongside of them to help them ardently love and faithfully serve their Creator. We do not view ourselves as "above" our counselees, or as experts. Although we are trained to use the Word, we do not look upon ourselves as having arrived. Because we continually confront ourselves with the Word, we are able to in "humility of mind . . . regard one another as more important than [ourselves]" (Philippians 2:3). We view ourselves as bondservants who hope to be used by our Lord to admonish the unruly, encourage the fainthearted, and help the weak (1 Thessalonians 5:14). We do this through verbal means in the counseling room and by the testimony of our daily life. In this process, we seek to establish a loving discipling relationship with our counselees, mercifully humbling ourselves to bear their burdens. We seek to understand their relationship with our Lord and their relationship with their neighbor. We seek to discern how those relationships affect and are manifest in every area of their life. Our prayer is that God will use us to guide them into a freer, more godly way of living so that our Lord will be pleased and glorified.

Biblical counseling, then, is the process in which believers seek to know, confront, strengthen, encourage, and disciple other believers to grow in their love for God and their neighbor, all for His glory.

A Brief Outline of How to Do Biblical Counseling

As I have already stated, biblical counseling is goal-oriented. The goal is to encourage Christians to live in a way that glorifies God through faithful service to Him. I understand that this goal is best accomplished by including these four elements in all our counseling:

1. Building a relationship of love, trust, and mutual respect with the counselee. This is accomplished by gathering data and seeking to understand the whole person, not just an isolated problem.

2. Building hope in her heart that true change is possible.

3. Teaching the counselee how to "put off" ungodliness and "put on" righteousness as she is renewed in the attitude of her mind and her motives are transformed.

4. Training the counselee to continually practice these new responses to life and thereby develop habitual godliness that will extend to all other areas of her life.

Building a Relationship Through Information and Understanding

Although each of the four steps are very important, I think that in some ways this first step is paramount. Everything that will happen in future counseling sessions hinges on the counselor's understanding of the person and interpretation of the problem(s) she faces. The thorough understanding necessary in good counseling is accomplished through careful listening and asking good questions.

The discipline of being a good listener is so very important that several warnings are given in Proverbs 18 about this. One appears in verse 13: "He who gives an answer before he hears, it is folly and shame to him." It is folly and shame to decide upon a course of action prior to spending time listening, understanding, and discerning. The counselor must not only seek to understand the scope and history of the difficulties faced by the counselee, but must also understand how the counselee has habitually responded to the situations in the past. What pre-suppositions does she hold that cause her to respond in a given way? For instance, it is not enough to merely learn that she was physically abused as a child—although that is extremely important. There are other underlying questions that need to be asked. How did she respond to the abuse? Who was responsible for the abuse? What has she come to think about herself, others, and the Lord because of the abuse? How does she presently respond to both difficulties *and* blessings in life because of the sinful or erroneous beliefs she developed as a child? What about beliefs or habits she has developed as an adult? She may not even be aware of her basic beliefs (or worldview) and habits because they are often formed intuitively or instinctively. She is merely accustomed to relating to life in a certain way, and her beliefs and values are continuing to be shaped as she interacts with her environment, which she interprets through the prism of her unique heart.

In addition, has she received other counsel that has influenced her toward more psychological thought? Does she view herself as a victim? Does she excuse sin in her own life because she has been told she is not responsible? Who significantly influences her?

Data must be gathered both *extensively* (in every area of life[3]) and *intensively* (in specific areas) before a course of action can be settled upon. Of course, that's not to say that you can't do any counseling at all before you have this kind of broad understanding. You will want to give hope through encouragement and homework even at the first session. In fact, some counselees won't open up and give you the kind of in-depth information you need until they see that you are seriously committed to this process. It's just that you must avoid making any concrete judgments about the appropriate direction to go in until you've done your work here. Even then, you must hold your judgments tentatively—after all, you may be wrong.

Another verse from Proverbs 18 that calls us to listen carefully is this: "A fool does not delight in understanding, but only in revealing his own mind" (verse 2).

We must continually guard against the temptation to play the role of "know-it-all." God calls this type of attitude foolishness. We must seek to understand others rather than "reveal" our own "great" thoughts. Of course, understanding others includes observing their external behavior—the things they do and say in varied circumstances. We know that frequently this external behavior displays the inner workings of the heart (Mark 7:20-23). But understanding also includes seeking to know a person's thoughts, desires, motives, and beliefs. "A plan in the heart of a man is like deep water, but a man of understanding draws it out" (Proverbs 20:5).

For instance, it is not enough to know that your counselee is overweight. It is not enough to say, "Stop eating so much." You must seek to understand her thoughts about food and eating. What did she learn about food from her parents? What does she believe about God's perspective on eating? Does she have motives or desires that are in conflict with God? For example, when worried, does she seek to comfort herself by eating when the Lord wants to be her comfort? Does she seek to demonstrate her independence by an attitude that says, "I can eat whatever I want"? Is she afraid of looking good to men? Is she testing her husband's love? You must take all of this information and interpret it in the light of biblical truth. Is it godly for her to give in to self-indulgence because she fears man? What changes in her inner and outer self must be made? Why?

Proverbs 18:2 may be paraphrased this way: "A woman is a fool if she does not find great pleasure in gaining insight into others; indeed, she is like an exhibitionist if all she wants to do is show off her own thoughts." Are you merely concerned with trying to impress with your knowledge and experience? Or are you sincerely interested in getting to know others so that you can help them?

The third warning from Proverbs 18 is this: "The first to plead his case seems just, until another comes and examines him" (verse 17). If you are gathering data about a relationship and only one member of that relationship is present, you must remember that you are not getting the full story. It is extremely important for you to try to get information from every person involved—spouses, children, employers, and so on. Even with the best intentions, you will hear things from very distinct points of view. How can you be sure that you are getting the whole story? Even though many husbands and children refuse to come in for counseling, they might be willing to speak with you over the phone, write a letter, or come in from time to time just so that you can get a clearer picture.[4]

Some Tools to Help You Gather Data   There are some tools that can help you gather data. First of all, it is important to have the counselee fill out a

Personal Data Inventory Form (PDIF).[5] This form will provide you with basic information that you will want to refer to over and over again. It will also help the counselee think in advance about the issues that need to be covered. If for some reason you are unable to have the counselee fill out a PDIF, then the following five questions (answered *before* the session begins) are helpful:

- What brings you here today?
- What have you done about it?
- How can I help you?
- How did you decide that now was the time to seek help?
- Is there any other information that I need to know?

As you can see, the answer to each question is vital. Not only will the answers give you critical information, they will also serve to focus the counselee's thoughts. You should take time to reflect on the answers to these questions, and use them as a springboard for more. In addition, you must also observe the manner in which they are answered.

Some Areas in Which to Increase Your Understanding

INVESTIGATE HER SPIRITUAL LIFE   You must ascertain the counselee's spiritual condition. It is best not to assume that anyone is a believer. The fact that your counselee is a member of your church's women's group doesn't guarantee that she is saved. Ask her to tell you her testimony. Does she have a basic understanding of her own personal sin? In our day of "Need Theology," many people attend church because they want God to perform some service for them or give them something. Does she recognize that she has sinned and that her sin is an offense to a holy God? If she does not acknowledge this, then her relationship with the Savior may be superficial. You might investigate further here by asking her to make a list of her sins during the week. If you determine that she may not be saved, the counseling room is a wonderful place to share the gospel.

Other questions you can ask about the counselee's spiritual life include: How long has she been saved? What kind of church does she attend? Is she a committed member? Does she serve there? Do other members of her family attend with her? How often does she attend? What about her personal devotions? Does she read the Bible? What is her favorite passage? What about her prayer time? Is she a witness to others? What does she believe about God?

For instance, some Christians have been taught to believe that only "good" comes from God while "bad" comes from Satan. Others believe that God is obligated to protect us from all suffering. What is her understanding of God's purpose in her life—specifically in the difficulties she is presently facing? What is her concept of herself as a "daughter of the King"? Finally, does she have hope in God's ability to transform and deliver her? The answers to these and other questions are vital in counseling.

DISCOVER HER RESOURCES   You must determine what resources are available to your counselee. If she doesn't have the power of the Holy Spirit or if she has a very limited or skewed understanding of God, her progress in counseling will be impeded. Homework assignments along these lines will give you insight into her level of spiritual growth. Ask her to read a pertinent passage of Scripture and interact with it. Don't just say, "Read 1 John." Tell her why you want her to read it and ask her to identify herself in it. Ask her to keep track of her devotional time. Knowing whether she spends time daily in prayer and Bible study is an important gauge of her resources. The Biblical Counseling Foundation's *Self-Confrontation Manual*[6] is an excellent resource that supplies forms for facilitating this kind of interaction, as are Wayne Mack's two volumes entitled *Homework Manual for Biblical Counseling.*[7]

CONSIDER HER PHYSICAL CONDITION   You must inquire into the counselee's physical condition. Physical problems can prompt emotional and spiritual problems. Also, emotional and spiritual problems can result in physical ones. That's why we must look at the whole counselee. This principle is illustrated in the Bible; for example, David was physically affected by his sin with Bathsheba (Psalm 32:3-4). Elijah's emotional state was at least partly affected by the great physical exertion he put forth running from Ahab. The Lord encouraged Elijah by sending angels to serve bread to him while he rested (1 Kings 19:1-5).

In your assessment, be careful not to assume that every problem is ultimately spiritual in nature. Perhaps your counselee has a new job that is very taxing physically. Perhaps she's working the night shift and isn't able to get good sleep. And what about hormonal problems? (see Chapter 20, "Medical Questions Women Ask Other Women"). It is a good idea to recommend a visit to the doctor for a checkup. At the least, you must determine whether the counselee is sleeping well, what kind of exercise she's getting, and how she eats. Sometimes just encouraging a change in diet and the addition of a recreational walking routine will be very helpful. Is she taking any medication? Has she been ill lately? Asking these kinds of questions is very important if you want to develop a precise picture of the counselee and truly understand her.

EVALUATE HER EMOTIONAL CONDITION   What is the counselee's emotional state? Some critics have accused biblical counselors of spiritualizing every emotion.[8] Although many emotional problems do stem from ungodly responses to life, some stem from physical problems, as mentioned above. Before assuming that depression comes from sinful responses to life, gather good data on your counselee's physical condition.

How should a biblical counselor evaluate emotions? Are all negative emotions sinful per se? Since the Bible makes it clear that God experiences emotions,[9] and also says that God is holy, it is incorrect to assume that negative emotions are always sinful. There are examples in the Bible of people who were angry without sin[10] as Ephesians 4:26 commands: "Be angry, and yet do not sin; do not let the sun go down on your anger."

You must evaluate emotions on several levels. First, what is the source of the emotion? Second, how does the counselee behave when experiencing this emotion? The fact that she is angry because her husband refuses to go to church with her is not enough information. Is she angry because God's glory is being diminished? Is she angry because her husband's sin is an offense to a holy God? Or is she angry because she's embarrassed about his laziness? There are very significant differences here based on what motivates the emotion. How has she acted this anger out? Does she nag or badger him? Has she threatened him? Does she withhold herself from him sexually? Or has she taken appropriate steps by contacting elders in her church who can help try to motivate him? Is the church actively involved in trying to win and disciple him? Does she accuse God of not helping matters?

Simply put, emotions tell you that something is going on in the heart. Because emotions are indicators of the condition of the heart, it is important to observe them. When I find myself experiencing negative emotions, I know it is time for personal evaluation. For instance, if I find that I am continuously irritable, it is time for me to attempt to understand what this reveals about the condition of my heart before God (or possibly my physical condition). If your counselee is frequently depressed you must seek to understand the thinking, beliefs, motives, and desires that are at work in her.

Emotions are also very powerful. Under the influence of anger, many people have done extremely wicked things.[11] But emotions can be controlled according to the book of Proverbs.[12] Paul's command from Ephesians to be angry without sin should give us hope. We recognize from this command that it is possible to control our emotions. "He expects of us only what He has Himself first supplied."[13] Remember, emotions, though powerful, merely signify the state of the heart.

We live in an era in which emotions have been elevated to supreme preeminence. Our speech commonly reflects this reliance on emotions as the ideal way to evaluate life. For instance, instead of asking, "What did you think about the message today?" we usually ask, "How did you feel about the message today?" I know this may seem like a trifling matter, but it does reflect our universal reliance on our emotional responses rather than our reasoning. This reliance on emotion is dangerous; for we all know that emotions come and go. We are never commanded to judge truth or error or our standing before God by the way we feel. Tozer points this out when he says that "we are . . . to live according to the high logic of spiritual truth, not according to our feelings and moods."[14]

When Edward Mote wrote the hymn "The Solid Rock" in 1834 he pointed out the folly of trusting either good moods or ill. Presently we refer to being in a "frame of mind," while it was common for people in Mote's day to refer to being in a happy or low "frame." Mote stated that he "dare not trust the sweetest frame [of mind], but wholly lean on Jesus' name." Even when he felt happy and felt that all was going well, he knew that he had to place his trust only on the truth of Jesus Christ and not in his own deceptive heart. We must all learn to live our lives according to the Word of God rather than according to emotions. Many counselees are experiencing problems for the simple reason that they are ruled by their emotions rather than by a will subjected to Scripture.

LOOK FOR HABITUAL BEHAVIOR PATTERNS   Another area to investigate is habitual behavior patterns. It is here that you will discover how the counselee normally responds to circumstances in her life. It is also here that you will uncover any recent changes that may have precipitated present difficulties. Gather data about how her parents normally responded to difficult circumstances. Ask her to keep a record of how often she worries, feels angry or depressed, and what specific event(s) trigger these emotional responses.

Habitual behavior patterns have a profound effect on us both emotionally and spiritually. Consider David's emotional and spiritual state after his sin with Bathsheba, or Judas's condition after the full weight of his betrayal fell upon him. As Wayne Mack writes,

. . . consider Cain, who was not only angry but also depressed . . . Cain sinned by bringing an inappropriate sacrifice to the Lord [Genesis 4:3], and the rest of the chapter indicates a direct correlation between that action and every part of his life. One disobedient action affected his relationship to God, produced various negative emotions, and led to further sinful action against his brother.[15]

ASK ABOUT HER PERCEPTIONS   Another area to assess is that of perceptions. First, what does she believe about God? Does she have a comprehensive understanding of His nature? Does she recognize His unchanging character? His omnipotence, omniscience, omnipresence, wisdom, and love? Does she believe that He is sovereign? Does she recognize that there is purpose and meaning to every trial? Does she understand and support God's intent and purpose? If there are errors in her perception of God, these misconceptions will influence all areas of her life. Second, what does she believe about herself in relationship to God? to others? to the church? to her employer? to her community?[16]

EVALUATE HER DESIRES   A final area to evaluate is that of her desires. What are the desires, motivations, or idols that rule her life? She may have a godly desire, such as to see her husband serving God, but if that desire rules her thought and actions, it has become too strong. It has become a false god. One way to help her ascertain whether her desires are too strong is to observe whether she sins when she is frustrated in them. If her whole life is geared toward getting her husband to do what she thinks he should do, then it isn't geared toward loving and serving God and her neighbor. Her good desire has become sinful. Whom does she trust? Upon whom is her security built? Is she manipulative or apathetic? Is she fearful or bitter? These responses may stem from a heart that is worshiping another god—her god.

Sadly, some women incorrectly interpret Psalm 37:4, which says, "Delight yourself in the LORD; and He will give you the desires of your heart." They believe that this verse is a promise from God that everything they desire will be theirs. Instead, this verse should be understood in the context of one's desires being shaped in the heart that is set upon delighting in Him alone. When our heart is fully set upon Him, He changes and molds our desires to please Himself. It is these desires that He loves to fulfill. Understanding not only your counselee's desires but also her beliefs about God's "obligation" to fulfill them is a significant part of your getting to know her.

Learning to be good at gathering data is a skill. Learning to ask questions and really listen to the answers takes discipline, patience, and love. Strive to ask questions that will give you information that you can readily use. Questions that begin with *why* call for speculation on the part of the counselee. Although this speculation may periodically be informative, the best questions begin with *what, how, when,* and *where.* As you strive toward excellence in this area, you will be rewarded in your counseling.

Building Hope That True Change Is Possible

Although hope is one of the hallmarks of the child of God,[17] it is frequently absent or waning in the hearts of those who need counseling. This may be because they have physiological problems,[18] faulty perceptions about God and His intentions,[19] or unfulfilled desires that are driving them.[20] It may be because they have been struggling in a trial for a long time and they have just given up. Christians often struggle in trials, trying this and that to resolve the problem, only to find themselves in a worse condition than before.

We must strive to teach our counselees the truth about God and thereby build a firm foundation for them to rest upon. Biblical hope is not some sort of wishful thinking, but is actually a confident expectation of good. This confidence is based on God's nature and His Word. It is not dependent upon others, possessions, or circumstances. It is the secure expectation that God, of whose character we can assured, is in control. Both the psalmist and Jeremiah echoed this thought:

> *Why are you in despair, O my soul? And why have you become disturbed within me? Hope in God, for I shall again praise Him for the help of His presence (Psalm 42:5).*

> *"The LORD is my portion," says my soul, "Therefore I have hope in Him." The LORD is good to those who wait for Him, to the person who seeks Him (Lamentations 3:24-25).*

The hope that is available to the believer is a life-changing force. It can bring assurance that sin no longer rules (Romans 6:14). It rejoices in ultimate victory through the death and resurrection of Jesus Christ (Romans 8:35-39). It furnishes a final expectation of good (Philippians 1:6). With the knowledge that God is watching over us, it comforts our hearts in the midst of trial:

> *No temptation has overtaken you but such as is common to man; and God is faithful, who will not allow you to be tempted beyond what you are able, but*

with the temptation will provide the way of escape also, that you may be able to endure it (1 Corinthians 10:13).

God sees us in our trials; He is in control of every aspect of our trials. He is able to change the circumstances of our trials and strengthen us to endure them. This verse assures us that we are never placed in a position in which we have to sin. God's never-slumbering eyes are watching over us and insuring our ultimate victory!

The hope that God supplies can be a driving force for change. Being assured that God is in control and that He has promised blessing to those who respond in faithful obedience[21] to Him is a powerful motivation. Romans 8:28-29 offers us this tremendously encouraging promise:

We know that God causes all things to work together for good to those who love God, to those who are called according to His purpose. For whom He foreknew, He also predestined to become conformed to the image of His Son, that He might be the first-born among many brethren (Romans 8:28-29).

Believers can rest assured that everything that comes into their lives is part of God's wonderful plan for good. Counselees are often confused when they read those verses because they wonder how their circumstances can be considered good. But it is not *our* perception of good that God is speaking of. It is *His* outlook on the situation and our ultimate change that He calls "good." As the Westminster Catechism states, "The chief end of man is to glorify God and enjoy Him forever." The ultimate purpose of life is not comfort and success (as secularly defined). It is our transformation into the likeness of Jesus Christ and the Father's glorification. When a counselee really grasps this truth, her heart can be filled with great hope and expectation. God will have His way. He will be glorified. Her trials will not be in vain. He has promised to be with her, hold her hand, and comfort her.[22] He has promised her ultimate victory in Him.

Here's one final exhortation regarding hope: Biblically, your counselee has no responsibility to change anyone other than herself. She doesn't have to wait for her husband or children or circumstances to change to enable her to grow in godliness. I didn't have to wait for others to "meet all my needs" before I could have joy and peace. I can walk in joy and peace for the very reason that the Lord is the foundation of my confident expectation. Even if I fail, I can be assured of my Father's loving guidance and forgiveness. God has promised to bring me to glory; that is all I need.

Now to Him who is able to keep you from stumbling, and to make you
stand in the presence of His glory blameless with great joy, to the only
God our Savior, through Jesus Christ our Lord, be glory, majesty,
dominion and authority, before all time and now and forever. Amen
(Jude 24-25).

If God is able to keep me from stumbling and make me stand before Him blameless and with great joy, I can have a heart filled with the hope that He is mighty enough to preserve me now. The trials that so frequently overwhelm us are nothing compared to the glory to be revealed in us.[23] Spend time building hope in your counselee. It will enable her to persevere and will encourage her to change.

Teaching the Counselee the Process of Change

God's intent for each one of His children is that they be sanctified.[24] Sanctification is "the process of God's grace by which the believer is separated from sin and becomes dedicated to God's righteousness."[25]

God's purpose is to cause each one of His children to become holy just as He is holy. God is in the business of change. When the Bible speaks of this change, it uses the word *sanctification*. As stated previously, the biblical counselor's goal is to facilitate change in the counselee's life so that his or her character is changed to conform to the likeness of Christ. God is glorified in the lives of Christians as they reflect His character. Nothing testifies any louder of God's reality than a changed life.

Change Explained

How does the process of change occur? Is it entirely God's project, or are we involved also? First, we can be certain that sanctification is God's project. It is accomplished in the atonement and made possible only by Christ's death and resurrection.[26] No significant change is possible before regeneration. It is only in salvation that a person's heart is changed to love and receive God's laws. God's intent in our lives is perfect holiness, which he commands.[27] Paul prayed that God would completely sanctify the believer (1 Thessalonians 5:23). At the same time, sanctification is also the responsibility of every believer.[28] The wonderful blending of God's effectual persuasion and our response to His grace is portrayed in Philippians 2:12-13:

So then, my beloved, just as you have always obeyed, not as in my presence only, but now much more in my absence, work out your salvation with fear and trembling; for it is God who is at work in you, both to will and to work for His good pleasure.

God is working in us. We are working because of His activity in us. It is both God and each individual believer striving toward sanctification.[29] As you read this book, don't be confused for an instant. None of our writers believe that we can accomplish any of the changes we are advocating apart from the sanctifying work of God. Not only would our change be impossible, we wouldn't even desire it.

So, how does the Lord accomplish this change in us? The Bible teaches us how this change occurs. The process requires putting off old, sinful attitudes and actions and putting on new, godly ones as Paul teaches in Ephesians 4:22-24:

You were taught regarding your previous habit patterns to put off the old person that you were, who is corrupted by deceitful desires, being rejuvenated in the attitude of your mind, and to put on the new person that you are, who is created in God's likeness with righteousness and holiness that come from truth . . . " (Christian Counselor's Commentary).

Does that sound simple? It is, but it is not simplistic. It isn't enough for a person to simply stop performing one action, or to merely change outwardly. The inner man, the attitudes and desires, must also be changed. Jesus' command that our righteousness supersede that of the scribes and pharisees demonstrates this point. Good behavior outwardly isn't enough. "This people honors Me with their lips [outward behavior], but their heart [inner behavior] is far away from Me," Jesus said (Matthew 15:8; *see also* Isaiah 29:13). Also, true sanctification is marked by new and righteous deeds, thoughts, and actions in place of the old. Ephesians 4:28 demonstrates this principle: "Let him who steals steal no longer; but rather let him labor, performing with his own hands what is good, in order that he may have something to share with him who has need."

In God's plan it's not enough to merely stop stealing. Anyone can stop stealing and yet not have a change in his heart and attitude. If there is no opportunity to steal anything, or if there is nothing worth stealing, a thief may stop stealing for a time. Does that mean that he is no longer a thief? No, it means that he is a thief without motive or opportunity. What will cause the nature of the thief to change? His nature will be changed by the power of the Holy Spirit as his mind is renewed and his actions conform to God's Word. Ephesians 4:28 teaches us what actions he must perform. First, he must perform honorable work with his own hands. In this way he will accomplish several things: He will provide for his own needs, thus making it unnecessary for him to have to steal to eat. He will learn the value and blessing of work and the wonderful sleep that is bestowed upon a hard worker.[30] He will no longer view himself as different or "above" others who have to work for a living. He will be able to enjoy peace instead of living in fear of discovery.

Second, he must give. He must learn to be generous and look upon others as having needs, rather than viewing them as "targets." As he practices habitual working and giving, his heart will be transformed, his mind will be renewed and he will grow in both his ability and desire to please God. He may not initially understand the full ramifications of God's displeasure or the new actions he must put on, but as he seeks to change, his attitude and understanding will change also.

Change Illustrated

I once counseled an older woman who had a problem with stealing. She had been a part of our church for quite a while, and she was in trouble with her employer for taking petty cash. She had done this on several occasions, and they were ready to fire her. She said that she felt an "overwhelming urge" to steal from others and she didn't think she could resist that urge. As we applied specific biblical principles to her life, we began to see change. First, she had to confess her sin to the Lord and to her employer and ask for forgiveness. It wasn't hard for her to confess because she had already been found out, but it was difficult for her to ask for forgiveness because she thought they wouldn't believe she really was sorry. They were very skeptical and kept her on staff only because she was getting counseling.

The next step was restitution. She and her employer figured out how much she had stolen and they agreed upon a plan for her to repay that amount along with an additional one-fifth.[31] Since she was already employed, all she had to do to obey God's commands was to start giving. In addition, because she was a member of my church's congregation, I asked her if I could monitor her giving over the next few months to be sure that she was being faithful in this area. She agreed that it would help her to know that she was accountable. As we discussed her financial obligations, I discovered that she was deep in credit-card debt. She was undisciplined in every avenue of her financial life, and we had to destroy her credit cards and write a budget for repaying her debts.

Because I knew that coveting other people's goods was part of her habitual thought life, we developed a contingency plan to help her when she felt the "urge" to steal. First, she would cry out to the Lord for help; God has promised to deliver us from temptation as we pray sincerely and turn from our sinful desires. Second, she would pray for the people from whom she wanted to steal. She would pray that God would bless them. Third, if she could, she would remove herself from the situation. Fourth, she would use her "thank list"[32] as a way to remember all the wonderful things that God had done for her. Fifth, she would think on the good things that God had given her and she would ask Him to help her be content.

At first she struggled with these steps, but as she habitually practiced them, she became more and more confident of God's ability to help her change. Because her habitual coveting was part of a lifelong pattern, this was no easy task. But the Lord was faithful to strengthen her, and eventually she was victorious.

Let's consider one more passage that demonstrates the principle of putting off and putting on:

> *Be anxious for nothing, but in everything by prayer and supplication with thanksgiving let your requests be made known to God. And the peace of God, which surpasses all comprehension, shall guard your hearts and your minds in Christ Jesus. Finally, brethren, whatever is true, whatever is honorable, whatever is right, whatever is pure, whatever is lovely, whatever is of good repute, if there is any excellence and if anything worthy of praise, let your mind dwell on these things. . . . practice these things; and the God of peace shall be with you. (Philippians 4:6-9).*

Worry is a significant problem for many women. It is the seedbed for many other sins, including unbelief, anger, and fear. Worry can also become habitual. What is God's process for overcoming worry? In the verses above, the apostle Paul wants us to recognize that God commands us to not worry. When we do worry, we are sinning, and we need to confess our worry and repent. But, once again, merely stopping the sinful action is insufficient. We must put on new attitudes and actions. How is this accomplished? First, we must pray about our concerns. A life of disciplined prayer will relieve the anxiety that engenders worry. To be beneficial, this prayer must be specific. In addition, saying this prayer at the beginning of the day will allow faith to be exercised before the concerns of life attempt to crowd faith out. And finally, this prayer must also be overflowing with thanksgiving. You see, it is impossible to worry and be sincerely thankful at the same time. That's why, as each day begins, you'll want to offer up a prayer that includes thanksgiving. This is an appropriate time to use the "thank list." Then during the day, as the worries of life try to crowd in, the knowledge that prayer has already been made for these concerns will raise up the standard of peace that will guard the heart.

I live near the Southern California coast, and during certain seasons the marine layer comes in and clouds everything up. By noon, however, the clouds disappear. I have often thought that the peace of God is like that marine layer—the clouds sort of float in and out and no one knows quite why. But the Bible teaches that the peace of God is present in the life of the believer who has been obedient to pray with thanksgiving instead of worrying.

Many Christian women do what I call "worry pray." By this I mean that they address their worries to the Lord all day long, never really praying in faith, never really finding peace. "Worry prayer" might sound like this: "Oh Lord, I'm afraid that I won't have money to pay the bills and then the utility company might shut off the gas, and then what would my parents think? And if that happened, I might have to move back in with them and, Lord, you know I don't want to do that!" This kind of worrying, addressed to the Lord, is more an exercise in fortune-telling than prayer. Instead of "worry praying," specific prayer should be made. When you are tempted to "worry pray," let your heart be calmed by the remembrance of obedient prayer. Philippians 4:8 tells us the kinds of thoughts we ought to have at all times, including in our prayers. I have heard Jay Adams call this verse, "God's leash law for the mind."

The worrier tends to have thoughts that go in many different directions. Instead of allowing the mind to spiral downward from one negative thought to another, the worrier must learn to discipline her thoughts. When an anxious thought comes in, she must remind herself that she has already prayed about this situation (if she has), remember God's promise to care for her,[33] and then think on things in line with Philippians 4:8. Careful records should be kept on a daily basis to determine the frequency with which the counselee resorts to worry and the new disciplines of prayer and thanksgiving.

Training the Counselee to Develop Habitual Godliness

I have found that one of the most difficult areas of change is that of continued practice. Paul, in Philippians 4:9, states the importance of practicing newly learned concepts. "The things you have learned and received and heard and seen in me, *practice* these things; and the God of peace shall be with you" (emphasis added).

Here again, we have the promise of peace as we walk in continued obedience to God's Word. In the original Greek text, the verb "practice" is in the present imperative tense, which renders it a command to do something in the future and involves continuous or repeated action. Jay Adams observes, "Notice that the verb . . . is not 'do' but 'practice.' Don't expect peace to arrive after the first attempt. When your *lifestyle* has begun to change with practice, then you can expect to find peace"[34] (emphasis added).

Although it can be difficult to change habitual behaviors, especially because new habits may feel uncomfortable at first, God will bless the effort and change will occur. If counselees become discouraged by their repeated attempts and failures, you will want to encourage them to persevere. Paul understood this propensity to capitulate to old habits when he wrote, "Let us not lose heart in doing good, for in due time we shall reap if we do not grow weary" (Galatians 6:9).

The counselee must learn to be patient in striving to become pleasing to God. I have had counselees repeatedly say to me, "Elyse, this is taking so long. Why can't I just change right now?" We hate to struggle with sin. We want a fairy godmother to sprinkle pixie dust on us and make us better instantly. We want someone to tell us "Five Easy Steps to Righteousness." We forget that we are in a battle. And the battle itself is God's plan to turn us from our sin toward Him. Many have forgotten what it means to struggle with sin; that's a sad commentary on the state of the modern church. Kay Arthur, in her book *Lord, Only You Can Change Me*,[35] discusses this shallowness of repentance in her chapter "Hungering and Thirsting for Righteousness." There she relates the story of a Hudson Taylor convert, Pastor Hsi. Hsi was converted from Confucianism to Christianity and was convicted that his opium habit had to be broken. He knew that he would suffer immeasurably as he withdrew from the drug, but he craved holiness and righteousness even more than opium. As he contended with pain and desire, he said, "Devil, what can you do against me? My life is in the hands of God. And truly I am willing to break off opium and die, but not willing to continue in sin and live!"[36]

In any kind of counseling that involves change, you need to encourage your counselee to hunger and thirst after holiness. Sadly, many counselees desire change simply because they believe it will make life more comfortable or it will relieve their sense of powerlessness. But as Christians, we are to desire change because God desires that change. If we are truly His, we will hate sin the way He does.

Change takes commitment—a commitment to practice, day after day, God's new way of living. It takes a commitment to continue even when we fail. It takes a commitment to continue even if the road seems to be getting rougher. Is the battle raging? You can assure your counselee that warfare is a sign of faith[37] and growth:

> The Christian who is satisfied to give God His "minute" and to have "a little talk with Jesus" is the same one who shows up at the evangelistic service [counseling office] weeping over his retarded spiritual growth and begging the evangelist [counselor] to show him the way out of his difficulty[38] (inserts added).

The marvelous truth is that God blesses our feeble attempts at change with His gracious power. James 1:25 tells us that "one who looks intently at the perfect law, the law of liberty, and abides by it, not having become a forgetful hearer but an effectual doer, this man shall be blessed in what he does." God is a loving Father, and our "baby steps" are a blessing and joy to Him. As A.W. Tozer writes,

> How good it would be if we could learn that God is easy to live with. He remembers our frame and knows that we are dust. He may sometimes chasten us, it is true, but even this He does with a smile, the proud, tender smile of a Father who is bursting with pleasure over an imperfect but promising son who is coming every day to look more and more like the One whose child he is.[39]

Our God is a gracious heavenly Father who encourages and enables us every step of the way!

As a counselee begins to cultivate new habits, continue to reinforce them. Don't stop prematurely, for old habits are hard to break and new ones are not really ingrained until they have been practiced over a period of time and in varying circumstances. The wonderful assurance that you may have however, is that the God of heaven is assisting your counselee in her attempts to change. God can take the vilest sinner and cleanse and sanctify him or her to become a vessel suitable for His use.

God Works His Will by His Word

Counseling that is genuinely biblical is grounded in the acceptance of several foundational truths. First, it is grounded in the belief that the Word of God is sufficient and authoritative. God has graciously provided everything needed to resolve any problem encountered by a child of God. Through the power of the Holy Spirit and in faithful and loving obedience to God's commands, all God's children can become pleasing to Him and live an abundant life. Because God's Word is eternal[40] and authoritative,[41] we can embrace it without reservation. As the psalmist wrote, "I esteem right all Thy precepts concerning everything, I hate every false way" (Psalm 119:128).

Second, it is grounded in the belief that man's heart is wicked and that his main problem is sin. As Solomon so wisely observed, "Indeed, there is not a righteous man on earth who continually does good and who never sins" (Ecclesiastes 7:20; *see also* Romans 3:9-20). As I stated previously, no other counseling method fully embraces the biblical doctrine of the fallenness of man. Man is not a good soul who has been poorly socialized, nor is he a blank slate that merely needs to be encouraged. He does not need to "recover"; *he needs to be remade.*

Man was created to worship, and in rebelliousness and proud independence he continuously chooses out for himself the idols of the land. Man consciously suppresses the truth of God, which has been made evident to him, and creates his own gods after his own image.[42] His problems do not stem from experiencing unmet needs, but rather from his own idolatrous lusting after those things that he perceives as needs. However, God has provided for man a "way of escape" from trials that seem to overwhelm. God has promised His presence and providential care to those who seek to please Him:

> *Why are you anxious about clothing? Observe how the lilies of the field grow; they do not toil nor do they spin, yet I say to you that even Solomon in all his glory did not clothe himself like one of these. . . . Do not be anxious then, saying, "What shall we eat?" or "What shall we drink?" or "With what shall we clothe ourselves?" For all these things the Gentiles eagerly seek; for your heavenly Father knows that you need all these things. But seek first His kingdom and His righteousness; and all these things shall be added to you (Matthew 6:28-29, 31 33).*

Third, biblical counseling embraces a comprehensive understanding of the character of God. It embraces a God who is immutable, sovereign, omniscient, omnipresent, omnipotent, eternal, loving, holy, patient, forgiving, just, and wise. The Lord God proclaimed this about Himself:

> *The LORD, the LORD God, compassionate and gracious, slow to anger, and abounding in lovingkindness and truth; who keeps lovingkindness for*

thousands, who forgives iniquity, transgression and sin; yet He will by no means leave the guilty unpunished, visiting the iniquity of the fathers on the children and on the grandchildren to the third and fourth generations (Exodus 34:6-7).

If any one of these attributes of God is missing or ignored in our understanding of Him, our relationship with Him and our neighbor will be skewed. A.W. Tozer observed that "our notion of God must always determine the quality of our religion."[43] Because the biblical counselor embraces this full view of God, he is able to offer hope and help, even in the midst of trial and suffering. He believes that "God causes all things to work together for good to those who love [Him], to those who are called according to His purpose" (Romans 8:28).

Suffering, then, is not worthless. Even our Lord learned obedience by the things He suffered. The biblical counselor does not look upon a person merely as a "victim"; rather, he views a person's sufferings as part of the preparation for his rejoicing with Christ.[44] The biblical counselor can encourage a counselee with the truth that even though he may be walking through the valley of the shadow of death, he does not need to fear evil, for God is with him. First Peter 4:19 reminds us, "Let those also who suffer according to the will of God entrust their souls to a faithful Creator in doing what is right."

The biblical counselor embraces a high view of God and His Word. He recognizes that man is a sinner, but he equally recognizes the glorious truth that man can be remade into the likeness of Christ. He is willing to involve himself in another's struggle with sin and believes that God has graciously provided all the tools necessary for this transformation. And finally, he recognizes that although he is involved in this process, he is not ultimately responsible for its success or failure. He knows that when change occurs, it is because of the Lord's work, and that the glory belongs to Him alone. The biblical counselor echoes the thought of the psalmist, "Not to us, O LORD, not to us, but to Thy name give glory because of Thy lovingkindness, because of Thy truth" (Psalm 115:1).

It is with these principles in mind that *Women Helping Women* was written. Our hope is that as you make use of this book, you will find that indeed, God's Word *can* change lives. In addition, we'd like to recommend resources you may want to peruse. Listed below are some excellent materials that will further help you. You'll also find listed some training opportunities that can help you to increase your effectiveness in helping others.

Recommended Resources

Jay Adams, *Competent to Counsel,* Grand Rapids: Zondervan, 1970.

Jay Adams, *The Christian Counselor's Manual,* Grand Rapids: Zondervan, 1973.

Jay Adams, *Ready to Restore: The Layman's Guide to Christian Counseling,* Phillipsburg, NJ: Presbyterian and Reformed, 1981.

John Broger, *The Self-Confrontation Manual: A Manual for In-Depth Discipleship,* Rancho Mirage, CA: Biblical Counseling Foundation, 1991.

Elyse Fitzpatrick, *Helper by Design,* Chicago, IL: Moody Publishers, 2003.

Elyse Fitzpatrick, *Love to Eat, Hate to Eat,* Eugene, OR: Harvest House Publishers, 1999.

Elyse Fitzpatrick, *Overcoming Fear, Worry, and Anxiety,* Eugene, OR: Harvest House Publishers, 2001.

John Kruis, *Quick Scripture Reference for Counseling,* Grand Rapids: Baker, 1988.

John MacArthur, Jr., *Our Sufficiency in Christ,* Dallas: Word, 1991.

John MacArthur, Jr., and Wayne Mack, *Introduction to Biblical Counseling,* Dallas: Word, 1994.

Wayne Mack, *Homework Manual for Biblical Living Volume I* and *Homework Manual for Biblical Living Volume II,* Phillipsburg, PA: Presbyterian and Reformed, 1980.

David Powlison, *Seeing with New Eyes,* Phillipsburg, NJ: P&R Publishing, 2003.

Lou Priolo, *The Complete Husband,* Amityville, NY: Calvary Press Publishing, 1999.

Paul David Tripp, *Instruments in the Redeemer's Hands: People in Need of Change Helping People in Need of Change,* Phillipsburg, NJ: P&R Publishing, 2002.

Edward T. Welch, *When People Are Big and God Is Small: Overcoming Peer Pressure, Co-dependency and the Fear of Man,* Phillipsburg, NJ: P&R Publishing, 1997.

Audio and Video Resources for Biblical Counselors

Five Star Conference Recording : 1-800-350-TAPE

Sound Word Cassettes, P.O. Box 2035, Mail Station, Michigan City, IN 46360

Training Opportunities

By furnishing this list the authors of *Women Helping Women* are not ensuring that everything taught in each of these institutions is consistently biblical. It would be wise to speak personally with the academic deans of each of these organizations before deciding to attend.

The Institute for Biblical Counseling & Discipleship (619) 462-9775 (www.ibcd.org)
  5333 Lake Murray Blvd., La Mesa, CA 91942—On-site as well as audio/video training available.
  (formerly known as The Christian Counseling and Educational Foundation West)

The Christian Counseling and Educational Foundation East (215) 884 7676
  1803 E. Willow Grove Avenue, Laverock, PA 19118

The Master's College and Seminary (805) 259-3540/(818)909-5627
  P.O. Box 221450 Santa Clarita, CA 91322

National Association of Nouthetic Counselors (317) 337-9100
  3600 W. 96th Street, Indianapolis, IN 46268-2905, info@nanc.org

Trinity Theological Seminary (800) 457-5510
  P.O. Box 717, Newburgh, IN 47629-0717

Westminster Theological Seminary (215) 887-5511
  P.O. Box 27009, Philadelphia, PA 19118

Westminster Theological Seminary (619) 480-8474
  1725 Bear Valley Parkway, Escondido, CA 92027

CHAPTER 3

The Essential Foundation: A Biblical View of Women

Carol W. Cornish, M.A.

You are probably familiar with these words from the Gospel of Matthew:

> *Everyone who hears these words of mine and puts them into practice is like a wise man who built his house on the rock. The rain came down, the streams rose, and the winds blew and beat against that house; yet it did not fall, because it had its foundation on the rock (Matthew 7:24-25 NIV).*

Some of us learned these words in Sunday school when we sang the song based on these verses. In this passage, Jesus taught that wise people build their lives on the foundational truths of God's Word, and foolish people build their lives on the sand of something other than the Word.

What have you built your life on? If you learned that song as a child, how do the words ring in your ears now? Have you built your life on that Rock? Or have you somehow found yourself living on shifting sand? I have had the delightful privilege of teaching many women how to build their lives on the Rock by thinking biblically about God, what He is doing in the world, who they are in relation to God, and where they fit in His grand plan. This chapter is designed to help you understand these things so that you will be thrilled with the person of God and strengthened to be His loving and faithful servant—to His glory and for your good. Let's begin with the story of Ted and Terri so that you can get a sense of what this knowledge can produce.

The Prevailing Confusion

A number of years ago, a pastor and I were team counseling a couple whom I'll call Ted and Terri. One day between sessions Ted called me because he couldn't reach his pastor. They were a young couple with four daughters, and Ted had expressed to us that he felt overwhelmed about shouldering the responsibility of leading and providing for his family. During the phone call, Ted sounded quite exasperated. He said, "I think it would be unwise for my wife and me to add another child to our family. Our resources—both financially and emotionally— are already stretched. Terri completely disagrees with me. She says she won't know what to do with herself this fall when our youngest daughter goes to nursery school. I'm beginning to think that Terri wants another baby just so she won't have to make the adjustment. She wants to continue to be the mother of an infant." Then with a weak laugh he added, "We can't do this forever."

As we met with Ted and Terri over the next few months, it became obvious that Terri identified herself almost exclusively with the role of mothering an infant. She had no idea how to think biblically about herself. She didn't realize that she needed to learn how to properly distinguish who she is from what she does. While it is certainly true that she is a mother and that being a mother is a wonderful blessing, motherhood is not her only—nor her foundational— identity.

It is essential for women to understand from the Scriptures who they are and what they are to do. Women, as well as men, need to understand what God is doing in the world and where they fit into His purposes. If you neglect these foundational issues in your discipleship and counseling, you may end up merely giving a woman the solution to *a* problem rather than a framework for thinking through *all* problems. As counselors, we need to help our counselees develop a biblical worldview. A worldview consists of assumptions that a person makes about what she sees and how she makes decisions. A biblical worldview equips a woman to see all of life (including herself) from God's viewpoint.

Many women are confused about the foundational issues of identity and role. Is it any wonder this confusion is present when such a wide range of ideas about these issues exists even within the church? Venture into your local Christian bookstore and go to the section called "Women" or "Women's Resourses." There you will find a potpourri of ideas and beliefs that can rival the countless variety of scents at the candle shop just down the street.

How important is it for you, as a discipler and counselor of women, to try to sort out what you believe about women in relation to God? Do you need to become an expert in theology? After all, even the "experts" differ widely in their views about a theology of women. While you need not be an expert on this subject, you do need a sound theological understanding of who women are and God's design for them in life. As you wrestle with specific manifestations of the problems that women face, you will need to possess a clear and accurate understanding of a woman's identity and role.

Understanding the Counselor's Role

Let me say a brief word at this point about whether there is a difference between discipling a woman and counseling her. *Discipleship* is a process in which you, as a mature disciple of the Lord Jesus Christ, teach another woman how to grow in her relationship with Christ so that she is obedient, faithful, and pleasing to Him. This process may or may not involve addressing specific problems in her life that do not seem to yield to the typical discipling process. When discipleship *does* involve addressing these difficult problem areas, its emphasis shifts to exhortation, or what we commonly call it: counseling. Thus, you can see that a definite line does not exist between discipling and counseling. Counseling should always be done in the context of a discipling relationship since the Bible does not separate them but rather assumes that exhortation and encouragement will be part of helping someone to grow in Christlikeness.

The various Bible translations use different but similar words to describe this process. For example, the NASB typically uses the word "exhort" while the NIV uses such words as "encourage," "appeal," or "urge." All these words communicate the idea of coming alongside someone to help him or her walk in faithfulness (especially when sinful habit patterns persist in preventing growth).

All Christians have the responsibility to exhort and encourage others. But some Christians are specifically gifted by the Holy Spirit (Roman 12:8) for a ministry of counseling within the local body of believers. These gifted men and women need to use their gift and gain experience in helping others so that they can offer wise, loving counsel to those who need their ministry.

Developing a God-Centered Perspective

Our understanding of ourselves must flow from God to us. The importance of a God-centered perspective is emphasized by Sinclair Ferguson: "Almost every problem or failure in the Christian life is in some way rooted in the fact that we do not understand or we forget who God is and who we are."[1] These are identity issues. When I say *identity*, I am referring to the real you—who you are in your essence (that is, your essential nature). When I ask a woman the question "Who are you?" the answer I typically receive is something like this: "I am a mother (or teacher, or secretary, or business executive)." But those words describe a role, not an identity. If you are suddenly injured or otherwise incapable of fulfilling your main role in life, then, do you lose your identity? Suppose you go into a coma. Who are you then?

You must understand who you are in your essential nature as a person. You need to know who you are as God describes you in His Word. That's important because we live our lives in God's presence; as Christians, we live in personal relationship to Him. Because He is God and we are His creatures, we are accountable to Him for how we live our lives.

You will not be able to help women much if you do not understand who God is and who you are. You may be thinking to yourself, *But I'm a Christian. I already know who God is.* Martyn Lloyd-Jones made this observation:

> We all start by assuming that our knowledge of God is all right, and if some-one tells us that that is the first problem, we feel it is almost being insulting. This is surely the central cause of so many of our subsequent difficulties, namely that we assume we know God, that we assume that this great knowl-edge is something at which we start. . . But my whole suggestion is that it is just there that we fail—and fail completely.[2]

Notice he said that making an assumption that we know God adequately is the *central* cause of many of our difficulties. You will be able to lead others toward increasing intimacy with God only as far as you yourself know Him. Examine your own intimacy with God before attempting to encourage another sister in Christ to a deeper, more intimate relationship with Him. Is God some vague idea to you, or do you relate to Him intimately as a child with a beloved Father? While we do not want to make a "buddy" out of God, still, God desires close fellowship with His people.

Every area of your life is affected by what you believe or don't believe about the person and work of God. "The only accurate way to understand ourselves is by what God is and by what He does for us, not by what we are and what we do for him."[3] And since God is our Creator, He is the only one who can accurately tell us who He is and who we are. Let's focus on specific portions of the Bible now so we can learn these essential truths.

The Essential Issues

Understanding Who God Is

By observing the created world, we can learn some things about God. This is what theologians call *general revelation*. While we can know some things about God from His creation, (*see* Psalm 19), the Bible is God's *special revelation* of Himself. Through the Holy Spirit, God speaks to us in His Word. The Bible tells us who God is and what He does. It tells us as much about God as God wants us to know at this time, and it's important for us to study God's Word so we can get to know Him better. Because God has revealed Himself primarily through His Word, the Bible is our best source of knowledge about God.

Some Christians object to thoroughly studying the Scriptures to get to know God. I've heard people say, "Theology (the study of God) is boring, academic stuff that has little to do with real life. I'd rather just experience God in my own way." But if we depend on our own experiences to "teach us" about God and neglect His Word, we are likely to shape our understanding of God in a way that suits our desires. The shape God takes in our minds will be marred by our imperfect or even sinful interpretations of who we think He is. We need to understand God as He reveals Himself in His Word—not as we perceive Him to be revealed in our subjective experiences.

Knowing God Through Scripture A great way to better understand God, ourselves, and others is through Paul's letter to the Ephesians. Our logical starting point is Ephesians chapter 1, where God reveals some truths about His nature. There, we learn that God is a triune being—He is three persons in one being: Father, Son, and Holy Spirit (the Trinity).

> *These are not three persons in the ordinary sense of the word; but rather three modes or forms in which the Divine Being exists. At the same time they are of such a nature that they can enter into personal relations.*[4]

All three persons of the Trinity are equal in their essence. This means that in their essential nature they are all the same. However, in terms of their function, some of the works of the triune God can be attributed more to one or another of the three persons.

> *God is triune; there are within the Godhead three persons, the Father, Son, and the Holy Spirit; and the work of salvation is one in which all three act*

together, the Father purposing redemption, the Son securing it, and the Spirit applying it.[5]

Theologians refer to these differences in function as a type of subordination. What is subordination? It is the willing placement of oneself under the authority or direction of another. With reference to God we know that Jesus Christ, the Son of God, willingly submits to the Father, and the Holy Spirit willingly submits to the Father and the Son. The Son of God does the will of God the Father, and the Holy Spirit does the will of the Father and the Son.

We also learn from Ephesians 1 that God is . . .

- a giver of grace (verse 2)
- the source of peace (verse 2)
- a source of blessing (verse 3)
- working out His plan (verse 4)
- loving (verse 4)
- an adoptor of children (verse 5)
- kind (verse 5)
- generous (verse 6)
- full of grace (verse 6)
- forgiving (verse 7)
- wise (verse 8)
- full of insight (verse 8)
- understanding (verse 8)
- purposeful (verse 9)
- a provider of knowledge (verse 9)
- sovereign (verse 11)
- provider of our inheritance (verse 11)
- worthy of praise (verse 14)
- giver of wisdom (verse 17)
- full of riches (verse 18)
- powerful (verse 19)
- omnipresent, or everywhere at once (verse 23)

You could continue this list by going through the rest of Ephesians to learn more about who God is. Do you understand and believe that God is like this? Unless you believe that God is who He says He is in His Word, you will have distorted thoughts about Him. Read, study, and meditate on portions of Scripture such as Isaiah 40, John 14, Colossians 1, Hebrews 1, and observe their detailed descriptions of who God is. Note carefully what these passages say about the nature of God.

Wrong thinking about God will both dishonor God and cause you to have a faulty understanding of who you are. For example, if you do not think that God is a faithful heavenly Father, you may conclude that you have no one to depend on but yourself. Or, you may develop idolatrous dependencies on other people.[6] To have a warm and vibrant relationship with God, you must know Him as He is. As you grow in true understanding of who God is, you will be able to gain a truer understanding of yourself as His child because He is your heavenly Father. (A child of God is one who has been chosen by God and who has surrendered her life to God's Son Jesus Christ as Savior and Lord. If you have done this, you are part of God's family!)

Hindrances to Knowing God   Are you politely bored by the subject of knowing God? When you read the statement that you are part of God's family, was yours a ho-hum response? Sinclair Ferguson says that,

> *Knowing God is your single greatest privilege as a Christian, and the one that sensitizes you to every other issue of importance. But is this the issue that lies at the center of your thinking? (emphasis in original).*[7]

I have had a number of counselees say to me, "I can't see God, so it's hard for me to believe He's real. And I can't touch Him. If only God could give me a hug." These statements are given as "reasons" for not seeking God. We want it easy. Reading, studying, and meditating on Scripture gets pushed aside because these activities require the work of concentrating and thinking. Now, it is true that to do these things for the sake of simply doing them is merely mechanistic. But when done in a spirit of quiet contemplation before the living God, these disciplines lead us into intimate fellowship with the one who loves and cares for us.

It's easy for us to let the demands and attractions of contemporary culture draw our attention away from these Christian disciplines. However, it is irrational not to seek the knowledge and intimate company of God. A.W. Tozer has called the Lord Jesus "utterly and completely delightful . . . the most winsome of all beings."[8] If you really believe that Jesus is completely delightful, will you not continually seek His company?

A reluctance to vigorously seek God is a common sin.[9] Sometimes people think that if they get to know God intimately He will ask things of them that they don't want to do or are afraid of doing. You know the fear—if I get close to

God, He may tell me to go be a missionary in Africa, or give up my boy-friend, or. . . . There are many reasons people give for why they are reluctant to seek God.

Disobedience, in general, creates a huge barrier in getting to know God. God tells us in His Word that He reveals Himself to those who are obedient to Him: "Whoever has My commandments and keeps them is the one who loves Me; and My Father will love the one who loves Me, and I will love him and reveal Myself to him" (John 14:21 *Christian Counselor's New Testament*[10]).

Our disobedience, then, hinders our ability to "see" God. Matthew 5:8 says it is the pure in heart who see God. It is vital that we understand repentance (that is, a sorrowful turning away from our sin because we know it offends God and grieves His heart) and how necessary it is to be cleansed of our sins by God so that we may see Him more clearly.

Other reasons why we don't seek God may include unbelief, ignorance, fears, distrust of God's goodness, selfishness, laziness, lack of interest, rebellion, unfaithfulness, suspicion of God, playing God by trying to be in control of our life, projecting negative experiences with an earthly father onto God, and following false gods.

The Blessings of Knowing God   We must be persistent in seeking to know God better:

> *Our creaturely limitations prevent us from knowing God fully, but they do not prevent an intimacy with our heavenly Father. While God through his Spirit draws us into a deeper relationship, we must also acknowledge our responsibility in knowing him. There is a necessary resolve of the will, a setting of the mind and heart, and an expectant attitude that we must cultivate. Pray today that you would have a great desire for God and his Word.*[11]

If you really love someone, if you really delight in that person, you will eagerly seek him or her out. The same is true of the person of God. If you really love Him and delight in Him, you will be an eager seeker of Him. "You will seek Me and find Me, when you search for Me with all your heart" (Jeremiah 29:13).

What are some of the blessings that come from seeking God?

- a right focus of the mind—on God, who is perfect
- a heart filled with joy and gladness
- greater desire to obey God
- deeper devotion to God

- increased resistance to temptation
- contentment
- spiritual strength
- greater spiritual understanding
- greater ability to see God at work
- greater concern for others
- ability to know what's really important in life
- diminished self-interest
- longing for heaven
- greater perspective in suffering

Rich fellowship with God is what you were designed for by God. He doesn't have favorites. You are as close to God as you want to be. "O God, Thou art my God; I shall seek Thee earnestly" (Psalm 63:1).

Understanding Who Women Are

The Big Picture   In the account of the creation of the world in Genesis chapters 1–2, we read that man and woman were created by God in His image. Genesis 1:31 tells us that at the end of the sixth day, "God saw all that He had made, and behold, it was very good. And there was evening and there was morning, the sixth day."

Men and women reason, create, use language, sense moral distinctions, make moral choices, exhibit religious capacity, and so on. All of these actions reflect God. Human beings carry out the actions and activities that are characteristic of personhood. All people, male and female, reveal God's image in a variety of ways.[12]

GOD'S WORD ABOUT WOMEN   A moment ago we explored what Paul said about God in his letter to the Ephesians; let's look at this letter in a similar manner to see what it says about who women are. Here's a sampling—you as a Christian woman are:

- blessed with every spiritual blessing in Christ	1:3
- chosen by God before the foundation of the world	1:4
- an adopted son (child) of God	1:5
- redeemed through the blood of Christ	1:7
- forgiven of your trespasses	1:7
- full of the riches of God's grace, which He lavished on you	1:8

- God's heir   1:11
- sealed in Him with the Holy Spirit   1:13

We could go on and study the rest of Ephesians and other portions of Scripture, but we don't have space for it here. Yet I hope this sample list encourages you to take a closer look at what Scripture says about you so that the thoughts you have about yourself will be based on God's Word. What marvelous, undeserved blessings God has bestowed on us! Think about these things. Have you taken time to meditate on them, to memorize them? Remember what Sinclair Ferguson said about our problem being that we forget who we are? He's right, isn't he? We do forget. And, we allow ourselves to get easily discouraged by earthly things. We let our circumstances pull our focus away from heavenly things such as these wonderful truths.

If we aren't thinking about ourselves according to the truths of God's Word, then we need to put off our old thinking and put on this new understanding about our identity. This requires a renewed mind. (See chapter 2, pages 47–56 for guidelines on renewing the mind.)

THE HISTORY OF REDEMPTION AND YOU   God chose you, Ephesians 1 says, before the creation of the world. God had you in mind way back then. He placed you in this world according to His purposes at His appointed time. All through history God has been working out His grand redemptive plan, and you are part of it. This is called the history of redemption.

| Creation of the World | Old Testament Saints | New Testament Saints | The Rest of the Saints Since About A.D. 100 | Present-Day Saints |

Do you see yourself in this grand sweep of history? You are part of the history of redemption! You are a present-day saint (the biblical definition of a saint is a genuine believer in Jesus Christ). God is doing something grand in the world. He is creating a kingdom of children to His praise and glory, and you are part of that!

If you haven't cultivated the habit of remembering what the Bible says about you as God's child, you will want to begin doing so. You are part of God's history of redemption; you are in the family of God. This is what is real about *you*. The little bit of personal history you have experienced is nothing compared to what God is accomplishing in His eternal plan. You'll find it extremely helpful to understand yourself from an eternal perspective so that the events of everyday life are not experienced out of proportion to their actual significance.

GOING FROM THE OUTSIDE IN   All people live in the presence of God whether they believe in Him or not. Hebrews 4:13 says, "Nothing in all creation is hidden from God's sight. Everything is uncovered and laid bare before the eyes of him to whom we must give account" (NIV). To try to separate man from God in order to understand him is like taking a fish out of water—he is no longer in his element. God made people to live in fellowship with Him, but our sin separates us from Him unless we are made new creatures in Christ (*see* 2 Corinthians 5:17).

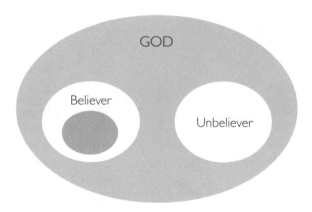

All persons, whether believers or unbelievers, live in the presence of the triune God, who is represented here as the large dark oval. The two smaller ovals represent, on the left, a believer, and on the right, an unbeliever. Notice that the believer is also indwelt by God the Spirit. There is no such thing as a "self" that can exist independent of God.

God is omnipresent; He is everywhere at once. God is our environment in the sense that He is not far from us and, in fact, all people live and move and exist in Him.[13] For Christians the news is even better: Not only is God all around us, He is also within us. John 14:17 says that "you know Him [the Holy Spirit] because He abides with you, and will be in you." Christians are indwelt by the Holy Spirit.

Do you think about yourself and your world in this way? God is both outside and inside of you. You are not alone; you will never be abandoned. God is a loving heavenly Father who is always with you.

A Closer Look

YOU ARE GOD'S CHILD   Most women whom I have counseled have built their self-concept based upon the model on the left side of the following illustration:

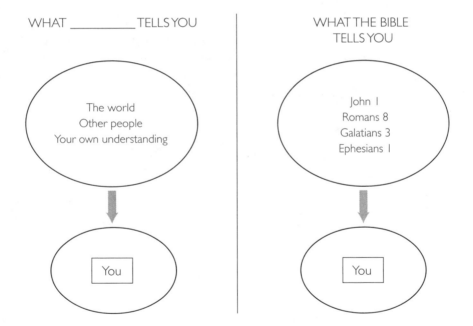

WHAT _____ TELLS YOU

The world
Other people
Your own understanding

You

WHAT THE BIBLE
TELLS YOU

John 1
Romans 8
Galatians 3
Ephesians 1

You

Women who use the model at the left allow their knowledge of themselves to be shaped by the opinions of others, which may come from family, friends, acquaintances, books, magazines, or TV shows. Or, they'll let today's cultural views or their personal perspectives shape their self-concept.

For example, Ann's co-worker, Nancy, criticized Ann's work behind her back. Ann heard the remark from someone else, and spent the next few weeks being miserable and thinking hateful thoughts about Nancy. She complained in a counseling session that she can never do enough to "make Nancy like me." Ann called herself a failure for not doing her work well enough to please Nancy. As a result she became depressed and considered changing jobs despite good reviews from her boss. When Ann sought counsel, we knew we needed to explore why Nancy's opinion was so important to Ann. There were many questions to explore, but the basic question involved Ann's understanding of herself as a person. Who did she understand herself to be? To whom was she accountable? In the course of several counseling sessions we discovered that Ann tried to please just about everybody because she thought she needed the approval of everyone around her. Even though Nancy was the office gossip and frequently tore down many other people, Ann still hoped that Nancy would speak highly of her.

Although it is true that Christians should desire a good reputation, Ann's desire for Nancy's approval was extreme. Ann was a lot less troubled by her hateful thoughts about Nancy than she was by her continued attempts to gain Nancy's approval. So Ann ended up sinning against God and Nancy by hating her (in her heart), while, at the same time, she did what she could to win Nancy's approval. Ann needed to build her self-concept using the model on the right-hand side of the illustration on page 70)—a self-concept that would be based on God's perfect truth!

We frequently need to remind ourselves that God made us and sustains us.[14] We live each moment of our lives in His presence. In terms of our understanding of who we are, it does not matter if we do not feel like the person that the Bible describes us to be. Feelings are an unreliable source of information. They can easily change depending on the many influences around us. We need to believe, appreciate, and live by our identity as God's child. When we do so, we glorify God because we are then freed to serve others rather than trying to manipulate them for our own purposes. Ann tried to get Nancy to like her so that Ann could "feel good about myself." But Ann needed to love and serve Nancy by lovingly confronting the gossip and assuring Nancy of her desire to work peacefully and helpfully with Nancy.

When Ann finally did this, Nancy was, at first, furious with her. Ann was scared by Nancy's response, but she persevered in serving Nancy in little ways that showed loving concern. Eventually, they were able to work well together, although Ann did have to confront Nancy's gossiping again. But this time, Ann's motivation was to demonstrate the love of Christ to Nancy—not to manipulate Nancy to like her. Ann could do this because she now understood who she was and she had developed a deep love for God and a desire to serve Him.

Identity Issues   As our culture shouts loud messages to us about who we're supposed to be and what we're supposed to do to be fulfilled, growing numbers of Christians are becoming confused about their identity and purpose. This confusion can be cleared up completely by learning how to think biblically about ourselves. Our self-concept must be in accordance with the teaching of Scripture to be correct. If it is not in accord with Scripture, we will come to wrong conclusions about ourselves. These wrong conclusions usually grow out of *our responses* to our life experiences. Anxiety, depression, hopelessness, compulsions, and other destructive attitudes and behaviors are often caused or influenced by thinking and believing wrong things about God and about ourselves.

Some Christians seem to have lost the ability to be discerning when they hear all sorts of psychological notions that masquerade as spiritual truth. In contrast, Acts 17:11 tells us, "Now the Bereans were of more noble character than the Thessalonians, for they received the message with great eagerness and examined the Scriptures every day to see if what Paul said was true." (See chapter 1, pages 16-18, 23-27 for more discussion on this topic.)

It is not unusual for the people whom I counsel to tell me that they suffer from low self-esteem. No counselee, however, has ever told me that she suffers from low *Christ*-esteem. That reveals for us the root of the problem: When we inadequately exalt God and instead exalt ourselves openly or subtly, aware or unaware, then we make ouselves vulnerable to wrong perceptions about ourselves.

You Are Complete in Christ   According to Scripture, if you are a Christian, you are in Christ and Christ is in you.[15] You are complete in Christ "and in Him you have been made complete" (Colossians 2:10). Nothing is missing. You are in union spiritually with the Lord Jesus Christ. Are you cultivating an awareness of this by filling your mind with the Word of God so that the Holy Spirit can use the Word to make you conscious of the Lord's presence in your life? Have you learned to be content with what you have and with who you are in Christ? You don't need to pump up your self-esteem if you are a Christian. You have a rich inheritance because of who you are in Christ. Don't let past hurts and disappointments make you think otherwise. Move beyond them and free your-self to serve others out of your fullness in Christ.

YOU ARE GOD'S SERVANT   Let's consider next what Christian women are called to do with their lives. In Ephesians 2:10, the apostle Paul states a key principle for all believers: "We are God's workmanship, created in Christ Jesus to do good works, which God prepared in advance for us to do" (NIV). We are to do good works. What does that mean? God has gifted each Christian—including women—through the Holy Spirit with spiritual gifts that fit them for specific ministry within the Body of Christ. God has prepared, in advance, for us to do good works that serve as evidence of our salvation. These good works are the fruit of the changes He has brought into our lives. Paul was not talking about good works as the means to salvation.

Loving and Serving   Romans 12 and 1 Corinthians 12 have much to say about the various ways that brothers and sisters in Christ can serve one another by means of their gifts through the power of the Holy Spirit.

The best way to determine how you have been gifted by the Holy Spirit is to try various areas of service in your local church. Pray and ask God to reveal to you what your areas of giftedness are. Ask for feedback from your fellow workers, and ask youself where your interests are. You will most likely find one or two areas in which your service bears the most prolific fruit. These will usually be the areas in which you most enjoy serving. Once you've determined where you can serve best, then get involved and serve with all your heart to the glory of God.

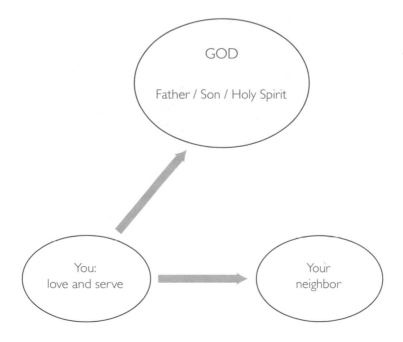

In addition to loving and serving God, we have been called to love and serve our neighbor. When these are the focal points of our life, then we take our attention off of self and free ourselves to serve in a way that glorifies God.

The Value of a Personal Mission Statement   You may want to develop a personal mission statement. A mission statement enables you to think clearly and set priorities so that you can more faithfully serve Christ. It will also help you to define the tasks and determine the areas of service on which God wants you to concentrate. A mission statement will assist you in living purposefully, guided by your beliefs rather than your feelings. It can help to keep you focused on the important things in life.

Remember the story of Martha and Mary in Luke 10:38-42? When Martha busied herself with housework, Jesus didn't say that she had done something wrong. He simply said that Mary had chosen what was better. We may consider many things important, but we must not let them keep us from pursuing rich fellowship with the Lord Jesus. Mary knew what was most important at the time; she chose to sit at Jesus' feet and listen to what He had to say because that was the best choice for that moment.

The Power Available to a Servant   You cannot serve God in your own strength; perhaps you have already found this out by experience. Thinking biblically about God and yourself and serving God and others comes about through the ministry and power of the Holy Spirit. In Ephesians 3:14-21, Paul offered this prayer for the believers at Ephesus:

> *I bow my knees before the Father, from whom every family in heaven and on earth derives its name, that He would grant you, according to the riches of His glory, to be strengthened with* power *through His Spirit in the inner man; so that Christ may dwell in your hearts through faith; and that you, being rooted and grounded in love, may be able to comprehend with all the saints what is the breadth and length and height and depth, and to know the love of Christ which surpasses knowledge, that you may be filled up to all the fulness of God. Now to Him who is able to do exceeding abundantly beyond all that we ask or think, according to the* power *that works within us, to Him be the glory in the church and in Christ Jesus to all generations forever and ever. Amen (emphasis added).*

The power and the strength you need to serve God and your neighbors comes from the Holy Spirit. It is available to you. But what will make you want to serve God and others?

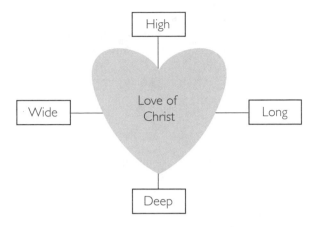

The premier motivator for the Christian is to grasp the magnitude of the love Christ has for him and for all who are His.[16] D. Martyn Lloyd-Jones wisely said:

> *The man who knows the love of Christ in his heart can do more in one hour than the busy type of man can do in a century. God forbid that we should ever make of activity an end in itself. Let us realize that the motive must come first, and that the motive must ever be the love of Christ.*[17]

The more we get to know God intimately, the more we will want to tap into His power and strength to serve Him and others.

We often fail to train ourselves to look for God approaching us in love.[18] An exercise that I frequently assign to my counselees is to keep a list of the ways they see God doing this. It is important to let the everyday, ordinary things of life remind us of God. Even our morning routine can be used this way. For instance, showering can remind us that God has cleansed us from all sin in Christ. Dressing can remind us that God has clothed us with the righteousness of Christ. There are many creative ways that we can see God approaching us in love!

We are enabled to do what God has called us to do because God gives us His power to do it. Feeling powerless should not deter us from the tasks God has given us to do. Human weakness provides the ideal opportunity for the display of divine power. We are dependent creatures—totally dependent on God, and God intended that by design. "The Son appears in the Gospels not as an independent divine person, but as a dependent one, who thinks and acts only and wholly as the Father directs."[19] Likewise, we can do nothing of any worth to God apart from Christ: "I am the vine, you are the branches; he who abides in

Me, and I in him, he bears much fruit; for apart from Me you can do nothing" (John 15:5). Apart from Him, we can produce nothing but plastic fruit.

The Mind of a Servant   If your mind is cluttered and preoccupied with all sorts of worldly concerns, you will likely be easily fatigued. No real and lasting joy is found in the things of the world because they are passing away and God did not design you to live for them. In contrast, setting your mind on God in heartfelt praise and adoration will help energize you. Recall that Nehemiah said to the grieving people around him, "The joy of the LORD is your strength" (8:10). If you have learned from the Scriptures to have a biblical self-concept, you will think biblically about yourself. You will then be enabled by the Holy Spirit to live more and more with your eyes on God and to overcome your circumstances to the glory of God.

Choosing Where to Set Your Mind   We get ourselves into trouble when we set our sights on what is happening around us rather than on the person of God. The Bible instructs us about the use of our minds: "Set your mind on the things above, not on the things that are on earth. For you have died and your life is hidden with Christ in God" (Colossians 3:2).

The Bible says we are responsible for what and how we think.[20] Therefore, if we spend our days worrying and fretting about life, we are in violation of God's Word. When we feel trapped by our circumstances, we need to readjust our thinking by the power of the Holy Spirit. We are "to put off your old self, which is being corrupted by its deceitful desires; to be made new in the attitude of your

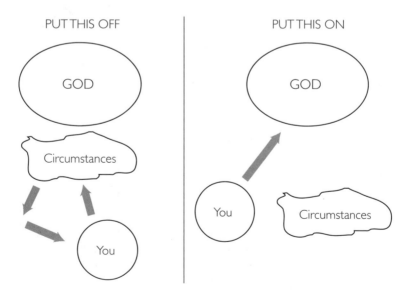

minds; and to put on the new self, created to be like God in true righteousness and holiness" (Ephesians 4:22-24 NIV).

When we allow ourselves to become preoccupied with our circumstances, they will obscure our view of God. Martyn Lloyd-Jones said this about the peace of God:

> *The final triumph of the gospel is seen in this, that whatever our circum-stances, we ourselves can be put right and maintained. . . . Paul does not say that the thing feared is not going to take place, he says that we shall be kept whether it happens or whether it does not happen. Thank God, that is the victory. I am taken above circumstances, I am triumphant in spite of them. . . . We all tend to be tyrannized by circumstances because we depend upon them, and we would like them to be governed and controlled, but that is not the way in which the Scripture deals with the situation.*[21]

We as Christians have the Holy Spirit living within us. Thus, we have the power to choose what we think about no matter what our circumstances. We may have to struggle to change our old thinking habits, but they can be changed. Paul spoke about such change to the Philippians and began by saying, "Rejoice in the Lord always; again I will say, rejoice! (4:4). Notice that he didn't merely say they were to rejoice; he said they were to rejoice *in the Lord.* Then in verse 8 he said they were to think upon whatever is true, honorable, right, pure, lovely, excellent, and praiseworthy, and that they were to let their minds "dwell on these things" (4:8). If we do not train ourselves by God's power to think upon these things, then our minds will naturally drift to the wrong things.[22]

Keeping a Thought Journal   What preoccupies your mind day in and day out? Do you know? Are your thoughts usually God-centered or self-centered? Many of us walk around all day unaware of what is going through our minds for the most part. How can you know what you think about all day long? One way to find out is to keep a thought journal. Divide each page into five parts: 1) waking, 2) morning, 3) afternoon, 4) evening, and 5) bedtime. Keep a pencil or pen with your journal. In the morning, record what you were thinking about as you woke up and began your morning routine. At noon, record what occupied your thoughts all morning. Continue recording your thoughts in the afternoon and evening. Finally, record what is on your mind just before you go to bed. If for some reason you miss recording a block of time, fill it in later the best you can.

Your journal will be most helpful if you do the recording at or soon after the period of time you're reflecting on. Keep journaling for a minimum of two weeks. At the end of this time, go back and look at what you've written. If you've been honest, your journal will reveal the things that preoccupy your mind. I have done this with many of my counselees with great success. They have been surprised at how much of their thought life was spent on earthly rather than heavenly things.

You may be thinking to yourself, *This will make me so heavenly minded that I won't be any earthly good.* But God won't be glorified if you are so earthly minded that you aren't any heavenly good. Besides, being heavenly minded in the *true* biblical sense will make you better able to do the ordinary things of life. Jesus said in John 8:29, "He who sent Me is with Me; He has not left Me alone, for I always do the things that are pleasing to Him." That is true heavenly mindedness: doing God's will in God's strength to God's glory totally dependent upon Him moment by moment.

Have you taken seriously the commands in Scripture to "set your mind on the things above, not on the things that are on earth"? Are you willing to trust God no matter what your circumstances? You may not know what is going to happen, but you can know the God who is absolutely sovereign (in control) over all things and who always works for your good (as defined by Him).

The Servant's Relationships and Roles   It is not my intent in this chapter to present lengthy arguments for or against particular views with respect to the place of women in the church and the home. There are several very good resources which can help provide a clear understanding on these issues, and they are listed at the end of this chapter.[23] For now I'd like to focus on some specific truths women can know with certainty about their roles.

Everyone who has been made a new creature in Christ is called by God to conform to the likeness of Jesus Christ (Romans 8:28-29). Because both males and females are included in this call, the gender of a person is not paramount in fulfilling God's highest calling for His children. When it comes to spiritual maturity or growth, men are not exhorted to be more "masculine," nor are women exhorted to be more "feminine."[24] Every Christian—whether man or woman—has a responsibility to work with the Holy Spirit in being made more and more like Christ.

Subordination in Relationships   The subordination in the Trinity and the relationship of Christ to the church are to be mirrored in human relationships. What is subordination in the Trinity? Earlier we learned that Jesus Christ willingly yields Himself to the Father, and the Holy Spirit willingly submits to the Father and the Son. Jesus, the Son of God, functions according to the direction of God the Father, and the Holy Spirit functions according to the direction of the Father and the Son. As for human relationships today, these patterns are not to be explained away as cultural anachronisms (something meant for another time and place). While men and women are clearly equal in terms of being persons made in the image of God (equal in essence), the Bible also teaches that they are different in function (both in certain areas of the physical and spiritual realms) according to God's design.

In Ephesians 5:15–6:9, we find some specifics about God's established order for relationships. Verse 21 gives us the general principle that we are to "be subject to one another in the fear of Christ." What follows is a description of how subordination looks in various human relationships: wives to husbands, children to parents, and slaves (employees) to masters (employers).

Equal But Different   In terms of their function in the church and the home, the Bible teaches that men are to *serve* in the church and the home as leaders. Do not think, however, that when Scripture assigns leadership roles to men that it is relegating women to inferior positions. The Lord Jesus certainly would not be considered inferior to God the Father just because He submitted to Him. It is a matter of differing functions: certain roles are carried out by certain individuals in order to accomplish specific goals and plans in an orderly fashion. The fact that women perform different roles than men does not in any way diminish their personhood. God's roles for men and women reflect the function of our trinitarian (three persons in one being) God. They are for our good and the good of God's kingdom. Righteousness and peace result when everyone carries out their assigned roles in a biblical manner.

Let's take a detour for a moment and address an issue that surfaces in the writings of some Christian authors. First Timothy 2 is a chapter that has challenged many Bible scholars over the centuries. It is a difficult task to determine exactly what Paul had in mind and how this particular passage is to be interpreted and applied today. I will not presume to settle the various arguments surrounding these verses. However, one thing is clear. Verse 14, which says, "It was not Adam who was deceived, but the woman being quite deceived, fell into transgression," is *not* teaching that women are more easily deceived than men. If we follow that line of reasoning, then we could just as easily say that because Adam (who was not deceived) knowingly rebelled against God, all men are more rebellious than women. We must keep in mind that Eve's deception was a one-time event that took place in the Garden of Eden. To conclude, then, that women are more easily deceived than man is unwarranted.[25] Nowhere in Scripture do we find that taught.

Even though men have the role as leaders in the church and the home, that does not mean women can not have any kind of influence in the affairs of those places. A wise male leader will take the time to seek the advice and perspective that a godly woman can provide.

In churches today, two extremes usually exist: no role distinctions by gender, or totally gender-segregated leadership. The latter seems to be more prevalent in conservative, evangelical churches. Yet there are no restrictions in the Scriptures that prohibit ruling elders from seeking wisdom from the non-elder members in a congregation. Surely mature, godly women can contribute wisdom to the church leadership in an informal way without holding the office of a governing or teaching elder. And giving a woman an opportunity to share her thoughts does not indicate that male leaders are shirking their responsibilities or giving in to cultural pressure.

For example, let's say a new congregation decides to build a church facility. The church elders agree that a building committee is needed. Do all the members of the committee need to be male? Because the committee members are not ruling nor teaching, they are not functioning as elders, so it would not be necessary for all the members to be men. In fact, it seems that it would be wise to have at least one woman on the committee because typically most church members are female, and their needs could be spoken to well by a woman committee member.

One area in which the Bible does make distinctions about women's roles is in the area of singleness and marriage. There are definite areas of service for both single and married women. Unfortunately, the place God has for single women is frequently ignored in today's church. In chapter 6, we discuss this and other issues of relevance to single women.

Some Thoughts About Women's Ministries　In Scripture, older women are strongly encouraged to disciple the younger women. While our culture may consider older women "over the hill," God considers them to be entering a most vital time of life.

Older (and spiritually mature) women can be used by God to help the younger women in your church and community. (By the way, some chronologically younger women fit the biblical category of "older women" because they possess spiritual maturity.) In churches that have no formal discipleship program, the spiritually mature, older women tend to be overlooked and their precious experience and knowledge lies dormant. They need to be given the opportunity to lead younger women in a discipleship ministry; they can have a significant part in building up the church by serving as "mothers" to the younger women.[26]

The Debate About Women's Roles   One of the most distressing aspects about the controversy over women's roles in the home, church, and society is that it focuses on what women are *not* to do rather than on what they *are* to do. Oftentimes the lines between actual church positions and positions in organizations that are not churches get blurred in such a way that women are denied roles they can rightly fill. Leaders must take care that they are not adding to Scripture by clinging to tradition and keeping women from positions biblically permitted to them.

So what can you do as a Christian woman? Vocationally, the following are all possibilities, and this list is certainly not exhaustive: doctor, lawyer, dentist, nurse, physician's assistant, senator, business executive, custodian, artist, scientific researcher, jet pilot, veterinarian, computer scientist, grocery store clerk, communications engineer, and on and on and on. What about in the church? Here are some non-elder roles women can fill:

- Christian education director
- music director
- director of women's ministries
- director of children's ministries
- youth worker
- counselor to women
- team counselor to women and their families

- computer consultant
- chief financial officer
- kid's clubs coordinator
- choir member
- Bible study leader
- small group coordinator
- missionary
- Sunday school teacher

The Bible clearly tells us that there are certain roles that only men can fill. However, this does not extend into the area of offering counsel to individual women. It is here that men have usurped an important ministry role given to women by God. As we saw in chapter 3 of this book, the biblical pattern is for women to counsel women, and for men to counsel man.

YOU ARE GOD'S SOLDIER   So far we've looked at two major aspects of the life of every Christian—being a child of God and a servant of God. Now we will look at a third aspect described by Paul in his letter to the Ephesians—that of being a soldier in God's kingdom. Because you are a child of God, you are an enemy of Satan. Satan is still waging war against the kingdom of God even though the final outcome has already been determined and Christ is the victor. Paul alerts us to the spiritual battle that is going on behind the scenes in the life of every Christian. In Ephesians 6:10-18, we are reminded that we as Christians are in a war. This is not the time to be sitting idly by, wishing that things could be different. Eternal life starts on earth (*see* John 17:3), but heaven awaits us in the future. Until then, whether or not we are aware of it, we are the targets of the devil's schemes because we are God's children.

Scripture tells us that we who are Christians are not only God's children and His servants, but also His soldiers. Paul said, "Endure hardship with us like a good soldier of Christ Jesus. No one serving as a soldier gets involved in civilian affairs—he wants to please his commanding officer" (2 Timothy 2:3-4 NIV). We are the soldiers, and God is our Commanding Officer.

Put on the Armor of God   "Therefore put on the full armor of God, so that when the day of evil comes, you may be able to stand your ground, and after you have done everything, to stand" (Ephesians 6:13). In the Sermon on the Mount, Jesus taught his disciples to not be anxious about what they would wear (*see* Matthew 6:25-43). A disciple trusts that God will provide what is needed for his physical well-being. But that's not all. God also promised to provide us with what we need for our spiritual well-being. We don't need to get anxious when the battle gets tough. We need to put on the armor of God. (For more details about this armor, you'll want to read the commentaries on Ephesians by John MacArthur, Jr. and D. Martyn Lloyd-Jones. Both are in the recommended resources list at the end of this chapter.)

Be Alert   Usually, assaults from the devil and his cohorts will be subtle. Are you alert? Are you ready?

> *Be self-controlled and alert. Your enemy the devil prowls around like a roaring lion looking for someone to devour. Resist him, standing firm in the faith, because you know that your brothers throughout the world are undergoing the same kind of sufferings (1 Peter 5:8-9 NIV).*

Do you take up the armor of God, resist evil, and stand firm? You can by God's grace. He has given you all you need to be able to stand against the wiles of the devil. Look to your Commanding Officer to guide you and give you strength!

The Benefits of a God-Centered Perspective

When you look in the mirror, whom do you see? Do you know that person looking back at you? Or are you like the person described in James 1:24 who goes away and forgets "what kind of person he was"? Don't forget who you are.

You are God's child, God's servant, and God's soldier. God created you uniquely as a woman. Remind yourself that this is the truth of who you are because of who your heavenly Father is.

At the end of the Sermon on the Mount, Jesus used an analogy to help His hearers grasp the importance of putting His words into practice. He said there are wise builders and there are foolish builders. Will you—and the women you help—build your understanding of who you are and what you are to do based on the sand of mere cultural thinking, or on the rock of solid biblical thinking? Only when you put your understanding of God and yourself into practice will you know true blessedness as a woman. Our hope is that you'll build your foundational thinking on the rock of biblical truth.

I waited patiently for the Lord; he turned to me and heard my cry. He lifted me out of the slimy pit, out of the mud and mire; he set my feet on a rock and gave me a firm place to stand (Psalm 40:1-2 NIV).

Recommended Resources

Books on women's roles

Susan Foh, *Women and the Word of God*, Phillipsburg, NJ: Presbyterian and Reformed, 1979.

James Hurley, *Man and Woman in Biblical Perspective*, Grand Rapids, MI: Zondervan, 1981.

Tapes

Mark Futato, Ph.D., "Feminism's Influence in the Church: In the Beginning Male and Female," parts 1 and 2, available from Five Star Conference Recording and Duplicating, P. O. Box 1261, Carlsbad, CA 92008, or 1-800-350-TAPE, # 615-OA.

Other Books

Jay E. Adams, *The Biblical View of Self-Esteem, Self-Love, Self-Image*, Eugene, OR: Harvest House, 1986.

Sinclair B. Ferguson, *A Heart for God*, Colorado Springs: NavPress, 1985.

_____, *Children of the Living God*, Colorado Springs: NavPress, 1987.

Susan Hunt, *Spiritual Mothering: The Titus 2 Model for Women Mentoring Women*, Wheaton, IL: Crossway Books, 1992.

D. Martyn Lloyd-Jones, *The Heart of the Gospel*, Wheaton, IL: Crossway Books, 1991.

D. Martyn Lloyd-Jones' series of commentaries on Ephesians, Baker Books, 1978.

_____, *Spiritual Depression: Its Causes and Its Cure*, William B. Eerdmans, 1965.

John MacArthur, Jr., *The MacArthur New Testament Commentary: Ephesians*, Chicago, Moody Press, 1986.

J. I. Packer, *Knowing God*, Downer's Grove, IL: InterVarsity, 1993.

David Powlison, *Power Encounters: Reclaiming Spiritual Warfare*, Baker Books, 1994.

John R. W. Stott, *Your Mind Matters*, Downer's Grove, IL: InterVarsity Press, 1973.

A. W. Tozer, *The Pursuit of God*, Camp Hill, PA: Christian Publications, 1995.

CHAPTER 4

Why Women Should Counsel Women

Carol W. Cornish, M.A.

The lecture hall was crowded. We listened attentively to the speaker, a biblical counselor. He described a counseling case in which a seductive female counselee had attempted to lure him into a physical relationship. He'd been counseling her for some time and knew her well. At one of their sessions, she arrived wearing provocative clothing. The counselor described how he defused the situation by meeting with her in his office but leaving the door wide open and having his secretary nearby. He then said that in the future he would address women counselees formally—by using their last names—to lessen the possibility that such a situation might arise again. All of his remaining comments then focused on the methods a counselor could use to protect himself from such counselees.

Who Needs Protection?

My response to this presentation was mixed.[1] On the one hand, I was grateful that the topic was brought out in the open and that the counselor resisted temptation. But on the other hand, something was missing. I wanted to know more about the counselee. What did they discuss during that session? How is she now? What was her comfort level when the secretary was within earshot? What motivated her seductive behavior? Was the compassion of Christ applied to her in this situation? Could the situation have been altered to ensure that the counselee received the most loving, wise, and compassionate help? Could the whole counseling process have been set up in a different way from the beginning?

When biblical counselors[2] discuss the risk of encountering temptation when counseling people of the opposite sex, they usually encourage one another to proceed with the counseling as long as the counselor is exercising self-control. Are we to conclude, then, that if the counselor is not troubled by temptation, then all potential problems have been resolved? Is protecting the counselor the whole story? Or is it equally important to protect the counselee from unnecessary exposure to temptation and the consequent turmoil? The means for protecting the counselor are helpful as far as they go, but they don't necessarily address what may go on within the counselee.

Sinclair Ferguson makes this observation in his book *Kingdom Life in a Fallen World*:

> God made men and women to be attracted to each other, to need each other, and to enter into relationships with each other that have physical, spiritual, and mental dimensions. . . . [Therefore] we must guard our heart and our actions, gestures and looks. . . . We will not play with our own emotions, and we will be scrupulous about the emotions of others.[3]

Ferguson's comment speaks to issues that relate to how we structure our counseling—that is, how we do it. Accordingly, when long-term individual counseling or discipleship is needed, I advocate that men counsel men and women counsel women. (When I say "individual" counseling, I am referring to situations in which someone comes alone for help.) While some problems can be taken care of with short-term remedial counseling, the process of bringing biblical change into a person's life usually occurs within the context of ongoing discipleship, friendship, and one-anothering relationships.[4] These long-term counseling relationships should be gender-specific (man to man and woman to woman).

Though my focus in this chapter is on situations in which a male counsels a female, the concerns I express are also applicable to females counseling males. I have not heard of any abuses in the female-to-male context, but a similar potential for sin or needless struggle is present. As you read, please keep these words from Elyse Fitzpatrick in mind:

> This is not an attack on male headship in the home nor is it an attack on male headship or eldership in the church. Wives are to submit themselves to

their husbands and female and male members are to submit themselves to their elders. I'm not saying that we ought to replace men in ministry. I'm just saying that there's a particular ministry that we would be wise to re-evaluate.[5]

Direction from the Scriptures

Even though same-gender individual counseling certainly seems like a wise path to pursue, some of us may be wondering what Scripture has to say about this issue. I realize that it is not possible to point to passages that absolutely forbid us from counseling members of the opposite sex. In fact, Jesus counseled the woman at the well (John 4), a woman who had a history of sexual problems. And Abigail spoke to David to counsel him against acting in a rash manner (1 Samuel 25). But in both of those cases, the one-to-one counseling was limited to one meeting.

However, in situations that call for long-term individual counseling, I believe I can show that Scripture directs us toward same-gender counseling. For example, in Titus 2:1-5, the apostle Paul calls for same-gender discipleship for issues that often arise in counseling men and women. For men these issues include being temperate, worthy of respect, self-controlled, and sound in faith, love, and endurance. And for women these include being reverent, not slanderers, temperate, teaching what is good, loving one's spouse and children, being self-controlled, pure, good managers of the household, kind, and submissive to one's husband.

As Christians, we usually take for granted the idea that a *discipling* relationship will be same-gender. If we understand counseling to be a specialized form of discipleship, then we will find help in Titus 2, which addresses the questions we're asking in this chapter. In fact, why don't you take some time right now to read Paul's letter to Titus? It won't take long because Titus has only three chapters. You'll want to pay attention to the things that are to be taught to men and women, and who is supposed to teach them.

Titus 2 Close-up

Let's take a closer look now at Titus 2 and investigate what Paul says about who should disciple/counsel whom. To establish the context, we should first note that Paul "left Titus to complete the establishment of the church and to rectify its errors."[6] The letter to Titus teaches much about orderly living, both individual and corporate. Notice in Titus 2:4-5 that Paul says,

> Then they [the older women] can train the younger women to love their husbands and children, to be self-controlled and pure, to be busy at home, to be kind, and to be subject to their husbands, so that no one will malign the word of God (NIV).

While we don't want to get mired down in a Greek lesson, a brief look at the original language of Titus can help our understanding of this passage, since the biblical Greek (at least in this passage) is more specific than English. In Titus 2:1 and 2:6, the commands to "teach" and "encourage" (Gk. *lalei* and *parakalei*) are in the second person singular; they refer to Titus' teaching older men, older women, and young men. But in Titus 2:4 the command to "train" (Gk. *sophronizosin*) is in the third person plural; the older women are the subject, not Titus.

Titus was not instructed by Paul to teach the young women; instead, he was to find mature women to whom he could teach sound doctrine. Given the cultural context, it seems likely that this would have been a group situation in which the authoritative Word was taught by Titus to women who had the potential to be mature leaders of other women. (A modern parallel would be a pastor who has oversight of a women's ministry in a church. He teaches or directs the women leaders so that they can lead other women.) These older women, in turn, were to teach the young women how to live godly lives. In his commentary on Titus, Hendriksen says, "One understands immediately that no one—not even Titus—is better able to train a young woman than an experienced, older woman."[7]

The teaching was to be same-gender because women were to be examples both as faithful Christians and as faithful Christian women for other women. Those who were to teach were to be good examples to those being taught. Therefore, those who were more spiritually mature were to teach and be examples for those of the same sex who were less mature. As you can see, then, God's Word gives us a framework for a discipling ministry to women. While the Bible doesn't talk about a distinct process called "counseling," it does couch counseling-type issues within discussions about ministry and discipling and body life within the church. Thus it seems reasonable to conclude that these principles from Titus still apply today in terms of who should disciple/counsel whom. Mature men are to counsel men, and mature women are to counsel women. In any situation where teaching, counseling, or discipling is being done on a long-term basis one-to-one, the biblical pattern is for such ministry to be same-gender.

A Recurring Theme in Titus

In a general sense, the book of Titus includes an indirect appeal for same-gender counseling. One of the recurring themes in the letter is an emphasis on doing good. In contrast to those around them, the Christians in Crete were to do good so that the spread of the gospel would not be hindered. We Christians have this same responsibility today. We must seek to do good so that others are not hindered from responding to the gospel. When Christians in ministry positions succumb to emotional and sexual temptation because of cross-gender counseling, they allow their reputations to be tarnished and the spread of the gospel hindered. Therefore, Paul's teaching demanding right conduct of all believers must be applied to counseling as well as discipleship so that godliness is encouraged and reputations are protected. Same-gender, long-term individual counseling is an effective way to accomplish this.

Other Pertinent Passages

There are other Bible passages that suggest the benefits of same-gender counseling. First Peter 3:5-6 reveals the benefits of woman-to-woman mentoring. Women are to follow the example of Sarah in doing good, not fearing disaster, and trusting God.

Another passage, 1 Timothy 5:9-10, lists "helping those in trouble" (NIV) as one of the good deeds to be done by widows. These widows were usually older women whose life experience and exercise of godliness over the years could benefit the troubled. While this verse does not limit their ministry only to women, the tasks listed in these verses were traditionally the functions of women. It seems as though this passage suggests same-gender counseling, even though it doesn't conclusively support it.

The "one another" passages found in the New Testament are not directed toward one sex or the other. So we can safely assume that encouraging, admonishing, teaching, rebuking and so on were being done by both men and women (*see*, for example, Romans 15:14; Galatians 6:1-2; Colossians 3:16). In the cultural environment of the first-century church, ministry to one another was probably occurring mostly within one-to-one, same-gender relationships. Even today, we assume that intimate friendships (outside of marriage) will be same-sex. We must be very cautious, then, about thinking that an office setting will remove or significantly minimize the innate dangers of cross-gender relationships.

Let's consider an Old Testament example: The woman in Proverbs 31:26 spoke with wisdom, and faithful instruction was on her tongue. The note on this verse in the *NIV Study Bible* says that the recipients of her instruction were her children and friends.[8] In light of the oriental culture, we can assume that these friends were women, giving us yet another verse that suggests same-gender ministry.

Scriptural Application or Cultural Accommodation?

How did the church and parachurch organizations (such as biblical counseling centers) reach the point where cross-gender counseling (especially male to female) is now accepted almost without question? It seems as though it has been permitted because of the pastor's role as a shepherd over all the people in a church congregation. Thus, the thinking goes, a male counselor is permitted to counsel both men and women. Or perhaps this view has been formed from portions of the Bible that were never intended to promote the kind of intimacy between unmarried persons that occurs in modern individual counseling. First Peter 5:2-4 is an example of the command to minister to the flock (with no restriction as to gender). Some might even see Galatians 3:28 as permitting it: "There is neither Jew nor Greek, slave nor free, male nor female, for you are all one in Christ Jesus" (NIV). But these verses do not intend to promote such an intimate relationship as is likely to occur in cross-gender, long-term counseling.

Secular Role Models

In contrast to these defenses, I wonder if biblical counselors have disregarded Scripture and simply followed secular models. In part, the issue of cross-gender counseling comes up because Christians have adopted secular models of professional psychotherapy into their ministries. In his book *A Theology of Christian Counseling,* Jay Adams remarks that you cannot "integrate pagan thought and biblical teaching. . . . Counseling may not be set up as a life-calling on a free-lance basis; all such counseling ought to be done as a function of the church, utilizing its authority and resources."[9]

Cultural Influences

During the First Century   A study of the culture of the New Testament era helps us to understand why the Bible is relatively silent on this issue. The cultural setting of the first-century church did not allow much non-spousal intimacy between the sexes. The writers of the New Testament did not need to address this issue because it would never have entered their minds. Men and women who weren't family members did not relate to one another in the ways that people relate in extended counseling situations. While the high status of women in the early church allowed them to interact with men, Scripture gives no examples of private meetings one-to-one for an extended period of time between persons outside of one's own family. No biblical mandate exists against cross-gender counseling relationships simply because it was understood to be highly inappropriate and unwise.

Although the Bible does not directly forbid or promote one-to-one cross-gender discipleship, it *does* promote same-gender discipleship. The burden of proof lies on those in favor of cross-gender counseling to show that it is appropriate from a biblical perspective. In the meantime, shouldn't we follow the more conservative course and seek to fulfill the patterns given to us in Titus 2? It is interesting that often in the evangelical church we opt for the more conservative road on many issues, but not on this one. It seems as though on this issue there may be a blind spot in the eyes of some evangelical pastors and many evangelical counselors.

Another cultural factor to consider is that in Bible times, people were much less private and more group- or household-oriented. Have we projected our culture of self-reliance and independence into our understanding of the biblical principles concerning counseling? *In Bible times you would find no private room behind a closed door where a man and a women (not married to each other) would meet repeatedly to discuss highly intimate matters.* If it did occur, it was probably for the purpose of pursuing an illicit relationship, such as Paul condemned in the Corinthian church.

Here and Now   Because I believe that long-term individual counseling should be same-gender, some people may wrongly conclude that I also believe in isolation of the sexes. This is not the case. I am simply calling for *prudence* and *wisdom* in situations where a man and a woman (who are not married to each other) may spend hours and hours together talking about matters that promote a high degree of intimacy and nurture strong relational bonds.

Particularly in modern American culture, with its rapidly crumbling moral base, this type of counseling is not wise. This is especially true if a woman comes for counseling about a problem involving her husband or boyfriend and he isn't a regular attender at the counseling sessions. Same-gender counseling in such a situation is preferable for two reasons: 1) more potential exists for a base of similar experience,[10] and 2) less potential exists for sinful outcomes or needless struggles with temptation.

Discussing this base of similar experience, Naomi Wright says that many pastors

see the female counselee as a helpless, defenseless, lonely, mistreated person. They feel protective of her. They can feel venomous toward her husband for mistreating her. They are often not quick to see that the woman may be part of her own problem.

[Female counselors] will recognize when a counselee may be part of her own problem. They can say things in love a man could never get away with. They will not be protective or transfer sexual affection to their counselee, although there may be a deep mutual appreciation.[11]

Sometimes men may justify counseling women because the woman counselee refuses to be referred to a woman counselor. But is her refusal a license to proceed? Perhaps you should think about why she doesn't want to be counseled by a woman. Naomi Wright accurately points out that a same-gender counselor often has insight into a person of the same sex that a cross-gender counselor is not likely to possess. Women counselees who are simply looking for sympathy will want to avoid women who possess keen insight. They want the special, exclusive attention from their male counselors that they may be lacking in their other relationships. This is a prescription for trouble. Why not give her a choice? Either she meets with a woman counselor, or she is team counseled by a man and a woman (preferably the male counselor's wife).

Some pastors and counselors object to team counseling on the basis that the counselee may feel "ganged up on." But if team counseling is done wisely, the counselee can overcome these feelings (if they are present). Humble attitudes on the part of the counselors and careful pacing of the counseling sessions can overcome the sense of being outnumbered. I have found that many counselees like team counseling because they get the benefit of two opinions and double the wisdom and encouragement.

What Experience Teaches Us

I have heard many accounts of heartache, confusion, and sin that have resulted from cross-gender counseling. When we examine the fruit produced by it, we uncover some disturbing things. Female counselees report having had fantasies involving male counselors. Some women have gone beyond fantasy to actual sexual sin with their counselor. Often the initial problem in these cases was a marriage that was falling apart. At the start of the counseling, the husband may have been willing to come. But if he loses interest or feels threatened and the wife continues alone, the stage is set for a dangerous situation. Wisdom, courage, and true kindness on the part of the counselor are necessary.

When a counselee who has specifically requested a female counselor comes to me, I ask about her reasons for wanting to counsel with a woman. Those who have had unhelpful or tragic experiences with male counselors have obvious reasons for their request. The rest of these women just consider it common sense that cross-gender counseling might create a situation ripe for trouble—a situation that can easily be avoided by going to a female counselor.

I've observed that some women who counsel with men at counseling centers develop a sort of rendezvous mentality. Going off to see their counselors has for them a measure of exclusiveness and intimacy somewhat akin to a tryst.

Several years ago a male counselor referred a woman to me because she revealed to him that she had begun to think about him in inappropriate ways. Her counselor displayed kindness and wisdom by sending her to a woman counselor. Initially she was concerned over the change in counselors. But after several sessions she wrote in her journal, "[I] cried all the way home in the car. Such a sense of God's leading me to Carol. This is a bright spot in a dark time."[12] She told me those tears were tears of joy for the hope she had received.

Don't Reach Out and Touch Someone

Perhaps it would be helpful to note that the above-mentioned counselor never physically touched his counselee—not even a handshake. He and I have both observed male counselors hugging their female counselees. I am concerned that male counselors have no idea of the effect that physical contact can have on a woman. If what I hear from my counselees is any indication of the general reaction to such physical contact, the impact is usually harmful to the emotional state of the woman being counseled.

As Lois Mowday observes,

> *... to assume that all is well because a man and woman are not touching each other physically can be overly simplistic. . . .* A man and woman can touch each other in very meaningful ways without ever being physically close[13] *(emphasis added).*
>
>   *Because we tend to say that nothing is going on when there is no physical contact, we may feel safe because we think we are still walking the road of obedience—when we are really not walking obediently at all.*[14]

Instead of working at the very edge of where right meets wrong, we need to be asking ourselves, *Is cross-gender, long-term individual counseling wise?* The Scriptures give no commands either positive or negative concerning cross-gender counseling in and of itself. On that basis, some people say there is nothing inherently wrong with it. But to defend this kind of counseling by saying there is nothing wrong with it ignores the crucial question: Is it wise?

Learning the Easy Way and the Hard Way

I believe that any defense of this sort of counseling should be examined carefully. Several years ago, part of my job as a resource staff person at a seminary was to sit in on internship classes for prospective counselors. One student in particular objected to the view being presented in this chapter. He remarked that it focused only on the negative outcomes of cross-gender counseling. He contended that a lot of good has resulted from it. For example, he thought that counselees increased their perseverance in difficulty and gained new understandings about relationships because of it.

I believe that any good result will also occur in same-gender counseling without the accompanying dangers involved and without exposing the counselee to unnecessary temptation. As a counselor/discipler, you need to exercise wisdom and weigh the potential for moral lapse or confusing your counselee rather than assume that both you and the counselee are immune to these things.

Another student observed that at the center where he was an intern, approximately 80 percent of the counselees were women who came alone and were seeing male counselors. He expressed concern that if counseling were to be made same-gender, the male counselors would lose most of their clientele. This same viewpoint was conveyed to me by a busy male counselor who had years of experience doing cross-gender counseling. However, anxiety over a perceived threat to one's counseling opportunities needs to be put aside (*see* Philippians 2:3-4). Uppermost in the counselor's mind must be the glory of God. Concern for the purity of both the counselor and the counselee and the cost to the counselee in terms of his or her spiritual, emotional, and mental well-being are also critical elements.

The situations that have ensued in the lives of the two students mentioned above are enlightening. The first student, who thought my views were somewhat negative, decided to take my advice and counsel males only. I urged him to pray that God would send him men that he could serve in his counseling ministry. He was delighted as God brought men to him for counsel. He expressed gratitude for being taught to trust God and to wait upon Him to bless his ministry.

The second student mentioned was, in his own words, "stubborn and unteachable" about this issue. During his internship at a counseling center, this student counseled a Christian woman who had been sexually abused as a child. His supervisor was present in the sessions at the beginning of the counseling. As the student seemed to grow in his ability to counsel, the supervisor left him to counsel her alone. The student reported in class that this counselee eventually began to demonstrate signs of dependency on him. He received feedback questioning the wisdom of proceeding with the case. Weeks later he described how she lunged at him and threw her arms around his neck. I strongly advised him to refer her to a female counselor. He chose to ignore my advice. Within several weeks his supervisor took him off the case. Subsequently, this student poured his heart out to me saying that he wished he had heeded my warnings. He is now a firm advocate of same-gender counseling; he learned the hard way.

Upon hearing the outcome of the latter student's case, I asked questions of some other people who had been involved with it. These questions were similar to the ones that arose in my mind at the counseling seminar mentioned at the beginning of this chapter: How is the counselee now? Where is she now? Who is counseling her now? What could have been done differently to help her? No one seemed to know. I wondered why the only concern being expressed was for the welfare of the student counselor. Why wasn't similar concern for the welfare of the counselee being expressed?

Where Are the Men?

Though this book has been written primarily for women, I am sure there are some men who are reading it. So, to you men I would like to respectfully make the following suggestion: Rather than passively accepting women counselees, why not encourage men to ask for help and teach men that they have a responsibility to be accountable to other men? Unsettle their western individualism, which results in sinful self-reliance. The statistics that I have seen on the gender of the counseling population indicate that 60 to 80 percent of counselees are women. It is hard for me to believe that problems manifest themselves overwhelmingly in the lives of women and not so much in the lives of men.

One well-known pastor wrote that many men are too proud to ask for help. He said:

> In general, women have an easier time developing accountability relationships than men do. There are several reasons for this. The biggest hindrance for men, however, is ego. God calls it pride. . . . The bottom line is that we don't like admitting our weaknesses to anyone else (as if those around us did not already know), especially to another man. At least with a woman there is a chance we will get sympathy and possibly a shoulder to cry on. But another guy? We think, He will see right through me. He may make me face myself as I really am. God forbid. I may look bad![15]

It is important for men to reach out to the men around them. Men need each other's mutual ministry, as Paul outlined for Titus in chapter two of that epistle.

Clearing the Way

Many of my women students and colleagues have observed the same problems with cross-gender counseling that I am describing here. They know female counselees who at one time were counseled by men and often had significant difficulties with attraction to the male counselor. For these women, the attraction became a serious problem that hindered the counseling process.

Several years ago a well-known biblical counselor wondered out loud why some women want to be pastors and elders when there is so much other work for them to do in the church. In response, it seems to me that if women counselees were routinely referred to women counselors, perhaps these gifted women would be less tempted to seek tasks for which they have no biblical call. Men who counsel women alone usurp the role given by God to mature women in the church: the older women are to disciple and counsel the younger women.

Perhaps some counselors may think that I am just trying to "drum up business" for women counselors. Let me reiterate again that my reason for raising these gender issues is that I have seen firsthand the great damage done to people and to the cause of Christ because of the unwise and sinful actions of both counselors and counselees in cross-gender counseling situations.

The Specter of Lawsuits

Influenced by the increasing number of lawsuits in America, counselees who have been sinned against by their counselors are choosing to take their grievances into court despite biblical teaching to the contrary in 1 Corinthians 6. Given the litigious society we live in, male counselors could easily find themselves being sued for breach of duty, meaning that they allegedly did something they should not have done.

Author Steve Levicoff, in his book *Christian Counseling and the Law*, defines the term "breach of duty" and then goes on to explain:

> *Doing something you shouldn't do generally takes the form of sexual involvement and often occurs in a marriage counseling situation. An individual or couple comes to you for counseling, and you have an affair with a counselee. While we don't like to admit that this happens in the realm of Christian counseling, the sad fact is that many successful lawsuits against counselors, including the clergy, have been based on seduction. This breach of duty is generally considered intentional in nature.*[16]

According to Marie Fortune's book *Is Nothing Sacred? When Sex Invades the Pastoral Relationship*, one reason for the increase in lawsuits against the clergy is alleged malpractice involving sexual misconduct.[17] Similarly, Jeffrey Kottler notes that

> *... malpractice suits against therapists for sexual misconduct are skyrocketing. In spite of the haughty indignity from a number of professionals who justifiably condemn such client abuse, it is so easy to see how it could happen, especially since 87 percent of practicing therapists admit to feeling sexually attracted to their clients. (Pope, Keith-Spiegel, and Tabachnik [1986]).*[18]

Rather than take comfort from the fact that Kottler addresses a non-Christian audience, we ought to heed the wise words of Lois Mowday:

> *The road to immorality involved a process, but the reality of this process is clouded because of two false assumptions about Christians and this particular sin: (1) that people in the pastorate or leadership or counseling positions are immune to succumbing to the temptation of immorality; and (2) that because I am a committed Christian I will never fall into immorality.*
>
> *Scripture warns us, "If you think you are standing firm, be careful that you don't fall! No temptation has seized you except what is common to man" (1 Corinthians 10:12-13).*[19]

What Other Writers Have Said

In some cases male counselors seem to be naive about the effects a counseling relationship can have on a female counselee. Psychiatrist Peter Rutter observes that ethical violations are often open to differences in interpretation with the violator, the woman, and those aware of the situation all being "skeptical about the true nature of the relationship. Therefore, to take the position that those involved or aware have to be more certain that client abuse is occurring before breaking the silence is not defendable."[20] In reference to the more extreme cases of counselee abuse, Rutter concludes that "the central psychological/spiritual/ethical flaw in the men [male counselors] who violate is that they do not perceive the damage done to the woman [counselee]. . . ."[21]

I have discussed these issues with a number of male colleagues, and I have been surprised to find that opinions about the wisdom of cross-gender counseling generally fall along two lines. Those who are or have been pastors believe that it is inappropriate and unwise; those who have not been pastors believe that it is appropriate. "We would balk at the suggestion that ministers should not include women in their counseling ministry," say Balswick and Thoburn.[22] On the other hand, Jerry Jenkins remarks:

> *[Too many men] think they can handle any temptation. Their resolve, their marriage, their spirituality will carry the day. These men are self-deceived, and we all know too many of them. . . . No one wants to admit he has a problem or weakness.*[23]

He goes on to say:

Pastors and other Christian leaders need hedges as much as if not more than the rest of us. If they counsel women at all—and they would, in most cases, do better to assign them to some wise, older women in the church— they should counsel with the door open and the secretary close by[24] *(emphasis added).*

Tony Campolo has said that when he was a young pastor and "no better looking than I am now," he was surprised that the women he was counseling were falling in love with him. They were coming to him with marriage problems; they were lonely because their husbands, they said, did not take the time to really listen to them. There he was, spending time alone with them on a regular basis and listening intently to what they had to say. Campolo says, "We always fall in love with someone who will listen intently and spend time with us."[25] Here is a man with the wisdom to perceive and the frankness to admit that the dynamics in this kind of situation are dangerous.

In his book *Can Fallen Pastors Be Restored? The Church's Response to Sexual Misconduct*, John Armstrong counsels pastors to take precautions as they minister. He says,

The pastor needs to decide how and when he will meet with women for counseling. It is commonly agreed that counseling women in long-term relationships is detrimental for both the pastor and the woman involved. I have found it best over many years of pastoral ministry to never meet a woman alone in her home, and never in my office unless others are present. Generally, I ask for the husband's presence. More times than not I meet a woman in my own home with my wife present. I find that godly women both understand and respect this approach. Paul counsels us to "make no provision for the flesh in regard to its lusts" (Romans 12:14b)[26] *(emphasis added).*

Dr. Armstrong is wise to ask for the husband's presence and to have his own wife present when he finds it necessary to counsel women. He also talks about the need to be cautious when working with women staff members. He reminds us that Scripture teaches us to avoid even the appearance of evil so that we do not provoke gossip and rumors. Again, notice that he says "it is commonly agreed that counseling women in long-term relationships is detrimental for both the pastor and the woman involved." This is also true for male counselors and the women they counsel alone.

Myths Inherent in Professionalism

Some unwise counselors seem to think that they can handle cross-gender coun-seling simply because they are "professional counselors." One counselor wrote this astonishing comment on the subject of counselee attraction for the counselor: "Having come to terms with our own sexuality, however, we can establish a professional relationship with the counselee."[27] This counselor claims that coming to terms with his own sexuality protects him from danger, but he never explains what that means. His vague argument represents the faulty traditional reasoning on this issue. This reasoning argues that if a coun-selor has properly dealt with issues in his own life, he will not be unduly affected by counseling a woman alone long-term. Even if this were always true, and it is not, it disregards the potential for setting up stumbling blocks for the counselee.

After admitting that cross-gender counseling is fraught with dangers, this counselor justifies it by saying that his duty was to relate to the counselee in a non-sexual way. His purpose is to have her experience a relationship with a man on a basis other than sex (as narrowly defined). She then, he says, can transfer this new understanding to her other male relationships.

This methodology of providing a corrective emotional experience is re-jected by David Powlison in his article "What If Your Father Didn't Love You?":

> *The psychological technique of using the therapeutic relationship to restructure experience simply puts a different false image of God into the person's life. The living and true God is no more like the benign all-accepting therapist than he is like the abusive all-rejecting father.*[28]

A "fatherless" counselee needs a warm, vibrant, precious relationship with her heavenly Father. This relationship grows out of a counselee's belief in God's Word and acting on those beliefs rather than trusting in her experience. God our Father is surely able to reveal Himself by His own Spirit and Word! The woman counselee can learn to know God with the help of a woman counselor—a counselor whose gender will not distract the counselee from wholeheartedly seeking God.

A counselee does not *need* an exclusive, intimate relationship with a man she can see and touch in order to improve her relationships with men and God. Elyse Fitzpatrick makes this observation:

> *For the male counselor with a female counselee, I think that there is a certain form of an improper bonding that happens between a counselor and his*

counselee. The very nature of counseling is to bond with another, isn't it? If you're doing good counseling, what's going on is that person is opening their heart to you and you in turn are opening your heart to that person and there is a sharing of intimate details. What happens out of that—a bonding happens, doesn't it?"[29]

This is not to say that good relationships with males are not helpful. But is long-term counseling or discipleship the place to experience this? Again, is it the wisest, most loving way?

Is our experience necessarily more real to us than the Word of God? The corrective emotional experience methodology denies the truth of Hebrews 4:12:

The word of God is living and active and sharper than any two-edged sword, and piercing as far as the division of soul and spirit, of both joints and marrow, and able to judge the thoughts and intentions of the heart (NIV).

The Holy Spirit is able to use His Word to enable us to experience our heavenly Father. James 4:8 says, "Draw near to God and He will draw near to you." Paul assures us in Romans 8:14-15:

All who are being led by the Spirit of God, these are sons [children] of God. For you have not received a spirit of slavery leading to fear again, but you have received a spirit of adoption as sons [children] by which we cry out, "Abba! Father!"

Counselees, then, must choose whether they will believe God's Word and walk by faith, or rely on human experience and walk by sight.

The corrective emotional experience methodology is not biblical; rather, this method is similar to that of secular "reparenting" techniques. These techniques lead the counselee to relate to the counselor as a daughter does to a father. The intended result is for her to gain the relationship that she perceives she missed as a child. In the Christianized version, counselors have concluded that she will also be aided in her ability to know her heavenly Father better. But we do not find a basis for this technique in the Scriptures. Instead, the following is said about God:

[He is] a father to the fatherless, a defender of widows, is God in his holy dwelling (Psalm 68:5 NIV).

You, O God, do see trouble and grief; you consider it to take it in hand. The victim commits himself to you; you are the helper of the fatherless (Psalm 10:14 NIV).

You hear, O LORD, the desire of the afflicted; you encourage them, and you listen to their cry, defending the fatherless and the oppressed, in order that man, who is of the earth, may terrify no more (Psalm 10:17-18 NIV).

The LORD watches over the alien and sustains the fatherless and the widow, but he frustrates the ways of the wicked (Psalm 146:9 NIV).

God is not limited to the use of human agents. *He has not abandoned His children nor forced them to attach themselves to strangers in offices in an effort to relate well to males, and especially to Himself!* God is still a compassionate, active, involved Father to His children. One of the aims of the counseling process should be to teach counselees how to see God approaching them in love. It is wonderful to watch a counselee's response when this happens.

Practical Implications

At least two questions come to mind in relation to a counseling or discipleship situation that involves a long-term cross-gender relationship:

- Is the counselor/discipler afraid or unwilling to face his or her own vulnerability?
- Is the counselor so insensitive to others that he or she may feel comfortable in a situation because it is not perceived to be a problem for the counselor, even while the counselee may be experiencing great difficulty?

Watch Out for Stumbling Blocks

Will the counselor be able to tell if the counselee is struggling with temptation or confusion because of their relationship? The counselor probably won't know unless the counselee tells the counselor. If she does, then both end up struggling because this knowledge might tend to feed the pride of the counselor. Being adored by a counselee sometimes makes it difficult for a male counselor to refer her to someone else. After all, being in ministry often puts a person in the position of being criticized rather than adored. Positive affirmation from a counselee tends to make her a precious commodity. A ministry that is patterned after Titus 2:4 will eliminate these kinds of problems.

It is naive to think that in a cross-gender, long-term individual counseling context deep attraction to the counselor is not a common temptation for the counselee. It is also quite likely that this kind of counseling breeds discontent in spouses whose partners, they think, do not compare favorably to the counselor. In addition to the original problem for which she sought help, the counselee may gain these new problems as a result of seeking help. Definite potential exists for the counselor to become a stumbling block instead of a helper. For these reasons, same-gender counseling is the wisest choice, as Paul directed Titus so explicitly.

In this regard, Randy Alcorn displays uncommon insight in unmasking his motivation with respect to a female counselee:

> *When meeting a woman for our third counseling appointment, I became aware that she was interested in me personally. What was more frightening was that I realized I had subconsciously sensed this before but had enjoyed her attraction too much to address the problem. Though I wasn't yet emotionally involved or giving her inappropriate attention, I wasn't deflecting hers toward me, either, and was thereby inviting it.*
>
> *I felt tempted to dismiss the matter as unimportant "knowing" I would never get involved with her. Fortunately, when God prompted me, I knew I was no longer the right person to meet with her. I made other counseling arrangements for her.*[30]

Notice that cross-gender problems were already surfacing in just the third counseling session!

To say, as some do, that because Christians have the Holy Spirit they are enabled to counsel those of the opposite sex alone and resist temptation may be to advocate testing God. When you test God, you are deliberately putting yourself in a difficult situation and placing the responsibility for faithfulness solely upon God. And you are also ignoring the situation's potential impact on the counselee as well as other people.

> *Deep pain is brought to the sexual partner in a clergy affair, and even deeper pain to the minister's wife. The minister [or counselor], given an honored office through which he is called to serve abused and vulnerable people, violates that very trust by becoming, himself, a violator.*[31]

Where potential for sexual sin exists, we are instructed by the Scriptures to *flee*, not to stay and try to resist (*see* 1 Corinthians 6:18; 10:14; 2 Timothy 2:22).

In addition, by not promoting the welfare of another, especially a brother or sister in Christ (*see* Galatians 6:10), we are sinning against him or her. Vera told her male biblical counselor that she was struggling with being attracted to him. He advised her to stay in the counseling relationship and resist the struggle. Many months later, he terminated their relationship by admitting that he was afraid he could no longer determine where the line was between brotherly affection and deep personal attraction for her. It was at this point that he decided to flee. Yet when *she* struggled with those same feelings, Vera was told to stay! Do we see a double standard here? When she later confronted him about telling her to stay even when she was struggling, he defended himself by saying that it seemed to him like the most loving thing to do. Because Vera had listened to his ungodly counsel, she experienced great confusion and serious personal consequences.

Caution and Concern

Although friendships and working relationships are somewhat different than counseling, both necessitate the application of wisdom, caution, and self-control. Some words of caution about these kinds of relationships can be found in Dennis Rainey's book *Lonely Husbands, Lonely Wives.* He says:

> . . . *people commit emotional adultery before they commit physical adultery. Emotional adultery is unfaithfulness of the heart. It starts when two people of the opposite sex begin talking with each other about intimate struggles, doubts, or feelings. They start sharing their souls in a way that God intended exclusively for the marriage relationship. Emotional adultery is friendship with the opposite sex that goes too far.*[32]

While sexual adultery is indeed very serious, emotional adultery can also be devastating to a counselee. Emotional adultery usually manifests itself initially in subtle ways, described by Peter Rutter as "ways that one looks, comments that one makes that may be framed as sort of standard generic social comments that you can make, 'You know, you're very attractive.' "[33]

The following is a specific example of applying caution in counseling. A pastor in our area got together with his church board to formulate a counseling policy for the pastoral staff. Part of the policy states:

> *No pastoral staff member will enter into extended sessions (more than one) of counseling with a woman.*
>
> *It is understood that this kind of a policy will necessitate the building up of other individuals within the local assembly for the purposes of counseling.*

This fits the biblical model of Ephesians 4 (equipping other saints for work and ministry). It also fits Titus 2, where the older women [are instructed to] teach the younger women.[34]

This policy not only provides the church staff with clear guidelines about who is to counsel whom, it has also given the pastors' wives an assurance that they need not concern themselves with vague uncertainties or serious problems that can arise from cross-gender counseling.

In Matthew 5:27-28, our Lord clearly stated that He is just as concerned about adultery of the heart as he is about adultery of the body. Counselors should be equally concerned about what might be happening in the hearts of their counselees. It's not enough to pay attention to outward behavior. Just because the person being counseled or discipled isn't displaying any outward misbehavior toward you doesn't mean that everything is fine. The absence of indiscreet behavior on the part of the counselee is sometimes falsely understood by counselors as a signal that the counseling relationship is edifying to the counselee. "Far from forbidding *some* acts of immorality, Jesus says God's law asks for purity and integrity in our hearts and in our thoughts about others."[35] A counselee who wants to keep the relationship intact will not risk exposing his or her attraction to the counselor.

As to the question of whether same-gender counseling is appropriate for counselees who struggle with homosexual desires, team counseling successfully solves this dilemma (two men counsel a man, and two women a woman).[36]

Power Imbalance

Another factor counselors need to keep in mind is that they usually have a great deal of influence over their counselees. While it's true that all believers are equal before Christ, in a counseling relationship, the counselee (particularly one who is inclined to idolize the counselor) may see the counselor as having more power. Because of the counselor's position and knowledge, the counselee may perceive him as having a certain amount of power over her, as frequently happens when one person asks another for help. This perception is usually not intentional, but it's very real. Power imbalance is one reason why women are reluctant to leave a male counselor even though the relationship may be growing increasingly difficult.

In considering whether "fallen" leaders should be restored to their positions, R. Kent Hughes and John Armstrong say this:

It saddens us that so few "fallen" leaders recognize the abuse of power inherent to pastoral adultery. And even fewer are willing to discuss the destruction of trust that their sins have effected. Many borrow psychotherapeutic concepts such as healing and recovery as rationales for returning to pastoral ministry, but with no genuine recognition of the pathology [deep sin pattern] that manifests itself in the abuse of power.[37]

A woman's previous experiences with males who abused, abandoned, or ignored her often predisposes her to vulnerability in counseling situations.

Gender Issues and Marriage Counseling

Although this chapter is primarily concerned with the effects of cross-gender issues in individual counseling, a brief word about the practical implications of cross-gender issues on marriage counseling may be helpful at this point. The most effective form of marriage counseling is team counseling, which can be done by a pastor and his wife, a pastor and a woman staff counselor, or a pastor and a mature woman from the church at either of their homes along with a spouse present.

It is common in marriage counseling to find that the spouse experiencing the most difficulty makes sinful comparisons between the counselor and the counselee's spouse. Thus, it is likely that having a woman meet alone with a male counselor will exacerbate the marital problems. The "husband perceives that his wife is being intimate with another man who understands her better than he does. . . . If she goes home and talks about how wonderful this man is that she's counseling with, what's going to make him [the husband] want to go in there?"[38]

Criteria for Deciding Who Counsels Whom

Is it ever wise for a man to counsel a woman alone or for a woman to counsel a man alone? The following factors should be considered as essential criteria for making this decision:

- What is the nature of the problem?
- Will it be necessary to meet more than once?
- What is the likelihood that all persons involved in the situation will be present in the sessions?

- Would the presence of a team counselor reduce gender problems?
- Does the church or counseling center have a policy against cross-gender counseling?

Some circumstances in which cross-gender individual counseling is appropriate are career, vocational, educational, and other kinds of counseling in which expertise of a specific nature is needed. These situations, however, are best limited to short-term counseling. If the number of counseling sessions cannot be limited, the counselee should be referred. His or her former and present counselors need to consult with one another to decide the best plan for helping the counselee.

Making the Teaching Attractive

Cross-gender individual counseling might be a biblical option, but only in very limited circumstances. It is particularly unwise when it involves long-term counseling. Individual counseling for marriage problems, for concerns of singles, or for divorce issues are situations in which long-term cross-gender counseling has significant potential to create difficulties. A counselor is unfair, unwise, and unloving to proceed with a counseling case in which he or she is not experiencing difficulty with sinful attraction but the counselee might be. Are you your sister's and brother's keeper? Yes. A twofold question must always be asked: Is it wise and is it loving for this counselor to counsel this counselee? A wise and loving counselor will refer the counselee to a counselor of the same gender as the counselee when long-term help is needed. Same-gender counseling is the best choice for 1) the sake of the kingdom of God, 2) the sake of the welfare of the counselee, and 3) the sake of the welfare of the counselor.

Church leaders have a responsibility to equip, advise, and oversee wise men and women as the men counsel other men and the women counsel other women. Biblical counseling centers need to take a hard look at the amount of cross-gender, long-term individual counseling being done and change their staffing to ensure that they can offer same-gender counseling. We should take these concerns to heart, just as Paul encouraged Titus to do so, with good reason: Paul did not tell Titus what to do without providing the motivation to follow through: "so no one will malign the word of God. . . . so that those who oppose you may be ashamed because they have nothing bad to say about us. . . . so that in every way they will make the teaching about God our Savior attractive" (Titus 2:5, 8,10 NIV).

Recommended Resources

Randy C. Alcorn, *Sexual Temptation: How Christian Workers Can Win the Battle* (booklet), Downers Grove, IL: InterVarsity Press, 1989.

John Armstrong, *Can Fallen Pastors Be Restored? The Church's Response to Sexual Misconduct,* Chicago: Moody Press, 1995.

Elyse Fitzpatrick, "Why Women Should Counsel Women," audiotape #421-12 available from Five Star Conference Recording and Duplicating, P.O. Box 1261, Carlsbad, CA 92008, or 1-800-350-TAPE.

Susan Hunt, *Spiritual Mothering: The Titus 2 Model for Women Mentoring Women,* Wheaton, IL: Crossway Books, 1993.

Susan Hunt and Peggy Hutcheson, *Leadership for Women in the Church,* Grand Rapids: Zondervan Publishing House, 1991.

PART 2

Addressing the Challenges Christian Women Face

CHAPTER 5

Counseling Single Teen Mothers

Mary Somerville, M.A.

Sue pleaded with great emotion in her voice. "Mary, I don't know what to do! Yesterday I ran into Chris, a friend of mine from high school. She led me to the Lord when we were working together at that time. Since then she's fallen away from the Lord, had a baby out of wedlock, and the father has custody. She can't even see her baby and she has so many problems that she is seeing a psychiatrist and is on more than a dozen drugs. She's totally incapacitated; she really needs help! Could you help her? Would you be willing to meet with her?"

Answering Sue's plea for help involved more than merely saying yes to a one-hour counseling session with her friend. I didn't know it then, but that day I was catapulted into a nine-year ministry working with young single mothers.

I knew God had answers for Chris. She agreed to meet with me and for the next two years Chris and I met together for weekly Bible study and biblical counsel. There were times before the Bible study that I would help her clean her squalid house. Frequently she was depressed. She dressed in old, out-of-style clothes that did not fit nor flatter her. She would readily admit that she was not at all lovable. Although my feelings were telling me not to help her, I knew what God wanted me to do. My love for her was coming from God Himself.

I tried to understand what it would be like not to be able to see my own child for two years. My heart ached for Chris. As she got her life right with the Lord, I helped her obtain an attorney to fight for visitation rights. Chris was finally allowed to see her child for two hours a week as long as I was on hand to supervise the meetings. I rejoiced in watching her get off all her drugs except lithium and become a God-reliant person. She also got a job, and now has a good relationship with her child and the child's father. She still calls me to let me know how things are going and to submit prayer requests. She has learned how to deal with her problems biblically—many of which were the result of her earlier sinful lifestyle.

Those two years of working with Chris required a tremendous commitment of time and emotional output, involving all of my spiritual resources. But I knew it was important to God. It would be His way of reclaiming a life that had been totally cast aside and lost. And it was a great way for me to see the changes God can bring about in a person's life. In Chris, God demonstrated His sufficiency. He saw fit to change her life as I took the time to work with her. The love paid off. She came back to the fold of the Good Shepherd. It was then that I knew *my* life had changed!

The cries for help did not end with Chris. I was subsequently asked to teach a Bible study in a group home for pregnant teens and teen moms. I did this for a year and a half. By that time, some leaders of an organization called Young Life had seen the need for a ministry to unwed teen moms. I was asked to set up a program. Since I was already discipling a teen mom from within our church, I set up a program to facilitate these kinds of discipleship relationships on a greater scale. I have been involved in directing this program, "Mentor Moms," for the last six years. We have mentored, on a one-to-one basis, 90 teen moms. Presently there are 20 mentors from 11 churches involved in our program.

Although I am working with a parachurch organization (Young Life), this ministry can be carried out just as effectively by any individual or church. One church in a small community set up a Mentor Moms program and recruited enough mentors within their own church to reach out to each of the teen moms in the local high school. (As you read this chapter, you'll see the ministry model that is used in the Mentor Moms program. My hope is that these principles will prove helpful to you.)

I do not purport to have even a fraction of the answers for the whole matter of teen pregnancy. It is a vast problem, involving a multitude of issues. I can merely attempt to present an overview of the problem our country is facing today. This is an opportunity for ministry that the local church must not pass up. Biblical mandate directs us to minister to these girls; let's see what we can do to help them. During the course of our ministry we have developed a model that you might consider adopting. Look around you. Do you see the need? Examine this model according to Scripture and use it if you think it's helpful.

How Big Is the Problem?

One million American teenage girls get pregnant each year, and half of these pregnancies result in the birth of a child. These numbers represent an average of more than four out of ten young women under the age of 20.[1] Of all babies born each year in America (almost 4 million), 12 percent are born to teens.[2] More than eight out of ten of these pregnancies are unplanned.[3] And 35 percent of all teen pregnancies end in abortion.[4] "Younger teenagers have abortion ratios near 1,000, which means that nearly as many pregnant girls 15 years old or under choose to have an abortion as choose to deliver the child."[5] The Centers for Disease Control and Prevention (CDC) of the Public Health Service reported that the national ratio of abortions rose rapidly from 180 for every 1,000 live births in 1972 (after Roe vs. Wade) to 359 in 1980, and subsequently dropped to 335 per 1,000 live births in 1992, the latest figures available.[6] Instead of ratios, let's look at the actual numbers of babies involved—from 586,760 babies aborted in 1972 to 1,359,145 aborted in 1992.[7] For every three babies born alive, one is aborted. Millions of lives are being taken!

Those who choose life for their children desperately need our counsel and support because the difficulties these young mothers face are extreme. Almost 75 percent of these teen mothers are unmarried, up from 15 percent 30 years ago.[8] "Half of teen mothers receive prenatal care compared to 85 percent of older mothers."[9] This often results in low birth weights, infant mortality, and future health problems. Most teen mothers struggle to finish high school: ". . . only 38 percent have a high school diploma and they are highly unlikely to have job skills."[10] The Congressional Budget Office reported that "three-quarters of unmarried adolescent mothers begin receiving Aid to Families with Dependent Children (AFDC) within five years after the birth of their first child."[11] Large percentages of juvenile and adult offenders were raised in homes headed by a teenage mother and an absent father. Teenage mothers, who often live in poverty-level households, contribute to the crime rate by having babies they are incapable of raising responsibly. This cycle of hardship and poverty is perpetuated because a large percentage of the daughters of teen moms end up becoming teen moms themselves.

This is not just "their problem." It is ours as well. We reap the consequences in high crime rates and welfare costs. The federal government spends $7 billion a year on social services to teens and their babies.[12] But most importantly, these teen mothers are our fellow human beings. Many of these women are suffering and perishing without the knowledge of Jesus Christ.

The world has tried many different "solutions" to remedy this situation. The kinds of help offered are sex education, free condoms, "family planning," and the National Campaign to Prevent Teen Pregnancy. Every year a month is set aside by the president as "Teen Pregnancy Prevention Month." These efforts have done little to help the problem; one out of every three girls has had sexual intercourse by the age of 16 and one out of two by age 18.[13] Three out of every four boys have had sexual intercourse by the age of 18.[14] The moral crisis remains even though eight out of ten teenagers have had sex education classes and eight out of ten know where to get birth control products. Who will offer a real and lasting solution?

What Is the Proper Response?

How is the church to respond to this dilemma? The church must make the teaching about God's view of sex attractive to teens and talk frankly with them about it. Perhaps you, as a godly woman, could be called upon to counsel girls in your church regarding abstinence. Young people need to be challenged to make a commitment to postpone sexual activity until marriage. They need to be encouraged toward a future built on a biblical lifestyle of one man for one woman for life, as God planned it.

But what about the young men and women inside and outside the church who get caught up in the sin of fornication? We cannot ignore them. What should we do with them? Reproach them? Shun them? Condone their lifestyle by doing nothing? Or is there a better course of action?

Since Christ is the head of the church, our first question should be, "What would Christ have us do?" Notice that when He saved us, He left us on earth to function as members of His body. He didn't call us home right away so that we could live pure, sinless lives with Him in heaven. Rather, when Jesus ascended into heaven, He gave us this mandate:

> *Go therefore and make disciples of all the nations, baptizing them in the name of the Father and the Son and the Holy Spirit, teaching them to*

observe all that I commanded you; and lo, I am with you always, even to the end of the age (Matthew 28:19-20).

If we were in heaven, we would not be able to show Christ's love and grace to a lost and dying world. The reason that we have been left on this earth is to carry out Christ's Great Commission. That is our principal task. Following the example of our Head, we must be willing to pursue those whom some in our culture and churches would tell us to shun—and that includes single teen moms. We must remember that the grace of Christ that was extended to us excludes boasting and a pharisaical attitude of self-righteousness. Our worst times are not beyond the reach of God's grace. In our best times we are never so good that we do not need God's grace. The grace of the gospel must reach out to young women in their sin, but not leave them there.

Jesus' Example

Let's take a closer look at Jesus so we can emulate our leader:

When the scribes of the Pharisees saw that He was eating with the sinners and tax-gatherers, they began saying to His disciples, "Why is He eating and drinking with tax-gatherers and sinners?" And hearing this, Jesus said to them, "It is not those who are healthy who need a physician, but those who are sick; I did not come to call the righteous, but sinners" (Mark 2:16-17).

We women must guard against self-righteousness and remember from what we were redeemed. God, in His divine love, took the initiative. He did not redeem us because of any good in us. He sent His Son to die for us while we were His enemies (Romans 5:8); He saved us by His grace (Ephesians 2:8-9). We did not merit salvation in any way. We were dead in our trespasses and sins. Only God could enliven us by His Holy Spirit (Ephesians 2:1). We are all on the same level because we have all sinned and are capable of sinning in every way. We must humbly say, "I am just one hungry beggar telling another beggar where to get bread."

In His own words, Jesus gave us a vivid illustration portraying His priorities. He told the story of a shepherd who had lost one of his many sheep. He left the other 99 safe in the fold and went after the lost one. When the sheep was found, the shepherd rejoiced over it more than over the 99 that had not gone astray (Matthew 18:10-14).

Jesus did not just talk about having compassion for sinners. He lived it. He seized every opportunity. He broke the cultural taboos of His time when He spoke to a Samaritan woman at a well. He wasn't put off by the fact that she had been married five times and the man that she was presently living with was not her husband. He knew she was thirsty and He offered her living water—eternal life. Jesus chose to minister to her even though He knew all about her sin. What's more He chose a woman who was on the lowest rung of the social ladder to be His messenger. She put her faith in the Messiah, the Savior of the world, and was so excited that she told the whole village. Many listened and were saved. Jesus taught His disciples as they returned with His lunch, "My food is to do the will of Him who sent Me, and to accomplish His work. Do you not say, 'There are yet four months, and then comes the harvest?' Behold, I say to you, lift up your eyes, and look on the fields, that they are white for harvest" (John 4:34-35).

Are we looking to the fields?

We see many similar instances of Jesus' compassion for stigmatized women throughout the gospels. Mary Magdalene, a woman with seven demons, was one of them. The religious leaders of her day avoided her. But she was important to Jesus. He set her free from Satan's hold on her life, and she joyfully followed Him to the end.

Jesus' feet were washed and perfumed by a woman who was a known sinner. He accepted her ministry to Him. His self-righteous friend wanted to stop her to protect Jesus' dignity, but He turned the tables and reprimanded His friend for not performing even a part of what this woman had done for Him. He then assured the outcast woman that her sins, which were indeed many, had been forgiven. He finished by noting that she loved much because she had been forgiven much, and that "he who is forgiven little, loves little" (Luke 7:47).

God took the initiative in providing the means of our salvation right where we were, just when we needed it. Jesus gave us numerous examples of seeking out the lost. Now we must take the initiative in reaching out to needy teen moms and their babies. Let's not wait for them to clean up their act; they can't do it on their own. Neither can the rest of us. We must remember that we are saved by God's mercy and grace. The whole Christian life is lived by grace. When we confess our sins, He forgives us, and we can rest in His cleansing power. So why can't we who have been forgiven offer mercy and grace to young women who need His love as much as we do?

A Substantial Grace

Offering grace does not mean excusing sin like the world does. Because our society can offer no real hope, it has resorted to offering consolation by lowering its standards. Our culture says that sex outside of marriage is to be expected and therefore we should just provide birth control. It says that having sex and children before marriage is acceptable. It says that a child doesn't need a father to help raise him. Rather, society says it's sufficient to provide government welfare. The humanists who make policy for our government consider man to be the highest order of animal. They reason that because animals are compelled to follow their natural urges, we shouldn't expect teens to suppress their urges. Rather, we should facilitate them so that they won't be hurt in the process.

But does grace simply dismiss sinful behavior? No! On the contrary, grace offers the forgiveness and assistance that is needed in order to answer the call to uncompromising holiness. We aren't called to accept the norms of the world (Romans 12:1-2). We are to lift up a righteous lifestyle as the standard for a follower of Jesus Christ.

Holiness is not an option. Remember, we are called to be holy because God is holy (1 Peter 1:15-16). We know what holiness looks like in the flesh because Jesus Christ was our perfect example. It is impossible to be holy on our own or through the law. Holiness is possible only as we yield to the Holy Spirit and He does His sanctifying work in us through the lifelong pursuit of obedience to God's Word.

So, how are we, as concerned women in the local church, to respond to the overwhelming problem of teen pregnancy? We don't want to shun nor reproach these young women, but neither do we want to condone their sin. We must share the gospel with them and restore them in love because God in Christ first loved us (*see* 1 John 4:19).

Putting Our Response into Action

Some Key Basics

How can we put our desire to minister to teen moms into practice? That's the question we'll answer as we go through the principles that comprise the rest of this chapter. As you read on, keep in mind that we must start with the restoration of those in our own body before we have a loving church home into which to bring teen mothers from outside.

First Establish Guidelines   What should a church do when a daughter of a family in the church becomes pregnant? Many people do not know how to react. Often they are at a loss to know whether to congratulate the prospective grandparents or avoid a touchy subject. They don't know whether to speak to the pregnant teen with enthusiasm about her coming child or ignore the matter. They don't know whether to express joy or grief. They think that if they express joy, then they are condoning sin. But if they keep quiet and say nothing, then they feel that they have let the family down.

When the expectant mother's situation becomes physically obvious, it often becomes a juicy morsel of gossip. People will take the liberty to express their concern or opinions to one another without any intention of becoming a part of the solution. Many times young women drop out of church as their bodies change shape so that they can avoid the stigma and guilt. They don't want to be the focus of gossip and scorn. Thus gossip destroys a church's ability to minister.

We must avoid the confusion and helplessness that lead to destructive, condemning talk. We can do this by establishing a policy that includes guidelines for loving involvement. But because "everybody's business is nobody's business," the church must appoint individuals to carry out these ministry goals. Unless someone is assigned to pursue the restoration process, the pregnant teen could slip through the cracks.

In addition, the elders or leaders of the local church should discuss its position on the whole issue of unwed pregnancy. They should draft a mission statement based on Scripture. These guidelines should be communicated to the church body. Then each case can by handled according to the guidelines, without partiality.

The Importance of a Mission Statement   Here's an example of a mission statement for ministering to single teen moms:

Our church, in the manner of Jesus Christ, extends grace to those who have become pregnant out of wedlock. We do not condone the sin, but we offer the grace of our Lord Jesus Christ. We will seek to minister to each one through the following means:

1. Provide a counselor (which could be the pastor, along with the pastor's wife or a spiritually mature woman) to meet with the pregnant teen and if

possible, the father of the baby, and give her/them biblical counsel that would include steps for repentance and restoration.

2. If repentance follows, they are assured of forgiveness. Then a supportive church body will seek to minister to her/them in the needs of the coming baby and will pledge to support her/them through prayer.

3. A mentor, as the Lord provides, will give continuing care, loving support, and ongoing discipleship.

4. A church shower will be given, under the condition that the mother is willing to forsake the sin of fornication and continue in the fellowship of the church.

5. Follow out the process of church discipline as found in Matthew 18 if she is a member and unrepentant (or if both she and the father of the baby are members).

Appoint a Counselor   The church elders or leaders should seek out and appoint a compassionate, godly woman who has a burden for ministering to teen mothers. As we learned in chapter 4, older women are commanded to disciple and counsel the younger women within the church; they are given very specific guidelines as to how to do this (Titus 2:3-5). If you want to be involved in this kind of ministry, tell your leaders of your desire. If you are married, it would be helpful if your husband wants to become involved as well so you can work as a team in certain situations.

The Church as a Haven for Teen Moms   The congregation must be informed through the church leaders that the pregnancy is not a matter for consternation and gossip, but rather is an opportunity for involvement. Women within the church can be appointed or may volunteer to be counselors or mentors. Great joy results when the body is assured that people are involved in the young mother's life, confronting her, helping restore her to a walk with God, and seeking to minister to the needs of her whole family. The church members are able to rejoice because they are free to encourage her without fear that they are condoning her sin. They can rejoice openly and praise her for making the right choice of not aborting the baby. She can be encouraged that God can use this situation in her life for good, and that this coming child will be a blessing as she continues to make the right choices. And those who do not choose to be directly involved can be reminded of their responsibility to lend loving support and prayer. Through all this the church becomes a haven in the storm—a haven desperately needed by the single teen mom.

A Practical Example

So that we can see how this kind of ministry takes place, let's look at a case study. Imagine that you are Jan, the counselor, who is the catalyst for bringing help and hope in this situation.

Stacy grew up in the church. After dating a sophomore at the local junior college for two months, she found out that she was pregnant. Stacy knew that her boyfriend was not interested in marrying her right then, and she didn't know what to do. Stacy had asked Jesus into her heart when she was very young and even though she had not been walking closely with her Savior, she knew that she belonged to Christ. She felt tremendously guilty about what she had done and didn't know who she could talk to. She avoided her parents at all costs, retreating to her room and her loud stereo whenever she was at home. She felt bad about letting down her parents, and her church family. For her, abortion was a very tempting option. Sometimes she thought that abortion was the best option because then no one would know about her sin and she could go on with her life. But she knew that the guilt of having an abortion would devastate her. So Stacy decided to have her baby because the other options—abortion and adoption—were unthinkable to her. When she could wait no longer, Stacy got up the nerve and told her parents.

"I can't believe you would do this to us," Stacy's father shouted. "After all we've done for you, giving you everything that you could want, raising you in the church, teaching you right and wrong, you should know better! I'll be disgraced in front of the whole church! You haven't told anyone else yet, have you?" Stacy shook her head between sobs as her mother, Sarah, tried to comfort her. "You better not until you've moved out! No daughter of mine is going to be an unwed mom! You can move out! You made your bed, now you can lie in it!" the distraught father screamed as he slammed the door on his way out. "John, how can you say such things?" Sarah shouted after him. "You know he doesn't mean it, honey," Stacy's mother said soothingly while crying tears of disappointment and compassion.

After the ordeal with her parents, Stacy felt even more desolate. She confided in her best friend, Laurie, for support. Laurie knew that the church had some kind of policy for helping teen moms, so she called the pastor to get his help. He then contacted the woman who had been appointed as a counselor over this ministry.

Ministering to the Teen Mom   After Jan, the counselor, got off the phone with the pastor, she reviewed the ministry's purpose statement from Galatians 6:1:

"Brethren, even if a man is caught in any trespass, you who are spiritual, restore such a one in a spirit of gentleness; each one looking to yourself, lest you too be tempted." After prayer for guidance and a time of self-evaluation, Jan contacted Stacy to let her know that she wanted to help her, not condemn her. She wanted to help her be restored to fellowship with Christ and the local body of believers.

Jan used utmost grace when the time came for her to meet Stacy. She took Stacy a rosebud—showing her the care and concern of the church family. She then told Stacy that God had allowed for the baby to grow within her. They read Psalm 139 together and praised God for being sovereign over all things. Jan told Stacy that God could use this situation for good in her life and that His grace was sufficient for her. Jan assured Stacy that the church wanted to minister to her at this time in a special way.

Jan then lovingly spoke to Stacy about forgiveness. Because of her knowledge of God's Word, Stacy realized that what she had done was wrong. Jan showed Stacy Jesus' response to the woman caught in adultery in John 8:1-11. She pointed out that Jesus showed compassion and grace to the woman. He told the pious religious leaders, "He who is without sin among you, let him be the first to throw a stone at her" (verse 7). They all walked away, demonstrating their guilt. Perhaps they were not guilty of adultery or fornication, but they knew they were guilty of other sins. Jesus, the only One who had the right to throw stones, gave her His grace—not judgment. He said, "Neither do I condemn you; go your way. From now on sin no more" (verse 11).

Jan mentioned to Stacy that Jesus, in His love and grace, forgave the woman caught in adultery, but He also commanded her to not continue in her sin. To continue in sin would be to break God's law, offending a holy God and causing damage to herself. Jesus wanted God to be glorified and desired the best for her; He wanted her to turn away from sin and practice righteousness.

Jan then asked Stacy if she was willing to ask God for forgiveness and turn away from her sin. She showed Stacy the wonderful promise of 1 John 1:9, which says, "If we confess our sins, He is faithful and righteous to forgive us our sins and to cleanse us from all unrighteousness." But Stacy rejected Jan's counsel. "I can't stop being with Brad. My dad is threatening to kick me out. Brad's the only one who really loves me right now. If you can't love me the way that I am, then I don't want to go to your church anymore."

Jan pointed out that the church was Stacy's as well. Stacy had grown up in this church. It was her family. The church members loved her. In fact, Jan felt that they might be able to find someone who was willing to let Stacy stay in their home.

In love, Jan pointed out to Stacy that the Bible makes it very clear that the true child of God will not continually practice sin (1 John 3:9). "It's a terrible thing not to have the assurance of salvation that God desires for us to have, or the fellowship with Him that is maintained as we confess our sin and walk in the light," she said. She pleaded with Stacy, stressing how much she needed God's help and blessing with a baby to raise. But Stacy was unmoved. Jan knew that if Stacy was God's child, God would discipline her. She had Stacy read Hebrews 12:6-13, which warned of coming discipline to those who continued in sin. Next, Jan showed Stacy Proverbs 28:13, which says that the person who confesses and forsakes her sin will find compassion, but the one who conceals her sin will not prosper.

Stacy, however, refused to accept this offer of hope through forgiveness. Jan, disappointed at Stacy's response, lovingly assured Stacy that God, like the father of the prodigal son, was waiting for her to come home. His arms were outstretched and ready to receive her, just like the father who welcomed his prodigal son with open arms (Luke 15). Jan told Stacy that she would be praying for her restoration to her Father.

Ministering to the Parents   Jan and her husband, Tom, set up a time to get together with Stacy's parents, John and Sarah. The purpose of this meeting was to offer counsel and express the church's support.

When Tom and Jan asked Stacy's parents how they were doing, John openly told them of their devastation. "Stacy has ruined her life!" he said, pouring out his pain and sorrow over the situation. Sarah joined in, "I can't even describe the overwhelming shock, disbelief, anger, helplessness, and disappointment we felt! It has caused such an upheaval in our lives. I just keep hoping that I'm going to wake up and all this will have been a dream. It seems that all we thought we had instilled in Stacy from childhood has gone out the window." "Yes," John added numbly, "I thought we had all our bases covered. Stacy knows God's plan—the blessings for abstaining and the consequences for sexual promiscuity. Where did we go wrong?"

John and Sarah were crushed by what their daughter had done. Their dreams and hopes for her seemed to have been dashed. They concluded that if they had been better parents, this would never have happened. They also felt that God was partly to blame. "If He is all-powerful, why didn't He prevent this from happening?" Sarah blurted out. Jan and Tom could see that bitterness was creeping into John and Sarah's hearts.

Jan and Tom encouraged Stacy's parents to thoroughly evaluate the situation before God. They explained that children frequently make wrong choices even when they have been raised by parents who endeavored to be godly role models. There are many examples of that in the Old Testament. They needed to recognize that each person is accountable to God for her own choices. Stacy was responsible for her sin, and they were responsible for their sin.

Jan and Tom then asked if John and Sarah had responded to Stacy in the way that they should have. Had they set an example to Stacy by evaluating themselves and making a list of the ways in which they may have failed God and their daughter (Matthew 7:1-5)? What was their foremost concern—how they would look in the eyes of others (fear of man), or how to help Stacy in her predicament? After they asked God for forgiveness, they needed to go to Stacy and ask for her forgiveness.

The counselors encouraged John and Sarah to avoid bitterness by thanking God for this trial and asking for His wisdom (James 1:2-8). God is the author of life, and He had allowed that new life to grow within their daughter (Psalm 139:13-16).[15] There are no accidents with God. This child was in God's mind before He made the world. God would sovereignly use this situation for good (Romans 8:28), and they had to cling to this truth along with God's other promises.

Jan and Tom also told John and Sarah that they could be glad that their daughter had made the right decision by choosing not to have an abortion. They could also be encouraged that God could use Stacy's sin (and the baby that resulted) to provide a much-needed focus in the life of their teenager. Stacy would be forced to take a serious look at her life and would have to take on many responsibilities that she had previously shunned. They could hope that the baby would cause Stacy to see that the responsibility of being a teen mother was too great for her to bear alone, and that she needed God's help.

It was also possible that God would use this circumstance to draw each member of the family closer to Himself. The child who would be born would be a new soul that they could influence for Christ. The child could bring blessing to the family and could have a great part in furthering Christ's kingdom. Indeed, God is a very present help in trouble (Psalm 46:1); He knew their heartache and He would comfort and sustain them. He would give them the strength to go through the whole ordeal one day at a time (2 Corinthians 12:9).

Jan then told John and Sarah about her meeting with Stacy and shared her sorrow over Stacy's refusal to repent and turn back to the Lord. She assured them that the church would be supporting them fully and would be praying for their daughter's spiritual condition before the Lord.

Jan and Tom also expressed concern about John and Sarah's marriage. They had seen couples break up because of the stress of having to constantly deal with the problems of a daughter's pregnancy and the birth of an illegitimate grandchild. A heavy weight of responsibility would now fall on their shoulders. They would have to care for their daughter if she became ill with morning sickness or she had complications in the pregnancy. They would have to cope with the stress of their daughter's emotional ups-and-downs in her relationship with the father of the baby. There would be new financial pressures from medical bills and the cost of supporting the new baby. With a baby in the house, there would be a loss of privacy, and a change in lifestyle because the baby would need attention day and night. There would also be the constant concern over their daughter and grandchild's future. All these factors can overwhelm a couple, and if the church family doesn't offer support, the results could be disastrous!

Over the following weeks and months, Jan and Tom and a few other close couples faithfully called upon John and Sarah to see how they were doing. They sent notes of encouragement and set up times to go out for dinner together. John and Sarah were encouraged to become part of their small group Bible study for support and accountability, and they were counseled to seek out other couples who had weathered similar circumstances.

Eventually, John and Sarah met another couple whose daughter had become pregnant. They said they were glad they had weathered the difficult situation, even though it had brought them to the brink of despair when it happened. But now, looking back, they could see how God had used this situation for good. Now they were able to comfort others with the comfort that they had received (*see* 2 Corinthians 1:3-7). The couple offered to be John and Sarah's prayer partners.

The church's loving support came as a tremendous relief to John and Sarah. Originally they had expected rejection from the church family because of the shame of their situation. But instead, they were becoming closer to the other members of the body than ever before! People were expressing love and support with mutual tears, hugs, and offers of prayer. All this spiritual help enabled them to focus on the one most important concern in this difficult circumstance: that Stacy would turn back to the Lord. Their prayers were to that end.

Following Jan and Tom's advice, John and Sarah sought Stacy's forgiveness for reacting sinfully to her situation and offered to support her by encouraging her to live at home. They had come to realize how patient God had been with them at the times when they had strayed away from him. They knew that it was God's kindness, forbearance, and patience that had led them to repentance (Romans 2:4). With that in mind, they wanted to extend grace to their daughter at this time of crisis in her life. They knew that if there ever was a time when she needed her parents, it was now! As a pregnant teenager, her body was going through tremendous changes. Not only was she still growing physically, but now she was also with child. They knew that the teen years are fraught with emotional instability, and that the stress of a pregnancy might compel Stacy to run away with her boyfriend or get into a worse situation. They had learned that some pregnant teens even struggle with contemplating suicide. Thus they encouraged their daughter to stay at home. Stacy agreed to stay at home, and everyone talked about the guidelines that would be necessary to ensure that all would go smoothly when the baby arrived.

Stacy's parents emphasized to her that they wanted to establish some house rules so everyone would know what to expect of each other. By clearly outlining both the responsibilities and privileges of living in the house, future conflicts would be avoided. Stacy, even though she was living at home with her parents, she was now an adult. Thus she had to carry the responsibilities of an adult, but she would also be given the privileges of an adult:

Responsibilities:
1) When you go out you must let us know where you are going and when you will be in.
2) Babysitting is not a given-it is an option that must be arranged for.
3) The care of the baby is totally your responsibility.
4) Certain household chores will be expected of you.
5) We, as a couple, will be taking time away from the family if possible.

Privileges:
1) Our home is your home and you are welcome here.
2) We will bear the financial burden of you and the baby, willingly and gladly because we love you. (If the father of the baby provides support, then that can be applied.)
3) We are here for you and want to support you and help you in any way that we can, as we are able.

4) You may make your own decisions as to how your baby is to be raised. We will respect your opinion.

5) You have the umbrella of protection as a woman living under your father, who is looking out for you.

6) Your child can grow and develop in the loving and stable environment of this home.

Ministering with the Message of Christ's Forgiveness   Shortly after Stacy gave birth to her baby, Jan went to visit. She gave Stacy a beautifully wrapped gift. After Stacy opened it, she started to cry. "I can't believe how much love my parents are showing for me now, and the way the people in the church really care. I have a whole stack of letters from people saying how much they have missed me at church. Now I have this new baby, and Brad is too busy with football to spend much time with me! I just can't understand it; this is his daughter, too. I know I made a big mistake, but I really want to be a good mom for Cassidy! I want a new start. Will you help me? I want to do things God's way."

Jan asked Stacy if she would like to receive Christ's forgiveness, and Stacy said yes. Jan then explained that Stacy needed to acknowledge her sin against God, and showed Stacy what David said about his sin of adultery in Psalm 51. Through tears Stacy acknowledged her sin to God and asked Him for the strength to live in a way that pleased Him. Then Jan prayed and thanked God for working in Stacy's heart and bringing her back to Himself. She also prayed for Stacy's continued obedience to His leading in her life.

Afterward, Jan rejoiced with Stacy—along with the angels of heaven (Luke 15:10)—over Christ's forgiveness and cleansing. Jan shared that there was now no condemnation for her sin (Romans 8:1). Then Jan added that although God's forgiveness had freed Stacy, she and her family would still have to bear the consequences of her behavior for many years to come.

The next time Jan met with Stacy, she told her that when we sin, we need to ask forgiveness from everyone who was hurt by it. That is God's method of restoration. It is not easy to do this, but the benefit is that when we think of how other people were hurt by our sin, we are deterred from repeating the same sin over again.

With that in mind, Jan asked Stacy if she felt ready to make everything right by asking forgiveness from those who had been affected by her sin. Stacy said yes, and immediately her parents, her boyfriend, and friends at church came to mind.

This was a big step for Stacy, but Jan was available to help and encourage her each step of the way. Stacy worked on what she should say and how she should say it. Jan helped her to realize that simply saying, "I'm sorry" wouldn't be sufficient nor fully biblical; rather, Stacy needed to say "I was wrong; what I did was sinful. Will you forgive me?" Once Stacy knew what she wanted to say, Jan prayed with her for God's strength and blessing.

When Stacy acknowledged to her parents that she recognized that her actions did not honor what she knew to be their will for her as their daughter, they recieved her with open arms. She then told them she knew she had caused them a great deal of heartache. "What I did was wrong. Will you forgive me?" she asked. They forgave her and all cried together and hugged one another. Then they commited the future to the Lord in prayer.

The next step for Stacy was to talk to her pastor along with Jan. Stacy humbly requested the church's forgiveness for sinning against the body of Christ. She acknowledged that she had caused the whole body to suffer (I Corinthians 12:26-27). The pastor, who was pleased about Stacy's change of heart, enthusiastically communicated the church's forgiveness. He told Stacy that she was not a second-class citizen in God's kingdom because of what she had done. He assured her that she would enjoy God's blessing on her life because she had chosen to follow Christ and obey His Word. Stacy left the church feeling much better, for the burden of guilt that she had been carrying for months had finally been lifted.

Stacy then went to her boyfriend, Brad, to ask for his forgiveness. Although the sin was his fault too, she knew she had to take responsibility for her part in it. She also told him that her commitment was to not have sex again with him as long as they were not married, because she wanted to do things God's way. Brad was touched by Stacy's willingness to come to him for forgiveness. He told her not to worry about it, and it was obvious that he didn't recognize his own sin. He said, "Stacy, I know how much we love each other and if you want to wait until marriage, we can." Stacy was surprised at Brad's positive response, but she knew that more changes had to take place in Brad's heart.

Stacy was now committed to living for Christ, and she began to go to church again. After the baby was born, the chruch checked with Stacy's family to see if they could welcome the baby the same way other babies were welcomed—with a rose on the pulpit and a notice in the bulletin. Dinners were brought to the house; cards and gifts were sent. Stacy was given help in securing needed baby items, such as a crib and a stroller. Other women offered to give her relief by babysitting.

Some ladies in the church offered to give Stacy a baby shower to help her care for the needs of her baby. This outpouring of love was a great encouragement to Stacy and her family. Stacy knew that life wouldn't be easy as a single mom, but she had learned that her family in the Lord was fully supportive.

The youth pastor welcomed Stacy back into the youth group. She was not able to go very often because she was in a different situation from the rest of her peers. Eventually she began to replace her old friends with new friends who had children.

Some weeks after Stacy had returned to church, she was asked if she could share with the youth group how God had used her circumstances for his glory. The young people listen attentively as she shared the valuable lessons she had learned through becoming a mother unintentionally. She emphasized that she had gone against God's intended order, but God had still used her situation for her good. She said she hoped that the young people would remember what she had gone through when they found themselves being sexually tempted.

Stacy's time of sharing allowed the youth pastor to talk to the young people about the whole issue of teen pregnancy outside of marriage. He explained that the church is a place for forgiven sinners who are pursuing God in their lives, not for people who think they have arrived. He encouraged the young people to reach out to other teen moms within the church and in their schools with the love of Jesus Christ.

The following Sunday, a few parents of the young people approached the youth pastor and complained that a poor example was being set for their children by allowing a teen mom to attend the youth group and speak before them. The youth pastor responded by telling the parents that the church was not putting their stamp of approval on sex before marriage by encouraging a teen mom to attend, but seeking to make the grace of the Lord Jesus Christ available. He reminded them that every Christian needs God's grace on a daily basis.

Having a teen mom in the church helps to serve as a good deterrent for other young people because then the consequences of sexual sin become obvious. The baby, as precious as he or she is, is a huge responsibility that curtails the freedoms enjoyed by most teenagers. After babysitting all day for a Mentor Mom group outing, one teenage boy remarked, "This is the best sex-ed class I've ever taken. I'm not having sex until I'm married!"

Ministering to the Father of the Baby   Brad had not intended for Stacy to become pregnant. Because he was in college, he wasn't ready to settle down and parent a child. He was very surprised when Jan and Tom, a couple from Stacy's church, invited him and Stacy over for dinner. During their time together, Brad and Tom had a good time talking about sports, which they both liked. Eventually, however, the conversation turned to deeper issues. Tom asked Brad if he understood what it meant to be a Christian. Brad said that although he accepted Christ as a child, he knew he hadn't really been living for God. But in recent months, because of the good changes he had seen in Stacy, he was interested in learning more about God. Tom asked Brad if he would like to get together weekly for a Bible study. "Oh sure!" Brad said without thinking.

But Brad wasn't very consistent. He let other commitments interfere. With school, sports, and a part-time job, his time was limited. However, Tom did not give up. His perseverance paid off, for Brad could see that Tom was not going to give up on him. Brad knew that Tom really cared. He was also at the receiving end of loving gestures of friendship from other church members. Eventually Brad was also confronted in the same way that Stacy was. He was taught about the reality of God's forgiveness and restoration when sin is acknowledged. Convicted by the Holy Spirit, Brad asked God for forgiveness. He confessed his sin against God, Stacy, her family, and his family. Ultimately he came to the realization that he needed to take responsibility for Stacy and the baby.

Jan was thrilled with the progress Stacy and Brad were making, but she knew that they would need ongoing discipleship. She knew that Stacy especially would need in-depth follow-up and support. Even if the teen mom's mother is supportive, it is still very helpful to have another woman involved for support. The father of the baby also needs a mentor, possibly the husband of the girlfriend's mentor.

In summary, based on this case study, we can see that a mentor will minister the love of Christ to the teen mom and her boyfriend (if he is still in the picture). She will do this through friendship and encouragement. She will follow Paul's example in not only imparting the gospel to the people, but her own life as well (1 Thessalonians 2:8-12).

Setting Up a Mentor Moms Ministry

Churches can set up a program to minister to the needs of the teen moms within their own church. They can also reach out to many who would never have entered the doors of their church in any other way. Evangelism is a large part of the Mentor Mom program; this program provides a perfect opportunity for troubled young women to learn about the love of Christ as they see it displayed in tangible ways during their time of need.

Steps to Starting the Ministry

Once the leaders in your church have agreed to minister to young single moms, here are some key steps to beginning a Mentor Moms ministry in your church.

1. Appoint a Director   The ministry needs to be organized and directed by a committed Christian woman who has a burden for unwed teen mothers. She may then want to divide up the responsibilities so that the workload isn't all on one person. Perhaps you are that woman, or you know someone who could be encouraged to take on this ministry.

2. Recruit Mentors   The director is responsible for recruiting caring Christian women who can mentor teen moms in a one-on-one relationship. These mentors will be asked to build bridges of friendship by sharing their lives and their faith with the teen women. Ideally, these mentor mom/teen mom pairs will meet once a week for friendship-building activities over a span of one year.

3. Conduct Mentor Meetings   The director plans and directs the Mentor Meetings, which are designed to help equip the mentors for ministering to the needs of the teen moms. In these meetings, the director disciples the mentors through the Word of God. These women must first and foremost be seekers of God who can have a godly impact on the lives of the teen mothers. The Mentor Meetings also provide the mentors with an opportunity to encourage and pray for one another.

4. Recruit Unwed Teen Moms   The director also helps to seek out teen moms who would like the support and encouragement of a mentor while they are pregnant or parenting. The director will initially want to recruit teen moms from within the church; then she will want to reach out to others—through friends of the teen moms, through the local Crisis Pregnancy Centers, and through school counseling programs. She then can match up the teen moms with the mentors for what could very well become wonderful, lifelong friendships.

5. Conduct Mentor/Teen-Mom Clubs   The purpose of the club is to allow all the mentors, teen moms, and their babies to get together once a month for fellowship and spiritual input. The babies are cared for in the church nursery so the teen moms can be free to enjoy the program, which usually includes a fun, mixer-type game, some praise choruses, and a time for sharing prayer requests and praying for one another. Then you can have a speaker give a presentation on how Jesus can make a difference in a teen mom's life. That can be followed by a craft activity and some time for refreshments and fellowship—allowing the teen moms the opportunity to talk with the speaker. This kind of meeting also lets a teen mom experience the loving support of all the other mentors whom she meets. And ultimately, it provides a friendly environment for sharing the gospel with teen moms who are not yet Christians.

The Task of Mentoring

Webster's dictionary tells us that a mentor is "an experienced, trusted friend and advisor." In our context, she is a woman who helps young moms achieve their God-given potential through sacrificially providing friendship, example, and teaching. It is an intentional, clearly defined relationship in which expectations are spelled out between the mentor and teen mom beforehand. And it is the kind of relationship in which in-depth time spent with one young woman can produce great and lasting results.

A mentor is a loving friend and a positive role model. She teaches more by her example than by her word, knowing that the teen mom will watch how she handles life. It is hoped that as the mentor displays Christ's love and grace, the teen woman will desire to have Christ in her own life in a vibrant and meaningful way.

A key goal in this relationship is for the mentor to demonstrate the love of Christ in very practical ways. She can do this by lending a listening ear and participating in activities with the teen mother. These activities may include homemaking activities or just fun things. The mentor can offer emotional support by listening to the young mother's thoughts, dreams, and hopes. She can encourage her to overcome difficulties, picking her up when she fails, and rejoicing in her successes. She can help the teen mom to get biblical answers and spiritual counsel for her problems.

The Mother of the Teen Mom

What about the teen mom's mother? Won't she feel that her role is being usurped by this mentor? No; she will likely welcome another caring person into her daughter's life. A mentor frees her from carrying the whole load of this trying circumstance. Of course, the mentor should assure the mother that she knows she could never replace her and that replacing her is not the mentor's goal. Also, if the mother is a Christian, she is probably already doing some of the things a mentor would do.

The mentor should never tear down a mother-daughter relationship—only supplement and encourage it. In the case of unsaved teen moms from non-Christian homes, the needs are great and the whole family can be impacted by the loving ministry of a Christian mentor-mom.

Expectations in Mentoring

In spite of the possibility of many wonderful blessings, a mentor should enter the relationship expecting nothing in return. If all expectations are relinquished at the start, there will be less room for disappointment. Don't expect to see a teen mother's tangled web of sin unravel quickly. Don't expect things to go smoothly. Don't expect many expressions of appreciation.

This ministry must be done as unto Christ Himself (*see* Matthew 10:42). Success in mentoring is defined as extending love and presenting Christ in the power of the Spirit. Leave the results to God. Keep in mind that you are sowing seeds of the gospel and planting love in the garden of this young woman's heart—all of which may bear fruit at some time in the future. We are told by Jesus Christ that some workers sow, and others reap, but all can rejoice together (John 4:36–37).

Remember, too, that by ministering to unsaved teen moms, you are invading Satan's territory. Satan doesn't want God to get the victory in these precious young women's lives. He wants to destroy them (*see* 1 Peter 5:8). We are in a spiritual battle; expect opposition! It is very hard to watch a teen woman reap the consequences of going her own way. In my nine years of working with teen moms I have witnessed many devastating consequences that have come as a result of their formerly rebellious lifestyle—including the death of the baby, babies born addicted to drugs, babies being taken away from their mothers and put in foster homes or given to the father, mothers being abused by their boyfriends, estrangement from families, poverty, and other untold heartaches.

I have also seen God work in remarkable ways. "Greater is He who is in you than He who is in the world" (1 John 4:4). I have seen teen moms commit their lives to Jesus Christ and get off drugs and take the mothering responsibility beautifully. I have watched them develop a hunger for God's Word and for pleasing Him. Some have married and are raising their children to know Christ. Others are working on difficult marriages by accepting biblical counsel. Some are going on to college or a trade school to prepare for a career. Some are already in a career. But the positive results do not necessarily come quickly or easily. We must learn to trust God's timing and provision.

Perseverance in Mentoring

Prayer and perseverance are the keys to success in this ministry. There may be times when your heart aches and you literally become sick because it looks like all you have invested in this precious young woman is to no avail. You may weep and cry out to God. "Why, Lord, has she gone back to her empty and fruitless way of life?" You may want to give up in utter discouragement and wallow around in the pit of despondency. Don't do it! Keep persevering, and trust God to work in answer to your prayers. Remember that whatever is accomplished is accomplished through answered prayer (James 5:16). Keep a record of your answered prayers so that you can better see God's faithfulness.

Remember, nothing done for Christ is ever wasted. We were created to do good works (Ephesians 2:10). He will abundantly reward service done to even the least. When we are serving a child, Jesus said, we are serving Him (Matthew 18:5).

Mentoring Activities

Here are just a few suggestions for different types of activities that can help build your friendship with the teen mom you mentor:

Friendship-Building

1. Take a picnic to the park.
2. Go out for frozen yogurt.
3. Make homemade cookies.
4. Take pictures of her baby and make an album.
5. Go for a walk in the woods or another pretty place.
6. Make a craft.
7. Go window-shopping in gift shops.
8. Work on a baby book.
9. Take a trip to the zoo.
10. Go to garage sales.

Discipleship

1. Read from the Bible and discuss the passage you read, or do a Bible study.
2. Take her to church with you.
3. Read a book together on parenting.
4. Offer to help her with a class that is hard for her.
5. Cook a meal together and teach her meal planning and budgeting.
6. Teach her a blessing or prayer to teach her child.
7. Write some thank-you notes together.
8. Go to an aerobics class together.
9. Have her over on housecleaning day or gardening day and let her share in the fun.
10. Show her how to make baby food and freeze it in ice-cube trays.

Bible Study   Mentors will want to encourage Christian teen moms to study God's Word, which will give them assurance of their salvation and help them to grow in the faith. It is in Bible study that teen mothers will discover how to live their life in a way that pleases God. As they hide God's Word in their heart, they will be kept from sin.

In addition, Scripture is sufficient for counsel in every area of a teen woman's life. As a mentor constantly takes her teen mom to the pages of Scripture for guidance and direction, she will gain valuable insights about how to face life. She will learn to look to God first when a problem arises. She will learn what God says about different problems, and how He promises to comfort her. She will find God's Word to be the only sure word in a world where there are no absolutes. It can be trusted in and relied upon.

Unfortunately, many people turn to psychology in their search for answers to the problems these teen mothers face. They assume that God's Word may address small problems, but that the big problems—such as sexual or physical abuse, and sins involving eating or the use of drugs—need to be handled by "experts."

But no problem exists for which God does not have a solution! You must become a student of the Word and dig out the answers. You may want to get training in biblical counseling so that you can gain confidence in handling difficult issues. God's Word is able to equip us for every good work (2 Timothy 3:16-17); if you need help, go to your pastor or a biblical counselor, and have him take your friend to God's infallible and sufficient Word for answers.

Issues Relevant to Teen Moms

Sexual Purity

Sexual conduct is one important area in which teen moms must learn to submit to the standard of the Bible. It is frequently hard for the teen mom to stop having sex with the father of her baby or to not get sexually involved with someone else when she and the father break up. She may feel that because the whole world knows what she has done, there's no use in being pure now. She may think it's too late! Also, once she is pregnant, she cannot get pregnant again for nine months, so it is easy to succumb to the temptation to have sex because there will be no other further consequences. Sexual activity can become a life-dominating sin that is difficult to break without the persistent encouragement and support of a mentor.

Returning to our case study, you'll remember that Stacy told Brad of her commitment to stay sexually pure. But that does not mean that she will no longer be tempted. Even though Brad was beginning to be discipled, there could come times when he would pressure Stacy into having sex again. She may think that to keep Brad in the picture, she will have to continue having sex with him or he will lose interest and find someone else. In addition, the sexual relationship offers many pleasures including the intimacy and security Stacy desires in her relationship with Brad. It would be much easier to continue than to resist. That's why it's essential for mentors to continually encourage teen moms to stay pure through Bible study, scripture memorization, and accountability.

One key reason that mentors need to spend time building the bridge of friendship is so that they can talk comfortably with teen moms about difficult issues. Discussions about sin and sexual purity are best approached in the context of a loving relationship. The mentor can remind the young woman that in God's eyes, she can be completely cleansed from her sin. She can have a new start and should remain pure until she can give herself to a husband who will be committed to her for life. A mentor can point out that even though she has taken the privileges of marriage prematurely, God can give her another chance. Through His forgiveness, she can begin anew and keep herself for her husband, whether it is the father of the baby or someone else. God will give her the strength to remain pure as she seeks Him.

Here are some good questions a mentor can use to get a teen mom thinking and talking about sexual issues:

- What does the Bible say about sex before marriage?
- Do you think God will give you the strength to do what He expects of you? How? What if you slip up?
- Do you know the physical and spiritual consequences of disobeying God in this area of sexual sin?
- Are you serious enough about your relationship with Jesus Christ to obey Him in this area of sex with your boyfriend?
- Whom do you want to please the most—God or your boyfriend?
- Do you think your relationship with your boyfriend is based on sex or a close friendship based on mutual interests, convictions, and concerns?
- Do you think your boyfriend would love you if you stopped having sex with him?
- Do you think your boyfriend would be willing to wait until after you are married to have sex? Would you be willing to talk to him about it and find out?
- How can you say no to sex so your boyfriend knows you mean it?
- How can you avoid getting into situations where it would be easy to have sex?
- If you are living with your boyfriend, are you willing to move out or have him move out? Do you need help making that happen?
- If the father of your baby is no longer in the picture, how do you plan to handle future relationships? How will you fortify yourself against temptation?
- Is it good for you as a Christian to date a non-Christian? Why?
- Are you willing to memorize (or at least read and write out) some scriptures that will help you during times of temptation? (Some helpful passages are: 1 Corinthians 6:9-20; Romans 12:1-2; 2 Timothy 2:19-22; 1 Corinthians 10:13; Colossians 3:5; Galatians 5:19-24; and Psalm 119:11.)

Marriage

The Scriptures must be our guide as to whether to encourage a teen mom to pursue marriage or not. We know that marriage is instituted by God (Genesis 2:18-24). In marriage, two individuals become one flesh. It is into this permanent, one-flesh relationship that God designed for a child to come into the world. However, when sin comes in and the order is reversed, how would God have us handle it? Exodus 22:16 says that if a man has sex with a young woman, he should marry her unless her father forbids her. God takes sexual union very seriously, and He expects a man to take responsibility for his actions. However, we must keep in mind that God gave this rule to His chosen people—to those who were committed to following Him. Thus the situation should be handled differently if the father of the baby is not a Christian.

In the New Testament, the biblical principal is that a believer is not to marry a non-believer (2 Corinthians 6:14). If the teen mother is a Christian who wants to do things God's way, she will not marry a non-Christian boyfriend, even if he is the father of their baby. She will wait until he makes a commitment to the Lord. Of course, if they are both non-Christians, then there would be no teaching that would be against them marrying. Again, let's return to Brad and Stacy. After several months of discipleship, Brad showed definite signs of growth in his spiritual walk with God. One day he approached Stacy's father, John, to ask if he could have Stacy's hand in marriage. John, unsure of what to say, went to his pastor for advice. He was glad that Brad wanted to take his rightful responsibility for his child, but he was also concerned about how young the couple was. How would Brad support Stacy and the child? What if they ended up being incompatible?

John's pastor pointed out that because both Brad and Stacy were Christians there was no biblical reason to forbid the marriage. On the contrary, men who fathered children needed to be encouraged to take their responsibility even if it posed a hardship and the couple had to start out poor. God intended for the family to consist of two parents for the stability and care of the children. And, with God's help, the couple *could* overcome any incompatibilities and choose to love each other sacrificially. With a relationship centered on Christ and grounded in God's Word, and with the body of Christ standing behind them, this young couple could achieve a lasting and happy marriage in which to raise their children.

At the close of their conversation, John's pastor offered to do extra premarital counseling to help the couple deal with all the strikes they had against them by entering into a marriage prompted by a pregnancy. John, greatly encouraged by what his pastor said, went home to tell Brad the good news.

After Stacy graduated from high school, she and Brad had a beautiful wedding attended by the entire church. During the ceremony, tears streamed down Jan's face as she thanked God for answering her prayers. As she watched the bride walk down the aisle in her white dress, she remembered the many days and months of agony she has endured—and knew that it had all been worthwhile.

Who Can Be a Mentor?

These "storybook endings" do not occur very often in our imperfect world. Our world is still very much affected by all the evil effects of sin. Perhaps you can attest to the pain and sorrow involved in being a single teen mom, or you are close to someone who has been there. Perhaps you or someone you know had been a teen mom with no knight in shining armor to come alongside. Perhaps you're still raising a child alone. Perhaps you were married because of a teen pregnancy and now you find yourself divorced. Maybe you have had to deal with the effects of a blended family. You could be a mother or grandmother of a teen mom or the father of the baby.

Perhaps you are thinking there was no one there for you in the church when you needed help. If at one time you were let down or deeply disappointed by a body of believers, don't let that influence you to give up on Christ or His church. Even though you might have lacked the help you needed some years ago, don't let that discourage you from offering help needed by someone going through the same struggles today. With sensitivity, you can minister to those who are where you have been.

If you can relate to teen mothers and the difficulties they face, then God can use all you have been through to help and comfort others (2 Corinthians 1:4). God has brought you to this point; you have seen His grace and power in ways that God wants to use for His glory.

Yet even if you cannot relate to teen moms in any way, you can still have a very valuable and fruitful ministry to them. Your happy marriage and Christian child-rearing perspectives can be a tremendous influence. Don't be hesitant to get involved with teen moms if you haven't been in their shoes; God will give you a heartfelt love that bridges the gap of lack of experience.

The Blessing of Being a Mentor

Jesus' last word to His disciples was, "Go." More correctly translated, this verb means, "As you go" you are to make disciples (Matthew 28:19). Women, don't miss this wonderful opportunity to obey this command wherever you are in your life now, no matter what your life has been like. As you go, you can reach out. If you are a young mom in your own child-rearing years or if you have an empty nest, you can go. If you are single or married, you can reach out. You can reach out if you think you did everything right, or you know you didn't. As you go, you can reach out, but you must put a priority on it.

God will richly bless those who follow Jesus' commands. Christ has promised to be with you in a special way. Your life will take on real joy as you see God use you to rescue a teen mom from Satan's clutches by the transforming power of Christ. As you reach this young mother for Christ, remember that you are not only influencing this generation, but the next. It would be well worthwhile even if only one life were saved, for through that one life, many other lives can be affected, and Christ's kingdom will be advanced.

Yes, you will need to make some sacrifices along the way. The going won't always be pleasant, and the rewards may be very few, if any. But remember, "God is not unjust so as to forget your work and the love which you have shown toward His name, in having ministered and in still ministering to the saints" (Hebrews 6:10). In our service, we are striving for incorruptible and eternal rewards—not temporal ones.

"Therefore, my beloved brethren [sisters], be steadfast, immovable, always abounding in the work of the Lord, knowing that your toil is not in vain in the Lord" (1 Corinthians 15:58). And when Jesus comes to receive us to Himself, may we hear the words, "Well done, good and faithful slave; you were faithful with a few things, I will put you in charge of many things, enter into the joy of your master" (Matthew 25:21).

Recommended Resources

Mary Somerville, *Mentor Moms, A Handbook for Mentoring Teen Mothers.* This guide may be obtained by writing 1819 E. Seeger Ct., Visalia, CA 93292, or calling (209) 734-7232. This handbook outlines how to set up a program from start to finish and gives 18 biblically based studies designed to help a woman be a godly mentor and serve Christ by serving teen moms.

Books on Mothering for Teen Moms
Sandra Aldrich, *From One Single Mother to Another,* Ventura, CA: Regal Books, 1991.
Helen Good Brenneman, *Meditations for the New Mother,* Scottsdale, PA: Herald Press, 1985.
Jean Fleming, *A Mother's Heart,* Colorado Springs: NavPress, 1982.
Tedd Tripp, *Shepherding a Child's Heart,* Shepherd Press, P.O. Box 24, Wapwallopen, PA, 18660, 1995.
Wes Yaystead, *The 3,000 Year-Old Guide to Parenting,*Ventura, CA: Regal Books, 1991.

Books on Sexual Purity for Teen Moms
Elisabeth Elliot, *Passion and Purity,* Grand Rapids: Revell, 1984.
Dawson McAllister, *You, God, and Your Sexuality,* Shepherd Ministries, 2845 W. Airport Fwy, Suite 137, Irving, TX 75062, (214) 570-7599.
Josh McDowell, *Why Wait?* San Bernardino, CA: Here's Life, 1987.

Pamphlets
Elisabeth Elliot, *Sex Is a Lot More Than Fun,* Gateway to Joy, Box 82500, Lincoln, NE 68501.
The Real Purpose of Life, Student Office, 3800 N. May Avenue, Oklahoma City, OK 73112, (405) 942-3800 ext. 246.

Books for the Mentors

Jay Adams, *How to Handle Trouble,* Phillipsburg, NJ: Presbyterian and Reformed, 1982.

_____, *How to Help People Change,* Grand Rapids: Zondervan, 1986.

_____, *How to Overcome Evil,* Phillipsburg, NJ: Presbyterian and Reformed,1977.

Jerry Bridges, *The Discipline of Grace,* Colorado Springs: NavPress, 1993.

_____, *Trusting God Even When Life Hurts,* Colorado Springs: NavPress, 1990.

John Broger, *Self Confrontation: An In-Depth Discipleship Manual,* P.O. Box 925, Rancho Mirage, CA 92270.

Evelyn Christianson, *What Happens When Women Pray,* Wheaton, IL: Victor Books, 1991.

Elisabeth Elliot, *Discipline: The Glad Surrender,* Grand Rapids: Baker Books, 1985.

Gene Getz, *The Measure of a Woman,* Ventura, CA: Regal Books, 1984.

Jeanne Hendricks, *A Mother's Legacy,* Colorado Springs: NavPress, 1988.

_____, *Women of Honor,* Gresham, OR: Vision House, 1995.

Lee Isel, *The Cinderella Syndrome,* New York: Bantam Books, 1985.

_____, *The Missing Piece,* Ann Arbor, MI: Servant Publications, 1991.

Barbara Johnson, *Count It All Joy,* Grand Rapids: Baker Books, 1981.

Paul Little, *How to Give Away Your Faith,* Downers Grove, IL: InterVarsity Press, 1966.

John MacArthur, Jr., *Our Sufficiency in Christ,* Dallas: Word Books, 1991.

Susan Olasky, *More Than Kindness—A Compassionate Approach to Crisis Childbearing,* Wheaton, IL: Crossway Books, 1990.

Anne Ortland, *Fix Your Eyes on Jesus,* Dallas: Word Books, 1991.

Doris Van Stone, *Dorie, The Girl Nobody Loved,* Chicago: Moody Press, 1979.

_____, *No Place to Cry—The Hurt and Healing of Sexual Abuse,* Chicago: Moody Press, 1990.

CHAPTER 6

Counseling Women Discontent in Their Singleness

Lorrie M. Skowronski, M.A.

"I'm lonely and depressed, and I'm having trouble motivating myself to do anything," Joan said as she sat crying in my office. "Lately I've been having trouble controlling my anger. I'm beginning to withdraw from my friends and from fellowship within my church. My friends are all married. People in my church keep asking me when I'm going to settle down and get married. I don't know what to say to them. I know they all mean well, but I always leave those conversations feeling more depressed. I feel like I don't fit in anywhere."

Joan is one of many women I have counseled who was suffering from the "side effects" of being single and not loving it. She is an attractive 38-year-old single woman who came to me for counseling when she began to see her singleness as a bad "condition" she had. She saw this "condition" affecting other areas of her life, and she didn't know what to do to stop it.

Instead of finding acceptance and encouragement from within her church, she felt pressure to find a husband and start a family so she would fit in with other people her age. Often she was matched up with a blind date that a well-meaning person would arrange with a sense of urgency because of her age. People would make unfounded promises, suggestions, and jokes relating to her singleness—all of which reinforced the negative thoughts she was having. Joan's problem was not that she was single, but that she was *not content* in that singleness.

As a 42-year-old single woman and counselor, I am frequently asked to speak at singles conferences and various church Sunday school classes. In many cases I have found that singleness is a term that seems to have a negative connotation. It is looked upon as a temporary condition that is acceptable only for a time. After a certain age is reached, red flags seem to go up warning that something must be done soon—before it's too late. The single person begins to ask questions like, "What's wrong with me?" and friends sometimes wonder if something is amiss in the single person's life.

What's Wrong with Being Single?

As you minister to single women, it is good to ask them what they tell themselves about their singleness. If a woman is struggling with being single, she may be telling herself some of the statements listed below—statements that ultimately say, "I'm deficient."

Personal Misconceptions

"I'm incomplete; there's something wrong with me." This statement is often supported by the church when marriage is offered up as the means to becoming complete. This perspective is usually based on Genesis 2:18, which says, "The LORD God said, 'It is not good for the man to be alone; I will make him a helper suitable for him.' " (*See* chapter 4, pages 15-16.)

"I don't fit in with others my age." Often I hear this from women in their thirties and forties, whose peers are all married and have children. As the woman becomes more focused on her singleness, she realizes she has different concerns and priorities than her married friends.

"I must be outside of the will of God. He is withholding marriage because of some sin in my life." This statement is commonly made by women who believe that their behavior determines whether or not God loves them. They often are perfectionists, thinking that God will withhold His blessing until everything is just right in their life.

"I feel like a child because I'm not married." This woman feels like she hasn't grown up because she doesn't have her own family. She is uncomfortable being "the odd woman out." She may be thinking that her adult life is slipping away while she waits to find "the right man."

"I must be incapable of handling marriage and family relationships." Some women conclude that God is keeping them from being married because He knows they couldn't handle the responsibility well.

"I'm a failure as a person." This woman tells herself that, in the ladder of life, the next rung up is marriage, and she can't reach it. She feels like a failure because marriage is the "norm" and she can't achieve it. It is a personal reflection on her.

"I'm wasting my life away. If only I was married . . ." Waiting has gotten this woman discouraged to the point that she believes marriage will solve everything. Yet, the longer she waits, the more life seems to be slipping by. Her whole purpose in life has become to be married.

"I would grow more as a Christian if I had a godly husband to spiritually nurture me." This woman has put the responsibility of her own relationship with God onto a husband. This indicates her poor understanding of the term *relationship.*

"God isn't who He says He is." After questioning herself for so long, this woman has now decided to question the very character of God. She has become bitter, blaming God for not doing what she wants Him to do for her.

In every one of those statements, the goal of the woman is clearly to get married. She has come to believe that marriage would meet all her "needs." Marriage is seen as the source of all peace, joy, love, comfort, strength, happiness, security, confidence, fulfillment, and so on. A single woman with the wrong perspective will think that marriage can provide the things that, in actuality, only God can. Thus marriage becomes her god. She lives for it, serves it, and waits for it to come. God calls this idolatry; we'll take a more in-depth look at that later in the chapter.

A single woman's thoughts about marriage aren't always her own; oftentimes other people are influencing her thinking.

Outside Influences

Parental—To some parents, marriage equals maturity. These parents feel that once marriage occurs, their job is finally done. For other parents, the goal is for their children to settle down and marry to begin the next generation. For them, the goal is grandchildren.

Sometimes parents long to become grandparents in the same way that a single woman longs to be married. There may be a wrong emphasis on the role and what it will do for them. I have seen parents put tremendous pressure on their single daughters, and many times the results have been disastrous.

Friends—A single woman may feel pressured when she goes to church and sees all her friends now married with families. They are looking at buying houses and deciding what school to send their children to, and she is not. Her married friends now have different priorities and interests than she does. Sometimes the status of the friendships changes on account of other people's marriages. The single women feel a sense of loss because the friendships aren't what they used to be.

Church—Within the church, marrying and having a family is considered the norm. Churches are family-oriented with good reason—the family was designed by God. We are the family of God. Believers are identified as brothers and sisters in Christ. We are part of a unique body, the body of Christ, with Christ as the head. As Ephesians 4:14-16 explains,

> *We are no longer to be children, tossed here and there by waves, and carried about by every wind of doctrine, by the trickery of men, by craftiness in deceitful scheming; but speaking the truth in love, we are to grow up in all aspects into Him, who is the head, even Christ, from whom the whole body, being fitted and held together by that which every joint supplies, according to the proper working of each individual part, causes the growth of the body for the building up of itself in love.*

Each of us is an important member of the body of Christ. Each one of us has a function, and is to grow up

> *. . . for the equipping of the saints for the work of service, to the building up of the body of Christ; until we all attain to the unity of the faith, and of the knowledge of the Son of God, to a mature man, to the measure of the stature which belongs to the fulness of Christ (Ephesians 4:12-13).*

However, some churches are so focused on the nuclear family that they neglect the discipling of the entire church family. Singles, widows, orphans, and others in the extended family of God may not be part of a nuclear family the way the church (and the world) defines it. They are, however, all a part of the family of God, which includes believers of all generations and nations. In some churches there is little or no intensive discipleship taking place within the church body to build up the individual members. The thrust is often world evangelism, while the members of the body of Christ limp along with only a few growing to maturity.

Many churches are guilty of focusing largely on family units and neglecting the needs of members who are single or widowed. We are *all* united to each other through Christ. However, that may not seem so if individual families become so self-focused that they don't nurture and care for their single brothers and sisters in Christ. In a family-focused church, singles may become influenced to adopt a wrong view of family as well as singleness. They may conclude that the only way to belong to a loving family is to marry and have their own. That, however, is not true.

Various outside influences, then, can contribute to a single woman's wrong view of singleness. She may see marriage as the answer to some of the pressures she feels from others, whether those pressures are intentional or not.

A Biblical View of Singleness

Singleness is a good gift

In 1 Corinthians 7:7, the apostle Paul states that singleness is a gift from God, just as marriage is a gift from God. (We will study this passage more later on in the chapter.) Both are good, and God can be glorified in both. Dependence upon God is essential for both to be lived out faithfully. The state of singleness is meant to be good, not negative, as so many people believe.

Singleness is God's will for me now, maybe even for life

A woman who is unmarried has the ability, by God's grace, to honor God in her single life. If she can bring glory to God now, she can do it for life.

My identity is rooted in Christ, not in marriage

As we learned in chapter 3 of this book, a woman must get her identity from her relationship with God, not from her role as wife. The woman who believes marriage will give her an identity grieves the Lord, who gives marriage or singleness as a gift. "Every good thing bestowed and every perfect gift is from above, coming down from the Father of lights, with whom there is no variation, or shifting shadow" (James 1:17). A single woman can trust that the Lord will either provide a mate or give her inner strength so she can continue as she is.

My contentment is not dependent upon my circumstances but upon my relationship with Jesus Christ

Paul states clearly that contentment comes through Christ alone. In Psalm 23:1 David states, The LORD is my Shepherd, I shall not want." He goes on to explain how his Shepherd provides for his every need. David's thankfulness to God for lovingly supplying all he needed produced a peace and contentment that was not affected by circumstances.

Our attitudes towards God's gracious provisions determine how content we will be. In 1 Thessalonians 5:18 Paul exhorted the believers to "in everything give thanks; for this is God's will for you in Christ Jesus."

Singleness allows for undistracted devotion to the Lord

In 1 Corinthians 7:32-35, Paul declared that people who are not married should strongly consider the option of remaining single because they can concentrate more fully on the Lord without the distractions of family life:

> *I want you to be free from concern. One who is unmarried is concerned about the things of the Lord, how he may please the Lord; but one who is married is concerned about the things of the world, how he may please his wife, and his interests are divided. And the woman who is unmarried, and the virgin, is concerned about the things of the Lord, that she may be holy both in body and spirit; but one who is married is concerned about the things of the world, how she may please her husband. And this I say for your own benefit; not to put a restraint upon you, but to promote what is seemly, and to secure undistracted devotion to the Lord.*

I am complete in Christ

Single people are often told that marriage "completes" them, leaving those who remain unmarried to assume they are "incomplete" until marriage takes place. This wrong belief was what brought a woman to my office one day in a state of serious depression. Her pastor had preached this viewpoint from the pulpit several weeks earlier and she couldn't get past feeling conspicuously "incomplete" in her church at the age of 37. This wrong viewpoint was reinforced when, after that sermon, the people in the church suddenly began to arrange dates for her, attempting to help her along in the process.

This desire to be "completed" by marriage sets up a woman to marry for the wrong reasons. Is she marrying because she needs to get something for herself from the marriage, or is she marrying so that she can give and serve?

In Colossians, chapter 2, Paul addresses every believer's completeness in Christ in verses 9-10: "In Him all the fulness of Deity dwells in bodily form, and in Him you have been made complete, and He is the head over all rule and authority." Every believer is made complete by the work of Christ in his or her life. If singleness is a good gift from God, and Paul encouraged the unmarried and widows to remain single, then how could single men or women be considered incomplete? "Well," you might say, "those who do stay single must have the gift of singleness." But what about those who are single even though they desire to be married? Has God given them the gift of singleness as well?

In 2 Peter 1:2-4, Peter writes:

> *Grace and peace be multiplied to you in the knowledge of God and of Jesus our Lord; seeing that His divine power has granted to us everything pertaining to life and godliness, through the true knowledge of Him who called us by His own glory and excellence.*

According to these verses, we have everything we need to live godly lives. God gave this to us when we became His children.

However, a single woman can misinterpret her desire for intimacy with God as a desire for a husband, a child, or anything else that she believes will give her complete and total fulfillment here on earth. We must remember that Scripture tells us there will always be a yearning in our hearts that will be fulfilled only when we are glorified and in the presence of our Lord:

> *We know that the whole creation groans and suffers the pains of childbirth together until now. And not only this, but also we ourselves, having the first fruits of the Spirit, even we ourselves groan within ourselves, waiting eagerly for our adoption as sons, the redemption of our body (Romans 8:22-23).*

Contentment and the "Gift of Singleness"

God's Gifts Are Good

If someone were to give you a gift, would you give it back because you didn't like it? Or would you look at the intent with which the gift was given, and accept it graciously? Perhaps the gift was given to you by someone who doesn't know you well, and your tastes are very different. Or, maybe the gift wasn't necessarily what you wanted, but the person knew of a particular need you had and sought to meet that need on your behalf.

Today, more emphasis is put on the recipient's desire for the gift rather than on the intent behind it. At Christmas, people frequently say, "If it's something you don't want, you can exchange it." We have become so self-centered that we receive gifts expectantly, as long as they are what we want. We may give gifts with the same selfishness, often with very little thought about why the gift is being given. What seems to be missing in both the receiver and the giver is love and a thankful heart.

In order for a gift to be given in love, you must really know the person who will be receiving it. Does God really know us? Yes, He knows everything about us because He created us. He knows exactly what we need in order to be drawn closer to Him so that we will get to know Him better and bring glory to His name. We often forget that *we* live for God, not He for us. We were purchased with Christ's blood. We were bought with a price. We were sealed in Him by the Holy Spirit, adopted into His family, and we now belong to God.

Why would we willingly accept the free gift of salvation but selectively reject the other good gifts God gives to us? I believe those who are single may be rejecting God's good gift because it's just not what they want. An unspoken expectation exists that "all" will marry. The verses in Scripture that say some people won't marry (such as 1 Corinthians 7:32-35) are ignored.

In his book *Deserted by God?*, Sinclair Ferguson said,

> *Spiritual contentment is rooted in and based on an inward relationship to God, not on external circumstances. . . . True contentment is not the same thing as getting whatever we want; it is submitting to the Lord's will and learning to desire what He does. Only then will we discover that His will is good, perfect, and acceptable.*[1]

Contentment is learned as we grow to know and love God as He is. A necessary ingredient is a thankful heart—no matter what circumstances we are in.

Discerning the Gift of Singleness

Often the question arises of whether or not a woman or man has the gift of singleness. I have read many books and articles that say the determining factor of single giftedness is a person's sexual drive. Some writers point to 1 Corinthians 7:7-9, where the apostle Paul wrote:

I wish that all men were even as I myself am. However, each man has his own gift from God, one in this manner, and another in that. But I say to the unmarried and to widows that it is good for them if they remain even as I. But if they do not have self-control, let them marry; for it is better to marry than to burn.

This burning, according to these authors, is what indicates that a person should marry. However, Paul later wrote to Timothy about younger women who were widows. These women were feeling "sensual desires in disregard of Christ" and wanted to get married. Paul said they were "incurring condemnation, because they [had] set aside their previous pledge" (1 Timothy 5:11-12). He then listed the behaviors exhibited by these women—behaviors that are characteristic of immature Christians. They had become idle gossips and busybodies, going from house to house talking about inappropriate things. Paul thus told Timothy,

I want younger widows to get married, bear children, keep house, and give the enemy no occasion for reproach; for some have already turned aside to follow Satan (1 Timothy 5:14-15).

It seems Paul was telling Timothy that the younger, more immature widows were prone to focus less on Christ and more on their sexual desires. As immature Christians, they were getting into trouble, living unfruitful and sinful lives. Paul's desire was for them to grow mature and be above reproach whether they stayed single or married. He wanted these women to live their lives in a way that served Christ.

These verses line up with what Paul wrote in 1 Corinthians 7—it seems he is saying that if a widow (or single woman) is struggling with sensual desires to the point of "burning" because of lack of self-control or spiritual immaturity, she should marry rather than put herself in danger of following Satan. However, this is not the highest good. Paul said, "I say to the unmarried and to widows that it is good for them to remain even as I" (1 Corinthians 7:8).

I don't believe Paul is teaching that all young widows and single women who struggle with sexual desires should just go out and marry. Struggling to control sexual desire, like all our trials, may be the road to greater dependence on God and a deeper knowledge of His grace and goodness. It seems Paul is saying to the widows that they should endeavor to mature to the point where they can consider remarriage with the right intent—to serve their spouses, rather than to go into marriage to get what they want from it. To marry with selfish motives would go against God's design for marriage, which calls for spouses to minister to one another, not to themselves.

Desire and the Will of God

Some people say that a woman can determine if she has the gift of singleness by examining the desires of her heart. For example, if her desire to have children is strong, then she may have the gift of marriage. If not, then her gift may be singleness.

The problem with this perspective is that a woman's giftedness is being determined by her own desire. Desiring to have children is good, obviously, within the context of marriage. However, a woman should not allow her desires alone to determine God's will. God's will must come to her from the Scriptures.

I've also heard people say that God wouldn't give a woman the desire to marry and have sexual relations if He wasn't going to provide a spouse for her. Therefore, if you have that desire, you can wait expectantly for God to "meet your needs." But it's important to note that God promises to supply all our needs as *He* defines them—not us. He didn't promise to simply grant our every request while we are here on earth.

It *is* possible for God to use our desires to guide us if we are living in obedience to Him. In Psalm 37:4, the psalmist writes, "Delight yourself in the LORD; and He will give you the desires of your heart." Notice that delighting in God is the focus in this verse, not getting what we want. If we delight in God and seek His guidance, He will give us desires that align with His desires for us. At times the Lord may even present us with several different options and leave the decision up to us.

Let's take a look at how we pray for the things we desire. Should I tell God that He owes me a husband because He gave me the desire for one? No, I mustn't tell God what I think I should have. If I do this, I am communicating to Him that I am trusting not in Him, but in myself. What I'm really saying is that I want my will to be done regardless of what His will is for me. As a Christian, however, I need to rest assured that I already have everything I need to live my life faithfully for God (2 Peter 1:3).

We run into danger when we let our desires become so strong that they control us. When that happens, we cross the line from having a normal desire to having an inordinate desire. Our want has become too great. Our thoughts have become so obsessive that every man we meet is immediately evaluated as a potential spouse. We end up forsaking the ministry of sister to brother out of love because we're "sizing up" to see what we can get for ourselves. This is idolatry, which, of course, offends God.

What are the characteristics of a content single woman? A content woman is . . .

- *confident* in the truth of God's Word, in His love, and in His plan
- *consistent* in her relationship with God and her daily walk
- *connected* to her church, using her gifts to serve God faithfully
- *committed* to accepting God's will with a thankful heart in all circumstances

In addition, she will seek to build godly relationships with her brothers in Christ for the glory of God and for their good. She will see single men as brothers to serve (1 Timothy 5:1-2) not as individuals to be manipulated to serve her (by marrying her).

Genuine Concerns and Fears

It is important for the church to understand the specific struggles single people have and to know how to effectively minister to them. When I ask people to name the number-one problem they think singles face, the answer is invariably, "Loneliness." However, that struggle is not unique to singles. I have counseled many lonely married women.

Some friends and I once got together and discussed the fears and concerns we had as single women. We decided to make a list of those fears and concerns. As the list grew longer, it became obvious that we all had a lot of the same ideas and experiences. The more we talked, the more we realized how the church needs to minister to single women. Here are some of the items that appeared on the list:

Missed Motherhood

We all had thought that by a certain age we would be married and have a family. As our biological clocks ticked onward, however, each one of us has had to come to grips with the possibility that we would never be able to experience the joys and stresses of pregnancy and give birth to a beautiful child created by God. Not all women want to experience motherhood, but each of us admitted to having a strong desire to have children.

As we talked about the different ways we coped with this frustration, we found that each of us had been faced with our own sinful periods of lust, anger, bitterness, and envy as we were challenged in our hearts by the Word of God.

Some of us also came to the realization that we had developed wrong motives for wanting children. A woman who has a child can feel "needed" in a unique way. Some of us weren't feeling very needed. We realized our assumption that having a child would give us an identity as a mother. A child would also enable us to fit in with society's expectation that people should be part of a family unit. We thus recognized that it's possible to want children for self-centered reasons. We shouldn't desire children merely because we think they will help us feel better about ourselves. We recognized selfishness and self-centeredness in our hearts. We thought it would ultimately make us feel better about ourselves, and that was a wrong motive.

Some of us were angry at God and ourselves for not getting what we wanted or what we thought we should have. We admitted to feelings of envy and times of avoiding fellowship in family-oriented situations. We all admitted to having struggles with this at different times in our lives, with some of those times being worse than others.

During our discussion we encouraged each other by remembering that we were God's children, and that we are in His family. We have been called to disciple His other children according to His will. We also remembered that every parent who brings a child into this world must keep in mind that his or her child belongs to the Lord. God entrusts a child into the care of the parents for only a short time. If we look to children for fulfillment, then our happiness will be short-lived, for children grow up quickly.

Financial Struggles

We talked about our concerns about financial planning. Retirement plan? Who is going to retire? Some of us were struggling to make ends meet daily with little, if anything, to put aside for the future. We decided that each of us needed to do some careful evaluating and budgeting to find ways to be better stewards of the incomes God had given us. Some of the women said they might find it helpful to see a financial counselor about planning wisely for the future.

Not only did future financial situations concern us; we thought about present ones as well. The fear that a major car repair, medical crisis, or other emergency could come at any time made a few of us shake on the spot. How would it get paid for?

The reminder that God is sovereign over all such situations brought calm and comfort as we began to reflect on the many ways He had provided for each one of us in the past. It is so easy in the midst of trials to allow our circumstances to cloud our vision of God. We must see our circumstances through His eyes, focusing on Him and not the momentary trial.

Illness

Some of us who live alone talked about the potential difficulties of getting sick or being on medication. If an emergency arose, would we be able to call for help? Of course, living with a female friend or with a family would take care of that problem, but for some of us, moving in with someone or sharing an apartment wasn't possible at the time.

We all assured each other that we would be available to call and keep watch over one another should such situations arise. However, some of us live quite some distance apart. Since we all don't attend the same church, we agreed we could also make ourselves accountable to people in our fellowship groups, Bible studies, or Sunday school classes. We would find people who would agree to be available to help should an emergency arise, and we would do the same for them. Out of love for God and one another, we would care for, nurse, feed, and minister to each other as needed for God's glory.

We also said we would encourage each other with the Scriptures, since pointing each other to God was most important. None of us wanted to become dependent on another person to the point that we forgot to depend on God. We did not want to create sinful dependencies, where we run to other people every time a problem arises and forget to look to God. We didn't want to put others before God in our hearts.

Dating

The subject of dating is often a controversial one among single women. Either they don't want to discuss it or it is all they talk about. Frustration, anger, sarcasm, apathy, and many other emotional responses will arise when you talk to single women about dating.

Women in their twenties often meet male friends in college or in a college and career group in their church. But as they get older, fewer opportunities exist to build friendships with single men simply because there are fewer men who are single.

As a student in seminary, I enjoyed great fellowship with men because we had a common goal and purpose in our studies. We encouraged one another daily, prayed for one another, and helped one another prepare for exams. Godly brother/sister relationships were developed and we all were blessed.

After seminary, however, those relationships dissolved as we scattered to different parts of the world. Also, some of the men became married, and the relationships we had as fellow students on the seminary campus didn't exist anymore. It would have been inappropriate to meet with them alone in a context outside the seminary.

My friends and I all agreed that having male friends was a special blessing, and we missed some of the past times when we could relate with men as brothers and sisters in a faithful, pure, and honest way.

The matter of dating becomes more difficult when women are in their late thirties or older. One advantage, of course, is that these women have a clearer picture of the type of person they would consider marrying. Yet, as time passes, when these women take their eyes off the Lord and focus on themselves, it's easier for certain temptations to enter in.

What exactly is dating? For years I thought dating was a means to an end—that end being marriage. There was another time when I thought dating was just going out with a man to enjoy his company. After becoming a Christian in my late twenties, dating seemed very strange. I thought it should be fellowship, yet some Christian men whom I dated weren't much different than the unbelievers I went out with when I was younger. As I got older, it seemed that no one wanted to call their times together "dates." Instead, we were "just friends doing things together."

In his book *Dating with Integrity: Honoring Christ in Your Relationships with the Opposite Sex,* John Holzmann gives a helpful definition of dating. He writes,

> *As far as I'm concerned, brother-sister dates merely require that you arrange to meet together and then, once you're in each other's presence, you share as many blessings as you can within the limits God has established for brother-sister relationships.*[2]

Biblically speaking, we are either brother and sister or we are husband and wife. In fact, if husband and wife are believers, they are brother and sister in the Lord. They have, however, made a covenant together with God to enter into the unique and exclusive marriage relationship.

The Bible has much to say about how Christian brothers and sisters should minister to one another. To better understand this kind of relationship, it is helpful to look up the words "one another" in a large concordance and write down all the commands God gives regarding interactions between brothers and sisters in Christ.

As the brother-sister relationship grows, it is possible that the man and woman may see themselves moving towards ministry to each other within marriage. Yet at all times, the ministry aspect of the relationship is most important. Are they friends? Are they serving others and encouraging one another to grow in their relationships with God? Is God first priority in each one's life, or are their minds consumed with thoughts of each another? Do they have the same ministry goals for the future?

Dating Unbelievers

One temptation any single woman faces is meeting a nice man who is an unbeliever. While it's possible to associate with an unbelieving male, it's impossible to have a dating relationship if we hold to the definition of dating as given by John Holzmann.

I firmly believe that Christians should not date unbelievers. I have had Christian friends try to interest me in dating an unbeliever whom they thought was "close" to salvation. Such dating, commonly known as "missionary dating," is dangerous and unbiblical. Second Corinthians 6:14 states clearly, "Do not be bound together with unbelievers; for what partnership have righteousness and lawlessness, or what fellowship has light with darkness?" Many of us have heard this verse quoted before. It all comes down to whether or not we choose to obey. Will we obey God, or do what we want to do? Clearly, the right choice is to obey.

A good portion of the counseling I do is marriage counseling. Many of my counselees are women who married an unbeliever. I have seen the pain and heartache involved when two people have absolutely nothing in common except possibly the children they have had. Loneliness and emptiness are every-day companions in this Christian woman's life. She desires a close, intimate, godly marriage but it eludes her. Hostility or apathy is evidenced by the unbelieving spouse. The unbelieving husband doesn't understand why his wife makes such a big deal about her faith. For more information about these kinds of relationships, see chapter 9, "Counseling Women Married to Unbelievers."

Inappropriate Expectations of Others

I once had a job that required me to work at night. I found out after a few nights that I would be the last person working in the building. Because I was the last person to leave, I was asked to check that the building was completely locked up before I departed. I went to my supervisor and asked, "Would you allow your wife to be put in this situation?" The man mumbled, "No," and walked away.

I was disappointed and hurt that I was expected to lock up a large, old building alone. This was not part of my job description, and it showed that my emloyer lacked any concern for my well-being. I then told my supervisor that he would have to find someone else to do that part of the job.

A friend of mine was asked to serve in a very time-consuming position in her church. When she said she didn't know if she had the time to put into the task, the person responded, "What do you mean? You're single. You don't have a family to take care of. You've got more time than a married woman would have."

Another friend was often "volunteered" for the clean-up committees (without being asked) by a woman in her church. This woman assumed that because my friend was single she could afford the time to stay for a while and work after church events.

In all these situations, people made assumptions about what single women can do—assumptions that were accompanied by inappropriate expectations. All of us in our discussion group had experienced these kinds of situations.

We reminded each other that this does not happen only to singles. Moreover, we knew that God designed for the individual members of the body of Christ to work together for the good of the whole. Each member needs to do his or her part. At the same time, single people need to let others know when unbiblical or unrealistic expectations are being placed upon them.

How to Minister to Single Women

It is the responsibility of all the members of the church to encourage and minister to one another. Hebrews 3:13 tells us, "Encourage one another day after day, as long as it is still called 'Today,' lest any one of you be hardened by the deceitfulness of sin." The Lord has given us a long list of "one another" verses in Scripture to help us know how we should care for the other members of the body of Christ.

Listed below are some ways you can minister specifically to single women within your local church body.

Be a mentor

Paul wrote to Timothy that older women are to encourage younger women—to mentor and teach them how to live godly lives (Titus 2:3-5). The idea of mentoring seems to have been lost over the years, yet this is exactly what discipleship is. I have heard many single Christian women express a desire for a discipler to talk with and learn from. The commitment level for the discipleship process can be whatever the two women decide, depending on their schedules. A woman who is willing to serve as a mentor can find a younger woman in the church and begin to get to know her and take interest in her. She will begin to see what some of the younger woman's needs are. An excellent way to begin this kind of relationship is to become prayer partners. If you choose to become a mentor yourself, be an example of the kind of woman you believe the Bible wants you to be. Be willing to be held accountable for your thoughts, words, and actions. You will find yourself growing even as you serve your disciple.

Adopt a single woman

Become aware of single women who may be without any extended family in the area. Bring her into your home for holidays, dinners, weekends, or special occasions. This is a blessing especially if you have children who want her to be there as well. She can become a great influence on your children; she will be another adult who can influence them toward godliness. Sometimes children like to talk about important matters with adults other than their parents.

Let me say a word of caution at this point. Some well-meaning Christians want the single woman to become part of the family to the point where they expect her to call them "mom" and "dad." Along with this, they make statements that intend to include her in the family—statements like, "You can just consider yourself part of this family, with all the privileges." Then when the woman acts on these statements, she realizes quickly that she is not really treated like the other members of the family. Hurt and confusion are usually the result.

It is important for the host family to be careful and honest when opening up their home to a single woman in the church. I've seen situations where a woman was "adopted" into a family without her really wanting to be a family member. Friendship was what she was looking for, but the family wound up appointing themselves her family. Along with that came all the expectations within a family, which made the woman uncomfortable and put a strain on the relationship.

If you are a married woman who wants to minister to a single woman, be sure to consult with your spouse before you make this kind of offer. Your husband may not be comfortable having a single woman walk in at any time. If your marriage is unstable in any way, you probably shouldn't adopt a single woman. It may cause confusion or misunderstandings that would be awkward and potentially threatening to your marriage.

Also, a single woman (or any woman) and your husband or older son should never be in the house alone for extended periods of time. Not only do you want to keep your spouse or son from being tempted, but you also want to help him "abstain from every form of evil" (1 Thessalonians 5:22).

Offer to be available to help in case a problem arises

Tell your single woman friend that she can call you any time a serious problem arises. Discuss what these situations might be so she knows exactly what you are offering. Be available if her car breaks down late at night or if she can't get home because of some emergency. Make sure you tell her truthfully what you would like to do for her.

Pick a single woman to encourage (appropriately)

I added "appropriately" because offering her promises of finding a marriage partner is just one of many inappropriate things to say to her. (Later in this chapter I will list several more things that result in discouraging single women.) Send cards, offer to pray for specific requests, or pass on good audio and video tapes (on spiritual growth, not on singleness, unless she asks for it!). It is the responsibility of the people in a church to nurture and build up one another in the faith.

Choose friends of all ages and positions in life, including single women

Don't let age or marital status determine who your friends are. Married couples don't have to fellowship only with other married couples, or widows with widows, and so on. The lives of single women, like everyone else, are enriched by having friends of all ages.

Also, be careful not to exclusively lump all single people together thinking that's the only place they want to be. If a single woman's avid goal is to get married, then most likely she will place herself in the presence of single men. In addition, by encouraging her to fellowship with others outside of the singles crowd, she will be better able to see whether she has made her goal of marriage an idol in her life.

Ask a godly single woman to become involved with your teenagers

As mentioned before, teenagers often benefit from the presence of another trustworthy adult whom they can talk to besides their parents. A godly woman in your church may be able to spend time with them and even disciple them or help with homework. If there are family problems, she may even be able to help facilitate better communication between you and your teens.

Choose a single woman to pray for throughout the week

Let her know you're praying for her and ask for specific needs she might have. If she is struggling with her status as a single, challenge her to check her motives for wanting to be married. Help her to look at the motives of her heart. Jeremiah 17:9-10 says,

> *The heart is more deceitful than all else and is desperately sick; who can understand it? I, the LORD, search the heart, I test the mind, even to give to each man according to his ways, according to the results of his deeds.*

According to this verse, my heart can easily deceive me. I can see this more as I examine the motives behind the things that I do.

Offer to host dinners or other social events for the singles in your church

This does not mean to play matchmaker. Ask a single woman if she has some friends she would like to have over for dinner. You may offer the use of your home if she has a small apartment or house. Perhaps you have a pool that could be enjoyed or a large living area that could be used by singles for a praise and fellowship time. Most of the single women I know are on tight budgets with small apartments. An offer like this might be a tremendous blessing.

Start a single woman's group to study the biblical view of singleness

If you know several single women who are struggling with their singleness, you might want to teach them how they can view their situation biblically. Start by helping them to be grounded in their knowledge of God and in their identity in Christ. Discuss their devotional lives. Then teach them to understand singleness in a way that's consistent with the Bible.

Or, perhaps you'll want to host the group and appoint a single woman to teach them. Whatever the case, you'll be helping to let them know that they can choose to look differently at their singleness and draw closer to the Lord through it.

Help a woman to build godly brother/sister relationships

It is important for a single woman to know how to relate to a single man in the family of God. Teach her to be a sister in the Lord who is faithful to minister to her brothers for the building up of the body of Christ. First Timothy 5:1-2 gives instruction about how to relate to various people in the body of Christ. It might be good to lead a Bible study on the "one another" passages in Scripture and discuss of how to put these commands into action. That could open up new opportunities for God-honoring male/female relationships for the single women in your church.

Hold a financial planning class or workshop

In your church, provide financial counsel that's designed specifically for singles so that their unique situations can be addressed. Approach members of the church who are trained in financial matters and ask if they can offer counsel about budgeting, saving for the future, getting out of debt, and so on.

Arrange a group of "caregivers"

Organize a group of women who can network together to serve as caregivers within the church. My church has a ministry like this, and the women serve by driving people to doctor's appointments, making phone calls to check on those who are ill, buying food and cooking for those who are ill, and so on. This kind of ministry can truly encourage a single woman who might have no one to turn to when she needs help.

Ten Statements That Discourage a Single Person (and the Assumptions Behind Them)

Throughout my 42 years of single life I've had many things said to me about my singleness. Some of them were embarrassing, some were irritating, and, quite honestly, some were frustrating. Some things said were untrue and without any basis whatsoever. Very few were encouraging to me.

My friends and I compiled a list of things we've heard that are unhelpful. We all agreed that most of these statements were made with good intentions, but they still had a negative impact.

I initially wrote this list for a Sunday school class I was teaching. I have since found it to be one of the most effective tools for helping people to understand how to think properly about what they say to single women. I hope you find this list helpful for avoiding discouraging words and the assumptions behind them.

1. How's your love life? (This question assumes it's okay to ask!)

I've been asked this question several times, and each time I've thought, *I wonder how you'd feel if I asked you the same question?* The person who asked was always married. I know I would never want to share the intimate details of my married life with someone. Would you be offended if I asked you this question?

2. Don't worry—you'll find someone. (Assumes there is someone.)

Virtually all single women have heard this statement many, many times. It is well-meaning, offered to give us hope. However, we have no assurance that this is a true statement. In fact, only God knows for certain if that statement is true. What we *do* know is that Scripture says we shouldn't worry. We don't know what God has in store for any of us. The hope we do have is that God promises to give us strength when we feel weak and are tempted to feel badly about our singleness.

3. Ask _____ to do it. She's single. I'm sure she has lots of free time. (Assumes singles have more free time in their day.)

I may be wrong about this, but the single women I know live by their appointment books. Some of us can hardly get together once a month because of full-time work, taking care of the apartment and car, doctor and dentist appointments, grocery shopping, church and ministry commitments and the need to put in overtime at work. I am not saying singles have less time in their day than married people do; they just aren't able to divide their workload between two people, as some married couples do.

I should add that both single and married women are responsible for making the best use of their time. As we learned earlier from 1 Corinthians 7:32-35, the single woman can devote herself more to the things of the Lord because she does not have to focus on pleasing a husband. However, if she is not careful, she can fill up her day with tasks that can pull her away from the "undistracted devotion to the Lord" spoken of in 1 Corinthians 7:35. If a single woman manages her time well, she will avoid making herself so busy that she is distracted and unable to serve the Lord wholeheartedly. In today's culture, overscheduling can be a constant dilemma.

4. Don't you get lonely? (Assumes married people don't.)

In my counseling ministry, I am amazed at how many lonely married people I see. The problems sometimes start during the honeymoon, and some two, five, or even ten years later, they are in counseling. For ten years, they have been two lonely individuals. Even in good marriages there are times when one or both spouses feel lonely, which I'm sure those of you who are married can attest to. Loneliness is something that affects married and singles. People who have been happily married for some time find it hard to imagine life without the other person, and therefore picture singleness as a lonely, solitary life without close, intimate companionship. However, my single friends and I constitute a network in which there are close, caring relationships. We overcome loneliness by serving one another in love. We are blessed!

5. When are you going to settle down, grow up, and get married? (Assumes singles aren't mature until they marry.)

This statement is a difficult one to hear because it assumes that no matter what your age, if you're still single, then you haven't grown up! It also assumes that you are wandering around from place to place somewhat aimlessly in life, unwilling to commit to one person for life.

6. Have I got a man/woman for you! (Assumes you trust their choice.)

This is usually said with a smile and a pat on the back, and also in a crowd so your face can turn beet red! It makes it sound as if the single woman was anxiously asking, "Have you found anyone for me yet?"

I've had some well-meaning people think they know what is best for me. They choose for me to meet someone whom they think I may eventually marry. That has led to some very awkward meetings and even some misunderstandings between me and my "date." I've come to trust only those who really know me well and who don't see it as their calling to match me up with a life partner.

7. Why don't you go to the mission field? You have no ties here. (Assumes family members are the only ties a single person has.)

Single women are frequently seen as potential missionaries. That's all right if people understand that everyone is a missionary in the sense that we're all to carry out the Great Commission. But sometimes single women who aren't dating anyone in particular are strongly encouraged to go into a foreign mission field. The idea is that a single woman is independent, unattached, and free to pick up and go at a moment's notice. However, single women have family ties, just as married people do. It is not necessarily easier for a single person to leave for overseas than it is for a family of four to leave the rest of their extended family home. In fact, it may be more difficult to travel to another country alone and start life in a new culture from scratch.

8. What are you waiting for? (Assumes you don't have to!)

This is another of the comments that is usually made in jest. There's really no way to answer the question except to say that God's timing is perfect! I've read some articles that encourage a woman to go after a man if she really wants him. Ruth is usually cited as an example of a godly woman who pursued Boaz until he asked her to marry him. However, we must remember that ancient Jewish law was such that a kinsman had a moral responsibility to marry and care for the widow of his relative, which Boaz did. That is *not* the same as a twentieth-century woman choosing a man to marry and pursuing him! I don't believe God wants single women to anxiously involve themselves in every Christian (or non-Christian) singles group they know of in order to track down and pursue a mate. God is able, in His power and providence, to bring a mate into the life of a single woman if He intends for her to marry. Her focus must be on loving and serving God and others; God will take care of the rest.

9. I met a guy on the mission field who's looking for a wife, and you would be just perfect for him! (Assumes going to the mission field to find a spouse is a legitimate "call.")

Should this be my "call" to go serve on the mission field? Is this the right motive for becoming a missionary?

10. You know, you're not getting any younger . . . (Assumes something can be done about that.)

This statement sends chills up my spine. Again, the notion that a single woman can get out there and fix her situation is erroneous. Certainly if a woman lives like a hermit and avoids men like the plague, she can change that. If a woman is not using proper hygiene and is offensive to be around, a loving friend should be willing to help her in these areas so she is not dishonoring God. But if a single woman does what is God-honoring and appropriate, then she shouldn't be pushed to get married before God's timing.

A Right Perspective of Singleness

In the beginning of this chapter I introduced you to Joan, a single woman whom I counseled. I determined that she was discontent with her singleness. At that point, Joan was willing to ask herself some hard questions about her motives for desiring marriage. In the process, she realized she was trying to be what everyone else thought she should be rather than what God wanted her to be. Her desire changed from wanting to be married to enjoying being single and learning to be content in her circumstances. She reached the point where she was able to consider her singleness as a good gift. As she recognized God's acceptance of her through Christ's work on the cross and the Holy Spirit's work in her heart, she grew to desire God's will more and more.

Out of love for God, Joan has learned new ways of relating to the single men in her church. She now sees them as brothers in God's family. Her contentment comes from knowing that God's love for her goes far beyond any human expression of love, and that her love for God is expressed to Him through her obedience to His Word and ministry to those whom He puts in her path. As counselors and Christian women, our hope should be that single women will choose to view their singleness in this same way, and accept whatever gift God has for them with grace and a grateful heart.

Recommended Resource

Sinclair B. Ferguson, *Children of the Living God,* Carlisle, PA: The Banner of Truth Trust, 1989.

CHAPTER 7

Counseling the Post-Abortion Woman

Eileen Scipione, B.S.

Her shoulders convulsed violently; her hands gripped her coffee mug tightly. Jenny's face was distorted with pain as sobs racked her entire body.

I slid off my chair at the dining table and moved to the chair next to hers, putting my arm around her shoulders. Words stuck in my throat. What could I possibly say to comfort my friend? My comments about wanting to volunteer at a crisis pregnancy center seemed to be the catalyst for this brokenheartedness. All I had said was that most women don't really want an abortion but aren't aware of the alternative help that is available. Maybe I should just let her cry for awhile to get it all out. But how long would that take?

Jenny and I had met in a women's Bible study in our church several years ago. Having much in common, with our children ranging in age from toddler to teenager, we struck up a friendship quickly. It soon became apparent that Jenny struggled sporadically with depression and that her marriage was filled with conflict.

Jenny had been raised in a believing home and "went forward" at a summer camp meeting while in her preteen years. However, by mid-junior high she was being heavily influenced by her friends in school. Her outward rebellion grew as their powerful and seductive pull influenced Jenny deeply. Her overly busy parents tried to exert tighter restrictions, but these were too little, too late. Jenny's relationships with her friends were stronger than they were with her parents.

Jenny had confided all this to me while lunching with our children at the playground after Bible study. For a long time she never mentioned to me what I would learn later as our friendship grew: that when she was in high school, she would sneak out of the house to meet her boyfriend Jason on most Friday nights in the summer. Later, by the time school resumed, Jenny noticed that she had missed two periods, an unusual occurrence for her. Marcia, her closest friend, said she knew where Jenny could get an abortion and that the state would pay for it. Jenny was not ready to think about an abortion. She couldn't imagine how she could be pregnant! She and Jason had gotten together only twice. He said he loved her and really needed her. They'd be together forever.

Many confusing thoughts darted through Jenny's mind. She couldn't focus or make a decision. Marcia took her to the drugstore to buy a home pregnancy test. When the plus sign appeared in the little well on the test kit, Jenny stared in horror. Mom and Dad would kill her! They'd never understand!

Maybe Jason would know what to do. He'd stand by her, wouldn't he? She counted the hours until she would see him at school. "We have to talk," Jenny whispered nervously as she pulled him to a quiet corner near the library. "I just took a pregnancy test. I'm pregnant!" Jason's eyes widened as he pulled his hands out of her grip. "What is your problem? You should have used something."

The tears in Jenny's eyes made it almost impossible to see his face. She pleaded, "What are we going to do?"

"Get an abortion. I can't let a baby ruin my football scholarship. I'm outta here!" Jenny's knees felt like mush as she watched Jason hurry away. She was overwhelmed with feelings of abandonment and loneliness.

Jenny struggled to compose herself while she looked for Marcia. When she arrived at music class, Marcia didn't seem surprised as she listened to Jenny's tearful account of Jason's walkout. "I told you where you can get rid of it. It's really no problem."

Jenny placed her hand on her abdomen. It felt no bigger than normal. Her breasts, however, were swollen and tender. She whispered to Marcia, "I can't have an abortion. It's killing a baby." Marcia flashed back, "No way! In our family life class last year a woman came from Planned Parenthood and said it was just a cluster of cells, like menstrual tissue."

Marcia went with Jenny the following day to Planned Parenthood. The people there never asked her what she wanted to do. The abortion procedure was briefly explained, and an appointment was scheduled for two days later.

Jenny was morose and frightened as she waited for the days to pass. Her parents never noticed. The school nurse drove her to Planned Parenthood's clinic. Marcia was not permitted to go with her. As Jenny waited in the waiting room with other silent, sad-faced young women, she tried hard to put all her fears out of her mind. "God," she screamed inwardly, "I don't have a choice. My parents would never forgive me."

Facts About Abortion

The preceding scenario is a composite of several true stories. With about one and one-half million abortions in this country per year since 1973 (a total of about 35 million since Roe vs. Wade was enacted into law), this story has been repeated thousands of times. It is even the story of many Christian women. Many professing believers have violated their own consciences and had an abortion when fear, anger, or ignorance overwhelmed them. You may already know a Christian woman who has had an abortion. Some have not faced this sin from their past; others have continuing problems related to their past abortion.

What's tragic is that many young women are not aware of the facts about the baby developing within their womb. The circulatory system begins to develop at 15-17 days; the brain and nervous system are established at 20 days; a tiny heart begins beating at just 22 days; brain-wave activity can be recorded at just 35 days; at 45 days the skeleton is complete (in cartilage) and movement begins; at 63 days the baby squints if stroked in the face, and tries to grasp objects placed in its hand.[1] Consider this testimony from an anesthesiologist:

Eleven years ago while giving an anesthetic for a ruptured ectopic pregnancy (at 8 weeks gestation), I was handed what I believe was the smallest living human ever seen. The embryonic sac was intact and transparent. Within the sac was a tiny human male swimming extremely vigorously in the amniotic fluid, while attached to the wall by the umbilical cord. This tiny human was perfectly developed, with long, tapering fingers, feet and toes. It was almost transparent, as regards the skin, and the delicate arteries and veins were prominent to the ends of the fingers.

The baby was extremely alive and swam about the sac approximately one time per second, with a natural swimmer's stroke. This tiny human did not look at all like the photos and drawings and models of "embryos" which I had seen, nor did it look like a few embryos I have been able to observe since then, obviously because this one was alive!

When the sac was opened, the tiny human immediately lost his life and took on the appearance of what is accepted as the appearance of an embryo at this stage of life . . .[2]

Although young women are taught in public school that the fetus is just a blob of tissue, the truth about life in the womb is an integral part of their facing the truth about their abortion. A woman who has had an abortion (or is considering one) must face the reality that the pre-born baby is a separate life—it is not merely a part the mother's body. Even though the U.S. Supreme Court ruled in 1973 that a pre-born baby isn't legally a person, medical facts and common sense prove them wrong.[3]

Who Should Counsel the Post-Abortion Woman?

Perhaps you don't know a pastor or elder who is competent to counsel post-abortion women. You might not have a biblically-based, post-abortion counseling group nearby to which you might refer a woman like Jenny. Although there are some workbooks[4] available in Christian bookstores and at pro-life pregnancy centers, they are not usually effective without someone to give personal care and to establish accountability on an ongoing basis. Where, then, should you begin? This chapter is designed to answer a few of the most basic questions about counseling post-abortion women. While there is much more to learn about counseling the post-abortion woman, this can at least help you begin the process.

A Godly Counselor

You are competent to counsel the post-abortion woman to the extent that you *know* and *live out* the principles of God's holy Word. First Timothy 4:16 teaches, "Watch your life and doctrine closely" (NIV). In addition to knowing and obeying God's Word, you need to be growing in humility, as Ephesians 4:2 says: "Be completely humble and gentle" (NIV).

Matthew 7:1-5 teaches that we are not to make the wrong kind of judgments. One such wrong judgment would be to proudly assume that we are not vulnerable to falling into the same kind of sin as others. Now, some people believe Matthew 7:1-5 says we shouldn't judge people at all. But a careful examination of this passage shows that we should not make proud and hypocritical judgments.

As a counselor, you need to be characterized by an ability to listen and to be slow in giving advice. James 1:19 admonishes, "Everyone should be quick to listen, slow to speak and slow to become angry" (NIV). Getting all the necessary data is crucial to offering effective help.[5] Avoid pat answers. Spend the time needed to understand the counselee's problems and circumstances completely.

A Woman Counselor

Aside from being a person who talks the talk and walks the walk, the person who counsels the post-abortion woman should be a woman. Titus 2:3-5 clearly gives older women the job of teaching and discipling the younger women. Although pastors and elders need to be quick to recognize the struggling post-abortion woman in their congregation, and these ordained men have the knowledge of God's Word and the power of the Holy Spirit, experience indicates that a woman's ongoing personal issues are best handled by a spiritually mature woman. An alert pastor or elder might start the counseling process, but would do well to quickly pass this woman on to another woman within the congregation. As we learned in chapter 4 of this book, grieving or sorrowing women are apt to become emotionally attached and even sexually attracted to men who listen to and counsel them for a long period of time; thus, female counselors are preferable.[6]

An Experienced Counselor

Experience is another prerequisite in godly counselors. The "older" woman of Titus 2 is "older" by way of her experience in applying Scripture to problems, not necessarily by way of her age. She does not need to be experienced in terms of having had an abortion. But having had one does enable her to understand the sorrow and shame of having made the decision to put one's own child to death. It is not a prerequisite, however. A godly woman counselor doesn't have to have faced a particular life-dominating problem in order to be a genuine help to someone who does. We all can identify with the experience of giving in to temptation and we all know the sorrow and shame that result when we fall into sin. It is this common experience, as well as a knowledge of the scriptural procedure for handling sin, that will equip a woman to counsel wisely.

In What Setting Should Counseling Occur?

Another question that often comes up is whether the post-abortion woman should be counseled one-on-one or in a group setting. Presently, most post-abortion counseling is done in one or two weekend marathons, or in weekly Bible study groups using workbooks. Some post-abortion manuals imply that effective post-abortion counseling must be done in a group setting led by a trained post-abortion counselor. The one main advantage of a group setting is that, upon hearing others speak openly about their abortion, a reluctant woman may begin to admit she has a problem and start to face the unresolved consequence of her own abortion. However, an individual counselor can facilitate this kind of honesty and openness by earning the trust of the counselee. The counselee's trust level is built on how well she knows the life and integrity of her counselor. But no matter what the setting, a counselee's willingness to admit the truth will ultimately depend on her faith in Christ's forgiveness and in His ability to change her.

Some Cautions

Many post-abortion women seek help at long weekend sessions. One problem with this type of counseling is that all the openness produced may be the result of the tear-filled stories and emotions of other participants rather than the power of the Holy Spirit bringing about true repentance. This is not to say that man-centered sorrow is always the result in these settings, but it is a danger we need to watch for. Second Corinthians 7:10 teaches that godly sorrow brings repentance that leads to salvation with no regret, but worldly sorrow brings death. Crying and grieving is beneficial only if there is true repentance and a commitment to faithful service. As a godly counselor, you should allow a counselee the freedom to express her repentance in crying and tears, but she must see that tears are not an end in themselves. Remind her that if these tears are from the Holy Spirit, true repentance and change will follow.

Another question frequently raised about the counseling setting is whether the post-abortion woman should be referred to her church or a parachurch organization.[7] It appears that parachurch organizations, which include post-abortion support groups, have sprung up largely because the church has failed to do its job. These post-abortion groups have been well-intentioned, compassionate, and diligent. Some have been effective, as well. But, after all is said and done, parachurch organizations *cannot* follow up, exercise accountability, or discipline the way the church can. The woman who has completed a weekend seminar or a Bible study has made some significant first steps. But many of these women must continue to wrestle with life-dominating problems. These habits don't go away in a weekend, nor even in 12 weeks. We all are aware that the evil one never quits bringing up our most distressing sins in order to steal away our freedom and joy in Christ.

But what if a church isn't willing or able to help with situations this extreme? No doubt there are many churches who do not offer help to post-abortion women. But how will they ever finally do their job if we don't come to them and prayerfully and humbly try to persuade them? If your church doesn't offer such help, perhaps you can help to begin such a ministry.

When and Why Does the Post-Abortion Woman Need Help?

If you know a post-abortion woman, or are one yourself, how do you determine whether counseling or help is needed? What are the signs that "all is not well"?

Understanding Forgiveness

Many post-abortion women say, "I don't know if I'm forgiven." "I don't know how I can forgive the other people who were involved." "I've asked for forgiveness, but I just don't feel forgiven. How can I know if I need to seek more forgiveness?" How should you respond to questions like that? All believers need to repent (Acts 17:30), be reconciled (Matthew 5:24), and restored (Galatians 6:1). How can a post-abortion woman know if she has accomplished all that in regard to her abortion(s)?

One way to help a woman with the issue of forgiveness is by asking her if she believes that her relationship is not right between herself and God or between herself and others. If she believes that she is still guilty before God or others, then it might not be Satan trying to steal her joy and freedom; it could be she has unfinished business. Perhaps she has not repented; perhaps she has not confessed her sin to others.

Taking Responsibility

The post-abortion woman may feel guilty because she has not truly repented. Repentance will involve taking responsibility for her part in the abortion. Some indicators of not having taken personal responsibility are blameshifting, rationalizing, and excuse-making. If the woman constantly blames her boyfriend, parents, or husband for her choice, she has not taken responsibility for it. Although others may have influenced her decision, she is ultimately responsible (unless she was physically forced to have the abortion). Perhaps her boyfriend did encourage her in the abortion; perhaps her parents were demanding and unforgiving; they do share some of the culpability, but she is responsible. If you notice that she blameshifts regularly, encourage her to write out the steps that were taken before the decision to have the abortion was made. What percentage of these steps was she responsible for? Did she have any other options? Gently lead her to recognize what part of the decision was her responsibility and encourage her to repent of that.

Another aspect of full repentance is that of confessing the sin to a key person or key people in one's life. There are many passages of Scripture that point out the necessity of taking responsibility for sin by confession. James 5:16 teaches, "Confess your sins to each other, and pray for each other so that you may be healed" (NIV). Proverbs 28:13 says, "He who conceals his sins does not prosper, but whoever confesses and renounces them finds mercy" (NIV). If a woman had a secret abortion while married, she must remember what 1 Corinthians 7:4 says, "The wife's body does not belong to her alone but also to her husband."

Whatever the situation, there may be other people who need to be approached. You and the counselee can prayerfully consider these possibilities as you work together to bring her to full repentance. For example, if she was living under the care of her parents or a guardian during the time of the conception and abortion, and has never asked for their forgiveness, then she has unfinished business. If she was married at the time of the abortion and didn't tell her husband, then she needs to talk to him. If the pregnancy was caused by someone other than her husband then she has unfinished business with her husband; however, she probably shouldn't contact the man who fathered the child. As you carry out this process you must be careful and sensitive, continually refreshing the counselee's heart and mind with reminders of God's abundant grace. She must be cautioned against telling others simply because she wants to establish her own self-righteousness or "feel better."

Emotional Difficulties

Another sign that a woman has not fully dealt with her abortion is the frequent presence of overwhelming sorrow. If she feels sorrow, anger, or guilt when someone brings up the subject of abortion, then she might not have handled her sin in a godly manner. Post-abortion women have been known to break into a sweat, become nervous and tense, and even express strong, unprovoked anger when the subject of abortion arises.

Uncomfortable feelings around babies or children that are about the same age that hers would have been is another indicator that help is still needed. Some women go out of their way to avoid holding, touching, or even seeing babies or children of comparable age. This response isn't necessarily a conscious decision; it may simply be an automatic response. Of course, this is not always true of unrepentant women, but it is not uncommon.

Another common problem is resentment toward those who were involved in the abortion decision. A woman may find herself filled with bitterness and anger toward those who were part of her life at the time. Some of these people may not have lived up to her expectations, and consequently they are the objects of deep and habitual anger.

Efforts at Compensation

Another sign of an unrepentant heart is when the woman has an obsession with pursuing the education, career, or relationships that would have been hindered by the birth of a baby. She may be trying to prove to herself and others that the sacrifice was worth it. This particular behavior is less obvious than the ones mentioned earlier. It is a way she can continue to deceive herself about the great value of the idol that demanded her child's life.

Other afflictions such as depression, anxiety over fertility and child-bearing issues, nightmares, flashbacks, hallucinations, anniversary syndrome (sadness at the time of year when the aborted baby would have been born), eating disorders, suicidal thoughts, and alcohol and drug abuse have been reported among women who have had an abortion.[8] This is *not* to say that some or all of these afflictions are always the result of an abortion. It is just that many women respond to their guilt in some of these ways.

Can You Counsel a Woman Who Does Not Want Help?

What if a woman you know shows many of the signs mentioned above and still does not admit her need for help? Most likely she will never seek help until she sees her need to do so. However, you still can confront her. Only God can change her heart, but you can speak the truth in love to her.

Start by examining your own heart to see if you have a "plank in your own eye" (Matthew 7:4). If you are not living in the same type of sin, then gently talk to her about what you see in her life. Invite her over for a cup of coffee or tea. You should describe carefully and tactfully the behaviors you see in her that may indicate trouble in her past. Give her plenty of time to express what she sees as contributing causes. After exploring other origins of these behaviors, you might ask if she might be experiencing difficulty because of a past abortion. If she admits to nothing, then assure her that you will continue to pray for and love her.

Beginning Steps for the Woman Who Wants Help

1. Help her *take responsibility* for her own actions as outlined earlier. She needs to be helped to own up to her participation in every part of the baby's conception as well as the abortion. Her responsibility needs to be emphasized at every stage of the counseling.

2. *Giving hope* is one of the most important steps in the beginning stages of counseling. The counselee must be assured from Scripture that no matter what ugly truth comes out about her life, nothing can separate the true child of Christ from God's love. Use Romans 8:37-39 to encourage her. Have her read the verses herself and then tell her that her homework is to memorize the passage. Assure her that no matter what she reveals to you about her past, you will continue to love her.

3. While giving hope through biblical promises, *gather as much data* as possible. The following events need to be faced (not necessarily in this order or in a short period of time):

   a. Facing the conception: "If you were single, how did you become sexually involved?" Unless she was raped, she needs to be shown her responsibility in the entire process. Ask her, "What kind of relationship did you have with the father of the baby? What went through your mind about the possibility of becoming pregnant?"

   b. Facing the abortion decision: "What was your first reaction when you realized you might be pregnant?" Discuss how she found out for sure that she was pregnant. Talk about who she told and the reaction of each person. Ask her to think about who she did not tell and why. Did she get any counseling from an abortion clinic or a pro-life pregnancy center? Who did she allow to have the biggest influence on her final decision? Discuss what she knew at the time about the three choices: parenting, adoption, or abortion. As you keep the counselee aware of her own responsibility, make sure you don't lose sight of Romans 8:1: "There is now no condemnation for those who are in Christ Jesus." Assure her that you do not condemn her either.

c. Facing the abortion procedure: The following questions should not be seen as avenues for reliving the pain, but purely for the purpose of discovering anyone toward whom the counselee may still be harboring resentment: "Who drove you to the clinic or doctor's office? What did the clinic staff tell you about the 'procedure'?" Discuss whether she had a sense of relief immediately after the abortion, as this is very common. Ask her, "Did anything else stand out in your mind regarding the whole procedure?"

d. Facing the results of the abortion: Discuss any physical, emotional, or spiritual changes that the counselee has observed in herself. Did she find that she began to get into a habit of suppressing the truth? Explore the possibility of one lie leading to another and eventually the problem of lying becoming a life-dominating habit. Have her read Luke 22:55-60 and write a paragraph about how Peter's denial of Jesus was a form of suppressing the truth. Then discuss what the following verse teaches about seeking the truth, and ask her the accompanying questions: "Surely you desire truth in the inner parts; you teach me wisdom in the inmost place" (Psalm 51:6 NIV). Is there anything else you are still not telling the truth about? How would learning to fulfill the command to "speak truthfully to [your] neighbor" (Ephesians 4:25 NIV) make changes in the way that you think and speak?

What Issues Are Most Important for a Post-Abortion Woman?

Struggling with Guilt and Depression

Pro-abortionists blame the pro-life movement for the guilt and depression women experience after an abortion. They claim it is our accusations that abortion is murder that makes post-abortion women feel so badly. Their counselors claim these women simply have *guilt feelings* rather than *true guilt*. They reject the idea that sin makes us truly guilty before a holy God. They teach that women just "feel" guilty when they have broken a standard that someone has laid on them or that they have accepted from others.

However, the biblical examples of those who sinned and then experienced a powerful sense of guilt and depression are revealing. These Bible characters *felt* guilty because they *were* guilty of sin. Remember that a person "feels" guilty because he has judged himself as guilty. In addition, the depressed post-abortion woman often has other issues in her past that contribute to her misery. Perhaps she was not only a victimizer of her child, but she was also a victim of grievous sins committed by others. Consider what these verses reveal about guilt:

- Lamentations 1:2: "Bitterly she weeps at night, tears are upon her cheeks" (NIV).
- Lamentation 3:20: "My soul is downcast within me" (NIV).
- Ezra 9:6: "I am too ashamed and disgraced to lift up my face to you" (NIV).
- Psalm 32:3-5: "When I kept silent about my sin, my body wasted away through my groaning all day long. For day and night Thy hand was heavy upon me; my vitality was drained away as with the fever heat of summer. I acknowledged my sin to Thee, and my iniquity I did not hide; I said, 'I will confess my transgressions to the LORD'; and Thou didst forgive the guilt of my sin."
- Psalm 38:17-18: "I am ready to fall, and my sorrow is continually before me. For I confess my iniquity; I am full of anxiety because of my sin."

Another reason the post-abortion woman struggles so intensely with guilt is her God-given mothering instincts and desires. We see evidence of a woman's mothering instincts in 1 Kings 3:16-28 (the two prostitutes before Solomon) and in Exodus 1:22–2:10 (Moses' mother and the Pharaoh's daughter). Isaiah 49:14-15 teaches that God's love is even greater than a mother's love. In spite of their fallen condition, women still have a natural desire to care for little ones and protect them from harm. When this desire is overruled through an abortion, a woman frequently experiences guilt.

One of the best ways to help a counselee overcome guilt and depression is to assign as homework the memorization and application of Bible passages that can help her "renew her mind"—such as Psalm 13; 51; 103; 38; Isaiah 55:6-7; and Romans 4:4-9. She also needs to be taught to rest in Christ. Following is a list of just a few of the verses that can encourage her to do so:

- Psalm 55:22: "Cast all your cares on the LORD and He will sustain you" (NIV).

- Psalm 126:5: "Those who sow in tears will reap with songs of joy" (NIV).
- Romans 8:26: "The Spirit helps us in our weakness. We do not know what we ought to pray for, but the Spirit himself intercedes for us with groans that words cannot express" (NIV).
- 2 Corinthians 4:17-18: "Our light and momentary troubles are achieving for us an eternal glory that far outweighs them all. So we fix our eyes not on what is seen, but on what is unseen" (NIV).
- Romans 8:1: "There is now no condemnation for those who are in Christ Jesus" (NIV).
- Galatians 5:1: "It is for freedom that Christ has set us free" (NIV).

By filling her mind with God's promises, the post-abortion woman who struggles with guilt and depression will have at her constant disposal the weapons she needs to fight Satan's accusations. For nightmares and hallucinations, she might play Scripture set to calming music. That is yet another way she can retrain her heart and mind to think God's thoughts.

Another way to help a counselee to beat guilt and depression is to have her get into and stay in close relationships with sisters in Christ who love her and will hold her accountable. That can help her to experience victory over other life-dominating sins. If her church is regularly preaching the full counsel of God's Word, and she participates in the life of the church on a consistent basis, she will gradually overcome her depression. In addition, she will need to be encouraged to fulfill her responsibilities no matter how she feels. Another valuable help would be for her to serve the Lord by getting involved with missions, abused children, teen moms, prison work, or nursing homes. Ministry to others will aid her in getting her focus off of herself.

Struggling with Anger

Anger is a very common response to an abortion. One of a counselor's most important jobs is to determine at whom the woman's anger is targeted. She may be filled with angry thoughts toward God, her spouse, her boyfriend, her parents, the abortionist's staff, or anyone else who was in her life at the time of the abortion. The anger could even be against herself. As you are gathering data during the counseling sessions, take care to note times when the counselee expresses anger in her tone or words. Pray for much discernment so that you will know when to focus in on any anger that the woman has that is sinful.

Assign as homework the study of scriptures about righteous and unrighteous anger. Compare Moses' unrighteous anger in Numbers 20:3-13 to Jesus' righteous anger in John 2:13-16. Another verse for further study is Ephesians 4:26, which teaches that Christians can be angry without sinning. Teach the counselee that most of the anger illustrated in the Bible is sinful and is accompanied by other sinful behaviors.

Pray that the "Wonderful Counselor" of Isaiah 9:6 will show the counselee the consequences of her anger. Unrighteous anger can cause her to become sarcastic, cynical, hostile, and even violent. Ask her to identify those with whom she is angry. Have her write out the reasons she is angry. Discuss whether she is sinning in her anger. Does she try to hide her anger? Does she feel justified in her anger even though she may be sinning? Have her describe how she typically exhibits her anger. Teach her how to put it off . She must learn that anger is an attitude of the heart that is rooted in pride. She will change when she learns humility and commits to humbly serving others and making use of proper conflict resolution skills.

Being Reconciled and Restored

If the post-abortion woman is to be truly reconciled and restored to God and to others, she needs to see that abortion is the taking of a judicially innocent human life. Gently review with her the beginning of this chapter, which looks at key facts about abortion. Take the time to study the following passages, which will help her to see that the Bible uses the same term for a prenatal child as a postnatal one. The Greek word *brephos*, used in Luke 1:41,44; 2:12,16; 18:15 and John 16:21, refers to both a fetus and an infant or young child. Psalm 139:13-16 and Luke 1:41 speak of the life in the womb as being a unique human individual.

Reconciliation with God   The first step in reconciliation is for the counselee to ask God to forgive her sin against Him. As we already know, 1 John 1:9 teaches, "If we confess our sins, he is faithful and just and will forgive us our sins and purify us from all unrighteousness" (NIV). Most of the women you talk to will probably have already made some move in this direction. For any number of reasons this seems to be easier to do than reconciling with people. Even though it appears to be easier to seek God's forgiveness rather than that of people, reconciliation with God needs to come first anyway. A person cannot truly forgive others without first knowing God's forgiveness.

In reconciliation, you want to make sure that the counselee knows the gospel message. If she is not truly born from above by the Holy Spirit, she will only be doing penance for her abortion. She may get the impression that her good deeds can atone or pay for her sins. You want to be careful that the post-abortion woman is reconciling with people solely because God in Christ has forgiven her, not for the purpose of causing God to forgive or love her. If she is not a Christian, then reconciliation with others will be impossible. How can she have enough love to truly forgive others if she knows nothing of Christ's forgiveness of her sins? (1 John 4:19).

Reconciliation with "Oneself"   One of the most common misconceptions taught in post-abortion counseling is the notion that the counselee must learn to forgive herself. Post-abortion women often lament, "I know that God has forgiven me, but I just can't forgive myself." In some ways that statement is understandable. A woman who must face the reality of her abortion may indeed struggle with guilt. Her abortion is a shocking testimony to the lengths to which she was willing to go to prevent the problems, humiliation, and shame caused by her pregnancy. She must be encouraged, however, that the Bible *never* teaches her to be concerned with whether she has forgiven herself or not. Rather, she is to be concerned about God's forgiveness and the forgiveness of those whom she has sinned against. She is to embrace God's lavish forgiveness in Christ (Ephesians 1), reminding herself daily of His mercy and grace, but she is not to become embroiled in psychological manipulations to try to "feel forgiven." Forgiveness is a matter of faith and belief in God's character and His Word, not feelings. She must believe that God will forgive her when she asks (1 John 1:9) and that His forgiveness is all that matters. His forgiveness is not based on her worthiness; in fact, just the opposite is true. His forgiveness is based on His goodness, which He extended to her even when she was His enemy (Romans 5:5-8). She cannot earn His love or His mercy; she must not seek to assure herself that, before God, she is somehow worthy. God is the only worthy One.

When a counselee feels condemned or is tempted to rehearse her sinfulness in her own mind, she should use that as an opportunity to rehearse passages about God's great grace, such as Ephesians 2:1-10 or Titus 3:5-7. She should remember the story of the woman who anointed Jesus' feet with her tears and costly perfume. This woman was a "sinner" (Luke 7:37). The Lord responded, "For this reason, I say to you, her sins, which are many, have been forgiven, for she loved much; but he who is forgiven little, loves little" (Luke 7:47). Notice that she didn't try to justify herself in her own mind and condemn herself with thoughts like, *How could I do such a thing?* Rather, she immersed herself in God's abounding love for sinners.

Help the counselee to think through this logically. *Her misconceptions about forgiving herself are making her standards for forgiveness higher than God's.* If God has forgiven her based on the substitutionary atonement of Jesus Christ on the cross, then she needs to be reminded to look to that cross constantly. Whenever the evil one accuses her of the awfulness of what she did to her baby, teach her to say to herself, "Lord, I thank you that my sin is under the blood of Jesus just like all my other sins. And nothing can separate me from His love!" Show her that having an abortion is not the unforgivable sin. It *is* possible for her to be reconciled to God and live at a much greater level of peace with herself.

Reconciliation with Others   The counselee needs to be shown that God both invites and commands her to repent (Matthew 4:17) and be reconciled and restored to Him, as well as to her brothers and sisters in Christ (Matthew 5:23-24; Romans 12:17-18; Colossians 3:12-14). For homework she should read and memorize these and other key passages. Dealing with reconciliation and restoration may be the most difficult part of the counseling process because the counselee is struggling with fearful, angry, or unforgiving attitudes.

You may need to help confess and repent of any unrighteous anger, bitterness, resentment, selfishness, rebellion, stubbornness, lying, substance abuse, or fornication (sexual sins). (To see all that is involved in confessing sin, see chapter 17 pages 16-24). Of course, in the counseling process, you may need to wait until her trust level in the Lord and in you has been solidly established. The freedom that forgiveness brings now and eternally will make the wait well worthwhile.

It may be prudent for the counselee to write letters to people who sinned against her or those against whom she has sinned. Matthew 5:24 and Luke 17:3 teach that we must make contact with the offended or offending party. Even if that does not seem to accomplish the expected reconciliation and restoration, God commands it and we must trust Him for the results. As the hymn writer penned, "Trust and obey, for there is no other way to be happy in Jesus but to trust and obey."[9]

The most painful reconciliations will likely involve a boyfriend, parent, or husband who did not offer the counselee the support she felt she needed to carry the child to term. She might need to ask forgiveness for years of bitterness toward those individuals, even though they haven't asked to be forgiven for their sinful failures. She might also hear other people discourage her with comments like, "That was so long ago"; "You'll never locate them"; or "Let them get on with their lives." Matthew 5:24 is a key passage for her to meditate on in that regard. (Of course, she can't seek reconciliation with people whom she has no way of contacting.) It might also be unwise for her to seek reconciliation with an old boyfriend if to do so would be harmful to her marriage or his (if he is married). Wisdom and caution must be exercised in these cases.

Assign as homework writing letters that express a request for forgiveness. Have her show them to you before she mails them. Help her to keep out blameshifting or accusatory comments that would move the responsibility for her sin from her shoulders to other people's. She should also avoid writing inflammatory comments such as "Forgive me for being angry and hurt and hating you for all these years, but you were such a jerk for walking out on me." She must let God do the convicting of other people's hearts. She can't change their attitudes; only the Holy Spirit can do that. She is only responsible to obey the Lord; she is not responsible for the outcome.

There may be another group of people who she believes failed her and sinned against her but against whom she has not sinned. She owes them no apology. This scenario is not common, but occasionally by God's grace we don't grow bitter and hateful to everyone who has hurt us. We are not called on to forgive those who have never asked to be forgiven, but we must be completely *ready to forgive* if they ask us to do so. Matthew 18:33,35 says, "Shouldn't you have had mercy on your fellow servant just as I had on you? . . . This is how my heavenly Father will treat each of you unless you forgive your brother from your heart."

You'll want to ask the counselee what her first response would be if her ex-boyfriend (or whomever she holds unforgiveness against) came into her life and asked to be forgiven for everything he did wrong to her. She needs to be ready to offer a forgiveness so deep that she will refuse to let the memory of those sins against her linger in her heart and mind. She may not be able to forget the past, but by God's grace she can try her best to not bring up the offenses that another person committed against her.

When another person's offenses do come to mind, the counselee should immediately pray that God would convict that person and bring him or her to repentance and faith in Christ. As she consistently practices this, she will learn to cultivate the godly kinds of thoughts that are listed in Philippians 4:8.

Is Reconciliation with the Child Necessary?

A BIBLICAL PERSPECTIVE   Some counselors teach that reconciliation can be accomplished with the aborted child, and they encourage women to write a letter to the child. These women are then assured that the baby forgives them. These counselors sometimes say that the "great cloud of witnesses" in Hebrews 12:1 includes a woman's unborn child. However, that is poor exegesis of the passage; besides, communication with the dead is forbidden in Scripture (*see* Isaiah 8:19). Thus it's wrong to encourage women in such a practice, which is pagan in origin, not Christian.

If the counselee wants to write a letter, she may want to write a prayer of repentance and thanks to God for His mercy and love for her. This letter can serve as a milestone that she can look back on to remind herself of her repentance and God's mercy.

QUESTIONS ABOUT THE CHILD'S ETERNAL HOME   It is inevitable that Christian women who have had an abortion will want to know where their child will spend eternity. There are a number of different ideas on this issue, and most are held to with great tenacity. I do not claim to have any great insight on this sensitive topic. However, if you are a biblical counselor, it is advisable that you make no dogmatic statement as to the eternal state of any aborted child. Our comfort must be in the justice and mercy of God, and not in any hard-to-defend teaching about "the age of accountability."[10] God is merciful, and when we reach our heavenly home, we will be praising Him (Revelation 19:1-3). Whatever the outcome is, we can be assured that we will praise God for His great wisdom and glory.

If the counselee brings up issues relating to the baby, she should be discouraged against asking God to reveal anything about that child other than what the Bible teaches. She might have a feeling about whether the baby was a boy or a girl, but unless she had a medical test or a visual sighting that indicated the gender, her feeling is only a subjective notion. In addition, this type of seeking after revelation gives in to the temptation to try to communicate with the dead and focuses on the child instead of God's mercy.

If your counselee struggles with accepting the reality that the fetus was actually a human being created in God's image, encourage her to review Psalm 139, Luke 1:41, and John 16:21. Ask her to prayerfully consider these passages and write out her reasoning on the subject. You may find that she is still wanting to avoid responsibility for her sin. If a woman has difficulty facing the fact that the fetus was, in fact, a baby, you might encourage her to keep a baby blanket or item of clothing as a reminder of its humanity and God's wonderful mercy in forgiving her.

Some women write a poem, compose a song, create a piece of art, or even plant a tree to remind them of God's great grace in forgiveness. These activities are to be God-centered and are not to focus primarily on the baby, whose existence she now recognizes. They are to serve as landmarks in her spiritual life—reminders that she has taken responsibility for her sin and received God's mercy. Creative possibilities abound; just be cautious to avoid any hint of idolatry. It is dishonoring to God for a woman to display worshipful expressions to the aborted child. She is not to create any kind of shrine. The post-abortion woman must be encouraged to "set [her] mind on things above" and fix her eyes on Christ (Colossians 3:1-2 NIV; Hebrews 3:1; 12:2). The temptation to morbidly focus on her baby and the abortion may be strong, but she must learn to say with Paul, "It is a trustworthy statement, deserving full acceptance, that Christ Jesus came into the world to save sinners, among whom I am foremost of all" (1 Timothy 1:15).

The counselee may find herself relating to the story of David and Bathsheba's illegitimate child (2 Samuel 11). Although this story does not deal with abortion, there may be similarities between the circumstances in the story and the counselee's life. The union between David and Bathsheba was secret and illicit; murder was a by-product of this union (the death of Uriah, Bathsheba's husband). The baby that she had conceived died because of their sin. Although God allowed the baby to die, its death was a direct result of David's sin. Note David's response to the death of the child in 2 Samuel 12:18: He arose from his fasting for the child, "anointed himself, and changed his clothes; and he came into the house of the LORD and worshiped." David didn't spend time focusing on the death of the child. Instead, he focused on God. He poured out his heart before God and worshiped Him. David's prayer of repentance in Psalm 51 is a perfect example of the attitude that God desires in us. David recognized that his sin was primarily against God, although others were involved. He prayed that God would restore to him the joy of His salvation and would sustain him with a willing spirit (Psalm 51:12).

Bringing Victory into the Life of a Post-Abortion Woman

Remembering the Priorities

Developing a disciplined life is of highest priority for your counselee. It goes without saying that it is equally important for you, too. Work with her regularly on her Bible study, prayer life, fellowship and accountability with other believers, communion, worship, and ministering to the needy. She should be held accountable by her counselor for each of the above-mentioned areas over a period of time that extends long after the initial weekly sessions stop.

One helpful homework assignment is to have her keep a diary of God's blessings, protection, graces, and provisions. As she pays attention to what God has done and is doing for her and her loved ones, she will cultivate a thankful heart and turn less and less to long-held sinful thought patterns.

Another very beneficial homework assignment is a study of God's character. She might study the names of God as well. She can utilize these studies in the praise section of her daily prayer time. This will aid her in keeping a vibrant walk with the Lord.

In addition, the counselee must seek to make ongoing peace with others a high priority. Next to Christ, her spouse (if she is married) is her greatest responsibility. She is to keep peace with him and with any children that she might have.

Remembering God's Promises

Satan, of course, will use the problems in her life as a means to whisper in her ear. The accuser of the brethren will tell her that because she "killed her baby," she'll never overcome her problems; she'll never be a strong Christian. When this happens, she'll need to put on the armor of God so that she can stand firm in Christ (Ephesians 6:10f).

"Where sin increased, grace abounded all the more," says Romans 5:20. The counselee will move from fear to freedom as she remembers that God's grace is greater than all her sin, both past and present.

Both counselor and counselee need to hold onto God's promises. "The old has gone, the new has come" is the teaching of 2 Corinthians 5:17. The counselee's sin is great, but she has a greater God who has promised to forgive, restore, and bless those who turn to Him in faith.

Not every post-abortion woman you counsel will be changed. Some will reject what you have to offer. But God is indeed able to use His Spirit and His Word to turn lives around. Maybe you will have the blessed privilege of being used by God to show the post-abortion woman and those in her world that she is no longer the victim or the victimizer. She is the victor in Christ!

CHAPTER 8

Counseling Women in Problem Christian Marriages

Martha Peace, RN B.S.N.

Three different women have come to my office this week seeking biblical counsel. Each one believes her problem to be her husband. According to Janet, her husband is weak, passive, and fails to lead their family. Janet says she feels frustrated and resentful. Peggy's husband, on the other hand, is domineering, easily angered, mean, and rules with an iron fist. Peggy says she feels hurt and afraid. Marsha's husband is a pastor who is a workaholic with time for everyone in their church and community except for her. Marsha says she feels overwhelming loneliness and resentment.

What should these women do? Some counselors would say, "Nothing, except pray." Others would say, "I wouldn't put up with that! God does not expect you to stay in an unhappy marriage." Still others would say, "You've got to do what you feel is right for you."

What should you do as their biblical counselor? The answer is . . . plenty! In each case, you must carefully gather data because "he who gives an answer before he hears, it is folly and shame to him" (Proverbs 18:13). You should keep in mind that you are hearing only one side of the story. Be careful not to judge a woman's husband too quickly (Proverbs 18:17). If you do, you will not likely give her objective counsel.

In addition to gathering data, you should *always* give her hope. I often say, "I don't know exactly how all of this will work out, but God does. Even if your husband may be a complete failure before God, you do not have to be. You can glorify God no matter what your husband does." Remind her of encouraging scriptures such as 1 Corinthians 10:13 and Romans 8:28-29.

After you gather data and give hope, begin your counsel by helping her first get the beam out of her own eye. Only then will she be able to see clearly to take the speck out of her husband's eye (Matthew 7:1-5). Ask her, "If I draw a circle on the board and the circle represents 100 percent of the problems in your marriage, how much would you say is your fault and how much is your husband's fault?" If she answers, "It's 30 percent my fault and 70 percent his fault," then you'll want to say, "All right. God wants you to take 100 percent responsibility for your 30 percent. So I will begin by helping you with your sin and then I will teach you how to respond biblically to your husband's sin." An often-insightful question to ask is this: "If I asked your husband what you are doing wrong, what would he say?" More times than not, a wife will give you a fairly accurate view of what her husband perceives as her problems. If she is accurate, you will have a better idea of what to cover in your counseling agenda.

Gathering data, giving hope, and helping a woman get the beam out of her own eye are basic biblical methods regardless of the husband's problems.[1] Certainly there is much more that could be said about the basics, but the purpose of this chapter is to prepare you as a biblical counselor to give wise, practical counsel to Christian women married to Christian husbands—Janet, whose husband fails to lead; Peggy, whose husband is an angry tyrant; and Marsha, whose husband is a workaholic pastor. If you need help with the counseling basics, there are several excellent books available to help you, and you can read chapter 2 of this book for a brief overview of basic counseling methods. Let's begin with Janet.

Counseling the Wife of a Passive Husband

As Janet shares her story, she is obviously struggling with frustration and resentment. She explains that she wants to be a godly wife and to be under her husband's authority. She believes that this is impossible for her because "Jim refuses to lead me or our family—spiritually or otherwise."

When asked for specific examples, she gives several recent incidents of Jim's indecisiveness even when "nicely" pressed for an answer. One such incident occurred when Janet asked Jim how much money to budget for certain items. He shrugged his shoulders and walked away. Other times, though he is a Christian, he steadfastly refused to pray with her or the children or have devotional times with them. He does read his Bible and pray, but does so privately. Another example of Jim failing to lead is the way he avoids conflict. Janet says, "He either ignores the problem or walks away saying little or nothing."

In dealing with the children, Jim is passive and Janet is left to take whatever disciplinary steps seem appropriate to her. When he is home and one of the children is disrespectful to him or Janet, he does not reprove or discipline that child. She cannot remember a time when her husband supported her because one of the children was being disrespectful. She also cannot remember a time when he stood up to her when she was sinning. He would, however, withdraw from her and seem to pout.

Imagine that you are Janet's counselor and you have already covered the previously mentioned counseling basics with her. Now it is time to teach her how to respond righteously to her husband. It is important that she place herself under the authority of her husband (unless he asks her to sin—Ephesians 5:22-24). This doesn't mean that he has to make all the decisions, but she should consult him in most matters and tell him, "I will do whatever it is you would like." If he still refuses to make the decision or even express an opinion, she should then make the decision based on what she believes to be biblically wise.

One word of caution: Take time to carefully explore the issue of biblical submission with her. Perhaps the problem is not that Jim refuses to lead, but that Janet does not permit him to when he tries. Ask her if there was ever a time during their marriage when he did lead. How did she respond? Was she critical of his mistakes or leadership decisions? Perhaps he used to try, but has finally given up.

Spend some time talking to Janet about the true beauty of a woman, one who is "precious in the sight of God" (1 Peter 3:4). This woman has the character of a "gentle and quiet spirit." In other words, she is humble and calmly confident in God and in His Word. She is beautiful like the "holy women of the past who put their hope in God" and adorned themselves by being "submissive to their own husbands" (1 Peter 3:5 NIV). Ask Janet if she is seeking to develop a confident, quiet heart, or if she badgers Jim about his failures. Give her Bible studies that explain these concepts to her.[2] Encourage her longing for God and her desire to please God. Remind her again and again, "Whether your husband serves God or not, you can serve God, delight in Him, and glorify Him by all you think, say, and do."

You should also hold her accountable to pray for her husband. Teach her to pray biblically. For example, she should pray that Jim will take on the role of head of their house and thereby obey God and glorify Him (Ephesians 5:23).

Instruct her, through counseling sessions and Bible study homework, to communicate biblically. If she clearly communicates in love what she would like for Jim to do, he may assume more of a leadership role than she thought possible. For example, she might ask him to take a lead in the discipline of the children when he is home, backing her up at times or intervening when one of the children is disobedient or disrespectful. In order to be very clear, she could calmly and nicely give him two or three concrete, specific examples.

Another example of clear communication would be Janet asking Jim to commit to a time to sit down with her to plan the budget. Also, she might tell him, "Sweetheart, I would love for us to have time to pray together. If I get up earlier, could we take a brief time to pray together before the children are awake?" Sometimes wives expect their husbands to somehow intuitively know what they want. Instead of expecting him to "just know," they should communicate their desire in a clear, gentle, godly tone (Proverbs 16:21).

Because Jim is a Christian, Janet should encourage him to develop an even deeper desire for the things of God (1 Peter 2:2; 2 Peter 3:18). She might want to give, as a gift, a book that is doctrinally sound and has a high view of God such as *God: Coming Face to Face with His Majesty* by John MacArthur (Victor Books).[3] She could also encourage him with testimonies of what God is doing in her life or the lives of others. To the degree Jim is in the Word of God, his desire for God will grow and he will become a stronger leader.

If, in spite of clear communication and encouragement in his desire for the things of God, Jim persists in failing to lead, then Janet should appeal to him. She should appeal based on the scriptural mandates to the husband, such as 1 Corinthians 11:3, which says, "I want you to understand that Christ is the head of every man, and the man is the head of a woman, and God is the head of Christ." Janet might say, "Honey, I would like to appeal to you to take a more active role in the leadership of our family. We want to come under your leadership and mature as a result. Scripture is clear that you are to lead and we are to follow. I will be glad to do anything I can to help you and make it easier for you. Is there anything I can do differently to help you? Would you think about what I've asked?"

Janet also has the freedom in the Lord to suggest good material to Jim that would help him, such as Lou Priolo's tapes, "How to Live with Your Wife in an Understanding Way" and "How to Be an Effective Spiritual Leader."[4] She could acknowledge that she needs to learn also. Janet should give him some time to think about what she said, perhaps a week or so. If he refuses or nothing changes, then she should again appeal to Jim and ask him (since they hold differing opinions) if it would be all right if they went together to talk to the pastor or one of the godly men in their church. The purpose of the meeting would be to seek help for both of them to learn how to carry out the roles that God intended. Again, Janet should give Jim time to think about what she has asked. If he still refuses or nothing changes, then Janet could consider going to the pastor to seek guidance. As a rule, it would be wise for her to inform her husband rather than "going behind his back." She can invite him to come along if he would like.

If in spite of Janet's appeal, Jim continues to neglect his responsibilities, their pastor and the male leaders in the church would decide how or whether it would be appropriate to proceed (*see* Matthew 18:15-18). In the meantime, you as a counselor will want to help Janet discern to what extent, if any, she should take on those responsibilities that her husband is neglecting. For example, she still has a responsibility to bring the children up in the "discipline and instruction of the Lord" (Ephesians 6:4). She is still responsible to plan a reasonable budget and adhere to it whether Jim expresses an opinion or not. This is part of her responsibility to manage her household, as Titus 2:5 commands.

In spite of Jim's negligence, Janet still has a responsibility to show respect and love to Jim. She can do this by fighting back with blessings (*see* 1 Peter 3:9). She can learn to think "kind . . . tender-hearted . . . and forgiving" thoughts (Ephesians 4:32) so as not to become embittered. She can strive to persevere in her prayers for him, to delight in her relationship with the Lord, and to glorify God by being a loving companion to Jim as much as Jim will permit. Remind her often that *her* obedience to God is not dependent on Jim's. Her ability to be pleasing to the Lord is not contingent upon Jim's godliness. Even though Janet's husband won't lead, she can still be like one of the "holy women of the past who put their hope in God" (1 Peter 3:5 NIV).

Counseling the Wife of a Domineering Husband

"I knew Stuart had a temper before we got married. His mother even told me privately that she was concerned about his anger and she suggested that I might want to reconsider the engagement. At the time, I was young and foolish and told her, 'He would never treat me like that. He loves me!' That was sixteen years ago and it has been far worse than I ever imagined."

Peggy explains further by telling about Stuart's moods, yelling and cursing, mean verbal attacks, and a few incidents where he pushed her down or hit her with his fist. Once she even called the police, but when they arrived she lost her courage and told them it was her fault and that everything was all right. So the police left. Another time she contacted her pastor, but she did not tell him the whole truth and he did not pursue it for fear Stuart would leave the church.

Stuart appears to be an exemplary church member. He is always arriving early to greet people. He cannot do enough for others, and he teaches the adult couples' Sunday school class. But after 16 years of marriage, Peggy is just going through the motions. She does not hear his Sunday school lesson, because she is bitterly replaying previous offenses in her mind. In despair, Peggy comes to you for counsel and says, "I'm so hurt and confused, I don't know what to do. Will you help me?"

Unfortunately, Peggy and Stuart's story is all too common. Peggy may mistakenly believe that God is pleased when she covers up Stuart's sin. Peggy is also afraid and bitter. She is afraid of angering Stuart and losing him. She is afraid that things will stay as they are perpetually. She is bitter because she harbors unforgiveness and believes that she is in a hopeless situation. The key to counseling her is to help her understand God's perspective of her problem. She must learn to biblically overcome her fear and use the resources that God has given to protect her.[5] This process will probably not be easy or pleasant, but it is possible for Peggy, with God's help, to respond to Stuart's anger in a righteous way.

"Do not be overcome by evil, but overcome evil with good" (Romans 12:21 NIV) is a command to all Christians. You will want to help Peggy seek to overcome evil with good in her married life. For instance, if Peggy is going to obey God, she may not choose the option of retreating and covering up for Stuart's sin. To respond biblically, she must take full advantage of all of the resources God has given in the Scriptures to protect her. As with Janet, you should instruct Peggy to pray for her husband and to communicate with him biblically; but because of the gravity of Stuart's sin, Peggy must go further.

Overcoming the Fear of the Wife

Exhort Peggy to begin responding biblically by overcoming her sinful fears with God's help. The key to overcoming fear is to stand firm in the Spirit.

Second Timothy 1:7 teaches that we as Christians don't have a spirit of fear but of power, love, and self-discipline. Through the Holy Spirit, Peggy has the power to do what is right—to truly love (1 Corinthians 13:4-7), and to be prepared to take biblical action. Begin preparing her to biblically confront Stuart by teaching her to think biblically. Consider the following examples of biblical thoughts that overcome fear:[6]

- "This is frightening, but I am going to do the right thing; and God will, no matter how my husband reacts, give me the grace to get through it."
- "If I have to feel anxious, I'll just have to feel anxious; but I am going to obey God and show love to my husband by responding to Stuart's sin with biblical 'good.' "
- "My responsibility is to do what is right and God will, at that time, give me the grace and wisdom to respond correctly" (1 Peter 3:6).
- "If I become confused or do not know what to say, I can always tell Stuart, 'Let me think about how to respond and I'll get back with you.' "
- "I am afraid Stuart will respond negatively, but I don't know that to be a fact. My responsibility is to confront him in a godly manner. When I do, God will help me."
- "If he leaves me or hurts me, it will be difficult and embarrassing; but if he does, I will be suffering for doing what is right and God will be glorified."
- "If he hits me, I will prepare a plan so it won't happen again for my sake and for his."
- "No one can perfectly guarantee my safety, but I can be assured that God will be glorified in my life if I obey His Word with the right heart attitude."

Offering Biblical Reproof to the Husband

After you prepare Peggy to think biblically, help her formulate a biblical reproof to be given to Stuart regarding his anger. To reprove a fellow Christian means to tell him or her how he or she is sinning. This step is based on Matthew 18:15, where Jesus said, "If your brother sins, go and reprove him in private; if he listens to you, you have won your brother," and Galatians 6:1, where Paul said, "Brethren, even if a man is caught in any trespass, you who are spiritual, restore such a one in a spirit of gentleness, each one looking to yourself, lest you too be tempted." Peggy is to do this gently, lovingly, and with the motive of restoring Stuart to a right relationship with God and herself. Peggy could respectfully and lovingly say something like this to her husband:

"Stuart, there is something I want to tell you. I love you and I am committed to you. You are my husband and my brother in the Lord. As Christians, we are to help each other become as much like the Lord Jesus as possible. That's why I want to talk to you about what I believe to be a pattern of sin in your life—the sin of anger. Because this is a long-standing habit, you will need help and accountability to change. I recommend that you and I go together to see our pastor. I know this is difficult for you. It is for me, too; but God will give us the grace to go through this and to grow together in love for each other. Stuart, you must change for the Lord's sake. 'He who conceals his transgressions will not prosper, but he who confesses and forsakes them will find compassion' (Proverbs 28:13). Please think about this and let's talk again to see what you have decided."

If Stuart agrees and cooperates (and he might), they should go together to see the pastor for counsel. If he becomes angry and begins blameshifting (and he might), Peggy must then be prepared to respond to a fool. Biblically, a foolish man is one who rejects the Word of God and does what is right in his own eyes (*see* Proverbs 1:7; 12:15). Anger is just one of the responses of a fool (Proverbs 29:11). Immature Christian husbands may act foolishly from time to time by responding angrily with harsh accusations, intimidation, or manipulation. Teach a wife to respond wisely to a foolish man: "Do not answer a fool according to his folly, lest you also be like him" (Proverbs 26:4).

The tendency for many wives is to respond to mistreatment by their husbands with sinful anger, fear, pouting, clamming up, yelling, going home to mother, crying, making brutal verbal attacks, or defending themselves. This is, in short, returning evil for evil because it is responding *to* a fool *like* a fool. Instead, teach Peggy to respond to Stuart's foolish behavior in a God-honoring way. Proverbs 26:5 says, "Answer a fool as his folly deserves, lest he be wise in his own eyes." In other words, Peggy should respond to Stuart's bullying with the wisdom of Scripture. Instead of saying nothing or defending herself, Peggy could *gently* say something like, "Stuart, your responsibility [the answer he deserves] is to speak to me with a gentle, loving tone and to humble yourself and admit that you are angry and need help."

Not answering back like a fool is easy to understand but hard to do in the heat of conflict. Peggy was concerned that she might become confused about what to say when she found herself in a difficult spot. Proverbs 15:28 teaches that a wise wife does not have to immediately give her husband a direct answer: "The heart of the righteous *ponders* how to answer." Therefore, you can instruct Peggy to tell Stuart, "I need to think about how to answer you, and I will give you a response as soon as possible. Would it be all right if we talk about this later?" If Stuart continues to rave and verbally attack Peggy, she should entrust herself to God and realize that she is suffering for righteousness' sake (1 Peter 2:23).

Many wives are reluctant to use Scripture when they answer their Christian husband's foolish accusations. They should remember that "the Word of God is living and active and sharper than any two-edged sword, and piercing as far as the division of soul and spirit, of both joints and marrow, and able to judge the thoughts and intentions of the heart" (Hebrews 4:12). The Word of God is the Christian's most effective weapon. The wife should use God's Word in a wise way in order not to respond like a fool and give her husband the answer that he deserves (*see* Proverbs 26:5). She must remember that "a gentle answer turns away wrath" (Proverbs 15:1), and pray for wisdom as to how to present the Word to him.

As Peggy learns to respond to Stuart biblically, her fear will gradually abate. She will be showing love to God by obeying His Word while at the same time showing love to Stuart because love "does not rejoice in unrighteousness, but rejoices with the truth" (1 Corinthians 13:6). Peggy's willingness to confront Stuart about his sin is an act of love.

Implementing Church Discipline If Necessary

If Stuart refuses to seek help and accountability, Peggy's next responsibility is to proceed with church discipline (*see* Matthew 18:15-18). She is to bring two or more witnesses with her to confront him. She should choose the witnesses wisely, such as two godly men in her church. She then would present the facts again to Stuart speaking in a quiet tone while giving well-prepared, clear examples. I would instruct her to write down what she wants to say ahead of time and practice it out loud several times. If Stuart still refuses to cooperate or continues to delay the accountability, Peggy should ask their pastor and church leaders (elders or deacons) to proceed (if upon investigation, they deem it appropriate) with the third and possibly the fourth step in church discipline as explained in Matthew 18:15-20. If you need further instruction about church discipline, I would recommend Jay Adam's book *The Handbook of Church Discipline.*[7]

Providing Protection and Encouragement

If Stuart still persists in his anger and abuse and refuses to follow the counsel of his pastor, Peggy has one additional biblical option. That is to call the police and press charges. This is an especially grievous and embarrassing action, but Romans 13:1 says, "Let every man be in subjection to the governing authorities." This includes Stuart. It is illegal for him to physically abuse Peggy. She may need to temporarily flee with the children for her and their protection. Both Proverbs 22:3 ("The prudent sees the evil and hides himself") and 27:12 ("A prudent man sees evil and hides himself") teach that it is wise for a woman to flee if she or her children are in danger. You should work with your counselee and the pastor to determine the occasion and procedure for leaving or staying and calling the police. It is important to prepare her because if the time comes for her to notify the police or flee, she will be much more likely not to be overcome by fear if she knows what to do. A plan similar to the following must be worked out with her: She needs to prepare where to go (friend's home, shelter, other); how to go; when to go; what to take; how to plan for taking her children; what to do about pets; how to prepare financially.[8] When the police arrive, Peggy should tell them the truth about what happened as calmly as possible and press charges. As drastic as this is, it is one of the ways that God has provided to protect Peggy and put pressure on Stuart to repent. She would be foolish not to take full advantage of this resource if she needs to.

It is understandable for any woman in Peggy's circumstances to feel frightened and hurt. She will need you to give her a lot of hope and encouragement, especially if her husband remains unwilling to repent. She does not have to live passively in fear and submit to her husband's sin. She can fight back biblically by seeking to overcome evil with good. She must be encouraged that what the Bible commands is good and right, even if it seems unpleasant or doesn't follow accepted cultural codes of conduct. Most of the time, when wives biblically (in love and truth) stand up to "bullies" like Stuart, the final outcome is much better than they thought possible. On the rare occasion that it is not, the wife will have the joy of knowing that she did "what was right without being frightened by any fear" (1 Peter 3:6) and that she suffered for doing what is right (1 Peter 3:17).

Counseling the Wife of a Workaholic Husband

Everyone in their church and many in their community believe Pastor John to be a wonderful, loving man. Everyone, that is, except his wife Marsha. Tears pour down her face as she expresses the agony she feels because of her loneliness.

"I feel trapped and don't dare tell anyone because I don't want to harm his reputation as a pastor. He's a good pastor to his people. In fact, no sacrifice would be too great. His work hours are from early morning to late at night every night. We almost never have a meal together as a family. We're there, but he isn't. He is so immersed in his work and "calling" that I may as well not exist. I've tried to talk to him but I end up angry and he says he'll do better, but it never changes. I can't take much more. I'm thinking about leaving him. What should I do?"

Marsha needs hope. Even though it will take more than one meeting to tell her everything she should know, you can begin by giving her hope. Help her turn her thoughts and heart to God. A good passage to share with her is Lamentations 3:21-25, which chronicles Jeremiah's struggle with despair and hopelessness:

> *This I recall to my mind, therefore I have hope. The LORD's loving kindnesses indeed never cease, for His compassions never fail. They are new every morning; great is Thy faithfulness. "The LORD is my portion," says my soul, "Therefore I have hope in Him." The LORD is good to those who wait for Him, to the person who seeks Him.*

You'll want to teach Marsha that even though she *feels* like she cannot take much more, God says she can. Her strength does not come from her own determination but rather from her knowledge that God's faithfulness is great. She must remember His faithfulness. He will not permit her to be tempted (pressured) beyond what she can bear. Somehow, some way, God will give her a way of escape (1 Corinthians 10:13). In the meantime, God will supply her with the grace to go through this and to endure her circumstances, even if her husband never changes.

Replacing Bitterness with Kindness

In addition to giving Marsha hope, realize that there are at least three areas of sin in her life—bitterness, anger, and coping with loneliness in an unbiblical manner. I recommend that you begin by helping her turn from her bitterness. Otherwise, she might be so focused on John's shortcomings that her progress in other areas will be hindered (*see* Hebrews 12:15-17).

Marsha's bitterness can intensify as she acts unlovingly, by "tak[ing] into account a wrong suffered" (1 Corinthians 13:5). In other words, as she meditates on the hurtful things her husband has done, she will feel more and more hurt and resentment. Encourage her to keep a self-talk log in which she writes down her thoughts whenever she feels hurt, resentful, or frustrated. Go over each recorded thought with her and help her formulate a biblically righteous thought that can replace the bitter thought. The righteous thoughts would be based upon Ephesians 4:31-32, which instruct us to put away all bitterness and anger and instead to be "kind to one another, tender-hearted, forgiving each other, just as God in Christ also has forgiven you." Consider the following examples adapted from the book *The Excellent Wife*.[9]

BITTER THOUGHTS	KIND, TENDER-HEARTED, FORGIVING THOUGHTS
He doesn't love me. He only loves his congregation.	He is not showing love to me as he should, but he may change (Colossians 3:14).
I can't believe what he has done to me!	What he has done is difficult, but God will give me the grace to get through it (1 Corinthians 10:13).
I will never forgive him.	After all the Lord has forgiven me for, this is the least I can do (Matthew 18:32-33).
I'll show him what it's like.	I'll give him a blessing instead (1 Peter 3:9).
We never should have gotten married in the first place. He's married to his church.	He is my husband and I am *committed* to him, no matter what.
God understands that I can't take this.	God will give me the grace and wisdom to hang in there.

Going the Second Mile

Bitterness is a sin. Marsha must repent. She repents by confessing her sin to God and to her husband, working at thinking godly, righteous, forgiving thoughts instead of bitter thoughts *and* going the second mile. Going the second mile involves giving John a blessing instead of retaliating in anger or bitterness. First Peter 3:9 says we are not to be "returning evil for evil, or insult for insult, but giving a blessing instead." In other words, each time Marsha feels like retaliating by entertaining vengeful thoughts or withdrawing from John, she should do something extra nice and unexpected. She could fill up his car with gas or leave him a special, encouraging note. She might ask to pray with him for God's favor and help. These are things which constitute "blessings." By acting contrary to her sinful feelings, she will be honoring the Lord and showing love to her husband. In addition, she will be overcoming evil with good (Romans 12:21) and will begin to experience God's grace to help her overcome her emotional distress.

More than likely, Marsha's anger will fade as she responds biblically regarding her bitterness. When she feels frustrated or resentful she will find it helpful to say to herself, "What does God want me to do? I know responding in anger is not the answer since 'the anger of man does not achieve the righteousness of God' " (James 1:20).

Instead of responding in anger, Marsha should make a godly appeal to her husband. Her tone of voice should be calm and gentle. Her motive should be to help him have a right walk with the Lord.

You can help Marsha prepare her appeal. She might say to something like this to John: "John, I love you and would like for you to consider something. I have thought about it a lot and believe that your work habits are interfering with the closeness of the relationship that God intends for us to have. What I'm talking about is the 'one-flesh intimacy' that is mentioned in Genesis 2:24. The closeness that God intends for us is not just a physical bond but a special bond that God gives only to husbands and wives. I believe we are to be close, spend time together, talk, and share personal things with each other. We should be closer to each other than to anyone else. In order to do that, could we plan some definite times to be together as a couple and also with the children? I thought perhaps you could schedule your time so that we have breakfast together each morning and supper together almost every night. Also, it would help if you would limit the number of nights out to two or three per week unless, of course, there is an emergency. I miss you and I love you. Please prayerfully think about what I have suggested and let me know what you think."

If nothing changes after Marsha gives John some time to think about what she has said, then she should speak with him again. (In the meantime, she should keep giving him lots of "blessings.") This time, the confrontation should be in the form of a loving, godly, gentle reproof using Scripture for its basis (*see* Galatians 6:1). For example, she could say, "John, I do believe your work habits and consequent neglect of us is sinful. You are not pursuing our 'one-flesh relationship' as you should (Genesis 2:24), you seem to be in bondage to your work habits (*see* 1 Corinthians 6:12), and you are not loving me biblically as you should (Ephesians 5:25-30). John, I love you and I am asking you for the Lord's sake to repent and turn from your sin."

If John does not repent after a reasonable length of time, then Marsha should calmly tell him that she believes his actions to be sin. Because sin is involved, she must bring in other witnesses. She should tell John that she will be talking to two or three of the elders or men leaders in the church and will ask them to come with her to talk with him (Matthew 18:16).

What Marsha should do from that point onward will depend on the circumstances and her church's government. One option she does *not* have, however, is leaving her husband (*see* 1 Corinthians 7:10). Likely, John will respond in a godly manner and her loneliness will subside (although this must not be her motive in confronting him). In the meantime, you'll want to help Marsha to understand her responsibility by giving scriptural examples of varying ways (right and wrong) to cope with loneliness.

Persevering in the Midst of Loneliness

One scriptural example of coping with loneliness is Elijah, who had a thrilling mountaintop experience as God rained down fire on Elijah's altar in direct challenge to the wicked prophets of Baal. Elijah had just witnessed an incredible miracle from God, but when wicked Queen Jezebel threatened to kill him, he panicked and ran for his life. Exhausted and hiding in a cave, Elijah began to feel isolated and alone. Instead of focusing on the power and protection of God, Elijah whined:

> *I have been very zealous for the* LORD, *the God of hosts; for the sons of Israel have forsaken Thy covenant, torn down Thine altars and killed Thy prophets with the sword. And* I alone am left; *and they seek my life, to take it away (1 Kings 19:10, emphasis added).*

Another example of a lonely person in Scripture is Jeremiah. Jeremiah was not a popular prophet. His sober warnings from God to the children of Israel went virtually unheeded. People pulled away from him. They thought he was a nut! They mocked him. Jeremiah struggled with intense emotional pain. He felt abandoned by God, forsaken, and isolated. He was burdened down, trapped, and despairing with no hope. Imagine how Jeremiah felt as he described his feelings:

> *In dark places He [God] has made me dwell, like those who have long been dead. He has walled me in so that I cannot go out; He has made my chain heavy. Even when I cry out and call for help, he shuts out my prayer (Lamentations 3:6-8).*

Jeremiah was lonely. Everyone was against him. No one believed him. He even felt abandoned by God! I cannot think of anything more desperate than to cry out to God for help and believe that even He has shut you out. There could not possibly be a greater sense of loneliness!

By far the most poignant and heart-wrenching picture of loneliness is that of the Lord Jesus Christ in the Garden of Gethsemane and later on the cross. Jesus asked Peter, James, and John to watch and pray with Him. Yet they slept as He agonized in prayer over His impending trial. His time of greatest need had come and His closest friends slept. He had done so much for them and they could not do this one thing for Him (Matthew 26:37-44).

On the cross, the Lord Jesus endured the most intense experience of loneliness possible. After having had perfect harmony with God the Father for all of eternity, He cried out in anguish from the cross, "My God, My God, why hast Thou forsaken Me?" (Mark 15:34). We cannot fathom His agony or His isolation as He bore the sins of the world.

Paul may have been tempted to feel lonely during his imprisonment in Rome. The prison was cold and damp and dark. Paul wrote to his beloved Timothy urging him to come and visit as soon as possible (2 Timothy 4:9).

Paul also warned Timothy to beware of those who had deserted and harmed him—Demas deserted him, and Alexander the coppersmith did Paul "much harm" (2 Timothy 4:14). At this time, no one supported Paul. Unlike Elijah, who could leave the cave he was hiding in, Paul was near martyrdom and in prison until the end. He knew he was already "being poured out as a drink offering, and the time of [his] departure [had] come" (2 Timothy 4:6-7). Paul was abandoned and he was cold. It is pitiful that he implored Timothy to bring him his coat before winter. He was going to die, his prison conditions were wretched, and he was alone.

Elijah and Jeremiah were overwhelmed by their loneliness. Jesus and Paul were not. The difference is that Elijah and Jeremiah felt sorry for themselves, while Jesus and Paul sought refuge in God. When Marsha feels lonely, she has a choice: like Elijah and Jeremiah she can choose to respond with self-pity, or like Jesus and Paul she can seek refuge in God.

A person's loneliness may be exacerbated by self-pity. Regardless of his circumstances, if he feels sorry for himself, he is likely to experience intense loneliness. Self-pity will throw a person into the pit of depression very quickly. The intensity of his self-pity can become much worse than his actual circumstances, and it will be because he has wrong thoughts about others or God.

Regardless of what John does, Marsha must seek refuge in God. She should begin with cultivating gratefulness to God and to her husband as she learns to be content in her particular circumstances. She needs to remember that God desires to mold her character to become more like the Lord Jesus Christ's (Romans 8:28-29). At the same time, she can rejoice with confidence because whatever God's purposes are in trying circumstances, they are good for her, or He would not have permitted them.

Seeking Fulfillment from God

You will want to question Marsha carefully and lovingly about her thinking and responses to John. If she is withdrawn and aloof from John, she may be expecting him to do for her what only God can do. She may be expecting him to be her constant companion, to know her perfectly, or to satisfy her desire for fellowship. Instead, she should seek refuge in God through prayer and meditation on His Word. She can show love to her husband whether she feels like it or not by studying the "one another" passages in the New Testament. She should also be open and honest with him and speak edifying words. If she has sinned against her husband due to her own bitterness, fear, or anger, she should clear her conscience through repentance and confession and then continue to do what is right (*see* James 4:8).

You'll want to help Marsha realize that it is not wrong for a wife to desire intimacy with her husband unless she desires it so intensely that she sins if she cannot have it. Then her desire becomes idolatrous. In that case, even if her husband attempts to be more open with her, she is likely to be disappointed no matter how hard he tries. He may give up trying, and then her idolatrous desire for intimacy will become even more intense.

Rather than allowing her "need" for intimate companionship to become idolatrous, a wife should long for and set her heart on closeness with the Lord Jesus. She can always talk to God and share everything with Him if her husband will not open up to her. She can have the heart of the psalmist, who wrote, "As the deer pants for the water brooks, so my soul pants for Thee, O God. My soul thirsts for God, for the living God" (Psalm 42:1-2).

Another example of a sinful idolatrous desire for intimacy is that of a woman daydreaming about having intimate conversations with other men. Ask your counselee if she does this. If she does, then exhort her to think about (and thus desire) pure and righteous things instead of sinful imaginations (*see* Philippians 4:8). Perhaps she is disrespectful to her husband because he does not meet her expectations. Instead, she should be grateful for whatever attention he gives her. As a result, she will likely be pleased with the attention he pays her instead of being resentful and disappointed. She should "in everything give thanks; for this is God's will for you in Christ Jesus" (1 Thessalonians 5:18). Check out whether your counselee believes she deserves an attentive husband. Let her know that her beliefs about what she thinks she deserves will give birth to thoughts and actions that are either godly or ungodly.

At the times that Marsha feels excessive sorrow because of lack of intimacy with her husband, she should instead worship and serve the Lord Jesus Christ. She can worship and serve the Lord whether or not she ever has an intimate relationship with her husband. Any Christian can "serve the LORD with gladness; [and] come before Him with joyful singing" (Psalm 100:2).

Looking to God for Comfort

What should Marsha do when she feels intense resentment towards her husband? Instruct her to give him a blessing instead of dwelling on past hurts. She is not to mull John's failures over and over in her mind because love "does not take into account a wrong suffered" (1 Corinthians 13:5).

The only way that Marsha will ever be joyful is for her to adopt a high view God. She needs to recognize that she is here to serve God, not vice versa. She should view her time alone as a gift from God. Encourage her to remember that she is never really alone. God is always with her; in Hebrews 13:5 He says, "I will never desert you, nor will I ever forsake you." Counsel Marsha to talk to God in her mind or aloud often during the day and lonely evenings. The more lonely she feels, the more she should let God talk to her through the Scriptures either by reading them, singing them, meditating on them, or recalling previously memorized verses.[10] Implore Marsha to long for God as King David did:

> *I remember the days of old; I meditate on all Thy doings; I muse on the work of Thy hands. I stretch out my hands to Thee; My soul longs for Thee, as a parched land (Psalm 143:5-6).*

You'll want to give Marsha hope that "the LORD is good to those who wait for Him, to the person who seeks Him" (Lamentations 3:25). Her responsibility is to biblically appeal to and confront John with his sin and to thank God— for her circumstances, for what God wants to teach her, and for how God wants to use her for His glory. Loneliness is painful, but it is not to become the occasion for sin. Being a pastor's wife gives Marsha many special opportunities to be like the "excellent wife" in Proverbs 31:12: "She does him [her husband] good and not evil all the days of her life." By God's grace, she and John can biblically solve their problem in a God-honoring manner and gain the closeness God intends for them to have.

Counseling Women Toward Completeness in Christ

I consider it a privilege to be used by God to give clear, biblical counsel to women. God has truly given Christians "everything pertaining to life and godliness" (2 Peter 1:3). What a joy it is to have counseled Janet, Peggy, and Marsha and to know that they are being sanctified in the truth, the Word of God (John 17:17).

As women pour out their hearts to you, pray for wisdom and work diligently in preparation for the counseling sessions. Exhort and teach them. Be patient and show love. Finally, have the passion of the apostle Paul, who proclaimed Christ, "admonishing every man and teaching every man with all wisdom, that [you] may present every man complete in Christ" (Colossians 1:28).

CHAPTER 9

Counseling Women Married to Unbelievers

Carol W. Cornish, M.A.

Wendy looked cheerful and composed as she began telling me what brought her to counseling. While describing her marriage of 20 years to Roger, tears began to glisten in her eyes and she found it hard to control her trembling lips. As tears spilled over onto her cheeks, I offered her a tissue. "Wendy," I said, "you seem to be hurting deeply. I want you to know it's okay to cry here." With that, Wendy broke into sobs and cried for several minutes.

"Roger is not a Christian," Wendy said as she breathed deeply and began to relax. "When we married, we were both unbelievers. We didn't really know what it meant to be a Christian and we didn't care. We were young and we wanted all the good things the world told us we should have to be happy. A decade went by before God brought me to the point where I realized I needed to surrender my life to Christ. Even Roger noticed changes in me after my conversion. Some of the changes he liked and others he didn't." I asked Wendy to give me some examples. "Roger liked it that I became kinder, more soft-spoken. But he didn't like how my tastes in movies changed. Roger likes action films and isn't offended by violence, nudity, or sexual themes. But I am offended by them. He thinks I've gone off the deep end. Our values clash over lots of things. It makes me feel isolated and lonely.

"We've had some counseling for our problems, but nothing seems to change. I'm really frustrated, too. I'm so tired of living with Roger. Most of the time I wish I could evaporate into thin air and go immediately to heaven. Can you help me? How am I going to live the rest of my life with this man I don't even like? Sometimes I don't know how to get through even one day with him much less the rest of my life!"

Wendy's description of her situation is similar to many I've heard in my counseling ministry. How do women get into this predicament? Typically, two unbelievers marry and later the wife becomes a Christian. Or less commonly, the woman finds out after marriage that her husband is not really a Christian. Some unbelieving husbands state openly they are not Christians. Others profess to be Christians but do not evidence the spiritual fruit necessary to be consistent with their claims.

Bearing One Another's Burdens

It is sad that people in the church often assume Christian wives of unbelievers willfully and rebelliously disobeyed God and married non-Christians. Some Christian women do disobediently marry unbelievers, but that is not the usual case. Living with this assumption by others that she has disobeyed God (and deserves what she got?) can provoke a woman to sorrow and discouragement. She is already in difficult circumstances and the wrongly judgmental attitudes of such Christians adds grievously to her burden.

Most churches have ministries to groups such as singles, married couples, and divorced people. But it is rare to find a church with a ministry that targets Christian spouses married to unbelievers. People in this category often suffer alone because of a lack of support. The near absence of such ministries is partly due to the delicate circumstance of trying to help the believer without offending the spouse. Nevertheless, with tact and wisdom it must be done.

An undue hesitancy seems to exist on the part of church leaders to get "tangled up" in a context where the person in a position of leadership in the home (the husband) is not a Christian. Rather than bearing one another's burdens (the local church for the wife), it is more comfortable to ignore the situation.

How can you help a woman married to an unbeliever? One way is to encourage men in your congregation to reach out to her husband. Perhaps an elder with the gift of evangelism could take particular interest in ministering to these husbands. What can you do to help the wife? Let's look at some portions of Scripture to find out.

Let Each Man (and Woman) Remain

In chapter 4, "The Essential Foundation" we said it is vital to see all of life from God's perspective. First Corinthians 7:12-17 gives God's view of the marriage of a Christian and a non-Christian. The church in Corinth had posed questions to Paul about several aspects of marriage perhaps including whether Christian wives and husbands should remain married to their unsaved spouses. Corinth was a pagan city when Paul brought the gospel there. Married men and women who became Christians suddenly found themselves facing this new situation if their spouses did not also embrace the faith. Paul counsels them by saying,

> *But to the rest I say, not the Lord, that if any brother has a wife who is an unbeliever, and she consents to live with him, let him not send her away. And a woman who has an unbelieving husband, and he consents to live with her, let her not send her husband away. For the unbelieving husband is sanctified through his wife, and the unbelieving wife is sanctified through her believing husband; for otherwise your children are unclean, but now they are holy. Yet if the unbelieving one leaves, let him leave; the brother or the sister is not under bondage in such cases, but God has called us to peace. For how do you know, O wife, whether you will save your husband? Or how do you know, O husband, whether you will save your wife? Only, as the Lord has assigned to each one, as God has called each, in this manner let him walk. And thus I direct in all the churches.*

Let's clear up some questions that arise over Paul's intent in this passage. By saying in verse 12, "I say, not the Lord," Paul is not merely giving his own opinion. He is saying that he is not directly quoting words that Jesus spoke while on earth. But Paul is speaking authoritatively as an apostle of the Lord under the divine inspiration of the Holy Spirit.

Application to Marriage

Verse 13 says that if an unbelieving husband consents ("is willing" in NIV) to live with his wife, she must not send him away ("divorce him" in NIV). The new Corinthian believers questioned Paul about whether they should stay married to their non-Christian spouses. Paul's teaching explains that God wants these newly converted Christians to remain married. Becoming a Christian is no reason to break up the marriage. Today, the same principle stands.

What does verse 14 mean when it says "the unbelieving husband is sanctified by his wife" and "otherwise your children are unclean, but now they are holy"? Sanctify (from the Greek verb *hagiazo*), *in this context,* means the husband is set apart for God's use because of his contact with his wife since she is considered by God to be holy in Christ. Her holy influence as a Christian extends to the husband and the children. "Sanctify" does not mean they are saved just because they are related to her. No one rides anyone else's coattails into heaven.

If the Unbeliever Wants to Leave

If the unbeliever is willing to remain in the marriage relationship with his Christian spouse, the wife must not divorce him, but rather be a holy influence in his life. But if the husband is unwilling to stay with her, what should she do? She is to let him leave (verse 15). She must not beg him or bargain with him to try to keep him from leaving. Why? Because "God has called us to peace." Listen to Jay Adams's explanation of what this "peace" is:

> Peace *means a final resolution of the matter. Too many counselors, meaning well but doing great harm, have advised Christian wives (for instance) whose unsaved husbands wanted out of the marriage to "just keep on praying." With no divorce, the husband, who may even leave the home, has the right to return at any time. The wife, still "bound" by marriage obligations, is required to have sexual relations. Having stayed long enough to have sex, a few good meals and his clothes washed, he may leave again, having gotten her pregnant. It is this sort of on-again-off-again uncertainty that Paul says God wants to put to an end: "God has called you to peace."*[1]

So if he wants to leave, she must let him leave. She is not to be bound to an unbelieving husband who wants out. She shouldn't try to manipulate her circumstances. Instead, she must trust God and be content in the circumstances in which God has put her whether her unsaved spouse stays or goes.

What Does It Mean to Be Unequally Yoked?

You've probably read or heard the term "unequally yoked" in reference to a Christian married to an unbeliever. This term comes from 2 Corinthians 6:14-15:

Do not be bound ["yoked" in NIV] together with unbelievers; for what partnership have righteousness and lawlessness, or what fellowship has light with darkness? Or what harmony has Christ with Belial, or what has a believer in common with an unbeliever?

Here in his second letter to the Corinthians, Paul is not directly addressing marriage. He is talking about the necessity of the believers in Corinth separating themselves from the practices of the pagan culture in which they lived and from the teaching of false prophets.

In a general sense, however, we could say these verses apply to relationships of any kind in which Christians will be held responsible for or significantly influenced by the attitudes and actions of unbelievers. For example, business partnerships and organizations requiring oaths of allegiance would fall into the category of relationships that need to have an equal yoke. Marriage relationships fit in here too. A believing single woman must not intentionally "yoke" herself to an unbeliever by marrying him. The principle of Paul's teaching in 2 Corinthians 6:14-18 is that binding relationships must occur between persons who are both in the Lord. He poses the question, "What has a believer in common with an unbeliever?" (verse 15).

Paul certainly does not mean that a woman, who is saved after her marriage to an unbeliever, should separate herself from her husband. To do so would be contrary to 1 Corinthians 7. Paul is not negating what he said to the Corinthians in his first letter to them. The principle he established still stands: Stay married unless the spouse wants to leave. However, to unmarried persons, the principle being taught in 2 Corinthians 6 applies: Do not marry someone who is not a believer.

If the Wife Wishes the Unbeliever Would Leave

Some women who are married to unbelievers may say, "I'd be glad if he would go. Life would be so much simpler." But they should beware of provoking him to leave. Sometimes women develop the attitude of not caring how their Christian values and activities affect their spouses. They may assume their Christianity gives them license to be demanding and inflexible. They may display behavior and attitudes that have little hope of communicating the love of Christ to their husbands. Being full of the truth but bankrupt of love is a sad state in which to find yourself.

God is grieved when His children fail to demonstrate His love to others as He has to us. Sometimes women are unwilling to love their husbands because they think they deserve someone better. Persistent refusal or seeming inability to love their husband calls into question their devotion to God. For God says in His Word a Christian can do all things through Him (Philippians 4:13), and nothing is impossible for Him (Numbers 11:23; Luke 1:37). If God can raise the dead, He can enable a woman to love her husband.

Often, women who are married to unbelievers are just plain tired—they feel weary of the whole situation. You'll want to encourage them to fortify themselves with God's Word. Tell them not to give up.

> Do you not know? Have you not heard? The Everlasting God, the LORD, the Creator of the ends of the earth does not become weary or tired. His understanding is inscrutable. He gives strength to the weary, and to him who lacks might He increases power. Though youths grow weary and tired, and vigorous young men stumble badly, yet those who wait for the LORD will gain new strength; they will mount up with wings like eagles, they will run and not get tired, they will walk and not become weary (Isaiah 40:28-31).

> And let us not lose heart in doing good, for in due time we shall reap if we do not grow weary (Galatians 6:9).

If a woman is weary of living with an unbelieving husband, have her talk to God about it. Have her ask Him for His help.

Remind your counselee that she can be faithful because God has empowered her by His Spirit to do good, to be obedient to Him. She needs to guard against allowing herself to slide into a swamp of dejection. Her circumstances are not insurmountable. Often a woman's response to this counsel is to say, "But it's hard." Yes, it is hard. It may be one of the hardest things she'll ever do. The difficulty of it doesn't absolve her of her biblical responsibility to love her husband and minister to him. Why? Because she has a powerful heavenly Father who can empower her to tackle even something this challenging.

If she doesn't love her unsaved husband, she can learn to love him. Biblical testimony and the experience of many women married to unbelievers testify to the truth of this statement. It's up to her. I'm not talking about having mushy, giddy feelings for him. I mean loving him in a truly biblical way. True biblical love is sacrificial service and affection. It is loving another person with the love God has poured out into her heart through the presence of the Holy Spirit in her (see Romans 5:5).

It is freeing when a woman realizes she doesn't have to be concerned with changing her husband. She can't change her husband. She can only change herself with God's help. She may be spending time daydreaming about how wonderful life would be if she didn't have to live with an unsaved husband. Perhaps she fantasizes about how useful to the Lord she could be if she weren't "shackled" to an unbeliever. She may also fantasize about Christian men whom she knows. These thoughts about greener grass are futile. It's a trap to believe God doesn't have her in exactly the best circumstances for her growth in Christlikeness.

Let your counselee know that changing her circumstances would not make her better able to serve God. She can serve the Lord best right where she is, even married to an unbeliever. Encourage her to be content and show her love to Jesus by being obedient to Him. The external circumstance of living with an unsaved husband need not spoil her inner contentment. She can have God's peace and joy even in the midst of troubling circumstances because nothing can ever separate her from the love of Christ (*see* Romans 8:35-39). *Her relationship with God must sustain her.* He gives "wings" to the weary.

The Reality of Spousal Persecution

A significant, but often overlooked, source of weariness in women married to unbelievers is persecution. *Persecution* seems like a very strong word. It may seem too strong to apply to the relationship between a Christian wife and an unbelieving husband. When we think of persecution, we tend to think of mammoth horrors such as being thrown to lions or herded into gas chambers. But there are degrees of persecution just as there are degrees of all other actions. Though what a Christian wife may be experiencing is less severe in degree, it could be the same in kind.

What is persecution? According to the dictionary, persecution is harassing "in a manner to injure, grieve, or afflict; specifically: to cause to suffer because of belief; to annoy with persistent or urgent approaches: pester."[2] Persecution includes hassling someone with petty irritations, getting on their nerves with persistent unpleasantness, irksomely interfering with someone's peace of mind, badgering, baiting, repeated teasing, and hounding. These are all forms of persecution. A synonym of persecution is the word "heckle." The word "heckler" conjures up in our minds the scene of someone in a crowd shouting out at a speaker. The dictionary says heckle "implies persistent interruptive questioning of a speaker in order to confuse or discomfit him."[3] I have seen this kind of behavior between husbands and wives right in my counseling office.

Why all this detail about the meaning of persecution? Because we need to understand that persecution is not always obvious or extreme in its manifestations. Subtle persecution can occur regularly in a marriage between a Christian spouse and an unbeliever. We just haven't thought about it in these terms. Failure to identify and *accurately* label the problem diminishes our ability to apply a biblical solution to it. Lack of insight into the true nature of the problem results in a vague sense of confusion and unrest. Let's clear away the fog and look directly at the problem.

An Example of a Persecuted Wife

Susan has been a Christian for ten years. Her husband, Jerry, is not a Christian. Susan loves to work with children and was asked by her pastor to teach the fourth-grade Sunday school class. Susan talked to Jerry about it at length and he agreed she could do it. Her teaching commitment was to be for a quarter (13 weeks). About halfway through that time, Jerry started grumbling and complaining frequently to Susan about her teaching commitment. Even though Susan was careful to plan her lessons when Jerry was not home and to minimize her commitment's effect on him, Jerry was quite unhappy about it. Jerry suddenly decided they should go away every other weekend so he could "escape" from work pressures. Susan gently reminded him that he had agreed she could teach. Jerry was unmoved by this reminder.

Susan is now torn between her desire to honor her commitment to her church (letting her "yes" be "yes") and her desire to end all the complaining, prodding, yelling, and sarcasm she has to endure from Jerry over this issue. Susan is suffering for doing good. She needs to rejoice *in the Lord*, fulfill her commitment to her church, and continue to be kind and loving to Jerry. In addition, she might try to find a substitute teacher for one or two Sundays as a way to show Jerry she is trying to accommodate his wishes even though he went back on his word.

In His Steps

Concerning suffering, the apostle Peter encouraged his readers with these words:

> *Even if you should suffer for the sake of righteousness, you are blessed. And do not fear their intimidation, and do not be troubled, but sanctify Christ as*

Lord in your hearts, always being ready to make a defense to everyone who asks you to give an account for the hope that is in you, yet with gentleness and reverence; and keep a good conscience so that in the thing in which you are slandered, those who revile your good behavior in Christ may be put to shame. For it is better, if God should will it so, that you suffer for doing what is right rather than for doing what is wrong (1 Peter 3:14-17).

A woman who is suffering can take comfort in knowing that God is in control and is well pleased with a godly response to suffering. Jesus suffered for her and she is to follow in His steps. He was persecuted for doing what was right, and His followers will be also.

Jesus spoke about persecution in the Sermon on the Mount with these words:

Blessed are those who have been persecuted for the sake of righteousness, for theirs is the kingdom of heaven. Blessed are you when men cast insults at you, and persecute you, and say all kinds of evil against you falsely, on account of Me. Rejoice, and be glad, for your reward in heaven is great, for so they persecuted the prophets who were before you (Matthew 5:10-12).

How should a Christian wife respond to such actions of her unsaved husband? Jesus said to consider herself blessed when she is persecuted because of Him. This means *suffering because she is obedient to God ought to be a source of encouragement.*

Some women may say, "Wow, this counselor is a glutton for punishment!" Let me explain why suffering for doing good ought to encourage a woman. First, she should realize I don't mean this is a barrel of fun. I'm not suggesting women should provoke their husbands to cause trouble so they can feel good about suffering so badly. The Bible means nothing like this when it talks about suffering for doing good. Suffering persecution because they've done what's right can produce a quiet, joyful kind of encouragement in them. It shows them they are truly different than they used to be. They are becoming more like Christ, who always did good and often suffered for it.

Suffering for Righteousness vs. Unrighteousness

If a woman is going to suffer, she should be sure it is the result of doing good not the result of doing wrong. Suffering because her response to evil is evil will not produce blessing or encouragement. Rather, it will lead to despair. For example, Janet's husband shouts at her for talking on the phone for five minutes to an elderly neighbor. He wants to use the phone and he wants to use it now.

Janet scowls at him and says goodbye to her neighbor. As she quickly walks away, she yells at him, "You're such a selfish pig, I don't know why I stay here." He yells back at Janet and a bitter quarrel ensues.

The suffering Janet experienced as a result of this interchange is certainly not from righteousness. She returned evil for evil. I'm not condoning her husband's behavior, but her response was not righteous. Her choice of words was sinful since she communicated disrespect, unkindness, and contempt. She is not suffering because of Christ, but because of her own failure to overcome evil with good. How could she have responded? Janet could have ended her phone call and then kindly, firmly, and calmly stated her displeasure with her husband's tone, timing, and demandingness.

Consider this example of a wife being persecuted for righteousness' sake by her husband. Wendy, the counselee mentioned at the beginning of this chapter, went with her husband, Roger, to visit some friends Roger met at work. During the evening, the topic of religion came up. Wendy was asked a question about where she thought people went when they died. Before she could reply, Roger let out a huge guffaw and said, "Don't get her started. She's thinks she has an inside track with God, and you'll be sorry you asked."

The friends laughed nervously. Wendy swallowed the lump in her throat and tried to answer the question. Her explanation was punctuated by Roger's sarcastic jokes about how Wendy was a saint, never did anything wrong, and thought herself above the average mortal. On the way home in the car, Roger ripped into Wendy for not changing the subject when asked her views about the afterlife.

Does Roger's behavior look like persecution to you? It is more subtle than a firing squad—nevertheless, it is persecution. The teaching of Jesus in Matthew 5 says Wendy should consider herself blessed. She will receive a reward in heaven for being persecuted for her faith. You may be thinking to yourself, "Oh no—pie-in-the-sky by-and-by." But Wendy can also reap immediate rewards for her faithfulness if her relationship with the Lord is a close, warm, personal one. The Lord through His Spirit can give her a sense of godly satisfaction that she has pleased her heavenly Father. Knowing that she has delighted God's heart through obedience can be a sweet and joyful reward here and now.

Me, Save Him?

Let's move on now and consider verse 16 of 1 Corinthians 7. The teaching in this verse seems like a mystery at first glance. What looks like its obvious meaning is plainly contradictory to other portions of Scripture. Let's try to understand what Paul is saying here. Clearly, a women is not her husband's savior. So then what does Paul mean when he says, "For how do you know, O wife, whether you will save your husband?" The Greek verb *sozo* is used here (and also in Mark 8:35; Luke 9:24; Romans 11:14; 1 Corinthians 9:22; and 1 Timothy 4:16) to mean saving from eternal death.

When we consider verse 16 in light of the whole counsel of Scripture, *sozo* here refers to those things which God uses; those influences through which God brings salvation to someone. That leads to two possible interpretations: 1) if a woman's husband wants to stay with her, she should not divorce him since she may influence him for Christ, or 2) a woman shouldn't force her husband to stay since she has no guarantee that his staying with her will bring about his salvation.

God chooses those who will be saved; the task of the wife in this situation is to be faithful to God. She can demonstrate the gospel by her life. She can be salt and light to others including her husband.

Whenever something is repeated in the Bible, we should pay special attention to it. Notice between verses 17 and 24 of 1 Corinthians 7 Paul says three times (verses 17,20,24) that each one should remain in the situation he was in when God saved him. Why all this repetition? Because it's part of sinful human nature to seek a loophole. Paul was emphasizing to the Corinthians that what is important is "keeping the commandments of God" (verse 19).

A woman must pursue *obedience* in her present circumstances rather than trying to change her circumstances. This does not mean that Christian singles should not get married, but rather that whatever state a Christian is in he/she must be content. Even to those who were slaves (verse 21), Paul urged a focus on the most important thing—obedience. Paul told slaves that if they could get their freedom it was okay to pursue it. But they must not forget their real freedom is in Christ. We are free to be Christ's slaves by obeying God.

Feeling Trapped

God Is a Protector

A woman shouldn't look for a way out if her unbelieving husband wants to stay married to her. (I am not addressing at this point women who are being physically abused by their husbands. We will speak briefly to those issues later in this chapter. Nor am I addressing those situations in which the husband is an unrepentant adulterer, in which case the wife has biblical grounds for divorce.) Many women feel trapped in this situation and want to escape. The way to "escape" is through obedience to God. Remember:

> No temptation has overtaken you but such as is common to man; and God is faithful, who will not allow you to be tempted beyond what you are able, but with the temptation will provide the way of escape also, that you may be able to endure it (1 Corinthians 10:13).

God has promised His abiding presence in the midst of trials. He won't allow the pressure to become so great that we have to give in to sin. He has graciously provided us with the ability to endure faithfully in any situation. A woman can love her husband as Christ has loved her and then leave the consequences to God. He is a faithful and loving Father. Whether a woman's husband stays or leaves, she is the Lord's. Therefore, she should glorify the Lord by being obedient to Him.

Jesus understands a Christian woman's feelings of entrapment when she is married to an unbeliever. Read the gospels and note how the Pharisees followed Jesus and looked for a way to trap Him by His words and actions. They were intent on His death. Yet Jesus endured their persistent attempts.

Psalm 142 was written by David when he was in a cave having fled from Saul. David writes in verse 3, "When my spirit was overwhelmed within me, Thou didst know my path. In the way where I walk they have hidden a trap for me." God knows the suffering woman's path too. He is intimately acquainted with all her ways (see Psalm 139). He grieves when she suffers and takes note of injustices done against her. God is also her Protector. David expressed this truth when he wrote, "The LORD is my light and my salvation; whom shall I fear? The LORD is the defense of my life; whom shall I dread?" (Psalm 27:1). God is her Defender too.

Having the Right Goal

A woman's goal must not be to change her unsaved husband. Some women I've counseled have responded to this question, "What brings you to counseling?" by saying, "I want to change so that my husband will change." This is a recipe for trouble, disillusionment, and disappointment. It is also displeasing to God and is unattainable.

A Christian woman can't change her unbelieving husband. Only the Holy Spirit can make lasting and godly changes in people. Her goal must be to be faithful to God to be the best wife she can be according to God's standards. Encourage her to trust God with the outcome that results from her obedience to Him. She must be motivated by a desire to please God rather than to change her husband.

Dealing with Spousal Jealousy of Jesus

Unsaved husbands are commonly jealous and suspicious of their wife's relationship to Christ. A husband may think Christ has replaced him in his wife's affections. Christ should certainly be first in a woman's devotion, but Christ's first place in her life should make her a better wife. She has the poured-out love of the Holy Spirit in her (Romans 5:5) and it must overflow to her husband. She is to love him as God loves her. When her husband experiences her increased love for him, his jealousy and suspicion usually will diminish.

Influencing the Husband for Christ

A woman would be wise not to place books, Bibles, tracts, verse cards, and so on around the house to influence her husband for Christ. She can better influence him by her pure, respectful, quiet, and gentle behavior (1 Peter 3:2,4).

She will want to be sensitive to how she spends her time when her husband is home. She should try to meet with God during a time when she and her husband don't usually do something together. It's best not to allow attendance at Bible studies and other Christian group activities to interfere with her time with her husband. She can arrange her schedule so that she can fellowship and grow in the faith without these activities being a hindrance to her marriage. However, Sunday morning services are an important time for her to worship God with other believers, hear authoritative teaching from God's Word, and fellowship with His people. Though she should not be legalistic about church attendance, she needs to be in church for Sunday services on a regular basis. This is non-negotiable. She may suffer persecution for attending church on Sunday morning, but God will bless her faithfulness.

No husband has the authority to command his wife to sin by neglecting corporate worship or for any other reason. Submission of the wife is limited to those areas in which God has given authority to the husband. Jay Adams comments on this by saying,

> *A wife, therefore, is to obey her husband in everything under his legitimate authority, but not without limits. The realm of authority is bounded by the*

Scriptures. . . . The idea that wives must obey their husbands even when commanded to sin is foreign to the Bible.[4]

He goes on to say, "All that a husband does as head should be for the sake of his wife. All decisions are to be made with her best interests and welfare in mind."[5] A wife, on the other hand, must not misconstrue God's will to include only those things she wants or doesn't want to do. If necessary, you may need to caution her against twisting her understanding of God's will to her own advantage.

Influencing the Children for Christ

Space limits what we can say about the effects on children of having one parent who is a Christian and one who is not. It is important to note that the Christian parent's response is crucial in this regard. A believing wife's loving, kind, patient response to an unbelieving husband can be a significant opportunity for the children to see the gospel lived out in real life. For the sake of Christ and the sake of the children, a wife should make it her goal to follow in Jesus' steps. Indeed, her presence in the home can have a sanctifying effect on her children.

Creating a Written Plan

In a marriage where one person has a biblical worldview and the other a secular one, conflict is more likely than in a marriage between two Christians. By "worldview" I mean the person's way of understanding life and how they make sense of the world. (See chapter 3, "Essential Foundations.") Since God has called us to peace, how will your counselee live peaceably in her situation? By having a written plan that she will use to guide her thoughts, attitudes, and actions.

The Need for Accountability

Your counselee's plan must be based on and flow out of the Scriptures. She should keep it in a safe, private place. Pray with her for strength from the Holy Spirit as she seeks to put her plan into action motivated by godly attitudes. Have her ask God to cleanse her heart of any bitterness, apathy, anger, rage, or malice she may have toward her husband.

At first, she will need to read her plan daily and keep a record of her progress in applying it. She will need a trusted friend who will hold her accountable to execute the plan. If she can arrange a discipling relationship with a mature, godly Christian woman, she should give that woman a copy of her plan and ask that she be held accountable to implement it. She should also ask her discipler for suggestions in implementing the plan.

The Joy Connection

Your counselee may find it hard or even discouraging to follow God's calling for someone who is married to an unbelieving spouse. Encourage her to ask God to give her the desire to change. Have her thank Him when she begins to see change in herself. She will want to keep a journal and record the changes she sees. She needs to persevere in doing good to her husband not chiefly for her good so that she will make it through (although that is wonderful), but rather for the glory of God and the furtherance of the gospel.

The goal of her perseverance must be to delight her Father's heart and to live before others a faith that is salt and light. How is it possible for her to do this? Remind her that the joy of the Lord is her strength (*see* Nehemiah 8:10). What is this joy? It includes, but is not limited to, the following: deciding to view her circumstances from God's perspective, learning to be content with what she has, choosing to think godly thoughts, cultivating a grateful heart, praying with a focus on who God is, keeping an eternal perspective on daily life, and fixing her eyes on Jesus and abiding in Him (keeping her thoughts centered on Him).

Saturating all her efforts must be an attitude and practice of prayer. She should use the Scriptures, particularly the psalms, when she prays for her marriage. You may want to suggest that she photocopy some of the psalms at an enlarged size and write her personal responses between the lines. Then she should pray accordingly. She needs the power and encouragement of the Holy Spirit to go through her days with joy. She should talk to God continually (*see* 1 Thessalonians 5:17). This is the way she can be joyfully connected to God.

Biblical Strategies for Living with an Unsaved Husband

A wise wife will develop biblical strategies to interact with her unsaved husband. When appropriate, she will also make plans to endure gracefully by respecting the unjust and loving the unlovely. In some extreme cases, she will need to plan to exit temporarily when it becomes necessary.

All of the strategies listed below center on one theme—that of doing good (as defined by God's standards and working toward His purposes). Each section begins with Bible verses to read and study. Have your counselee read the verses in several translations and write out the ones that are especially helpful to her. Then have her write down what she will do in response to God's Word. She may want to keep all of her materials in a notebook or folder.

Strategy #1: Build your relationship with God.

SCRIPTURES TO READ AND STUDY: Isaiah 40; Matthew 11:28-30; 1 Corinthians 6:17; Ephesians; Philippians 4:4-5; Hebrews 12:3; and 2 Peter 1:2-3.

Your counselee must know who God is, who she is in relation to Him, and what He wants her to do. She also needs to remember how far God has brought her. She was once dead in her sins. Have her study the entire letter to the Ephesians in order to strengthen her knowledge of God and to understand herself as His child. See chapter 4, "Essential Foundations," for help in doing this. Meditate on God's promises.[6]

A wife's union with Christ is an even higher union than the marriage bond. She is not alone. She is complete in Christ (*see* Colossians 2:10)—Jesus is her closest companion. If she does not believe this, have her: confess her sin of unbelief, ask God to forgive her, and repent. Repent, in this sense, means that she will work diligently with God's power to live out the reality of her special union with Christ as God's child.

Strategy #2: Don't return evil for evil or provoke.

SCRIPTURES TO READ AND STUDY: Proverbs 26:4; 2 Timothy 2:23–26; 1 Peter.

Dealing with sins of retaliation and provocation may be one of the hardest things your counselee will ever do. In 1 Peter 2:13–3:17, notice Jesus' response to persecution: He didn't retaliate (actively or passively), He made no threats, He entrusted Himself to God. In the same way, your counselee must not retaliate or insult. If she needs to be silent in order to get control of herself, she can humbly explain to her husband why she cannot talk. She'll need to acknowledge the hurt this may cause her husband. She can say something like, "I'm sorry I can't talk right now. I'm finding it hard to control myself. So I'll need to be quiet for a while." Encourage her to model her response after the response of Christ to His persecutors: commit herself to the One who judges justly and continue to do good. Have her take her hurt to the living Savior and pour out her heart to Him because He cares for her. She can entrust her deepest feelings to Him.

Proverbs 26:4 gives instruction in how she can listen and respond to what she hears. If her husband is speaking foolishly to her, she will want to avoid answering him with more foolishness of her own. She'll want to learn to act out of obedience to God rather than reacting to foolish words or actions.

Second Timothy 2:23-26 overflows with wise advice for wives who are responding to husbands who oppose them. They shouldn't quarrel or argue. Husbands are not won with fine-sounding theological arguments. A wife should go to God confessing any resentment she may have toward her unbelieving husband. Remind her to get the log out of her own eye before she tries to gently point out the speck in his eye (see Matthew 7:1-5). Support her in her endeavors to be kind to him. If he asks her a question, she can gently explain her point of view calmly. She can pray for him according to 2 Timothy 2:23-26. She can pray that God will grant him repentance leading him to a knowledge of the truth, and that he will come to his senses and escape from the trap of the devil, who has taken him captive to do his will. She can sympathize with him, be tenderhearted, and regard him as more important than herself (see Philippians 2:3-11). She should not constantly try to correct him.

Women typically fluctuate between two sinful extremes in their responses to difficult husbands:

anger  appeasement

Women who are angry try to overpower or outmaneuver their husbands while women who merely appease them simply give in to all sorts of demands. While we often recognize the former as sinful, we may be less apt to see that the latter is also sinful. Why? Because it is sinfully self-protective. It keeps the peace (the status quo) rather than making true peace. It is not ministry-oriented.

God is quite displeased and grieved at both of these response patterns. He wants a woman to be quiet, gentle, reverent, and pure. He doesn't want her to give way to fear. First Peter 3:1 says, "In the same way . . ." In the same way as what? Look at what the Bible says in 1 Peter 2. God is asking her to do what Jesus did. Jesus knows exactly what it is like for a believing wife to live with an unbelieving husband. He wants her to do the same thing He did. She shouldn't look at her marriage to an unbeliever as a "cross to bear," but as a wonderful opportunity allowed by God in which she can practice being like Jesus. Women who do this gain valuable insight into what it is like for God to put up with them. They need to have mercy on their husbands the way God has mercy on them.

I haven't lost sight of the fact that some Christian wives live with "tyrants." Later in this chapter we will talk about what to do in such a situation. But for now, I want to help us try to appreciate the fact that we wives can be hard to live with too. God has shown great forbearance on our part and He wants wives to do the same for husbands.

Strategy #3: Think biblically about the demands made upon you.

SCRIPTURES TO READ AND STUDY: John 8:32-33; Acts 5:1-33; Galatians 5:13.

If a women who is a child of God responds to difficulty according to the truth, she will be set free from confusion and despair. Have your counselee ask herself, in a morally questionable situation, if she needs to submit to her husband's authority as leader in her home or if this is a case where God wants her to obey Him rather than her husband (Acts 5:29). For example, if her husband asks her to sign a fraudulent tax return, she must refuse. Her refusal should be made in a polite way with an explanation if her husband wants to hear it. Any behavior that is *clearly* contrary to God's Word must be refused. At the same time, she needs to be careful that she doesn't abuse this principle and make issues out of things which are unclear in Scripture.

A believing wife must minister to her unbelieving husband while being faithful to God at the same time. She must not merely give in to all of his wishes or demands; rather, she should discern whether his request is reasonable (consistent with biblical principles) or whether it will feed his sin.

Strategy #4: Develop a forgiving, forbearing spirit.

SCRIPTURES TO READ AND STUDY: Matthew 18:21-35; Mark 11:25; Ephesians 4:32; Colossians 3:12-13.

Unbelieving husbands who act foolishly or abusively must be forgiven. (Later in this chapter we will address wife abuse.) A wife may need to hold this forgiveness within her own heart if telling her spouse she has forgiven him will only result in a defensive, angry response.

There is a difference between attitudinal and transacted forgiveness. Attitudinal forgiveness means within a wife's own heart before the Lord she commits to not holding the sin done against her to her husband's account. She releases him from the debt against her. "Forgive us our debts, as we also have forgiven our debtors" (Matthew 6:12). She must bear no ill will toward him. On the other hand, transacted forgiveness means she respectfully confronts her husband with his sin, he acknowledges his wrongdoing, and asks for her forgiveness. In this case, she must grant forgiveness to him. Jesus told Peter that forgiveness would need to be granted each time a person asks for it even if he asks repeatedly (*see* Matthew 18:21-22).

Have your counselee study the parable of the unmerciful servant in Matthew 18. Her debt against God, for which Christ paid the price, was much greater than any debt against her by another human being. If she refuses to forgive her husband, she shows evidence of not understanding or appreciating the debt Christ paid on her behalf. Persistent unwillingness to forgive should raise doubts in your mind about her salvation (see verse 35). A true child of God will forgive. She can do this because she has been forgiven and is able to be comforted and strengthened by God to release the sinner from the debt of his sin against her.

Remind your counselee that God is absolutely sovereign (in control) over all things. This includes her husband. Sometimes women do not want to forgive because they think their husbands will be more prone to repeat the same sin. They reason that "if I let him off easy, he'll hurt me again." She needs to forgive and she may need to lovingly confront. But she must not hold a grudge against him. (This does not mean that she should remain in the home with a husband who threatens or batters her. Even if he repeatedly asks for her forgiveness, she is not obligated to stay. In fact, she must leave at least temporarily. See the section later in this chapter about exiting.)

Strategy #5: Do good.

SCRIPTURES TO READ AND STUDY: Romans 12:14-21; 1 Thessalonians 5:15; 1 Timothy 6:18; Titus; 1 Peter 3:11.

Look at the treasure of wisdom the verses in Romans 12 contain, including, "Never pay back evil for evil to anyone" (verse 17). Why is this so hard? Because our sinful nature wants revenge. We want those who hurt us to hurt as badly as we are hurting. In fact, we want them to hurt worse—to pay for what they did to us. However, God has not given us permission to retaliate. God says we are to leave room for His wrath. You see, He is the only One who can be impartial. Only He can decide what is just repayment. Therefore, God tells us not to seek vengeance. Your counselee will need to resist the temptation to play God by seeking vengeance. She can trust God to bring about vengeance in His way, in His time (*see* 2 Thessalonians 1:6-8).

In the midst of suffering persecution in her marriage, encourage your counselee to put herself to work doing good for her husband. "Bless those who persecute you; bless and curse not" (Romans 12:14). Even small things can communicate good to him. Point out that she can make an effort to minister to him with loving action. Help her write a list of specific ways she can do good to him. Suggest that she try to anticipate times when he may need extra help from her. This is an opportunity for her to be creative and study her husband and figure out ways to be helpful to him.

At this point your counselee may be sighing because she thinks she is already doing too much just by trying to live with him. The book of Nehemiah in the Old Testament tells the story about the wall of Jerusalem being rebuilt by people who worked with one hand and held weapons with the other to ward off their enemies. Nehemiah reminded them that "the joy of the Lord is your strength" (8:10). A Christian wife can build up her unbelieving husband on one hand while she receives joy in her relationship with Jesus in the other. She can receive great strength from her relationship with the Lord. She truly can "do all things through Him who strengthens [her]" (Philippians 4:13).

Strategy #6: Respect your husband.

SCRIPTURES TO READ AND STUDY: Romans 13:7-8; Ephesians 5:33; 1 Peter 2:11– 4:19.

Wives of unbelieving husbands are often strongly tempted to be disrespectful to them. They observe their husband's behavior and are sometimes at the receiving end of actions and attitudes that are selfish, hurtful, and demeaning. Instead of acting in righteousness, wives often react and return evil for evil by being disrespectful in attitude or action. But Ephesians 5:33 says, "Let each individual among you also love his own wife even as himself; and let the wife see to it that she respects her husband." It's very clear isn't it? A wife must respect her husband.

"But," your counselee may be saying to you, "he's supposed to love me. And if he'd love me the way he's supposed to, then I'd be able to respect him." I'll admit that kind of reasoning is very appealing. In essence it says if he does "a" then I can do "b." Although this kind of thinking is appealing, it is a trap. She is making her obedience dependent on the actions of someone else by following this line of thinking. She is tying her experience of God's peace and joy to her husband's actions. In addition, this kind of thinking ignores the fact that the Bible holds each of us responsible for our own actions. There is no room in Scripture for blameshifting or attributing our failure to obey God to someone other than ourselves. No matter what a woman's husband is like, she, as his wife, must respect him.

How is she going to be able to do this with a husband who screams, throws things, withholds love and affection, sulks, complains excessively, or who generally seems to make her circumstances miserable? There is only one way—she respects the position of authority given to her husband by God as the leader, the head of her home. God isn't asking her to respect selfish, vile, or ridiculous behavior. That would be irrational. But He is asking her to respect the position of "husband." What does *respect* mean in this context? It means she honors her husband by treating him well, speaking to and acting toward him in a kind, courteous, considerate, polite, and mannerly way. It means she regards him highly by speaking well of him to others, and she does things for him that communicate care and affection.

Strategy #7: Act wisely and decisively.

SCRIPTURES TO READ AND STUDY: Judges 13:2-24; 1 Samuel 25; 2 Kings 22:14–20.

One of my favorite stories in the Bible is the account of the actions of Abigail in 1 Samuel 25. It is too long to quote here. I suggest you read this chapter several times. Notice that Abigail took action for her husband's good without consulting him because he was in no condition to make a rational decision. Abigail waited to tell Nabal the truth until he was able to hear it. I recommend you study what she did and when and how she did it.

Nabal had a reputation for being surly, foolish, and mean. Abigail knew David's reputation and that he was the Lord's anointed (God had picked him to succeed Saul as king). She demonstrated great love for God by risking her husband's wrath and intervening on his behalf with David. Her courage is displayed in her willingness to go directly both to David and to Nabal. Notice she acted in a decisive and timely manner. We have no indication she was either fearful or proud. In fact, there is no negative comment at all about her actions.

What does this mean for your counselee? Sometimes she may have to act swiftly and wisely and against her husband's wishes in order to do him good as

Abigail did for Nabal. For example, Lucy's husband, Bill, went to the doctor about a relatively simple problem. While there, the doctor decided to do some routine tests since he hadn't seen Bill in several years. The doctor was concerned about other symptoms Bill was experiencing. Several days later, Lucy asked Bill if he had received the results of the tests. Bill told her he wasn't going to call for the results because he didn't want to know what they were.

Since Lucy was also concerned about the symptoms Bill was experiencing, she decided to call the doctor herself to ask about the test results. The doctor told her some of the tests indicated a need for further attention. Risking Bill's anger, Lucy urged him to consult again with the doctor. She tried to assure Bill of her love for him as her motive for calling the doctor. Bill was furious with Lucy. He told her she was nosing into matters where she didn't belong. He never went back to the doctor. Lucy demonstrated faith in God by leaving the consequences of her actions in God's hands.

Strategy #8: Persevere and endure.

SCRIPTURES TO READ AND STUDY: 1 Corinthians 4:6-17; 2 Thessalonians 1:1-12; Hebrews 12:1-3; James 1:1-4.

A wife can persevere and receive joy from doing what is right under difficult circumstances. God is not nearly so interested in changing her circumstances as He is in changing *her* in the midst of the circumstances. His goal is to make her more like Christ. She shouldn't seek a burden-free life. It's not realistic. Rather, she should seek a life focused on God and commit herself to a life of joyful obedience.

Strategy #9: Challenge tyranny appropriately.

SCRIPTURES TO READ AND STUDY: Proverbs 26:5; Acts 26:1-32; 1 Peter 2.

What is tyranny? Tyranny is the effect of the actions of a tyrant. Tyrants are people who use their authority or power in harsh ways. Some husbands act like tyrants. They are excessively demanding and oppressive in effecting leadership in the family. These men usually have insatiable felt needs. Sometimes godly resistance to their idolatrous demands is appropriate. A wife is not required by God to "feed" his idols. For example, she may rightly refuse to go to the liquor store to buy alcoholic beverages for a drunken husband; she does not need to agree to sexual practices she finds demeaning or disgusting; she does not need to exhaust herself lavishly entertaining friends every weekend because her husband gets bored and feels insignificant if his social calendar isn't filled (especially if he doesn't assist her with the work involved).

It is not uncommon for unbelieving husbands to abuse their power and authority, sometimes in subtle ways and other times in more obvious ways. For example, Wendy's husband, Roger, bought a new car every year even though the family could not afford it. He kept borrowing more and more money to finance his lust for new automobiles. When it got to the point where he needed to borrow against the equity in their home, he approached Wendy and asked her to sign for the loan since they share joint ownership of their home. Wendy refused to do so because she considered it foolish spending. She knew going into debt unnecessarily is a sign of poor stewardship, but she did not verbalize that to Roger. Besides, they needed to save money for repairs to their house. Roger was furious. But two weeks later when a storm ripped most of the shingles off their old roof, he was glad he hadn't gone further into debt for a new car.

You may be thinking Wendy should have signed the loan and let Roger reap the consequences of his decision. But remember that overspending on new cars was a pattern in his life. Also, Roger was asking Wendy to sign a legal document (a car loan) obligating and binding her to its stipulations. The Bible calls a wife to be a helper. It also calls her to submit. Part of submission includes giving the best help she can offer. In this case, we decided together that what was honoring to God and in Roger and Wendy's best interests was for her to refuse to sign the loan. She did this with respect and a certain sense of sadness that she could not agree to Roger's wishes. She was not overbearing or self-righteous. She did her best to communicate love to Roger even though she knew he would be sorely disappointed.

Showing someone his sin is not a mean, hardhearted action. It is loving to stop a blind person from falling into a ditch (*see* Luke 6:39-42). But sin must be pointed out in a wise and humble manner. Proverbs 27:6 says, "Faithful are the wounds of a friend, but deceitful are the kisses of an enemy." False tenderness is really self-protection and lack of love in disguise. A wife should be wise in her application of this proverb; a wise woman will discern whether her husband can hear her words and profit from them. She will keep in mind that her unsaved husband "does not accept the things of the Spirit of God; for they are foolishness to him, and he cannot understand them, because they are spiritually appraised" (1 Corinthians 2:14). So she will need to consider carefully what she says and how she says it.

Tyrants have an inordinate desire to exercise control over people and circumstances, to display and consolidate power, and to ensure their own pleasure often at the expense of others. A Christian wife in a relationship with such
a husband must gently resist his sinful agenda. She should love him, but wisely
and graciously resist his attempts to be a tyrant. If she merely acquiesces to his
sinful agenda, she enables it to continue and is not truly serving him. In pointing out these things, I am not encouraging your counselee to make wrong
judgments. I'm trying to help her see the situation in a clear way so you can
help her apply biblical solutions to it.

Many times the persecutory actions of tyrants are subtle. For example, persistent, unrelenting teasing is a way some husbands undermine their wife's
peace. It is a way to indirectly harass someone. I am not talking about the occasional time when any sensible person would be willing to laugh at herself. This
other destructive kind of teasing is an attempt to provoke to anger, resentment,
or confusion. Some people are masters at this and deny any responsibility for
causing trouble in the relationship by saying, "Oh, I was just teasing. Can't you
take a joke?"

Strategy #10: Know the limits of your responsibility.

SCRIPTURES TO READ AND STUDY: 1 Corinthians 4:1-5; 2 Corinthians 1:12;
Galatians 6:1-5.

The wife of an unbelieving husband should seek to understand the limits of
her responsibility before God. She should have realistic expectations of people,
including herself. Some people will be disappointed with her and critical of
her. Her unsaved spouse may be one of them. A wise woman will listen to criticism to a point; she can almost always learn something from it.

On the other hand, a woman shouldn't allow herself to be devastated by
undue criticism from her unbelieving husband. Rather, she should take his
criticism and examine it against the standard of Scripture. For example, he
may complain about the way she looks. She should consider his comments and
then go to the Bible and ask herself if she needs to take his words seriously.
She'll find that the Bible talks about dressing modestly, not overdoing outward
adornment, and so on. While it is right for her to look nice for her husband,
she does not need to give in to extreme requests such as having a face lift or
liposuction. Encourage her to do her best to stay fit and look pleasant and
appealing, and leave the rest to God.

Strategy #11: Build rest and recreation into your schedule.

SCRIPTURES TO READ AND STUDY: Psalm 37:1-8; Matthew 11:25-30.

Living with an unbeliever often results in the wife being unusually fatigued. The need to be constantly mentally processing what's going on is quite tiring. Proverbs 27:3 says, "A stone is heavy and the sand weighty, but the provocation of a fool is heavier than both of them." What does this proverb mean? It says that though physical labor may be tiring, being provoked by a fool (someone lacking wise judgment or prudence) is more tiring than physical labor. Living with a person who disregards the Lord is very tiring. You'll want to help your counselee learn to anticipate those times when she may be especially subject to provocation by a husband who foolishly disregards the Lord. For her to be self-controlled and alert will require energy. She will need to get proper rest, proper nutrition, and exercise.

It is easy for a woman to grow weary when she shares a house with an unbeliever who acts foolishly. Two people joined together and pulling in opposite directions quickly wear themselves out. A wife in this situation needs to find appropriate time to spend with other Christian women who will build her up in the Lord and pray with and for her. But while she's with them, she should be very careful that she does not gossip about her husband. She should not run him down in their eyes.

Suggest that your counselee pursue sports or hobbies that uplift her and challenge her in good ways. Perhaps, she will like to take long walks or play golf with her friends. She should be careful, however, not to fill her schedule so full that she is always on the run. When she plans her schedule, you may want to suggest that she take one thing out of it if possible so that she has room for emergencies or just a few minutes rest instead of always trying to function at full steam.

Strategy #12: Meet regularly with a mature Christian woman.

SCRIPTURES TO READ AND STUDY: Romans 15:14; 1 Corinthians 12:25; Galatians 6:2; Colossians 3:16; 1 Thessalonians 4:18, 5:11; Titus 2:3-5; 2 Timothy 3: 16-17; Hebrews 3:13; James 5:16.

It is essential that your counselee meet regularly with a mature Christian woman or a small group of mature Christian women who will hold her accountable to being a faithful wife. She needs someone to hold her accountable to be growing in her relationship with Jesus and in her relationship with her husband. Perhaps you can help her choose women who are understanding and who will uphold biblical confidentiality. Your counselee will then be able to share her concerns with them in a discreet manner so that her husband's privacy is not compromised. She can ask these women to pray for her and teach her how to glorify God in her marriage.

Strategy #13: Actively use your spiritual gifts to serve the Lord.

SCRIPTURES TO READ AND STUDY: 1 Corinthians 12:1-7; Galatians 5:13; 1 Peter 4:7-11.

Help your counselee find a way to minister her gifts to the body of Christ. Her service does not need to interfere with her time with her husband and family. She could find a way to serve from her home. For example, she could have a ministry of cards and notes to sick people. She could make local calls to shut-ins. Help her be creative and find ways to serve. Start with an area of service that does not require a big commitment. As she serves, she will be able to decide whether she can take on more responsibility in the future.

Organize a Wise Exit Plan, If Necessary

Difficult circumstances require difficult choices and responses. When physical abuse is occurring in a marriage, exiting the home may be crucial for the sake of the wife, the abusing husband, and their children. If a wife is being abused by her husband, she is facing a complex problem that has no single right answer. Only she can determine what is best in her situation. It is important to realize that leaving a truly abusive spouse is not an act of rebellion against God. A wife's exiting can be an act of loving ministry to her husband. Leaving her home does not necessarily lead to a divorce; just because a woman removes herself from danger does not mean her marriage is over. (*See* chapter 8 for more discussion about wife abuse.)

The Glory of God and the Godly Wife

I hope your counselee is increasingly able to see why her relationship with God is so vital and why it is essential for her to eliminate distortions in her understanding of who God is. It all comes back to her relationship with Him. God is sovereign. He is her creator. The clay doesn't say to the potter, "Your expectations of me are ridiculous."

I hope it is easier now for your counselee to see why she needs a plan to live to the glory of God and for the good of her unbelieving husband. Her desire to be a godly wife must be a high priority in her life. It's more important than a committee at her child's school, a political caucus meeting, the garden she wants to plant, or the class she wants to take. The glory of God is at stake in *her* marriage!

If she persists in her efforts to grow in Christlikeness as a wife, she is in for an adventure that will thrill her soul. Why? Because God will use her efforts at being a godly wife to an unbelieving husband to show her more of Himself. Knowing God is the sweetest, most fascinating, most glorious experience she will ever have. Her devoted obedience can put a smile on the face of God.

Recommended Resources

Jay E. Adams, *How to Overcome Evil*, Phillipsburg, NJ: Presbyterian & Reformed, 1977.

James and Phyllis Alsdurf, *Battered Into Submission*, Downers Grove, IL: InterVarsity Press, 1989. (Caution is advised when reading this book. While the description of the problem of wife abuse is helpful and some of the suggestions for change may be useful, this volume derives its basic understanding of people from psychology, not from Scripture.)

Charles Bridges, *Proverbs*, Carlisle, PA: Banner of Truth, 1979.

Jerry Bridges, *The Discipline of Grace*, Colorado Springs: NavPress, 1994.

Elisabeth Elliot, *Discipline: The Glad Surrender*, Old Tappan, NJ: Fleming H. Revell Co., 1982.

Sinclair B. Ferguson, *Kingdom Life in a Fallen World*, Colorado Springs: NavPress, 1986.

John MacArthur, Jr., *The Power of Suffering*, Wheaton, IL: Victor Books, 1995.

Kay Marshall Strom, *Helping Women in Crisis*, Grand Rapids: Zondervan, 1986. (See chapter 10 on "Wife Abuse." This chapter is generally very helpful but it contains a few references to concepts that are not wholly biblical, such as self-esteem.)

CHAPTER 10

Counseling Women Considering Adoption

Carol Almy, M.D.

I had known Jenny well since she was in my junior high Sunday school class. I had watched with joy as she had blossomed into a lovely and godly young woman. The commitment that she had made to the Lord in those early years had kept her during her high school days and she was an example and leader to the other young people. Five years ago the church delightedly celebrated her marriage to a fine young man from the church, Karl. It seemed to be a perfect match—both of these young people had a fervent love for the Lord and were a pleasure to be around. They seemed to be happily married and were very involved in children's ministries and the choir. Everyone at church agreed that they were going to make wonderful parents.

Sometime later, however, I began to notice that the joy that was so common in Jenny's manner seemed to be fading. She seemed angry and depressed and on several occasions I had noticed her crying during the worship service. I knew that I needed to approach her and ask her if there was something that I could help her with. Like a bubble that was ready to burst, Jenny dissolved into tears at my mention of trouble in her life. She was so upset that she didn't want to talk then, but we scheduled a time to meet later that week.

At our meeting, I could barely get through our time of prayer before she began crying again. "I just don't understand it," she sobbed. "All my life I've tried to do what I thought God wanted me to do. I didn't run around with the guys in high school like all my friends. I've tried to honor my parents, and I love Karl. I really thought that God would bless my life and that I would have a family like everyone else. But after Karl and I started trying to have children three years ago and were unsuccessful, I went in to my gynecologist. She ran some tests and had us try all sorts of different things for the last two years. And now, finally, she's told us that we should really begin to consider the possibility of adopting or trying other, more expensive procedures. It seems that my body just doesn't function properly—and there's nothing anyone can do."

Jenny paused, and began to cry again. "Why did God make me this way? Is He punishing me for something? I know that He could heal me if He wanted to, but we've prayed and prayed and still nothing happens. It's gotten to the point that I don't even want to have sex with Karl any longer. It has become so frustrating and humiliating. I wanted to have children with Karl. We've talked many times about what they would look like and what we would name them. We had even planned to homeschool them and laughed about how we would put them in the toddler's choir at church. But now," she wept, "that's all over. I know that we could adopt sometime later—and Karl is willing—but I just don't think that I can go through with it. I know that it's almost impossible to adopt children that look biologically similar and it's very expensive. Besides, I've read that most of these children have psychological problems. Karl has a good job, but we just can't afford to spend $10,000 to adopt a child or to try some special procedure that may or may not work. It's just hopeless. I feel so empty and meaningless. Why can all these other women get pregnant—even drug addicts who don't even want children? It just doesn't seem fair. I've always hated the thought of abortion, but now it infuriates me. Why is God doing this to me? The Bible talks about children being a blessing, doesn't it? Why is God cursing us?" When Jenny finished she put her head down on my desk and cried and cried. I joined her.

What could I say to her? How would you answer her? What is the biblical view of infertility and adoption? Was God punishing or cursing her? She seemed so angry, envious, and hopeless. How should I minister to her?

The Statistics on Infertility and Adoption

The difficulties associated with adopting children is of great concern in America today. Indeed, you may be personally acquainted with a couple who is unable to conceive and wants to adopt children but has had to endure long waits for one reason or another.

Infertility rates in this country appear to be on the rise. Recent figures show that "one couple in four cannot have children."[1] This means that approximately 2.3 million couples in the United States are infertile.[2] This rise in infertility is thought to be due in part to two factors: sexually transmitted diseases (causing infertility in approximately 150,000 women annually[3]) and a social trend in which people are delaying marriage and childbearing until they are older (and thus less fertile).

> *For example, the proportion of first-time brides who were between 25 and 39 years of age rose from 11 percent in 1970 to 41 percent in 1990. In addition, the percentage of women reaching age 35 who were still childless increased from 15 percent in 1980 to 21 percent in 1991. These statistics are significant because age is positively associated with elevated risks of infertility and miscarriage[4] (emphasis added).*

Though these two factors contribute to the growing number of American couples considering adoption, others like Jenny and Karl may have reasons unique to them.[5] The National Council for Adoption (NCFA) conservatively estimates that there are at least "one million infertile and fertile couples who are waiting to adopt children. For every one adoptable infant available, there are at least 40 couples hoping to adopt."[6] The latest available published data are from 1986, and in that year 51,157 American children were adopted.[7] Of these approximately one-half (24,589) were healthy infants of all races. The remainder were adoptions of older or what are termed "special needs" children. In addition to the children born and adopted here in America, several thousand foreign-born children have been adopted by Americans. Records show that in 1994, 8,195 foreign-born children were adopted by U.S. couples. "Korea was the greatest source for intercountry adoptions, followed in descending order by Russia, Guatemala, Colombia, Paraguay, the Philippines, India, China, Ukraine, Peru, Honduras, Brazil, Bolivia, Bulgaria, Vietnam, and El Salvador."[8]

As these statistics indicate, many couples desiring to adopt an infant must wait for some time before their wishes can be fulfilled. In the United States, this shortage is primarily due to abortion. Forty-one percent of out-of-wedlock pregnancies in 1991 ended in abortion.[9] This amounts to the staggering number of 1.5 million babies killed annually (4,400 every day) while millions of infertile couples long for a child to become available for adoption. Although the majority of Americans view adoption as the most preferable outcome to an out-of-wedlock pregnancy, the figures we've just examined show that they do not act on this stated belief.

Another factor in the increasing scarcity of adoptable children is the rise in the acceptability of illegitimacy. In 1991, 44 percent of out-of-wedlock pregnancies were carried to term. However, "only 2 percent of those children were placed for adoption":[10] Before 1973 when abortion was legalized, about one in five non-marital births to white women, for example, were placed for adoption. *But by the late 1980s, the number of children placed for adoption dropped drastically to one in 30"*[11] (emphasis added).

Most birth mothers are choosing to keep the babies born out-of-wedlock rather than place them for adoption. Data for 1990 shows that over 1.1 million babies are born illegitimately in the United States, with 21 percent of all births to whites and 65 percent of all births to blacks being illegitimate.[12] While these statistics surely indicate devastating consequences for our culture, the government financially rewards these decisions. More and more unwed mothers are keeping their babies, including Christians.[13]

Alongside these statistics are more figures that suggest that approximately one out of four married couples in your church may be trying unsuccessfully to have children. Are you willing to "fulfill the law of Christ" (Galatians 6:2) by carrying the burden of others like Jenny? Are you willing to "weep with those who weep"? (Romans 12:15). Surely we should be prepared to help these couples in a biblical way.[14]

Numerous complications are involved in the discovery of infertility and the process of adoption. Many Christian women view infertility with more than a little distress and think of adoption as second-best—as a last resort. Let's review the Word of God together and try to think clearly about these issues; God guides those who are His, and He does it primarily through His revealed Word. We will be looking at Scripture as a whole, making sure that we look at the context of each passage and seek to understand its meaning in light of the entire Bible. Second Timothy 2:15 calls believers to correctly handle the Word of truth; failure to do so can result in discouragement and confusion. Viewing infertility as a "curse" from the Lord as Jenny did is one such discouragement.

A Biblical Perspective on Infertility

How a Christian Woman Should Look at Infertility

For the chosen nation of Israel, the material blessings and the allotment of the land came primarily through bloodlines. Childlessness was therefore viewed as a withholding of blessing because the inheritance was to be passed from parent to child. Although many "foreigners" were adopted into the nation (such as Rahab the harlot and Ruth the Moabitess), the primary avenue of Israel's growth as a nation was through the biological family. Children, particularly sons, were needed to perpetuate the clans and their occupation of the Promised Land.

However, it is important to understand that the true church, the family of faith, was never propagated along bloodlines. The increase in what are called "the children of Abraham" (Galatians 3:7,28,29) is not dependent on anyone's fertility. Although family structures are a part of God's plan, we must never view the faith as propagated by way of bloodlines. God's blessing to Jenny does not depend on her ability to conceive a child. Jesus established this understanding of family in Matthew 12:46-50. In this passage we read that someone came to Jesus while He was teaching and reported that His family was waiting outside to see Him. He answered, "Who is My mother and who are My brothers?" (verse 48). He stretched out His hand to His followers and said, "Behold, My mother and brothers! For whoever does the will of My Father who is in heaven, he is My brother and sister and mother" (verses 49-50). Jesus was establishing the fact that relationship with His Father did not rest on genetic ties, but rather on spiritual ones.

Those who believe, trust, and obey are part of God's family. God's blessing to you is not determined by your genes. It is determined neither by what genetic material has been passed to you nor by what genes you may pass on to future generations. God's blessing is based on His grace and extends to those who are part of His family. Jenny's infertility was not a curse; as part of God's family, all of His gifts to her were good (James 1:17).

God's indictment of this misunderstanding is stated clearly in Luke 3:8: "Bring forth fruits in keeping with repentance, and do not begin to say to yourselves, 'We have Abraham for our father,' for I say to you that God is able from these stones to raise up children to Abraham." Jesus then added, "The axe is already laid at the root of the trees; every tree that does not bear good fruit is cut down and thrown into the fire" (verse 9). Jesus was not referring to the fruit of the womb; He was rebuking the Pharisees for their self-righteous confidence in their biological heritage.

An Infertile Woman Can Please God

Jesus makes the same sort of statement again in Matthew 10:34-39:

> I did not come to bring peace, but a sword. For I have come to turn a man against his father, a daughter against her mother. . . . Anyone who loves his father or mother more than me is not worthy of me; anyone who loves

his son or daughter more than me is not worthy of me; and anyone who does not take his cross and follow me is not worthy of me. Whoever finds his life will lose it, and whoever loses his life for my sake will find it (NIV).

If we understand what Jesus has done in redeeming us from sin and what the Bible calls the "second death," He will be the primary focus of our love. Jenny and Karl need to learn to love Him more than their parents, more than siblings, more than the idea of having children. "We love because He first loved us" (1 John 4:19 NIV). The right priorities will always place the Lord above our families in our lives. We must fight against the prevalent practice of making idols of the family, motherhood, and children. This is a choice that must be made by every believer, not just infertile couples. Jesus' commands to an infertile woman are no different than to any other believer: "Love the Lord your God with all your heart, and with all your soul, and with all your mind . . . [and] love your neighbor as yourself" (Matthew 22:37,39), and, "Go therefore and make disciples of all the nations" (Matthew 28:19). Even though Jenny was despairing, she could still fulfill the Great Commandment and the Great Commission.

If you still doubt that you can be pleasing to God while infertile, the New Testament refers to one infertile couple, Zacharias and Elizabeth, in glowing terms. Luke writes,

They were both righteous in the sight of God, walking blamelessly in all the commandments and requirements of the Lord. And they had no child, because Elizabeth was barren, and they were both advanced in years (Luke 1:6-7).

Listen to those words. God doesn't merely say that Zacharias was righteous, He says that they *both* were. God considered Elizabeth a righteous woman; her barrenness was not on account of anything that she did wrong, nor was it because God was withholding His blessing.

Jenny's confusion about her standing before God was based on her ability to perform. She thought that she was worthless before God because she was unable to conceive. We can know with certainty that Elizabeth's righteousness was not based on her ability to have a child. Rather, it was based on her faithful service to God.

God wasn't punishing Elizabeth by her infertility. He was mindful of it and the New Testament records that Zecharias' prayers had been heard (Luke 1:13). Both Karl and Jenny can rejoice that God knows their situation and hears their prayers. God's plan for Elizabeth and Zecharias was unknown to them during Elizabeth's many years of barrenness. God's plan for Karl and Jenny is also unknown, but they can rejoice that even though all seems hopeless, their loving Father is in control.

For Jenny, change begins with the "renewing of [her] mind," as Romans 12:2 instructs. She must not be conformed to the world in her thinking, but must be transformed by God's renewing work in her mind. In any area where Jenny is embracing the idols of this age by worshiping motherhood and family, she needs to renew her mind and embrace the truth that her righteousness is based solely on Christ's righteousness, not her ability to conceive.

In addition, Jenny needs to wrestle with the reality that her loving Father gives different women different gifts and callings, and she should thank Him for that. No matter what our circumstances, He can give a peace that passes all understanding (Philippians 4:7). Only He can give that—a baby cannot do so.

The Idol of Motherhood

Living to please and glorify God will prevent the Christian woman from elevating fertility to a godlike status in her life. When she puts God first in her life, she will no longer see motherhood as her source of peace and joy, nor will she always be glancing with envy or anger at women who have children.[15] She will be protected from falling into self-pity like Hannah in 1 Samuel 1, who wept bitterly and would not eat because she was barren.

The natural desire for children can become a lust for a woman and one for which she is willing to sacrifice almost anything. She can throw her marriage into turmoil and spend tens of thousands of dollars on a myriad of questionable techniques to aid fertility. Artificial insemination and in-vitro fertilization range from $6,000 to $12,000 per procedure.[16] In the United States, procedures to overcome infertility constitute a $2 billion-a-year business. There are 250 to 300 fertility clinics facilitating approximately 4,000 births per year.[17] However, caution should be used when consulting fertility specialists because this industry is essentially unregulated and there are ethical concerns about many of the procedures used. For a woman who takes right-to-life beliefs seriously, questions about the use and treatment of embryos must be answered before any procedures are agreed upon.[18]

God's Definition of True Religion

James 1:27 says, "This is pure and undefiled religion in the sight of our God and Father, to visit orphans and widows in their distress, and to keep oneself unstained by the world." In our society there are many children who are not orphans in the strict sense of the word. They have living parents, but these parents are either unable (usually because of actions by the State) or unwilling to raise them. Some have had their parental rights terminated by the State; other have willingly relinquished them. Although not orphans in the strict sense of the word, they are without parents and need the protection, comfort, and nurturing that a believing couple can offer. Believing and obeying this passage can quickly take a couple from despair and self-pity to facing their responsibilities and opportunities. A couple can take an orphan and teach him or her about the love of Jesus. Remember, it is in service that we lose our life for His sake and thereby find it. It is in service that our real blessing comes, and it is in service that we find our real joy. Fertile or infertile, single or married, we are called to look after orphans and the fatherless. Although there is a shortage of adoptable babies, there are other avenues available, such as foster-parenting.

God declares that He is "the great, the mighty, and the awesome God who . . . executes justice for the orphan and the widow, and shows His love for the alien by giving him food and clothing" (Deuteronomy 10:17-18). We are encouraged to be like Him—to love not only with "word or with tongue, but in deed and truth" (1 John 3:18). We do this when we seek to meet another person's need instead of closing our heart against him (see 1 John 3:17).

God's blessing is not promised as a by-product of having children. His blessing, however, is the result of obediently caring for those God brings to you (James 1:25,27). Joy comes from obedient submission to a loving Father, whether He chooses to bring children to you biologically or through other means, such as adoption or foster parenting.

Scripture's directives toward caring for others should urge the infertile Christian woman toward more than paying her taxes to cover welfare costs. Contributions to the local homeless shelter or sending money to mission agencies are legitimate avenues for such caring, but God may well have something else for her. She should not view adoption, foster parenting, or becoming the legal guardian of an orphan as second-best.

Every Christian Is an Adopted Child

Every Christian is an adopted child of God. Although adoption is seldom mentioned in the Old Testament (as in Pharaoh's daughter adopting Moses), caring for the fatherless and orphans is mentioned frequently. In addition, adoption is a major theme in the New Testament. Romans 8:15 tells us, "You have not received a spirit of slavery leading to fear again, but you have received a spirit of adoption as sons by which we cry out, 'Abba! Father!' " The term "Abba" is an Aramaic word that "corresponds to our 'Daddy' or 'Papa.' "[19] This shows the closeness of the relationship between ourselves and our adoptive Father, God. In Galatians 4:6, Paul uses the word "Abba" again in relation to adoption: "Because you are sons, God has sent forth the Spirit of His Son into our hearts, crying 'Abba! Father!' " In Romans 8:23, we are encouraged to eagerly await the fullness of our adoption.

Our adoption as God's children wasn't some accidental happening or a second choice, last-resort decision on God's part. Scripture clearly states that God chose us and sought us. "He predestined us to adoption as sons through Jesus Christ to Himself, according to the kind intention of His will" (Ephesians 1:5). Adoption was always part of God's plan for us. None of us are in God's family by our own merit or bloodline. He sought us and bought us with His own precious blood. God took good pleasure in adopting us. Likewise, we should take pleasure in caring for orphans.

Jesus teaches that caring for others in distress is one of the hallmarks of a true believer. In the parable of the sheep and the goats (Matthew 25:31-46), the Lord separates true believers from false ones, noting that the true ones cared for the hungry, the thirsty, the naked, the sick, those in prison, and those who appeared as a stranger in need. We were "strangers and aliens" before we were adopted by God, but now we are "fellow citizens with the saints, and are of God's household" (Ephesians 2:19). The point is clear: Surely God expects us to care for those outside of our biological family as a part of His bringing strangers into the Father's house.

Only by His Righteousness

We need to remind ourselves that it is only when the righteousness of Jesus is placed on us through His blood shed at Calvary that God can look on any one of us. Romans 5:6 says, "While we were still helpless, at the right time Christ died for the ungodly." Paul says in Romans 3 that we were worthless. A woman who is wrestling with the issue of adopting children should think about God's love for her when she was completely worthless and lost. God cared for you when you were His enemy. Is she willing to care for children who are not her own, who may be racially mixed or physically handicapped? Encourage her to give over to her Savior the cares and doubts brought on by the world. He will strengthen, encourage, and help her to become a mother to the motherless.

Some Godly Examples

C.T. Studd was a wealthy, handsome graduate of Cambridge University who had all that this world has to offer, yet he chose to spend his life as a missionary in malaria-infested African jungles. He said, "If Christ be God, and He died for me, then let nothing I might ever do be called a sacrifice." Surely that should be the heart-cry of every believer. Again, real and lasting joy lies in losing our life for His sake; it does not lie in preserving our mortal flesh nor even in propagating it. Although there is joy in childbearing, this joy simply cannot match the eternal joy that comes from service to God.

Jenny could study the history of Amy Carmichael, who left England in 1895 for India and remained there until her death in 1951. Depending solely on the grace of God, she rescued one child after another from the pagan temples where they were to be sacrificed or used as prostitutes.

How God Measures a Successful Woman

Encourage your counselee to pray that she will be used of God in whatever way He chooses. Success for the Christian is not to be measured in the world's terms; God measures success in terms of faithfulness. Some women may believe and even tell you that birthing a child is the *only* satisfying project a woman can ever undertake. As we have already seen, Scripture contradicts this view and urges us to look after the orphan.

God has given each one of us certain gifts and talents. He gives these gifts according to His good pleasure (1 Corinthians 12:11). He knows your heart much better than you do, and His plans for you may differ considerably from what you had in mind. Jenny may indeed shed tears now, but she must look to Jesus' example in Scripture as He prayed, "Not as I will, but as Thou wilt" (Matthew 26:39). A believer must trust the One who redeemed him. Are you willing to do so?

Sometimes using our gifts and talents is risky and painful. Unlike Jesus, we want to opt for comfort. God hasn't promised us ease, but He has promised us strength and endurance to perform the task along with joy in obedience. As Paul learned when he was despairing of life and burdened excessively, "we should not trust in ourselves, but in God who raises the dead" (2 Corinthians 1:9). Keeping these truths in mind daily will free a woman from the overwhelming burdens laid on her by the world and fellow Christians regarding motherhood.

The Blessings of Adoption

Adoption holds many benefits for both the "birth-mother" and the child born to her. Fortunately, the U.S. Congress is attempting to encourage adoption by initiating a tax credit for the adoptive parents and by outlawing the practice of limiting adoption to a family of the same race as the child.

Benefits of Adoption for the Child

A recent study of adolescents who had been adopted found that adoption benefited them in a number of ways:[20] First, it provided for them a loving, intact family. Ninety percent of these adopted children live in two-parent families (a better average than the general populace). Second, they have come to develop deep child-parent attachments. Adopted adolescents are as deeply attached to their parents as their non-adopted siblings. Ninety-five percent of adoptive parents experience strong attachment to their adopted child. Third, a majority of adopted children (75 percent) seemed to be functioning well in their tasks and relationships with others. Finally, in relation to adequate financial provision for the child, 54 percent of adopted children live in homes with family incomes three times higher than the poverty level. According to government studies, children who are raised in single-parent families (such as an unwed mother who keeps the child) show a higher incidence of problem behavior.[21]

Benefits of Adoption for the Single Mother

Certain studies indicate that young single mothers who choose to give up their babies for adoption reap many personal benefits. These young women are more likely to complete high school and advance further educationally than those who choose to keep their babies. They are more likely to be employed and have a higher income. They are less likely to live in poverty or receive public assistance. In fact, 60 percent of welfare recipients are, or were at one time, teenage mothers. They are more likely to subsequently marry. They are less likely to have a repeat out-of-wedlock pregnancy than the teenagers who choose either parenting or abortion.

Misleading Ideas Concerning Adoption

Children Given Up for Adoption Are Unstable

Unfortunately, there is much confusion over adoption in the church today. A typical evangelical children's home describes the children there as having "serious behavioral and emotional problems which require professional staff intervention on a regular basis." But we need to remind ourselves that children have been successfully adopted by Christians for many hundreds of years! Do the children in this evangelical children's home have a more extreme history of abuse than the children rescued in India by Amy Carmichael? No, the only difference between these children and the many others available for adoption is our view that they are somehow damaged or different from other children.

You Must Find a Biological Match

Scripture can free couples from the desire to match their prospective child to themselves in hair color, eye color, and in general genetic background. Encourage them to review what Scripture teaches about their heritage and see whether that might affect their adoption decisions. Romans 5 is one of many passages that reveals that we are all of the same bloodline. We are all Adam's children. We are fallen, each one a sinner by our very nature. Each one of us is condemned and without hope if we have not accepted Christ's substitutionary atonement. That is why Jesus defines the family as he does in Matthew 12: 46-50. A couple need not grieve, then, because the infant who is available doesn't look like them. Remember Jesus' parable of the good Samaritan: he crossed racial and sociological divides to care for someone in need.

Part of the duty of every Christian is to honor his father and mother; that should be an outstanding and notable characteristic of the believer. It is right that we express gratitude to our parents for all they have done for us—especially if they have given to us a godly heritage. However, this does not erase the clear teaching of Scripture that we are in the line of Adam and have inherited an empty way of life from which we must be redeemed if ever we are to know real life.

When you counsel a woman considering adoption, have her compare God's view of her inherited traits and her adoption as His child with the way she has been thinking about adoption. This will help her to clear her mind of the world's teaching about adoption, which so often has the effect of manipulating people's emotions and confusing the issues. A couple does not need to be concerned about finding a biologically-matched child for adoption; they and their prospective child have the same nature because we all have Adam as our father.

Fears About "Ancestral Demons"

A biblical understanding of our shared heredity will help erase the fears couples may have about adopting a child that might bring "ancestral demons" into their home. If ancestral demons really were a problem, wouldn't James have warned the church about it when he defined true religion as caring for orphans? Were the children of which James spoke somehow different from the orphans available today? Scripture does not teach that children carry ancestral demons. This teaching has its basis in eastern mysticism, not in Christianity. What's more, the Bible does not assign to any human being the task of diagnosing, analyzing, naming, and commanding demons.[22] Scripture warns against such arrogance. Read Jude 8-10, and remember that even the archangel Michael left the devil in the hands of the Lord and did not try to claim authority over other celestial beings.

Fears About Ancestry

Many verses clearly state that a person's biological ancestry has no bearing on his standing before the Lord. Ezekiel 18:20 says,

> *The soul who sins is the one who will die. The son will not share the guilt of the father, nor will the father share the guilt of the son. The righteousness of the righteous man will be credited to him, and the wickedness of the wicked will be charged against him (NIV).*

Look at Deuteronomy 24:16: "Fathers shall not be put to death for their children, nor children put to death for their fathers; each is to die for his own sin." Jeremiah 31:29-30 says, "People will no longer say, 'The fathers have eaten sour grapes, and the children's teeth are set on edge.' Instead, everyone will die for his own sin; whoever eats sour grapes—his own teeth will be set on edge"(NIV). Paul encapsulates this thought in Romans 14:12: "So then, each one of us shall give account of himself to God." The clear teaching of Scripture is this: Each person stands condemned before a holy God for his own sins regardless of his heredity. Only the perfection of God's Son sacrificed for those sins will save that person, and it does so regardless of heredity.

Concerns About Self-Esteem

The unscriptural teaching of the importance of self-esteem is another area in which the church discourages couples from looking after orphans. If a couple takes this teaching to be the scientific fact it is claimed to be, they will be overwhelmed with fears about whether they can care for the "needs" of the adopted child's self-esteem.

According to self-esteem teaching, even a newborn is seen as damaged goods because he has a vacuum (empty love-tank) that will remain forever unfilled because of the biological mother's failure to "bond" with the child. This confused mixture of pseudoscience and sentimentalism further says that the older the child is when you bring him into your home, the more therapy he will need to raise his self-esteem and thus heal his "wounded inner child." Prospective adoptive parents worry that their medical insurance won't be enough to cover the years of therapy needed to attain good self-esteem, relive the wounding, gain insight into the abuse, and in some ill-defined way, come to "healing."[23]

Couples will never find such teaching in Scripture, nor is it scientific in any real definition of science. Encourage them to search the Scriptures and fortify themselves to reject such teaching. It is important that they don't avoid looking after orphans on the basis of such deception.

Resting in God's Word

As a couple feeds on God's Word and prayerfully separates themselves from the teaching of the world, they will be freed from confusion and discouragement in the task before them. They won't have to attend seminars and support groups that make unwarranted claims about the special problems of the adoptive family or the unique emotions of adopted children. In addition, they won't be filled with fear and despair if the birth-mother should unexpectedly appear and seek to have input into the child's life. As they daily sort out their thinking with the help of God's Word, they will no longer be impressed, seduced, or deceived by this type of wordly "knowledge."

Remind the prospective mother that she and her husband can trust the all-knowing Creator who redeemed them and promised never to leave them. He is more than able to redeem an orphan or adoptive child, no matter what happened in the child's past. Help the woman to discern between God's truth and what Paul called "hollow and deceptive philosophy, which depends on human tradition and the basic principles of this world" (Colossians 2:8 NIV).

Some of the greatest blessings that can come to adoptive parents in all of this earthly life will be theirs as they struggle to serve God in caring for their adopted children. As they spend each day in care and nurture of these children, they will be reminded of God's gracious adoption and care for them, too.

Karl and Jenny now realize that their plans to raise a family for God may be fulfilled in their ministry to adopted children. Although this wasn't their first choice, they are now able to rest assured in the knowledge that God is indeed good, wise, and loving. Upon committing themselves to their heavenly Father, they began to pursue adoption as an avenue of blessing for children other than their own.

Practical Suggestions for Women Considering Adoption

As a counselor, here are some encouragements and practical helps you can offer to a woman who is considering adoption. These suggestions are written as if you were speaking to the woman yourself:

- Once you have concluded through medical diagnosis that you will be unable to conceive children, spend time in prayer. Humbly submit yourself, your entire life, all your plans and dreams to the purpose of your God. This may be a time of deep sorrow for you. Remember that Jesus Christ is called a "man of sorrows, acquainted with grief." First Peter 2:21 tells us that we are to walk in His footsteps. Study His prayer for you in the Garden of Gethsemane. Understand that His plans for you are for your good and His glory. Even though this may be one of the darkest moments of your life,

Christ's light can shine on you. He can take each of your sorrows and use them for His glory. He can cause you to serve Him with joy and gladness. He knows your heart. Turn it towards Him in faithful submission and service. In your suffering, you can begin to learn how God comforts you so that you can learn how to comfort others (2 Corinthians 1:3-10).

- Read Isaiah 53:10: "The LORD was pleased to crush Him, putting Him to grief; if He would render Himself as a guilt offering, He will see His offspring, He will prolong His days, and the good pleasure of the LORD will prosper in His hand." Even though Jesus was crushed and grieved, later He was rewarded with the knowledge of His Father's good pleasure. You may be crushed and grieving now, but you can rejoice in the fact that someday, if you are faithful, you will be rewarded with the experiential knowledge of God's blessing in your life.

- Study Psalms on the topic of sorrow. Grapple with your own heart and desires as you learn to say, "Why are you in despair, O my soul? And why have you become disturbed within me? Hope in God, for I shall yet praise Him, the help of my countenance, and my God" (Psalm 42:11).

- Get a concordance and find all the uses of the words "orphan," "fatherless," and "stranger" in Scripture, and prayerfully seek God for what these passages might be saying to you in your considerations regarding adoption. What is God's attitude toward orphans? How does God view those who care for orphans? Are you willing to be like Him, seeking out the lost?

- Prayerfully consider whether your desire to have a child has become an idol in your life. Are you disregarding God's commands in your efforts to conceive? Are you falling into self-pity and concluding that God is unfair to you? Do you accuse God of wrongdoing? Study Isaiah 40. If you suspect that you may be idolizing having a child, confess this sin to God, repent of it, and humbly submit to His will and service.

- Keep track of your thoughts on a daily basis. Would you say that you are generally thankful and content though sorrowful, or are you angry and bitter? Seek to say with Paul, "I have learned to be content in whatever circumstances I am" (Philippians 4:11). Paul knew that God was strengthening him in every circumstance (Philippians 4:13). Make a list of the things you are thankful for. Thank God for His adoption of you. Thank Him for forgiving your sin and giving you the indwelling presence of the Holy Spirit. Thank Him for giving to you His precious Word to enlighten your path and encourage your heart daily. Are you thankful for each of these things? What about your temporal blessings? Are you thankful for health? For a husband and home? Seek to focus on His blessings rather than on what you perceive to be your misfortune. Focus on what you have, not on what you lack. While this may sound trite, it is, nevertheless, true: "In everything give thanks; for this is God's will for you in Christ Jesus" (1 Thessalonians 5:18). Trust God, as His plan is always best.

- Study the lives of Christians, such as Amy Carmichael, who have cared for orphans. Read her book *Toward Jerusalem*.[24] Read Elisabeth Elliot's book *A Chance to Die: Life and Legacy of Amy Carmichael*.[25] Pray Carmichael's poem, *Make Me Thy Fuel*:

From prayer that asks that I may be
Sheltered from winds that beat on Thee,
From fearing when I should aspire,
From faltering when I should climb higher,
From silken self, O Captain, free
Thy soldier who would follow Thee.

From subtle love of softening things,
From easy choices, weakenings,
Not thus are spirits fortified,
Not this way went the Crucified,
From all that dims Thy Calvary,
O Lamb of God, deliver me.

Give me the love that leads the way,
The faith that nothing can dismay,
The hope no disappointments tire,
The passion that will burn like fire,
Let me not sink to be a clod:
Make me Thy fuel, Flame of God.[26]

- Go with your husband to the church elders or leaders to discuss the possibility of adoption. Consult with older women in your congregation who may be able to counsel you about adoption. Ask them to pray with you.
- If you decide to adopt, contact organizations that may be able to help educate you. See if your denomination recommends an adoption agency for

Christians. Contact the Family Research Council for the names of Christian agencies.[27] Get a list of agencies from the National Adoption Information Clearinghouse.[28]

- Consider whether you prefer an open adoption, in which you are personally acquainted with the birth mother, or whether you prefer an adoption where you and the birth parents never meet. Select an adoption agency, either public or private. Public agencies are less expensive, but they have very long waiting lists.

- Consider adopting a "special-needs child." These children may have medical problems, are older, or may have siblings that must be adopted along with them. Usually these children are in a state's foster care system. Both public and private adoption agencies are involved with placing special-needs children.

- Consider adopting a foreign-born child. Some agencies deal primarily with international adoptions.

- Consider becoming a foster parent. Although children are placed with foster parents to give birth parents a chance to improve their situations, many foster children eventually become available for adoption. "Foster/adoptive parents are willing to be foster parents while that is the need and understand that the agency will make all efforts to reunite the child with the birth parents. However, if the child is freed for adoption, the foster/adoptive parents are given priority consideration as his potential adoptive parents. All things being equal, you would be able to adopt that child."[29]

- Be prepared to wait. While you are waiting, guard your heart against the idolatry of believing that a child will be the answer to everything in your life. Ask God to give you patience.

- Redeem the time. Look for opportunities to serve others in your community who might not be as fortunate as you. Remember God's commands to care for those who are naked, hungry, sick, and in prison.

God Created, Knows, and Loves You

Even though adoption may not have been a woman's first choice and desire, she needs to look at the events in her life as God's gift to her. She can pray Psalm 139 back to God, thankfully rejoicing in His good pleasure:

"O LORD, Thou hast searched me and known me.
Thou dost know when I sit down and when I rise up;
Thou dost understand my thought from afar.
Thou dost scrutinize my path and my lying down,
And art intimately acquainted with all my ways.
Even before there is a word on my tongue,
Behold, O LORD, Thou dost know it all.
Thou hast enclosed me behind and before,
And laid Thy hand upon me.
Such knowledge is too wonderful for me;
It is too high, I cannot attain to it. . . .
For Thou didst form my inward parts;
Thou didst weave me in my mother's womb.
I will give thanks to Thee, for I am fearfully
    and wonderfully made;
Wonderful are Thy works,
And my soul knows it very well.
My frame was not hidden from Thee,
When I was made in secret,
And skillfully wrought in the depths of the earth.
Thine eyes have seen my unformed substance;
and in Thy book they were all written,
The days that were ordained for me,
When as yet there was not one of them.
How precious also are Thy thoughts to me, O God!
How vast is the sum of them!" (verses 1-6,13-18).

Jenny and Karl learned along with the psalmist that God is their creator. They learned to differentiate between their own desires and God's perfect will for them. They learned to rejoice—even in the midst of sorrow and disappointment—and to trust God's plan for their lives. Every Christian woman must learn to place her hopes and expectations in the hands of her loving Father. As she does this, she will find precious fruit growing out of the fertile soil of a heart that is wholly His—fruit that brings glory to Him.

CHAPTER 11

Counseling Mothers of Children with Learning Difficulties

Kaleen Chase, M.A.R.

There are many mothers today who are discouraged and concerned about their children's seeming inability to succeed in school. They may feel alone in their distress, but they are not. Many children struggle with their schooling. These struggles may be sporadic or chronic, and are experienced by children in a wide variety of educational settings and family situations. Oftentimes it's not easy to find the answers about why a child is having difficulty in school, and a mother may wonder if her child's struggles will be chronic, become afraid that her child may never succeed, or suspect that there is something physically wrong.

Whether a child's struggle is physical, academic, behavioral, social, or emotional, *ultimately it is also a spiritual struggle.* A mother may say, "Wait! My kid hates math! What does that have to do with spiritual matters?" Truthfully, the one has everything to do with the other. *Spiritual matters are matters of belief and truth, and they invade every aspect of life, including education.* What a mother *believes to be true* of her child and his situation is of utmost importance. What she conveys to her child about who he is and how he may best glorify God is one of her primary responsibilities as a parent. Because of this responsibility, her beliefs—and those of her husband—must be true.

Parents can understand and interpret life, including a child's educational struggles, in the light of the Bible. Paul's words in 2 Corinthians 4:8 were written for all believers: "We are afflicted in every way, but not crushed;

perplexed, but not despairing." They were written to exhibit the godly example set by Paul and his ministry partners, who knew hope in the midst of perplexing and difficult circumstances. A Christian parent whose child struggles educationally is not alone. God is present. A Christian mother can hope in Him; she needn't despair.

In this chapter we will look at three basic categories of school difficulties: those that are primarily physical in origin; those that are primarily academic in nature; and finally, those that are caused by behavioral, social, and emotional factors. Within each category we can find hope based on God's Word. Mothers need hope for themselves that can come from the truth; with this hope mothers will be able to comfort and better understand their children.

Physical Considerations

Examining Health-Related Difficulties

There are many physical or health-related problems that can cause children to have difficulties in school. Some are chronic, others are temporary. Let's look at several of them.

Vision   Vision problems in children are not always apparent before a child enters school. As an educator at the elementary level I have made an annual practice monitoring the visual needs of the students in my classroom. The parents of a school-aged child should be sure of their child's ability to see.

Pediatricians and ophthalmologists advise that school-age children be taken for eye examinations on an annual basis starting at age 5.[1] According to the American Optometric Association, "one out of six children between the ages of 3 and 17 need glasses."[2] Wisdom dictates, "An ounce of prevention is worth a pound of cure." Before looking for more complex answers to a child's educational difficulties, a mother will want to check and make sure that the problem isn't visual in nature.

Hearing   A loss of hearing, whether it be mild, moderate, or profound, can significantly hinder a child's learning. Besides a child's sense of touch, his sense of hearing is his most important link to the environment in which he lives and learns.[3]

The detection of hearing losses in children is a delicate matter. It is made more difficult by the sad reality that small children do not realize that they have a hearing loss. *A child that is not hearing the world around him has an injury that cannot be seen and does not draw attention to itself.*

In addition, parents (and teachers) are unlikely to recognize even profound hearing loss in a child unless they are specifically looking for it. Nonetheless, early detection is crucial. If a mother suspects that a child might have hearing loss, she should contact a pediatrician for an auditory screening.

Nutrition   Jonathan lives in a comfortable house in an upscale neighborhood. Each morning he is hurriedly dropped off from his family's luxury car onto the elementary school campus, well-dressed and groomed. He seems distracted and frazzled by the morning's routine. He's irritable and argumentative. It is only 10:17 A.M. and already his teacher has reprimanded him twice for being uncooperative. Laura, a pale, withered-looking girl of seven, walks ten blocks to school every morning. The shoes on her feet are a size too small. She wears the same faded dress three times a week. Her hair is unkempt and her face is smudged with dirt. She falls asleep at her desk at 10:05 A.M.

It would be easy to assume that these children have nothing in common. One is rich, the other poor. One is cared for; the other neglected. One has every advantage, the other has few. What is their shared connection? Both skipped breakfast and are hungry, which has affected their ability to learn. Undernourished children like Jonathan and Laura are not uncommon; in fact, "in 1992 an estimated 12 million American children consumed diets that were significantly below the recommended allowances of nutrients established by the National Academy of Sciences."[4]

There are a variety of ways that children miss the nutrients they need for the demands of their day. Some children skimp on or even completely skip breakfast. Other children eat a breakfast that is not substantial enough to support them throughout their morning's activities. Some forget their lunch money or were never given any in the first place. There are some adolescents who skip buying a nutritive lunch to buy a chocolate-covered donut and a soda instead. Teenage girls may even choose to avoid food altogether (anorexia), or will force themselves to vomit (bulimia) to escape what they believe to be the "loathsome" effect of eating—weight gain!

Other reasons that a child is undernourished may include poor eating habits, unhealthy food choices, a fast-paced lifestyle, financial strain, or unbiblical beliefs concerning food and body image.[5] Poor eating habits are most often "inherited" from the family; that is, a child probably has eating habits similar to that of his parents. If the parents habitually skip breakfast, then their child probably doesn't see breakfast as "the most important meal of the day."

The fact that malnourished children have difficulty learning isn't surprising. These children are often inattentive, irritated, or sluggish in the classroom setting. They are also more susceptible to illness. As a result, their attendance in school is poor. On average, their educational experience is inferior to that of their well-nourished classmates.[6]

A mother who is concerned about her child's nutrition should check the contents of her refrigerator and pantry to see if they are stocked with an ample supply of milk, orange juice, fruits, vegetables and grains. These foods will help supply the calories a child needs during the day. The Department of Agriculture has found that a child needs to consume about 2,200 calories per day. These calories should be available in the following food-group servings: 9 servings from the bread group; 4 from the vegetable group; 3 from fruit; 3 from milk; and 6 from the meat group. If a child drinks a large amount of caffeine-filled drinks, such as soda, he may feel nervous, irritable, agitated, and nauseous.[7] A child should have caffeine only occasionally, it should not be a routine part of his diet. Being sure that nutritious food is available for a child is one way to enhance his ability to learn.

A fast-paced lifestyle can also affect a child's nutritional health. Children who constantly eat on the run usually are not getting all the nutrients they need to stay healthy. Nutritional considerations are often sacrificed to the god of convenience. Of course, sometimes families are so busy running from school to soccer games to gymnastics that eating at a fast-food restaurant becomes a necessity. Parents should question whether their fast-paced lifestyle is godly or not. If parents must use the convenience of fast food, then they can ask the fast-food restaurant for a nutritional guide to their menu and help their children pick items that are lower in fat and higher in nutrients.

A child's nutritional health can also be supported by having good snacks available. To encourage good snacking habits, a mother should have healthy snacks on hand, such as peanut butter, dried fruits, crackers, cheese, cottage cheese, cereal, fresh fruits and vegetables, and yogurt. Most importantly, both parents need to set a good example in the way that they eat. They also need to pray with the children and thank God for the food so the children will see Him as the Sustainer of life.

Tight finances may limit a family's ability to provide a nutritionally balanced diet. This is especially true for single mothers. A single mother should learn to read labels and purchase foods that are less expensive but nutritionally sound. Whatever she chooses to do to meet a child's nutritional needs, she does not have to choose it alone. The Bible gives many examples of the abundant provision of God. One such example appears in Acts 2:44-45:

All those who had believed were together, and had all things in common; and they began selling their property and possessions, and were sharing them with all, as anyone might have need.

God still meets the physical needs of His people through the church. A single mother should let her physical needs be known to her brothers and sisters in Christ; they want to help. She could go to her pastor and ask about sources of assistance.

Asthma   If a child experiences shortness of breath, tightness in his chest, wheezing, or excessive coughing, he may have asthma. Although there is no known cause for asthma, it is the most common chronic illness in childhood. If a mother notices these symptoms, she should take her child to a doctor immediately for a checkup.

Asthma is a leading cause of absence from school, according to the American Academy of Pediatrics.[8] *A child struggling to breathe is not concerned about spelling or mathematics; nor should he be.* A doctor can help prescribe asthma medications and give advice for handling asthma attacks.

Allergies   Many school-age children are allergy sufferers. Dust mites, pollen, a variety of molds, tobacco smoke, pet dander, and poor air quality are just some of the things that can trigger allergic reactions that impinge upon a child's learning. Even certain types of food, such as peanuts and cow's milk,[9] can complicate a child's school day. Severe allergic reactions are rare, but the nagging, persistent irritation that mild to moderate allergic reactions impose often considerably hamper a child's ability to perform at his educational best. If a child has unremitting cold-like symptoms, a mother may want to have him tested for allergies.

Medications   Medications, like everything else, can be good or bad. Consideration must be given to the impact of medications on a child's learning. Benadryl is a prime example. This popular over-the-counter medication asserts it provides relief for "sneezing; itchy, watery eyes; runny nose and itchy throat due to allergies and colds." But then the back label states, "May cause excitability especially in children," and "May cause marked drowsiness." This antihistamine, then, can be good for a child's health, but bad for his education. A medication that can cause excitability and/or drowsiness can also cause a problem in a child's ability to pay attention to what he is being taught in the classroom.

A mother should make her children's medications and their side effects her business. The local pharmacist can help her. She should learn to be conservative about giving medications. She should read labels, front and back. As much as possible, she should try to restrict giving a child medications that might adversely affect him during school hours. In fact, as a rule of thumb, *a child who is in need of medicine should stay home from school*. However, if it does become necessary to give medicine to a child prior to or during school hours, the teacher should be informed of the type of medication given and of its possible side effects. Of course, when using prescription medications, a pediatrician's advice should be followed closely.

Sleep   According to Leslie Tadzynski Shur, a leading pediatric expert, there are no specific guidelines about how much sleep is required at any stage of human development. However, eight to twelve hours daily is recommended from toddlerhood through adulthood. As most mothers know, sleepy children usually exhibit signs of inattentiveness, excessive silliness, and grouchiness. The energy required of them in a schooling situation exaggerates the tendencies.

A mother may guard her child against sleep deprivation, even if it is only of the mild variety, by establishing a regular sleep schedule in her home. Each child is different, so the amount of sleep needed for one will differ from that of another. She should know how much sleep each child needs, and personalize their bedtimes so that they get a good night's sleep. If possible, the hour before bedtime should be a quiet time in the home. Specific bedtimes, whatever they may be, are better than vague ones.[10]

Mothers should make a commitment to enforce the bedtimes they establish. The child who makes a big fuss about going to bed at night has been taught to view it negatively. Unpleasantness may be avoided by giving a child's bedtime a personal touch. Sending a child to bed and tucking a child into bed are two different things. As often as it is possible, a mother should take time to personally escort her child to bed. She should talk to him, especially concerning the things of God (*see* Deuteronomy 6:7). She can listen to him and pray with him. If he is having difficulty in school, she should take the time to pray specifically about this problem. She can pray that the Lord will give her wisdom and give the child the desire to do his best.

The common, ordinary task of putting a child to bed each night can be changed into the wonderful task of setting Christ before him. As a mother seeks to do this consistently, her child will not only get the rest that's necessary for school, but he will also learn to say with the psalmist, "My soul finds rest in God alone; my salvation comes from him" (Psalm 65:1).

Overcoming Health-Related Difficulties

In this first section we have looked at some key physical or health-related barriers that can keep children from learning. Sometimes these limitations can be removed. For example, glasses can be purchased for a nearsighted child. Nutritionally balanced meals can replace fast-food frenzies. However, sometimes the obstacle to learning is of a more permanent nature. The deaf child, or the child with chronic asthma, must learn to view his physical problem biblically. He must come to trust in the wisdom of his Maker. He must learn to express, as did the psalmist, "I will give thanks to Thee, for I am fearfully and wonderfully made; wonderful are Thy works, and my soul knows it very well" (Psalm 139:14). A mother of such a child has been given the awesome task of expressing and affirming this truth to him.

Academic Considerations

There are a number of issues involving a child's education that are of the more academic sort. These are related to concerns about educational philosophy (why educate or learn?) and pragmatics (what? when? and how?). They are the foundation upon which a child's education is constructed.

The Purposes in Learning

God's Purpose and Ours   Everything fundamental to education is answered by two questions: Why educate? and, Why learn? Parents must be able to answer these questions for themselves and for their child. Their answer to these questions will have a strong influence on their child's educational experience. It can mean the difference between a contented, happy education and a frustrated, boring one.

For the Christian, the purpose of educating a child is the same as it is for doing anything in life: the purpose is to glorify God (1 Corinthians 10:31). The mother, father, educator, and Sunday school class teacher are called to teach a child to honor God. All teaching must reflect this purpose if it is to be pleasing to the Lord. What is taught and how it is taught should always demonstrate biblical integrity. Above all else, we must guard ourselves against educating for education's sake! The knowledge we impart ought to be applicable and useful to the child. It should be meaningful. Possession of knowledge without application is vain for both the child and the adult.

The Child's Purpose   The purpose for learning is similar to that of educating, but here the focus is the student rather than the teacher. A child is to learn in a way that brings honor and glory to the One who made him. A mother who teaches her child to learn for God, and to please Him in every aspect of his education, has endowed her child with one of life's most precious gifts. God commended Solomon's request for knowledge and wisdom, saying,

> *Because you had this in mind, and did not ask for riches, wealth, or honor, or the life of those who hate you, nor have you even asked for long life, but you have asked for yourself wisdom and knowledge, that you may rule My people, over whom I have made you king, wisdom and knowledge have been granted to you. And I will give you riches and wealth and honor, such as none of the kings who were before you has possessed, nor those who will come after you (2 Chronicles 1:11-12).*

The Lord was pleased to grant Solomon's request for knowing how he might better serve God and His people. A wise person desires to learn; in contrast, "a fool does not delight in understanding" (Proverbs 18:2). For him, learning is the most boring of all life's endeavors. A mother should teach her child to learn for God and encourage him to take pleasure in all that is made known to him.

Variables Related to Learning

A Child's Individuality   Any mother who has more than one child knows that children differ greatly from one another. She realizes that each child is an individual. This individuality remains constant, even within an educational setting. Consider these children:

- Lily, a plump girl of ten, is very bright for her age. She enjoys art and music. She is confident of her abilities.
- Ralph, a handsome young man of twelve, struggles in school. He has a hard time making friends. He cheats.

- Melissa is five. She has braces on her legs to help her walk. Kids make fun of her. She thinks they're mean.
- Andrew, who is seven, is the tallest child in his class. He smiles and laughs a lot. He enjoys a challenge.

All children are unique individuals in the sight of God. They each possess their own strengths and weaknesses. Their life experiences are particular to them. Their personal and educational interests, in most instances, are more different than similar. That's why they should each be treated equally, but never the same.

It's important that the individuality of a child not be ignored by parents, administrators, or educators. Parents who fail to discern a child's educational strengths and weaknesses may burden the child with unfair and unrealistic expectations. "Parents should not impose standards and expectations on their children that their children developmentally or characteriologically are unable to perform unless those standards or expectations are clearly delineated in Scripture. The emphasis should be on character, not achievement. For example, godly character is shown in doing you best for God's glory, not by getting straight A's."[11] Administrators, who are often made inflexible by district guidelines and policies, may require classrooms to be uniform in such a way that it chokes the individuality of both teacher and student. Educators, who are routinely guilty of using outdated and ineffective methodologies, may have failed to ask, "How does this student best learn?" Parents, administrators, and educators who are serious about supporting each child's individual educational development must ask and answer this question: *Who is this child?*

The Report Card   The report card is a communication device that goes from the school to the home. *Its purpose is to inform.* It fulfills this purpose by spotlighting the peculiar academic strengths and weaknesses of a child. As such, it is meant to be used as an instrument for good.

Unfortunately, there are many parents who mishandle the assessment data recorded for them on the report card. Both the excelling child and the one who is faltering may be equally cheated in the process. Each is deceived into believing that his academic performance, as reflected on his report card, is the basis for his self-identity and for gaining or losing the acceptance of his parents. The report card, which is designed to serve as a communication piece from teacher to parent, may be twisted into a scale used to measure the quality or value of a child. Tedd Tripp writes,

Parents typically send their children to school and pressure them to get good grades. Are good grades a biblical objective? What passages would support this objective? Then parents may add to the unbiblical objective of unbiblical incentives. "I'll pay you one dollar for every 'A' you get on a test." Or perhaps parents say, "If you work hard you will be able to get a good job and earn lots of money when you grow up." A biblical objective? Hardly! The Scriptures say the opposite. "Do not wear yourself out to get rich." I am not denying in any sense that those who are faithful will be richly rewarded. Of course, that is true, but one cannot work simply for that reward as his goal. In contrast, you should send them off to school with no pressure for good grades at all. Grades are unimportant. What is important is that your child learn to do his work diligently for God. God has promised that He will reward the faithful. Knowing that gifts and abilities are a stewardship from the Lord, your child's objective should be faithfulness. You need to train your child to find in Christ the strength and power to work for God's glory. Anything else is training him to think and act unbiblically.[12]

In light of the principles of biblical stewardship (Matthew 25:14-23), it is inappropriate for parents to use their child's report card in any way other than as an informational device. The excelling child should receive praise from his parents not because he has gotten excellent marks on his report card, but because his grades reflect that he has used his intellectual talents wisely. In the same manner, the faltering child, whom God has entrusted with lesser academic talents than his excelling classmate, should also receive praise from his parents if he has been a faithful steward of his abilities.

When a child's poor grades are due to a lack of effort in the classroom, then parents have reason to be concerned and disappointed. Unsatisfactory grades that are *due to a lack of effort* show that a child has not used his talents, however limited, to the best of his ability. A child who routinely refuses to work up to his academic ability should not be excused. Idleness and indifference are not acceptable traits before God, nor should they be before parents. All work, even the schoolwork of a child, should be done in service to the Lord. (Colossians 3:23-24). Discerning parents, reading their child's report card, will ask, *What do these grades tell me about my child's use of his abilities.*

Parental Acceptance   Most parents, at one time or another in their child's educational development, will grapple with the issue of acceptance. Parents of the bright child, or of the overachiever, are just as likely to have difficulty accepting their child as are the parents of the slow learner. The parents of the bright child are often unprepared to handle the occasional failure or, more pointedly, the underachievments (a "B" instead of an "A") of their child. They wrongly presume that because academics have always come easily to their child, that they always will. This is not always the case. At times, for any of a number of reasons, a bright child may have difficulty grasping the most elementary of concepts. Ironically, it is not usually the child, nor his academic performance, which causes a lack of acceptance by the child's parents. Rather, the struggle usually lies within the parents themselves. All parents have hopes and aspirations for their child, whether their child is overachieving, average, or academically slow. These expectations, if they are not reasonably fitted to their child's abilities, will lead to a lack of acceptance on the part of many parents. Thankfully, the answer to the problem is given in the pages of Scripture. The apostle Paul, in view of the abiding grace and mercy of God, writes these words of exhortation:

> *Now we who are strong ought to bear the weaknesses of those without strength and not just please ourselves. Let each of us please his neighbor for his good, to his edification. For even Christ did not please Himself. . . . Wherefore, accept one another, just as Christ also accepted us to the glory of God (Romans 15:1-3,7).*

A godly mother will bear with the weaknesses of her child, including those that are academic in nature. She can encourage him how to be content with his gifts and abilities even though he is struggling academically. Such encouragement will help to edify him.

Unfortunately, some parents withhold acceptance and thus spawn a fear of failure in the academic life of their child. This child usually hasn't been taught how to be content and thankful. A child already struggling academically usually stops taking educational risks, such as participating in class discussions or raising his hand to ask for help. Parents who continually disapprove of a child even though he is trying his best will hinder rather than encourage their child's education. Godly parents who humbly consider their child's strengths and weaknesses will be granted the grace to be content with their child and will pass along to their child the contentment that they have found for themselves.

Failure What is failure? What makes it unacceptable? Why is it feared? The Christian's perspective on failure must be different from the world's. *Academic failure is not the enemy of the child; it is his tutor.*

Academic failure means different things to different parents. Most parents recognize that when a child fails to pass a particular grade or subject, he has failed it—academically speaking. He must go back and try again a second time.

Academic failure "proper" (or retention) is not the failure most of today's parents face. Most children do not fail in this sense. However, many children do fail in one area or another. Typically their failure is isolated to a few academic areas. For example, an artistic child may struggle in mathematics, or a child competent in science may be an atrocious speller. A mother should ask herself whether or not it is ever acceptable for her child to receive an "F" on his report card. If it is never acceptable, then perhaps she has some rethinking to do. Let's assume for a moment that her child has given the subject area his best "college try," and yet has failed it. The "F" on his report card, *if unrelated to his motivation or effort,* merely says that he lacks understanding in that subject—nothing more!

Some parents who are overly concerned about grades may even come to think of failure not in terms of "Ds" and "Fs," but as "Bs" instead of "As." Since most children are of average academic ability, which means that most are "C" rather than "A" students, this is unwise. Parents should allow for grades below "As" as long as they know their child is not being lazy or indifferent.

Children are taught to fear failure by parents who have unrealistic expectations. A child who is expected to live up to the unrealistic opinions of others is bound to fear failure. Proverbs 29:25 states, "The fear of man brings a snare, but he who trusts in the LORD will be exalted." Rather than criticize their children when they fail, parents must lovingly teach their children how to respond to failure. A child should be taught how to evaluate his efforts and motivations. If he has sought to please the Lord and if he has not been lazy or indifferent, then he can be content in the knowledge that his work is pleasing to the Lord—even though he may not have been successful.

Christian parents who are loving and wise know that education is not about grades but about learning. These parents work to transform their child's academic failures into something good. They train their child to lean on God for strength in the midst of weakness. They teach him to say with the apostle Paul, "I am well content with weaknesses, with insults, with distresses, with persecutions, with difficulties, for Christ's sake; for when I am weak, then I am strong" (2 Corinthians 12:10).

When a parent decides to view academic failure as a tutor and teach the child to view it this way as well, then failure can never be the child's enemy.

This parent will take the time to ask, *What does my child's failure teach me about my child?*

Promotion vs. Retention   When parents are faced with deciding whether to promote or retain a failing child, they should prayerfully consider the options and seek to make informed decisions. Before a final decision is made, the parents should consider seeking counsel from a wise parent or teacher in their church.

I believe young children (K-3 grade[13]) who are failing in school should be *promoted* to the next grade only when the following conditions exist:[14]

- This child's intellectual ability is in the low to low-average range. (Special education services at a child's school can determine this quite easily with a minimum of testing.)
- This child displays average to above-average maturity for a child of his age.
- This child's teacher does not believe retention is in the child's best interest.

Children who fit the above descriptions probably should not be held back. A child with low intellectual ability probably won't be more successful when he repeats the grade. If immaturity does not seem to be a problem, the failing child is probably doing the best that he can in school. A child's teacher can be a source of good counsel because she has spent the most time with him academically. If she advises that retention won't help, it probably won't.

Children who are failing in school should repeat the grade only when the following conditions exist:

- This child has been evaluated by the special education team at his school (this evaluation should include a full battery of tests), and has failed to qualify for any special-education services.
- This child's primary language is English (more on this in a moment).
- This child is socially or developmentally immature for his age. (The child's teacher can help provide insight regarding this.)
- This child has been affected in the past year by something that has hindered his normal education—for example, parental divorce, death, critical personal illness, sexual or physical abuse, arrest of a parent, transience, and so on.
- This child's teacher recommends retention.

A child who fits this profile will probably benefit most from repeating the grade. Disqualified from special education services, he would probably face greater failure if promoted to the next grade. The language spoken by a child is also an important consideration. If his primary language is not English, it is most often the language, and not the child, which presents the barrier to learning. An immature child typically needs more time to appropriate academic skills. Another year in the same grade cannot do him any harm. It will give him what he needs—time. Retention of a child who has been affected by certain circumstances is recommended because it gives him time to deal with what has happened to him and it removes the academic pressure that would accompany a promotion to the next grade. Be aware that teachers rarely recommend retention; if a child's teacher recommends it, she probably has good reasons for thinking it to be in the best interest of the child. Parents should ask her for those reasons—they may find them helpful for understanding how they can better help their child.

Some parents try to avoid having their child retained because they feel that it might adversely affect their child's self-concept. However, modern society's beliefs about self-concept are not biblical.[15] The Bible teaches that a person is to view himself soberly (Romans 12:3); this includes children. If a child is failing because he has been lazy or indifferent, he should not be encouraged to "feel good" about himself. He must learn to confess his sin and to put on the habits of self-discipline and diligence. If, on the other hand, the child has tried diligently but has not succeeded (for whatever reason), he should be lovingly told that God has allowed this failure as an opportunity to bless and teach him. This will enable the child to face the future with confidence because he knows that God has him in His loving hands.

Retention and failure are neither good nor bad; they are neutral occurrences. The reasons for them and the way a parent interprets them are what determines whether they are positive or negative experiences for a child. Ultimately, the decision to retain rests with the parent who must answer the question, *What is in the best interest of my child?*

Classroom Setting and Placement   Placement, a key element in a child's education, is rarely discussed because educational placement in most American schools is based on chronological age. The discussion is closed before it begins.

Grouping children chronologically does have its advantages. Generally, children of the same age have a lot in common. They tend to think, communicate, and interact similarly to one another. The academic differences between the high and low students in a classroom are usually minimal.

Though children of the same age are generally alike, it is unwise to assume that all children of the same age are suited to the same educational placement. What may be generally true of children may not be specifically true of a particular child. Remember, each child is still very much an individual even though he may share many similarities with others his age. If a child is struggling to succeed academically at his chronological level of placement, it may be necessary for the parents to pursue a placement that more correctly fulfills his educational needs.

For example, some children are immature for their age. A strictly chronological placement may not be the best for these children. A kindergarten placement test, usually administered to children in the summer before they enter kindergarten help will give some idea of a child's academic maturity level or "school readiness." If a child scores poorly on such an assessment, it is usually advised that formal education be delayed for another year. This is especially true for boys, because boys usually develop mentally and physically at a rate slower than girls. Indeed, most cases of academic failure might have been avoided if parents had put off their child's formal education for an additional year. Parents must ask and answer the question, *When is the best time for my child to start school?*

Learning Style   Children learn in a variety of ways. Some have learning styles that are significantly different from those of their peers. Educational difficulties are common among these students because their chronological placement has failed to allow for their style of learning. Some children learn through mostly visual means; others are mainly auditory learners; still others are tactile, learning through means of touch and hands-on experience. Some children learn best in interactive learning environments that call for extensive cooperative learning among students. Many children learn best in a quiet, self contained setting. Children who are easily distracted may be best suited for this kind of educational environment. There are many students who, for one reason or another, are best taught at home.

External Influences   The issue of placement is very important in circumstances involving children who are not successful in a regular classroom setting. Many of these children are labeled "learning disabled." Some learning disabled children, however, are made, not born. Educational success may be hindered in the lives of these children because of external factors. Although these children are average to above-average in intelligence, some are unable to learn successfully in a regular classroom because of the distractions of their home life, including poverty and family turmoil. Many are ADD-labeled children. A mother of a learning disabled child must decide whether his disability is physiological or if it is the product of other factors.

Internal Influences Some children who are designated as learning disabled have true learning disabilities. Most of these children suffer in their learning because of neurological processing difficulties. They tend to visualize, process, and communicate in ways that differ from most of their school-age peers. They may have difficulty with left-to-right orientation. Sometimes these children read and write words and numbers backwards instead of forward. Some of these learning disabled children suffer from memory problems. Barbara Novick writes that "memory disorders in children occur frequently. They, however, often are not recognized."[16] These memory disorders may be auditory or visual, sequential or spatial. Such children tend to be poor spellers or have difficulty memorizing math facts. They do not normally do well in test situations. Other children have language-specific disabilities. Novak comments, "In the majority of language-disabled children, the disorder is of the developmental variety, referred to as dysphasia."[17] She adds that dysphasia "may be manifested by failure to develop language, delay in language acquisition, or development of deviant language."[18]

Identifying Children with Learning Disability Characteristics

If a mother suspects that her child may have a learning disability, whatever its particular manifestation, identifying it is a relatively simple procedure. If the child attends a school with a special education team, a request for a full psychological screening may be made. If your child does not attend a public school, you may need to contact the local Board of Education to find an office where these tests can be given. (Testing, by the way, cannot be done without a parent's permission.)

This screening differs in kind from "personality" psychological testing, which is a questionable practice. Educational psychological screening is focused on academics, not personality. Tests like the WISCIII and the Woodcock-Johnson Revised are two tests typically used by educational psychologists to determine whether or not a sufficient gap exists between a child's cognitive ability and his individual achievement. A significant gap must exist between these two areas in order for a child to be considered learning-disabled. If it is found that a child is learning disabled, he can be given a special education placement in the areas where he is significantly below the achievement of his peers. Special education placement will usually include an Individualized Education Program (IEP) that is tailored to meet his educational needs.

Placement is an important issue in the educational life of a child. Parents are responsible for determining what type of school and grade placement they believe is best for their child. Many parents find home schooling to be the best option, while others believe that private or Christian education is preferable. Still others believe that the public school in their area is fine.

Whatever the situation, parents should carefully and prayerfully make decisions about the educational training of their children and not just follow the crowd. Parents must be involved in their child's schooling no matter what venue they choose. Parents need to take the matter of educational placement seriously, especially if a child is having a great deal of difficulty in school. Every parent must answer the question, *Where will my child best learn?*

The Teacher's Impact on Learning

Everyone can remember a teacher who has positively (or negatively) influenced his or her life. Each teacher adds or subtracts something from each life she touches. A child's teacher, for good or evil, will influence his educational welfare this school year. Depending on the beliefs and practices of the teacher, the educational setting can be ordinary and ineffective or extraordinary and educationally dynamic. In an article entitled "The Teacher as Encourager," Alan J. Watson states the difference between these two educational settings: "The difference was the show of teacher concern for individual students, the absence of favoritism, good peer esteem and appropriate task difficulty."[19] Although math, science, reading, and the creative arts are being taught in both types of classrooms, they are being overseen in a completely different manner. One teacher cares about her students; she leads through service. The other does not.

In situations where parents can choose a child's teacher, parents should look for the quality of servanthood. A teacher who is a servant will view each child as an individual. A Christian teacher who has this quality will encourage children to learn for God. She will teach them to be humble and helpful to other students whose strengths and weaknesses are different from their own. An encouraging teacher can teach a child to be an encouragement to others in their learning and will make a child's educational experience manageable and meaningful.

Classrooms being overseen by teachers who lack the quality of a servant may be harmful to the children who occupy them. Children who are struggling in their education need more from their teacher than reading, writing, and arithmetic. They need to be encouraged and cared about as individuals. Above all else, whether through the teacher or the parents, children need to be inspired to glorify God in the midst of their educational difficulties. When choosing a teacher, parents must first ask and answer the question, *Who can best encourage my child in his learning?*

Behavioral, Social, and Emotional Considerations

A Key Behavioral Factor

In this section we will look at three additional factors that can contribute to a child's educational difficulties. We will look at a key behavioral factor, known as Attention Deficit Disorder (ADD) and Attention-Deficit Hyperactivity Disorder (ADHD). We will also look at two key social and emotional factors that can affect a child's performance at school.

The "Characteristics" of ADD/ADHD   A considerable number of young children—many whose lives have been adversely affected by difficulties in the home—are labeled as having Attention Deficit Disorder (ADD) or Attention-Deficit/Hyperactivity Disorder (ADHD). Labels, however, although sometimes useful, are often misleading. Jay E. Adams warns,

> *The difficulty with labeling isn't that diagnosticians call names. The trouble comes (1) when they carelessly gum the wrong label on someone's file, (2) when they don't warn about the fact that labels often refer to temporary, changeable states of being, and (3) when they substitute labeling for genuine help as though a label were an end in and of itself rather than a means to an end. Labels identify, direct, classify, and enable us to understand and communicate.*[20]

ADD/ADHD is "the best-known psychiatric diagnosis ever."[21] A technical definition of ADD/ADHD has evolved over the last few decades. Its present form highlights two symptoms: *inattention* and *hyperactivity-impulsivity*. When a physician is considering making an ADD/ADHD diagnosis, he will look for the following behavior[22] in specific frequency:

Inattention is usually characterized by frequent careless mistakes in school work or other activities, having difficulty paying attention to work or play activities, not listening when being spoken to directly, lack of follow-through, and failure to finish schoolwork or chores. A child who receives this label is usually forgetful and disorganized, losing things necessary for tasks, and is reluctant to engage in tasks that require sustained mental effort. He is easily distracted.

Hyperactivity is usually characterized by fidgeting or squirming, inability to remain seated; inappropriate or excessive running about or climbing, having difficulty playing games quietly; seeming to always be on the go and talking excessively. *Impulsivity* is characterized by blurting out answers before hearing the whole question, difficulty in waiting to take turns, and often interrupting or intruding on others.

A Proper Understanding of ADD/ADHD   As an educator, I have taught many children who have been diagnosed as having ADD. However, I use the word *diagnosed* with a great deal of caution. *ADD is not a medical diagnosis; it is a behavioral one.* "Most discussions about ADD assume that the list of descriptions is equivalent to establishing a medical diagnosis. The popular assumption is that there is an underlying biological cause for the behavior, *but the assumption is unfounded*"[23] (emphasis in original). ADD/ADHD is not a "disease" like tuberculosis or diabetes. It is a classification of a certain type of behavior.

I know this might seem confusing because it is most often a medical doctor who gives the diagnosis. But ADD/ADHD diagnoses are usually made without any medical testing at all. This label is given by a doctor after he observes and inquires about the child's behavior. *Behavior* is used to support a diagnosis of ADD/ADHD, not any established biological or neurological evidence uncovered in the doctor's office. *ADD is simply a way to describe behavior rather than explain it.* Saying that a child has ADD/ADHD is like saying that a youngster has a bad temper. The label tells what he does—not why he does it.

Understanding ADD/ADHD as a behavior rather than a disease is complicated by the fact that most of these children are the recipients of medical treatment. Edward T. Welch writes,

> *The vast majority of ADD-labeled children will have normal physical
> exams, but many physicians suggest a medical treatment anyway. The treat-
> ment is typically stimulant drugs such as Ritalin or antidepressants such as
> Norpramin (Desipramine) or Prozac.*[24]

Lawrence H. Diller discloses this about Ritalin:

> *A comparison of 1993 Ritalin production with the latest figures available for
> 1995 suggests that 2.6 million people currently are taking Ritalin, the vast
> majority of whom are children ages five through twelve.*[25, 26]

Because of this confusing set of circumstances, parents of these young children—and the children themselves—may wrongly believe that the remedy for
ADD/ADHD is primarily medical. This creates other problems as well because
parents and children who believe that ADD/ADHD is a medical problem frequently ignore other factors that may be influencing the child's behavior. One
of these factors is that these children might be missing structure in their life.
Welch explains,

> *Structure refers to boundaries, guidelines, reminders and limits. It is a fence
> that can help contain and direct. Since some children have a style of thinking
> that is chaotic, disorganized and unreliable, structure compensates by
> providing external controls. Without structure, the constant change and
> ambiguous expectations aggravate every small difficulty.*[27]

Many ADD-labeled children have been raised in homes lacking in structure.
The only constant for them is inconsistency. They need structure that, for one
reason or another, their home environment has failed to provide. The tendency
to view this behavior as a medical problem also fails to take into consideration
development, learning disabilities, emotional status, family interaction, classroom size, and other environmental factors that may be relevant.[28]

Choosing to treat an ADD-labeled child medically may not be sinful,[29] but it
must not be the first or only thing parents do to address their child's behavior.
Welch emphasizes, "The most important principle to maintain is that your
quest for medical treatment must not outdistance your diligence in spiritual
nurture."[30] Parents who view their child's behavior solely as a medical

condition and ignore the more important spiritual aspects of it teach the child to believe that his behavior is something beyond his control. He is the child that shouts, when reprimanded for striking another student, "It's not my fault! I forgot to take my medication!"

What are the spiritual aspects of a child? We are reminded that "there is not one area of life that is not religious (Deuteronomy 6:1-9). All activities of life (1 Corinthians 10:31) are to be done to God's glory."[31] In other words, all aspects of a child's life, inward or outward, are religious or spiritual in nature. A child must be encouraged to offer every facet of his life—especially his behavior—to God in faithful worship (Romans 12:2).

God Can Help the ADD/ADHD Labeled Child   Help for the ADD-labeled child is not beyond the Bible's scope. God is the creator of all people; David proclaimed, "Thou didst weave me in my mother's womb" (Psalm 139:13). The child with ADD/ADHD can claim these words to be true of himself. God created him, and as a created being, he is finite or limited. Finiteness brings with it limitations and weaknesses of all sorts. One child's ability to pay attention may differ from that of his classmates. Another may struggle with memorization or following oral directions. These limitations, in and of themselves, are not sinful. But the mother of an ADD-labeled child must keep in mind that her child is not only finite, he is also sinful (Romans 3:23). Sometimes it is extremely difficult to distinguish between a child's natural limitations and his sinfulness. It is very important that a godly mother provide her ADD/ADHD child with a biblical perspective that will take both his limitations and his sinfulness into account. She must teach her child to cultivate the practice of self-examination as recommended in 2 Corinthians 13:5 and Matthew 7:3-5. Only God truly knows the inner heart of a child. The child who learns to seek God's face and to know His Word is the child who will come to discern for himself the difference between the good and bad fruit on the tree of his life.

Assisting the ADD/ADHD Labeled Child

BUILD STRUCTURE INTO HIS HOME LIFE   Structure can be built in an ADD/ADHD-labeled child's life in a variety of ways. In building this structure, the expectations of parents, teachers, and administrators must reasonably coincide with the child's natural limitations in areas of attention, impulsivity, and hyperactivity. Wise parents must strive to be both fair and consistent. For instance, rules should address only the area of sin. Selfishness is always sinful, but squirming in a classroom chair is not. A child should be held responsible when he clearly transgresses God's law. In all other matters, when a child fails to do what is requested, you first decide if the expectation was reasonable. Did the child understand the request? Was it presented to him in a way that he could understand it? Was the child capable of performing the task? Some children find it helpful to have a clearly written list of tasks, assigned in sequential order. Other children should be given only one task at a time. At heart, a parent should try to discern whether the child is being rebellious and lazy, or if he simply cannot comprehend and follow through. Parents need to be as flexible as God's grace enables them to be.

CHOSE THE CHILD'S TEACHER CAREFULLY   Finally, if the parents of an ADD/ADHD-labeled child are able to do so, they should choose their child's teacher carefully. She should manage a very organized classroom. Her discipline should be consistent, fair, and loving. The feature that would distinguish the right teacher's classroom from those of her colleagues is summed up in one word—structure.[32] Finding such a person to instruct this type of child may help prevent him from becoming discouraged. With discouragement cast aside, the child becomes free to experience the genuine enjoyment and encouragement that can come with learning.

Social and Emotional Factors

Discouragement can greatly affect a child's educational welfare. While there are many possible causes of discouragement, I will touch on the two that I see most commonly: parental divorce and a transient lifestyle.

Parental Divorce   "Divorce has become one of our society's greatest threats to children."[33] Divorce may result in profound and lasting discouragement for some children. These children are usually struggling with disillusionment, fear, anger, and grief. This should not be surprising, for God never designed for the family unit to be broken. Divorce was not God's original intention for man (Mark 10:6-9), but was allowed only because of the hardness of our hearts (Mark 10:5). Even so, many parents disregard God's counsel, and frequently their children suffer for it. Some children, because of their temperament or God's grace, are able to weather the storms of a family breakup quite well. Others suffer some or all of the problems we're about to look at. (For a fuller discussion of divorce, including examples of both righteous and sinful divorce, see chapter 13. This chapter is concerned only with how divorce may affect a child's ability to learn.)

Up to a generation or two ago, many parents in difficult marriages stuck together "for the sake of the kids." That is no longer the case today. In addition, though few divorcing parents may take into consideration that their actions do have a direct and lasting effect on children, please keep in mind that this section is not meant to condemn any divorced person; rather, I am writing with the hope that parents will come to understand the serious consequences of divorce and what can be done for the child. [Editor's Note: Of course, there are times when a Christian mother or father will try to keep their marriage together only to find that their partner goes ahead with the divorce anyway. Or, perhaps a Christian is married to an unbeliever who wants out. The Christian is commanded to "let him leave" (1 Corinthians 7:15). In these cases, the parent who cares for the children will want to do what he or she can to minimize the possible effects on their children.]

EFFECTS OF PARENTAL DIVORCE

Disillusionment A child of divorced parents may be a disillusioned child. He may not be able to understand what is happening in his family. An unbiblical divorce is especially likely to cause confusion and bewilderment.

Learning is usually the last thing on the mind of a child whose parents have divorced. In class, he may spend much of his time trying to make sense of his circumstances. His preoccupation and worry may lead to difficulty at school. He may wonder, *Who will take care of me if my parents can't even take care of themselves?*[34]

If you are counseling a divorced mother who has custody of her children, you'll want to encourage her to talk to her children about the choices she has made. If she has purposely disregarded God's counsel, then she needs to ask her child (and others) for forgiveness. If possible, she should seek to be reconciled with her husband. This is a good time for her to counsel her child about the mistakes she has made and the way to live a more godly life.

If the divorce was a righteous one on a mother's part, she must take the time to explain, in terms that her child can comprehend, the decisions that had to be made. She should encourage him that even though he may be struggling with confusion and disillusionment, God will help them together as they seek to serve Him.

Fear Fear may also be apparent in a child whose parents are divorced. One of his parents has already left; he may begin to wonder whether the remaining parent will leave. He may fear abandonment. At school, he may sit at his desk and brood. His mind may be disquieted by nebulous schemes to appease his custodial parent or to manipulatively entice the other. His teacher's words might seem unimportant and distant. Why should he care what she is saying? *His parents are divorced. He may fear that his life will never be the same.*

A godly mother can help calm her child's fears. She can direct him to Bible verses that affirm that God is a "father of the fatherless" (Psalm 68:5; *see also* Psalm 146:9). She can seek ways to reassure him that her love and concern for him will not change. Ultimately, however, she must teach him to put his trust in God alone, who has promised that He will never leave nor forsake His children (Hebrews 13:5).

Anger   A child of divorced parents may also be an angry child. Sometimes this is especially true when the divorce involves an older child or an adolescent. Although some adolescents recognize the ultimate good that may come out of a righteous divorce, others think that it is a dreadful decision with which they are forced to cope. A child may feel that his parents' divorce is unjust or unfair, and he may be angry about the changes that will take place in regard to his housing and possibly even his schooling. His anger may yield to sinful bitterness, or he may feel ashamed.[35] The respect he once had for those in positions of authority may erode. His moods and disposition may change considerably or fluctuate wildly. His anger may compel him to skip some homework assignments or even to skip school. *His anger may end up eating away at him to the point that he sinfully allows the anger to devour his desire to learn and grow.*

Sorrow   A child of divorce is sometimes a sad, grief-stricken child. The loss of a parent due to divorce may occasion greater sorrow in the life of a child than is found when a parent is lost through death. A parent who dies, barring suicide, does not leave the child behind willingly. Sometimes a divorcing parent does. Some children recognize this and grieve over it. A significant portion of the child's mourning is derived from the painful realization that the divorcing parent seems to have chosen to leave him behind. The heartbroken child has no interest in books or numbers; frequently, his thoughts are of a father or mother who is not coming home again.

In her book *Children Without Childhood*, Marie Winn gives this warning:

> *In many ways a family breakup increases a child's vulnerability to the stresses of modern life. Statistically, children of divorce are more likely to become involved with alcohol and drugs, to commit suicide, to get in trouble with the law, to fail in school. . . . [these children] showed lower achievement and substantially more school problems than children from families in which both mother and father lived in the home; these problems included*

infractions of discipline in the classroom, absenteeism, truancy, suspensions, dropouts, and expulsions. . . . children in one-parent families were more likely to defy their teachers' authority. . . . achievement-test scores and school grades of children being reared in single-parent homes tend to be lower than those of children living with two parents.[36]

Each child, as an individual, will respond to parental divorce in an individual way. Many will exhibit, to a greater or lesser degree, the characteristics of discouragement that I have mentioned. Others will not. The circumstances surrounding the divorce, the support given to the child during the divorce, and the child's own interpretation of and response to the divorce are all pivotal factors. A child should see that the mother (or father) is striving to please God and protect him throughout the divorce proceedings; that will help to minimize the negative effects of the divorce.

SUPPORTING A CHILD OF PARENTAL DIVORCE   Supporting a child through a divorce is a weighty endeavor. It is too heavy a burden for one parent to bear alone. Jesus beckons, "Come to Me, all who are weary and heavy-laden, and I will give you rest" (Matthew 11:28). This offer of comfort includes a divorcing or divorced parent. Jesus bids that parent to come. He is the Man of Sorrows; He is well acquainted with grief. Yet, there is one qualification for the parent: Jesus insists, "Take My yoke upon you, and learn from Me, for I am gentle and humble in heart; and you shall find rest for your souls. For My yoke is easy, and My load is light" (Matthew 11:29-30).

If you as a counselor find that the parent sinned in the divorce (and this is not always the case), you can encourage that parent to turn to the Lord for forgiveness and peace. The Lord will help that parent and encourage him or her as he or she seeks to become more pleasing to Him. And if reconciliation is possible, encourage the parent to seek it. Above all, the parent is to seek God's blessing as described by Peter:

Let him who means to love life and see good days refrain his tongue from evil and his lips from speaking guile. And let him turn away from evil and do good; let him seek peace and pursue it. For the eyes of the Lord are upon the righteous, and His ears attend to their prayer, but the face of the Lord is against those who do evil (1 Peter 3:10-12).

A child of divorce is an interpreting and responding child. We must keep in mind that divorce does not merely happen to a child. A child is not a passive participant in the ordeal. His social, emotional, and behavioral responses are active. They are the fruit (good or bad) of the interpretations he has made. It is not only the hearts of divorcing parents that are laid bare in divorce; the thoughts and attitudes of their child's heart are exposed as well. The following scenario illustrates this.

A fourth-grade boy (I will call him George) discovers that his parents are divorcing. One Thursday evening, around 9:45 P.M., he is awakened by an argument between his parents. It is not the first time his sleep has been disturbed in this way. His mother's ranting and raving drive him from his bed to the living room doorway. His father, a man of minimal aspiration, is hardly stirred by his wife's berating comments. It seems a strain for him just to make eye contact with her. He is irritated. She is blocking his view of the television set. George's mother notices her ten-year-old son standing in the doorway, and harshly directs him to get back to bed. Startled by her discovery of him, with tears in his eyes and fear in his heart, he darts down the hallway to his room. He crawls into bed, wipes the tears from his eyes, and worries himself to sleep.

In the morning George is told that his mother has gone to live with an aunt, and that she has asked his father for a divorce. At breakfast, he sits at the dining room table staring blankly into a bowl of cereal. Although he usually has a healthy appetite, this morning most of his cereal is still in its bowl when he catches the bus for school.

The day's activities do not hold much meaning for George. His mind is occupied with family troubles. Although he has often been overlooked by his mother in the past, he still finds it disheartening that she would leave without saying good-bye. He wonders, *What did I do wrong that she would leave me behind?* His heart is filled with anxious thoughts. He is scolded by his teacher for not finishing his morning assignments. He dares not explain his distraction. He does not want his friends to find out what has happened. He is ashamed, and fears that they may reject him if they know what has happened in his house. His fretful thoughts convert to angry ones. He swears to himself. He thinks of his father as an imbecile and his mother as the Wicked Witch of the West. He hates them both. His heart cries out in agony, *How could they do this to me!* At that moment, a classmate cuts in front of him in line. In a rage, George throws the boy to the ground. This is the first day of what he believes to be the rest of his miserable, worthless life.

George is a puzzled, apprehensive, embittered, and despairing child. His reaction to the divorce of his parents is what many would call normal. As a biblical counselor and an educator, I believe that to say George's response was normal is not to say enough to help this child. Bewilderment, fear, anger, and heartache are not *normal* experiences in divorce; they are *typical* ones. They are common to tragedy. A word like *normal* is misleading. It suggests that these experiences are as they should be and therefore, are justified. Only in a limited sense is that true.

Divorce, though not always sinful, is always the result of someone's sin. A child who has been sinned against may recognize the wrongness of the divorce. He may feel uncertain and sad. Reactions such as these are justifiable. A child left with no biblical guidance in the matter is abandoned to his own skewed interpretation. If he has an unbiblical interpretation, that will lead to an unbiblical response. Pondering leads to perplexity, fear to panic, anger to rage, and grief to despair.

George felt oppressed by the divorce of his parents, and he didn't recognize that God could comfort him. And as a child of divorce, he also became an oppressor. George, disregarding the welfare of his classmate, threw him to the ground.

Jesus wants all children, oppressed and oppressing, to come to Him. In Mark 10:14 Jesus told the disciples, "Permit the children to come to Me; do not hinder them; for the kingdom of God belongs to such as these." Children who have been hurt by divorce can be transformed into hope-filled, joyful children of the living God as they believe the good news of Jesus Christ. The gospel can transform children like George and take them from misery to blessing.

Making a Difference   You and other Christians within the church family of the divorced parent can make a difference in the life of the child. Your time and attention can help to fill the void that may have been left by one parent. King David sings, "A father of the fatherless and a judge for the widows, is God in His holy habitation. God makes a home for the lonely" (Psalm 68:5-6). As a member of God's family, the body of Christ, you can offer encouragement to the child abandoned by divorce. As a helping hand, you can take hold of a lonely or sorrowful child. As an ear, you can listen as he conveys both the heartaches and joys of his life. As a foot, you can walk in the place of the missing parent, teaching the child to observe the statues of the Lord (Deuteronomy 6:7). As a mouth, you can instruct him in the wisdom of Proverbs. If it is the child's father who has left, you can help sustain his mother through what may be a financially impoverished period of her life (Acts 2:4). Follow in the footsteps of our Lord as you seek to "bring good news to the afflicted; [and] bind up the brokenhearted" (Isaiah 61:1).

We are to be imitators of God, living selflessly for the sake of others (Ephesians 5:1-2). Pure and undefiled religion, as James speaks of it, presumes the tender care of orphans and widows in their distress (James 1:27). In a sense, a child of divorce is functionally an orphaned child because one parent is missing from the home and the other is usually away working.

Educational Help   A child of divorce can be given educational support in any number of ways. Volunteer to provide or arrange for child care while the custodial parent works. Assist the child with his homework assignment so he can maintain educational stability. Attend special events involving the child, such as plays or sports activities, to express your care and concern for the child. "Adopting" a child in any of these ways will help to undergird his life and enable him to better handle the educational context in which he finds himself.

In my personal experience as an educator, I have observed nothing more devastating in the life of a child than the divorce of the parents. You can have hope, however, that as the remaining parent seeks to diligently follow the Lord and teach his or her child the ways of the Lord, He will work in the parent for both the parent's and child's ultimate good.

Transient Lifestyle   Each year at my school I instruct an increasingly larger number of children who are new to the school and the district. Upon checking their permanent record cards, I discover that many of these children are perpetually new. Some have moved from place to place so frequently that the number of teachers by whom they have been taught actually outnumbers their chronological age. The educational welfare of some of these children has been and is being compromised by the transient lifestyle of their parents.

There are a variety of circumstances that contribute to transience in families. Divorce, financial strain, death, and job changes are common causes for many family moves. Some parents, military families in particular, are unable to avoid moving frequently. In the majority of cases involving joint-custodial divorce, although the child's schooling situation remains constant, the child's living arrangement is fluid. Sometimes a child may actually be toted back and forth between two houses as many as two or three times in the course of a week. This kind of continuous displacement may hinder some children's ability to learn. If given the option, an adult would rarely choose to live life from a suitcase. Does it seem reasonable to expect such a thing from a child? Although joint custody is the typical decision of most courts across our land, it would be better, if possible, for a believing parent to avoid sharing custodial rights with an unbelieving parent.[37] Although this is usually unavoidable, it may not be in the best interest of a child.

Transience, whatever its cause, is sometimes detrimental to the education of a child. Habitual moving from school to school sometimes breeds social detachment, loneliness and asocial or antisocial behaviors. A child may become more selfish and ingrown because he has come to view himself more as an individual than part of a community. He may not feel that he is responsible for doing his assigned work or homework, and thus he might fail academically.

Parents who make long-term plans about their housing are helping their children enjoy a better educational experience. If it is at all possible, parents should make their planned moves before their children reach school age. If a move must take place after the children have already begun their schooling, the most convenient time would be during the summer.

Some parents move for the sake of their children; they want to put them in a better school or school district or move them away from dangerous neighborhoods. Just remember that every effort (within reason) should be made to avoid moving a child during the school year. If it does become necessary to move, a mother should be aware of the fact that her child may be discouraged by this and extra time will need to be spent encouraging a child to adjust to these changes in a godly way. Leaving friends and comfortable surroundings for someplace new is both exciting and frightening. A mother will want to spend time talking with her child about his concerns and praying with him. By doing this, she may be able to keep him from becoming discouraged.

Recognizing Discouragement in Children   Discouragement has been the umbrella under which I have chosen to expound two social and emotional pitfalls that I believe to be most prevalent and harmful to children and to their education. Of course there are other behavioral, emotional, and social considerations that have been left unaddressed. Some children have both parents in the home but are ignored or neglected because the parents have made other things their priority. Some parents are very loving and attentive, yet they have children who refuse to respond in godly ways.[38]

Parents have a God-given obligation to bring up their children in the "discipline and instruction of the Lord" (Ephesians 6:4). Fathers are told on two different occasions to avoid exasperating or provoking their children to anger (Ephesians 6:4; Colossians 3:21). Parents who seek to encourage their children to think about and respond to their education in godly ways will usually find that their children flourish in the classroom setting. Ultimately parents are responsible for setting a godly example for their children. They cannot take the "educational" speck from the eye of their child when there is a "log" of folly or disinterest in their own. But thanks be to God! Though all parents will at times fail to remain faithful to their calling as servants in the lives of the children (there are no perfect parents!), God is always faithful to them. All children, especially those who are discouraged, can turn to the God of all comfort, knowing that He will care for them.

Looking at All the Factors

A mother whose child has learning difficulties needs to look at all the factors influencing his life. Is he healthy? Has she taught him how to think about his education? Are there any behavioral, social, or emotional issues that may be interfering with his learning?

Parents of children with learning difficulties can be comforted by the understanding they glean from a right interpretation of the Bible. They can rest in the knowledge that their heavenly Father will encourage and teach them as they strive to please Him. They can also rest in the knowledge that God can cause even their mistakes to work for good in their children's lives. Instead of fearfully seeking to manipulate their children, or giving up their position of authority in frustration and indifference, parents can encourage and comfort each other for God's glory.

And, a godly mother can rejoice in the Lord as Hannah did at the birth of her son, Samuel: "My heart exults in the LORD; my horn is exalted in the LORD, my mouth speaks boldly against my enemies, because I rejoice in Thy salvation. There is no one holy like the LORD, indeed, there is no one besides Thee, nor is there any rock like our God" (1 Samuel 2:1-2). This mother can hang onto the Rock, trust and walk in His Word, and joyfully and confidently love her children and encourage them for His sake.

CHAPTER 12

Counseling Mothers of Rebellious Teens

Mary Somerville, M.A.

"I can't communicate with my son anymore. Ever since he entered high school he has retreated into his own world and wants to talk only to his friends. He doesn't seem to care about our family anymore! He goes into his room and listens to his music, and has his walls decorated with pictures of his new heroes. He stays on the phone for hours with his friends. When he's not on the phone they go cruising around, wasting their lives away! Is this just a phase or should I do something?"

*

"I was afraid that my daughter was messing around but I didn't know what to do. Now she's pregnant! I feel like it's my fault for not stopping it from happening. I brought her up to love God. Sure we weren't perfect parents, but we did our best. Then as soon as she started dating that 'loser' we lost all control."

*

"How can my son be into drugs? We've never even had a drop of alcohol in our home! Where did I fail? What do I do now?"

*

As a counselor, you may have heard these or similar concerns expressed by mothers. I have personally struggled with these issues and have counseled many other women who have as well, and have written this chapter so that you as a counselor can help discouraged mothers who are looking for answers. However,

I want to say at the outset that I don't believe that there is a set formula to follow to bring a child out of his rebellion. Each child is unique and his rebelliousness may take many forms. I don't purport to have all the answers, but I know God's Word does contain all we need for life and godliness (2 Peter 1:3). I will set forth some general biblical principles that apply to rebellious teens, but because each situation is unique, you and the teen's mother may need to adapt the answers so that they fit the particular situation at hand. If the mother is willing to obey God, He will show her the way to walk as she seeks Him in His Word (Psalm 119:105). We can have this confidence because we serve a sovereign God who is powerful enough to change lives. We serve a living God who is worthy of all our love and devotion. And we can bring glory to Him in this battle whether or not a rebellious child ever comes around to serve Him.

As soldiers in this battle, we need to know our enemy. We must have God's perspective on rebellion so we don't ignore it, excuse it, run away from it, or become overpowered by it.

Knowing Our Enemy

Rebellion Defined

Rebellion is defined as "open opposition to any authority." To be rebellious is to "defy authority or control," "to disobey or oppose someone in authority."[1] Although *rebellion* is the proper word to describe the behavior of staunchly disobedient children, many in our society view this term as offensive or accusatory. They prefer to use euphemistic labels for rebellion, such as "dysfunctional behavior." Some people think of rebellious children as victims; others use varied and contradictory psychological theories to explain the problem. These theories fall into categories such as a self-esteem deficiency, the fear-of-becoming-adults theory, and the chemical imbalance theory. Yet these theories and all the others have one thing in common: they fail to address the issue at its root—the heart, the inner self of the person.

It is true that there are many hormonal changes taking place within teens and we need to take these into account. But, if bizarre behavior is taking place, a doctor should be consulted because the parent may be seeing signs of physiological problems or drug use. Also, many young people have had terrible sins committed against them, and may show it in their behavior. But what is really at the heart of the issue is the response of the child. In order to help solve a young person's problems, we must not confine our understanding of the problem to the past and what cannot be changed. The first step in learning to solve problems God's way is to classify them the way that God does.

Unfortunately some childhood "experts" have written books that demand that children be raised according to their philosophy of child-rearing. Frequently mothers feel guilty because they have failed to live up to these authors' recommendations. Just remember: God is the only one a mother needs to please, and He is very merciful and gracious. God's Word is to be the Christian's guide for child-rearing. Thus parents need to immerse themselves in the Word so that they may understand their teenager's problem and obtain guidance to solutions through biblical principles.

According to God's Word, rebellion is a heart issue. It is a sin. It occurs in a heart that refuses to recognize and submit to God or other God-ordained authorities. Rebellion is not a disease that can be cured by a psychological diagnosis and medication. When psychological counselors encourage their teen clients to blameshift (by labeling their rebellion as a problem with self-esteem or chemical imbalance), they only disguise and complicate the problem. Encounter groups that encourage teens to speak negatively about their parents or blame others for their problems lead to excusing and desensitizing them to their sin. In these groups the teens receive more sympathy and approval than help (*see* Romans 1:30-32).

At its base, rebellion is idolatry. It is love and respect of self above love and respect of God. All the secular labels and theories offered outside of God's Word simply lead to more idolatry. In order to help a child who does not submit to authority, we must identify his attitudes and actions as rebellion—the root of all sin against God. All rebellious idolatry must be forsaken in submission to God. Let's begin to meet the problem head-on with God's Word.

Rebellion Today

Is there more rebellion today than in other times or generations? It seems that today rebellion is more widespread than ever. The only thing that stops all-out rebellion and anarchy is the Christian virtue of submission. We are now in what historians call the post-Christian era. More and more people are doing what is right in their own eyes and the family structure is disintegrating. Consequently, children are raised without recognizing legitimate authority. Because the media is driven by what the market will consume (and by its own ideology), it portrays and celebrates every form of rebellion. Movies, television, MTV, and rock music depict illicit sex, drugs, violence, and flaunting of authority. Just spend a few minutes watching the afternoon talk shows that are tailored for teens, and see if you doubt what I say. I wouldn't even recommend watching MTV for the purpose of analysis; it is a cesspool of evil. This generation is unshockable when it comes to wickedness.

Rebellion is rampant today. Is God shocked? Certainly not! History is unfolding according to His plan. Someday His reign will be evident and rebellion will be put down.

Rebellion is nothing new; since the dawn of history there has been rebellion against God and His laws. In my personal study of Scripture I once found 84 verses that included the words *rebellion, rebel,* or *rebellious.* In addition, there are other additional terms in the Bible that describe rebellion: stubborn and unrepentant heart (Romans 2:5), and disobedience and transgression (Ephesians 2:2; Hebrews 2:2; 4:11).

We can also trace numerous cases of rebellion that are recorded in the narrative of God's dealings with man. Our first parents, Adam and Eve, acted in rebellion against God, their loving Creator. He had given them everything they needed; they lived in a perfect environment. Through their disobedience to the one prohibition He had given them, they introduced the whole human race to sin (Romans 5:12). We are not rebels only by inheritance, however. We rise to mutiny every time we fail to love and obey God fully. None of us are innocent of rebellion. We are rebellious people, and we have rebellious children.

God's View of Rebellion

What is God's response to rebellion? He pronounces woe to His rebellious children (Isaiah 30:1). Rebellion provokes Him to utmost wrath (Deuteronomy 9:7). He equates it with the abominable sin of witchcraft (1 Samuel 15:23). He does not minimize, excuse, or overlook rebellion; He hates it and pronounces judgment on it.

In the Bible the punishment for rebellion is extreme. When Israel was a country ruled by God, He instructed His people how to handle a stubborn and rebellious child who would not obey his parents. They were to stone him to death (Deuteronomy 21:18-21). When the nation of Israel rebelled against God, He said this to them through His prophet Jeremiah:

> *This people has a stubborn and rebellious heart; they have turned aside and departed. They do not say in their heart, "Let us now fear the LORD our*

God. . . . Shall I not punish these people?" declares the LORD *(Jeremiah 5:23–24,29).*

God followed through on His threats. Jeremiah lived to see the Temple and the holy city destroyed and the people taken into captivity by the Babylonians. Even while they were in captivity the people still had not learned their lesson. God, through His prophet, Ezekiel, promised further discipline:

I shall purge from you the rebels and those who transgress against Me; I shall bring them out of the land where they sojourn, but they will not enter the land of Israel. Thus you will know that I am the LORD *(Ezekiel 20:38).*

Unfortunately, there may be consequences for the entire family if one member is rebellious. For instance, an elder is disqualified from service if his child has a reputation for rebelliousness (Titus 1:6).

Disobedience to parents is one of the heinous sins listed in Romans chapter 1 (verse 30). The list is followed by these sobering words: "Although they know the ordinance of God . . . those who practice such things are worthy of death, they not only do the same, but also give hearty approval to those who practice them" (verse 32).

Whose Fault Is Rebellion?

The Bible warns that parents who live in sin will affect future generations. Thus they must continually allow the Holy Spirit to convict and cleanse them. In Exodus 20:5, God said:

You shall not worship [idols] or serve them; for I, the LORD *your God, am a jealous God, visiting the iniquity of the fathers on the children, on the third and the fourth generations of those who hate Me.*

God does allow the sins of the parents to be visited on the children in one sense—they learn their parents' sinful habits by watching them. Now God doesn't visit punishment or death on children for their parents' sins, but for the children's own sin, or for following in their parents' sinful ways:[2] "The person who sins will die. The son will not bear the punishment for the father's iniquity, nor will the father bear the punishment for the son's iniquity" (Ezekiel 18:20). On the positive side, God graciously promises to show lovingkindness to thousands—to those who love Him and keep His commandments (Exodus 20:6).

Eli the priest is an example of a case where the sins of the father influenced the choice of the sons to rebel. Eli had sons who were referred to as "sons of

Belial" or sons of the devil because of the way they were living. They despised the offering of the Lord and acted wickedly. Tragically, their father didn't rebuke them (1 Samuel 3:13). A prophet of God informed Eli of the judgment that would fall upon him for honoring his sons above God (1 Samuel 2:29). Eli's sons would also be disciplined because they, too, had honored themselves above God (1 Samuel 3:13).

As prophesied, their lives were taken prematurely in a battle. The most dreadful part of it all was that their death led to eternal separation from God. There was no atonement for Eli's house through the sacrifices or offerings that they had despised (1 Samuel 3:14). The folly and wickedness Eli displayed by idolizing his sons brought him a broken heart and then physical death. This is a sobering example for parents; they must never honor their children above God by looking the other way or excusing their rebellion. They must never seek to please their children or make them their "friend" in lieu of pleasing God. They must never deny their children's sin by saying, "My child would never do that." If they do, then they are taking the rebellion lightly, and they may suffer harsh consequences for doing so.

It's important to realize that rebellion is not necessarily the parent's fault. There is no biblical basis for the assumption that a child's rebelliousness must be the parents' fault. Parents must praise God for His mercy and grace if their children follow the Lord for all of their lives; they must take care not to become "puffed up." They must never judge other Christian parents whose children do not follow the Lord. None of us want to fall into the sin committed by Job's "comforters": Because Job was suffering so much, they accused him of having some hidden sin in his life.

A mother of a rebellious teen most likely is in grief over her child. Solomon wrote, "A wise son makes a father glad, but a foolish son is a grief to his mother" (Proverbs 10:1). A mother feels agonizing grief when one of her children becomes rebellious. She also feels shame (Proverbs 29:15). It's difficult to know that a child has rebelled after so much attention and care has been given to him. A mother feels great disappointment when she feels as if all her efforts, prayers, and her very life seem to have been wasted.

Rebellion Is a Choice

All children have a propensity to sin and rebel. If they appropriate God's grace and live in obedience to Him, then the parents can praise the Lord. If the children rebel and choose to go their own way, that is their decision. The parents must not feel they should shoulder the blame for their children's sin. God will not hold them accountable for the sins of their children. "The soul who sins will die" (Ezekiel 18:4). Parents will be held accountable for their own sins, including their sins in parenting, but they will not be held accountable for the sins of their children.

Moses set before God's chosen people a choice:

> *I have set before you today life and prosperity, and death and adversity; in that I command you today to love the LORD your God, to walk in His ways and to keep His commandments and His statutes and His judgments, that you may live and multiply, and that the LORD your God may bless you in the land where you are entering to possess it. But if your heart turns away and you will not obey, but are drawn away and worship other gods and serve them, I declare to you today that you shall surely perish (Deuteronomy 30:15-18).*

No Guarantees Against Rebellion

Understanding What Scripture Says   Some parents say, "I thought God promised me that my child wouldn't rebel. What about Proverbs 22:6, which says, 'Train up a child in the way he should go, even when he is old he will not depart from it'? I trained up my child in godly ways—doesn't God guarantee that he will not depart from those ways and rebel?"

Dr. Iain Duguid, Associate Professor of Old Testament at Westminster Theological Seminary, writes, "We must remember that by definition a proverb is a succinct general truth or rule of conduct. It is not a promise."

He continues:

> *The Book of Proverbs is not a collection of promises or prophecies but (as the name suggests) of proverbs. Proverbs, by their nature, are the collected observations of the wise on the way the world operates. Thus the key to the wise use of proverbs is not simply knowing a proverb which is "true" (as all biblical proverbs are, by definition). Rather, one needs to perceive the correct situation to which the proverb applies. Using a proverb to guide action in an inappropriate situation is highly dangerous; that is why Proverbs 26:9 reminds us that a proverb in the mouth of a fool is like a thornbush in the hand of a drunkard (likely to inflict injury on himself and all around him!).*

Moreover, wise behavior itself carries no guarantee of maximal "success." It is wise to plan prudently for the future and work hard rather than to trust in buying lottery tickets. Most people are more likely to prosper in that way. Yet that does not mean that you will never meet people who have become rich through buying a lottery ticket. Wisdom deals with the ordinary, normal use of means rather than the unusual, unique distortions of circumstances.

Thus the first question for Proverbs 22:6 is, For what situation is it designed? I would suggest it is an encouragement to parents to take seriously their responsibilities towards the young, since (in general) the road you start out on is the one you will end up following. Furthermore, since the way (same word) of the wicked is encompassed by thorns and snares (Proverbs 22:5) and humility and the fear of the Lord bring wealth and honor and life (Proverbs 22:4), which way you go is a matter of considerable importance.

That does not guarantee that every child started off on the right way will automatically become a Christian, any more than the preceding verse guarantees that every wicked person will find life difficult. In general, sin does complicate life and frequently leads to difficulties because this is a world designed by God. But through His common grace we do not all experience the full consequences of our sin. Likewise, as the proverb asserts, early training and discipline is incredibly important. Many people have cause to give thanks for the example and instruction of godly parents. But who would seriously want to claim this proverb as a promise? All of us as parents are seriously flawed by sin; at best, we pass on to our children a mixed message. If my child's salvation depends entirely on my ability to start them off right, then he or she is certainly doomed! Fortunately God's grace works in spite of our sin, calling to Himself His elect, redeeming the flaws small and great in our own backgrounds through the work of his indwelling Holy Spirit. And no matter what we once were, whether through our own rebellion or through our parents' sin, we do not have to remain that way (1 Corinthians 6:9-11).

On the other hand, what the proverb does do is to hold us accountable for our responsibility to give our children training in the ways of the Lord. In the mysteries of providence, one common way in which the Holy Spirit may work is through the influence, teaching and discipline of parents from the earliest of days. Our society adheres to a different "wisdom," which is why so many people are untroubled at handing even the youngest children over into the hands of others to raise. But the Bible teaches that early learning is vital not merely in the intellectual realm but in the moral realm also.[3]

Influencing Our Children's Lives   When we train our children to know God, He uses His Word in their lives to mold them and shape them. His Word never returns empty; that is why God told His people to put His commands on their hearts and teach them continually to their children. Yet although the sons of Israel had every kind of spiritual advantage, they constantly turned from God. Parents, then, are to be responsible to obey God in the nurture and discipline of their children, but their children are responsible for their own decisions.

God hasn't guaranteed our success as parents. However, He has given us the responsibility of training our children to know Him. He is able to use His Word in their lives to mold and shape them. We can be confident of His blessings as we are faithful to Him, for His Word never returns empty.

The church is one place where parents can acquaint their children with the ways of the Lord. Part of their responsibility is to make sure that the family is faithful in church attendance and that their children attend youth activities. Parents can then hope that the years of church training have equipped their children to take on the world with all its snares and temptations. But remember, there is no guarantee that the children will benefit from these advantages and follow Christ. Parents need to remember that they are responsible for submitting to God's directions on parenting—no matter whether the children respond in a godly way or not. Parents are to seek to please God, not attempt to manipulate their children into godliness.

The teen years are a time of transition between childhood and adulthood. It is a time in which the child must determine whether he will cling to the faith of his parents. During this sensitive time, parents should seek to maintain biblical standards of conduct in the home to protect their child. They should not try to force their child into an external Christianity in which the heart is not converted. A child's external conformity is no guarantee against rebellion of the heart. Insisting that a child who is not converted pray or worship will breed hypocrisy. Parents may insist that their child attend church and youth functions, but to expect participation in the spiritual disciplines is something different.

When a child shows outward rebellion, he may be revealing an unconverted heart. A parent needs to thank God for his or her child's rebellion even though it hurts. They can pray that he will be caught in every harmful act and realize that rebellion is a dead-end street.

Good Parents Don't Always Have Good Kids   Contrary to popular opinion, environment does not predetermine how a child will turn out. That is a matter of God's election. Each child is an individual and has his own unique desires. Many children from very abusive and wicked families turn out, by God's amazing grace, to be godly people. Through the working of the Spirit in their lives, they choose to accept the grace offered them in Jesus Christ and submit to Him in obedience. Sadly, the opposite is also true: Children with godly parents may choose to go their own way in rebellion.

The Bible chronicles the lives of good and bad children who come from both godly and wicked parents. The kings of Judah are prime examples. Hezekiah, one of the best kings, was succeeded by his wicked son, Manasseh, who led the nation into idolatry. Manasseh's son, Amon, followed him in his wickedness. Yet by God's grace, Amon's son, Josiah, served God and brought about great reforms (2 Kings 19–22).[4]

Dorie Van Stone[5] is an example of a godly person who grew up in a terribly wicked environment. She was abandoned by both of her parents and terribly abused by the people in the orphanage in which she was raised. Her life is a testimony of God's redeeming grace. She came to know Christ as her Savior and realized that He was all she needed. She became a missionary to the Dani tribe in Borneo and ministered to people who had also been mistreated by their pagan parents.

If it were true that we are predetermined by our environment, then Dorie never would have been saved and evangelism would be a "mission impossible." Remember, there are *no sinless parents,* and we live in a sin-cursed world. As it is, God elects people from every kind of background. Each person will one day stand before God and be held responsible for the choices he made (Romans 14:12).

Even if you could be a perfect parent, that would be no guarantee that your children wouldn't rebel. In the parable of the prodigal son, whom does the father represent? The father is God. Jesus portrayed God, the perfect Father, as having a prodigal son, rebellious mankind. I believe that we may assume from this that the perfection of the parents does not guarantee against rebellion. Rebellion is a choice.

That is freeing news for parents who sought to set a godly example, pray, and raise their children in the things of the Lord—only to see them rebel. God has seen the parents' faithful service. They are not alone. God understands their sorrow. They are not to blame themselves for their children's sins. They are to persevere in love and faithful obedience.

Rebellion Allowed for the Glory of God

Parents of rebellious children can become easily discouraged when they consider the prevalence and consequences of sin. They must remember that even the wrath of man can praise God (Psalm 76:10). For instance, God allowed Adam and Eve to rebel in the Garden of Eden so that He could demonstrate His glorious grace by sending His Son to the cross. God hardened Pharaoh's heart so that He could gloriously deliver the Israelites through the Red Sea. God broke off the branch of Israel so that He could graciously graft in the Gentiles. Parents should not lose hope by focusing on temporal tribulations.[6]

> *In this you greatly rejoice, even though now for a little while, if necessary, you have been distressed by various trials, knowing that the proof of your faith, being more precious than gold which is perishable, even though tested by fire, may be found to result in praise and* glory *and honor at the revelation of Jesus Christ (1 Peter 1:6-7, emphasis added).*

God is sovereign and He is in control even when a child is out of control. A parent can know that his or her child is still loved by God even more than he is loved by the parent. Remind parents that they can trust that God is at work in their child's life to bring him to repentance. It is the Holy Spirit's job to convict of sin, not the parents'. They don't have to cajole and manipulate their child to try to get him to return to the Lord. They can release him to the heavenly Father's care, knowing that He is fully capable of bringing their son or daughter to repentance. They can rest in the peace and joy that comes from knowing that God is sovereign. They are to fast and pray, wait patiently, and remember how patient God was with them.

Glorifying Christ in the Battle

Now that we've seen our enemy, rebellion, for what it is from God's perspective, let's look at how to respond to it in everyday life. When the mother of a rebellious teen comes to you for counsel, she may be experiencing anger against God—anger which can result in bitterness, hopelessness, depression, or tremendous fear. Here are some practical strategies you can offer to mothers who want to bring glory to God in each arena of their battle.

Glorifying God in Your Relationship to Christ

"I don't know when I last got a good night's sleep. When our son is out with his friends who use drugs, I can't get to sleep until he's in, and even then I lie awake thinking about the direction Kevin's life is headed. I don't see any ray of light ahead for him. His life is bound up in his friends who are all losers going nowhere. How could he not be using drugs when he is constantly with them and seems to have no strength to stand alone? His grades have gone down. I don't know if he will even graduate. Why couldn't Kevin be like our other children, who have followed the Lord? Why? Why?"

Has God forgotten to be gracious to this mother? Does all the love she has invested into her child's life amount to nothing? A resounding *no*! God is still gracious. He has seen the love and devotion that the mother showered on her son or daughter. God is sovereign in this trial. He has hand-picked this trial to come into the mother's life for His purpose: her growth in Him. She can be assured of God's love. She can rest in it and draw close to Christ. It's in this time of trial that she will want to focus on her relationship with Christ. As a counselor, you can help facilitate this mother's growth in maturity by getting her to focus in faith on the following steps:

1. Glorify God by thanking Him for the trial (Romans 8:28; Philippians 4:4-8; 1 Thessalonians 5:18; James 1:23).   Christ is glorified in our lives as we trust Him in our trials, knowing that He will use them for good. It dishonors Him when we worry and fret, because every situation we encounter passed through His loving and sovereign hands. If a mother finds herself becoming anxious, she should confess it as sin. Have her thank God for the trial, then pray. God promises to give her an incomprehensible peace that will guard her heart and mind. It is just amazing what thanksgiving does; it can help the mother to see the things that He wants to teach her as she exercises her faith and releases the trying circumstance to God. Her destructive worry becomes constructive, passionate prayer. Have her thank God for the occasion to know Jesus better through sharing in the fellowship of His sufferings as she is driven to talk to God many times in the night watches.

2. Glorify God by coming before Him and asking if He is disciplining you (Joel 2:12-17; Hebrews 12:6).   God told His people to return to Him with all their heart, with fasting, weeping, and mourning—to rend their hearts.

Likewise, God wants to see that the mother is serious about this situation—her sin and the sin of her child. She needs to come before Him in ways that demonstrate this. She probably has been doing plenty of crying about her child, depending on the severity of the rebellion. Now she should cry unto the Lord, "for He is gracious and compassionate, slow to anger, abounding in loving-kindness, and relenting of evil. Who knows whether He will not turn and relent, and leave a blessing behind Him . . . ?" (Joel 2:13-14). He wants to show Himself strong on the mother's behalf in answer to her prayers. "Why should they among the peoples say, 'Where is their God?' " (Joel 2:17).

If a mother has sins in her life, God will reveal them to her as she seeks Him in His Word. Have her ask God for the strength to put off her sins and put on right attitudes and actions (Ephesians 4:22-24). It is never too late to begin obeying the Lord.

Have the mother examine the way she raised her child. If she sees that she has failed in any area, have her confess by agreeing with God that she has sinned against Him. Have her specifically name each sin, and He who is faithful will forgive her and cleanse her from it (1 John 1:9). Some areas where a mother may have sinned against her child are:

- *Love (prayerfully study 1 Corinthians 13)*
  Is God's love evident in the mother's home? Is she patient, kind, not jealous or prideful or easily provoked? Does she rejoice when her child does something good and truthful? Does she bear all things? Does she believe the best? Does she have hope in all situations? Does she endure all things? This kind of love is only possible as the mother yields to the Holy Spirit and allows His supernatural love to flow through her.
- *Spiritual leadership (Deuteronomy 6:4-9; Ephesians 6:4; 1 Timothy 4:7-8)*
  Does the mother bring Christ into her home through natural sharing of what He is doing in her life? Does she read the Word and discuss it with the family? Does she pray together with the family? Does she encourage her children by her example of self-discipline for the purpose of godliness? Does she teach them how to have their own quiet times with God if they are Christians?
- *Time (Titus 2:4-5)*
  Is the mother too busy to spend time with her child? Are other things of first priority? Does that time include play as well as work? A mother needs to be available in all kinds of circumstances to develop rapport, to

be an example, and to teach. There is no substitute for time in the discipling process.

- *Discipline (Proverbs 29:15)*
  Does the mother faithfully set down standards and carry out discipline consistently and fairly? Is she too permissive? Spoiling on the one hand and punishing unjustly on the other are both wrong.
- *Authoritarianism (Ephesians 6:4)*
  Is the mother too much of an authoritarian? Young people can be provoked to anger by many things, but this is perhaps the most frustrating for them. Parents can either be dictators or loving leaders in their homes. Teenagers need space to think for themselves and room to fail. They need to be respected as individuals. They are not extensions of their parents. Thus, parents must see them as separate persons whom they are called by Scripture to respect (*see* Romans 13). Teens should be taught how to come to their own conclusions based on the Word of God. Parents can sometimes be overbearing, critical, and intolerant. These traits definitely limit communication and openness. Parents are not to try to create their children in their own image. God has a plan for each individual child, and He alone can shape that child's life into that plan.
- *Humility (Philippians 2:3)*
  Is the mother seeking to portray a false sense of perfection? Is she trying to make it look like she doesn't struggle with sin in her life? Young people pick up on hypocrisy like a satellite dish catches a signal. Do they see their mother's sorrow for her sin and see her repentance? Does she allow them to see how she struggles to walk with Christ? Is she approachable? Is she a servant to her family, or does she expect her children to serve her? Does she ever seek forgiveness from her children or from her husband in front of the children?

3. Glorify God by seeking the child's forgiveness (Proverbs 15:33; Matthew 7:1-5). We are instructed by Jesus to deal with our own sin before we can see clearly enough to deal with the sin of others. If a mother has been unfair, unloving, authoritarian, or if she has not taken spiritual leadership, she needs to confess it. If she has been too busy to deal with issues that needed to be handled long ago, that is no excuse to continue to avoid them. Encourage the mother to admit her failure, ask forgiveness, and boldly make the change in faith. Her child may not choose to forgive her right away; that is his responsibility before God. She is responsible only for asking for forgiveness and modeling a forgiving spirit.

Then have the mother pray that as her child experiences God's forgiveness, he will choose to give up his bitterness and forgive her.

4. Glorify God by being malleable (Romans 5:3-5, 8:29; Galatians 5:22-23; Philippians 3:10; 1 Thessalonians 5:17; James 1:3-4). God is in the business of conforming us to the image of His Son. The trials we experience will help us learn His love, joy, peace, patience, kindness, goodness, faithfulness, gentleness, and self-control in ways that we would never learn them otherwise. What better way for God to teach a mother His kind of love than to give her a child that is hard to love? What better way for God to demonstrate His triumphant joy in the midst of pain than to give her a child whose shameful behavior brings her sorrow? What better way for God to show His peace to be beyond understanding than by giving her a child who is slowly destroying his own life? Does she need to learn patience? Wow! This will give her plenty of practice! What better way for God to teach her His kind of patience than by giving her a child that tests her patience every day? Does she need to learn kindness and goodness? What better way for God to teach her to practice His kindness and goodness than by giving her a child who is acting in an evil way? What better way for God to teach her His kind of faithfulness than by giving her a child that she feels like giving up on because the problems are overwhelming? What better way for God to teach her His kind of gentleness and self-control than by giving her a child who may be driving her wild?

It may sound impossible for the mother—or for *anyone* to appropriate these godly responses. It *is* impossible—in the flesh. Jesus said, "Apart from Me you can do nothing" (John 15:5). But we are new creatures in Christ. We have "crucified the flesh with its passions and desires" (Galatians 5:24). Paul gives us this command accompanied by a promise, "Walk by the Spirit, and you will not carry out the desire of the flesh" (Galatians 5:16). How does a person walk by the Spirit? By putting off the deeds of the flesh and yielding to the Spirit. Encourage the mother to begin meditating on passages of Scripture that deal with her specific areas of weakness.[7] Help her devise a plan for putting off the old ways and putting on the new ways. Let her know that as she goes through her day, the Holy Spirit will convict her when she yields to the flesh. She needs to be sensitive and quick to change. If she asks for the Holy Spirit to produce His fruit in her life, He will: "If you abide in Me and My words abide in you, ask whatever you wish, and it shall be done for you" (John 15:7).

This sanctifying process will not be comfortable. It hurts to be broken and shaped and molded. God never promised an easy road. Jesus said, "If anyone wishes to come after Me, let him deny himself, and take up his cross daily, and follow Me" (Luke 9:23). The mother needs to commit to obedience. Remind her to not be controlled by passing feelings, but to remain obedient by abiding in God's Word. As she reads it daily, she will be learning the valuable lessons that God wants to teach her at this time. In this way, she will prove herself to be a true disciple and bring glory to God. "By this is My Father glorified, that you bear much fruit, and so prove to be My disciples" (John 15:8).

Glorifying God in Your Relationship to Your Husband

"My husband Bill and I just can't get it together," Lori blurted out. "All we ever do is fight about how we're dealing with our son. Shane doesn't want to go to church or youth group anymore. Bill thinks it's okay for him to stay home. He thinks that if he doesn't want to be at church, it won't do him any good. But I think that at least he would be exposed to the Word and God could use it. I think we should call the parents when he goes to someone's house for a party. My husband doesn't think it's necessary. I think we should require him to get rid of his evil posters but Bill disagrees. All we do is fight, fight, fight. I hate it. Can you help?"

For couples, trials are an opportunity to draw closer together. But like Lori, many women are frustrated because trials like these seem to drive a wedge between the spouses. Why is the trial causing division? Here are some questions you can ask your counselee: Are you concentrating on the problem and forgetting about your spouse and your biblical responsibility to him? Are you blameshifting? Blameshifting might sound something like this: "If only you had spent more time with our son," or "If only you hadn't been so lenient with our daughter," or "If only you had taken more spiritual leadership." When a wife attempts to shift the blame, then she not only has the difficulty of the rebellious child, but she may also have the difficulty of a strained relationship with her husband. They must stay united. How can this be accomplished? Here are some suggestions you can give to the mother:

1. **Pray together for your child (James 5:16) if your husband is a Christian.** The couple needs to examine their hearts together as outlined above. They should seek to know where they may have failed as a couple and come humbly before God together. God alone can change the heart of their child; He works in answer to prayer.

Encourage the couple to pray Scriptures back to God together. When we pray in accordance with His revealed will, He will answer (1 John 5:14-15). For instance, I know a father who wrote a list of 40 Proverbs that he has prayed through for his son for four years. Some of the fruits are just beginning to be demonstrated. The book of Proverbs contains much good wisdom for our children, and parents can personalize the verses with their child's name. For example, they could pray like this from Proverbs 4:20-27: "Dear Lord, may _____ give attention to Your words. Help him to incline his ear to Your sayings. Do not let them depart from his sight. Keep them in the midst of his heart, for they are life to him and health to his whole body. Help him to watch over his heart with all diligence, for from it flow the springs of life. Help him to put away a deceitful mouth, and put devious lips far from him. Let his eyes look directly ahead. May he watch the path of his feet and may all his ways be established. Help him not to turn to the right nor to the left, but turn his feet from evil."

Have the mother pray together with her husband for wisdom for how to respond to the trial (James 1:5-8). God will give them insights on how to minister more fully to their child. He will give them insights from others who have experienced God's grace in similar situations. As they humble themselves together before the Lord, they will grow closer to Christ and to one another.

2. Submit to your husband's leadership (Ephesians 5:22-24).   God holds the husband accountable for the family and the training of the children. As the head of the family and the head of the whole human race, it was Adam's sin that was imputed to mankind even though Eve sinned first (Genesis 3:11; Romans 5:12). The husband is the head of the wife, and he is called to care for her as for his own body. Peter instructs the husband to live with his wife in an understanding way (1 Peter 3:7). If a woman wants her husband to understand her, she must tell him what she is thinking. Have your counselee share with her husband any insights or ideas that she may have about their child's problems. Have her talk things over with him and let him know her thoughts. If she thinks that her husband's decision is unwise, she can appeal to him to reconsider. After all that, she must step back and allow him to make the final decisions, unless his decisions are sinful.

While the counselee awaits her husband's decision, she can pray for him and trust God to direct him. If she disagrees about a course of action, she should commit it to the Lord. If God allows her husband to make an unwise decision, he will learn from it. The important thing is that she and her husband will have stayed united. Unity is vital. They must respond as one, especially in disciplining their children. If they negate each other's discipline, a rebel will use this to avoid further correction. If she and her husband continually argue and fight, their child may become fearful. Satan would like nothing better than to divide and conquer their home. He will do it any way he can; he will use their children to divide them if they let him.

Remind your counselee that she is modeling submission to her child by her submission to her husband. Have her think about that. Could a lack of submission in the past be a factor in her child's behavior?

3. Love your husband (Titus 2:4).   It is very easy for a woman in this situation to put her child before her husband. Although she should not be concerned with earning her child's approval, she may try hard to win back her own child's affection and obedience. She may pour her life into the child with little thought for the man she was created to help (Genesis 2:18). God, however, puts first priority on the husband-wife relationship. It is above the parent-child relationship. While a woman's children will leave home someday, her relationship with her husband is until death.

Does your counselee welcome her husband at the door at the end of the day, seeking to bless him, or does she bombard him with a litany of problems for him to fix? Have her evaluate her life. Is she seeking to show her husband how much she loves and respects him (*see* Ephesians 5:33)? Is she concentrating on loving her husband with all her heart? Encourage her to bring the romance back into their marriage if it has slipped away. She can make home a place where music and laughter is heard again. She can seek to build up her husband and thank and praise him for all he is and does. She can let her rebellious child see that her husband comes before him.

Perhaps your counselee is married to a man who does not know the Lord.[8] She cannot pray together with him, nor does she feel like submitting to him because he is not seeking God's wisdom. What should she do? The Bible tells how a husband who is disobedient to the Word may be won: "You wives, be submissive to your own husbands so that even if any of them are disobedient to the word, they may be won without a word by the behavior of their wives, as they observe your chaste and respectful behavior" (1 Peter 3:1-2). God can use a wife's love and godly example as a way to convict her husband and possibly bring him to Himself. Your counselee can still set an example of submission even though her husband is not submitting himself to the Lord. She needs to love her husband and submit to his God-given leadership in the home. You'll also want to point out that even the unregenerate usually want the best for their children, so perhaps her husband will have good common-sense ideas for raising their child. Remind her that as she stays in her marriage, her unbelieving husband and children are set apart in a special way for God to bless them (1 Corinthians 7:14,16).

Glorifying God as a Single Mother

If your counselee is a single mother with a rebellious child, then obviously she cannot follow some of the suggestions we've just considered. You'll want to pray together with her and have her claim the promise that "God is faithful, who will not allow you to be tempted beyond what you are able, but with the temptation will provide the way of escape also, that you may be able to endure it" (1 Corinthians 10:13).

God has promised to be a father to the fatherless (Psalm 68:5). There are many references to the fatherless in the Scriptures. God has a special place in His heart for children without fathers, and He cares about the children of a single mother. He wants to care for those children and provide for the mother's needs (Isaiah 40:11). He does this tangibly through His body, the church.

In the early church the office of deacon was created because certain widows were being overlooked (Acts 6:1-3). In addition, the apostle Paul gives instruction for the care of widows and guidelines for their conduct (1 Timothy 5:3-16). Those mothers who are suffering from the consequences of a righteous divorce[9] are in the same situation as widows, and they can rest assured that God will be their provider.

A single mother should be given the opportunity to avail herself of the ministries of her brothers and sisters in the local church. It may be humbling, but she should ask for assistance from other families in the church. A home Bible study is a good place for her to share her needs and receive help. She can ask other families to do things together with her and her children. Suggest that she not wait for others to offer help, but that she make her needs known.

If your counselee has a son, help her to find adult Christian men who can serve as role models for him. Ask your pastor or elder if he knows of a man who would be willing to reach out to your counselee's son and establish a one-on-one discipling relationship with him. Depending on the teen son's receptivity, this may or may not mean going through a Bible study once a week. The discipler might want to start by taking the teen son out for a soda or attending an activity in which he is involved. He may also be able to develop rapport by having the teen son spend time with him as he does some aspect of his work or recreation. However, utmost caution must be exercised. A single mom and her child should never spend time with a married man unless his wife is there too. Satan would likely try to use such a situation to draw a generous man away from his own wife and family.

If the single mom was never married or she did not have biblical grounds for her divorce and this has deprived her child of a father, then she needs to ask her child for forgiveness. Her child may have bitterness because of the inconsistency he has seen in her life. Her disobedience to God and His Word may be what precipitated her child's rebellion, but as has been noted, it is not an excuse for it. She can share with her child that the difficult situation she is in is a consequence of her rebellion against their heavenly Father and His guidelines for marriage. She should tell her child that she wants to follow God's example in applying consistent discipline so that the child understands that there are moral consequences to rebellious behavior. When a mother makes herself humble and transparent in this way, the child is able to learn from her mistakes and may be spared untold heartache.

A single mother may fear being a disciplinarian because she thinks that her child will not love her if she is firm with him. But if she loves her child more than herself, she will discipline him diligently, teaching him that there are consequences for his actions. According to Proverbs 13:24, the parent who is not disciplining his or her child is acting hatefully.

A single mom may be tempted to indulge her child for fear that he will turn to the other parent (in the case of divorce) or to his peers. The child may be all she has left, so she may settle for peace at any price. But that will be a dear price to pay, because it could result in her child giving in to peer pressure, flunking out of school, turning to drugs for thrills, or ending up in jail because he lacks discipline. If the mother hasn't insisted on upholding God's standards, then she needs to repent of this sin. It will not be easy for her to start disciplining a child who is not used to it. But encourage her to be diligent. Pray alongside her as she strives to make and keep biblical standards. Hold her accountable to you in applying discipline consistently. In the long run, as the child sees his mother's consistent love, he will come to love and respect her more.

Glorifying God in Your Relationship to Your Child

Susan was confused and pled for help. "I found some marijuana in Brent's room last night. So now we know he's using drugs. We have to get him away from his friends, but we don't know how. Do we pull him out of the public school and put him in a Christian school? That may not help either because he's lost interest in the things of the Lord. I know that kids at the Christian school use drugs, too. What can we do? I just love him so much, and I can't understand how God has let this happen!"

In their confusion over a child's rebellious behavior, parents sometimes think that they love their child more than God does. But God's perfect love is always present; He is at work in the child's life. The parents must remember that from the time that their child was born, he has been on loan to them. They were entrusted with an important stewardship, but their child belongs to God first. When a mother expresses sorrow and fear over her child, remind her that God is in control and He loves her child. He will do whatever it takes to work in the child's life to accomplish His will. In the meantime, the mother is to look to God for the grace to:

1. Love the child (Titus 2:4) Acting in love may be hard at this particular time. Your counselee will need to ask God for the love that comes from above. His love is better than "unconditional" love. Even though He loved us while we were unlovable sinners, He did not allow us to remain in our sin. "God so loved the world, that He gave His only begotten Son, that whoever believes in Him should not perish, but have eternal life" (John 3:16). His love seeks to change us. His love gives us what we need. What does the child need right now?

Some have said that love is spelled T-I-M-E. Encourage the mother to spend time listening to her child. She will probably have to draw him out through thoughtful questions. Caution her to be slow in giving advice at every turn. She should just be there for him. She can also plan times away with her child. She can plan time to get to know him away from his peers, siblings, and other demands. She should also encourage him in all the ways she can. She could leave notes on his dresser, make special things he likes to eat, do crazy pranks to let him know she is fun to be around, and invite his friends over for dinner or snacks. If he is involved in sports, she should go to his games. If he is into drama or music, she should go to his plays or musicals. She should take interest in his interests. Encourage her to do these things in faith; she doesn't need to have feelings to accompany deeds of love.

A rebellious child is not fun to be around. There is often no response to gestures of love. Many times the teen has no desire to be around his parents, no matter what they do. But love is a fruit of the Spirit and is not based on reciprocation. Anyone can love those who love back, but Christians are called to love even their enemies. Pray with your counselee that God's love, as described in 1 Corinthians 13, will flow through her. Even if she feels as though her child is her enemy, she is to love him and minister to him. When she acts in this way she will demonstrate God's love for him.

One way your counselee can show love is by talking to him about his rebellion and asking what God thinks of it. She should not rest in the assurance that he is a Christian because he prayed a prayer at a young age. Have her exhort him to test himself to see if he is in the faith (2 Corinthians 13:5). She can tell her child that she loves him enough to tell him that he may be headed to destruction. She should let him know that Jesus died on the cross to forgive all rebellion and sin. He can be forgiven, cleansed, and begin a new life as he lives in obedience to Christ.

If the child doesn't respond to his mother's urgings, she should not continually preach or nag. Rather, she needs to pray for him and trust the Lord to bring him to repentance in His time. Remind her that the goal is for the child to genuinely respond to the Holy Spirit, not merely seek to placate his parents.

2. Set standards for the home and parent-child relationship (Ephesians 6:1). As a child gets older, the parental control should lessen. The child should be given more and more opportunities to make his own decisions. Parents must move from being authorities to being advisors. There should be room for a child to learn to make good choices within the framework provided by the parents. When choices are made that are against the parents' beliefs, some authority has to be taken back. They may have to make decisions for their child until he has demonstrated that he is trustworthy and has matured.

Even though they may fight vigorously against them, young people need boundaries. They may rebel against the parents' "narrow-mindedness." That's why it's wise for the parents to draw their lines biblically. Fads come and go. The parents should avoid making big issues over such things as clothing or hairstyle. These things are temporal and external. They may or may not accurately express the heart. Parents should focus instead on the root of the problem by drawing their battle lines at sin. Advise your counselee to not set standards of conduct or appearance simply because she doesn't want to be embarrassed. Her fear of man and her pride will be a detriment to her child's understanding of God's desire to work in his inner man. God is looking at the child's heart, and she should, too. Remind the mother that her goal is her child's conversion and sanctification. She should choose her battles carefully;

she is to fight against sin. She should not bend standards just to avoid conflict, but pick her conflicts wisely.

The mother may find it helpful to discuss the purposes of her standards with her adolescent. If he demonstrates an understanding of the spirit of the law, she may be able to grant him more freedom. For instance, she may not need to have a set curfew if the teen agrees to let it be known where he can be reached and what time he will be home. If he understands that he must not set his mind on perverse or ungodly lyrics, perhaps he could be allowed to choose his own music. If he likes a style of music that is distasteful to your counselee but is not sinful, she should let him have his way. When it comes to choices, have your counselee continually ask herself: Is this sinful, or just different from my personal preferences?

On the other hand, if the child refuses to see the value of the rules your counselee has set, she may have to maintain them sheerly on the basis of loving authority. Because she loves him, she will not allow him to pollute his mind or body while he is in her home. She will not allow him to mistreat others under her roof. She may require him to disassociate himself with certain friends. She might not be able to monitor all of his actions, but at least if he is caught in disobedience she can enforce consequences of a set standard. Once he moves out he can live by his own standards and face the consequences of his decisions.

Help your counselee to determine what substances (such as drugs, tobacco, or alcohol) can and cannot be brought into the house. Because her desire is to honor Christ in her home, she will want to prohibit occult paraphernalia and games. She can also set standards of speech and conduct. She should prohibit disrespectful or vulgar speech, but she should do so in a calm and controlled manner. She should say, "You may not speak to me with those words and in that manner," not, "How dare you speak to *me* in that way!" She needs to make it clear that repeated violence or illegal drug use may be reported to the police.

The guidelines—and the consequences of disobeying them—can be spelled out in writing with appropriate Scripture references. These can then be easily referred to as indisputable. Remind the mother that the issue is sin, not preference. If her child is breaking either God's laws or man's laws, he must be stopped.

3. Discipline the child for disobedience (Hebrews 12:6). A child of any age who is living at home must know there are consequences to disobedience. If the parents neglect their responsibility to discipline him, then God will discipline the rebel Himself. God's discipline, of course, may be much more severe than the parents'. God will use the established authorities to discipline a rebellious child. If the child ignores the authority of the parents, the church, or the state, then eventually God Himself will discipline him.

Point out to your counselee that discipline must be done with a purpose. Consequences should affect young people in a way that shows them that there are natural consequences to their behavior. The punishment should fit the crime and have a remedial effect. If he is being irresponsible with the car, driving privileges can be revoked. If she is not coming in on time, curfew can be shortened. If he is negatively affected by television or music, his listening and viewing can be monitored. If she is tempted by being with certain people at certain times, her activities with those friends can be restricted. If his actions have caused monetary consequences, he must be responsible to make restitution. I do not recommend indiscriminate grounding for all misbehavior, especially if it includes exclusion from activities that would be spiritually beneficial. Children become hardened and bitter when they do not see the correlation between their sinful behavior and the consequences.

There are times when a mother must go against her natural instinct to protect her child and allow the natural consequences of his actions to ensue without interference. In answer to prayer, God often allows harsh consequences to follow sin. There is not to be peace at any price. Susan and Bill may need to call the police when they find the marijuana in their son's room. Of course, this is assuming that Brent has previously been warned that this will be the consequence of this kind of behavior. One of the consequences may be that Brent is put on probation for a period of time. This shame to the parents and to the child is necessary as a deterrent. Brent needs to see what the inside of a prison cell is like. He needs the stern warning that this is where he is headed unless he changes.

Once it is determined that a situation calls for discipline, the parents must commit to carrying it out in a godly manner. Confrontation must take place in the spirit of gentleness (Galatians 6:1). If discipline is administered in anger, it takes the focus off of the young person's offense onto the fault of the parents. If they blow up, they are giving the devil a foothold (Ephesians 4:26-27, *see also* James 1:19-20). Firmness and sinful anger are two different things. The parents should not be afraid to show the grief that their young person's actions are causing them. They'll want to explain to their child that he has hurt them and grieved God by his actions. They have no reason to hide their tears; this will let their child know they are longing for his repentance and stand ready to forgive.

Is there a time for grace? Is it ever legitimate for parents to avoid bringing down punishment for every infraction of their guidelines? Yes; God gave the church at Thyatira time to repent (Revelation 2:21). He waits patiently for people to come to Him in repentance (Romans 2:4; 2 Peter 3:9). In certain cases, the parents can explain to their child that his actions merit punishment but they believe that he can learn his lesson without consequences in addition to those he has already suffered. But they should keep in mind that if there is a repeated removal of the consequences to sinful behavior, the young person will not change. Consistency is important. As noted previously, God deals with rebellion very severely.

A time may come when the parents have to put their son or daughter out of the home because he or she is not submitting to their authority and is living in total rebellion. This is especially true if there are other younger children who may be harmed or influenced for evil. In most states the parents are legally responsible to care for the needs of their child until he turns 18. If he is 18 or over, he can be told that since he has chosen the path of rebellion, he is not welcome at home any longer. He will have to find another place to live and will have to support himself. The parents can tell him they will no longer be able to support him in his particular lifestyle. In that case, the choice is clear-cut—the way of rebellion, or the way of submission. If the child chooses to leave, the warning should be given from God's Word, "the way of the treacherous [or transgressor] is hard" (Proverbs 13:15). It won't be easy. If he is God's child, he will receive discipline. If your child is not a believer, God's wrath rests upon him (John 3:36; Ephesians 2:3). For the parents, this estrangement may cause much heartache. They need to have objective support from God's Word and wise counselors that they have taken the right course of action. They will be able to fall back on this assurance when doubts arise. Most importantly, remind your counselee to *not* make the decision to ask a child to leave in the heat of an argument. She and her husband need to make the decision wisely, after committing the matter to prayer and seeking godly counsel.

4. Seek Godly Counsel (Proverbs 11:14; Romans 15:14). Let your counselee know that her problem is not too big for the church to handle. If her son or daughter is into drugs or alcohol, Alcoholics Anonymous or Narcotics Anonymous is not the answer. This is a spiritual problem. She will probably say that these problems are too big for her and her husband to handle alone. She is right, and you can tell her that is why God put all of us in a body. If she hasn't had success in getting her child to lay aside his sin, then she should seek help. She can look to the pastor, the youth pastor, her brothers or sisters in Christ, or biblical counselors as good sources of godly wisdom. She may also want to seek out a wise woman in her church who can advise her in this time. In addition, her teenager may need some long-term discipleship with someone in the church who is maturing in Christ. He needs to see that it is possible and necessary to put on godly behavior to break the life-dominating sins of lust or physical self-indulgence. If he is unwilling to get help, then the teen can be told that seeing a godly counselor is a requirement if he wants to stay at home. If he is a member of the church, the parents and the church leaders may need to carry out church discipline as outlined in Matthew chapter 18.

5. Pray and Persevere (James 5:16).   Pray with your counselee that God would reveal her child's sin so it can be dealt with. God's Word says, "Be sure your sin will find you out" (Numbers 32:23). God has His ways of bringing to light a person's sins so he can be helped.

Encourage your counselee to never stop praying and never lose hope. "Let us not lose heart in doing good, for in due time we shall reap if we do not grow weary" (Galatians 6:9). God loves to answer our prayers as we seek Him. God is glorified as we bring our needs before Him and trust Him to answer our prayers according to His will. Because God causes all things to work together for good, it is with confidence that we can say, "Weeping may endure for the night, but a shout of joy comes in the morning" (Psalms 30:5).

Comfort your counselee by reminding her that tribulation brings perseverance (Romans 5:3). God treasures the development of perseverance in the lives of His children. Does she want to grow, or would she rather remain weak and immature in faith? God honors perseverance. He blessed Job's life in the end because Job remained faithful through the severe trials that he faced. Peter tells us the reason that we can rejoice in trials: ". . . that the proof of your faith, being more precious than gold which is perishable, even though tested by fire, may be found to result in praise and glory and honor at the revelation of Jesus Christ" (1 Peter 1:7).

Did the father of the prodigal son give up and stop loving his son when he went into the far country and lived in sin? No! He waited patiently and expectantly. He did not frantically pace back and forth. When the rebel son came to his senses and returned in penitence, the father ran to embrace his son and showered him with compassion. What rejoicing followed! The father killed the fattened calf and had a party with music and dancing (Luke 15:11-32).

Have your counselee place her son or daughter in God's hands. Sing this song of praise and dedication, "Father, I Adore You,"[10] as I have often done, to the Lord. Fill in the name of your beloved rebel as you lay him or her before the triune God, whose glory you seek. Wait patiently but expectantly!

Recommended Resources

Ruth Bell Graham, *Prodigals and Those Who Love Them*
Bibliography
Jay E. Adams, *Christ and Your Problems*, Phillipsburg, NJ: Presbyterian & Reformed, 1971.
_____, *Christian Living in the Home,* Phillipsburg, NJ: Presbyterian & Reformed, 1972.
_____, *From Forgiven to Forgiving,* Wheaton, IL: Victor Books, 1989.
_____, *Ready to Restore*, Phillipsburg, NJ: Presbyterian & Reformed, 1981
_____, *The War Within,* Eugene, OR: Harvest House, 1989.
Ron Alchin. *Ripening Sonship: A Wise Father's Counsel to His Son,* Reminder Printing, (708) 398-3529.
Henry Brandt & Kerry Skinner. *The Word for the Wise,* Nashville, TN: Broadman & Holman, 1995.
John Broger. *Self-Confrontation—Biblical Counseling Training Program*, Biblical Counseling Foundation, P.O. Box 925, Rancho Mirage, CA 92270, 1991.
Ruth Bell Graham, *Prodigals and Those Who Love Them*, Colorado Springs: Focus on the Family, 1993.
Franklin Graham, *Rebel with a Cause,* Nashville, TN: Thomas Nelson, 1995.
Tim and Beverly La Haye, *Against the Tide*, Portland, OR: Multnomah Press, 1993.
Wayne Mack, *Strengthening Your Marriage*, Phillipsburg, NJ: Presbyterian & Reformed, 1977.
Bob Phillips, *What to Do Until the Psychiatrist Comes,* Eugene, OR: Harvest House, 1995.
Lou Priolo, *How to Help Angry Kids,* S.E.L.F. Publications, 220 Wall Street, Alabama City, AL, 35904, 1996.
Bruce Ray, *Withhold Not Correction,* Phillipsburg, NJ: Presbyterian & Reformed, 1978.
Robert Savage, *Pocket Prayers,* Wheaton, IL: Tyndale House, 1982.
Tedd Tripp, *Shepherding a Child's Heart,* Wapwallopen, PA: Shepherd Press, 1995.

CHAPTER 13

Counseling Divorced Women and Single Moms

Diane A. Tyson, M.A.

Julie and Dee were sitting across from each other in Julie's counseling office. It was their first counseling session, and Dee was feeling a little foolish and more than a little nervous because she didn't really know what her problem was. "What brings you here for counseling today, Dee?" Julie asked. "Well, we were encouraged in our counseling internship class to consider counseling for ourselves as a step in training us to counsel others," Dee replied.

"Is there a problem you want to work on?" Julie asked.

"Ever since I started seminary, every class has highlighted some aspect of divorce," said Dee. "It has even come up in Hebrew class! I was divorced two years ago, and thought I had come to terms with it. But, my feelings have been so raw, I know the Lord wants to expose something I overlooked. I just don't know what it could be."

When Julie asked Dee what caused the divorce, Dee burst into tears. When she was finally able to speak, she told a sad tale of a faithful wife of 26 years rejected by her husband. "I've always believed it is unbiblical for a divorced person to be in a position of ministry. When my divorce occurred at the end of my first year of Bible College, I almost decided to quit school," Dee explained. "I sought godly counsel at the time, and the Lord seemed to be directing me to continue my education. But I feel so worthless, and I'm not really sure how to think about divorce. Not only that, I just can't understand why

God would punish a person for being divorced by never allowing them to remarry, even if that person didn't want the divorce in the first place!" Dee finished plaintively. Wisely, Julie gave Dee a Bible study on divorce as her first homework assignment.

God's Word on Marriage, Divorce, and Remarriage

What Is Marriage?

Contrary to what some people think today, marriage was not initiated by man; it was instituted by God in the Garden of Eden (Genesis 2–3). It is the foundational institution of all human society. Since God Himself instituted marriage and designed the rules and principles for entering into and maintaining this relationship, people cannot disregard or set aside His guidelines in favor of their own preferences. He is the one who judges whether marriage, divorce, or remarriage is sinful or righteous. Although some disagreement exists among Christians about the correct interpretation of God's directives about marriage, divorce, and remarriage, still, there are some very clear truths to which we must adhere. They must not be deliberately set aside or altered to suit our own purposes. Additionally, marriage is more than a venue for procreation, although procreation is a sub-purpose of marriage. Sexual relations do not establish a marriage, nor does adultery necessarily dissolve a marriage. The importance of this point will be demonstrated later.

Marriage is established by participation in a ceremony where the contractual elements of the marriage are placed on public record. In our day, public vows are taken and the God-ordained institutions of church and state usually recognize these vows as binding. "In biblical times, a marriage did not require approval and licensure by the state . . . contracts were drawn up and executed by the parties in concern with witnesses. . . ."[1] A truly biblical marriage always involves the making of covenantal vows and promises. These covenantal vows involve the leaving of one's home, the cleaving to one's spouse for life, and the weaving together of two separate lives into one, all for the glory of God. As Genesis 2:24-25 says, "For this cause a man shall leave his father and his mother, and shall cleave to his wife; and they shall become one flesh." This oneness and service is to model the relationship of Christ and His church to the world (Ephesians 5:22-32).

Resolving Conflicts and Learning to Forgive

A good marriage is a union or covenant between two sinners who have learned to forgive each other for the Lord's sake. We're all sinned against by others, and all of us sin against others. This is true for husbands and wives as well; conflict in close relationships is inevitable. But that doesn't mean we have to allow conflict to divide us. God, in His mercy and wisdom, has given us guidelines for resolving conflicts[2] (*see* Matthew 5:23-26; 18:15-17; Romans 12; Colossians 3; James 4:1-12).

God's ideal for married men and women is to stay together for life, growing in Christlikeness[3] and learning to resolve conflicts in a God-honoring manner. Unfortunately, most people enter into a marriage with no idea of how to solve conflicts, and when they arise (as they always do), divorce is sometimes the outcome. Indeed, many newly married Christians are shocked when their spouse sins against them, and unfortunately, many of these same people have not yet learned how to forgive. That the current divorce rate among Christians is about the same as that among non-Christians is a sad commentary on the lack of teaching about the seriousness of covenants and the inevitability of offenses. The number of divorces among believers might be drastically reduced if pastors and counselors spent more time teaching about the proper way to resolve conflicts.

What Is the Purpose of Divorce?

The whole purpose of divorce is to dissolve a marriage. By definition, it is a cutting, putting, or sending away. God hates divorce (Malachi 2:16) because it is always a result of sin and brings misery and destruction with it. Divorce was not God's plan for man, but as Jesus teaches, came about because of the hardness of man's sinful heart (Matthew 19:8).

Although God hates divorce, He recognizes and regulates it. Divorce terminates the marriage contract, as Deuteronomy 24:1-4 illustrates:

> *When a man takes a wife and marries her, and it happens that she finds no favor in his eyes. . .and he writes her a certificate of divorce and puts it in her hand and sends her out from his house, and she leaves his house and goes and becomes another man's wife, and if the latter husband turns against her and writes her a certificate of divorce and puts it in her hand and sends her out of his house, or if the latter husband dies who took her to be his wife,*

then her former husband who sent her away is not allowed to take her again to be his wife.

In this passage, God is not commending the practice of putting one's wife away because she "finds no favor in his eyes." Rather, he is regulating a practice that was already occurring in Israel. It's apparent that the woman in Deuteronomy 24:1-4 was not "still married in God's sight" to her first husband. She not only became another man's *wife*, but the Lord God refers to her first husband as her *former* husband. Jesus also made it plain that marriage could be destroyed when He cautioned people not to separate what God had joined together (Matthew 19:6; Mark 10:9). Just as marriage is a binding contract between two people, divorce is a breaking of the contract and is so recognized by God and His ordained authorities.

Divorce Is Not Necessarily Sinful

"I hate divorce," said God in Malachi 2:16. Since God hates divorce, and we know that He hates sin (Psalm 45:7), then it must follow that all divorce is sin, right? That's faulty logic. The Bible never says all divorce is sin. A good student of the Bible will not make the mistake of looking at only one passage of Scripture to determine biblical truth. The Scriptures comment on and interpret themselves, and must be considered as a whole.

In Deuteronomy 22:13-29 and 24:1-4, God *regulates* rather than *forbids* divorce. Since sin is repugnant to God, and Deuteronomy 25:16 says, "Everyone who acts unjustly is an abomination to the LORD your God," God wouldn't regulate divorce if it were always sinful. While Malachi 2:16 testifies that the Lord hates divorce, we must also keep in mind, Jeremiah 3:8, which says, "I [God] saw that for all the adulteries of faithless Israel, I had sent her away and given her a writ of divorce, yet her treacherous sister Judah did not fear; but she went and was a harlot also." Since God cannot sin, and since God divorced faithless Israel, it follows, therefore, that divorce *per se* is not sin.

The Cause of Divorce Is Sin

The God who created us and instituted marriage says that the only legitimate grounds for divorce are unrepentant, sexual adultery (Matthew 5:32; 19:9) and desertion by an unbeliever (1 Corinthians 7:15-16). When two Christians are married to each other, divorce is allowable, and is not sinful, on two grounds: 1) if a spouse has committed adultery and is unrepentant; and 2) for desertion if one spouse is declared an unbeliever through church discipline because he or she deserted the family. Divorce is allowable and is not sinful for a believer married to an unbeliever on two grounds as well: 1) if the unbeliever leaves (which is desertion); and 2) for unrepentant adultery.

In these allowable cases, sin is the root cause of the divorce, but divorce initiated by either of these two causes is not sinful itself. If a divorce was for reasons other than sexual adultery or desertion by an unbelieving spouse, it was a sinful divorce. Lust in a person's heart is *not* grounds for divorce. Although lust is sin, it is not the same as physical adultery.

What If a Divorce Was Sinful?

Even a sinful divorce can be forgiven. If the woman you are counseling was sinfully divorced before she became a Christian, her sin (including the divorce) is forgivable. This is confirmed in 1 Corinthians 6:9-11, as observed by Jay Adams:

> . . . *adulterers, fornicators, and homosexuals, as well as others with notorious records, are said to be "cleansed, washed, and sanctified." It seems well-established that once a believer was forgiven and had forsaken a sin, he was no longer considered a fornicator, a drunkard, etc. Why then should we continue to call the breaker of the covenant [of marriage] such?*[4]

If a woman is born again, there is no condemnation because of Christ (Romans 8:1). If she has confessed her sins, she has been cleansed (1 John 1:9). Whether she became a believer before, during, or after her divorce, God will forgive her when she prays for forgiveness out of a sincere, repentant heart. Divorce is not an unforgivable sin.

We are all people broken by sin. Only Christ's death and resurrection can mend us. None of us is innocent—not the married nor the single, not the divorced, separated, nor widowed, not the young nor old. David says, "I was brought forth in iniquity, and in sin my mother conceived me" (Psalm 51:5). Our hearts are deceitful above all things and desperately wicked (Jeremiah 17:9), and all our good deeds are like filthy rags (Isaiah 64:6).

If, as some have been taught, a person can be forgiven for divorce only if it happened *before* salvation, then Christ died in vain, and there is no such thing as salvation by grace and grace alone.

Must You Reconcile with Your Spouse?

The Bible clearly states that Christians are to seek reconciliation when a negative matter has affected a relationship:

> If therefore you are presenting your offering at the altar, and there remember that your brother has something against you, leave your offering there before the altar, and go your way; first be reconciled to your brother, and then come and present your offering (Matthew 5:23-24).

The Lord counsels us in Matthew 18:15, "If your brother sins, go and reprove him in private; if he listens to you, you have won your brother."

We are always responsible, as much as it depends on us, to be at peace with everyone around us (Romans 12:18). According to the whole counsel of God, then, we must be willing also to reconcile a broken marriage. For instance, if after a divorce the erring spouse truly repents and seeks reconciliation, then re-marriage is a preferable option (as long as neither former spouse has married another person in the interim). Remember, God reconciled with faithless Israel not because she begged Him, but at His initiation because of His great grace (Jeremiah 3:11-14). There was no "need" for God to seek reconciliation with Israel. But He loves perfectly, and set an example for us to follow. However, a believer may not remarry an unbelieving spouse unless the latter has repented and become a Christian (1 Corinthians 7:39).

Is Divorce Mandated When Lawful According to Scripture?

Even though God allows divorce for sexual sin, and we have Jesus' explicit words on the subject, divorce on the grounds of sexual sin cannot be understood to be a scriptural precept (command intended as a general rule of action), but instead a possible option. Remember that sexual relations do not constitute a marriage and adultery does not invalidate it. Even though adultery has a devastating affect on marriage, it does not nullify it. Because of the costly forgiveness we have received from our Lord, we can, and must, forgive repentant spouses who have sinned against us, even to the point of adultery. Hosea and Gomer's story in Hosea chapters 1-3 demonstrates how love and forgiveness *are* possible in such a circumstance.

First Corinthians 7:15 gives us the basis for legitimate divorce by an unbelieving spouse: "If the unbelieving one leaves, let him leave; the brother or sister is not under bondage in such cases, but God has called us to peace." This is not a scriptural precept for believers to divorce unbelieving spouses, but rather, God is giving permission for the believer to consent to the unbeliever's divorce action. That's because it is futile to try to hold unbelievers accountable to upholding scriptural principles. If a believing wife has done all she can to keep her marriage together and her unbelieving husband still desires to leave, she is not to fight against him, *but to live in peace.*[5]

We as counselors may feel it is loving to excuse a believing woman for initiating a divorce against her unbelieving, difficult-to-live-with husband, but we must be careful to hold up the "living and active" word of God as final authority in such situations. The believing spouse is free to consent to divorce *only* if the unbeliever initiates it. A believing wife must be careful not to do anything to try to force the situation. This is *not* to say that she can't initiate a divorce if the unbelieving husband is a repeat adulterer.

No scriptural precept or principle supports the idea that we can initiate divorce solely because we have been sinned against. Indeed, our Lord Jesus Christ taught at the end of the disciple's prayer, "If you forgive men for their transgressions, your heavenly Father will also forgive you. But if you do not forgive men, then your Father will not forgive your transgressions" (Matthew 6:14-15). The basis for our forgiveness of others is the grace of God in His forgiveness of us. We are demonstrating sinful hearts when we fail to forgive others, and blatant unforgiveness is evidence of not being saved. Paul reinforces to us the necessity of imitating Christ through demonstrating a forgiving spirit in Ephesians 4:31-32:

> *Let all bitterness and wrath and anger and clamor and slander be put away from you, along with all malice. And be kind to one another, tender-hearted, forgiving each other, just as God in Christ also has forgiven you.*

Remarriage Is Legitimate

Remarriage for widows is perfectly acceptable to God, as noted in Romans 7:3 and 1 Corinthians 7:8-9,39. First Timothy 5:14 encourages remarriage: "Therefore I *want* younger widows to get married" (emphasis added). Is it possible, then, that the Lord would approve a second marriage for a divorced woman? Let's review some of the biblical facts about marriage and divorce: 1) God instituted marriage (Genesis 2); 2) divorce is not necessarily sinful;

3) divorce always breaks a marriage; 4) God will forgive a sincerely repentant sinfully divorced person. In light of those principles, what does God have to say about remarriage after divorce, and why is there so much controversy?

The controversy surrounds Jesus' words on divorce in Matthew 5:32, 19:9, Mark 10:11-12, and Luke 16:18, where He issues warnings against committing adultery. Adams, however, points out that it is possible to remarry without committing adultery.[6] He says that the question, "Who may remarry?" is answered in this way: "All persons properly divorced may be remarried." By properly divorced he means those who are "released without obligation."[7]

Those who have been divorced according to the biblical provisions we have discussed are free and able to remarry. A woman who has been righteously divorced has no obligation to seek reconciliation with her former spouse and remarry him, although she may do so if he is repentant. If, however, a sinful divorce has occurred, a woman does have an obligation to seek reconciliation and remarriage if her former husband is a believer. Aside from these two obvious facts, the topic of remarriage after divorce is too lengthy for us to tackle here. I strongly urge you to search the Scriptures and investigate the whole counsel of God before adopting any position (Acts 17:11; 2 Timothy 2:15). Jay Adams' book *Marriage, Divorce, and Remarriage in the Bible* and John Murray's *Divorce* are helpful in this regard. In addition, it would be wise to counsel with godly advisors and talk with the elders of your church whenever you have a counselee who needs to make a decision related to these matters.

Almost all of the divorced women I have counseled do not know what God has to say about divorce. You'll want to establish a firm foundation for your counseling by starting with a careful examination of what Scripture says about marriage, divorce, and remarriage. Then you can determine what steps should be taken by the woman you are helping. Ultimately, your goal is for her to submit to God's guidelines.

HEART ISSUES

Emotions and Relationships

Let's begin our discussion of emotional and relational issues by listening to David, the psalmist:

> *Be gracious to me, O LORD, for I am in distress;*
> *My eye is wasted away from grief, my soul and my body also.*

For my life is spent with sorrow,
And my years with sighing;
My strength has failed because of my iniquity,
And my body has wasted away.
Because of all my adversaries, I have become a reproach,
Especially to my neighbors,
And an object of dread to my acquaintances;
Those who see me in the street flee from me.
I am forgotten as a dead man, out of mind,
I am like a broken vessel.
For I have heard the slander of many,
Terror is on every side;
While they took counsel together against me,
They schemed to take away my life.

Psalm 31:9-13

Written by David when he felt the deep need for God's protection, this psalm is a remarkable biblical characterization of the grief experienced by the woman who has gone through an unwanted divorce. It captures the essence of her experience in vivid word pictures.

"For I Am in Distress"   What does it mean to be a woman "in distress"? Imagine that you have been put under great mental—and perhaps even physical—stress or strain. Assume that intense emotional distress and deep sorrow are your constant companions. Imagine yourself in dangerous circumstances or in desperate need. Suppose you routinely experience suffering, misery, and agony. These are the afflictions of a woman "in distress."

Suffering divorced women will accept the distress and often become stoically indifferent to all emotion. Misery underscores the unhappiness that accompanies her loss. She may find in her misery that she has developed sinful behaviors or repellent characteristics such as a critical spirit, an angry attitude, or greed and immoral thoughts or behavior; or she may have become absolutely hopeless, engulfed by a dullness and total lack of energy or motivation. Sometimes in agony, the distress will seem too intense to be borne.

Yes, the divorced woman is a woman in distress: full of emotional turmoil and confusion, doubts and recriminations. One of my counselees, Dinah, vividly remembers that confusing time because she had to work hard to make even the simplest decisions. She was terrified because she believed she was almost totally incompetent and would never be able to survive on her own.

Do you see how our discussion of distress parallels the graphic description of the psalmist's anguish of body and mind? The divorced woman also experiences grief and sorrow, many tears, emptiness, and constant weariness. David's words speak of the connection between the physical pain and the emotional distress: "my soul and my body also. . . my strength has failed . . . my body has wasted away." Depression and anger are hinted at in the weariness and physical involvement, and are, indeed, quite prevalent in the divorced woman's experience.

"My Strength Has Failed Me Because of My Iniquity"   Psalm 31:10 reminds us that the *sin issues* of the divorced women's situation must also be addressed. Is there unconfessed sin in her life? Was her divorce biblically legitimate? Is she guilty of unforgiveness, bitterness, or vengeance?

These are essential considerations when we are endeavoring to restore a divorced woman to a right relationship with Jesus Christ. Unless we identify sin as sin, she may continue to walk in deception or confusion. Be sure to think through sin issues with the woman you counsel so you can help her learn how to identify sin and to distinguish between true guilt and false guilt.

However, before you confront a divorced woman's sin issues, remember the compassion, grace, and love the Lord shows you when He confronts your sins (*see* Matthew 7:1-5). Remember His grace, which makes it possible to stand before Him now, and His love, which is so poignantly exemplified in the parable of the lost son (Luke 15:11-32).

"I Have Become a Reproach"   Psalm 31:11-12 acknowledges disintegrating relationships. Does the divorced women have enemies—such as her ex-husband and in-laws? Do her neighbors ridicule her? Do her friends avoid and ignore her? Is there slanderous talk circulating about her?

When Bobbi's neighbor found Bobbi crying on the back porch, the neighbor said, "What do you want with a bum like him? Didn't you know he was running around on you for years? You're better off without him. I don't know what you're crying about!"

After Dinah's divorce, the couples in her former Sunday school class neglected to return telephone calls. The women literally turned their backs to her and walked in the opposite direction when she came toward them.

A friend of another counselee, Nettie, told her that the people at her husband's new church were saying that she locked her husband out of her house, refused all attempts at reconciliation, and refused to allow her poor husband to see his children. Although all the allegations were untrue, Nettie soon began to hear the same things at her own church. (Some of this slander could have been avoided if Nettie's church had been involved in the divorce proceedings and had kept good records of her lack of culpability in the break-up.)

A divorced woman may be bereft of personal relationships as well as church affiliation because of the divorce. For instance, Dinah's family had been very active in their local congregation, and all their socializing took place at church activities. Her church also took a strong stand against divorce for any reason. When her husband deserted her, she wanted to continue to worship there, but soon found it impossible. The shunning was obvious, even towards her children. She had to find a more nurturing environment for them.

Considering the brokenness that characterizes divorce, isn't it understandable that a woman would hesitate to reach out for counsel or friends? (*see* Psalm 31:12). Dinah expressed a typical response when she said, "I was embarrassed, and felt that since I was thrown away I must be a horrible wife and person. . . . "

Unless a divorced woman is a member of a Bible-believing, discipline-practicing church, she will probably end up being very confused. She won't know what to believe. She might be made to feel like a second-class citizen; those who once were her peers may make her feel very much out of place. After my own divorce, I made the wrong choice: I believed my *feelings* rather than the truth of God's Word. In following my feelings, I was walking in darkness and hopelessness. Since my feelings were constantly changing, I was tossed off course continually. I was getting nowhere fast. We can be grateful that God's truth never changes and is the only firm foundation upon which we can build our lives.

In addition to her own personal struggles, the single mom must be aware of her children's struggles in the area of relationships. How will she help them relate to their dad? How is she going to relate to all of them while emotional issues are roiling around inside of her?

Dinah worked hard at keeping herself together in front of the kids so they wouldn't be alarmed. She made excuses to them for their father. After they went to bed, she broke down from the weight of the responsibility of caring for them. Keeping her own anger in check over the emotional trauma the children were experiencing was very difficult. Unfortunately, some hurting single moms make no attempt to protect their children from their emotional turmoil and speak slanderously about the children's father.

"I Have Heard the Slander of Many"   Psalm 31:13 confronts the divorced woman's fear and confusion over her true identity; that is, who she is in God's eyes. There are Christians and churches who treat divorce as the unforgivable sin and refuse to have anything to do with a divorced person. She wonders: Are they right? Have I committed the unforgivable sin? Am I dead spiritually? In addition, she is left to wrestle with questions about her purpose in life. Does the failure of her marriage also render her useless to the Lord?

Many women believe that when they lose their marriage they lose their identity. Who is a woman once she is divorced? How should she define herself? Is she single and able to marry another, or is she eternally married in God's sight? Does she still have spiritual gifts? If so, is she able to use those gifts for God's glory? How, and where?

"They Schemed to Take Away My Life"   Even if the divorced woman is not in danger of losing her physical life (and she may well be), she is not in full control of many of the most important decisions of her life. Other people will force changes on her that she neither wants nor has the power to avoid. It's like driving a bumper car at the amusement park: She turns the steering wheel, but the car doesn't go where she wants it to. She's trying to steer through the situations in her life, but the steering wheel seems disconnected from the car! Frequently a divorced woman is not accepted in her church and is unable to continue to socialize with people because they have ostracized her. Sometimes these people are friends who know her character, but even they are unwilling to examine their own prejudices. Her words have no effect on them. No one seems to care about what she has to say about herself or her situation. She is divorced; she is suspect.

A divorced woman often feels as if her life has been taken from her. Her losses can include her closest friend and confidant, her sexual partner, her church, her home, her job, her ministry, her friends, her social status, her financial security, her dreams, her family, her direction, her sense of self, and life as she has known it. Fears of neglect, abuse, rape, or even murder may overwhelm her.

Nettie, a single mom, often thought she and her children were in a state of danger. She was fearful for her family's safety as well as their emotional well-being. All too frequently her ex-husband made threats, trying to intimidate her into giving in to his demands. She was often afraid to ask for help whether from the local police department, family, or church friends. She believed the problems were really her fault, and she felt that reporting the threats would increase the likelihood of her losing her children. Not until Nettie came to understand the difference between true and false guilt was she able to respond to her situation wisely and with confidence.

When Dinah's husband ordered her out of their home, it was her first time completely on her own. She was terrified. She had no financial resources and three very young children. Where would she go? How would she be able to provide for them? She felt vulnerable and unprotected. Three years later, she is able to attest to the Lord's faithfulness in supplying all their needs.

Even though Bobbi had held responsible positions in the workforce before her marriage and was an experienced decision-maker, money concerns were her constant companion. When one of her children came home from school with the news that she needed a couple of dollars for a party the next day, Bobbi sometimes had to call the teacher to explain that she didn't have even that much to spare. She tried to avoid letting people know just how desperate her financial situation was, but in time she found that people were willing to help when they knew there was a need. The Lord refined Bobbi through her times of need and taught her to trust Him. She also learned that being vulnerable and honest kept her from looking for approval and acceptance outside of Christ. Bobbi realized that her reluctance to ask for help came from her deep fear of rejection. As she focused on the character of Jesus Christ and God's plan for her life, she was humbled and grateful, and no longer felt the need to protect herself from the possible rejection of others.

Identity Issues

Let's return to Dee and Julie, whom we met at the beginning of the chapter. As Julie continued to counsel Dee, Dee discovered that she had an unbiblical view of herself. She saw herself primarily as a divorcee and was allowing her past to define her identity rather than Christ. She wanted to be a wife more than anything in the world; that spelled s-u-c-c-e-s-s to her. She believed that she and God had a covenant still intact and that as long as she was faithful, she was still married in God's sight. Since divorce *always* nullifies a marriage, she was refusing the truth. It was too distressing, too humiliating. Besides, if she wasn't a wife, who was she? By insisting upon seeing herself as a wife, she was 1) denying her true identity in Christ; 2) rebelling against God by refusing to walk in the truth; and 3) putting marriage first in her life before all else.

Dee's unbelief was most obvious when she believed her feelings of being un-forgiven rather than believing what Scripture says about God's forgiveness. Pride and idolatry of self—elevating her feelings, intellect, plans, and desires above God and His truth—were evident when she gave in to self-pity and played the martyr. Dee's marriage had failed, and she was angry at God for not restoring it. After all, she'd worked so hard and prayed for so many years. Pride was evident in the shame that she felt. It was only as Dee became aware of her own personal sin, repented of it, prayed for a renewed mind, and put on thankfulness and a servant's heart that her life began to change in wonderful ways.

Now That I'm Divorced, What About My Ministry? Although many Christians desire to be gracious and loving, they struggle with accepting divorce or a divorced person for fear of compromising the sanctity of mar-riage. Even in cases where the divorce is scripturally permissible, some Christians struggle. They say, "If a divorced person is put into a position of ministry, aren't we putting our stamp of approval on divorce? Wouldn't that be inviting other people to consider divorce as an option for troubled marriages?"

Church leaders, such as pastors and elders, are responsible for deciding the fit-ness for service of those who desire to hold positions of influence in their local congregations. While all Christians, including those who are divorced, must love and serve others, the Bible gives guidelines for determining who is fit for certain ministries. For example, portions of 1 Timothy and Titus describe who is fit to serve as an overseer (elder) or deacon in the church. Titus 2 describes some of the characteristics that should be true of women in leadership.

So, biblical guidelines concerning ministry positions (biblically open to women) are to be applied the same to divorced women as for those who are not divorced. However, the circumstances surrounding the woman's divorce must be taken into consideration. On a case-by-case basis, church leaders should make a decision as to whether the woman is qualified for the service she desires to per-form. In those cases in which the woman was biblically justified in being divorced, she should be held to the same standards that any woman would have to meet.

If the divorce was not scripturally permissible and was due to continuing sin in the woman's life, then she should be considered ineligible for the ministry position. However, if the woman is truly repentant, the elders would need to determine her present fitness for the position.

We want to promote a decision about her fitness for ministry based on biblical standards. We want to avoid the two typical extremes: a legalistic view that says no divorced woman under any circumstances can hold any position in the church; or the other extreme, in which people are allowed to hold positions without careful consideration given to their spiritual fitness for such a position.

The idea that a woman's ability to preserve a marriage automatically makes her fit for service in the church is fallacious. We need to ask, "What sort of wife is she?" A faithful, humble, divorced woman may be better qualified spiritually to teach that junior high girls' Sunday school class than a married woman who quarrels constantly with her husband, is careless about training her children, and runs roughshod over the members of the church committee she leads.

There are many divorced women who desired very much to preserve their marriages for the Lord's and their children's sake, yet found themselves divorced by a wayward husband. These women are deeply hurt and discouraged when they are told (by word or action) that they are not fit to serve in Christ's church simply because they are divorced. These women need to be encouraged to use their spiritual gifts to the serve church.

If you are counseling a divorced woman who is unjustly being shut out of ministry at her church, caution her to trust the Lord's leading and timing. She should cultivate a submissive attitude and not give way to grumbling or complaining. Remind her that God does not need our service. Serving in the church is a Christian privilege, not a right. She must not demand an opportunity to minister her gifts. She can present her situation to the church leadership and respectfully ask them to help her understand how they view her role in the church. She needs to trust the Holy Spirit to work in her church leaders as they counsel her, and "be subject to [them] in the fear of Christ" (Ephesians 5:21).

God is never glorified when we take matters into our own hands and try to engineer outcomes to our liking. Counsel her to wait on the Lord and be patient with those in authority over her. Even if she is unjustly shut out of a formal ministry position, she can still serve her brothers and sisters in the Lord in other ways. "So then let us pursue the things which make for peace and the building up of one another" (Romans 14:19).

When we consider a divorced person's role in the church, we desperately need for God to open our minds to understand grace. In accepting divorced women, then, we are not compromising God's principles. Divorce is grievous and hurtful, but it is not always sinful. When it is sinful, it is forgivable.

By saying this I do not in any way intend to diminish our need to obey God and serve Him with faithfulness. When we are walking in unrepentant sin (whatever that sin may be), then we should be excluded from ministry. But if we have truly repented of sin (whatever that sin may be), God can use us for His glory. The ways He chooses to do this will, of course, be consistent with His Word.

Fitting the Pieces Together Again

Beginning by Renewing the Mind

Whether a woman initiated her divorce or was the passive recipient of a divorce decree, the counselor's job is to help her examine the broken pieces of her life and fit them together so she can faithfully serve God. God's Word speaks primarily to her mind, which can be renewed as she studies the Word and obeys it through the power of the Holy Spirit. She must follow the instructions found in Romans 12:2-3 (NIV):

> Do not conform any longer to the pattern of this world, but be transformed by the renewing of your mind. Then you will be able to test and approve what God's will is—his good, pleasing and perfect will. For by the grace given to me I say to every one of you: Do not think of yourself more highly than you ought, but rather think of yourself with sober judgment, in accordance with the measure of faith God has given you.

Let's consider four actions that are involved in renewing the mind; you'll want to share these principles with your counselees:

1. Decide to believe the Word. The counselee's situation at this moment comes directly from the hand of God for her (ultimate) good and for His eternal glory, no matter how upsetting or inexplicable it is (Romans 8:28-29). Share with your counselee the Lord's declaration in Isaiah 55:8 "My thoughts are not your thoughts, neither are your ways my ways"(NIV). This means she must choose to believe God and repent of any unbelief or disobedience. Repent means "to turn around, to change." The following scriptures on repentance and humility should help her to understand the importance of this step: Psalm 147:3; Isaiah 57:15; 61:1; Luke 13:1-5; 15:11-32; Romans 12:3,10,16; 2 Corinthians 7:9-11; James 4:6-10.

2. Know God's promises and assurances to His children. Read through each of the following scripture passages and write down the essence of what it says: Psalm 138:7-8; Isaiah 43:7; Romans 8:28-29; 2 Corinthians 3:18;

Ephesians 4:24; Philippians 1:6; 3:21; Colossians 3:10; 2 Timothy 1:7; 2 Peter 1:4; and 1 John 3:1-3. For example, Psalm 138:7-8 shows that the Lord has a plan for your counselee's life, regardless of her current difficulties, and He will see that plan through to completion.

As she decides to trust God and believe His Word, she will learn to wholeheartedly embrace God's will for her. Pray that she will be uplifted and fulfilled by doing God's will, like Jesus in John 4:34: "My food is to do the will of Him who sent Me, and to accomplish His work." Remind her that God intends our sufferings as gifts to make us more like Christ (Romans 8:17,28-29; Philippians 1:29). Since that is true, she can praise God and give thanks in *all* circumstances (Philippians 4:6; 1 Thessalonians 5:19). She will then know a peace that passes all understanding (*see* Philippians 4:7).

3. Replace wrong (sinful) thoughts with godly thoughts (2 Corinthians 10:3-5).

   - Have your counselee examine her responses to the verses listed in point #2 above and identify the discrepancies between what she is believing and what God has said.
   - Have her find a particularly meaningful verse and begin to commit it to memory.
   - Have her write the opening statement in point #1 on an index card to remind herself during the day of the truth of her situation. Have her keep it in her purse or pocket, or place it strategically in areas where she is likely to see throughout the day (i.e., over the kitchen sink; on the dashboard of her car; on the bathroom mirror; in her top desk drawer at work).

4. Make the Bible the only standard of truth for faith and action. Encourage your counselee to make God's Word the measurement of what is true and what is false, right and wrong, good and bad, wise and unwise. She should act on what she knows to be true and right. Remind her to be thankful no matter how she feels. She can pour her heart out to God like the psalmists did. But don't let her merely "follow your heart"—don't let her move forward in life based on her feelings. She needs to follow Jesus by being obedient to His Word (*see* Hebrews 12:2; 1 Peter 2:21).

   A study of the many passages related to suffering (such as Romans 8:17 and Philippians 3:10-11) invites us to persevere through the hard times so we can become like Christ and to learn more about God the Father. Matthew 5:3-12 defines happiness and tells us how it is obtained.[8]

As your counselee perseveres in doing what is right, her feelings will eventually catch up to the truth and will be appropriate to the reality of her situation. Therefore, have your counselee . . .

- Acknowledge her feelings to herself and to God. Have her read some of Psalms [chapters 6, 7, 13, 25, 51–57, and 140–143 are good to start with]; Isaiah 53; Hebrews 2:3, 9-18; and 4:14-16. These verses emphasize the fact that God cares about how she feels and wants her to learn to come to Him for and with everything. He also wants her to trust, believe, and obey His Word.
- Be encouraged by God's Word on the importance of obedience, and *be obedient!* Have your counselee read Deuteronomy 28; Matthew 19:17; Luke 13:6-9; John 13:17; 14:15–15:17; Romans 12:9-21; Philippians 2:1-18; and Colossians 3:12-17.
- Be encouraged by God's Word on the importance of thankfulness, and *be thankful!* Have her read Philippians 4:4-9; 1 Thessalonians 5:15-22.
- Have your counselee repeat the actions listed in point #3 (on the previous page) whenever she is thinking or believing something God has not said.

Remind your counselee: *This is a process!* Change does not happen overnight. It is vital to persist and persevere.

As your counselee's mind is renewed, she will acquire God's perspective on her situation. This will lead her into a grateful acceptance of His plan for her life and will dispel the confusion and emotional turmoil from her daily existence. This strategy will help her to focus on the Lord rather than on her disturbing emotions. When she makes decisions according to how she feels, she in essence is saying: "God cannot be trusted. I do not believe Him. I believe my feelings. They are my standard of truth, not God's Word. I will come to God on my own terms. His terms are too harsh, too hard, too humiliating. There is an easier way, a better way, a more satisfying way than the one God has provided."

The truth is, "There is a way that looks harmless enough; look again—it leads straight to hell" (Proverbs 16:25, *The Message*). Your counselee needs to believe the Word of God and Jesus Christ, who said, "I am the road, also the truth, also the life. No one gets to the Father apart from Me. I am the bread of life"(John 14:6, *The Message*), and "The person who aligns with Me hungers no more and thirsts no more, ever" (John 6:35, *The Message*).

Gaining Strength by Acknowledging Sin

With your counselee, go back and review the sin issues surrounding biblical and sinful divorce. Does she need to seek forgiveness from her former husband? If so, she should not resist being obedient by justifying her position in her mind.

Recognizing true guilt brings tremendous relief to the person who has been broken by divorce. Sin has a remedy. The sinner can confess her sins to God and know that she is forgiven and totally cleansed (1 John 1:9)! In Lamentations 2:14 the false prophets refused to expose the Israelites' sin, thus keeping them in captivity. If the prophets had been faithful to expose the sins of the people, the Israelites would have had the opportunity to confess and repent and thereby be restored from the captivity.

It is not truly kind to avoid mentioning a woman's sin as you counsel her. Don't condemn her, but do help her live a pure life before the holy and just Judge of the universe.

Drawing Closer to God by Building Godly Relationships

Our relationship to God is the central relationship in all of life; any distortion in our understanding of this relationship impacts how we relate to everyone else in our world. Many Christians do not have a thoroughly biblical understanding of God, and therefore, they have no idea of what it means to "image" Him. Consequently, they cannot possibly know who they are. This leads to believing and acting upon lies about themselves and about God.[9]

As your counselee develops a biblical relationship with the Lord, she will see her other relationships begin to change. Here are some specific actions she can take to improve her relationships:

1. Find a mature Christian woman to disciple her and share in a relationship of mutual accountability and follow through with your commitments to each other (Matthew 18:18-20; Titus 2:3-5).
2. Study David's and Jonathan's friendship (1 Samuel 18-20; 2 Samuel 9); study Paul, Philemon, and Onesimus. What can she learn from these friendships?
3. Learn to be a peace*maker* rather than simply a peace*keeper*. How? Read *The Peacemaker* by Ken Sande and work through the questions at the end of each chapter.

4. Study Ephesians 4:17–6:9 and put into practice what she learns.
5. Become a forgiver. Remind her to trust God, the righteous Judge, to do the right thing at the right time concerning those who have sinned against her (*see* Luke 18:7-8; Romans 12:17-19). By granting forgiveness, she promises never to talk again about the forgiven sin to the person who sinned against her, never to talk about it to anyone else, and never to dwell on it herself.
6. Decide to concentrate in a godly way on her friendships with other women, especially while she is learning about relationships.
7. Learn how she contributed to the broken relationship with her spouse.
8. Take all necessary biblical steps to address her sins.
9. Learn to praise the Lord. Praise develops her relationship with Him and her knowledge of Him. It keeps her focus where it belongs.
10. Read *31 Days of Praise* by Ruth Myers.[10]

As your counselee commits herself to improving her relationships, have her consider these wise words from J.I. Packer:

> It is only as one gives oneself in human relationships, in the home, in friendships, with neighbors, as members of Christian groups and teams—in relationships that sometimes go right and sometimes go wrong, as all our relationships do—that experiential knowledge of God becomes real and deep. . . . Only the Christian sharer, who risks being hurt in order to take and give the maximum in fellowship and who sometimes does get hurt as a result, ever knows much of God Himself in experiential terms. [11]

Godly relationships give us a glimpse of relationship in the Trinity—Father, Son, and Holy Spirit. Thus we learn to know God better through them.

Persevering by Being Content as a Single . . . Again

The transition into singleness is very often fraught with rebellion, anger, and fear. Sexual purity becomes a cogent issue. Also, many divorced women are single moms—custodial parents—which can add another dimension to their stress. Life as they knew it has been drastically altered. In many ways, it is as though they have been transported from all that is familiar and comforting, and deposited in a foreign land where they don't know the language or the customs.

While a divorced woman might not have much control over her circumstances, she is free to choose how she will respond to them. For example, consider how Paul and Silas responded to being jailed in Philippi (Acts 16:16-28). They didn't let their imprisonment drive them to despair.

In some cases, a divorced woman's lifestyle may not change much from how she lived when she was married. However, she will most likely make changes in how she thinks and plans for the everyday, mundane events in her life. Becoming single again is an exhausting transition that can make her grief more poignant every time she needs to adjust her thinking. She may get discouraged and want to give up. You must gently encourage her to do the difficult things, to make the hard decisions. You may need to lovingly remind her often that a believer's goal in *pressing on*—for being persistent and persevering—is to bring glory to God by becoming like Christ. You will want to encourage her that her motivation must come from Christ's love for her and her love for Christ (*see* 2 Corinthians 5:14-15). If she perseveres, she will one day hear her precious Lord say, "Well done, good and faithful servant!" (Matthew 25:21,23 NIV). Direct her to Hebrews 12:1-3, and give her this exhortation:

> . . . *keep [your] eyes on Jesus, who both began and finished this race we're in. Study how He did it. Because He never lost sight of where he was headed— that exhilarating finish in and with God—He could put up with anything along the way: cross, shame, whatever. And now He's* there, *in the place of honor, right alongside God. When you find yourselves flagging in your faith, go over that story again, item by item, that long litany of hostility He plowed through.* That *will shoot adrenaline into your souls!*[12]

Back in the days when I struggled with my newly acquired singleness, I realized that I hated being single and kept telling the Lord that I did not have the gift of singleness. Then I happened to hear Elisabeth Elliot contend on her radio program that if someone is single, God has indeed given that person the gift of singleness . . . for today. What a freeing—and humbling—truth! Praise God, He's given us all we need to live in sexual purity (2 Peter 1:3). The Holy Spirit can produce self-control in us (Galatians 5:22-23) and give us the power to do what He requires (Romans 8:11; 1 Corinthians 10:13).

Our sexuality, however, is not to be confused with sexual expression. We are sexual beings because God created us as such. Being celibate in no way neuters or diminishes womanhood. All of us can rejoice in God's good design in creation, the beauty of His gift of sex, and the wisdom of His restrictions on the use of that gift. Most of all, we can decide to honor God by presenting our bodies "a living and holy sacrifice, acceptable to God which, is [our] spiritual service of worship" (Romans 12:1).

Becoming Faithful by Submitting to God

How does a divorced woman go about reshaping a life? *One step at a time.* The single most important move she can make is to submit herself totally to the Lord and His plans for her life. She needs to embrace her life as He designed it; she must die to self—her own plans, desires, methods, and so on—and live for Christ (John 12:24-26; Galatians 5:24; Philippians 1:21).

Will she trust Him? Does she believe that God is in this? Does she believe that His plans are for her welfare, to give her a future and a hope (Jeremiah 29:11-14)? Or does she think that her ideas and plans for her life are the only acceptable ones?

Isaiah 29:16; 45:9-11; 64:8; Jeremiah 18:1-10; and Romans 9:21 encourage us to think correctly about God, our "Potter," and our position as "the clay." We must be completely surrendered to the Potter, accepting His workmanship in our lives. Remember, the Lord is *committed* to conforming us, His children, to the image of Christ—with or without our cooperation—because He is a faithful God. As we meditate on the truth that God is the Potter, recalling Isaiah 55:9-11 may give us a better perspective of who we are and who God is: "As the heavens are higher than the earth, so are my ways higher than your ways, and my thoughts than your thoughts" (NIV).

God's ways do seem strange to us at times. They are so different from our ways! We need to depend on the Lord and we need to do our part, as clearly portrayed in Philippians 2:12-13: Though we are to "work out" our own salvation, God is working in us not only to do His will, but also to give us the desire to do His will. God is at our side; we're not left on our own. What more could we possibly need?

Faithfully yielding ourselves to the heavenly Potter will cause us to begin a process in which virtually every piece of our lives will need to be examined. This may require not only adding new pieces, but reshaping or disposing of old ones, with these questions in mind:

- What are my overall responsibilities and long-term goals?
- Will this time in my life help me accomplish them?
- What are my responsibilities concerning this time in my life?
- Am I thinking biblically about where I am in life now?
- Does what I am planning bring glory to God?

Dealing with Loneliness by Remembering God's Promises

God has promised that He will always be with us (Matthew 28:20), that He will *never* leave us nor forsake us (Hebrews 13:5). He is true to His Word.

Regardless of how we *feel,* we must walk in the Spirit, not in the flesh; that is, we must act on the truth rather than on our feelings.

Oftentimes we forget that a woman can be more lonely married than single. Being alone does not necessarily mean we will feel lonely. While God created us for relationship, Romans 12 helps us in addressing situations that can lead to loneliness. Verses 10-13 are the key:

> *Be devoted to one another in brotherly love; give preference to one another in honor; not lagging behind in diligence, fervent in spirit, serving the Lord; rejoicing in hope, preserving in tribulation, devoted to prayer, contributing to the needs of the saints, practicing hospitality.*

If a divorced woman applies these precepts to her life, she will be so involved in faithfully serving others she will not have time to focus on herself. Tell her that when those lonely feelings do visit that she can tell God about them because He cares. Suggest that she follow her prayer with praise for Him. She'll be surprised how quickly her perspective changes!

Remaining Sane by Establishing Priorities

Whereas a married woman might have some help with the workload around the home, a divorced woman suddenly finds herself having to do it all: bill-paying, decision-making, cooking, shopping, and cleaning. Even the maintenance and inspection of the house, car, and appliances is now up to her. And, if she's a mom, it's possible that all the child care falls on her as well. For example, prior to my divorce, even though I was accustomed to being alone with my sons, their dad was usually home at dinnertime. He was "in charge" of the discipline whenever he was present. It took several weeks and the pointed remarks of several friends until I realized that I had to be in charge at dinnertime!

In our culture, as well as in the church, women are encouraged to be involved in causes, activities, and organizations. We're exhorted by television messages to "be all you can be." And our churches may clamor for our help, especially with ministry to children.

In light of the increased demands at home and possibly elsewhere, a divorced woman must choose wisely and prioritize. She may have to learn to be satisfied with "good enough." She shouldn't be afraid to say, "Not this week" when she must. When she's exhausted by her workload, she needs to put off what can't be done today. She may have to give up choir for a year or so. In helping her to know when to say yes, remind her that in Luke 10:38-42, Jesus praised Mary for choosing the "good part" by sitting at His feet. Mary understood on that occasion what was high-priority. If your counselee needs help in deciding about her priorities, invite her to seek counsel from you and other godly women. A good rule of thumb for her is, "When in doubt, don't." Encourage her to say yes to one less thing than she thinks she can do. She may need to lower her expectations, at least temporarily, of what she can do in one day, one week, one month.

The single mom must be willing to shelve her own activities while her children are young. Right now, her children come first. Remember this assurance in Ecclesiastes 3:1: "There is an appointed time for everything. And there is a time for every event under heaven." There will be time for other ministries in the future; her ministry now is her children. No more important job exists than for her to bring up her children in the "discipline and instruction of the Lord" (Ephesians 6:4). She will never regret the time she spends with her children. It is all too short. I know; I've been there.

Comfort for a Single Mom's Fears

The single mom is usually most fearful about how she will support her family financially, as well as the possibility of losing custody of her children. The legal battles can become vicious. At the very least they are emotionally draining, costly, and stressful. Will her former husband bring the children home when he is supposed to, or will he flaunt the agreement? How long should she wait before notifying the authorities? There are many other worries and fears faced by a single mom; the list could go on and on.

All these pressing issues can leave a single mom feeling anxious, weary, and hopeless. Where can she go with the stress? At the risk of seeming trite or simplistic, you as her counselor need to encourage her to go to the Lord.

The suggestions I'm offering here are valid for all single moms. I cannot, however, address every situation because they are all so different. But God can. Consider David's plan in Psalm 31:1-5:

In Thee, O LORD, I have taken refuge; let me never be ashamed; in Thy righteousness deliver me. Incline Thine ear to me, rescue me quickly; be Thou to me a rock of strength, a stronghold to save me. For Thou art my rock and my fortress; for Thy name's sake Thou wilt lead me and guide me. Thou wilt pull me out of the net which they have secretly laid for me; for

Thou art my strength. Into Thy hand I commit my spirit; Thou has ransomed me, O LORD, God of truth (emphasis added).

David looked to the Lord for wisdom, protection, strength, and guidance. And He received it. Why? He tells us: "For Thy name's sake." God knows about secret plans, dirty tricks, lying lips, and so on. For the glory of His name, He will deliver you, too. Sometimes He will take you into the midst of the battle, and sometimes He will leave you on the sidelines. But He will always be true to His word and His righteous character.

The Divorced Mom, Her Children, and Their Dad

"Why isn't Dad here anymore?" "Why did we have to move to this awful/ little/ugly place?" "Why don't you live with us anymore, Mom?"

How does a divorced mother answer her children's honest questions without turning them against their dad? And what should she do if she discovers her ex-husband is lying to the kids about her? How can she be honest yet kind, fair, and appropriate? Don't her children deserve to know the truth . . . the whole truth?

In the "best" of divorces (what an oxymoron!) there is at least sadness and grief. In most divorce situations, many deep and distressing emotions are evident. Is it appropriate for the mother to share these feelings with her kids? How can she keep from playing the "blame game" with her children? And when the desire for revenge kicks in, how can she resist the temptation to use the children as pawns or bargaining tools?

The question of all questions for a divorced woman, however, is this: What is my relationship to the father of my children now? The way she answers that question can have a profound effect on her children's relationship with their father (and with her).

Let's be more specific. A divorced woman's relationship with her ex-husband is that of "co-parent" to their children. She doesn't have to like him or pretend that they are friends. She must, however, love him as a neighbor (Matthew 5:43-46; Mark 12:31; *see* 1 Corinthians 13:4-8 for a definition of love). She must respect him for his role as the children's father. Encourage her to bless him, pray for him, and live at peace with him as much as it is possible for her to do so. She should never take revenge.[13]

If she practices God's precepts for relationship as described above, she will be able to protect her children from the brunt of her own distress. They will know when she is upset. She can tell them, when they ask, that she feels sad because of all the changes and she misses daddy (if she does). She should be careful about telling them she doesn't trust their dad. It may be wise, though, for her to give the children instructions about how to get in touch with her. She should also teach the children how and when to call 911, information, and other important sources of help.

She can let her children know she loves them by her hugs, words, facial expressions, and her use of time and money. She can teach them all she is learning about God—His love, protection, strength, faithfulness. This will demonstrate to them that they can trust God no matter what happens. As the children watch their mother's example of faithful dependence on God, they will learn that they can trust Him, too. If her children challenge her beliefs, she can respond by: 1) explaining why she holds those beliefs; 2) reading them the Scripture verses that encourage her; 3) telling them about God's work in her past; and 4) reminding them of how He has answered her prayers for them. If the children don't understand their mother's confidence, trust, or joy, she can calmly invite them to go to God with their questions; she can help them as they wrestle with establishing a robust and vital relationship with the sovereign and holy God.

As the mother lives out her faith, she should keep communicating with her children. She can share with them scriptural principles and verses about the situations she faces. They will then learn how she approaches her problems and see that God is involved in all her decisions. This will help the children to think more biblically about their own situations and decisions. The mother will want to be honest and humble with her children when they have witnessed her failures; she will want to confess and repent, and ask her children for forgiveness when appropriate. When they witness her confession of failure, they will understand that their mother has sinned. Remember, *repent* means "to change direction." The mother should let her children see her change. Nothing will demonstrate the power and beauty of the Gospel message more convincingly to them. They will find stability and strength in their mother's vulnerability with them. Remind her to "keep fervent in your love for one another, because love covers a multitude of sins" (1 Peter 4:8).

Making a Difference as a Counselor

As a counselor, ask the Lord to help you gain an understanding of the changes, emotions, and difficult situations a divorced woman must confront as she adjusts to being single again. Help her to think biblically about her situation. Help her to implement godly changes in her life. And encourage her to keep on loving the Lord enough to care about His precepts. Your love and care for her in these ways will make a real difference in her life.

Recommended Sources

Jay E. Adams, *Marriage, Divorce, and Remarriage in the Bible,* Phillipsburg, NJ: Presbyterian & Reformed, 1980.

Elisabeth Elliot, *Loneliness,* Nashville: Oliver Nelson Books, 1988.

Sinclair B. Ferguson, *Children of the Living God,* Colorado Springs: NavPress, 1987.

Susan Hunt, *Spiritual Mothering,* Wheaton, IL: Crossway Books, 1993.

Andrew Murray, *Absolute Surrender,* Fort Washington, PA: Christian Literature Crusade, 1978.

John Murray, *Divorce,* Grand Rapids: Baker Books, 1961.

J.I. Packer, *Knowing God,* Downers Grove, IL: InterVarsity Press, 1973.

Tedd Tripp, *Shepherding a Child's Heart,* Wapwallopen, PA: Shepherd Press, 1995.

CHAPTER 14

Counseling Women Abused as Children

Elyse Fitzpatrick, M.A.

Marcia first came to me because she had a problem with overeating. She was about 100 pounds overweight. Although she had gone to her physician and had tried many diets, she just couldn't seem to overcome her problem. She also seemed unhappy with the relationships in her life, particularly with her husband. As I sought to understand her problems and the issues she faced, I was touched by her suffering and sorrows. Marcia was a victim of child abuse. Her divorced mother, who had been promiscuous while Marcia was young, had married a man who was to become Marcia's stepfather and abuser. At first, she enjoyed her relationship with him as he flattered her with gifts—dolls and special favors—and she grew to trust him. He began touching and kissing her, and although she felt uncomfortable, he assured her this was a normal relationship for a daughter and stepfather "who really loved each other." This secret activity became more and more pronounced and Marcia, at age twelve, found herself functioning in the role of her mother. She was the caretaker. She was the lover. Her brother, Adam, was terribly abused by both her mother and stepfather—being beaten with belts and locked in closets. Although Marcia felt badly for him, she was confident she wouldn't have these same problems because she was "special." Nevertheless Marcia experienced a double tragedy: Her stepfather used and manipulated her while her mother, who should have protected her, turned a blind eye.

As time went on, Marcia and Adam found life more and more unbearable. They were not allowed to call anyone on the phone, go to friends' homes, or invite anyone over after school. Frequently they missed school because their parents needed them to stay home and care for things in the family business. If they failed to be compliant, both their mother and stepfather would punish them. Marcia's complaints about their situation earned her a three-month summer vacation in her room. During this time she was allowed visits only from her brother and stepfather. Marcia and Adam tried to discern how to please their parents. In humiliation, Marcia became a "doormat," increasingly seeking ways to comply with her parents. Because Adam was more angry, he gave up trying to please and developed a defiant and rebellious lifestyle. Marcia became increasingly aware that her physical relationship with her stepfather was very wrong. As she began to resist his advances, he became more and more violent, threatening to send her to Juvenile Hall if she resisted or told anyone about them. He frequently beat her brother to punish her for noncompliance. She could recall many times during her early and mid-teen years when she was raped. Daily she faced the probability of having to unwillingly acquiesce to her stepfather's perverted demands so she might purchase peace at any price. (To this day, Marcia's mother claims that she was unaware of the sexual abuse.)

Although she was not a Christian, she began to pray that "god" would come to the aid of her and her brother. It was during this time that the Lord opened Marcia's heart and gave her faith to believe. Marcia was 16. A Christian friend at school spoke to her about Jesus and Marcia began to experience a peace she had never known before.

She also knew that she had to escape her home situation. Soon, the Lord opened the door. Although Marcia had knowledge about sexual relationships that were beyond her years, she was extremely naive about the workings of the world. One afternoon, while watching television, she discovered she could make collect telephone calls. To ensure that her stepfather would not find out, she called the operator and asked if records were made of collect calls. Assured that she could make a call without her parents' knowledge, she found her birth father's phone number and called him. Pleading with him to keep their conversation secret, Marcia poured out her heart to him, describing the ghastly situation she and Adam were in and begging him to rescue her. He assured her that he would take care of her. She went to sleep that night, for the first time in many years, with hope for the future.

In school the following day she was called to the principal's office. There she found police officers waiting for her. They informed her that her mother and stepfather had accused her of lying and being incorrigible. They asked that she be kept in Juvenile Hall until she could be made a ward of the state or other arrangements could be made. Marcia, who had always tried to be a "good girl" in school, was led out of the principal's office in handcuffs. Crushed, despairing, and humiliated, her mind was filled with one haunting thought: Her stepfather had carried out his threat. She spent an entire month in Juvenile Hall, feeling like a criminal, while her mother, father, and stepfather fought over who was going to have the responsibility for this rebellious troublemaker.

She eventually went to live with her grandmother, who made it clear that she only took Marcia to get her out of "jail." Marcia was thankful for a short rest. Adam had been sent to another relative and she would not see him again for many years. Marcia was made to feel guilty for breaking up the family and for causing her mother trouble. Her grandmother never let an opportunity pass without reminding her that she had been the cause of this difficulty and of her mother's subsequent divorce. The truth became evident to Marcia—no one was going to believe her or rescue her.

As Marcia recounted this story to me, she made this astonishing statement, "Elyse, the abuse wasn't the worst thing that happened to me. It was being led away from school in handcuffs. That was the worst." Being betrayed and humiliated by her father, doubted and deserted by her mother, disgraced and mortified before her classmates, this was true abuse indeed.

Eventually Marcia married and gave birth to three children. Both she and her husband are Christians and are seeking to serve the Lord. Yet, she still struggles. From time to time she has sought counseling, but never found lasting victory.

What would you say to Marcia? If you have a history like hers, how do you perceive yourself, your relationships with your neighbor, and your relationship with God?

A Godly Response

As women who desire to love and serve others, we must be prepared to help women who have been abused. Although there is much disagreement about how many actual cases of child abuse there are. The U.S. Department of Health & Human Services states that there were 342,548 substantiated cases of physical and/or sexual abuse of children 18 or under in 1992. This number rose to 371,387 in 1992.[1] We can be certain there are many women who have experienced abuse. We need to be prepared to help them—with love, insight, and wisdom.

The Bible Speaks to the Weak and Oppressed

How can I discover what the Bible has to say about victims? The Bible uses terms such as "afflicted," "fatherless," "weak," "needy," "oppressed," "helpless," "broken-hearted" and "humble" to describe those who have been sinned against or who are, because of persistent difficult circumstances, worn out or strengthless. Since it is helpful to know that the Bible speaks[2] about people who have been sinned against in these ways, I've listed the terms with their definitions for you:

"Afflicted"—to be brow-beaten, depressed, oppressed, ravished (*see* Psalm 9:12)

"Fatherless"—to be lonely, bereaved, orphaned (*see* Psalm 82:3)

"Weak"—to be worn out, grieved, put to pain, strengthless (*see* Psalm 82:3-4)

"Oppressed"—to press, distress, afflict, crush, force to rage, be violent against, bruise, discourage (*see* Psalm 10:18)

"Helpless"—to be weak, thin, needy, poor (*see* Psalm 41:1)

"Brokenhearted"—to burst, break, crush, destroy, or quench the heart (*see* Psalm 34:18; 147:3)

"Humble"—to humiliate, depress, bring low, be made low (this word is often used with a sexual connotation: "He humbled her" i.e., "He forced himself upon her") (*see* Deuteronomy 21:14)

The Bible Commands a Response

When you see these words or others like them in your Bible, view them as terms that describe people who have been perpetually sinned against in unusual ways. How are we to respond to people who have had these kinds of experiences? The Bible teaches that we are to be compassionate and sympathetic: "We urge you, brethren, admonish the unruly, encourage the fainthearted, help the weak, be patient with all men" (1 Thessalonians 5:14).

All Sunday school teachers can quote Acts 20:35, especially when it comes to offering time, but I think there may be something more to learn from this verse: "In everything I showed you that by working hard in this manner *you must help the weak* and remember the words of the Lord Jesus, that He Himself said, 'It is more blessed to give than to receive' " (emphasis added).[3]

We are to work hard at helping the weak. In doing so we will be following in our Lord's footsteps and obeying His command. We will also find blessedness—that wonderful state of knowing that God's good countenance is resting upon us.

Finding a Biblical Answer

Let's prepare ourselves first by looking at a few preliminary precautions.

Offer Biblical Help

What kind of help are we to offer? We all know of situations in which Christians have offered pious platitudes to those who are suffering. There have been times when I didn't respond to another's suffering because I wasn't sure what to say. We repeat cultural catch phrases such as "work through your pain," "learn to love and forgive yourself," and "heal your inner child," without thinking about what they mean or whether this counsel is biblical or even helpful. We want to say something to let our friend know we care, but sincere advice is not enough. We must give biblical advice or we will give wrong advice and miss the blessing of God. Jeremiah 6:13-14 illustrates this problem: "And from the prophet even to the priest everyone deals falsely. And they have healed the brokenness of My people superficially, saying, 'Peace, peace,' but there is no peace."

Let's be careful that we are working to help the weak by giving them strong, loving, biblical counsel, and not just glossing over their problems by saying, "Peace, peace" without showing them how to attain that peace.

When you are dealing with someone who has a history like Marcia's, it is necessary to empathize with her sorrow, but you must be careful not to allow her suffering to hinder your counsel. (This is one instance where a woman's counsel to another woman is especially helpful.) As C.S. Lewis states in *The Problem of Pain*, "Indignation at other's sufferings, though a generous passion, needs to be well-managed, lest it steal away patience and humility from those who suffer and plant anger and cynicism in their stead."[4]

Guard Your Heart

It is easy to take up another's offense and get wrapped up in their pain and emotions. As a counselor it is very hard not to carry these cases around with me. I am angry at the sin that people commit against one another. I am mourning and weeping with Marcia over the wrong she has suffered. But I must be careful. I could become so upset by her story that I shrink back from presenting her with the whole counsel of God. How dare I inquire into her own sin when she's been so wronged? How could I seek to hold her accountable when her weakness is so obvious? I can't ask her to behave like any other child of God, can I? These doubts, and others like them, will hamper your ability to offer godly counsel. If, because of misplaced sympathy for Marcia, I shrink back from giving her the whole truth, *how will her life ever change?* As friends who offer counsel, we must avoid falling into the trap of believing that we can right all wrongs. Fortunately, the job of Savior has already been filled.

Adequate to Counsel?

Sometimes we labor under the false assumption that we can't counsel or help anyone if we haven't experienced their problems ourselves. You may not have been physically abused, but the Lord taught us in Luke 17:1-2 that we are all sinned against in one way or another: "It is inevitable that stumbling blocks should come." Perhaps you have never known sexual or physical abuse, but I'm sure you have experienced betrayal or abandonment of some sort. You may never have been used sexually, but it's very probable you have been used in one way or another. The pressure that some have endured may be greater than what you have faced, but you know what it is like to be misused, betrayed, neglected, disappointed, or abandoned. We all have experienced the disappointment of having significant people let us down, break promises, or even sin against us. You can use this common suffering as you think about what it would be like to be seriously abused. These experiences will make you a stronger, more compassionate, and more balanced counselor.

A Victim?

I have another caution I want to share with you. However, before I do I must ask you to put aside preconceived ideas about biblical counselors being callous or any tendency you might have to being overly melodramatic.

I wonder how appropriate the term *victim* is. Now before you slam this book shut, let me explain what I mean. I do not mean that children and women (and men) aren't sinned against. Nor do I mean that abuse does not occur or that it is not significant. I just wonder if the word *victim* is an appropriate label for a Christian who believes in a sovereign God. *Victim* is synonymous with other words such as *casualty* or *fatality*—accidents. *Christians believe there is a God and He is in control.* Some Christians believe God *allows* certain events, while others believe God *ordains* everything. Whichever you believe, the reality for every Christian is that there is a God who is able to control every circumstance and could have prevented or stopped the abuse if He had chosen to do so. Of course, He has not obligated Himself to do so and therefore anger at God is not justified. The sovereignty of God should stop a person from believing that he or she is inherently a "victim." Let me illustrate what I mean with these verses:

> The LORD has made *everything for its own purpose,* even the wicked *for the day of evil (Proverbs 16:4).*

> *The poor man and the oppressor have this in common:* The LORD gives light to the eyes of both *(Proverbs 29:13).*

Let's face it—God allowed Marcia's father to live. God is sovereign, which means He is in control. The word *sovereign* means "ruling, free, or independent." As Kay Arthur states in *Lord, Only You Can Change Me,*

> *When I speak of God's sovereignty, I am referring to the fact that God rules over all. He is totally, supremely, and preeminently over all His creation. Nothing escapes His sovereign control. No one eludes His sovereign plan.*[5]

God allowed the events in Marcia's life for a reason. Although it is impossible to fully know the reasons for her suffering (remember the story of Job), it is my goal to help Marcia find some of those reasons and to help her see herself and the abuse through the sovereignty of God. If you give in to referring to her or treating her solely as a "victim," you may be thwarting the very work that God wants to accomplish in her life.

False Memory Syndrome

One last caution: Be sure what you're dealing with is *real abuse.* Without getting into a long discussion on False Memory Syndrome,[6] it is wise to investigate the situations surrounding the memory of the abuse.[7] For instance, just because a woman has a problem with habitually overeating, you shouldn't assume she is the victim of abuse, especially if she doesn't remember being abused. We all have besetting sins (Hebrews 12:1) or what the world euphemistically labels "dysfunctions." Let's not speculate on anything "deeper" than our own sinful hearts and our propensity to please, promote, and protect ourselves when wondering why. We don't need a *reason* to sin—we are sinners by nature. We must be very careful not to suggest that abuse is the cause of ungodly behavior. It is right to ask if there is any abuse and to gather extensive data on the family's history. However, we must be careful not to assume a link between sinful behaviors or difficult relationships as an adult and repressed memories as a child. This link (Freudian in nature) has never even been scientifically established. "...Neither Freud nor any of his successors has ever proved a cause-and-effect link between a repressed memory and a later neurosis or a retrieved memory and a subsequent cure."[8]

God's Goals, Your Goals

Let us assume now that your counselee has truly been grievously sinned against. As you begin to counsel her you need to be sure you are seeking to accomplish God's goals. As has already been discussed (*see* chapter 2), biblical counseling is more than just "lending a listening ear." Biblical counseling is goal oriented.

Restoring Her to Faithful Servanthood

The goals of a biblical counselor are primarily oriented toward the glory of God. We are interested in helping those we counsel glorify God in their lives— possibly in ways that are new for them. Before you begin your counseling, ask yourself two pivotal questions: 1) How has this woman's faithful service to the body of Christ been damaged by this abuse and her response to it?, and 2) How has the glorifying of God been thwarted by the abuse *and* her response to it? Before you can proceed with any counseling, you must have a goal: Where are you going? More importantly, where do you think the Lord wants you to go? Do you have a goal? How will you know when you have reached it? Biblical counseling is not mere listening; nor do biblical counselors believe that mere talk without a plan of action is helpful.[9] Your overriding goal must be to restore her to a place of faithful service to her Lord, as you are instructed to do in Galatians 6:1-2:

> *Brethren, even if a man is caught in any trespass, you who are spiritual,*
> *restore such a one in a spirit of gentleness; each one looking to yourself, lest*

you too be tempted. Bear one another's burdens, and thus fulfill the law of Christ.

You must determine how to mend or restore your counselee's ability to serve God and others faithfully. For instance, is she unwilling to sing in the choir, although she has a beautiful voice, because she's afraid she might fail or be embarrassed? Is she unwilling to have regular sexual relations with her husband (as 1 Corinthians 7 commands) because she believes that sex is dirty? Is she overprotective of her children, not allowing them to participate in youth group or school functions because she wants to shield them from all harm? Does she self-indulge (with food, alcohol, drugs, or shopping) to bring pleasure to herself and numb her heart? Does she frequently overcommit herself and become frustrated and angry because she is afraid to say no for fear of rejection? Is she always trying to prove she's okay instead of resting in the grace of God? Does she have problems sustaining loyal friendships with others in the body? The answers to these questions, and others like them, will help you determine how her service to her Lord is being hindered.

Building Hope

For the victim of child abuse, hope is the one quality of life that seems elusive. In Psalm 9:18, David expresses these thoughts: "The needy will not always be forgotten, nor the hope of the afflicted perish forever." David recognized that the afflicted struggle with lack of hope. Think of Marcia's hope that her father would rescue her and then the crushing of that hope as she walked away from her school in handcuffs. The book of Proverbs teaches us that "hope deferred makes the heart sick, but desire fulfilled is a tree of life" (Proverbs 13:12). The Hebrew word for "sick" in this verse may be translated "sick" or "weak." Frailty, cynicism, despair, and dejection are the fruit of a heart that has no hope. Vigor, strength, courage, and confidence are descriptors of a heart that is full of hope.

It's safer for Marcia not to hope. Why dream about the day things will be better when, in her innermost being, she doesn't believe anything will ever change? I'm not saying this is a godly attitude for her to adopt, just one that is understandable. As a counselor, you must invest much time in building her hope.[10]

Guard your heart against impatience. You are commanded to "mourn with those who mourn." Contrary to some teaching, mourning isn't sinful or faithless—just read the psalms. Patiently and lovingly direct her to Bible verses on hope to memorize and write about. Encourage her to talk about her grief with the Lord. Hope will grow as she begins to believe that God loves, hears, and cares. You can also recommend attainable short-range goals that will demonstrate that her life really can change.

Build hope by teaching her about the sovereignty of God. There is nothing more comforting than to fully embrace God's sovereignty. If life is truly left in the hands of abusers, if it is chaotic and filled with accidents, how can we ever hope for anything? As Michael Horton writes, "The sovereignty of God comforts us in crisis and curbs our pride in triumph."[11] Kay Arthur echoes this thought in *Lord, Only You Can Change Me*:

> *We must accept His sovereign rule. We must grapple with the character of this One who rules over the affairs of men and the hosts of heaven.* Of all the truths I have ever learned, none has brought me more assurance, boldness, calmness, devotion, equilibrium, gratitude, and humility than . . . the sovereignty of God.[12] *(emphasis added)*.

We must teach Marcia that there is hope because there is a sovereign God. He may allow suffering and sorrow, but He always does so for our ultimate good and His glory:

> *We know that God causes all things to work together for good to those who love God, to those who are called according to His purpose. For whom He foreknew, He also predestined to become conformed to the image of His Son, that He might be the first-born among many brethren (Romans 8: 28-29).*

These verses offer strong hope to the weak at heart. Whether you believe God ordains or merely allows trials, you must believe God will work out His glorious plan in your life if you love Him and have been called by Him. His plan does not necessarily include earthly comfort or protection from suffering. We have hope because we know it includes something better. Nothing in life is chaotic or meaningless. Under the care of the Master's loving hand every tear, every sorrow, every bruising is meant for our ultimate good. What is the good that He has in mind? That our lives might be conformed to the image of His perfect Son. God wants us to be like Christ. That's His goal. Hope grows in the light of this glorious thought! God ordains events so that we are continually turned toward Him and away from idols, self-protection, self-indulgence, man-pleasing, and manipulation. He is continually working to free us, not for ourselves (although we do benefit), but for His ultimate glory. Amazing grace!

The wickedness of man is brought into the service of God and establishes His glory and righteousness.

Doris Van Stone, author of *No Place to Cry*,[13] describes her perspective on the heinous, almost unbelievable abuse she suffered as a child,

> *I can honestly say that there is nothing in my life I would change. Not because all my scars have healed or because my hatred of abuse has dissipated, because neither has happened. But I can say I wouldn't change anything for this one reason: God has been glorified through my suffering. And He has used me to give hope to others whose scars are as bad or even worse than mine.*

What Christian doesn't want to hear the Lord say, "Well done, good and faithful servant"? We all desire the shining of God's good countenance upon us and it is in the middle of suffering that He shines upon us most. As Doris Van Stone writes,

> *Regardless of the heartaches I have endured on earth, I know that this present suffering cannot be compared with the glory that will be revealed in us. . . . Eternity is a long time. Someday I shall speak to my Savior, who stood with me when no one else did. Maybe He will tell me why I had to endure all those tears. And maybe He will point to some people and say, "Dorie, these are here because you told them about My grace and power." Just a word from my Savior will make up for the past.*[14]

There is hope in God for Marcia. Her life can change; she can change. She doesn't need to be shackled to the sin of her parents. As she responds in faith and obedience through the power of the Holy Spirit, the darkness of the sin of her past will cause the brightness of her life to shine even more. There is a God and she can trust Him. She can hope in His loving plan.

Helping Her Face the Past Honestly and Fully

Some of you may be wondering, *Why is it important to even talk about abuse? It's all in the past. Why can't Marcia just get with the program and go on with life?"*

Every person is a compilation of many elements. What happened in our past is important. What is more important, however, is how we responded to those things in the past. Our hearts are revealed by our responses to both the suffering and blessing in this life. Good experiences don't necessarily make good hearts, nor do wicked experiences make wicked hearts. As Christian women, we have the moral capacity to respond both sinfully and righteously. Of course, before our conversions, we did not have the capacity to act righteously, but now that God has given us new hearts and written His law upon them, we can react in new, godly ways.

An important reason for discovering personal history is to uncover habitual patterns of response, in both thoughts and actions. How does your counselee respond to disappointment, frustration, or criticism? The answers to these questions are important as you seek to replace sinful responses with godly ones.

In addition, it is important for women like Marcia not to hide from their past. It is important for at least two reasons. First, our God is a God of reality and not fantasy. His reality includes His sovereign rule, love, and grace. Philippians 4:8 commands that we think on certain things:

> *Finally, brethren, whatever is true, whatever is honorable, whatever is right, whatever is pure, whatever is lovely, whatever is of good repute, if there is any excellence and if anything worthy of praise, let your mind dwell on these things.*

When we are commanded to think on things that are true, that means that we are not to live in our imaginations, such as False Memory Syndrome or when women pretend abuse didn't happen or doesn't matter. Once again, I'm not talking about women with repressed memories, but those who know they were abused and pretend it is not significant. The question that must be asked is, "How is this woman's life and service for the Lord presently being impacted by the past?" If she appears to be functioning in a godly manner and she does not *pretend* that everything in her past was rosy, then don't force the issue. If it's obvious, however, that she is still troubled by the abuse, not functioning in her role in the church, or if she is responding to life as though she still thought of herself as a victim, then she must accept the truth of the abuse in her past. Yet this is not the only truth God wants her to accept. God wants to use her past for His glory. He wants to take her weaknesses and turn them into strengths both for herself and for the rest of the body of Christ. If she pretends nothing happened, how is she or anyone else to be helped by her experiences? She will be unable to comfort others as Paul describes in 2 Corinthians:

> *Blessed be the God and Father of our Lord Jesus Christ, the Father of mercies and God of all comfort; who comforts us in all our affliction so that we may*

be able to comfort those who are in any affliction with the comfort with which we ourselves are comforted by God (2 Corinthians 1:3-4).

The abused woman is not to make-believe—she is to believe. God wants to redeem this suffering. He wants to change her by revealing her heart and by teaching her to be compassionate and comforting to others. She is to train her mind to think godly thoughts, to think about truth, and to not allow her vain imaginings to become her idol of the past. Paul puts it this way in 2 Corinthians 10:5, "We are destroying speculations and every lofty thing raised up against the knowledge of God, and we are taking every thought captive to the obedience of Christ." Whenever she allows herself to pretend her past was something it wasn't, she is denying the ability of God to redeem it. She is refusing to embrace His plan for her life. Acknowledging the past is important. Seek to help her do so for God's glory.

Answering "Why?"

It is not possible, in these few pages, to give a full treatment of the purposes of God in bringing suffering to His children. In some ways I have already touched on this subject, but let me direct you to several avenues for continued thought.

The Life of Joseph   The life of Joseph is a perfect example of God accomplishing His good goal through the temporary suffering of His servant. A review of Joseph's life with your counselee would be beneficial. Point her to Genesis 50:20: "And as for you, you meant evil against me, but God meant it for good in order to bring about this present result, to preserve many people alive." At the end of his life Joseph realized the evil intent and actions of his jealous brothers were part of God's ultimate plan to bring good to many people. God's plan benefited not only those who enjoyed the provision of grain, but all who have read Joseph's story and been given hope because of it.[15] God held Joseph's brothers accountable as they sinfully exercised their free will by selling Joseph into slavery. It is a mystery how their free will worked in concert with God's sovereignty, but let us be content to realize that God had a plan for Joseph's life that his brothers fulfilled.

In the same way, God had a plan to use Doris Van Stone and even my friend Marcia to bring deliverance and testimony. God has a plan to use every adverse circumstance in the lives of His children for His ultimate purpose and glory. The Christian can learn to rejoice in the knowledge that there is not one tear shed nor one instance of suffering that is outside God's purpose or authority. Although adversity may originate from others, "by the time suffering gets to us, it is God's will."[16] Our personal struggles, as we view them in the light of God's providential care and concern, can become well-springs of blessing and life. Such was the case with Joseph. Press your counselee to think about ways in which her suffering could be a blessing to others. Encourage her to view her life in the light of this rich and inspiring story.

The Blessings of Suffering   There are a number of verses in the New Testament that speak to the reasons and benefits of suffering. For instance, Romans 5:3-5 states,

> *We also exult in our tribulations, knowing that tribulation brings about perseverance; and perseverance, proven character; and proven character, hope; and hope does not disappoint, because the love of God has been poured out within our hearts through the Holy Spirit who was given to us.*

Along these same lines, consider the words of James, the brother of our Lord:

> *Consider it all joy, my brethren, when you encounter various trials, knowing that the testing of your faith produces endurance. And let endurance have its perfect result, that you may be perfect and complete, lacking in nothing.*[17]

Ask your counselee how much she values her growth in perseverance, character, hope, and endurance. Does she want to become mature and whole? Paul and James teach us that sufferings and tribulations, when embraced in faith, are the gateway to these qualities.

Paul speaks in two passages of the wonderful blessing accrued to us through suffering:

> *The Spirit Himself bears witness with our spirit that we are children of God, and if children, heirs also, heirs of God and fellow heirs with Christ, if indeed we suffer with Him in order that we may also be glorified with Him. For I consider that the sufferings of this present time are not worthy to be compared with the glory that is to be revealed to us (Romans 8:16-18).*

Second Corinthians 4:16-17 says,

> *Therefore we do not lose heart, but though our outer man is decaying, yet our inner man is being renewed day by day. For momentary, light affliction is producing for us an eternal weight of glory far beyond all comparison.*

Suffering is so obviously part of what it means to be a fellow heir with Christ that it is astonishing that we are often surprised by it. We know that as we suffer for the Lord we are attaining incomparable glory in heaven. As Mother Teresa said, "From heaven, the most miserable life on earth will look like one bad night in an inconvenient motel."[18]

Let me remind you of Romans 8:28-29 and 2 Corinthians 1:3-11 and the wonderful teaching on suffering found there. First, we know God causes everything that happens to us to work for our ultimate good and His glory. God's purpose is to transform us. This transformation is best accomplished in the furnace of suffering. In addition, we can use this suffering and the comfort that God brings to us in the midst of it to help and comfort others.

There is one more point to be made from the 2 Corinthians 1 passage. Notice verses 8-9:

> *We do not want you to be unaware, brethren, of our affliction which came to us in Asia, that we were burdened excessively, beyond our strength, so that we despaired even of life; indeed, we had the sentence of death within ourselves* in order that we should not trust in ourselves, but in God who raises the dead *(emphasis added).*

The Lord put Paul and his companions in the furnace of affliction for a purpose. What was that purpose? That they should trust not in themselves, but in God who, even if they were to die, could raise them from the dead. Now, if Paul and his companions needed to learn this lesson, why is it surprising that we should also? God uses suffering to drive us to His mercy and to free our hearts from self-deception. Our hearts deceive us as we think we can rely on ourselves. How often we would forget that we must trust in Him and His grace to be fruitful (*see* John 15).

Let us teach our counselees to be thankful for their suffering because they serve as sweet alarms that wake us from hazy dreams of independence and self-sufficiency. They motivate us to trust and rely solely in God. They remind us of the transitory nature of this earthly home and cause us to long for our heavenly one. They turn us toward the cross and the innocent suffering Servant who died there at the hands of abusers for our sin.

The Sources of Suffering Our typical response to suffering is to blame. In the story of the man born blind in John 9 we have a perfect example of how suffering brings glory to God and comfort to millions. The disciples revealed their theology of suffering when they asked Jesus, "Who sinned that this man was born blind?" They believed suffering was always a punishment for some-one's sins, but Jesus answered this question in an astonishing way, "It was neither that this man sinned, nor his parents; but it was in order that the works of God might be displayed in him" (John 9:3).

We want to blame other's sins, as the disciples did, or God, as Job's wife did. We frequently overlook other causes. While it is true that there are causes to our suffering, we must be careful as we seek to distinguish them. In Ed Welch's article, "Exalting Pain? Ignoring Pain? What Do We Do with Suffering?" he pinpoints five causes of suffering: 1) Others, 2) Me, 3) Adam's sin, 4) Satan, and 5) God. He illustrates these causes in the following way:[19]

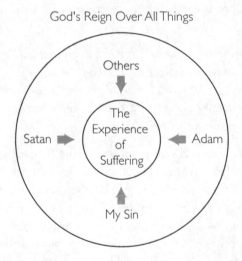

While it is true God reigns over all our suffering, we must also remember God's sovereignty "does not rob creatures of their will."[20] Because of Adam we live in a sin-cursed world. We sin against God and others and are sinned against. Also Satan tempts us to sin, although he cannot cause us to do so. "God is over sin and suffering, but He is not their author."[21] It is important for your counselee to differentiate between suffering that is her responsibility (continually covering for a drunken husband), other's responsibility (her husband's habitual drunkenness), or is part of living in this sinful world influenced by Satan's schemes. Although she may not be able to immediately discern the precise cause of her suffering (as was the case with Job and Joseph), she must live faithfully and obediently before God. Over all, we must strive to help our counselees see beyond fault and guilt to a God who orders everything after the counsel of His own will.

Encouraging Confession, Repentance, and Forgiveness

Differentiating Between Personal Sin and Being Sinned Against   If you have allowed yourself to become overly sympathetic to a counselee's suffering, you might have a difficult time with what I'm about to say. We have heard so much about how a victim tends to believe her abuser's sins were her fault that we shy away from addressing her personal sin. First, let me remind you the Bible clearly teaches that we all sin.[22] You must spend time gently teaching her the difference between her sin and the sins of others. The truth that will set her free must not be compromised by false compassion. How is she presently sinning? Is she sinfully worried, angry, or afraid? Does she try to manipulate circumstances or function as super mom so she might control the future? She is not responsible for being sinned against, but she is responsible for her response to that sin. You must point her to verses on confession and repentance of sin such as 1 John 1:9. You must also teach her that before she can confront her abuser (or anyone else who has sinned against her), she must remove the log from her own eye:

> Why do you look at the speck that is in your brother's eye, but do not notice the log that is in your own eye? Or how can you say to your brother, "Let me take the speck out of your eye," and behold, the log is in your own eye? You hypocrite, first take the log out of your own eye, and then you will see clearly to take the speck out of your brother's eye (Matthew 7:3-5).

The point of this passage is clear: All of us sin. We all are in need of forgiveness and grace. Your counselee will grow as she realizes the ways in which she sins against others. There is no position so far from grace as the moral high ground that ignores personal sin and claims victimhood.

Determining Culpability   Your counselee must understand and believe the Bible's teaching about culpability for sin. We find the Old Testament case law particularly helpful in this regard. Although this is a long passage from Deuteronomy 22, I believe it would be helpful for you to ponder:

> If there is a girl who is a virgin engaged to a man, and another man finds her in the city and lies with her, then you shall bring them both out to the

gate of that city and you shall stone them to death; the girl, because she did not cry out in the city, and the man, because he has violated his neighbor's wife. . . . But if in the field the man finds the girl who is engaged, and the man forces her and lies with her, then only the man who lies with her shall die. But you shall do nothing to the girl; there is no sin in the girl worthy of death, for just as a man rises against his neighbor and murders him, so is this case. When he found her in the field, the engaged girl cried out, but there was no one to save her (verses 23-27).

As we seek to attain understanding of the implications of this passage, notice some assumptions that are made. The first assumption is that the girl (in this case a girl old enough to be engaged) understands that sexual relations with a man outside of marriage are wrong. It is assumed that the knowledge of this impropriety prompts her to cry out for help. Most young girls do not have this understanding. Frequently, they are told by their abuser that this relationship is a normal one. Until instructed otherwise, they believe it. They may sense there is something uncomfortable about this relationship, but do they know enough to cry out?

The second assumption is that there is someone listening. Numbers of girls have told their mothers that abuse was happening, but their mothers chose to ignore them or, as in Marcia's case, punished them for telling. In the case of Doris Van Stone, there was no one to whom she could cry for help, since she was a virtual prisoner in a foster home or orphanages.

Ask the following questions to help your counselee determine her culpability in the matter: Did you know the activity you were involved in was wrong? If you knew it was wrong, was there someone to whom you could cry for help? If you did cry out, were you believed and protected? If your counselee answers negatively to any of these questions, you must show her what the Bible teaches—*"There is no sin in the girl."* Explain to her that although she has been sinned against, God's Word teaches that children are not responsible for the sins of parents.[23] "God reminds us that we do not cause the sin of other people. They are responsible for their own sin."[24] This is an important truth for those who might be tempted to take the blame for another's sin. Women will sometimes take on responsibility for sin that is not theirs, while ignoring sin they are responsible for. Many women struggle in this area because they don't want to believe that a person they loved and who was responsible to love and care for them, could act in such a wicked way. It is easier to believe they did something that caused the abuse rather than believing the person they loved and trusted was wicked. You must gently help them to believe the truth.

Let us assume, however, your counselee was older at the time of the abuse and knew the activity was sinful. Let's assume she knew she could have told someone without fear of retaliation, but didn't. Ask her specifically if she believes she sinned. If she is aware of her sin and you can discern that she is not taking on someone else's responsibility, counsel her to handle her sin in an appropriate way. Don't be afraid to allow your counselee to confess and repent of any sin that she thinks she has committed. We have a wonderful Savior who is willing to forgive all sin. Be careful not to negate any work the Holy Spirit might be doing in her heart. It's not as though we are unbelievers who have no answer for sin except to shun responsibility for it. The despair that comes from recognition of sin is overcome in the shadow of the cross. Teach your counselee the depths of Christ's redeeming work.

True Guilt, False Guilt   We often hear about "true guilt" and "false guilt" and there may be some confusion here. True guilt is an acknowledgment of culpability before a holy God. We have transgressed the law of a holy God and we are judged guilty before Him. But is there such a thing as "false guilt"? We tend to think of "false guilt" as feelings of guilt that are not justified by reality. Let me try to illustrate this point: I get angry and push my child. He accidentally falls down the stairs, breaks his neck, and dies. I recognize that I am guilty before God (and the State) of manslaughter. In faith, I confess my sin to God and ask for forgiveness, and God forgives me. But, I still feel guilty. I can't get over the fact that in anger I killed my child. I rehearse the scene over and over in my mind. I can't believe God has forgiven me. I am afraid to approach Him for fear that He condemns me, even though I have repented and asked God's forgiveness. Although this is typically how we think of false guilt, is this guilt false? No, it's true guilt, but guilt of another kind. The guilt of my sinful anger has been forgiven. Now I am guilty of something else. I am guilty of the sin of unbelief and doubting God's Word. This is important for your counselee to understand.

If, as you discuss the abuse with her, it is probable that she didn't sin, then you must show her what the Word says. If then you notice a reticence on her part to give up her "guilt," you must talk to her about believing and embracing the liberty God has bestowed on her. On the other hand, if she is convinced she has sinned and she has asked the Lord's forgiveness, but still seems to struggle with guilt, you must teach her that her struggle with God's graciousness is unbelief.

Struggles with Forgiveness   Sometimes we struggle with forgiveness because we have a hard time believing we are capable of sinning in these ways. We are more concerned about our inability to live up to our own standards than we are about sinning against a holy God. It doesn't matter that God has forgiven us because we can't forgive ourselves. Fortunately, *the Bible never commands us to forgive ourselves.* Our focus in forgiveness must always be on the Lord and those we have sinned against.

Some women say, "I just don't feel forgiven." Happily, forgiveness is not a feeling. Forgiveness is a *promise* that God makes to us (and we may make to others) that He does not hold our sin against us any longer (*see* Isaiah 43:25). Our feelings must flow from our belief in God's unchanging character. If He promises to forgive us, He has. Your counselee must consciously force herself to embrace the truth of God's Word and ignore any habitual self-condemning and faithless self-talk. This may take some time to work through, so be patient and kind and continue to draw her back to God's mercy and His standards.

Confronting the Abuser

If you have done a good job pointing your counselee to her own sinfulness, the topic of confronting and forgiving her abuser will be more easily accepted. If she has experienced the joy of God's forgiveness, she should be more willing to forgive others. Confronting abusers and extending forgiveness to them is also an important part of the growth in grace. There is much confusion about these topics in Christianity, so let me make a few brief comments and refer you to a book that treats the topic at length.[25] First, confrontation and forgiveness are always to be for the sake of the Lord and the offender—never so that the one forgiving will feel better. Although obeying the Lord does bring about blessedness or a knowledge that one is pleasing to the Lord, our motivation in confrontation and possible eventual forgiveness is not so that we can vent or unload. Luke 17:3 teaches that if we are sinned against, we must rebuke the one who sinned against us so that person may have opportunity to be made aware of his sin and repent, receiving God's and our forgiveness.

It is important to be very careful here. Caution is advised when making any accusations of abuse, especially if there is any question as to whether the abuse actually took place. According to Dr. Jay Adams, the word "rebuke" in this passage means to "rebuke tentatively." You must rebuke with the thought in mind that you might be wrong, you might have misunderstood.

Forgiveness is to be granted to the offender *only* if the offender asks for it. Our forgiveness is to be patterned after God's forgiveness (Ephesians 4:32). He does not extend blanket forgiveness to all men, but only to those who request it. Since the possibility exists that your counselee might need to bring charges against the offender either in the church or the state, forgiveness must not be granted unless the perpetrator is repentant. This is because forgiveness is a promise made, "I will not hold this against you any longer. I will not bring it up again to anyone, including myself."

Forgiveness is not a feeling. It is not forgetting. It is an act of the will in response to God's command to forgive the repentant. Although Christians must always have a heart that is ready to forgive, praying that God will not hold this sin against the perpetrator (rather bringing him to repentance), actual forgiveness can only be granted the way that God grants it—in response to confession and repentance.

Although forgiveness is not to be granted to the unrepentant, you must grant forgiveness to those who ask for it (Matthew 18:21-35). We must recognize our own wretchedness before a holy God and remember the overwhelming grace He lavished upon us. We must not take this grace for granted, but must allow it to permeate our heart so that we are willing to forgive others. Remember Luke 17:3-4: "Be on your guard! If your brother sins, rebuke him; and if he repents, forgive him. And if he sins against you seven times a day, and returns to you seven times, saying, 'I repent,' forgive him." The Lord has made a wonderful promise to us: "If you confess your sins, I will forgive your sins."[76] Now He asks that we prove our gratitude by extending the same promise to others. Granting forgiveness will seem difficult only if we minimize our sin and maximize others'.

Marcia will never completely forget what happened to her. But she can view her past as being redeemed by the Lord and as an eventual blessing to others. Joseph had this same attitude in Genesis 41:51. "And Joseph named the first-born Manasseh, 'For,' he said, 'God has made me forget all my trouble and all my father's household.'" Joseph wasn't saying he forgot his past completely. He recognized his brothers when they arrived in Egypt and was overcome with emotion. God had caused the sting of his suffering to be forgotten.

Predictable Areas of Personal Sin

As a counselor you will probably encounter the following arenas of sin, but keep in mind that people respond to being sinned against in many different ways.

Sinful Anger, Righteous Anger

An Understanding of Anger   Once you begin working to restore your sister to faithful service in Christ, it is likely you may discover a deep well of anger and bitterness in her heart. It is important for you to help her examine this anger to determine if it is pleasing to the Lord. Some Christians mistakenly teach that all anger is sinful. Others teach that venting anger is beneficial. I believe the Bible teaches anger is neutral. It may be either pleasing or displeasing to the Lord. The bottom-line question is: "Are you angry because the sin being committed is diminishing the glory of God?" In addition, you must ask, "Have you responded in any sinful way because of your anger, righteous or unrighteous?"

Scripture teaches that God the Father and Jesus Christ were both angry, yet without sin. There are also cases recorded in Scripture where a person who loved the Lord was angry without sinning, such as Moses (Exodus 16:20; Leviticus 10:16-20), Saul (1 Samuel 11:6), Jonathan (1 Samuel 20:34), Elisha (2 Kings 13:19), and Nehemiah (Nehemiah 5:6). Ephesians 4:26-27 teaches, "Be angry, and yet do not sin; do not let the sun go down on your anger, and do not give the devil an opportunity." We learn from these examples that it is possible to be angry without sinning, yet these occurrences are rare. Indeed, the Proverbs teach us that there are many dangers associated with anger. "A fool always loses his temper, but a wise man holds it back" (Proverbs 29:11). "An angry man stirs up strife, and a hot-tempered man abounds in transgression" (Proverbs 29:22). Foolishness and transgression go hand-in-hand with anger. Rather than venting or stuffing our anger, we must learn to respond without sinning when we experience anger. It is likely that your counselee has developed habits of sinful anger. She was probably never taught how to handle anger in a godly way as she was continually enraged at the betrayal and wickedness of her abusers. You must spend time teaching her how to put off anger and put on kindness and appropriate confrontation (Ephesians 4:14-15).

The Leprosy of Bitterness   One of the most nefarious results of anger is bitterness. Bitterness is a leprosy that consumes the soul and eats away at grace, forgiveness, and mercy. It is variously translated "rebellious," "discontented," and "disobedient." Ephesians 4:31-32 instructs us to put off anger and bitterness and put on kindness, tender-heartedness, and forgiveness:

> Let all bitterness and wrath and anger and clamor and slander be put away from you, along with all malice. And be kind to one another, tender-hearted, forgiving each other, just as God in Christ also has forgiven you.

Women like Marcia must be taught that the sin of bitterness is just as sinful as the abuse that initiated it. The writer of Hebrews states that bitterness is a root that grows more pervasive as it is allowed to flourish. It causes trouble, defiles many, and is associated with immoral and godless persons, such as Esau, who thought nothing of selling his birthright to satisfy his cravings.[27] Bitterness shouldn't be embraced, worked through, or understood—it needs to be repented of.

Fear of Man and Man-Pleasing

"The fear of man brings a snare, but he who trusts in the LORD will be exalted" (Proverbs 29:25).

Differentiating between a righteous fear of God and sinful fear of man is important in all our lives, but particularly in the life of a woman who may have spent her entire childhood in terror. Many victims can recall trying to figure out how to please their abusers. They wondered over and over again what they could do to avoid the abuse. They took the blame for their abusers' sins. Habitual man-pleasing and fear of man is the result of this kind of training. Again an abused woman is not culpable for another's sin, but she is for her own.

Ask questions to determine whether your counselee is sinning by man-pleasing or fearing man. Are the energies of her heart and life focused on trying to please those around her, rather than living to please the Lord? Is she overly concerned about what others think of her? Does she worry and fret that she might have made someone angry with her? Consider how she responds to criticism. The answers to these questions will help expose one area of her heart that may need light.

The fear of man is bondage. Proverbs says it brings a snare—it entangles, trips, and binds those caught in it. Life is to be lived for God alone. Although His standards are high, He is not unreliable nor unstable. He doesn't say one thing one day and something different the next. If, through the work of the Holy Spirit you can convince your counselee to say, "In a primary sense, I don't care whether I am pleasing to anyone else or not. I must first be pleasing to the Lord," you will have helped her immensely. Worrying about what others think, "walking on eggshells," and compromising God's truth so that no offense is ever given is a bondage from which God desires to deliver her. It is idolatry. She needs to join with Paul in saying,

> *Just as we have been approved by God to be entrusted with the gospel, so we speak,* not as pleasing men but God, who examines our hearts. *For we*

never came with flattering speech, . . . nor did we seek glory from men, . . .
but we proved to be gentle among you, as a nursing mother tenderly cares for
her own children (1 Thessalonians 2:4-7, emphasis added.).

Flattery, glory-seeking, fear of man, and man-pleasing are indications she is more concerned about man's opinion than God's. It will be difficult for her to be "gentle as a nursing mother" when she is motivated by the responses and approval of others. This brings too much self-imposed pressure to perform and impress others —too much fear. In the final analysis the opinions of others become the god she serves. "Others' Opinions" is a demanding taskmaster. She can hardly help but become demanding herself as she seeks to please her god and forces others around her to do so. Her idolatrous craving for approval continually subjects her to the question, "How do you think I'm doing?" When she fails to receive another's approval, she may be quick to judge and condemn (or may continue to try to gain the sought-after approval). She has become both a slave (to others' opinions and approval) and a slave driver (expecting others to try to please her).

God desires to free her from this bondage. She must recognize her manipulation, demandingness, and conniving for what they are, worship of a foreign god. In a pathetic effort to maintain peace and control the future, an abused woman might demand perfection from her children while putting up with abuse from her husband. "I'll do anything to avoid problems" is her life focus. Teach her to ask herself, "Is what I am doing pleasing to God?" As she studies the Word and grows in His grace, she will be able to differentiate between her own standards and gods and the true and living King. Even though pleasing God will bring her into conflict with the world (and possibly even with Christians around her), she can be encouraged that she is walking in the footsteps of her Lord.

Rebelliousness

Another facet of man-pleasing is rebellion. The woman who is thoroughly rebellious and angry, seemingly "despising" the opinions of others, is just as much a man-pleaser as her more compliant sister. Craving for the approval of others has driven her for so long that she has decided to show her disdain of others through rebellion. Why is she rebellious? Why is she wasting her life in various forms of dissipation? Because she wants what she cannot attain—the approval of others. She may use sex as a form of control over men, laughing in her heart over their weakness and her power over them. In anger and frustration, she thumbs her nose in the face of those she inwardly desires to please and adopts a life of self-indulgence. Obviously, these habits eventuate in more and more rebellion, anger, and self-worship, but at heart the two women are the same. This woman must be brought to repentance on several levels. Rather than merely focusing on the more outward rebellion and self-indulgence, urge her to look at her idolatrous man-pleasing and rage as the seedbed for her more overt forms of sin.

The Desire for Safety and Security

The psalms speak about the desire for safety and security of those who are afflicted and about God's promise to satisfy: " 'Because of the devastation of the afflicted, because of the groaning of the needy, now I will arise,' says the LORD; 'I will set him in the safety for which he longs' " (Psalm 12:5). "But I am afflicted and in pain; may Thy salvation, O God, set me securely on high" (Psalm 69:29).

Safety and security are driving desires of someone who has been abused. Although this is understandable, if this desire has taken on the form of an idol, it must be confronted. Help your counselee determine the importance that safety and security hold in her life. Try to discover if she has sinned in order to maintain her own safety or security. She may not know the answer to that question and you could illustrate it for her in this way. A woman might be coerced into lying for her husband to his boss, saying he is sick, when in fact he is drunk. She doesn't want to rock the boat. Habitual lying to avoid confrontation displays a heart bent on preserving its own security. If she does this sort of thing, she must be taught to put her trust in the Lord, obey Him, and rely on Him alone for her security. Self-protection is at heart, self-love. Covering for her husband's sins is not a loving thing for her to do. It encourages him in his sin and demonstrates her desire for security and safety more than the blessings of God. Teach her about the grace and goodness of the Lord. Although she may have felt abandoned before, God has promised never to leave or forsake her: "For He Himself has said, 'I will never desert you, nor will I ever forsake you,' so that we confidently say, 'The LORD is my helper, I will not be afraid. What shall man do to me?' "[28]

Fear of rejection, trouble, and resultant insecurity have driven many women to put up with the most atrocious sins. It is one thing to choose to suffer as a Christian; it is quite another to grasp at security and endure abuse out of weakness. The suffering of a Christian is one of strength, not neediness.

Self-Indulgence and Worry

All of the forms of idolatry we have been discussing will eventuate in self-indulgence and worry. For instance, I find many Christian women, who wouldn't even think of getting drunk or using drugs, use food as a panacea to soothe their hearts and comfort themselves. If your counselee seems to have a problem in this area, please refer to chapter 16 on overeaters and bulimics. In addition, she may struggle with overspending or sinful sexual relations (masturbation, promiscuity, or frigidity). This type of self-indulgence always results in worry, as our Lord taught in Luke 21:34: "Be on guard, that your hearts may not be weighted down with dissipation and drunkenness and the worries of life." Every time she seeks to soothe her heart by buying something she can't afford, she gives herself cause to worry. "How will I hide the bill from my husband?" "How will I cover my sin?" "How can God ever change me?"

Worry and self-indulgence go hand-in-hand, one causing the other in a cyclical maelstrom of guilt and hopelessness. Teach her that she must put off her self-indulgence through structured living. If she is tempted to use credit cards, have her give them to her husband or better yet, have her destroy them. Teach her to use a budget, to allow God to comfort and reward her, and to become a giver. Also teach her to handle her worry, using Paul's writing in Philippians 4:6-9 as specific steps in putting off and putting on.

Of course, there are many other areas in which you may have to help her. She may be consumed with self-pity, isolation, and loneliness. Teach her to become a servant. She may be easily discouraged. She may feel forgotten and unloved. Help her to grasp a more realistic view of life. Even people with great parents get discouraged, have failures, feel alienated.

You must focus on how she is functioning in the church. Is she using her gifts for others or merely waiting for them to come to her? Does she use her "victim badge" to elicit sympathy in others and excuse her from responsibilities? No matter how misused she was as a child, she can still serve God. Point her again to Joseph, who named his first child Manasseh because God had taken the sting out of the memory of his trouble, but who also had another son, "And he named the second Ephraim, 'For,' he said, 'God has made me fruitful in the land of my affliction' " (Genesis 41:52). God desires to make your counselee fruitful in her affliction. Is she suffering? Let her learn to pour out her soul to her loving Father, and then weep with others who are weeping. Does she ache with the loneliness she felt as a child? Encourage her to disciple others who are alone. My friend Marcia has a wonderful ministry to international students.

She takes them into her home, witnesses to them, brings them to church, and has "adopted" many of them. She understands what it is like to feel alone, and she uses this understanding to comfort others.

Counseling Points to Remember

Of course, if you are not already trained in biblical counseling, I recommend you pursue it. In the recommended resources section at the end of chapter two there is a list of resources and schools which offer training. However, by way of reminder, let me list some suggestions you may find helpful for your counseling endeavors:

- Get all the data. Who was the perpetrator of the abuse? What kind of abuse took place? What was the duration of the abuse? Were other people involved? How was secrecy enforced? Did the woman ever tell anyone? What was the reaction of her parents, particularly of her mother?
- How does her history affect her present life and ministry? How does she view the future? What are her habitual ways of handling difficulties, disappointments, trials, betrayals? Is she willing to address her own sinfulness?
- You are to set the agenda. Your goal is to restore her to faithful servant-hood for God's glory. In that process, she will experience increased positive feelings, but good feelings are not your primary goal.
- Is she willing to commit herself to a program of change that may not be comfortable? Is she willing to be accountable to you or a church leader for her growth in discipleship? Does she really desire change, or does she just want someone to complain to?
- Are you willing to invest time in her life? She does not need someone else who betrays or disappoints her. Of course, you are to teach her to put her whole trust in Christ, but you have an obligation to commit to helping her over the long haul. Do you want a new friend? Are you willing to bear her burden? If you are, then you can have the assurance that you are fulfilling the "law of Christ"[29]—you are loving your neighbor as you already love yourself.

As a woman who counsels and disciples other women, it increasingly has become my goal to work toward the model of the virtuous woman described in

Proverbs 31, especially verse 25: "Strength and dignity are her clothing, and she smiles at the future."

If I observe weakness, manipulation, complaining, or a lack of confidence in God's ability to handle the future, then I know the Lord's gracious plan for her life has not been fully realized. God can change weakness into strength. He can remove her garments of shame and humiliation and replace them with grace and confidence. He can teach her to smile at the future. The brokenhearted are the special ministry of the Messiah. In His providence, the Lord is now teaching you to minister to the afflicted. Are you willing to be His hands extended?

> *The Spirit of the Lord* GOD *is upon me, because the* LORD *has anointed me* to bring good news to the afflicted; He has sent me to bind up the broken-hearted, to proclaim liberty to captives, and freedom to prisoners (*Isaiah 61:1, emphasis added*).

Recommended Resources

Jay Adams, *The Grand Demonstration: A Biblical Study of the So-Called Problem of Evil*, Santa Barbara, CA: EastGate Publishers, 1991.

_____, *How to Handle Trouble*, Phillipsburg, NJ: Presbyterian & Reformed, 1982.

Jerry Bridges, *Trusting God*, Colorado Springs: NavPress, 1988.

Ed Bulkley, *Only God Can Heal the Wounded Heart*, Eugene, OR: Harvest House, 1995.

Elisabeth Elliot, *Through Gates of Splendor*, Wheaton, IL: Tyndale House, 1986.

C. S. Lewis, *The Problem of Pain*, New York: Macmillan Publishing, 1977.

Joni Eareckson Tada and Steven Estes, *A Step Further*, Grand Rapids, MI: Zondervan, 1990.

Doris Van Stone, *No Place to Cry: The Hurt and Healing of Sexual Abuse*, Chicago: Moody Press, 1990.

Ed Welch, "Exalting Pain? Ignoring Pain? What Do We Do With Suffering?" *The Journal of Biblical Counseling*, vol. XII, no. 3, Spring 1994. *The Journal of Biblical Counseling* may be ordered by contacting The Christian Counseling and Educational Foundation, 1803 E. Willow Grove Avenue, Laverock, PA 19118.

CHAPTER 15

Counseling Women with Addictions

Penny J. Orr, M.A.

Beth could be anyone's daughter, sister, mother, or friend. She made a profession of faith in Jesus Christ as soon as she was old enough to understand the gospel. Growing up, much of her life revolved around church activities. She was a model child. She obeyed her parents and excelled in her studies at school. Adults were impressed with her maturity and her peers were drawn to her warm, caring personality. Even though Beth believed that God had forgiven her sins, she still struggled with a persistent sense of inadequacy, failure, and guilt. She worked harder, excelled all the more, and was applauded by her family and friends at church.

After graduating from college, Beth met and married a wonderful Christian man. She pursued her career for a few years until she had her first child. Three other children arrived rather quickly. Beth wasn't prepared for the challenges of motherhood; the responsibilities were overwhelming. The sense of inadequacy that had always troubled her consumed her. She felt hopeless and trapped. No one knew about her silent struggle, not even her husband Brad. She and Brad arrived at church every Sunday morning with their children in tow all polished and smiling.

As Beth's friend, however, you've noticed a change in her. Physically, she's lost weight and there are dark circles under her eyes. She no longer attends the young mother's group on Tuesday mornings. In fact, Beth has not seen nor talked with even her closest friends the last few weeks. She almost seems irresponsible these days; she's not following through on committee responsibilities and becomes agitated when she is graciously reminded of her obligations. Initially you attribute Beth's change to the increasing demands of her young family.

Later, Brad finally breaks his silence. Things are falling apart at home. The house has become cluttered and dirty, the children are unkempt most of the time, and Beth doesn't seem to care. Recently she started leaving supper for him to prepare when he arrives home from work. They don't really fight; in fact, he wishes she would communicate more. She has grown sullen and distant. These changes took place gradually and were barely noticeable, but now they are too apparent to ignore.

Brad is suspicious. Beth had surgery on her knee to repair a recurring injury from college sports. It was uncomfortable and inconvenient, but she healed quickly. She came home from the hospital with prescriptions for painkillers and sedatives that helped her to rest comfortably. That was almost a year ago. Brad thought Beth had stopped taking the medication because she told him the prescriptions had run out. However, he found unfilled prescriptions in her purse from a clinic in the neighboring town. When Brad confronted Beth about the prescriptions, she blamed the family doctor for not believing that her knee still hurt. She accused Brad of being insensitive and not helping her more with the housework. She also claimed the women at church were too petty and demanding.

Yes, Beth was abusing her prescription medication. Not only had the medication relieved her physical pain, she discovered it also relieved her emotional turmoil—at least temporarily. She enjoyed the artificial calm the medication induced. The doctor had instructed her to take the drugs when the post-operative pain bothered her, but after her knee healed, she began taking the drugs when she had a headache, when she needed help falling asleep, and when she felt tense as a result of the children. Beth was surprised to hear herself asking the family doctor to renew the prescription even after her knee healed; he reluctantly agreed. The third time she asked, he refused. Beth found a doctor who didn't know her, and he obliged her request. She then went to another doctor, and then another. Despite her denial and defensiveness, Beth knew what she was doing was wrong. That added to her sense of failure and guilt. She had wept and prayed to God many times in penitent cries of confession. She promised to stop tomorrow, but Tomorrow never came.

Let's suppose that Beth isn't married and doesn't have four children tugging at her skirt demanding her attention. Maybe she is single and finds her job boring and her social life unexciting. Her on-again, off-again engagement holds no promise for a future of wedded bliss. She spends her lonely evenings finding solace and gratification in smooth, creamy chocolate desserts from the local bakery or entire bags of salty, crunchy snacks. It's ridiculous, but Beth (who lives alone) has hidden junk food throughout her apartment. Beth's friends notice the increase in her weight, but she denies having a problem and points to family members who are overweight and says with indifference, "I'm doomed." The truth, however, is that Beth is miserable.

Beth could be a compulsive shopper. Her attic and closets are full of shoes and dresses that don't fit. She proudly rationalizes, "What a bargain, I couldn't resist!" She buys collectibles and the curio cabinets to display them. When she tires of looking at them, she gives them away and starts a new collection. She pays for most of her treasures with credit cards. The monthly bills are so high that she and her husband haven't been able to save a cent. They argue about every shopping spree and every bill.

Maybe you're reading this chapter because you know a "Beth" who is addicted to a substance or activity. You look at her life and see the irrationality of her actions—the denial, the lying, the withdrawal, the broken relationships, and the guilt and remorse. Tough questions fill your mind.

- Why does she continue to do this when she knows she's neglecting her family and responsibilities?
- Aren't the consequences of her sinful behavior enough to make her stop?
- What does she mean when she says that she feels "out of control"?
- Are problems with addiction genetically predetermined or caused by a chemical imbalance, as some researchers suggest?
- How can I help her? What biblical counsel can I offer her?

Scripture holds answers to the tough questions of life. Second Peter 1:3-4 affirms,

His divine power has granted to us everything pertaining to life and godliness, through the true knowledge of Him who called us by His own glory and excellence. For by these He has granted to us His precious and magnificent promises, in order that by them you might become partakers of the divine nature, having escaped the corruption that is in the world by lust.

God has given us everything we need to know about life and godliness. In His Word, He vividly describes the difficult experiences of our lives, including addiction. He doesn't stop with the description, however, He also exposes the root cause of the sin and sorrow and gives us solutions that are effective and sure. God wants us to know and understand addictions so that we can be wise helpers in the lives of our sisters.

Describing and Defining Addiction in Biblical Categories

Characteristics of an Addicted Person

Addiction is a useful word. When someone uses the term *addiction*, we all have an idea of what he means. Even though drugs, alcohol, gambling, and pornography tend to get most of the press, there are other kinds of addiction, too. To be an addict is "to devote or surrender (oneself) to something habitually or obsessively."[1] That something could be just about anything. *Addiction*, however, is not a biblical term. The *problem* existed in Bible times; many descriptions of and warnings against drunkenness and gluttony appear in the Scriptures. We'll be taking a closer look at some of them. But if we are to understand God's solutions, we must be able to define man's problems on God's terms. To do this, I want to approach the task using a biblical analogy. Matthew 7:17 says, "Every good tree bears good fruit; but the bad tree bears bad fruit." We'll begin by doing some "fruit inspection" and answering the question, What are the characteristics of someone who is addicted? Then we'll dig deeper to expose the roots that produce the fruit. How do the Scriptures account for what is happening in the life of this person? What does Scripture call the problem that twentieth-century man has labeled "addiction"?

You will discover, as I did, that the broad foundational principles in Scripture that describe and define the addict are true whether the individual is addicted to drugs, alcohol, exercise, food, or shopping. Later in the chapter, we'll look at the various addictive substances and activities. Some addictive agents present unique concerns that you'll want to be aware of. With the problem thoroughly defined on God's terms, we'll then turn our attention to God's solutions.

Carefully read the following verses:

> *If any man has a stubborn and rebellious son who will not obey his father or his mother, and when they chastise him, he will not even listen to them, then his father and mother shall seize him, and bring him out to the elders of his city at the gateway of his home town. And they shall say to the elders of his*

city, "This son of ours is stubborn and rebellious, he will not obey us, he is a glutton and a drunkard" (Deuteronomy 21:18-20).

Wine is a mocker, strong drink a brawler, and whoever is intoxicated by it is not wise (Proverbs 20:1).

Do not be with heavy drinkers of wine, or with gluttonous eaters of meat; for the heavy drinker and the glutton will come to poverty, and drowsiness will clothe a man with rags (Proverbs 23:20-21).

Who has woe? Who has sorrow? Who has contentions? Who has complaining? Who has wounds without cause? Who has redness of eyes? Those who linger long over wine, those who go to taste mixed wine. Do not look on the wine when it is red, when it sparkles in the cup, when it goes down smoothly; at the last it bites like a serpent, and stings like a viper. Your eyes will see strange things, and your mind will utter perverse things. And you will be like one who lies down in the middle of the sea, or like one who lies down on the top of a mast. They struck me, but I did not become ill; they beat me, but I did not know it. When shall I awake? I will seek another drink (Proverbs 23:29-35).

It is not for kings, O Lemuel, it is not for kings to drink wine, or for rulers to desire strong drink, lest they drink and forget what is decreed, and pervert the rights of all the afflicted (Proverbs 31:4-5).

Woe to those who rise early in the morning that they may pursue strong drink; who stay up late in the evening that wine may inflame them! And their banquets are accompanied by lyre and harp, by tambourine and flute, and by wine; but they do not pay attention to the deeds of the LORD, nor do they consider the work of His hands (Isaiah 5:11-12).

These also reel with wine and stagger from strong drink: The priest and the prophet reel with strong drink, they are confused by wine, they stagger from strong drink; they reel while having visions, they totter when rendering judgment. For all the tables are full of filthy vomit, without a single clean place (Isaiah 28:7-8).

Do not get drunk with wine, for that is dissipation, but be filled with the Spirit (Ephesians 5:18).

I created a list of "fruits" or characteristics of addiction from these verses. Not every fruit will appear in the life of a woman who is struggling with an addiction. The extent to which these bad fruits are apparent is dependent on the woman, the circumstances of her life, the substance or behavior in which she chooses to engage, and the length of time she has pursued the addictive agent. Consider these characteristics:

- sorrow
- discontentment
- lack of wisdom
- forgetfulness
- laziness, lacks motivation
- financial trouble
- stubbornness
- poor judgment
- delusions
- hallucinations
- suspiciousness
- lying
- pursuit of pleasure and entertainment
- irresponsible lifestyle; neglects good nutrition, rest, and exercise
- poor physical appearance; bloodshot or dull eyes, disheveled, weight loss or gain
- long-term physical impairment
- contentions and arguments, strained or broken relationships
- withdrawal from others
- mistreatment and abuse of others
- disrespect of authority (God, civil, parental, or employer), or law-breaking
- rebellion, passive indifference or open hostility
- disregard for punishment and the natural consequences of wrong behavior
- endangerment of self and others
- lack of concern for the things of the Lord

Biblical counselors must pray for and develop the ability to be keen and discerning observers. An accident, a brush with the law, an overdose of drugs or alcohol, ill health, or broken relationships may have precipitated your "Beth's" cry for help. Often, the fruit isn't as obvious and we must seek to bring clarity to that elusive sense that something is wrong. The characteristics I've listed are an excellent place to start in formulating questions that will assist you in gathering data. How much time and money has Beth spent on her addictive agent? Is she in debt as a result? How has Beth's behavior brought sorrow to her family or brothers and sisters in Christ? Is Beth neglecting any of her responsibilities? What characterizes Beth's interaction with others: argumentativeness, self-absorption, indifference, disrespect, ill treatment? Has she lied to you or others about her whereabouts or activities? What changes have you noticed in Beth's spiritual life? How often is she seeking to fellowship with the body of believers? What commands or principles of Scripture has she broken or ignored? How does she view God and His sovereign work in the affairs of her life?

The Origin of an Addiction

Let's turn our attention now to the root from which these fruits of unrighteousness draw their life. This root is not found in the dysfunction of an addict's family of origin, it is not found in her biochemical make-up, nor is it found in her environment. Isaiah 5:11-12 says that those who pursue drunkenness and pleasure "do not pay attention to the deeds of the LORD, nor do they consider the work of His hands." Herein lies the key. If a woman is not paying attention to the deeds of the Lord or considering the work of His hands, she is not truly worshiping Him. More than likely, she is worshiping the object of her addiction. God's first commandment to Moses on Mount Sinai was, "You shall have no other gods before Me. You shall not make for yourself an idol, or any likeness of what is in heaven above or on the earth beneath or in the water under the earth. You shall not worship them or serve them; for I, the LORD your God, am a jealous God" (Exodus 20:3-5).

In the Old Testament, idolatry was most closely associated with the worship of tangible objects made from wood, metal, or stone. The Old Testament prophets made it perfectly clear that the object was not so important as the significance ascribed to it in the heart of the worshiper. Consider Ezekiel 14:1-4:

> Some elders of Israel came to me and sat down before me. And the word of the LORD came to me saying, "Son of man, these men have set up their idols in their hearts, and have put right before their faces the stumbling block of their iniquity. Should I be consulted by them at all? Therefore speak to them and tell them, 'Thus says the Lord GOD, "Any man of the house of Israel who sets up his idols in his heart, puts right before his face the stumbling block of his iniquity, and then comes to the prophet, I the LORD will be brought to give him an answer in the matter in view of the multitude of his idols, in order to lay hold of the hearts of the house of Israel who are estranged from Me through all their idols." ' "

For the elders of Israel, the thought of idols was not one which they casually considered and dismissed. It was a seductive thought which they embraced and to which they gave great forethought. Preoccupation with a substance or behavior—doesn't this describe the addict? Paul, in the New Testament, broadens our understanding of idolatry when he includes intangible idols in the definition: Consider the members of your earthly body as dead to immorality, impurity, passion, evil desire, and greed, which amounts to idolatry" (Colossians 3:5). Addiction is a problem of misdirected worship that issues from an idolatrous heart. Simply put, addiction is idolatry.

God created man to worship and to serve Him and to experience intimate relationship with Him. That relationship was severed by the Fall, and mankind's darkened hearts longed for something to worship. Even though God has since redeemed His own through Christ's atoning work on the cross and has restored our relationship with Him, sin persists and our hearts continue to deceive us. Even then, God lavishes His grace and mercy on us and grants us His precious and magnificent promises. We are not in need of any good thing. Yet we persist in seeking fulfillment in things that we think we can control, things meant to serve us that we eventually come to serve. In fact, these things enslave us and become evil taskmasters bent on our destruction. One secular author was quite insightful in defining addiction as "a pathological love and trust relationship with an object or event."[2] For the child of God, that relationship of love and trust ought to be with a gracious and loving heavenly Father.

A Detailed Look at the Problem of Addiction

Isaiah 44:6-23 is an extremely helpful passage for understanding the addict's experience at the levels of both "root and fruit." With Bible in hand, I invite you to read along as we carefully consider the insights this passage holds.

The prophet Isaiah begins his teaching about idolatry by painting a vivid picture of the one true God whom we should worship (verses 6-8). God is the King, the Redeemer, the Lord of hosts, the first and last. He existed before the world; He created the world and all that it contains; He rightfully rules over His creation of which we are a part; and He has redeemed us from bondage to sin. The challenge then comes, "And who is like Me?" (verse 7). Though God is indeed a great God, we are admonished not to fear for He has made His character and His works abundantly known to us in His Word.

The addict is someone who does not know the character of God or has chosen to doubt and ignore the truth about God that she may already know. She has forgotten that He alone is worthy of worship and able to redeem her from her sorrows. Because she is selfishly demanding and unwilling to come before God on His terms, apply His solutions, and wait on His timetable, she turns to gods of her own design.

As Isaiah begins to speak directly about the issue of idolatry in verse 9, the folly of it becomes even more stark when contrasted against the background of God's character. Isaiah says that the idolater is futile and the idol unprofitable. They are both void of life and power. Why? Because the one who crafts idols is a mere man. The creature is ascribing to the work of her own hands attributes that belong to God alone. How does the addict do this? Consider Beth, the subject of our case study earlier in this chapter. Beth sought release from her overwhelming feelings of inadequacy, failure, and guilt. Rather than deal with the cause of her feelings by acknowledging her sinfulness and claiming by faith the forgiveness and freedom that God has provided in the cross of Christ, Beth looked to drugs as a "savior" from her feelings. The release, though immediate, was superficial and temporary.

Isaiah tells us that the addict is so entrenched in her misunderstanding that she doesn't fully recognize what she is doing. However, eventually she will meet with confusion and shame because idols are, as we've already established, void of life and power. They can't save. And isn't that what ultimately happened to Beth? Her problems were compounded. Isaiah 44:9-11 tells us that the addict is proud and arrogant in her misunderstanding: "Let them all assemble themselves, let them stand up" (verse 11). Some addicts may demonstrate a little more finesse in their expressions of pride, but it will be present. So as a counselor, you'll want to watch for it.

In verses 12-17, Isaiah gives us a long, detailed description of the addict's behavior. John Calvin, in his commentary on Isaiah, offers us some insight into these descriptive verses, which provide a starting place for considering solutions to the problem:

> He might otherwise have condemned this wickedness in a single word or in a few words; but this catalogue points out the fact, as it were, with the finger, and places it before our eyes, while he details the tools and labors and industry and care of workmen, so as almost to bring it actually before us. Men who have their error deeply rooted by nature in their hearts are more deeply affected in this manner than by simple doctrine; for they cannot be roused from their lethargy but by loud and continual cries. Every part must be delivered to them, and broken into small fragments, and even chewed and put into the mouth, as they do with infants, that they may receive the doctrine, which would otherwise appear to them strange and uncommon.[3]

Our expressions of worship can be laden with rituals. Whether you participate in a church that is traditional or contemporary in its Sunday morning worship style, if you observe carefully, you'll recognize that some ways of doing things seem not to change. That doesn't necessarily mean rituals are wrong; in the proper places, rituals can offer a sense of order and familiarity. But in relation to an addiction, the addict's behavior can be very ritualistic. Addictive rituals can be anything from sneaking snack cakes from the freezer and rearranging them so no one will notice to snorting cocaine in a certain place with certain music playing in the background. If we try to identify and expose—fragment by fragment, as Calvin advises—the rituals the addict has built around getting and using her idol, we may break through her blindness and help her to recognize the reality of what she is doing. Simply telling her that she has a problem is not enough.

Addicts can expend great mental thought and physical energy in the pursuit of their idols. Often, as Isaiah 44:12 states, this is to the neglect of things essential for life. Since an idol is lifeless, it must be sustained by the life of the one who created it. As a result, addicts may end up experiencing hunger, thirst, and exhaustion. If an addict is responsible for others, those individuals may be affected as well. For example, malnutrition can be an issue among women who abuse drugs and alcohol heavily. Much of their money is spent on the substance, leaving none to purchase food. Or, their minds are so preoccupied with the thought of their idol that they do not plan and prepare nourishing meals for themselves and their families. This can be true for women who are addicted to soap operas. Their afternoons are wasted in front of the television indulging the pleasures of romantic fantasies and adventures. Their husbands and children, on the other hand, learn to savor the "pleasures" of microwave meals and junk food.

We read in Isaiah 44:14, "Surely he cuts cedars for himself, and takes a cypress or an oak, and raises it for himself among the trees of the forest. He plants a fir, and the rain makes it grow." What Isaiah teaches us is that idolatry starts small and grows. Since this growth can take time, the idolator is often very persistent and obstinate. For example, when Beth's doctor denied her request for refills, she started to visit other doctors. Some prescribed physical therapy for the imaginary aches and pains in her knee, while others prescribed painkillers. Beth became relentless in her search for doctors who were willing to prescribe painkillers. Commenting on Isaiah 44:14, John Calvin said, "As soon as we have been led away by foolish desire to the practice of false worship, there is always reason to fear that we shall be plunged into that whirlpool."[4] It's easier to uproot a sapling than it is to cut down a full-grown cypress or oak tree. When you see a sister struggling with idolatry, don't "wait and see" what happens. The problem usually doesn't go away by itself. Rather, it gets worse.

Isaiah exposes the irony of idolatry in verses 15-17. Often the things that the addict idolizes are good things that God has given for humanity's benefit: food, exercise, medicine, and so on. When we use them properly, we demonstrate that they are indeed subservient to us. Yet we exalt them as gods when we look to them for assistance or a salvation that they cannot give. At the outset, idols become trusted friends because they do indeed deliver what the addict may be seeking. The pleasure of a luscious slice of chocolate-chip cheesecake makes one forget the stress of a challenging day at the office. But day after day, piece after piece, the cheesecake teaches nothing about how to respond biblically to the source of the stress.

The addict, enticed by her own lusts, embraces the lie that this false god is somehow profitable. In the process, she closes her heart to the truth and opens it to deception and delusion. Her heart is deceived and her eyes are spiritually blinded. Isaiah says in verse 20 that she "feeds on ashes." Sadly, she is satisfied with this as her portion. Deceit is a hallmark of addiction; addicts are chronic liars. They lie to themselves, and they will lie to you. The lie may be boldfaced. She may lie to you or family members about her whereabouts or activities. Or the lie may be more subtle. She may secretly reduce the amount of time she spends exercising. She may rationalize and justify her most recent credit-card purchases. The discerning counselor will anticipate such lies, listen for them in the addict's conversation, and hold her accountable to speak the truth.

Summarizing the Rituals of Addiction

Before we begin to consider biblical solutions, let's pull together some basic principles and look at the idolatrous ritual that characterizes every addict.

Stage One: Challenges. We live in a sinful world. We are sinned against and we sin. Every day we are confronted with difficulties, suffering, temptations, and battles. The addict attempts to accomplish one or more of the following things as she lives out her life day by day:

- Avoid responsibility that is rightfully hers
- Dull emotions she deems unpleasant, such as loneliness, fear, grief, rejection, failure, guilt, anger, stress, and so on

- Satisfy a consuming felt need; that is a lustful desire
- Escape the reality of genuinely difficult circumstances

Stage Two: Choices. Being morally responsible creatures before a holy God, we can choose to serve and glorify God when confronted by responsibility, unpleasant emotions, lustful desires, and difficulties; or we can choose to serve ourselves. The addict chooses to serve herself and accomplish her purposes. She does this by choosing to use the substance or engage in the behavior that has become her idol.

Stage Three: False Comfort. The idol delivers, almost immediately, what the addict is seeking to gain: a mental or emotional shift away from the realities of life in a sinful world. She experiences relaxation, fulfillment, euphoria, gratification, pleasure, or comfort.

Stage Four: Immediate Consequences. At first, the consequences of idolatry aren't very noticeable. The idolater can easily dismiss the subtle feelings of guilt with simple rationalizations: "I drank just a little too much the other night—It's never happened before. I don't have a problem," or "My clothes still fit. I haven't pushed the limits yet. When I do, I can always diet." The benefits of idolatry certainly outweigh any risks, or so it would seem. As time passes, however, the consequences of worshiping an idol begin to mount.

Stage Five: Long-term Consequences. Not only is the addict confronted by the challenges, difficulties, and temptations of life, she adds to that burden the guilt, shame, fear, self-disgust, and complications that accompany the use of her addictive agent. (We listed many of these "bad fruits" earlier in the chapter.) What does she do? She blindly turns again to her idol—the addictive agent—for comfort, pleasure, or relief, and the idolatrous ritual begins again. Choice after choice, repetition after repetition, she eventually discovers that she is in downward spiral. Yet the ritual is sacred to her. She will build around it a defensive wall of denial, rationalization, blameshifting, and justification, each brick held in place by the mortar of pride.

The Idols of Addiction

We've already referred to many of the substances and activities that can become the idols of addiction. Below is a thorough yet hardly exhaustive list of them.

- drugs
- alcohol
- exercise
- anger

- cigarettes
- prescription medication
- nose spray
- over-the-counter drugs
- chocolate
- coffee
- sex
- homosexuality
- pornography
- gambling
- shoplifting

- food
- spending money
- relationships
- ministry
- work
- television
- romance novels
- entertainment
- self-exaltation
- gossip
- perfectionism

When I think about the substances and activities of addiction, it is helpful to do so in light of a basic biblical truth about how God created us. Scripture teaches that human beings are made up of two components: the physical part, which we can see—the body, or the "outer woman"—and the unseen spiritual part, or the "inner woman." The inner woman is described in Scripture with the words *heart, soul, spirit,* or *mind,* but they all refer to the same thing. The outer woman and inner woman are separate and distinct components, yet they function as a unity and influence one another. The Scripture calls the body weak in that it is subject to illness, injury, and decay. However, the Scripture makes it very clear that it is the "inner woman" that is morally responsible before God. It is the heart that is sinful or righteous as it makes choices in response to the influences of the body.[5]

We've all heard stories about uncommon displays of superhuman strength in the face of danger. For example, a petite mother lifts the front end of a station wagon to free her injured child. This feat was enabled by the rush of a chemical that her body produces in response to the danger. This chemical quickened her sense of alertness and gave strength to her muscles; it's called *adrenaline*. Our emotions, whether a mild sense of pleasure or euphoria, are also influenced by biochemicals that are released by our central nervous system in response to various stimuli.

The Effects of Chemical Addiction

At the top of our list of idols we have chemical substances. These trigger the desired emotional shift through artificial means—that is, the drug or alcohol replaces the chemical the body would normally produce. People who abuse street drugs usually experiment until they have discovered which chemicals and how much of them produce the emotional effect they are after. As we move down through the list of idols, we see activities that trigger the desired emotional shift by stimulating production of the body's own biochemicals. Thus when we counsel someone struggling with an addiction, we cannot ignore the interaction of the body and the heart. This is especially true if the individual has chosen drugs or alcohol as her idol.

If a drug is regularly present in a person's body over a long enough period of time, the central nervous system will shut down production of its own biochemicals or somehow compensate for the presence of the drug. Entire chapters in books on physiology and pharmacology are devoted to explaining this phenomenon on a molecular level. It is quite fascinating reading if you are scientifically minded. Truly, we are fearfully and wonderfully made! But for our intent and purpose, we need to understand three concepts that result from this biochemical interaction in the body, *tolerance, physical dependence*, and *withdrawal*.

Tolerance simply means that repeated exposure to the drug results in diminishing effect. The abuser will eventually need to use larger amounts of the drug to achieve the same emotional shift she experienced in the early days of her idolatry.

The following graph helps us understand what is happening. Let's say that the solid line represents a normal level of biochemical and emotional functioning. When the chemical abuser uses a drug for the first time, she experiences the sought-after emotional "high" with little, if any, aftereffects. As her body compensates for the presence of the drug, the high isn't quite as "high" as it used to be. The aftereffect of using the drug is a "crash" characterized by depression, fatigue, body aches, and a variety of other symptoms. The crash is caused by the depletion of the chemical in her body. You can see that as time goes on, the chemical abuser will reach a point where she has to use the drug just to "feel normal." By this time her body has developed a *dependence* on the drug in order to function.

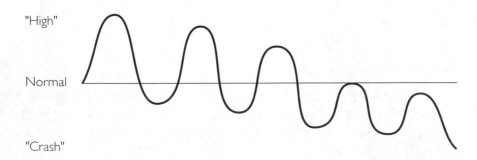

When counseling a woman who has been using drugs or alcohol extensively, you may pose a danger to her if you suggest that she quits "cold turkey." *Withdrawal* can occur as her body readjusts to the absence of the chemical. Withdrawal can be as mild as a high fever, runny nose, and flu-like symptoms, or as serious as a rapid pulse rate, high blood pressure, convulsions, or hallucinations. You should begin by encouraging your counselee to have a thorough medical examination. In some cases, hospitalization may be required to carefully monitor the detoxification process. In other cases, a gradual reduction in dosage over time may be required. This needs to be medically supervised.

Counselors should be familiar with the drugs that counselees use, the side effects of those drugs, and the potential withdrawal symptoms. In addition, people who abuse street drugs generally use more than one drug, so counselors need to be on the lookout for potentially dangerous drug interactions. A drug plus alcohol is the typical combination. An extensive discussion of these problems is beyond the scope of this chapter; you will want to continue your research at the local public library once you know what your counselee has been using.

The Types of Addictive Drugs

As a framework for your research, here is an overview of the five classes into which drugs of abuse are generally categorized. Each class of drugs is defined by the effect of the drug on the user.

1. *Stimulants* produce a heightened sense of awareness and energy in the user and include caffeine, amphetamines, and cocaine. Stimulants also include diet pills.

2. *Depressants* have a depressive effect on the user. Their use may result in relaxation, lack of coordination, slowed reaction time, recklessness, and unconsciousness. Alcohol, barbituates, benzodiazepines (Ativan, Librium, Valium, and Xanax), and methaqualone ("quaaludes" as it is known on the street) belong to the class of drugs known as depressants.

3. *Narcotics* are painkillers that can induce sleep at high enough dosages. They tend to dull the user's sense of awareness and alertness. This class includes opium, morphine, codeine, heroin, Demerol, Percodan, and Talwin.

4. *Hallucinogens* induce altered visual and auditory perceptions. LSD, mescaline, phencyclidine ("angel dust"), and certain derivatives of the amphetamines are all hallucinogens.

5. Marijuana and hashish seem to defy classification according to their effect on the user and are placed in a class by themselves called *cannabis* (the

scientific name for the marijuana plant). Marijuana can be a relaxant in low doses and can cause altered perceptions in high doses.

The likelihood of physical dependence is greatest with depressants and narcotics, possible with stimulants, and very low with hallucinogens and marijuana. Consequently, the greatest possibility of withdrawal symptoms exists with depressants (anxiety, delirium, convulsions, death), narcotics (watery eyes, loss of appetite, chills, sweating, nausea), and stimulants (depression, apathy, irritability, disorientation, excessive sleeping).

Biblical Solutions for Addictions

Addiction—that is, idolatry—is a life-dominating sin. No matter how hard she tries to prevent it, every area of your counselee's life is touched by her worship of a false god. Her idol dictates the friends she chooses or abandons. It rules her checkbook, distracts her from responsibilities to her family or employer, and may fill her empty hours with pleasure. The idol is the ruling principle of her life.

When we as counselors and disciplers work to dislodge the false god in an idolator's life, she may respond with the sense of grief, emptiness, and anxiety that is associated with losing a lifelong, inseparable companion. Therefore, we cannot think simply in terms of removing the idol; we must think in terms of reconstructing a whole life from the ground up. Ephesians 4:22-24 describes this substitutionary principle by commanding us as believers to "lay aside the old self" and "put on the new self." This must happen at both the "root" level of beliefs, attitudes, and thoughts and the "fruit" level of behaviors.

We must understand that this biblical reconstruction is a process, and not a simple one at that. If we are to be faithful, responsible counselors, we must be prepared to carefully examine and understand how each stage of the idolatrous ritual has developed and played out in the counselee's life. We must be creative in bringing the truths of Scripture to bear on the circumstances of her life and in formulating decisive steps of intervention. We must be prepared to meet with resistance from our friend as we attempt to chip away at her self-protective wall of lying, denial, rationalizing, and blameshifting. In other words, we must be willing to make a commitment to demonstrate the patient, longsuffering love of God toward our friend for the long haul.

No set formula exists for how to go about this process of biblical restoration. You will never be able to check off "step one," then "step two," then "step three." *I prefer to think in terms of biblical principles applied in the context of the idolater's life.* For example, Mary watches soap operas obsessively, and our friend Beth abuses prescription drugs. Soap operas do not involve the "inner woman/outer woman" principle of Scripture to the same extent that drugs do. My first concern for Beth would be to get her to a physician to assess the potential for physical dependence and withdrawal. With Mary, however, we can jump right to strategizing ways for her to escape the temptation of turning on the television in the afternoon according to 1 Corinthians 10:13. Beth might not be ready for these strategies right away. With both women, I want to eventually understand what challenges of life have provided them with the temptation to choose idolatry. I want to help them "put on" a new understanding of God and the proper biblical response to the temptations they face. This process won't be the same for everyone; depending on the situation, the application of some principles will naturally take precedence over others. The need to begin addressing one may arise while working to apply another.

You may be asking yourself, "How do I know where to begin and what to do when?" My response is twofold: Know God, and know the woman whom you are trying to help. Your friend has been looking to a false god and has lost sight of the one true God. You are His ambassador in her life. Your sister can learn of Him as you are faithful to minister His grace and mercy in her life and to model Christlike behavior in your own life. You are able to do this to the extent that you know and serve God yourself. Ambassadors not only represent a king, they are servants who do his bidding. God is very much in control of this process of restoration in your friend's life. Your role is to pray for her and to serve her as God grants discernment and direction. Having read this chapter, you now know a lot more about your friend. You know some important facts. Do you know these facts as they find unique expression in the life of your friend? She will be increasingly open to you and receptive to your involvement if she perceives that you are genuinely concerned about her and intent on ministering the grace of God to her. Tackle the more immediate issues first, and doors will begin to open to the deeper concerns.

Here are some key overarching principles for helping someone with an addiction:

Principle #1: Understand fully the nature of your friend's idol worship. We cannot help someone sever a relationship with an idol without first understanding the "little" rituals she has established around the worship of it. Ask your friend the following questions about her thoughts, feelings, and actions:

- In what circumstances do you find yourself when you are tempted to sin?
- What happens?

- What are you thinking?
- What are you feeling?
- What do you do in response?
- What are you trying to achieve?
- When do you do it?
- Where do you do it?
- Who is with you when you "indulge," or are you alone?

Don't be afraid to ask for details. If you can't get a clear picture of what she is doing, have your friend keep a journal. She should record answers to the who?, what?, where?, when?, why?, and how? questions every time she is tempted or actually sins. Recording the day and time these temptations occur is also important. What the two of you want to look for are patterns in the worship of her idol.

Principle #2: Help your friend sever her relationship with her idol. Having identified the behaviors that need to be "put off," you can begin to plan behaviors to "put on." For example, maybe your friend passes a bakery or liquor store on her way home from work and she frequently stops there. The "put on" may be as simple as taking another route home from work. Scripture calls us, in 2 Timothy 2:22, to "flee from youthful lusts." Some temptations come upon us unexpectedly, others occur in situations that can be anticipated and avoided. Help her to be prepared for both kinds of temptations.

Not only should we watch for pattern behaviors, we should also watch for patterns in thought and attitude. These often find expression in the idolator's manner of speech. Idolatry is deceitful, and idolators have trained themselves to selectively forget the harsh realities of their sinful lifestyle. They will often glamorize their experience by speaking with fond remembrance of the "good times" and enjoyable aspects of their sin. They may develop their own special language around the idolatry. Or, they may dwell on the idol and speak about it incessantly. Listen to your friend carefully. Graciously repeat back to her what you just heard or how you perceived it. Your faithfulness to speak the truth in love will help her gain an awareness of what she is doing and open a window to her heart. Philippians 4:8 admonishes,

Finally, brethren, whatever is true, whatever is honorable, whatever is right, whatever is pure, whatever is lovely, whatever is of good repute, if there is any excellence and if anything worthy of praise, let your mind dwell on these things.

Memorizing relevant passages of Scripture is a helpful way for your friend to stop dwelling on her idolatry.

The Scripture commands us in Matthew 5:29-30 to practice "radical amputation" where sin is concerned. The "put offs" in an idolater's life may include people—friends with whom she engages in her idolatrous behavior or an individual who has become the idol. Seeing the necessity of breaking ties with "bad company" (1 Corinthians 15:33) is obvious. Seeing the necessity of breaking ties with good, moral, upstanding citizens, which is sometimes the case, isn't so obvious. Either way, it's difficult. The fear of severing emotional ties, of offending someone, or of experiencing loneliness can be strong. You must encourage your friend to make cultivating the fruits of righteousness and honoring the Lord the top priorities in her life. "Nevertheless many even of the rulers believed in Him, but because of the Pharisees they were not confessing Him, lest they should be put out of the synagogue; for they loved the approval of men rather than the approval of God" (John 12:42-43).

Principle #3: Help your friend re-establish her relationship with God. Let's return to Isaiah 44 for a moment. Verse 20 says, "He [the idolator] cannot deliver himself." Carefully executed blueprints for restoration in an idolator's life will not work apart from the Master Builder. "Unless the LORD builds the house, they labor in vain who build it; unless the LORD guards the city, the watchman keeps awake in vain" (Psalm 127:1). How many times has your friend determined to do better tomorrow? How many times has she promised to smoke one less cigarette? How many diet plans are posted on her refrigerator door or tucked away in the pantry?

An idolator's feeble efforts fail because they do not address the root issue—sin. Her failed attempts at restoration are caused by her lack of brokenness and grief at the realization that she is sinful and has offended a holy God. Rather, she is harboring a selfish desire for relief from the emotional turmoil and consequences of her sin. The very thing that opened the door to her idolatry in the first place is what motivates her efforts to change, guarantees her failure, and holds her captive. That thing is a self-absorbed focus on her own desires and pleasures and a forgetfulness of God. She must begin the restoration process by submitting to the lordship of Christ in her life.

Isaiah calls the idolator to "remember these things, O Jacob"(44:21). What things? The things he said about the one true God (verses 6-8) and the folly of worshiping a false god (verses 9-20). The way to help your friend re-establish her relationship with God is by reminding her of who He is. (*See* chapter 3

"The Essential Foundation.") You do that by modeling for her, as we've already discussed, the Christlike qualities of mercy, patience, longsuffering, and truthfulness. I appreciate Sinclair Ferguson's definition of mercy: It's "getting down on your hands and knees and doing what you can to restore dignity to someone whose life has been broken by sin (whether his own or that of someone else)."[6] You also help your friend re-establish her relationship with God by pointing her to the Scriptures—especially passages that speak of God in relation to the present circumstances of her life. "Error and delusions can never prevail," John Calvin wrote, "so long as the remembrance of God is rooted in our hearts."[7]

When delusion and error are recognized through the remembrance of God, brokenness, confession, and repentance should follow. Be mindful that addicts can be guilt-ridden and full of shame. Help your friend understand the difference between sorrow or guilt that produces true repentance and the sorrow of the world, which produces death (*see* 2 Corinthians 7:6-12). Sorrow that produces repentance remembers God and embraces His grace, demonstrated on the cross of Christ, as the only solution for man's sinful condition. Sorrow that produces death forgets God and in pride embraces futile self-effort in an attempt to save oneself. Humility and submission to God must replace pride and self-effort (*see* James 4:6-10). Help your friend understand also that repentance is not a one time act. She must make choices each day and each hour to serve God rather than herself through her idol.

In her striving against sin, your friend may have times when she fails—perhaps even repeatedly. Rather than become introspective and focus on her sin, she must be encouraged to focus on the cross of Christ and the riches of grace that belong to the children of God. (A very helpful work on this topic that offers a companion study guide is *The Discipline of Grace* by Jerry Bridges [Colorado Springs: NavPress, 1994].) When Isaiah contemplated the redemption of God, he broke forth into praise:

> *Shout for joy, O heavens, for the LORD has done it! Shout joyfully, you lower parts of the earth; break forth into a shout of joy, you mountains, O forest, and every tree in it; For the LORD has redeemed Jacob and in Israel He shows forth His glory (Isaiah 44:23).*

Help your friend praise God by cultivating a grateful heart. Praising God not only helps her express gratitude to God, it is also a reminder to her that He indeed does desire to show forth His glory in her life.

The ways in which your friend can re-establish her relationship with God are through daily meditative Bible reading and earnest prayer, Scripture memorization, church attendance, and reading Christian literature. You can serve as a facilitator in this process; you can encourage her to meet daily with God. You might accompany her to the weekly worship service and other church activities. Recommend biblically sound reading material, or have a weekly Bible study with her. Remember that it is the Spirit of God who is responsible for bringing about the changes that you long to see take place in her life.

Principle #4: Help your friend reconcile any broken relationships and build strong relationships with her family, friends, and the church community. We are all familiar with the greatest commandment: "'You shall love the Lord your God with all your heart, and with all your soul, and with all your mind' . . . The second is like it, 'You shall love your neighbor as yourself'" (Matthew 22:37,39). Not only should your friend strive to cease serving herself and start serving God, she should also consider how she can start to serve others.

Depending on the addiction, the sin an idolator commits against her friends and family by serving herself can have a variety of consequences. A home-maker addicted to romance novels or soap operas may neglect her household duties. Her husband and children may feel uncomfortable in a dirty, cluttered home and resentful that she places an unfair amount of responsibility on them to do the cleaning. A woman who has been entrenched in drug and alcohol abuse for some time may have done what seems to be irreparable damage to her relationships. Serving others may need to begin with humbly confessing sins committed against the other persons and asking for forgiveness. She may also need to learn what it means to forgive. An improper response to sins committed against her may have been one of the challenges of life that provoked her to choose idolatry.

Remind your friend that trust takes time to rebuild. The sincerity of her intentions must be demonstrated in tangible acts of love. The "one another" and "each other" verses of Scripture will provide a starting place for her to think about how she is to love others. (*See* "one another" verses NIV: Romans 12:10, 16; 13:8; 14:13; 15:7; Galatians 5:13; Ephesians 4:2,32; 5:19,21; Colossians 3:13; 1 Thessalonians 5:11; Hebrews 3:13; 10:24,25; James 4:11; 1 Peter 1:22; 3:8; 4:9; 5:5; 1 John 3:11,23; 4:7,11,12; 2 John 5. *Also see* "each other" verses NIV: John 15:12,17; Galatians 5:15,26; Ephesians 4:32; Colossians 3:9,13; 1 Thessalonians 3:12; 5:11,15; Hebrews 13:1 James 5:9,16; 1 Peter 4:8.) For each of the verses that contain the phrase "one another" or "each other," have her write down two or three tangible ways that she can extend to her family and friends what the verse commands. For example, James 5:16 commands us to "confess your sins to one another." She may need to approach her husband, children, or friends, confess specific ways she has sinned against them, and ask them to forgive her. She will then need to plan how she will be devoted to her family or friends in brotherly love (*see* Romans 12:10). This may find expression in getting up in the morning to prepare breakfast for her family and see them off to school or work. Or, it may mean supporting her children by attending their extra-curricular sports activities and programs.

Not only should your friend be learning to serve others, the body of Christ should come alongside of her to strengthen her as she strives against sin. According to Titus 2:3-5, the older women of our churches are responsible to teach the younger women about serving God and their families. It is also interesting that the older women are to model for the younger what it means to not be "enslaved to much wine." Identify spiritually mature women in your church with whom your friend can cultivate relationships. This can be in the context of a women's Bible study, a discipleship relationship, or a prayer partnership. One or two other woman in the church should be ready to help your friend with accountability and prayer when she is facing temptation and struggles.

Building a variety of relationships with other women is essential when a woman's idol is another person. This is a caution to you as a helper. If a network of relationships is not being built, you may become the next object of idolatry. A relationship idolator is masterful at creating the illusion of having a relationship. At the outset, she will listen attentively to your counsel and appear to be open and genuine. In reality, she may be suppressing her true thoughts and feelings and looking to you to meet her needs. She will strive to please you. She will endeavor to spend increasing amounts of exclusive time with you. Watch for her responses when your attention is turned to other people or responsibilities. She may attempt to control the situation through accusations or emotional appeals. Minister to her as a sister in Christ, but do not give in to the temptation to rescue her. Hold her responsible for her reactions and behavior. Don't allow her to become dependent on you in an idolatrous way. If you need to be needed, then you will not be helping her.

Principle #5: Help your friend to be truthful in all things. Ephesians 4:14-15 says,

> *. . . we are no longer to be children, tossed here and there by waves, and carried about by every wind of doctrine, by the trickery of men, by craftiness in deceitful scheming; but speaking the truth in love, we are to grow up in all aspects into Him, who is the head, even Christ.*

Idolatry is deceitful; it pulls a person into a world filled with lies. Your friend may be so convinced of the lies she has concocted that she has lost sight of the truth. If so, then someone needs to lovingly bring that to her attention.

We've already mentioned many of the situations that you may encounter which will be an invitation for you to speak the truth in love to your friend. They are important, so let's review them. Take careful notice of her:

- blaming her actions on something or someone else
- rationalizing the extent of her sin
- justifying why she did what she did
- intellectualizing her behavior in order to ignore the consequences or painful emotions
- glamorizing her sin or recalling only the good times
- lying about what she has been doing
- using pet phrases to describe her sin in order to avoid the reality of what she has done; for example, a rendezvous rather than adultery
- avoiding people or circumstances that remind her of the consequences of her sin

There are many ways you can help your friend recognize the truth about what she is doing. When you catch her rationalizing her behavior or blaming someone else for the choices she has made, you can point out what she is doing. You or a loved one can significantly influence the addict by expressing how you feel in response to her behavior or words. All too often, we ignore our own feelings and respond with accusatory statements that may end up putting her on the defensive. Responding with, "Beth, when you're taking the pills, you seem so distant. I feel alienated from you and the children are confused. The kids asked me the other day if you still love them because you don't spend time with them anymore" is an invitation for her to examine the consequences of her actions.

Principle 6: Build a network of accountability for your friend. A strong network of accountability is very important. As we've already mentioned, older women in the church can help nurture your friend's devotional life and be available for prayer and encouragement when she is tempted. Having your friend keep a journal can be an effective means of accountability also. In it she can record how often and how much time is given to her idolatrous behavior or quantities of substances used. Journaling can help reveal whether your friend is minimizing the situation or avoiding the truth. For example, what does she mean when she writes, "I had a few potato chips this afternoon." Did she, in fact, eat the whole bag?

Your friend's spouse or close family members are an important part of her support system as well and shouldn't be overlooked. They can be a tremendous help in holding her accountable to be truthful in word and deed. Remember, your friend may not always present an accurate picture of her life outside of the counseling room. Family members will often speak with greater detail and honesty about her idolatry. When you consult them or enlist their help, be sure that your friend is aware of what you are doing and why you are doing it. Avoid all appearances of gossip. If your conversation with your friend's loved one exposes any lying, minimizing, or avoidance of the truth on her part, you and the loved one should lovingly confront her as soon as possible according to the principles in Mathew 18:15-17.

Principle #7: Help your friend establish a regular daily schedule. Involvement with an idol can disrupt a person's normal daily routine and interfere with her responsibilities. Street drug abusers tend to party all night and sleep most of the day. Truancy or cutting classes is common among school-aged women as is time lost on the job for employed women. Women who are extremely obese from overeating can become depressed and sedentary. Their inward focus results in neglect of their appearance and environment. Those who spend excessive amounts of time with romance novels, television, or another person are allowing themselves to be distracted from the things that really matter.

In 2 Thessalonians 3:10-11, Paul said, "Even when we were with you, we used to give you this order: if anyone will not work, neither let him eat. For we hear that some among you are leading an undisciplined life, doing no work at all, but acting like busybodies." The goal we want to keep in view is a disciplined, productive lifestyle to the glory of God. Knowing what needs to be accomplished and when it needs to be done aids in developing discipline.

Work with your friend to plan a weekly schedule. Have her list her responsibilities—a job, grocery shopping, housecleaning, cooking, laundry, and so on. Set aside blocks of time on the schedule for each of these responsibilities. Don't forget to include time with her children and spouse (if she is married), time for personal devotions, time for exercise (whether it's a walk around the neighborhood or 20 minutes of an exercise video), and time for church. Be mindful of the little things. Encourage your friend to eat meals at regular times. She should also go to bed in the evening and get up in the morning at the same time each day.

Consistency is important. And point out that the purpose in planning a schedule is not to provide her with a standard of perfection that instills guilt every time the mark is missed. Life can be unpredictable. The schedule is a merely a guideline, a very useful one. Its purpose is to provide needed structure and order to a disorderly life.

As you work on the schedule, anticipate unexpected empty hours and plan for them. These times can be open invitations for your friend to engage in her idolatry. With some idolatries such as drug and alcohol abuse, dependent relationships, and "workaholism," women do not know how to use their leisure time. They cannot relax and have fun apart from the idol. We may have to help these women discover leisure activities that will honor God. In any case, a plan with several options should be in place.

Principle #8: If appropriate, help your friend improve her physical health. Principle #8, in many ways, goes hand in hand with Principle #7. Proper rest, exercise, and nutrition are essential for everyone. However, it will be of more concern for some idolatries than for others—specifically drug and alcohol abuse, overeating, and sexual promiscuity. Women who fit these categories should be encouraged to have a thorough medical examination. Drug and alcohol abusers will need to assess the extent of damage done to their bodies by the chemicals. Overeaters will need to be approved by a physician prior to starting any weight-management program. Women who have been sexually promiscuous will need to determine if they have exposed themselves to sexually transmitted diseases, including AIDS.

A nutritionally balanced diet and proper exercise are essential. The interaction of the "inner woman" and "outer woman" discussed earlier in this chapter is truly complex. What goes—or doesn't go—into our mouths can affect our mood. Many drug and alcohol rehabilitation centers serve the residents meals that are free of excess sugar, caffeine, and white flour. These substances trigger cravings that chemically dependent people can interpret as cravings for their drugs of choice. The benefit of exercise is that it releases substances into our bodies called *endorphins,* which generate a feeling of energy and well-being. In appropriate levels, exercise is a good preventive to the depressive moods that tempt some women to turn to their idol.

Principle #9: Help your friend understand biblical alternatives for dealing with the challenges of life and distressing emotions. We live in a fallen, sinful world. We sin and we are sinned against. God has done something about sin and suffering; He has won the victory over it through the death, burial, and resurrection of Christ on the cross. Unfortunately, an underlying belief that gives momentum to the behavior of most idolators is, "I shouldn't have to suffer." But such an assumption is inconsistent with truth of Scripture.

Suffering is a thread that runs through the fiber of Scripture.[8] Examples of men and women who have suffered abound throughout the Bible. We can learn from their examples. Scripture also abounds with God's precious and magnificent promises; we can claim them by faith. Be diligent to direct your friend to passages of Scripture that speak to her past and present sufferings. Help her to understand that through suffering, God desires to mature her in Christlikeness and bring glory to Himself. "After you have suffered for a little while, the God of all grace, who called you to His eternal glory in Christ, will Himself perfect, confirm, strengthen and establish you" (1 Peter 5:10).

Suffering can be defined as having something you don't want and wanting something you don't have. An inordinate amount of "wanting" leads to lustful desire and idolatry. Wanting the wrong things, wanting them so that they may be spent on selfish pleasures (*see* James 4:2-3), and wanting them immediately are all characteristic of idolators. Help your friend learn to have faith in the God who "comforts us in all our affliction" (2 Corinthians 1:4). Teach her from the Scriptures how "our comfort is abundant through Christ" (2 Corinthians 1:5).

Principle #10: Give your friend hope. Read Romans 5:1-8. We can blame addiction on a supposed "dysfunction" in the addict's family of origin, on environmental influences, on genetics or physiology or disease. These "explanations" certainly sound kinder to the ear of the hearer than the explanation of Scripture. But addiction is sin, and the addict is a sinner. It's a harsher reality to hear and receive, but it is the only one that offers true and lasting hope. God Himself has provided the solution to sin: "Hope does not disappoint, because the love of God has been poured out within our hearts through the Holy Spirit who was given to us. For while we were still helpless, at the right time Christ died for the ungodly" (Romans 5:5-6). The Bible speaks well and speaks adequately to the problem of addiction. Be confident that the Word of God contains all that is needed to loose the addict/idolator from the bonds of her sins.

From Addiction to Freedom

The first step for Beth was to admit that she had a problem. She was resistant at first. However, her husband Brad and her closest friend at church, Laura, lovingly and graciously persisted in confronting her with the truth about what she was doing and how they felt in response to her actions. Concerned for their children's safety, Brad made arrangements to have a relative care for them while he was at work. He explained to Beth that he could not trust her judgment as long as she was taking the medication. She was heartbroken and finally realized that she needed help.

Laura did some reading about the medication Beth was abusing. She learned about the potential for side effects and difficulties during withdrawal. She first advised that Beth make an appointment with the family doctor. In fact, she accompanied Beth to the appointment and listened to the doctor's instructions for discontinuing the medication. The plan was to gradually cut back on the dosage over a period of time.

Laura was a faithful friend. She prayed for Beth daily and called her regularly. They met twice a week to go for walks or to just talk and pray together. She sent timely notes with verses of Scripture to encourage Beth. Sometimes Beth was very moody and short-tempered as her body adjusted to taking decreasing amounts of the medication. Beth was also experiencing the emotions she had tried to dull with the medication. They seemed more intense than ever. Laura didn't personalize Beth's moodiness or remarks; she consistently demonstrated forgiveness and grace.

During their walks, Laura asked Beth all the who, what, where, when, why, and how questions. She learned a lot about Beth. Beth eventually admitted her "need" to "be perfect" and her struggles with feelings of inadequacy, especially as a mom. Laura introduced Beth to Mrs. Webster. Mrs. Webster knew about managing a busy household; she'd raised five children. Mrs. Webster also knew God. She had a vibrant faith and intimate relationship with God that was contagious. Beth agreed to meet with Mrs. Webster regularly to learn how to be a better mom. Along the way, she also learned how to live as a child of God.

Some days, Beth didn't "feel" very victorious, even when she'd been obedient. Other days, she failed miserably. She'd ignore her responsibilities or withdraw from Brad and treat him with indifference. But she learned to rest on the grace of God and not on her feelings or performance. Laura and Mrs. Webster were careful to remind Beth about God's grace. As Beth's understanding of God grew, so did her desire to please Him through her obedience. She came to experience the joy and blessedness that can come only through worshiping and serving the one true God. May *your* "Beth" also come to know the joy of worshiping and serving the one true God!

Recommended Resources

Jay E. Adams, *You Can Kick the Drug Habit,* Grand Rapids: Baker Books, 1975.
Jerry Bridges, *The Discipline of Grace,* Colorado Springs: NavPress, 1994.
Margaret Clarkson, *Destined for Glory: The Meaning of Suffering,* Grand Rapids: Eerdmans, 1983.

Sinclair B. Ferguson, *A Heart for God,* Carlisle, PA: The Banner of Truth Trust, 1987.

_____, *Kingdom Life in a Fallen World: Living Out the Sermon on the Mount,* Colorado Springs: NavPress, 1986.

Gary S. Shogren and Edward T. Welch, *Running in Circles,* Grand Rapids: Baker Books, 1995.

Edward T. Welch, *Addictive Behavior,* Grand Rapids: Baker Books, 1995.

_____, *Counselor's Guide to the Brain and Its Disorders,* Grand Rapids: Zondervan, 1991.

CHAPTER 16

Counseling Women for Overeating and Bulimia

Elyse Fitzpatrick, M.A.

I am unceasingly amazed at the number of Christian women for whom eating is an area of confusion or even slavery. Many books have been written recently on the subject of disordered eating. Overeating and bulimia are topics of concern to many people. Women spend millions of dollars a year on weight-loss programs. Mothers grieve over their daughters' obsession with weight and are distressed as they discover their bulimic behaviors. Christian women search for help in the latest prescription drugs and across the land. "Fat Burner" classes at private gyms are full. Both secular and Christian publishers have had input in this area. What's going on here? Why do so many Christian women struggle with overeating or give into binging and purging?

"Obesity is a serious problem for Americans," says Dr. F. Xavier Pi-Sunyer, a professor of medicine at Columbia University. A 1991 study found that one-third of U.S. adults are obese. To be classified as obese, a person must be 20 percent or more over their ideal body weight.[1] For a 5'4" woman, this would amount to about 25 pounds. In addition, "a whopping 42% of women ages 45 to 54 are 20% over a desirable weight."[2] According to the U.S. Food and Drug Administration the weight-loss industry is a booming business. "Americans spend an estimated $30 billion a year on all types of diet programs and products, including diet foods and drinks."[3] An estimated 50 million Americans will go on diets this year. Sadly, only 5 percent of those who lose weight will manage to keep it off in the long run. Women are looking for help in many different venues. According to a Weight Watchers® fact sheet, more than 600,000 people are presently attending 15,000 weekly meetings in the U.S.[4] In addition to these support groups, there are also about 8,500 commercial diet centers offering structured weight loss programs. These programs involve liquid diets, special diet regimens, medical or other supervision. About 8 million Americans a year enroll in these programs.[5]

Why do women overeat? Why would a woman binge or force herself to vomit? Why do women resolve to control their eating, only to find themselves slipping back into the same old patterns time after time? Are these problems initiated by low self-esteem? What should a Christian think about "compulsions"? Does the Bible address these kinds of behavior? Should Christians even be concerned with their eating habits or their weight?

In this chapter I propose to answer these questions. First, let's take a brief look at what the Bible has to say about food and eating. Second, let's look at what it says to the woman who habitually overeats and how she is helped. Finally, we'll examine what the Bible says to the woman who practices habits of binging and purging and how she can be helped.

Biblical Principles on Food and Eating

It's interesting that the subject of food comes up in Scripture almost immediately. In Genesis 1:29 God declares, "Then God said, 'Behold, I have given you every plant yielding seed that is on the surface of all the earth, and every tree which has fruit yielding seed; it shall be food for you.' " God originally gave man seeds and fruit for food, but after the flood He gave animals as well. "Every moving thing that is alive shall be food for you; I give all to you, as I gave the green plant" (Genesis 9:3).

God Created Food for Nourishment and Pleasure

God purposely created food for man and pronounced it good. Both the Old and New Testaments illustrate this also:

> He causes the grass to grow for the cattle, and vegetation for the labor of man, so that he may bring forth food from the earth, and wine which makes man's heart glad, so that he may make his face glisten with oil, and food which sustains man's heart (Psalm 104:14-15).

He did not leave Himself without witness, in that He did good and gave you
rains from heaven and fruitful seasons, satisfying your hearts with food and
gladness (Acts 14:17).

God, out of His love for us, created food to satisfy and gladden us. Eating
was meant to be pleasurable. God made it that way. Pleasure in eating and
rejoicing because of God's provision are part of God's good gifts to us. The
psalmist said, "Thou dost give them their food in due time. Thou dost open
Thy hand, and dost satisfy the desire of every living thing" (Psalm 145:15-16).
God delights in giving us food and satisfying our godly desires. Christian
women should seek to develop thankful hearts in response to His provision.
Paul encouraged Timothy and warned him about false teachers,

Men . . . will advocate abstaining from foods, which God has created to be
gratefully shared in by those who believe and know the truth. For everything created by God is good, *and nothing is to be rejected, if it is received*
with gratitude; for it is sanctified by means of the word of God and prayer
(1 Timothy 4:3-5, emphasis added).

The Lord graciously created food for our pleasure and it is to be received with
gratitude. But as with all His creation, we must regulate our pleasures under
His guidance.

God Gives Commands Concerning Eating

Beginning in the Garden and continuing to the post-flood world, God gave
commands concerning eating. Take time to read the following verses from
Genesis on the fall of man.

Now the serpent . . . said to the woman, "Indeed has God said, You shall not
eat from any tree of the garden'?" And the woman said to the serpent, "From
the fruit of the trees of the garden we may eat; but from the fruit of the tree
which is in the middle of the garden, God has said, 'You shall not eat from it
or touch it, lest you die!' " And the serpent said to the woman . . . "You surely
shall not die! For God knows that in the day you eat from it your eyes will be
opened, and you will be like God, knowing good and evil." When the woman
saw that the tree was good for food, and that it was a delight to the eyes, and
that the tree was desirable to make one wise, she took from its fruit and ate;
and she gave also to her husband with her, and he ate (Genesis 3:1-6).

Aren't those verses loaded with insight and instruction? Let's look at the principles we can learn from them:

- *All the trees except one were lawful for food.* Adam and Eve could eat from any tree they desired—God had provided wonderfully for them! Can you imagine what that "fruit" must have been like? I'm sure it is beyond our comprehension. They were restricted from only one tree. Would they be obedient to His command and enjoy His provision?

  God tested Adam in the same way He would later test Israel in the desert.

  > *He humbled you and let you be hungry, and fed you with manna which you did not know . . . that He might make you understand that man does not live by bread alone, but man lives by everything that proceeds out of the mouth of the LORD (Deuteronomy 8:3).*

  Would Israel be willing to enjoy His provision and be obedient to His restrictions? Would Adam trust that God had given him everything he needed? Or would he "lean on his own understanding," conceitedly thinking he knew best?

  In the post-flood world, God gave additional laws about eating. "Only you shall not eat flesh with its life, that is, its blood." This command was reiterated in the New Testament in Acts 21:25: "Abstain from meat sacrificed to idols and from blood and from what is strangled." The Lord continues to regulate our eating today.

- *Independent eating appeals to us.* Adam and Israel gave into the "lust of the flesh and the lust of the eyes and the boastful pride of life" (1 John 2:16). As we saw in Genesis 3, food appeals to the lust of the eyes ("it was a delight to the eyes"), to our flesh ("it was good for food"), and to the boastful pride of life ("it was desirable to make one wise"). The Israelites complained because they didn't have any food to *look* at besides manna. Forgetting their cruel slavery they longed for the "wonderful" food of Egypt (see Numbers 11:6). Both Adam and Israel succumbed to the deception that God was denying them something needful for life. They took the provision for life into their own hands. They demanded more than God had provided.

- *God was to be their source.* In the Garden as well as in the wilderness, God was teaching His children that He was to be their source. The Lord Jesus recognized God as His source during His temptation in the wilderness. He had been fasting for 40 days and nights. He was hungry. Satan came to Him, tempting Him to change stones into bread—to unlawfully use His power to provide for Himself. Jesus answered Satan's temptations with, "It is written, 'Man shall not live on bread alone, but on every word that proceeds out of the mouth of God' " (Matthew 4:4). Our Lord succeeded wonderfully in ways that both Adam and Israel failed. He was unwilling to fall for Satan's deception. He refused to rely on His own power to provide for Himself. Instead, He leaned on His Father and trusted in His word. In response, God provided angels to minister to Him.

- *They responded in unbelief.* Instead of believing God had graciously given them everything they needed, they craved more. Even though God had given them every tree in the Garden for food, Adam and Eve craved fruit from the tree of the knowledge of good and evil (*see* Genesis 3:6). In spite of the fact that God provided bread from heaven for His children, Israel craved meat (*see* Psalm 78:17-20). The continual cry of their hearts was, "Give me more! Give me better! I'm not satisfied with what You have provided!"

Many times we respond in the same ways. We aren't satisfied with the Lord's provision, so we move outside His will for us and seek to satisfy ourselves.

Many of the sinful eating problems we see in counselees mirror these same struggles. Sometimes our counselees use food to declare independence from God's commands—"Don't tell me what to eat!" Other times, they use it to satiate their own desires for pleasure—"I can't stop eating this; I just love the way it tastes!" They frequently worry about food and drink, disregarding Jesus' command by being anxious saying, "What shall we eat?" or "What shall we drink?" (Matthew 6:31). They fail to prioritize their desires by seeking to fulfill their needs before His kingdom and righteousness. They forget Jesus' words that "life is more than food, and the body than clothing" (Luke 12:23). Sometimes they overlook the fact that God is aware of their needs: "For all these things the Gentiles eagerly seek; for your heavenly Father knows that you need all these things" (Matthew 6:32). Hasn't God provided abundantly? I wonder why we are still enslaved to our desires, wanting more or better or creamier or hotter or crunchier? I wonder why we're never satisfied (*see* Ecclesiastes 6:7)?

Greedy Desires

I think the answer to those questions lies in our hearts. Our palates have grown accustomed to eating greedily. The children of Israel also had greedy desires, craving meat in the wilderness. You remember how they complained about the manna that God had provided for them. "Oh that someone would give us meat to eat!" they grumbled, "For we were well-off in Egypt" (Numbers 11:18). They rejected God's abundant provision for them and cried about their food. They even wanted to go back to Egypt so they could get good food again. "We remember the fish which we used to eat free in Egypt, the cucumbers and the melons and the leeks and the onions and the garlic" (Numbers 11:5). Their memory was corrupted by their hunger for more tasty food. They forgot about making bricks without straw and the annihilation of their children. Their mouths were watering. So God gave them meat. He gave them meat for a whole month until it became loathsome to them. In fact, our patient Lord was so angry with their craving hearts that He even killed some of them. "While the meat was still between their teeth . . . the LORD struck the people" (Numbers 11:33). The dead were buried at Kibroth-hattaavah—in "graves of craving." Psalm 78:29-31 identifies those buried in the "graves of craving" as the "stout" ones. They were the people who were enslaved to their palates. The greedy eaters.

We believe it is our right to have any kind of food we want, whenever we want it. There is such an abundance of food in America it is hard to comprehend the fact that we shouldn't eat it all.[6] We rarely consider that God might want to regulate this area of our lives. C.S. Lewis pinpointed this problem in *The Screwtape Letters*. Read the way in which gluttony is spoken of by the demon, Screwtape:

> *"The contemptuous way in which you spoke of gluttony as a means of catching souls, in your last letter, shows only your ignorance. One of the great achievements of the last hundred years has been to deaden the human conscience on that subject, so that by now you will hardly find a sermon preached or a conscience troubled about it in the whole length and breadth of Europe. . . . Your patient's mother . . . is a good example. She would be astonished—one day, I hope, will be—to learn that her whole life is enslaved to this kind of sensuality . . . what do quantities matter, provided we can use a human belly and palate to produce querulousness, impatience, uncharitableness and self-concern?"[7]*

Chilling, isn't it? I wonder what Lewis would say about today's obsession with fat-free eating. Some people look at fat-free food as the way to eat gluttonously without gaining weight. Please understand, I'm not saying that watching how much fat you consume is sinful. I'm just wondering whether we are striving to submit all of life to God's authority or if we are merely concerned with externals. For instance, how do our desires interfere with God's command to love our neighbor? Are we are uncharitable when someone offers us cookies made with butter? Are we uncharitable when we discover all the cookies are gone? The Lord is to be King over every area of life.

God gives commands about our eating and cares about our obedience. He wants to free us from our greedy desires. Remember, Colossians 3:5 defines greed as idolatry. Wanting more and more and never being satisfied is the worship of a false god. This god's name is Taste, Pleasure, Self-Sufficiency.

The Heart's Mirror

We need to understand that the whole arena of food and eating is simply a mirror of the heart. Are we thankful? Are we willing to deny ourselves? Do we fast? Are we willing to submit even this area to the Lordship of Christ? Eating a cookie isn't a sin *per se*. It is a sin if it is done as an act of defiance, self-indulgence, or unbelief. Let's put off shallow thinking about eating and embrace a fuller view. Yes, the Lord created food for our nourishment and our pleasure. Yes, we can enjoy it as long as we receive it with gratitude. But, He wants to regulate our consumption and use food to train us to become like Him. Please understand, I'm not advocating some sort of righteousness based on harsh treatment of the flesh. Paul taught that "severe treatment of the body [is] of no value against fleshly indulgence" (Colossians 2:23). I am encouraging the development of habits that *faithfully consider God and His kingdom*. It's perfectly legitimate to eat and enjoy food, as long as this eating is not done in rebellious disregard for His preeminence in our lives. Deuteronomy 14:26 advocates feasting in response to God's good provision:

> *You may spend the money for whatever your heart desires, for oxen, or sheep, or wine, or strong drink, or whatever your heart desires; and there you shall eat in the presence of the* LORD *your God and rejoice, you and your household.*

Rejoicing on Thanksgiving Day isn't sinful in itself. But it *is* sinful if you habitually overeat and never fast. It is sinful if your love for God and others is hampered by your desire for certain foods. Your eating habits are sinful if they master you. You must strive to remember that you already have a Master. *What do your eating habits say about the condition of your heart?*

Help for the Overeater

Developing Biblical Motives

Before we begin this discussion, there are a few foundational truths to establish. First, *God never commands us to be thin.* For those of us who have spent a
good part of our lives dieting, that's quite a shocking statement. Many of us
have spent too much time being consumed with what we consume. Think
about it—there is no command to be conformed to the image of Christie
Brinkley. God never dictates what size is godly. He never said weighing over
150 pounds is a curse. God isn't concerned about our size—*except as it reveals
our hearts.* God's plan is to conform us to the image of Christ. I'm convinced
maturing in Christ has a lot to do with our willingness to be obedient in every
area of life, including our eating habits.

We live in a society in which thinness is a prevailing unhealthy obsession. We
are continuously bombarded with media images of the "perfect woman." Today's
models weigh 23 percent below the national average, while 25 years ago they
weighed only 8 percent less than the average.[8] Weight control is a $30 billion a
year enterprise. Many businesses seek to create a market for their products by
continuously assaulting the public with depictions of the "ideal, happy woman."
She is always very thin. What they fail to tell us is the majority of us will never
look like a model, even if we diet and exercise continuously. For the Christian
woman, seeking to look like a model is an ungodly and futile pursuit. Let's start
now to put off this worldly thinking. We must put off the belief that being thin is
equal to being happy. As Romans 12:2 teaches, "Do not be conformed to this
world, but be transformed by the renewing of your mind, that you may prove
what the will of God is, that which is good and acceptable and perfect."

Joy comes from being in right relationship with God, not from wearing a
size 6. Mothers of daughters must be particularly careful that they do not
overemphasize the ideal body. The majority of girls who practice behaviors
associated with bulimia and anorexia come from homes where worth is
measured by adherence to certain external standards, such as body image.
Christian women must learn to think about their bodies in more biblical ways.

Godly Motive #1—Being Conformed to the Image of Christ   The fundamental motive for developing a godly perspective on eating is that of transformation. God's goal is to transform us—not from a size 16 to a 6, but from our
old nature to the nature of Christ.

We know that God causes all things to work together for good to those who love God, to those who are called according to His purpose. For whom He foreknew, He also predestined to become conformed to the image of His Son, *that He might be the first-born among many brethren (Romans 8:28-29, emphasis added).*

We should share God's goal. We can be encouraged that God will use everything—even our slow metabolism—to change us into the likeness of Christ. I have a dear friend who put it this way: "I'm glad God has given me this problem. He uses something as simple as my vanity to teach me about Himself." For some of us, this struggle is the arena God has chosen for our growth. *No, God does not command us to be thin. He commands us to be holy.* The New Testament is filled with injunctions and illustration about change. We must see our eating habits as just one part of our hearts that God wants to change. Remember, He doesn't look at the outside, He looks at the heart (1 Samuel 16:7).

Godly Motive #2—Everything for the Glory and Pleasure of God   The only satisfactory motive for anything we do is the glory and pleasure of God. We must strive to bring our eating into line with His commands. But this must be primarily for God's sake, not ours alone. We must learn to subjugate both desires for thinness and for comfort foods to the one desire that God commands: "Whether, then, you eat or drink or whatever you do, do all to the glory of God" (1 Corinthians 10:31). We must learn to eat in a way that will be pleasing to God. Merely accomplishing weight loss isn't enough. We want to be careful not to exchange the sin of gluttony for that of vanity or pride. Our hearts must be focused on hearing these words: "Well done, good and faithful servant."

Godly Motive #3—Your Body Is the Holy Spirit's Home   You must begin to see your body as the home of the Holy Spirit. Being obese is a health hazard and may limit your effectiveness for Christ. If your service to the kingdom is hindered by weight-related health disease, such as high blood pressure or joint injuries, you are abusing God's temple. If you are the Lord's, you don't own your body. It has been purchased with the precious blood of Jesus and the Holy Spirit now indwells.

Do you not know that your body is a temple of the Holy Spirit who is in you, whom you have from God, and that you are not your own? For you have been bought with a price: therefore glorify God in your body (1 Corinthians 6:19-20).

As Paul argues for a holy, disciplined life, notice the four elements in his reasoning:

- In contrast to the pagan temples of prostitution and idolatry, your body is inhabited by a *Holy* Spirit. Your temple is to be used for holiness rather than self-indulgent sin.
- The body of the believer is owned by the Lord. You are no longer free to do whatever you please with your body. The Lord owns you for two reasons: He created you (*see* Genesis 1:27) and He redeemed you.
- God has purchased your body with the precious blood of the Lamb (*see* Acts 20:28; 1 Peter 1:18-19). God has demonstrated His great love for you (*see* Romans 5:8). You can be an overcomer! He is for you (*see* Romans 8:31).
- The Lord has called you to glorify Him with your body. You are to live every day conscious of the truth of His abiding presence (*see* Hebrews 13:5).

It is astounding to think we can glorify the God of heaven with our bodies, which were made from dust. As Romans 12:1 says, "I urge you therefore, brethren, by the mercies of God, to present your bodies a living and holy sacrifice, acceptable to God, which is your spiritual service of worship." It is a matter of worship for you to bring your eating habits under the lordship of Christ. Learning godly eating habits isn't about whether you are "feeling a little fat," it is about learning to glorify and worship God.

Godly Motive #4—All of Life Is His   You must begin to see that *every part* of your life belongs to Him. Everything you do, everything you are, and every thought you think belongs to God and is either holy or sinful. In many Christians' lives there exists a dichotomy between the sacred and the profane, the sanctified and the secular. You may think, for example, that prayer, church attendance, giving, and Bible reading make up your spiritual life, while everything else is secular. I don't believe that's what the Bible teaches. I believe God is concerned with every facet of your life. Everything you are, every deed you perform, every word you speak, every meal you eat are all either acts of worship or acts of irreverence. As Romans 14:23 plainly teaches, "whatever is not from faith is sin." Do you demonstrate grateful faith in everything you do?

Godly Motive #5—He Redeemed You from Slavery   Much of the sixth chapter of Romans explains the truth that Christ has purchased freedom for us. In response to this freedom, we must be careful not to allow any sin to master or overcome us. Instead we are to walk in freedom, as Romans 6:12-13 teaches:

> *Do not let sin reign in your mortal body that you should obey its lusts, and do not go on presenting the members of your body to sin as instruments of unrighteousness; but present yourselves to God as those alive from the dead, and your members as instruments of righteousness to God.*

Jesus paid a dear price for our freedom. We must be careful not to fall back into any slavery once we have been freed. As you begin to develop correct motives, you must remember that although these habits seem overpowering at times, you can change because of the work of Christ. Remember that one of the results of the work of the Holy Spirit is "self-control" (Galatians 5:22-23). The Holy Spirit will teach you not to give into the desires of the flesh, but rather to walk in self-disciplined conformity to the Word.

What Motivates Sinful Eating?

Many women use food to comfort them in times of trouble or stress. Some women eat because they are angry and want to prove they have control over at least one area of their lives. Some women eat because of boredom or loneliness. In any case, you should spend time considering your counselee's motives. For instance, if she always eats when she is worried, have her study Philippians 4:6-9.[9] As a first step, I suggest using a form such as Jay Adams's[10] "Discovering Problem Patterns." This form is divided into seven days, with each day divided into morning, noon, and evening. On this form your counselee should record every instance of undisciplined eating and the emotional dynamics that were present. Circle the situations that occur two or more times. These are areas where your counselee will need to work the put-off/put-on dynamic. Of course, there may be sinful eating habits which are not tied to emotional responses, and in these cases you don't need to try to find them. Sometimes people eat just because it's 3:00 and they have always eaten at 3:00.

Steps to Take in Counseling

As I've previously stated, proper motivation for change must be at the heart of any biblical counseling. You should continue to challenge a counselee to grow in her understanding of a spirit-controlled life. In addition to this, there are some disciplines she should be encouraged to put on immediately. The following should be recorded on a daily basis so you will be able to examine her progress. This daily diary is also helpful for your counselee in that through it she will see that she can overcome her sinful habits.

1. *Memorize Scripture Weekly.* You should choose verses on the topics we have discussed and encourage her to begin to memorize and meditate on them right away. You could start with Romans 8:28-29. After she memorizes this passage, tell her to write a paragraph about what God is teaching her through it.

2. *Read Scripture Daily.* The Lord taught us "man is to live by every word that proceeds out of the mouth of God." We are to do this rather than give in to the illicit desires of the flesh to have more and more "bread." Encourage your counselee to read at least two chapters in the Bible daily and keep track of what she has learned through her reading.

3. *Daily Prayer.* Praying every day will bring your counselee into a closer walk with God and will encourage her to keep her eyes on the Lord rather than the scale. She is to make a prayer and thank list that she should use on a daily basis. She should make notes about her time of prayer in her daily diary.

Along with this daily prayer time goes the injunction to thankful prayer before every meal. God commands that food be received with prayer and thanksgiving (1 Timothy 4:4-5). Before she eats anything (snack or main meal), she should stop and calm her heart by giving thanks to God. This will assist her in avoiding complaining about food, will avert binge eating, and will demonstrate a loving trust that God has provided everything she needs.

4. *Exercise.* Exercise, along with controlled eating, is one of the two great keys to weight loss. A sedentary lifestyle is one cause of obesity. Studies have shown that the average U. S. adult watches between four and five hours of television per day.[11] If you can convince your counselee to turn off the television for just one hour and go for a walk instead, she can begin to see results. Once again, the focus has to be on caring for the temple of the Holy Spirit.

If your counselee is not accustomed to exercise, she must begin slowly with walking. She will burn approximately 100 calories for every mile walked. She should try to work up to about 1,000 calories burned through exercise per week. Aerobic exercise three times per week for 30 to 40 minutes is sufficient for good health. It is now also recommended that some form of resistance training to develop muscles be incorporated into your routine. I'm not suggesting a woman try to look like Arnold Schwarzenegger. She probably couldn't even if she tried. But strong muscles can be developed by consistent training with small weights. A combination of these exercises will help in raising the rate of the metabolism so that fat will burn more easily. For menopausal women exercise is crucial. Bone loss begins almost immediately with the loss of estrogen.[12] Exercise, particularly resistance training, helps build strong bones. It also reduces the risk of heart attack, the number-one killer of post-menopausal women.

There are many reference materials available on this topic that will help your counselee find an exercise she enjoys, can be consistent at, and will help her lose weight and become more fit. The amount and type of exercise should be recorded in her daily diary—for instance, "Monday—walked two miles, 200 calories burned."

As with anything, exercise can be carried to extremes. All women, but particularly those who practice anorexic or bulimic behaviors, should have their exercise monitored if there is a possibility of overexercising. The American College of Sports Medicine has issued the following guidelines for physical activity:

- Frequency—3 to 5 days per week
- Intensity—50 to 85 percent of estimated maximum heart rate
- Duration—15 to 60 minutes of continuous aerobic exercise
- Resistance Training—moderate intensity, minimum of 2 days per week[13]

5. *Controlled Eating.* There are many eating plans that are readily available and easily understandable. Your counselee should be encouraged to go to the library and review the different types of eating plans, such as those produced by The American Heart or Diabetes Associations. You must encourage her to avoid faddish diets promoting quick weight loss, which appeal to her fleshly desire to look better without addressing the more significant issues of the heart. Most quick weight-loss diets cause a loss in water weight that is immediately regained when the regimen is concluded. Before your counselee decides on any eating plan, she should consult her physician.

Remember that one pound of fat contains approximately 3,500 calories. The body stores excess protein and carbohydrates in the form of fat. In order to lose one pound in a week, your counselee will need to lower her caloric intake by about 500 calories per day, which equals 3,500 calories in one week. The basic nutritional needs of most women are 1,800 to 2,000 calories per day. If she consistently eats 1,300 to 1,500 calories per day, she will have a slow but consistent loss of fat, not muscle or water. In addition, if she is also increasing her calorie usage by exercising, she can be assured of a greater loss.

Since your counselee is interested in maintaining her body for the Lord's sake, she should be sure that she is eating nutritiously. Instead of eating only bananas for two weeks, she should learn healthier ways of normal eating. She should choose a diet with plenty of grain products, vegetables, and fruits.[14]

After a suitable eating plan is chosen, she must begin to record *everything* she eats in her daily diary, specifically noting types and amounts of foods. This practice of recording is important for several reasons. First, she may not be aware how much food she eats, and recordkeeping will help inform her. Second, it will cause her to become more aware of the types of food she should eat, enabling her to measure her progress. Third, you will be able to determine the areas of her eating where she consistently gives in to self-indulgence. Studies have shown that cutting caloric intake is more important than exercise.[15] Some women exercise thinking they can eat whatever they want. Others starve themselves and never work out. Both exercise and calorie-cutting are important to maintain good health.

Remember, body size is not the issue here. The issue is the heart. Is she seeking to glorify God? Is she seeking to care for her body, the Holy Spirit's home?

6. *Goal-Setting.* What changes does your counselee think God wants her to make in her disciplines? Does she have a realistic weight goal? A slow weight loss of one to one and a half pounds per week is best. You'll have to be careful that neither of you get hung up on weight loss except as it reflects how she is progressing in her quest for the temperate, godly life.

I recommend you plan to meet with your counselee on a weekly basis. At this meeting, she should bring in her daily diary with all of her disciplines recorded. You should also weigh her at each meeting.

Help for the Bulimic

A Biblical Perspective on Bulimia

Everything that I have written up to this point about eating, food, weight control, and methods of counseling must be understood before you consider what is said about bulimia.

An Understanding of Terms   A recent Gallup Poll projected that about 2 million American women ages 19 to 39 and about 1 million teenagers are affected by some symptoms of bulimia or anorexia.[16] "Ordinarily, bulimia begins between ages 17 and 25."[17] By way of introduction, bulimia—literally "ox-like appetite"—is a habitual, voluntary cycle of behavior characterized by secretly eating huge quantities of food and then inducing vomiting or some other form of purge, including overexercising. Bulimia and its sufferers have received a lot of press lately, especially high-profile celebrities such as Princess Diana and Jane Fonda. As the behaviors and dangers of bulimia are glamorized by models and ballerinas who confess they have used these procedures to control their weight, many young women will try it out for themselves. Talking about it, "educating" the public, ironically will probably cause more young women to experiment with it. In my weight-loss groups I have heard women jokingly say, "I've been praying I would get bulimia." Since it seems popular to be bulimic now, we will see more and more of it in our counseling rooms. We need firm, clear, biblical answers that speak to the heart.

Over the next few pages, I will define the physiological and behavioral indications of bulimia. I will describe the various common, overriding motives present in most bulimics. I will identify wrong standards and habits and those that should replace them and will outline a specific plan that you, a biblical counselor, might employ with your "Princess Di's."

Before I do, though, I think I need to clear up a few misconceptions about labels such as "bulimia." What is the truth about labels? In some ways, labels can be useful. For instance, I have used the term "bulimia" in this chapter and you know without a great deal of explanation, what I mean. However, there are certain innate problems which can arise that cause me to resist using the label "bulimia" with counselees.

The Problems with Labels   First, a label tends to promote the idea of a disease model. A counselee may think that because she has a problem with a medical-sounding name used in the medical community, she has a disease. "I have bulimia," may be used by some people in the same way as, "I have diabetes." Instead of saying, "I practice behaviors of bulimia," which is more accurate, she speaks about her bad habits as though they were something over which she has no control.

Disease terms are obviously useful and appropriate in describing somatic problems or organic abnormalities that impair normal physiological functioning. In many cases one is not responsible for being ill. In other cases, the illness or disease is caused by certain harmful behaviors. Even in these behaviorally generated cases, however, the disease will have an organically based diagnosis, prognosis, and pathology. Presently in the U.S. there are many behaviors which are being popularly classified as diseases. Behaviors such as alcoholism, anorexia, and bulimia are thought to be real diseases by the general populace.

True, there are certain physiological effects of continually practicing bulimic behaviors, but there are no known chemical agents, genes, viruses, or bacteria that *cause* this behavior. My point is this: Bulimia is *not* a disease. It is a behavior. The label "bulimic" tends to cloud this issue.

Second, the use of labels may subtly deceive the counselee into believing she has an excuse for her behavior. "I can't help it. . . . I can't stop . . . I have a disease . . . I have bulimia . . . the counselor said so." None of us need excuses for our sin. We're quite proficient in thinking of excuses without the aid of a label. The Bible teaches we are responsible for our behavior (Romans 14:12), whether that behavior has a certain medical-sounding name or not. Excuses not only excuse, they condemn. If your counselee believes she has a disease with no known cause and no known cure, she may easily become hopeless or fall prey to quack remedies.

Third, the use of a label may cause some counselees to believe God needs to "heal" them for change to occur. Your counselee may believe that since she suffers from a "disease," the only path to freedom from this "pain" is to experience a supernatural encounter with the Lord. The process of becoming free from enslaving habits is indeed supernatural and occurs in the context of fellowship with God. However, a desire for a special "healing" of behavior is unbiblical. She may futilely run from one deliverance or inner-healing ministry to another, seeking someone with enough faith and power to heal her. She will typically end up frustrated, disillusioned, and hopeless. The Bible is clear about how to handle problems of wrong thinking and living. This process of change, or "sanctification," is discussed fully in chapter 2 on the methods of biblical counseling.

Fourth, labels turn our eyes away from the truth and toward a deceiving euphemism that is more palatable. Disease is not quite so hard to look at as sin. I would rather think that I have a bacteria that causes me to act in unkind ways than recognize that I am self-centered and self-serving.

Fifth, some women may take a sort of perverse pride in the fact that they are unique and have a disorder. "Bulimia almost has a celebrity status, the 'in' thing to have," says Dr. Sue Bailey, director of the Eating Disorders Clinic at the Washington (D.C.) Hospital Center."[18] These women must be taught to think about their behavior in biblical terms, not as a way to uniqueness or even popularity.

There are dangers in using labels with counselees unless both you and they are very clear about what you do and do not mean. I have used the term *bulimia* in this chapter only for the purpose of convenience. I define it as a certain type of *sinful behavior*, not a *disease*.

Defining This Behavior

Bulimia is a habitual behavior pattern characterized by frequent times of binging, usually terminated by stomach pain, sleep, social intervention, vomiting, or other forms of purging. Binges are normally planned, secret, and rapid. A feeling of lack of control occurs during the binge. Purging may include self-induced vomiting, use of laxatives, or rigorous dieting, exercising, or fasting in order to counteract the effects of the binge-eating. I have seen a report of a woman who consumed 54,000 calories of food in an eight-hour period with intermittent times of self-induced vomiting. There are also documented cases of women who have taken up to 200 laxatives before a binge or who eat "markers" (small, colored pieces of plastic) so they will know when they have purged thoroughly. These behaviors are most common among women, with no specific ages defined, although bulimia ordinarily begins between the ages of 17 and 25.[19] Oftentimes teenage girls begin this behavior in high school to lose or control the 14- to 16-year-old weight gain. They then will employ it from time to time in college or after childbirth in adulthood. Statistically, many bulimic women come from families in which the parents are obese. "Bulimics often spend $50 or more a day on food and may even steal (food or money) to support the [behavior]."[20]

The habitual practice of bulimia has many serious physiological effects: the erosion of the esophagus and teeth; increased inability to digest food; involuntary vomiting; bowel irregularity or extreme diarrhea; absence of menstruation; slow heartbeat; subnormal body temperature; and growth of a coat of delicate, downy hair. Although weight is usually maintained within normal ranges, there are frequent fluctuations depending upon binges, purges, diets, and fasts. If a counselee comes to you with the problem of bulimia or any of the above physiological symptoms, your first order of business is to get her to a physician. It is important for you to be sure what you are dealing with is behaviorally caused and not a physiological problem.

The following are four common dominating motives in the life of a bulimic. Not every bulimic will have these desires ruling her life, and there may be other motives I haven't listed here. I believe these to be the most common. Use these as a place to begin thinking about people who go through the cycles of binging and purging.

Habits of Greed and the Desire for Instant Gratification: *"Craving in the Wilderness"* In the life of the bulimic you will find certain behaviors she may describe as "compulsive." She will identify a strong physical feeling of being compelled to binge. As she begins the binge she may not even taste the food. She may not consciously think about what she is doing as she crams food into her mouth. She may lose track of time and how much she has consumed. She may sit in front of the television and concentrate on some meaningless program while she shovels in baked potatoes, cartons of ice cream, boxes of cereal, or bags of cookies. She will experience a certain pleasure (euphoria) from eating. This pleasure is not simply from the taste or texture of the food, or the chemical reaction of raised blood sugar levels, but it is an experienced release and calm that comes after a hurried and frantic self-indulgence. This time of binging may be short-lived, especially if she is interrupted by her family. A recent study showed the average binge to be slightly less than 75 minutes long with an intake of slightly more than 3,400 calories (an entire pecan pie, for instance).[21] Or it may continue over many hours with intermittent times of binging, remorse, hopelessness, and purging.

Make no mistake—this compulsion to binge is as strong as any faced by the habitual heavy drinker. It is probably fairly common among women in your congregation, especially among the younger ones. You should gather data carefully here as you uncover the "triggers" of this behavior. What precipitates these binges? You may discover lusts of both the body and mind (Ephesians 2:3). Perhaps binges are aroused by worry or anger or stress. They may be associated with feelings of fatigue, weakness, premenstrual syndrome,[22] or nervousness.

A TYPICAL EXAMPLE OF THE DYNAMICS OF BULIMIA   One woman confessed that if she ate a piece of candy or cake at work, she would binge later that evening at home. In her case, violating her personal law, "Thou shall not eat sweets," would result in condemnation and guilt. She would use her "failure" ("I ate a brownie at work") as an excuse to binge, which would normally be followed by a self-atoning purge. She grew when she began to understand that her god, "I must look better than my sisters," had certain laws, "Thou shall not eat sweets." When she violated her weak, idolatrous conscience, she felt guilty, gave in to her sin, and then sought for atonement through purging. She swung back and forth on a pendulum, the fulcrum of which was her own god, "I must look better than my sisters." Let me illustrate her problem this way:

"I must look better than my sisters."
Her god

Legalism   Self-indulgence
"I can never eat sweets."   "I failed so I might as well give up."

We worked to halt this process at its root, which was her worship of a perfect body. We replaced her false worship with worship of the Living God and obedience to His commands.

"I desire to love and serve God and others for His glory."

Obedience to His commands
"I want to develop self-control
for His glory."

Humble reliance and confession of sin
"I failed but I can confess my sin and
rejoice in God's grace and love."

Once again, let's not underestimate the power of the media to influence our thinking. We must put off the world's ideal of the perfect woman and put on the mind of Christ. Worship always carries the idea of obedience to law with it, and a means of atonement for violation of that law. Once my counselee began to see how these principles functioned in her life, she still had to struggle to overcome ingrained habits, but we made definite progress down the road to her freedom and God's pleasure.

UNDERSTANDING COMPULSIONS   I am convinced that in some cases a feeling of "compulsion" would be more biblically defined as habitual greed. Greed is a rapacious desire for more than one needs or deserves. Since the Bible broadly addresses greed, solid help may be offered to your counselee. First, taking the behavior out of the mystical ("compulsion") and placing it in the realm of daily understandable experience gives hope. You can point out that she is not isolated in her struggle with greed (*see* 1 Corinthians 10:13). Remind her that the children of Israel struggled greatly in the desert: "And the rabble who were among them had greedy desires; and also the sons of Israel wept again and said, 'Who will give us meat to eat?'" (Numbers 11:4).[23] Psalm 78:17 and the following verses speak of rebelliousness, testing, speaking against God, and unbelief: "Because they did not believe in God and did not trust in His salvation." This psalm plainly speaks of cravings as being both common to all and a by-product of trusting in one's self for satisfaction and salvation instead of trusting in God.

When your counselee is nervous, angry, unhappy, or worried, she seeks ways to save herself and placate her discomfort with food. Instead she needs to turn to her gracious Savior. Clearly she must learn to trust in God, as Jeremiah 17:5-8 states: "Cursed is the man who trusts in mankind . . . and whose heart turns away from the LORD. . . . Blessed is the man who trusts in the LORD and whose trust is the LORD."

The New Testament also speaks expansively about greed and trust. Our Lord warns us, "Beware, and be on your guard against every form of greed; for not even when one has an abundance does his life consist of his possessions" (Luke 12:15). He continues, "For this reason I say to you, do not be anxious for your life, as to what you shall eat, . . . for life is more than food . . . and do not seek what you shall eat . . . and do not keep worrying" (Luke 12:22-23,29). Notice the way the Lord links greed, worry, and self-indulgence with food and drink.[24] Worry is a by-product of trusting in self and must be addressed in the context of these habits of greed.

Again, when my counselee transgressed her personal standard, "Thou shall not eat sweets," she worried about it all day and finally gave in to greedy self-indulgence in the evening. The apostle Paul addresses greed in Colossians 3:5, stating that greed amounts to idolatry and is part of the old nature. We are to consider the old nature as dead. My counselee had to be taught that her worry and greed fed off each other and were the fruit of her self-trust and self-worship (idolatry). As with any idolatry, what may start out as a harmless, pleasurable excursion becomes an enslaving trap—a "grave of craving." As a counselor, it will be helpful for you to use the term *greedy habits* in place of the euphemism *compulsion*.

A Desire for Surface Perfection and Pride: *The Pharisee Within*   In the bulimic a particularly wicked and deadly combination of motives reign. Coupled with these overwhelming habits of greed, worry, and self-indulgence is a desire to appear in control and beautiful. The natural consequences of habitual binging are weight gain and discomfort. The bulimic is not willing to pay the price for her self-indulgence. She hides, is dishonest, and blameshifts to avoid the resultant weight gain. She purges. She may fast for several days to make up for the binge or overexercise to burn the extra calories. In any case, she's avoiding the truth about her self-indulgence.

Matthew 23 speaks about living for outward appearance. In this chapter Jesus confronts the Pharisees and scribes about their hypocrisy and pride: "They do all their deeds to be noticed by men" (verse 5). "You clean the outside of the cup and of the dish, but inside they are full of robbery and self-indulgence" (verse 23). "Even so you too outwardly appear righteous to men, but inwardly you are full of hypocrisy and lawlessness" (verse 28). How clearly the Lord speaks to our hearts. Unless the Lord delivers us, we are all Pharisees, man-pleasers, wanting to cover up our sin so that others will think well of us. Like Eve in the Garden, your counselee is sewing fig leaves together. "Don't see me as I am!" Only the humble, transparent, and trusting heart will be freed from this bondage. To this end your counselee must commit to confess any binge or purge to her husband (if married), parent, roommate, or you as her counselor. No more covering it up! She must commit to recording *all* the food she eats daily for perhaps six months or so.

Because there are no commands to pursue thinness, when the bulimic purges she is pursuing an unbiblical goal. It is never the proper goal to merely look good on the outside. The proper goal is to please God with a heart that is in submission to Him. Loving and seeking after the standards of the world,[25] "looking good," and seeking after man's approval have no place in the heart of the believer. Judging ourselves or others according to the flesh is sinful and foolish.

Since your counselee is wrapped up in how she looks to others, she will probably be judgmental of others who look overweight. She may be like the Pharisee in Luke 18:9: "He [Jesus] also told this parable to certain ones who *trusted in themselves* that they were righteous, and *viewed others with contempt*" (emphasis added).

How does your counselee view others who struggle with their weight? Does she crave the respectful greeting, "You look great!"? Does she enjoy flirting? She must be taught to look at overweight women as sisters, not rivals or "pigs." She should be encouraged to pray for them. She must learn to look at men as brothers, not conquests. In other words, she needs to begin to love her neighbor as she loves herself. She should get involved in women's groups and learn to share the Lord with them. She should confess her pride to others and ask for prayer.

Penance in Place of Atonement: *She's Her Own Personal Savior*   In some ways purging is an act of penance or self-flagellation—trying to make up or atone for sins. This penance, in itself, is illustrative because it exposes a heart that is trusting in self instead of Christ and His provision. The stumbling block of the cross is that we cannot save ourselves. Any attempt to do so tramples underfoot the precious blood of Jesus. Spend time with your counselee and discuss the difference between repentance and penance. A study of Philippians 3:8-9 is important: "I count all things to be loss in view of the surpassing value of knowing Christ Jesus my Lord . . . [that I] may be found in Him, *not having a righteousness of my own derived from the Law*" (emphasis added), and Galatians 2:16: "since by the works of the Law shall no flesh be justified."

When your counselee seeks to establish her righteousness through obedience to Old Testament Law or her personal legalism flowing out of the worship of her god, she isn't progressing in her walk with Christ. She is serving her own law rather than rejoicing in grace.[26]

Humble repentance and confession, including meditating on passages such as 2 Corinthians 7:9-10 (in which the difference between worldly and godly sorrow are contrasted), will be important.[27]

Instant Solutions and Laziness: *Putting on Diligence*   Your counselee may indeed want to be free from the discomfort of the binge or the embarrassment or "guilt" of the purge. But when you outline the diligent work that must be done it will not seem very inviting. Why should you expect resistance, even in a counselee who sees her sin? Notice how Proverbs links laziness and craving: "The soul of the sluggard craves and gets nothing" (13:4). "The desire of the sluggard puts him to death, for his hands refuse to work; all day long he is craving" (21:25-26).

Part of bulimia is a greedy craving for food. Another part is the willingness to short-circuit the system with the purge. Your counselee will need to learn that taking the lazy way (the purge) will only lead to more craving (the binge) and ultimately, death. Diligently working at putting off habits of self-indulgence by practicing a wise diet and living thankfully in response to the true God will eventually bring real change in your counselee's life.

This process of sanctification is not only a matter of learning specific eating patterns. Godly change must occur in other areas of her life as well. Further, this change will be a slow, steady *progression* toward conformation to Christ, not an overnight transformation. The Lord often uses these habits to reveal other areas of distrust and unbelief. Your counselee will need to be encouraged to work with patient diligence, knowing that the Lord is also at work in her to bring about her ultimate freedom for His glory.[28]

There are many wonderful passages extolling the reward of diligence. Consider these from Proverbs: "Poor is he who works with a negligent hand, but the hand of the diligent makes rich" (10:4). "The hand of the diligent will rule, but the slack hand will be put to forced labor" (12:24). "A slothful man does not roast his prey, but the precious possession of a man is diligence" (12:27). "The soul of the sluggard craves and gets nothing, but the soul of the diligent is made fat" (13:4). Although the temptation to take the easy way out through purging will be strong, you must encourage your counselee that God will bless her efforts as she struggles diligently.

You should also be aware that Ephesians 4:28 speaks of dishonesty (stealing) in the context of the slothfulness and distaste for work. Many women actually steal food from stores or others and lie about what they have eaten. Your counselee's slothfulness, laziness, and desire for the "easy way" in her eating patterns may be pervasive in unrelated disciplines in her life. Learning to be completely honest about what she eats and where she gets the food will be a big step toward sanctification for her in other areas.

Steps to Take in Counseling

Here is a plan you might follow as you consider how the preceding information characterizes your counselee.

- Be sure of your counselee's salvation. Check the state of her relationship with God. Is there conviction of sin? Assurance of God's mercy and power? As in all counseling, the mere fact that she came to you through the church doesn't mean you can assume she is a believer.
- Gather data about the following:
  A. The onset of these behaviors.
  B. Family history: How are her relationships with her parents and siblings? Is there competition or emphasis regarding physical appearance or weight? Are there other family members with weight problems? Is there a history of dieting and unhealthy eating behavior in the family?
  C. Current exact weights and average weight over the last few years.
  D. Current behaviors of eating. Keep a journal recording everything eaten over a period of several weeks, including the times she binges.
  E. Current physiological problems as corroborated by a physician.
- Set the agenda. Any goal less than that of pleasing God is unacceptable.
- Plan to deal with resistance. Remember Proverbs 26:16.
- Build hope!
- Establish accountability for all of the following as well as the disciplines listed in the section on overeating:
  A. The family's involvement in prayer, encouragement, and accountability.
  B. Confession of all binges to the Lord and you, the counselor.
  C. Removal of all laxatives, diuretics, and weight scales from the counselee's home.
  D. Commitment, if possible, never to eat alone. Eating alone makes it easier to binge. In any case, she should remember she is not alone— Jesus is always with her.

E. Identification of her "god." Her god may be being thinner than her sister or never wearing anything larger than a size 10. She must also learn to identify her personal ten commandments, such as, "Thou shall not eat any sweets." How does she react when she violates one of her commandments? Teach her to put off this idolatry and self-worship and put on worship, service, and obediece to the Lord. She must realize her standards are not God's standards (*see* Isaiah 55:8-9). Assume she will struggle in this area. She may believe God wants her to obey her own commandments rather than sinning by being a glutton. She must understand the motive of her heart is wrong when she is obeying her laws. Even though God wants her to be disciplined, it must be for His glory and according to His standards, not hers. The true motives of her heart will be exposed when she violates one of her laws and turns to the purge rather than Christ. She must also be taught that the purge (including exercise and laxatives) is not to be her savior. Rather, she must embrace Jesus Christ and His atoning sacrifice for her sins. Her legalistic perfectionism is exposed by the statement, "If I eat one wrong thing, I'll eat everything." This must be identified as self-serving pride rather than godly self-control.

F. Guarding of her heart so she doesn't spend time fantasizing about foods.

• Teach her to handle temptation. When faced with a strong temptation to binge, her contingency plan to overcome it might include the following:

A. In humble trust, cry out to God for help.

B. Confess any idolatry or obedience to her own laws as sin.

C. Ask for help from her husband, a godly co-worker, or a counselor.

D. Identify the motives that are drawing her into this sin (*see* James 1:13-16).

E. Draw near to God for both mercy and help (*see* Hebrews 4:16).

F. Move, Move, Move! She should change her position and location. For instance, she could get out of the house and go for a walk, or go to a room other than the kitchen and read the Bible.

G. Remember that she is accountable to report her binge. She should grab a pen and her diary and start writing down what she has eaten.

H. Remember that the option of the purge is no longer open to her. She must call upon the Lord Jesus as her Savior, the true way of atonement from the penalty of her sin.

I. Worship the Lord with a favorite chorus or hymn and review her thank list.[29]

J. Write down portions of Isaiah 53 on cards and place them in her purse, car, or on the refrigerator door. She can meditate on the suffering of Christ in her behalf and His bountiful grace to her.

K. Stop a binge already in process by crying out for God's help.

Finally, as a biblical counselor, do not belittle your ability to help women who struggle with these problems. The heart attitudes of the bulimic are the same as your own. The Bible speaks richly and piercingly to us all.

Powerful Hope for Change

Even though it may seem habitual ways of eating and thinking are too ingrained to change, be assured your counselee can be victorious through God's power. Over the years I have watched God's grace strengthen and free numbers of women from sinful eating patterns. It is not too much to hope that a complete transformation of life can be attained. The Lord is more interested in freeing your counselee than you are. Remember Paul's words in Philippians 1:6: "I am confident of this very thing, that He who began a good work in you will perfect it until the day of Christ Jesus." You too, can be confident that God will complete His work in His child. It may seem like an uphill struggle all the way, but God is patient and omnipotent.

A good place to start with your counselee is Romans 12:1-2:

With eyes wide open to the mercies of God, I beg you, my [sisters], as an act of intelligent worship, to give him your bodies, as a living sacrifice, consecrated to him and acceptable by him. Don't let the world around you squeeze you into its own mold, but let God remold your minds from within, so that you may prove in practice that the plan of God for you is good, meets all his demands and moves toward the goal of true maturity (J.B. Phillips).

Recommended Resources

Elyse Fitzpatrick, *More Than Bread,* San Diego: The Christian Counseling and Educational Foundation, 1992. (A workbook on overeating, bulimia, and anorexia.)

_____, *Uncommon Vessels,* San Diego: The Christian Counseling and Educational Foundation, 1990. (Videotape and detailed plan for organizing a program of discipline for women in your local congregation.)

C. John Miller, *Repentance in the 20th-Century Man,* Fort Washington, PA: Christian Literature Crusade, 1975.

CHAPTER 17

Counseling Women Involved in Sexual Sins

Diane A. Tyson, M.A.

Heather came to me for counseling several years ago because she wanted to learn how to develop godly relationships with people. As she described some events from the past, it became evident that Heather's decision to seek biblical counsel was a wise decision.

During her four years at Bible college, Heather engaged in a sexual relationship with her roommate and best friend, Abby. Heather called it "an affair." Abby was the one friend Heather could depend on.

After graduation, job opportunities separated them so their relationship was interrupted. A year later, Abby married Jim and moved to another state. Heather was devastated not so much because Abby married, but because Abby was now so far away. While they no longer spent large amounts of time together, both Heather and Abby spent a lot of mental energy on their relationship. They talked frequently by telephone and often sent cards and gifts to each other.

Jim's mother lives in the same town as Heather. So whenever Abby and Jim come to visit his mother, Abby spends at least one night with Heather. The two women have continued in this way for ten years apparently without Jim's knowledge.

But now Heather is dating Ron and she's kept it a secret from Abby. When Abby came to town the last time and wanted to spend the night with her, Heather very reluctantly told Abby she couldn't spend the night because Ron would be there. Abby screamed and cried and called Heather all sorts of names.

"I don't know what I'm going to do," said Heather. "Abby's my best friend. I don't know what I'll do if I lose her. I want you to help me patch up my friendship with Abby. What should I do?"

Confused Thinking About Relationships

In today's cultural setting, Heather is in the majority. No one was really being hurt by her choices, she thought. Besides, isn't it dangerous to repress your sex drive and abnormal to deny yourself sexual expression in any form that pleases you? Heather believed these things and acted on them. Supposedly great humanistic thinkers have said it is impossible to expect people to abstain from sexual expression and cruel to even suggest it.

Our culture is so confused on these issues that euphemisms have been coined to explain away sinful behaviors. A *euphemism* is a word or words that substitute for other terms or phrases that might be offensive to some people. An example is using the word *gay* instead of *homosexual*. Political correctness requires us to call by another name a behavior that God calls sin. We who are Christians are labeled judgmental and harsh if we use the term *homosexual*. Likewise, it is not unusual to hear pastors and other Christian speakers use the word *affair* instead of the term *adultery* because they don't want to sound harsh. So euphemisms have crept into the church where clear, biblical terminology would be much more helpful.

In this chapter, I will strive to use biblical terms for sexual sin not to be harsh and unloving, but because I desire to bring the clarity and freedom of biblical thinking to problems that have the potential to destroy lives.

If we say that the Bible is our standard for faith (what we believe) and practice (what we do), we must learn to use its vocabulary. Let's consider Heather's story and substitute biblical terminology for her cultural language.

We never see any mention of "affairs" in Scripture. Instead, the "affair" to which Heather referred is what the Bible calls "homosexuality." Abby's marriage added the dimension of "adultery" to that liaison since Abby was sexually involved with someone who was not her husband. In her twisted thinking, Abby believed she was not betraying Jim because her involvement with Heather started before her marriage. Since Heather admitted to me that she and Ron were "sleeping together," Heather was participating in what the Bible calls "fornication." Some of you may be thinking, "Oh, what an ugly, old-fashioned word!" But that's what the Bible calls voluntary sexual intercourse involving an unmarried person.

According to the terminology of psychology, both Heather and Abby are *bisexual*. This term refers to persons who are involved in sexual relationships with both male and female partners. Heather's relationships with Abby and Ron were immoral. This means that they were not in line with the Lord's commands concerning sexual purity.

Some people may say, "Who cares what we call it as long as we know whether it is right or wrong." But knowing right from wrong requires knowing what God has to say about the issues. If we don't know what label the Bible puts on these behaviors, we won't be able to make the distinctions necessary to decide on a person's morality or immorality.

If you are a keen observer of our culture, you know that playing with and distorting language is one way to significantly influence how people think about issues. For example, in the abortion debate, pro-abortionists call themselves "pro-choice" because that term sounds more positive. In this chapter we will use biblical terms and categories to discuss sexual sin so that we are clear on the issues. Using biblical language and categories will also enable us to rightly arrive at God's solutions for dealing with sexual sin.

The Major Ways Women Sin Sexually

Let's look now at the major ways that women sin sexually against God and others. We will begin with the outward behaviors, and then investigate sin that is more subtle because it occurs primarily in the mind.

Adultery

Adultery is, in its most technical sense, voluntary sexual intercourse between a married person and a person who is not his or her spouse. Most of us probably know that one of the Ten Commandments says, "You shall not commit adultery" (Exodus 20:14). Leviticus 20:10 tells the penalty for Israelites who committed adultery: "If there is a man who commits adultery with another man's wife, one who commits adultery with a friend's wife, the adulterer and the adulteress shall surely be put to death."

The message from God is crystal clear: adultery is sin of a most serious nature. The message from television or the movies, however, is completely the opposite. Adultery is portrayed as fun, something that just happens when the "chemistry" between two people is right. But the biblical equation says that while the sin of adultery may be pleasurable for the moment, there is a big price to be paid for indulging in it. Sooner or later the price will be death. While the laws of the United States don't call for putting adulterers to death, people who indulge in this sin pay the price through broken relationships, splintered families, sexually transmitted diseases (what used to be called venereal disease), and eventually eternal death.

You may be thinking, *But Christians are under grace and can even be forgiven for the sin of adultery.* Yes, that's true. However, committing adultery ought to flash giant red lights in the conscience of a person who calls himself or herself a Christian. John said in his first epistle,

> The one who says, "I have come to know Him," and does not keep His commandments, is a liar, and the truth is not in him; but whoever keeps His word, in him the love of God has truly been perfected (1 John 2:4-5).

We can't engage in sexual sin and claim to be Christians if it doesn't bother our consciences and lead us to confession and repentance. We will talk later in the chapter about the way out of sexual sinning.

Proverbs was written to "give prudence to the naive" and to increase the learning of the wise (*see* Proverbs 1:4-5). So along with the naive and the wise, let's look at what Proverbs 6:32 says about adultery: "The one who commits adultery with a woman is lacking sense; he who would destroy himself does it." People who commit adultery don't set out to destroy themselves, do they? No, they think they are pursuing something that will bring them pleasure and happiness—and it may, for a short time. Both Proverbs 14:12 and 16:25 say the same thing: "There is a way which seems right to a man, but its end is the way of death." For some reason the Holy Spirit included this proverb twice in Scripture. Perhaps it is because we don't listen very well and need to hear it more than once. While adultery may seem right, it leads to death. How? Because this sinful behavior affects a person both physically and spiritually. While modern medicine has kept most adulterers from dying physically from their sin, eventually they will pay the price spiritually unless they repent of their sin and are forgiven by God.

Suppose someone merely *thinks* about committing adultery rather than actually committing the act. Is that person off the hook? Is he or she pure in the eyes of God? It is interesting that in his first sermon, Jesus chooses to address this issue among others: "You have heard that it was said, 'You shall not commit adultery'; but I say to you, that everyone who looks on a woman to lust for her has committed adultery with her already in his heart" (Matthew 5:27-28). God's standard for us is high, isn't it? No adultery—not of the body, not of the mind. All adultery begins in the mind. So, if you control your thoughts and do not entertain adultery in your mind, you will not commit adultery with your body.

We should be very thankful that God's standard for us is so high. God wants the very best for us; God asks the very best from us. Is this fair? Yes, because He can enable us to do it. We can reach and maintain God's holy standards if we will trust in Him for the strength and power to do so. Since none of us does this perfectly, we are still in need of God's grace and mercy.

Fornication

There's that word again. It really does sound strange to our ears, doesn't it? About the only time we hear this word used anymore in our culture is in movie dialogue stereotyping Christians as uptight hypocrites. But *fornication* is a biblical term so we want to understand what it means. Here's how theologian Millard Erickson defines fornication in *The Concise Dictionary of Christian Theology*:

> In the broadest sense, [it means] sexual immorality of all kinds; in a nar-rower sense, voluntary sexual intercourse between unmarried people. The narrower sense contrasts with adultery, which is similar action by a married person with someone other than his or her spouse.[1]

The way we determine the sense of a word in Scripture is by looking at the con-text of the passage in which it is found. Sometimes the Bible uses fornication to refer to sexual immorality of all kinds, while at other times the Bible refers specifically to the physical act of sexual intercourse involving at least one un-married person. Because we've already looked briefly at adultery, let's consider fornication in its narrower sense.

How prevalent is the sin of fornication in our culture? It's all over the media, isn't it? Our public school systems have virtually given up any semblance of teaching the sanctity of sex within marriage. It is only recently, probably with the advent of AIDS, that public officials have even thought of encouraging young people to be abstinent. For many years, so-called "safe sex" has been the byword of public discussions about sexuality. The concept of "safe sex" would be laughable if it weren't so devastatingly serious both in its physical and spiritual consequences.

How prevalent is fornication, in its narrow sense, in the church? How about the kids in your church's youth groups or the college and career Sunday school class? "Not in our church," you say? I'm afraid you may be mistaken. Fornication is a serious problem among Christians, mostly young people. They often seem to think it's not a big deal and wonder why anybody wants to "hassle" them about it. Sexual purity seems to them like an outmoded idea.

But the Bible has a different view of fornication. While the Bible speaks positively about sexual intercourse (which God designed), it does so only within the context of a faithful, heterosexual marriage. (For some examples, see Genesis 4:1,2; Ruth 4:13; 1 Samuel 1:19; 2 Samuel 12:24; Song of Solomon 6:11–8:14; 1 Corinthians 7:3-5; Ephesians 5:25-33; 1 Timothy 3:2 [implied]; and Hebrews 13:4.) Speaking of the discipline of the body, Elisabeth Elliot says,

> Like every other good gift that comes down from the Father of Lights, the gift of sexual activity is meant to be used as He intended, within the clearly defined limits of His purpose, which is marriage. If marriage is not included in God's will for an individual, then sexual activity is not included either. . . . To offer my body to the Lord as a living sacrifice includes offering to Him my sexuality and all that that entails, even my unfulfilled longings.[2]

Fornication is a sin, according to the Bible. It is considered immoral. God did not design sexual intercourse for those who are not married to each other.

Jesus described fornication (sexual immorality) as an act that causes defilement (*see* Matthew 15:19-20). And Paul says to the Corinthians,

> Do you not know that the unrighteous shall not inherit the kingdom of God? Do not be deceived; neither fornicators, nor idolaters, nor adulterers, nor effeminate, nor homosexuals, nor thieves, nor the covetous, nor drunkards, nor revilers, nor swindlers, shall inherit the kingdom of God (1 Corinthians 6:9-10).

Hebrews 13:4 says that God will judge "fornicators and adulterers." Not a pretty picture, right? Whom we have sexual intercourse with is very much God's business. He has made it plain that unless we are married, sexual intercourse is off limits. And if we are married, our only biblically legitimate sexual partner is our spouse.

Homosexuality

The word *homosexual* refers to a sexual inclination towards or exhibiting sexual desire for persons of one's own sex. You will notice in 1 Corinthians 6:9-10 that homosexuality is another behavior that is prohibited by God. Engaging in homosexual behavior ought to cause a person to examine whether or not his or her profession of faith is genuine.

Because some people distort God's Word (2 Peter 3:16-17), some Christians put themselves in the precarious position of trying to justify homosexuality. In a misguided effort to avoid seeming intolerant, these Christians either willingly accept the misuse of Scripture or simply do not take the time to carefully study God's Word.

Yet the Bible clearly states that homosexual behavior is sin. We would need to twist Romans chapter 1, in particular, to come to any other conclusion. Being tempted is not sin, but *acting* on temptations by keeping them in our thoughts or by carrying them out in our activities with others is clearly sinful. Paul says this in Romans 1:22-27:

> *Professing to be wise, they became fools, and exchanged the glory of the incorruptible God for an image in the form of corruptible man and of birds and four-footed animals and crawling creatures. Therefore, God gave them over in the lusts of their hearts to impurity, that their bodies might be dishonored among them. For they exchanged the truth of God for a lie, and worshiped and served the creature rather than the Creator, who is blessed forever. Amen. For this reason God gave them over to degrading passions; for their women exchanged the natural function for that which is unnatural, and in the same way also the men abandoned the natural function of the woman and burned in their desire toward one another, men with men committing indecent acts and receiving in their own persons the due penalty of their error.*

Some Christians have bought into the myth of the "unique" spiritual needs of the homosexual in an effort to avoid appearing harsh or extreme. In showing biblical love, however, we cannot discard the truth. But, it is good to remember that we must present the truth in a loving manner.

The other extreme is to put homosexuality in a class all by itself as far as sins go. Too many times in the church we are horrified at hearing of someone's homosexual sin but merely shrug our shoulders at reports of heterosexual sin—namely adultery. Even when adultery involves pastors, it often is not taken seriously enough.[3] God calls homosexuality "an abomination" in Leviticus 18:22 and "detestable" in Leviticus 20:13. But Deuteronomy 25:16 says, "For *everyone* who does these things [using dishonest weights, for example], *everyone* who acts unjustly is an abomination to the Lord your God"(emphasis added). Whether sexual immorality involves homosexual acts or heterosexual acts, they are both condemned as sin.

Masturbation

This subject is a frequent topic of television sitcoms. Masturbation is self-stimulation of the genital organs usually for the purpose of producing an orgasm. You can take a concordance and search hard, but you will not find *masturbation* or any other forms of this word in the entire Bible. So can we conclude, then, that there is nothing morally wrong with it? If the Bible is silent on this topic, can we participate in it?

First, arguments from silence are weak because they rest on what the Bible *doesn't* say rather than on what it does say. In the case of masturbation, some people say that because the Bible does not refer to masturbation nor explicitly prohibit masturbation, it is an acceptable practice for a Christian. But we have to be extremely careful about arguing from silence, for that doesn't necessarily mean God approves of the practice. Second, simply because the Bible does not use the word *masturbation* does not mean it fails to speak about this issue.

Masturbation fits under the biblical categories of lust, selfishness, and perversion. Why is that so? Because God designed the human genital organs for sexual purposes within the context of a marriage. Any other use is a perversion of God's design. People masturbate seeking pleasure for themselves rather than to give pleasure to a marriage partner. Therefore, selfishness is one of the roots of this behavior. (We will say more about what motivates all forms of sexual sin later in the chapter.) In addition, lust drives the sexual fantasies that almost always accompany masturbation.

Celibate Marriage

The word *celibate* refers to a person who abstains from sexual intercourse. You may be surprised to learn that refusing to minister to your spouse sexually is sinful. Now, I'm not saying that every single time a husband wants to have sexual intercourse with his wife she has to agree. Obviously, illness or truly urgent responsibilites may delay her ability to minister to him this way. In such situations, the husband should be sensitive and ready to help her.

Unfortunately, the usual reason that married women refuse to have sexual intercourse with their husbands is bitterness and resentment at them.[4] Resentment will kill sexual desire like nothing else can. Resentment is a sort of smoldering ill will. It can fester just below the surface of a relationship for many years. It is important for a woman to take her resentments to God and ask Him to forgive her sin of unforgiveness.

For some women, this may be hard to do. They can't take anymore of this "do your duty" stuff. They've read 1 Corinthians 7:3-5 and heard the admonitions about being a faithful wife. They know this passage says they should fulfill their marital duty to their husband and that their body does not belong to them alone but also to their husband.

To these women, this seems like a bitter pill to swallow. *Perhaps,* they think, *the feminists are right and Paul was a male chauvinist who just had no clue what it was like to be a woman.* But remember that Paul wrote under the inspiration of the omniscient (all-knowing) Holy Spirit. God didn't make a mistake here. He was warning the Corinthians that celibacy has no place in marriage as some of them were claiming it did.

Resentment can involve such issues in the husband-wife relationship as the couple's premarital sexual history, abortions, adultery, unconfessed sin, or un-reconciled sin. If you are counseling a woman who does not have sex with her husband because of resentful feelings toward him, you must determine if she has any unconfessed sin—especially sin that may stem from premarital sex that influenced her to feel used by her husband-to-be. In addition, some women use sex to elicit a marriage commitment from a man. This sexual manipulation sometimes results later in resentment on the part of the wife. Other women use sex as a way to control men before marriage. But after marriage, they feel a loss of control when they have to submit to their husband's desires.

Resentment at a husband's lack of help with child care and housework is also a fairly frequent problem. Many women complain that their husbands come home from work, plop themselves in front of the television, and barely lift a finger to help with the kids or the house. If the wife works full-time outside the home, her situation is even more difficult because she is faced with her "second job" when she gets home. Surveys indicate that in households with two full-time income earners, the wife usually does a larger proportion of the housework and child care. Many of these employed women are just plain exhausted by the time they turn in for the night. Women who work part-time also experience this "second job" phenomenon but to a somewhat lesser degree.

So, what does all this have to do with celibate marriage? Well, when the husband desires sexual intercourse, these women are often resentful because they are tired and didn't get to rest earlier in the evening like the husband did. They often have little interest in having intercourse by the time they go to bed. In addition, they're already concerned about their workload for the next day.

The solution to this problem is for a wife to respectfully describe to her husband the nature of the problem and some possible solutions. She should try to enlist his help. Women often must make a choice between accepting the husband's lack of help (and refusing to harbor resentment), or cutting back on their employment outside the home so that they are not so tired. If the wife continues to work, she needs to be able to delegate some of her tasks to other members of the family.

Sexual Fantasy

A fantasy involves the creation of mental images in the mind. These images are shaped by the desires of the person creating them. Fantasizing is daydreaming; it is indulging in the condition of being lost in thought. Not all fantasy is sinful; sometimes our daydreaming can be productive if it helps us to shape godly ideas about our service for God.

But we are considering here fantasizing that involves illicit sexual thoughts. This is where sexual sin is born. "Each one is tempted when he is carried away and enticed by his own lust. Then when lust has conceived, it gives birth to sin; and when sin is accomplished, it brings forth death. Do not be deceived, my beloved brethren" (James 1:14-16). Many women, even Christian women, watch soap operas or movies that encourage this type of fantasy. Some women even employ these fantasies to help them feel more sexual with their own husbands. If the fantasy involves a man other than a woman's own husband, it amounts to adultery of the heart.

Dependence upon fantasy to feel sexually motivated with a husband ought to be a warning sign that something is wrong with the wife's perspective on marital sexual relations. Perhaps she sins by lusting for inordinate romantic feelings. Because she may see her husband or her circumstances as less appealing than a scenario from a movie or television program, she may indulge in fantasies that end up perpetuating her disappointment with her husband. Women who do this can get caught in a trap of failing to appreciate the real husband whom God has provided for them. Such women would find it profitable to study the Scriptures to gain a biblical perspective on the joys, privileges, and responsibilities of marital love, including sex.

Motives Behind Sexual Sin

Heart Issues

When Jesus taught about discipleship in Luke 6:39-49, He made it clear that we can truly understand our actions only by seeing what's in our hearts. (Remember that "heart," in the Bible, means the inner person—that part of you that is not physical.) In verse 45 Jesus said, "The good man out of the good treasure of his heart brings forth what is good; and the evil man out of the evil treasure brings forth what is evil; for his mouth speaks from that which fills his heart." Mark 7:21 also illustrates this truth:

> *For from within, out of the heart of men, proceed the evil thoughts, fornications, thefts, murders, adulteries, deeds of coveting and wickedness, as well as deceit, sensuality, envy, slander, pride and foolishness. All these evil things proceed from within and defile the man.*

When the inner person—mind, emotion, will, strength, soul, spirit—is filled with godly thoughts, imaginations, and attitudes, then godly actions are produced in the life of that person. But when that inner person is filled with sin, sinful actions are produced.

The Fruit of Wrong Thinking

What is happening in a woman's heart when she decides to engage in sexual sin? Notice I used the word *decides*. Though people involved in sexual sin say that they "fell in love," suggesting a response outside their control, every person has the ability to choose his or her actions. Choosing to sin sexually generally results from pursuing a feeling of closeness to another person without risking true intimacy or responsibility. In such a sexual relationship, three problem motives crop up repeatedly. Let's take a brief look at them.

Selfishness   Selfishness is when a person puts herself first or insists on her own way. It demonstrates a disregard for another person's best interests. It is the opposite of servanthood. People who selfishly enter into a relationship usually bail out when they feel the relationship has become inconvenient, dull, or unfulfilling. The phrase counselors most often hear as justification for sexual selfishness is, "My needs weren't being met."

Selfishness is self-centeredness. When we are at the center of our world, we, usually unknowingly, worship ourselves. Self-worship crowds out worship of

God with the result that the first two of the Ten Commandments are broken (*see* Exodus 20:3-6). We are now guilty of idol worship—the idol of self. We have set ourselves up as god in our lives. We decide what's right for us. God's instructions for sexual purity and servanthood are ignored because of our own sinfulness.

Anger   A common underlying motive fueling sinful sexual expression is anger. Situations in which a person feels oppressed, stifled, trapped, or controlled can generate angry feelings that need to be acknowledged and dealt with in a godly way. But if these feelings are handled in a sinful way the result can some- times be sexual sin. Women who sin sexually report feeling so out of control of the circumstances of their lives that they respond with bitterness, resentment, and anger.

This anger is usually directed at the persons involved (such as a spouse) and often also at God. These women conclude that God is unloving, unmerciful, and unkind. After all, they reason, if God is ultimately in control of everything, why does He leave them in such frustrating circumstances? They believe that God should provide what they want. They have a keen sense of having been be- trayed, and in their minds, God is the greatest betrayer of them all. A loving God, they say, shouldn't allow His children to suffer.

These women have a strong sense of entitlement; they think that they deserve something or someone better. They get angry at God for not giving them what they want or what they think they deserve. Their anger at God is rebellion, which usually leads to further rebellion. However, anger at God is *never* justified. God is perfect and never does anything at which man can be righteously angry. You may hear some Christians promoting the idea that God is "big" and He can take your anger, so just be honest with Him and let it out. That is blasphemy. If a person is angry at God, he needs to reverently repent of his anger at Him.

People who are angry at God often seek comfort in sexually sinful relationships. "I deserve" is the ruling attitude of their hearts. But their concept of God is unbiblical. They have never known or have forgotten the true and living God of the Bible. Because they measure love by unbiblical standards, they blame God for failing in His "duties" to them. Sometimes people, particu- larly singles, blame God for His supposed lack of providing a marriage partner so they won't have lustful thoughts. If you have a counselee who is involved in sexual sin, be sure to look for the attitudes that lie behind the outward sexual behaviors. When you try to decern a person's motives, anger, lust, and selfish- ness are the roots you will find behind sexual sin.

Anger at God is sometimes provoked by severe trauma such as incest, rape, or sexual abuse. These are highly distressful issues requiring the light and comfort of God's Word tenderly applied to them. At the same time, the counselor must lovingly correct the counselee's understanding of God. The counselee must be taught to believe that God is who He says He is in the Bible: compassionate, just, and an avenger of evil. Our life experiences must not dictate our view of God (see chapter 3, "The Essential Foundation"). Knowing God and experiencing His comfort requires obedience to Him (*see* Matthew 5:17-20; John 14:21; 2 Corinthians 1:1-11).

The trials a woman faces do not remove her responsibility to obey God's commands. In fact, 2 Corinthians 1:9 tells us that trials come so that "we should not trust in ourselves, but in God who raises the dead."[5] The woman who sins sexually must be held accountable to a firm commitment to sexual purity no matter what her past experiences have been.

A compassionate heart is necessary for any counselor ministering to people who have been sinned against. Past sexual abuse often influences present sexual choices, but cannot be understood as a cause of sinful sexual behavior. Simply identifying past abuse, understanding where ideas about sex originated, or gaining insight will not change people in a God-pleasing way. Such counselees need God's help; only with God's power can they change.

Lust   Lust is an acute desire or craving whether sexual or nonsexual. *Lust* is one of the Bible's words for *addiction.* (*See* chapter 15 for a definition of addiction.) Sexual sin is usually accompanied by inordinate sexual desire or intense cravings for physical closeness. Lust can include an urgent felt need for someone—anyone—to care.

Prolonged lusting for relationship can result in what pop psychology calls "co-dependency" or "emotional dependency."[6] We'll look at co-dependency more closely later in this chapter. The Bible calls these dependent behaviors lust, which is a form of idolatry. Thus craving relationship—that is, inordinate desire for relationship—is sin; it is the sin of idol worship. Only God may properly receive our adoration, our complete devotion.

As Heather progressed through the counseling process, she recognized that lust was at the root of her problems. She came to realize that she had established an idol in her heart.[7] This idol was not made of wood nor stone, as pictured in Isaiah 44:9-20. Our idols today are mostly ones we form in our hearts in response to inordinate desires. The idol of sexual pleasure usually starts with fantasy and progresses to masturbation. Because people tend to become hardened to a specific kind of pleasure, they are continually searching for new, different, and more intense pleasures.

This process is similar to drug addiction in that a more intense experience is sought as old thoughts and behaviors become customary. Paul described this downward spiral when he wrote, "Having lost all sensitivity, they have given themselves over to sensuality so as to indulge in every kind of impurity, with a continual lust for more" (Ephesians 4:19 NIV). The essence of addiction is "a continual lust for more." Heather and Abby were caught in that trap, and Heather found it difficult to get out. But, getting out is not impossible. Let's look next at the way out of sexual sin.

Achieving and Maintaining Sexual Purity

Change Is Possible

Like Heather, your counselee might be discouraged and say, "Wow, I'm a bigger sinner than I thought I was. I can't justify what I've become. It's hopeless." But I reminded Heather, and you can remind your counselee, that there *is* a remedy for sin. She *can* change. She doesn't have to stay the way she is no matter what behaviors she has adopted. God is greater than her weakness. Her hope for change must reside in his Holy Spirit.

> I pray that the eyes of your heart may be enlightened, so that you may know what is the hope of His calling, what are the riches of the glory of His inheritance in the saints, and what is the surpassing greatness of His power toward us who believe. These are in accordance with the working of the strength of His might which He brought about in Christ, when He raised Him from the dead, and seated Him at his right hand in the heavenly places (Ephesians 1:18-20).

God raised Christ from the dead. Is anything too hard for Him? Is anyone beyond His reach, His power? Never. "What is impossible for mortals is possible for God" (Luke 18:27 NRSV).

If a woman's sexual sin starts with the fact that she is darkened in her understanding because she is not a Christian, God can save her from her sin and bring her into a saving relationship with Him. Or, if she is a Christian, she can be cleansed even from sexual sin because she has a High Priest who intercedes for her. Confession and repentance is the way out.

The Way Out

First Corinthians 6:9-11 gives hope to those caught up in sexual sin and other habitual sins. When we looked earlier at verses 9-10, we saw that they contained a list of sinful behaviors that have no part in the kingdom of God. Then, Paul shone the light of gospel hope on the subject when he said in verse 11, "That is what some of you were. But you were washed, you were sanctified, you were justified in the name of the Lord Jesus Christ and by the Spirit of our God" (NIV). This is what some of you *were*—past tense! If the people in first-century Corinth could change from those sinful patterns, then people can change today, too! God can change your counselee. Will she let Him?

Your counselee's situation is not hopeless. She can change with God's help and in God's way. Let's examine the three aspects of God's way out of sexual sin.

Washed by God To put off sexual sin and put on sexual purity, your counselee needs to be washed clean in the blood of Christ. She cannot be permanently freed from the stain of sin if she has not been cleansed of her sin by the blood of Christ.[8] What does that mean? Everyone is a sinner by birth and by practice and needs a Savior to redeem him or her from sin. Your counselee must surrender control of her life to Jesus Christ and ask Him to forgive her for her sinfulness. Have her ask Him to enable her to give her life to Him because He gave His life for her (*see* 2 Corinthians 5:15).

Remind your counselee of the truth that if she is born from above (John 3:3), she is clean in the sight of God because of the work of Christ on her behalf. God is pleased with His children and delights in them; He has done for her what she could not do for herself. She does not need to try harder to please God in order to be saved from her sin. She needs to trust what Christ has already done for her. God's love is not a reward for good behavior; it is a gift (*see* Ephesians 2:8-9)!

Heather was visibly relieved when we discussed this truth from Scripture. She was beginning to understand God's marvelous grace. Perhaps the whole concept of grace is as vague for your counselee as it was for Heather. She may understand the *idea* of grace, but not its reality. Grace is God's favor shown to us sinners purely out of His mercy. We cannot earn God's favor. He gives it to us freely. We who have been reconciled to the heavenly Father through His Son, Jesus Christ, receive grace lavishly poured out into our lives (Ephesians 1:3-10).

Does this mean that God winks at a Christian's sexual sin and doesn't consider it serious? No, not at all. Such sin grieves God's heart. Consider God's response to man's sin during Noah's time:

Then the LORD saw that the wickedness of man was great on the earth, and that every intent of the thoughts of his heart was only evil continually. And the LORD was sorry that He had made man of the earth, and He grieved in His heart (Genesis 6:5,6)

We grieve God's Holy Spirit when we sin (*see* Ephesians 4:30). God takes sin very seriously. But He knows that we are sinful, weak people greatly in need of His grace, and so where our sin abounds, grace abounds all the more (*see* Romans 5:20). All the help we need to overcome sin is provided for us by God.

If we confess our sins to God and ask for His forgiveness, He is "faithful and righteous to forgive us our sins and to *cleanse us from all unrighteousness* (1 John 1:9, emphasis added). Psalm 51 is David's song of confession and repentance after he was confronted by Nathan about his adultery with Bathsheba and his guilt in the murder of her husband. This psalm provides an example of what it means to confess sin:

- recognize God's holiness, compassion, mercy, and grace (verses 1-2)
- tell God how you have sinned against Him and against others (verses 3-6)
- grieve and mourn as you see your sin in relation to God's holy standard given to us in His Word (verses 3-6)
- agree with God that you have offended Him (verses 2-5)
- acknowledge that only God can take away your sin (verses 7-9)
- ask God to give you a pure heart, a renewed spirit, and to restore your joy (verses 10-12)
- praise God for His righteousness and rejoice in His cleansing (verses 13-17)

When your counselee first begins to change, she *may* find herself still falling back into sin repeatedly and therefore having to confess her sin to God repeatedly. As days and weeks go by, if she is faithful to confess each time she sins, God's Spirit will continue to work in her and bring about change. Yes, she *may* go through times when she falls back into sin. But encourage her not to give up. She can keep going to God, asking for His help and forgiveness. Though this may feel humiliating, it will help her to develop a humble spirit. Eventually, the habitual sin will have less of a grip on her as she battles against it in the Spirit's power. In some instances of habitual sin, a counselee can give it up immediately. But do not be surprised and do not give up on your counselee if she struggles with failure in the beginning of this process. (*see* Romans 7:7-8:17; 1 John 1:1-3:10). Remind her that God, who raises the dead, can enable her to put off even the worst kind of sin. God's power is sufficient for all of our needs. He who calls us to be holy will surely provide "everything we need for life and godliness" (2 Peter 1:3 NIV). Confession goes hand-in-hand with repentance, which is the next step.

Sanctified by God   *Sanctification* refers to being set apart by God for a holy purpose through the sacrificial death of Jesus Christ. When we surrendered our life to Christ we were sanctified. In one sense, this work is already done. However, another aspect of sanctification is that God *continues* to make us more like Christ. This is called *progressive sanctification.*[9] In simple terms, it means that God loves us too much to leave us the way we were when He brought us into His kingdom. He is busy making us new creatures in Christ (*see* 2 Corinthians 5:17). God is holy, so His children must also be holy.

Repentance is the key to sanctification. Second Timothy 2:22 admonishes us to "flee from youthful lusts, and pursue righteousness, faith, love and peace, with those who call on the Lord from a pure heart." And 1 Corinthians 6:18 warns, "Flee immorality." Don't play around with sexual sin—flee!

Your counselee must show God she is serious about wanting to change. *Repent* means to change direction—she needs to turn away from her sins and run to the Lord. Let your counselee know that the Lord compassionately invites idolatrous and faithless people to return to Him.[10] Have her memorize appropriate Scripture passages so she can quote them to herself when she is weak. God's Word will help sanctify her and renew her mind so that she can be transformed and not follow her old sinful ways.

APPLYING REPENTANCE   In repentance, your counselee will admit that she is wrong and that God's way is good and right and best. She will humble herself before Almighty God and grieve over her sin and how it has offended God. Matthew 5:4 says, "Blessed are those who mourn, for they shall be comforted." When your counselee genuinely mourns over her sin, God Himself will comfort her.

It is important for your counselee to die to what she wants and to wholeheartedly seek what God wants for her. Jesus said, "If anyone wishes to come after Me, let him deny himself, and take up his cross daily, and follow Me" (Luke 9:23). What does this mean? In order to follow Jesus, it is necessary every day to die to those things that have no part in Christ's kingdom.

Sometimes a woman will have such compelling feelings for another person that she thinks she can't survive without that person. She may be reluctant to give up that person because she has made him (or her) the center of her world. But God hates this. Only He deserves that kind of adulation, devotion, worship. Agonizing though it may be, the idol must go. Therefore, the Bible tells such an individual to put off old attitudes and behaviors and put on new ones:

> You were taught, with regard to your former way of life, to put off your old self, which is being corrupted by its deceitful desires; to be made new in the attitude of your minds; and to put on the new self, created to be like God in true righteousness and holiness (Ephesians 4:22-24 NIV).

Heather personalized Colossians 3:1-17 in order to give structure to the change process. We put her name right in the verses so that they spoke specifically to her. That helped her to be obedient to God. We made a chart with two columns—one was titled "Put Off" and the other was titled "Put On." This helped Heather to pay attention to the things that needed to go out of her life and put into practice the godly attitudes and behaviors that she needed to adopt. In this way, Heather saw God's Word as directed not only to all Christians, but also specifically to her and her situation.

Remind your counselee of Paul's words in 1 Corinthians 6:11: "That is what some of you *were*"(emphasis added). Sexual sin can be past tense in your counselee's life. If she was involved—whether in mind or body—in fornication, adultery, masturbation, celibate marriage, or homosexuality, *God can set her free!* With God's powerful help, she can fight her way out of sexual sin. She can live a life pleasing to God. She does not have to be enslaved to sinful sexual attitudes and behaviors.

WRITING A PLAN   If your counselee seriously desires to overcome a sinful pattern of sexual behavior (whether in heart or in both heart and behavior), she needs to write out a plan for herself detailing how she will change. It must be specific and must include pertinent Bible references. She will need to refer to her plan as often as necessary. At first she may need to read it several times a day to remind herself how to put off the old and put on the new and why she is doing that in accordance with God's Word.

Remember, human willpower is no match for the sin nature in a person or the influences we are under from the world around us and from the devil. A person needs the Spirit of God to enable him or her to repent of sexual sin. Philippians 2:13 encourages Christians to "work out [their] salvation with fear and trembling; for it is God who is at work in [them], both to will and to work for His good pleasure." Christians are new people who are *gradually* being changed into the likeness of Christ (*see* Romans 8:29).

Here are some steps you may want to help your counselee incorporate in her plan:

1. Remind your counselee that temptation *will* come.

2. Identify the circumstances under which your counselee is likely to be tempted to sin. Include times, places, and persons who present difficulties for her. For example, one of my colleagues notes that a surprising number of women she has counseled for sexual sins say that the Friday afternoon drive home from work is a time of intense temptation to indulge in sinful sexual or romantic fantasies.

3. With your counselee, identify the reason(s) for the temptation. In the preceding example, the drive home is a situation vulnerable to temptation because the woman's concerns about work are not as immediate and therefore she is more likely to let her thoughts drift. A passive mind is a mind in danger. Maybe a particular song or type of music reminds your counselee of the past she wants to leave behind. Figure out the situations in which your counselee feels most vulnerable: unstructured time, fatigue, loneliness, unpleasant relationships at home or no one at home, weekends, holidays, and so on. Help her determine how to handle each of those situations.

4. Exhort your counselee not to frequent places that increase the temptation.

5. Help your counselee find ways to keep her mind occupied with good things. Let's consider that Friday afternoon drive home again. If that is a time when her mind wanders to fantasies, she can play some books on audiotape or listen to tapes of Christian teaching that would edify her mind. She could play praise tapes or make her own tape reminding her to pray for friends, missionaries, ministries, and so on.

6. Help your counselee learn how to control her thoughts. Have her study some verses in Scripture that teach a Christian how to use her mind. Here are some verses she can start with: Joshua 1:8-9; Psalm 16:8; Proverbs 3:5-8; Isaiah 26:3-4; Romans 8:5-17; 12:1-3; Ephesians 4:22-24; Philippians 4:4-9; 2 Corinthians 10:5; Colossians 3:1-3; and Hebrews 3:1; 12:1-3. Have your counselee choose some verses to memorize. While it may not seem like a person chooses what she thinks about, it is, nevertheless, true. Your counselee can choose to change her thoughts. It will be hard at first, but as she forms new thinking patterns, it will become easier to do.

7. Have your counselee develop godly relationships with mature Christian women. Ask your pastor or perhaps another biblical counselor to put her in touch with women who can disciple her. Encourage her to be part of a small group that can help her grow in godliness.

8. Remind her that perseverance and faithfulness are what God wants from her. When she sins, she is not condemned (*see* Romans 8:1). She can totally honest with God about her feelings and fears of falling back into sin. God is omnipotent (all-powerful). He can enable her to succeed in giving up sinful patterns in her life.

9. Have a trusted friend or discipler (which might be you) hold your counselee accountable to her plan. She must have someone asking her on a regular basis (at least every two weeks—preferably once a week especially in the beginning) whether or not she is being faithful to carry out her plan to put off sexual sin and put on sexual purity. Have your counselee show this woman her plan and ask for suggestions. If your counselee struggles with homosexual desires, have her meet with two or more mature Christian women rather than one-to-one so that she can avoid temptation.

For your counselee to be accountable to someone means that she is willing to take responsibility for her actions and be answerable to another person for what she does. *This is a vital part of growth in Christlikeness.* She must be totally truthful with you about her feelings, desires, beliefs, and actions.

We were not meant to live out our faith in isolation. Read the following verses to see the importance of Christians being involved in one another's lives: Proverbs 27:17; Malachi 3:16; Romans 15:14; 1 Corinthians 12:25; Galatians 6:2; Colossians 3:16; 1 Thessalonians 2:7-13; 5:11-15; Hebrews 3:13; 10:24-25; and James 5:16. Do you see how important it is to develop relationships with other believers? Consider the prophet Nathan's involvement in David's life. When Nathan rebuked David for his adultery with Bathsheba and the murder of Uriah, he was holding David accountable for those sins. Read this story in 2 Samuel 12:1-25. David's response is found in Psalm 51. What would have happened to David if Nathan had not been willing to be faithful and hold David accountable for his actions?

God wants our accountability/discipling relationships to have depth. He wants us to share our hearts, our lives with a few trusted Christian friends. We need to be transparent so we can spur one another on to be like Christ. Our tendency to deceive ourselves won't be corrected if we are unwilling to be completely truthful.

Keep in mind that I'm not talking about a "checklist" kind of accountability.[11] I'm not referring to a list of "do's" and "don't's" that merely prompt people to change their outward appearances. We don't want to be like the Pharisees, of whom Jesus said,

Woe to you, teachers of the law and Pharisees, you hypocrites! You are like whitewashed tombs, which look beautiful on the outside but on the inside are full of dead men's bones and everything unclean. In the same way, on the outside you appear to people as righteous but on the inside you are full of hypocrisy and wickedness" (Matthew 23:27-28).

Jesus warns us against being overly concerned with outward appearances and exhorts us to look at our hearts. How can you tell if a counselee's heart is changing? There are two ways: ask her, and watch for the signs of heart change in her outward behavior. If you know her well and see her in different contexts (home, church, school, and so on) over a long enough period of time, the counselee's real nature will reveal itself.

10. Encourage your counselee to develop a grateful spirit. Her heart ought to overflow with thanks for all that God has done for her. A thankful spirit will result in a Christlike attitude that joyfully proclaims God's greatness and humbly obeys His commands. If your counselee has a grumbling, complaining spirit, talk to her about cultivating a grateful one. The old saying "Count your blessings" may sound trite, but having that mindset truly does help to change the heart.

When your counselee puts these ten action steps into practice, she will be well on her way to overcoming sexual sin.

Justified by God What does it mean that God justified us? It means that we have been restored to a state of righteousness because Christ paid for our sins. We are trusting in His work on our behalf and know that our own accomplishments will never get us into heaven. When God looks at a Christian, He sees the righteousness of Christ because the Christian is *in Christ* (*see* Romans 6:1-14). Our sin debt is *paid in full,* and we are not guilty before God. But we are debtors to the grace of God. We owe Him our lives. Remember Paul's words to the Corinthians:

Flee sexual immorality. All other sins a man commits are outside his body, but he who sins sexually sins against his own body. Do you not know that your body is a temple of the Holy Spirit, who is in you, whom you received from God? You are not your own; you were bought at a price. Therefore honor God with your body (1 Corinthians 6:18-20 NIV).

What if someone suddenly came along and paid all your counselee's debts—every last one of them—so that she didn't owe anyone anything? What would her response be? She'd probably jump up and down for joy! Well, she can go ahead and jump because, spiritually speaking, that is precisely what Christ has already done for her. She is no longer weighed down in sin. She's free! Encourage her to live out what she is—washed, sanctified, and justified in the Lord!!

"Co-dependency" and Sexual Sin

Near the beginning of this chapter, we talked about euphemisms. *Co-dependency* is a euphemism for relationship idolatry. This kind of idolatry involves two people who believe that they need each other in ways that the Bible says are sinful.

It is clear from Scripture that we all need each other in order to carry out ministry in the church. First Corinthians 12 describes how the different parts of the body of Christ (the church) interact with and help each other. And it is true that we need the farmers, the doctors, the engineers, and many other people who provide goods and services to support human life.

But the kind of need that surrounds co-dependency is a need that is displaced onto the wrong object. What do I mean by this? People caught up in relationship idolatry have lost their lives for someone other than God. The person they "love" is to them what only God can be in their lives. Their substitute god receives from them worship, honor, glory, and devotion that only God can rightly receive because of who He is.

It is important to note that Jesus instructed His disciples with the following words:

> *Anyone who loves his father or mother more than me is not worthy of me; anyone who loves his son or daughter more than me is not worthy of me; and anyone who does not take his cross and follow me is not worthy of me. Whoever finds his life will lose it, and whoever loses his life for my sake will find it (Matthew 10:37-39 NIV).*

These verses teach us at least three truths about the place the Lord Jesus should have in the life of a Christian:

- loving anyone more than Jesus renders you unworthy of Him
- denying yourself (taking your cross) and being totally committed to Jesus means that you choose to do His will and not yours
- losing your life for anyone other than Jesus means that you're seeking life outside of relationship with Christ (and that is idolatry)

The woman who is a co-dependent violates all three of these truths. She loves the person she "needs" more than Christ. This love is usually a highly intense infatuation. In these dependent relationships, the person actually being loved the most is the person's own self. Basically, co-dependency is self-worship or idolatry of self. The person who is the object of intense affection is usually manipulated to meet the desires of one's self. Thus there is an attempt to control the idol to make it worship one's self.

In Heather and Abby's relationship, Abby was the one who appeared to be the most needy. Abby tried to make everyone her best friend. She would gush over and flatter others. By constantly seeking their help with her many problems, Abby tried to connect with other people. Once in a while Abby would develop a friendship only to see it end abruptly and unpleasantly as the friend got tired of her neediness. Abby tried to hold on too tightly to anyone who seemed willing to get involved with her. She monopolized the friend's time. And if her friend made other plans, Abby would always find a reason to appear on the scene. Her friends felt suffocated. Unsuccessful in her attempts to resolve these situations, Abby experienced a continuing series of lost friendships—until she met Heather.

A Mutual Attraction

Heather seemed to "have it all together," but she was just as "needy" as Abby. She longed for a close relationship but didn't reach out to others. The worst fate she could imagine was being rejected. She feared that if anyone got to really know her, they wouldn't like her anymore. Being aloof was less risky. She had an intense desire for people to think the very best of her. Letting them get close meant having them know the worst, and Heather couldn't live with that.

When Heather and Abby met, it was like bringing two pieces of velcro together. Abby, soft and fuzzy, immediately "stuck to" Heather, rigid and stiff. You know the rest—they were inseparable. Being assigned as roommates seemed to them a match made in heaven. Heather was organized and a good student, while Abby was undisciplined and struggled with her studies. She "needed" lots of help. Although Abby's constant flattery made Heather uncomfortable, and it often seemed insincere, Heather longed for someone who would appreciate her abilities and make her feel worthwhile. Abby filled the bill. And besides, Abby really knew how to have fun.

A Vicious Cycle

Their mutually dependent friendship eventually deteriorated into physical sin. At times they would repent of their behavior and promise each other not to do it again. But they did. They were ensnared in the cycle of idolatry. Here's how they were enslaved to the cycle of homosexual sin:

- they experienced intense sexual feelings along with an overwhelming yearning for an intimate relationship to the point of feeling consumed by their passion
- they gave in to their longings, allowing feelings to rule their hearts and bodies
- they experienced the emotional and physical pleasure of their encounters
- they recognized their sinfulness and felt guilty, ashamed, fearful, and disgusted
- they determined never to let it happen again
- they tried to pay for their sin by reading two extra chapters in the Bible every day, and praying for 30 minutes three times a day
- they experienced intense sexual feelings along with an overwhelming yearning for an intimate relationship to the point that they *felt* consumed by their passion

At this point the cycle is repeating itself. (*See* chapter 15 on addiction for further discussion about addiction and idolatry.)

The idol a co-dependent establishes and tries to control soon controls the co-dependent. In fact, she finds out to her dismay that she never did have control over it. Throughout this process of establishing an idol in her heart, she is an active participant in sin; she is *not* a passive victim. This same cycle operates in heterosexual adultery and fornication; it is not exclusive to homosexuality.

Not all idolatrous relationships end up in overt sexual sin, but the probability that they will do so is high. These overt behaviors result from prior heart sins. Eventually, the condition of a person's heart always works its way out into his or her behavior. If you recognize these sins brewing in a counselee's heart, it is essential that you immediately point out the counselee's need to repent of them. She can do this with you or along with another mature Christian woman who can help hold her accountable to be faithful to God and become pleasing to Him in every way—both in mind and body.

An Appropriate Response

If a woman confides in you about her struggle with sexual sin, pray for gracious words to use in showing her the truth of God's Word. Pray that this sister will be convicted in her own heart by the Holy Spirit to repent of her sin and change in ways pleasing to God. If you, the counselor, have an ungodly attitude toward this person, your exhortation may not influence her to repent of her sin. If you are self-righteous or make wrong judgments, she is likely to avoid you or to pay little heed to your counsel. You will lose the trust of the person you want to help. Remember, our Lord said that we should get the log out of our own eye before we attempt to take the speck of out of our sister's eye (*see* Matthew 7:1-5).

If the woman you are counseling must break a sinful relationship, help her prepare to experience the grief that will result from this loss. She may experience both godly and worldly sorrow as the result of separating herself from a sinful relationship. She may exhibit symptoms of depression. God will comfort her in her sorrow if her repentance is real. He will cleanse her; He will be to her "the Father of compassion and the God of all comfort. . . . For just as the sufferings of Christ flow over into our lives, so also through Christ our comfort overflows" (2 Corinthians 1:3,5 NIV). God can turn her sorrow into joy. God is so incredibly compassionate. Psalm 103 tells us that "he does not treat us as our sins deserve or repay us according to our iniquities. . . . for he knows how we are formed, he remembers that we are dust" (10,14 NIV).

Obedience Produces Blessing

The mercies of God are wide and deep. God's mercy will meet a repenting heart. He will restore a woman who has turned from sexual sin and give her a heart of joy instead of sorrow. The road to blessedness through obedience may seem long to her, but the Lord will walk with her if she will love Him, trust Him, and obey Him. This is the only way to true joy.

When your counselee grasps the truth of her washing, sanctification, and justification from sexual sin, the result is freedom in her mind and the potential for better health in her body. Remind her of Paul's words in Romans 13:13-14:

> *Let us behave properly as in the day, not in carousing and drunkenness, not in sexual promiscuity and sensuality, not in strife and jealousy. But put on*

on the Lord Jesus Christ, and make no provision for the flesh in regard to its lusts.

God is not a cosmic killjoy waiting to rain on anyone's parade. His commands produce safety and blessing for His children. When human sexuality is expressed in godly ways within the parameters set down by God, it is able to bloom in its most beautiful form.

Recommended Resources

Horatius Bonar, *God's Way of Holiness,* Phillipsburg, NJ: Presbyterian & Reformed, 1979.

Elisabeth Elliot, *Discipline: The Glad Surrender,* Old Tappan, NJ: Fleming H. Revell Co., 1982.

————, *Loneliness,* Nashville: Oliver Nelson Books, 1988.

Sinclair B. Ferguson, *A Heart for God,* Colorado Springs: NavPress, 1985.

Erwin Lutzer, *How to Say No to a Stubborn Habit,* Wheaton, IL: Victor Books, 1979.

C. John Miller, *Repentance and Twentieth-Century Man,* Fort Washington, PA: Christian Literature Crusade, 1993.

Lois Mowday, *The Snare,* Colorado Springs: NavPress, 1989.

John R. W. Stott, *Your Mind Matters,* Downer's Grove, IL: InterVarsity Press, 1973.

A. W. Tozer, *The Knowledge of the Holy,* San Francisco: Harper, 1978.

Counseling Women in the Afternoon of Life

Elyse Fitzpatrick, M.A.

Women in the afternoon of life? What does that mean? Although this is merely an arbitrary designation, I thought it would be helpful to look at the life of a woman as a single day. The present life expectancy of an American women is 79 years. If we divide these expected years into six 15-year segments, and correlate it to a day, it looks something like this: 0-15 Dawn, 16-30 Morning till Noon, 31-45 Noon, 46-60 Afternoon till Twilight, 61-75 Evening, 75+ Nightfall. As a woman who falls into the 46-60 age range, I'm encouraged as I think about my life in these terms.

I had never heard Margie so upset. When she called me in the early afternoon she said, "I have to talk to you. My whole life is falling apart. I just don't think I can take it anymore." We made an appointment for that evening. I wondered what could have upset her so. Sure, we had recently celebrated her forty-ninth birthday, but she seemed to enjoy the light-hearted kidding about being "over the hill." She had seemed pleased that her youngest child, Jennifer, had been accepted at a Christian college in the northern part of the state. Margie's girls were blessings to us all. She was one of those women who seemed born to nurture. Her daughters had responded well to their mom's teaching and care—she had homeschooled them all. She and her husband, Chuck, had been members in our congregation for many years. They were involved in missions projects and Margie lead the women's prayer group frequently. What could be going on?

Margie arrived early looking disturbed and disheveled. After we prayed together for God's wisdom, I asked her to explain what the problem was. "I can't believe my life is over," she cried. "We dropped Jennifer off at school on Thursday. I woke up this morning with the realization that all my girls are gone. It's not that I'm unhappy about any of them leaving; it's just that now that they're gone, I know my life is over. On top of all of this, I went to the gynecologist yesterday and he says I'm perimenopausal.[1] I can't believe it! I was even thinking about having another baby! I can't believe this is happening to my body. I won't be able to have more children! I guess it's finally dawning on me that my life is finished. What am I going to do with myself?"

I waited quietly while she cried. Then Margie continued, "And the worst thing of all is that Chuck just doesn't get it. I think he's actually glad the girls are gone. He thinks I should be happy not to have to homeschool them any longer. I just can't imagine spending the next 20 years in an empty house with no one to talk to but him. You know," she whimpered, "he has never really understood me. If we don't have the girls to hold us together, I just don't think we're going to make it."

Have you heard women say these kinds of things before? Are you aware of the issues that a woman faces in the afternoon of her life? Would you know how to counsel Margie? What would you say?

The Aging of a Nation

In case you've never heard this kind of thing before, you may hear it soon. The American population is aging. As larger segments of our society enter what I'm choosing to call the afternoon of life, more and more thought will have to be given to the age-specific problems we're about to examine. On July 1, 1996, there were 16.5 million women in the 45 to 54 age group. In addition, there are 10.5 million women who are 40 to 44 waiting to join their ranks! Let's assume the percentage of committed Christians is around 10 percent.[2] This means that there are 1.6 million committed Christian women facing these issues *now*. Let me try to demonstrate this in another way. If your congregation loosely resembles the demographics of the population, a full 30 percent of the women in your congregation will be 50 or over by the year 2000!

The Problems Faced in Aging

Many problems are intrinsic to a woman who is an "afternooner." Physiological problems include menopause, infertility, and the general loss of youth. The Baby Boomer generation doesn't seem to be prepared to face the realities of physiological aging. "Empty nest" issues are present for some women with an apparent loss of purpose that sometimes accompanies it. Marital problems may surface at this time. In addition, the burden of caring for ill parents becomes a new concern. Let's take a brief look at the dynamics of each of these issues and then seek to uncover God's wisdom for them.

Physiological Problems

Shirley Galucki has written on these issues in chapter 20 from a medical perspective. I want to illustrate these issues from a more personalized level.

The Biological Clock Has Struck Twelve   Although women know they won't remain fertile forever, still, the transition to infertility often comes as a shock. Gail Sheehy, in her interesting (though thoroughly secular) look at the process of aging, *New Passages: Mapping Your Life Across Time*,[3] does a good job of capturing the surprise and dismay of women who are just discovering the clock has indeed struck 12:00. These women face the difficult task of grasping the fact that their bodies no longer function the way they did when they were 20. She cites statistics from the National Center for Health, which found that ". . . of women between 35 and 44, *half* had difficulty conceiving or carrying a child to term. The chances of a 44-year-old's being able to get pregnant naturally and have a healthy child *are 3 to 4 percent*"[4] (emphasis added).

These realities come as a devastating shock to the 30 million women aged 30 to 44 who have never had children.[5] Of course, of these women, many are unmarried,[6] but among families with married couples, there are 24 million households *with* and 27 million households *without* children under the age of 18.[7] What all this means is that there is a significant number of women who presently have no children and who may be under the delusion that they will be able to give birth to children whenever they so choose. Sheehy cites the rage women who embraced feminism may feel and quotes essayist Anne Taylor Fleming, who wrote, ". . . movingly of her own obsession with making up for lost time in her forties, failing to conceive and feeling betrayed by the feminist message to her generation."[8]

She continues,

Almost invariably these anxiety-ridden women confess to doctors the same regret: "Why didn't I start trying to get pregnant earlier?" Many bemoan having put career first. They fall into the same guilt cycle common among women who have had therapeutic abortions and later find themselves infertile: I'm being punished for my past. *Yet typical of their generation, they believe that if they just work hard enough they can make anything happen."*[9]

In America, infertility is a $2 billion-a-year business! Women, many of whom are past the age of having children naturally, are desperately spending around $8,000 in unregulated clinics *for each* in-vitro fertilization procedure.[10]

The Arrival of Menopause   Menopause often comes as a surprise to women. Even though we have a general knowledge that it eventually will happen, many of us are uninformed and ill-prepared for its arrival.

In Sheehy's chapter "Wonder Woman Meets Menopause," she states that in the year 2005 22.7 million women will be entering the age of perimenopause.[11] Think about it—22.7 million women who will be menopausal. Even though you may not have experienced any of the symptoms associated with this transition, you can be sure that at some time between the age of 46 and 52, you will. And the likelihood you will meet or get to know women in this in this stage of life is very high.

The Loss of Youth   Not only does the physiology of a woman's body begin to change in the afternoon of her life, so does her appearance. I live in Southern California, and the pressures here to be fit and strong and *alive* are enormous. Women are spending billions of dollars enrolling in fitness clubs, buying roller blades, discovering new anti-wrinkle fruit acid cremes, and practicing biofeedback and meditation to slow aging. I have friends who read fitness magazines to discover "How to Burn 800 Calories Per Hour!" "Have Abs, Legs, Hips like Rocks!" and "Eat Only 1200 Non-fat Calories Per Day (without missing out on anything)"! Some women fear they are being bulldozed toward a dark and terrifying chasm wherein arms and legs turn to cellulite and one's best friend is a facial sculptor.

Even women who have refused to rely primarily on appearance to attain goals may find these years difficult. Since some men (and women) consider aging and particularly menopause as the "end of life," women in this age group frequently feel insignificant, out-of-step, and obsolete. Women who have focused solely on their careers may look at their prospects and worry about who will take care of them as they age. They frequently envision themselves as the bag ladies of the future. They see bright, young, pretty girls climbing up the corporate ladder to take their place. As they observe the interaction between their male counterparts, younger women, and themselves, they frequently report feeling "invisible." On the other hand, women who have not pursued a professional career find this a difficult time also. Many of these women feel older than they are. Some feel trapped in dead-end positions, with few or no choices. Many of them are going through divorce or the empty-nest struggles. More than 40 percent of them are overweight[12] and find it difficult to be motivated to change or take chances. Many of them struggle with depression.

Of course, not all women experience these difficulties. For instance, women in Asian communities, where elders are venerated, don't worry so much about obsolescence. It is commonplace in many cultures that the grandparents live with their children and participate in the raising of their grandchildren. Although this is the model we see in the Bible, it is not the accepted cultural norm in America. Because of this, many women anticipate the loss of youth with trepidation.

The Empty Nest

At the same time physiological changes are occurring, a woman's children are leaving home. Although for many of us this event has been anticipated for a long time, the unsettling emptiness and unfamiliar quiet that now fills formerly chaotic halls is discomforting to say the least. No one is fighting for the shower before church! There are only two loads of laundry to do! Who is going to take out the trash now? What are we going to do with our time? For the average Christian woman who has chosen to devote herself to the propagation of the faith through her children, this may be a time of seeming loss of ministry and meaning.

For me, the grief over the empty nest came as an eye-opener. I thought I would be unscathed by this sorrow because I had never viewed myself as a "super mom." There are women who, like Margie, are born to nurture. I think that this is the best way to be, but I never thought about myself in those terms. I did homeschool my two youngest children at different times during their education, but I was never the Kool-Aid mom on the block. That's why I was shocked by my own response to the realities of the empty nest.

My eldest son joined the Navy in 1987 upon graduation from high school. I mourned and wept over his absence, but I still had other children demanding my time. My middle child (and only daughter) was married in July of 1995. Both my husband and I were happy about the marriage and grateful to God for her choice of a godly young man. I enjoyed planning the "wedding of the century," and though I was weepy from time to time, I was still in control. My daughter and her husband live close by and although I felt the loss, it wasn't devastating.

Then, in August of the same year, my youngest child was accepted at a Christian college. My husband and I drove into the parking lot for freshman orientation and when I read the welcome banners hanging over the school entrance, I burst into tears! I was sobbing. Fortunately, my husband, whose humor has kept me balanced through the years, came through. Quoting Tom Hanks's line from *A League of Their Own*, he said, "Elyse, there is no crying in college." I started laughing and was able to make it through the day. Now I understand the sorrow that other parents have experienced through the years. The word *empty* means "abandoned, uninhabited, unoccupied." I'm not used to thinking about my home in these terms. It is painful. Consider this touching poem by Cliff Schimmels in *And Then There Were Two: Empty Nesting After Your Kids Fly the Coop.*

The Empty Nest

The crying has stopped now.
No longer do the sobs seep out beneath the door.
No longer do we listen lying in our beds,
     trapped between our need to sleep and their need to weep.

No longer do the sighs start soft
     and grow into a roar
          resounding through the house
          and into our attention.

No longer do we need to summon one wee one into our room
     to console and comfort and show deep concern
          for the big problems—the day the guppies died,
        the day the boyfriend liked someone else,
        the day another was chosen for the honor.

No longer do we kiss away the tears and
        make it right with promises of a far-away future—
                "Someday, my little man, you will be a man
                and have a fish and a car and a job all your own."
                "Someday, my little girl, you will be a woman
                with a child all your own."

The crying has stopped, now that we are only two.
        And the far-away future has come—
It's a happy time; the laughter leaks through the phone lines—
        and we celebrate together the new child, the new job,
        the new house, the new achievement.

Those are big moments   those moments of rejoicing—
        because they tell us where we have been
                and where we are going.
And this is why we live.

The crying has stopped, now that we are only two.
And there is nothing left
        of the sobs and sighs behind the door.
Nothing left except the ache of remembering.[13]

Marital Difficulties

Partly due to the strains we have already mentioned and in part due to others,[14] the highest incidence of divorce occurs among people ages 40 to 54. William L. Coleman illustrates this problem with an amazing statistic: "About 40% contact a divorce lawyer soon after the last child moves out."[15] Among those getting divorced, more women than men are the ones choosing the single life and choosing to stay in it. "Among divorced couples between the ages of 45-54, it is women who are choosing to stay single more than men."[16] Many women have already achieved financial independence and once the constraints of children are past there seems little incentive for the woman who is apart from the Lord to stay in a relationship that, to her, seems to have outlived its relevance long ago. Of course, for the believing woman, the constraints of vows to a living God outlive all other considerations.

For many couples, like Margie and Chuck, the focus of the relationship has always been the children. Many women sinfully use children to replace the husband as best friend. Then, when the children move out, they feel isolated and alone. They may use this discomfort as the impetus to spur them on to new ministry, career, or educational ventures, or they may seek out a new source of companionship.

Caring for Ill Parents

As if all this weren't enough, it is usually around the age of 50 or so that our parents' health begins to decline. As our parents reach their seventies, the chances that they will need part- or full-time health care multiplies.

> In 1993, 28% of older persons assessed their health as fair or poor. . . . In 1986 about 23% . . . had health-related difficulties with one or more activities of daily living (including bathing, dressing, eating, transferring from bed or chair, walking, getting outside, and using the toilet). . . . Most older persons (65+) have at least one chronic condition and many have multiple conditions."[17]

Unfortunately, most people have not even thought about their parents' death, let alone organized the legal and financial instruments necessary to conduct business in a God-honoring way for them. (*See* chapter 19 for more on this.) The care of parents usually comes to rest on daughters. Women are customarily the caregivers and are more in tune with the physical needs of their parents. Some women may have recently gotten used to freedom from child-rearing responsibilities only to find themselves once again in the role of nurturer. Indeed, many women spend more time nurturing a parent than they did their own children. Two stories that illustrate the heartaches intrinsic in caring for an ill parent follow.

Carrie's Story　Carrie was the first of my friends to care for an ill parent. She, her husband, Don, and three sons took over the care of her mother, JoAnn. JoAnn had left the family home after her husband had divorced her, and moved closer to her daughter Carrie and her family. JoAnn continually complained about not feeling well, but the doctors couldn't discover the cause of her distress. They accused her of alcoholism and being a hypochondriac. Finally, they decided she was suffering from Cushing's Syndrome. Cushing's Syndrome is a rare hormonal disorder marked by upper-body obesity, severe fatigue and muscle weakness, high-blood pressure, backaches, elevated blood sugar, easy bruising, and bluish-red stretch marks on the skin. Over the course of the next three years Carrie and her family were either on-call to visit JoAnn in the hospital or convalescent center or she lived with them. Although the physicians performed numerous surgeries, they could not discover the precise source of her hormone imbalance. Carrie was forced to stand by helplessly as she watched her gregarious, outgoing, independent mother perceive her own growing frailty. JoAnn was required to spend six weeks in intensive care because her respirator couldn't be removed. She suffered for weeks with a staphylococcus infection and could not receive any visitors. In the meantime, Carrie's family moved to another part of the city to try to give JoAnn a nicer home environment. Because of the move, Carrie was isolated from her usual church supports and had trouble making significant connections in their new church. Carrie recalls it was hard for her to carry on typical after-church conversations with the ladies when her heart was breaking. She wanted to shout, "My mom is dying! Where is the fairness of God in this? Why would God allow this to happen to my mom, who has always been so kind and good? Why would God allow my father, who left her, to get off scot-free? Where is God?" Unhappily, these kinds of questions tend to make parishioners scatter. Even if her new friends had offered to help, Carrie was too overwhelmed to articulate what her needs were. She needed someone to nurture and care for her.

Carrie's mother passed away in 1990; she was 61.

Joy's Story   Joy's mother, Barbara, was diagnosed with Alzheimer's disease[18] seven years ago. Barbara was able to live on her own and with Joy's grandmother for the first three years of her illness. But eventually, she got to be too much to handle and moved in with Joy, her husband Carl, and their three girls. Joy's family also changed residences to better accommodate her mother. At first, Barbara's illness was only mildly noticeable, and some of the silly things she did made the family smile. She was also able to go once or twice a week to an Alzheimer's family care facility so that Joy could have time to work in her home-based business or care for the needs of her three homeschooled children.

I hadn't seen Joy for almost a year when we met to discuss her situation. I was astounded by the change in her. She seemed hopeless and the bubble of joy and sweet giggle that had always been present, even when she struggled, were missing. She was despairing and angry. Her mother had transformed into a demanding, vicious child in an adult's body. Joy had to care for her mother 24 hours a day. She bathed her, dressed her, and changed her diapers. She fed her, cutting her food for her and reminding her how to eat. She listened to her incessant demands. She endured her abuse. Barbara was becoming more and more violent. This was particularly painful to Joy because Barbara had seriously abused Joy as a child.

"I can't believe I'm living through this again. I thought that part of my life was finally over," she wept. I asked why she didn't put her in a nursing home or get some help. Joy patiently answered the question that she had been wrestling with for years. "My mom isn't old enough to receive Medicare. She'll be 62 next year and I'll have to wait until she's 65 before I'll be able to put her on a waiting list to get into a nursing facility. Most of these places cost $3,000 per month or more, and you know we just can't afford that. I can't get her into a day-care facility now because she has deteriorated too much. I can have a home health-care nurse visit for $12 per hour, but even when the nurse is there, my mother doesn't leave me alone."

Tragically, Joy was a slave to her mother's demands. I asked whether she was getting any help from her church. She explained that when her mother first came to live with the family, she thought it was best to devote herself to her care. She slowly dropped out of all her fellowship groups and was attending church only on Sunday mornings. "They just don't know what's going on. They don't know how bad it's gotten." "Why don't you tell them?" I asked. "I have, but they don't know what to do." Like Carrie, Joy needs someone to give care to her. She needs someone to nurture her. Joy doesn't even know how to communicate her needs. She feels isolated, alone, and trapped.

Woman are usually the ones there by the bedside. Women are the nurturers, the caregivers. It has always been this way. As the population continues to grow older and live longer, the numbers of women who will be taking care of an ailing parent will grow. In 1994, "about 13% of seniors over 65 were not living with a spouse but were living with children, siblings, or other relatives."[19] As the numbers of those 65 and over grows from present figures (33.2 million in 1994) to 35.3 million in 2000 and 40.1 million in 2010, the very real probability will exist that significant numbers of Christian women will be involved in some facet of caring for a parent. In addition to the graying of the population, the growing specter of the probable bankruptcy of the government medical system looms ahead. These issues must be anticipated by the church as it fulfills its call to practice true religion: caring for widows and orphans (see James 1:27).

As you can see, the age-specific dilemmas associated with this time of life are legion. The church must not miss the opportunity to help and counsel these women. How would you counsel Margie? Does the Bible speak to her problems? How would you counsel Joy or Carrie? Is your church equipped to support and encourage such women?

A Biblical Response for "Afternoon" Women

Many of the problems Christians face stem from a misunderstanding of who God is and who we are before Him. If a woman is defined only in terms of her fertility/child-rearing potential, what is she to do after her children are grown? If she is judged by her outward appearance and her ability to be alluring to her husband, what is she to do when she loses those fleeting outer charms? If she believes God has called her to a life of prosperity, and she has the ability to speak healing and everyone immediately is well, what will happen to her faith when she is faced with parents who have Alzheimer's disease? What will she do if she believes her husband's approval echoes God's approval and he leaves her for a younger woman?

All of these questions and others like them must be answered. Let's start with God's view of aging. In each of the following areas I will list pertinent verses to study and homework to assign to counselees.

God's Perspective on Aging

Some Key Observations Even a superficial review of God's counsel on aging and the aged portrays a perspective very different from that of modern America. Our antipathy toward people over 65 and our subconscious assumption that they are no longer useful is demonstrated in spades by the media's hits on 1996 presidential candidate Bob Dole. "But he's so old!" many whined. Political affinities aside, the Lord instructs us to value, cherish, and honor the aged. Typically, our culture's thoughts and ways are by nature opposed to God's. "For my thoughts are not your thoughts," the Lord declared through Isaiah (Isaiah 55:8). The thoughts in the heart of man haven't changed much in the past 4,000 years, have they?

Solomon recognized there would always be tension between those who favored youth over maturity. "The glory of young men is their strength, the honor of old men is their gray hair," he wrote (Proverbs 20:29). Yes, young people may have physical strength, but older people often have strength of character. This maturity and strength of character is developed only in the crucible of real-life experience as lived out under the hand of God. The woman who has lived out God's counsel through years of toil and trial has resilience, stamina, and a faithful perspective. Godly wisdom supersedes any loss of physical prowess she may be experiencing. Therefore, Paul instructed Titus to raise up mature, godly women to counsel other women.[20]

A Key Quality   Wisdom is not mere acquisition of knowledge. Any child can learn formulas, dates, and grammar. The biblical perspective of wisdom is quite different from academic learning. Biblical wisdom is the "ability to judge correctly and to follow the best course of action, based on knowledge and understanding."[21] Godly wisdom means insight, prudence, understanding, and discretion. It tells us how to live—what decisions to make, how to respond in any given circumstance, how to achieve certain tasks (*see* Exodus; 28:3, 31:3). It is practical rather than merely theoretical. Wisdom is always associated with a relationship with God: "The fear of the LORD is the beginning of wisdom, and the knowledge of the Holy One is understanding" (Proverbs 9:10). It is attained by obedience to God's commands: "See, I have taught you statutes and judgments . . . so keep and do them, for that is your wisdom " (Deuteronomy 4:5-6). Job stated, "Wisdom is with aged men, with long life is understanding" (Job 12:12). The Lord places great worth on this quality and commands we honor those who possess it: "You shall rise up before the grayheaded, and honor the aged, and you shall revere your God; I am the LORD" (Leviticus 19:32). Of course, being old is not a guarantee of being wise. Wisdom is available only to those who are willing to search it out (*see* Job 28:12-23; Proverbs 8, especially v. 17). The wise, such as David, have experienced a lifetime of knowing God (or if not a lifetime, have sought to make up for lost time by seeking God with intensity[22]). "I have been young, and now I am old; yet I have not seen the righteous forsaken, or his descendants begging bread" (Psalm 37:25).

David knew that those who put their trust in the Lord were secure in Him. This knowledge informed his actions and dictated his beliefs. David possessed a wisdom acquired through the passage of time. He knew about the blessings of God; he also knew of His discipline. He understood that God was faithful, even when David failed to be. He knew God was loving and merciful, but also holy and not to be trifled with.

Experiential wisdom is obtained as it flows out of the hand of God through His dealings with His children. These dealings may take many forms. They are all for our ultimate benefit and God's glory. He wants to bless us with wisdom, for His sake and ours. We ought to embrace His dealings in our lives as channels through which His loving wisdom is flowing to us. As A.W. Tozer wrote, "It is doubtful whether God can bless a man greatly until He has hurt him deeply."[23] God's gift of wisdom comes to us through joys and sorrows, filtered through our loving Father's hand, as we seek to live according to His Word. James describes this wisdom as "pure, then peaceable, gentle, reasonable, full of mercy and good fruits, unwavering, without hypocrisy" (James 3:17).

The Lord also understands that the aged may feel less secure because of their loss of strength. He has promised His continued care all through life: "Even to your old age, I shall be the same, and even to your graying years I shall bear you! I have done it, and I shall carry you; and I shall bear you, and I shall deliver you" (Isaiah 46:4). God's everlasting love rests securely on the man or woman who has, by His strength, served Him faithfully, weathered the storms, grown in grace, and matured in love.

Cast off the thinking of the world! Embrace the mind of Christ! The loss of youth is not something for us to fear. Rather, it is something to be welcomed. With it comes the wisdom that pleases our King.

Physiological Problems   The macabre comedy, *Death Becomes Her,* is not too far off the mark as it portrays America's greed for youth and beauty. The leading female roles portray rich, vain women obsessed with their image. In a telling scene, a middle-aged woman returns to her cosmetic surgeon, begging for more treatments to slow the inevitable aging process. He is unwilling to perform them because they are unsafe. She doesn't care. She is willing to sacrifice her health for her beauty. As the story progresses she and another woman "sell their souls" to the devil in exchange for the promise of eternal youth and beauty. The movie ends with the two of them squabbling over who has the super glue so that they can reattach severed body parts. They are grotesque caricatures of women whose sole purpose in life is to be worshiped for their beauty. Like Oscar Wilde's Dorian Gray, they discover too late that the nature of the soul reveals itself, no matter how good one might look on the surface.

In contrast we are given the portrait of the woman of excellence in Proverbs 31. "Charm is deceitful and beauty is vain, but a woman who fears the LORD, *she shall be praised*" (Proverbs 31:30). Here, in my opinion, is the heart of the matter. Many women worry about the loss of beauty because they love and crave the praise of men (and women). They love those admiring greetings: "You look great! Don't you ever age?" They love the way other women look enviously at them. They love to turn heads. This self-love and desire for worship from others is from the flesh, the sinful nature. Ezekiel gives us insight in the fall of hell's master, Lucifer: "Your heart was lifted up because of your beauty; you corrupted your wisdom by reason of your splendor" (Ezekiel 28:17). Lucifer was corrupted by an inordinate appreciation of his own beauty, as many women are today.

In contrast to these displays of self-love and self-worship is the excellent woman of Proverbs. Her beauty doesn't stem from how she looks. Rather, it flows out of a heart that is centered on trusting God. Rather than trusting in her own beauty as the harlot Jerusalem did,[24] she trusts in her God. She knows that charms, especially a woman's sexual attractiveness, are deceitful. The word *deceitful* is a powerful word, meaning "illusive, deceptive, misleading." She knows that outer beauty is a mere breath. It is like a vapor, which appears for a little while and then vanishes away. What will she have left when the wind blows her beauty away? On the other hand, if she has revered the Lord and sought to conform her heart to His law—if she has loved what He loves and hated what He hates—she will receive praise! Isn't that interesting? The woman who seeks after the praise of men by being consumed with her beauty will find futility. But the woman who seeks after the Lord, desiring His approval, will have praise![25]

I'm not saying it is godly or ungodly to wear make-up or to try to look good by exercising, buying nice clothes (as you can afford to), or learning new ways to fix your hair. I'm not called to judge anyone else's spirituality by the outer body. The Lord taught this truth to Samuel as he was seeking after a king to replace the handsome Saul: "Do not look at his appearance or at the height of his stature, because I have rejected him; for God sees not as man sees, for man looks at the outward appearance, but the LORD looks at the heart" (1 Samuel 16:7).

We women need to put off our self-righteousness and judging. Don't think you are righteous just because you don't wear make-up or jewelry. On the other hand, don't think you are righteous because you have the liberty to wear anything you want. God is looking at your heart. What are your motives? Are you seeking after the praise of men? Are you loving your brother and doing everything possible to avoid tempting him to lustfulness? Are you trying to draw attention to yourself, either by wearing or shunning cosmetics? Are you overspending your time and money in the pursuit of beauty? These are the questions every woman must prayerfully answer. On the other hand, a woman may be legitimately concerned about her appearance so she may minister to her culture, a culture that is obsessed with appearance (1 Corinthians 9:19-23).

Rejoice in God's wonderful promise that no matter what features you were born with, you and any other woman can be beautiful and praiseworthy.

> *Let not your adornment be merely external—braiding the hair, and wearing gold jewelry, or putting on dresses; but let it be the hidden person of the heart, with the imperishable quality of a gentle and quiet spirit, which is precious in the sight of God. For in this way in former times the holy women also, who hoped in God, used to adorn themselves (1 Peter 3:3-5).*

The Lord teaches women where they should focus their efforts. They shouldn't focus on the externals, such as attention-getting hair styles or finding the "perfect accessories." Instead, women must concentrate on the adornment of lovely qualities that remain unaffected by the passing of time and the deterioration of the body. These qualities are gentleness and quietness. At first glance, 1 Peter 3:3-5 may seem it's saying that God places the highest value on women who are "wallflowers." But Peter's words are far richer and don't describe a woman who has no opinion about anything. The word "gentle" (or "meek") is commonly misunderstood and needs clarification. It is the

> *inwrought grace of the soul* . . . it is the temper of Spirit in which we [women] accept His dealings with us as good, *and therefore without disputing or resisting. . . . This meekness, being first of all a meekness before God, is also such in the face of men, even of evil men, out of a sense that these, with the insults and injuries which they may inflict,* are permitted and employed by Him for the chastening and purifying of His elect. . . . *It must be clearly understood, therefore, that the meekness manifested by the Lord and commended to the believer is the* fruit of power. *The common assumption is that when a [wo]man is meek it is because [s]he cannot help [her]self; but the Lord was "meek" because he had the infinite resources of God at His command. Described negatively,* meekness is the opposite to self-assertiveness and self-interest; *it is equanimity [composure] of spirit that is neither elated nor cast down,* simply because it is not occupied with self at all[26] *(emphasis added).*

This woman also has a "quiet" or tranquil heart. Imagine a lake in the morning—glassy, unaffected by wind, beautifully reflecting the surrounding hills, tranquil. Do you get the picture? Instead of being demanding or trying to manipulate others by the way she looks outwardly, a woman should be seeking to adorn herself with graces that are unaffected by the passage of time. Meekness is the character of a woman whose heart is serenely resting in God's providence and has ceased to trust in herself. This woman has opinions and knows there are times when it is godly for her to voice them. She loves and serves from a position of strength. She willingly submits to her Lord because she knows she can trust Him. She doesn't have to worry about getting old or not being "pretty" any longer. These inner qualities are precious, very expensive. A woman can spend all her time adorning that which is passing away if she likes. Or, she can invest herself in developing character qualities that will never decay and are of great worth.

Inner beauty is developed by spending time with the Lord. In frequent prayer, meditation of Scripture, and obedience to His way, the heart is conformed to the beautiful, winsome character of Christ. Inner beauty is a quality of both strength and godly condescension. It is strong enough not to be overly concerned with other's opinions, but at the same time condescends to be all things to all people so that it might win some. It is a heart of dignity.

As your counselee seeks a gentle and quiet spirit, ask her the following questions. If she answers yes to them, have her begin to put on the actions indicated.

- Are you consumed with your troubles? Do you strive to control your circumstances through sinful means (badgering, nagging, manipulating others)? Pray instead that your heart would be consumed with the love of God. Pray with Augustine, "Hide not Thy face from me. Oh! that I might repose on Thee. Oh! that Thou wouldst enter into my heart, and inebriate it, that I might forget my ills, and embrace Thee, my sole good."[27]
- Are you frequently anxious and fearful? Put on thankful prayer and godly action instead (*see* Philippians 4:6-9; Psalm 16:11).
- Do you spend more time working on your appearance than your heart? Begin today to more spend time in the Word, in prayer, and in service (*see* Psalm 90:17).
- Do you try to manipulate others to your way of doing things? Seek instead to serve and lay down your life (*see* Luke 9:23).
- Do you seek positions of respect? Begin to pour out your life in faithful service to others (*see* Matthew 20:20-28).

An afternoon woman can change the focus of her life. She can relax in His grace and mercy, sitting at His feet as Mary did. She doesn't have to attain the world's standard of perfection. Discourage her from trusting in her ability or seeking to establish her goodness by trusting in her abilities. She can trust in her faithful heavenly Father, who has promised to provide everything she needs and surround her with His lovingkindness. As she grows older, she can do so with grace—embracing the lessons of a life well lived under the shadow of His wings. She can rest in the knowledge that God has promised to care for her all of her days, even in her old age.

Here are some suggestions for personal study and homework for you or your counselee:

- Study Bible verses that mention the aged or gray-haired.
- List the adjectives the Lord uses to describe them.
- Make a list of the phrases you hear or see in the media about youth. Compare them to Scripture.
- Make a list of your personal beliefs about aging. Compare them to Scripture.
- Make a list of the ways you have grown in wisdom since you were saved. What changes have you made in your life as you have learned the ways of the Lord through the passing of time? For instance, I used to fear the loss of financial security. The day before our daughter Jessica was born, my husband lost his job. God worked in my life over the next year and a half to free me from this fear and demonstrate His ability to provide. Study Proverbs to see what it says about wisdom and foolishness. Make a list of the blessings and characteristics of each.
- Prayerfully meditate on your fear of aging. Ask the Lord to reveal your fears so you can put them to rest. Are you afraid of illness? Death? Loss of beauty? Is vanity, pride, or unbelief the root of these fears? Confess any known sin. Seek to put off any ungodly actions or attitudes (such as using credit cards to purchase expensive cosmetics or spending more time at the gym than in the Word). Seek to discover what godly actions God wants you to put in their place (such as ceasing extravagant expenditures for cosmetics or clothing, tithing regularly, volunteering at a convalescent home, memorizing Scripture so you can encourage elderly people about God's care).
- Study passages on death and the believer's assurance. Read *Pilgrim's Progress*. Note Pilgrim's passage through the Dark River and into the Celestial City. Ask God to encourage your faith with a true understanding of heaven. Read John MacArthur, Jr.'s, *The Glory of Heaven* and Joni Eareckson Tada's, *Heaven, Your Real Home*. Read Revelation chapters 21–22. Try to imagine the beauty of heaven. Ask the Lord to give you a longing for it and to turn you from love of the world. Read Hebrews 12

and list the heroes of faith who have gone there before you. What was their attitude about the world? What was their perspective? Review chapter 19 of this book, which addresses death and dying.

- As a godly, maturing woman, what wisdom do you possess that you might share with other women? Have you raised children? Have you learned to balance career and home and ministry? Have you learned what it means to submit to your husband even when you don't want to? This wisdom is needed by your sisters. If you weren't older, you might not have it.

- Research and study the problems that go along with aging. Investigate proper health practices that can help prolong well-being and begin now to practice them. Learning to eat well and exercise in moderation are helpful keys to fitness. Although Paul teaches that bodily discipline is of little profit, he acknowledges there is some profit in it (*see* 1 Timothy 4:8).[28]

- Spend time with older women in the church. Get to know them. Learn about their desires and trials. Glean wisdom from them. Begin to consciously seek to honor them. What place do seniors hold in your congregation? In our youth-crazed society, many churches focus on youth ministry and ignore seniors or relegate them to second-class status. You can help to foster communication and fellowship between the younger and older women in your congregation. You might start a "seasoned sister" ministry by planning a women's luncheon at which several older women give their testimonies. Younger and older women could be paired up for mutual fellowship, prayer, and mentoring over a period of a year or so (as many churches do with "secret pals"). At the end of the year another luncheon might be planned at which the younger women give testimonies of appreciation for the older women's influences. Your church, like many others, may be overlooking one of its most valuable assets. Perhaps several older women who have experienced the difficulties mentioned in this chapter could be invited to speak. A woman who has raised children might be encouraged to disciple young mothers. A woman who has gone through sorrow, such as the loss of a child, might encourage younger women not to fear and to trust in God. A woman who has spent 30 years keeping house can give a lot of insight to newlyweds. Women who have had a consistent life of prayer and Bible study could mentor young Christians. These things do not have to be done publicly. In fact, one-on-one mentoring and discipleship is probably best. There are many exciting possibilities and opportunities for older women to season the younger ones!

- Study 2 Corinthians 4:16-18. Are you losing heart because your "outer man is decaying"? What are you doing to renew your inner man? Do you recognize the "eternal weight of glory" God is producing for you? Ask the Lord to illumine your heart to these things.
- Study 1 Peter 3:1-7. Even if you don't have a husband who is disobedient to the Word, take time to evaluate its emphases in your life. Are you concerned more with how you look outwardly or inwardly? Are you seeking to develop a gentle and tranquil heart by frequent prayer and meditation on God's Word? When you are displeased about your circumstances, how do you respond? Do you put your trust in your ability to look good outwardly or in contentment in your inner beauty? Do you judge other women by their physical appearance and compare yourself with them? Are you seeking to obtain the costly qualities God says He loves, or are you settling for mere shadow?

The Empty Nest   As Carol Cornish stated in chapter 3, "You need to understand who you are as God describes you in His Word." Women are defined first as persons before God. If they have husbands and children, then their roles as helpers and nurturers are secondary to their relationship with God. Sadly, many Christian women believe their only ministry is to their children. Hence, when the children leave home, they feel like they are out of a job. What will they do with the rest of their life?

About 30 percent of children who leave home return. In addition, children are staying home and putting off marriage longer. It's not unusual for a child to be 28 or even 30 before he commits to a relationship and moves away. "Of unmarried American men between 25 and 34, more than *one-third* are still living at home."[29] Perhaps these figures should make you glad you're struggling with an empty nest!

As I have thought and read about empty nesting, I have identified two common areas of difficulty. They are "change of ministry" and "change of relationship."

CHANGE OF MINISTRY   Many women look at ministry to their families as their primary calling. I believe this is an appropriate perspective considering Paul's exhortation to young women in Titus 2:4 "to love their husbands, to love their children, to be sensible, pure, workers at home, kind, being subject to their own husbands, that the word of God may not be dishonored."

All women, including those who are married and have children, must arrange their priorities according to the Lord's teaching. If a Christian woman chooses to marry or have children, then she must arrange her priorities accordingly. She is to be discipled by wise older women who can teach her how to faithfully fulfill these responsibilities. First, she must learn to love her husband and children. Because the biblical perspective on love is different from the world's perspective, let me define what I mean. She must demonstrate a heart of commitment and service to her husband and children, no matter how she feels. That's biblical love.[30] She must desire the best for them and do everything she can to encourage them to grow and mature in Christ. Loving her husband and children, however, does not mean she no longer considers herself an individual before God. It does not mean becoming a slave or doormat so she can manipulate others for her own personal interests. A woman must be encouraged to serve her husband and children *in the Lord*. This means her service springs from a heart that strongly trusts that the Lord will be pleased.

Loving her husband and children is her first priority. Caring for small children may indeed occupy every waking hour. When children are young it is especially important for her to be with them, although the Bible assigns the primary responsibility for child-rearing to fathers. Being a "worker at home" may mean she spends most of her time there. This Greek compound word, *oikourgos*, is a compilation of two words: *house*, and *work, deed*, or *worker*. A married woman is responsible to maintain the household. A woman is free to determine what this means, although at the least it should mean she oversees the smooth operation of the home, whether she does the work herself or can afford to hire a maid. First Timothy 5:14 encourages women to rule or govern the household. Both the Titus 2 and 1 Timothy 5 passages speak to a woman's work at home in contrast to wasting her time by flitting from house to house gossiping. Rather than being a restriction upon a woman who might want to work part-time outside the home, Titus 2:4 is an injunction against gossip, idleness, and laziness.[31] If a woman desires to stay at home full-time, this option is open to her. But, what about the older woman, who because of her gifts and inclinations, is able to manage her home and love her husband and children and still have hours left during the day? Is she prohibited from being involved in other activities? I think Proverbs 31 demonstrates that an excellent woman may be involved in many endeavors as long as she has her priorities straight. Certainly the Proverbs 31 woman was not censured in any way for being involved in business endeavors outside the home.

When our children were young, I was involved in teaching at their Christian school. We wanted the kids to get a Christian education and since it would have been a financial hardship for us, we decided I should work in the school. I had about the same hours as they did and my work there partially fulfilled my responsibility to love them and manage their care. As they matured and home-schooling became a viable option, we decided I would stay home and teach them. I'm thankful for the years we had together; they were beneficial. I was able to fulfill the mandate to love my husband and children and manage my home while homeschooling. As my children matured and demanded less of my time, I decided to get training in biblical counseling and fulfill the mandate to disciple younger women through biblical counseling. Eventually I was able to earn a graduate degree in counseling. The Lord has been gracious because in all of this He kept my priorities straight and reminded me my first priority had to be my husband and children. I have pursued my areas of interests and gifts within the bounds of godly submission to my husband.

Now that the raising of my children is practically complete, at least on a day-to-day basis, I have more discretionary time. Still, the same questions must be applied to every endeavor I consider. Will this enable me to fulfill my responsibility to love my husband or will it diminish my service to him? Will this add to or detract from the smooth functioning of my home? Extra money from a new job may enhance the operation of the home. Will this enable me to fulfill my ministry and gifts?

I believe it's important for women to know they have responsibilities and opportunities besides child-rearing. I think there is confusion on both sides of this coin. Some women may be confused because they don't recognize that God (not man) graciously requires prioritizing family first. Others may be confused because they wrongly believe the only place they can serve is in their own home with their own kids. In our zeal to protect the home and encourage women to care for their children, let's be careful that we don't subtly teach women to idolize the family.

Women who face the empty nest have splendid opportunities to serve. In some ways they have been freed like the single woman in 1 Corinthians 7:32 to pursue the pleasure of the Lord. Now is a good time to get involved in service. Interests can be expanded and broadened. Women who have entered this phase of life have wonderful experiences to share with others. A woman can be involved in anything she and her husband believe to be worthwhile. Each of the writers of this book is involved in special ministry. A woman at this stage in life could organize a mentor mom group[32] in her church for unwed mothers, work in a center for unplanned pregnancies, volunteer time in a convalescent home or hospice, or set up a seasoned sisters ministry in her congregation. The opportunities, like the needs, are endless.

Perhaps she wants to finish her education or pursue a seminary degree. Perhaps she wants to get a real estate license and, like the excellent woman, "consider a field and buy it." Why not teach or start a business? Why not write a book? All legitimate work is honorable and glorifying to God as long as godly priorities are preserved and godly motives maintained.

Why not encourage your counselee to take up a new hobby? Learn another language so that she can minister to those in her congregation from other countries? Learn to sign for the deaf? Who knows, perhaps God will bring deaf people to her church. Why not revisit the piano she started playing 20 years ago? You get the picture—a woman can now prayerfully choose how to spend the next 30 to 40 years, as God allows. Look at things this way: Her *change* of ministry has now turned into a *chance* for new ministry.

CHANGE OF RELATIONSHIP   Comfortable relationships change during the empty nest years. A woman's usual ways of interacting with her husband will change. They'll have more time together. This can be a blessing or a challenge (we'll discuss this more in a moment). Her usual ways of interacting with her children will change. For example, it's sometimes hard for her to remember that her children are adults; especially when she sees the goofy things they still do. But her kids are adults. Even if they move back in with her for a time, the relationship must change. She is no longer the one responsible to train them. She is not responsible to be sure they are choosing the right friends, jobs, or spouses. Her adult children are responsible before God for their choices. However, she can advise them, when they request it. She can offer help but she cannot insist they do things her way. She must not shield them from the consequences of their sinful choices as she might have done when they were young. She must not try to live her life vicariously through them. They are adults.

I have done some premarital counseling. When I counseled the prospective brides and grooms, I would go over Genesis 2:24 point-by-point: "For this cause a man shall leave his father and his mother." I would then emphasize to them that as a married couple, they must sever any unbiblical ties with their families. Not that they shouldn't see them any more, but those relationships must change after they are married. They must not bring into the marriage sinful habits of their parents. They are to leave anger and bitterness behind. They are to seek to establish a new home with new goals. I asked my counselees each to write a letter to their parents explaining this change and thanking them for all their help. When my daughter was married, it dawned on me it was *my* family she was leaving! She was to sever ties with *me!* *I* was now the mom who had to keep her nose in her own business! Our relationship changed.

These kinds of changes work out in little ways all through the year. Where will the children spend the holidays or their birthdays? What will family vacations be like without them? What will we do with all the leftover food? Who will be responsible to take out the garbage and walk the dog? What if they move out of town? Will we plan our vacation time around theirs so we can visit? What will we do with the extra rooms? Convert them to an office, study, or guest room? While at one time the phone never stopped ringing, now it rarely rings.

All of these changes in relationships will be uncomfortable at first, like a new pair of shoes. But over time, a woman will get accustomed to the peace and quiet and she'll wonder what the big fuss was about. But make no mistake—for many this is a difficult time.

Understand that sorrow and grief over a child's absence are normal. I miss my children's comedy routines. I miss the affectionate hugs and watching them while they sleep. I miss the easy banter and being up on everything that's new and cool. I miss their spontaneity and zest. I miss little pajamas with feet in them and Osh Kosh B'Gosh® overalls with snaps. I miss bonnets and curls at the nape of the neck. I miss drying tears and telling them, "It's going to be all right, because Jesus will help you." I miss singing with them and listening to their dulcet voices. I miss smelling their sweet baby breath. I could go on and on. But the Lord is here in this time of my life, just as He's always been. I don't have to pretend I don't miss them. God understands my sorrows and bears me up in my griefs. Jesus was concerned about the suffering of His mother, Mary, even as He hung on the cross. He gave her another son to care for her in her old age. "Woman," He said, "behold, your son!" (John 19:26). One of the last services our Lord performed was to care for His mother. He knows a mother's sorrow; He can be her refuge. He can turn her mourning into laughter. She just needs to give Him and her heart a little time. "Missing our children is part of loving them. But part of loving them is letting our lives continue after they have left us."[33]

Here are some suggestions for personal study and homework for you or your counselee:

- Study sorrow in the book of Psalms. List God's promises to those who are suffering righteously.

- Study God's place as your refuge in times of trouble. What kinds of problems has He carried and protected you through? Memorize pertinent passages such as Psalm 46:1-3 and 62:7-8.
- Keep a journal of your thoughts so you can share them later with younger mothers.
- Clean out your children's rooms and box up the things they left. Don't erect any shrines. Don't let yourself sit around hugging their teddy bear.
- Ask them to tell you if you are interfering or being obnoxious. Don't be angry when they do.
- Get involved in other types of ministry. Begin to prayerfully consider areas of interest you have stifled. Look into a new career. Investigate. Get counsel. If you miss having teenagers around, volunteer in your church's youth ministry.
- Ask your husband or a close friend to tell you when you're obsessing about them. If every other sentence begins with, "I remember when the kids . . . " ask them to tell you. Broaden your conversation base. Read books. Go to plays. Listen to "Book Notes" on C-Span and discuss what you learned with a friend without mentioning your children.
- Put off attitudes and actions that demonstrate self-focus. Put on thanksgiving and praise that God gave you the opportunity to raise children at all. Begin to thank God daily for the new horizons He will open to you.

> We should never take any blessing for granted, but accept everything as a gift from the Father of Lights. Whole days may be spent occasionally in the holy practice of being thankful. We should write on a tablet one-by-one the things for which we are grateful to God and our fellow men. . . . In trying to count our many blessings the difficulty is not to find things to count, but to find the time to enumerate them all.[34]

- Read one or two of the books in the recommended resources list at the end of this chapter and take notes. Share your new insights with your husband or a close friend. Ask them to hold you accountable to put your new insights into practice.

Marital Problems   Have you ever done much thinking about the kinds of marriages women in the Bible had? As I ponder the kinds of relationships women have with their husband and children, I am reminded of Rebekah and her family in Genesis 24 to 27. Rebekah exhibited the heart of a servant and was willing to become Isaac's wife. Although she was loved by Isaac, the Bible says she was barren. Finally, she conceived twin boys, and the Lord told her that the elder would serve the younger. Later, in Genesis 25:28, we see that there was conflict in the family: "Now Isaac loved Esau, because he had a taste for game; but Rebekah loved Jacob." Isaac's natural affinity for hunting and savory food drew him toward his robust son Esau, while Jacob's peaceful nature appealed more to Rebekah. Think about the conflict that must have been present in the family for Rebekah to be willing to receive her husband's curse in order to acquire his blessing for her favored son. She didn't care if he cursed her. She was going to do what she wanted, no matter what happened. Have you ever noticed there are very few conversations recorded between Isaac and Rebekah? In two of them she is complaining about Esau's wives. "What good will my life be to me if Jacob marries like Esau?" she whines. So she arranges the deception that would eventuate in the loss of her favored son, Jacob. We never see Jacob and Rebekah together again.

Some couples have lived like Isaac and Rebekah for years. Fighting over the children, manipulating and being deceptive, complaining about one another's favorites. Fathers favoring one son over another because they enjoy football together. Mothers favoring one daughter over another because they both like to swim. Fathers and mothers favoring their children over their spouses and using these relationships to illustrate the resentment and abiding disappointment they feel toward each other. Mothers are not the only parents who replace spouses with children.

God, however, intended marriage to be a covenant that includes companionship.[35] This means that the husband and wife are to have rich, intimate fellowship. They are to seek to provide companionship and fellowship to one another, working together to accomplish God's will. They are to cleave to one another (*see* Genesis 2:24). This does not mean they have to be in one another's presence all the time, or that they can't be separated for a time (1 Corinthians 7:5)—it's just that a lifestyle of isolation isn't God's plan for spouses. Both spouses have the opportunity to love and serve the other and to provide companionship. If a woman has distanced herself emotionally from her husband and substituted the children as companions, God can help her. First, by God's grace, she must repent. Second, she must ask God to renew her mind as she seeks to be obedient to Him. Finally, she must actively seek ways to serve her husband and reestablish companionship with him.

Here are some suggestions for personal study and homework:

- No marriage, no matter how long it's been let to lie fallow, is totally hopeless. Study passages in the New Testament about "one anothering" and begin to practice them with your husband. Remember, God will lovingly restore your marriage relationship if you are seeking to be pleasing to Him. You might study 1 John to determine how to think and act in a loving way toward your spouse.
- Study the passages in the endnotes on the covenant of companionship (*see* note 35). In what ways have you failed to be a friend to your spouse? Have you substituted friendship with the children for friendship with him? It's easy to do; it's easy to enjoy a little child's acceptance and trust. They just love and give. What do you need to do to recommit yourself to your covenant? Make a list of five things and begin doing them today.
- Put the Lord first. Ask Him to help your marriage become pleasing to Him. Ask Him to reveal your heart to you and to give you the grace to want to change. Remember you have only a few more years and then you'll have eternity. Will the Lord be pleased? Will your work stand the test of His blazing gaze? Review 1 Corinthians 3:10-15 and 2 Corinthians 5:10. I know that trying to rebuild a marriage can seem overwhelming. I know that sometimes it's hard to have the desire to do so. You must remember the comparative shortness of your life here and the meagerness of your sacrifice in comparison to Christ's.
- Was there a child that you particularly favored? Did you and your husband have only one thing in common—fighting about the children? Perhaps you should write letters to each of your children and ask them to forgive you for the example you set. Be wise, however, when you do this. In your zeal to reconstruct your marriage, don't hurt the children. It would probably be best just to point out the fact that you didn't set the kind of example a wife should and you are working to rebuild your friendship with their dad.
- If you desire to do so, you can "fall back in love" with your husband, even if he doesn't change. You might wonder how to do this. Just begin acting the way you did when you were first in love! Hold his hand. Leave little notes around for him. Think of three things you know he would appreciate and do them. Your emotions will follow your actions. If you persevere through the first few weeks of acting in a way you are unaccustomed to, you are likely to experience love once again.

- If, over the years, the two of you have developed different interests, change some of yours! I have read *Sports Illustrated* so I would be able to carry on a semi-intelligent conversation with my husband about something he enjoys. I took up golf so I could be with him. The way I play adds humor to his day. These are not things I would choose for myself. But I chose him for myself, and I want him to know I like being with him. I have only a short time to love him. It's not as difficult as it sounds. I've just made some little choices that don't really cost me much. My husband has reciprocated by going to plays and musicals and watching the sunset with me. Recently, we have begun a collection of sunset pictures from our travels. These are some of the cords that hold our covenant together.
- Don't give in to self-pity or manipulation. Now that your children are gone, resist the temptation to seek to fill the empty spaces in your heart with other people. The Lord has given you an opportunity to start over. Seize it!

Caring for Ill Parents   Perhaps for you the thought of having to care for an ill parent is inconceivable. Perhaps your parents are energetic and lively. Every person I have counseled about this topic had one thing in common: They weren't prepared. They didn't know what kinds of medication their parents were taking, what medical insurance they had, or who their doctors were. They didn't know where the will was or if there was one. They didn't know what insurance policies their parent had sacrificially provided for them. They didn't know what bank accounts there were so that on-going care could be provided. They had never discussed their parent's wishes regarding funeral arrangements. I know that if your parents are healthy, it seems morose to talk about these things. Sometimes we avoid them because we don't want to look like vultures, waiting for the end. I believe it is prudent and loving to discuss these kinds of things in advance so your parents can rest assured their affairs will be arranged in a way that would honor God and please them. Perhaps you have never considered what the Bible says about caring for parents. Does the Bible even address these issues? What are the obligations of a child?

A BIBLICAL PERSPECTIVE ON CAREGIVING   I believe the Bible teaches that it is the responsibility of children to care for their parents. It is filled with admonitions to care for the widow. God is very obviously concerned about the rights of those who are no longer able to care for themselves, such as widows. He calls Himself a "father of the fatherless and a judge [defender or advocate] for the widows" (Psalm 68:5). He states that He "protects the stranger; He supports the fatherless and the widow," in contrast to the way of the wicked, whom He "thwarts" (Psalm 146:9). When instructing wicked Israel about repentance, doing good, and seeking justice, He tells them to "reprove the ruthless; defend the orphan, plead for the widow" (Isaiah 1:17). Those who do not fear God are described as oppressing the wage earner, widow, and orphan (Malachi 3:5). The Lord isn't merely interested in widows as a class—He is interested in the protection of all those who cannot protect or provide for themselves (the stranger or alien, the worker, the orphan, the widow).

The New Testament also speaks to the care of widows. As I have already said, Jesus cared for his widowed mother from the cross. He ministered to widows and used them as examples of piety on numerous occasions.[36] The office of deacon in the New Testament church was established primarily to oversee provision for widows.[37] Paul gives explicit instruction on the care of family members in these verses from 1 Timothy 5:

> Honor widows who are widows indeed; but if any widow has children or grandchildren, let them first learn to practice piety in regard to their own family, and to make some return to their parents; for this is acceptable in the sight of God. . . . But if anyone does not provide for his own, and especially for those of his household, he has denied the faith, and is worse than an unbeliever. . . . If any woman who is a believer has dependent widows, let her assist them, and let not the church be burdened, so that it may assist those who are widows indeed (vv. 3-4,8,16).

In a time when there was no assistance available from the state, believers individually and as a church were taught it was their responsibility to care for the elderly. Widows were in circumstances in which they were unable to provide care for themselves. The family and church were to care for them, or they would have had to beg. Children are instructed to "honor" their parents. This word means not only respect but also to offer material assistance.[38] This is demonstrated by Paul's piercing statement, "Let them practice piety in regard to their own family."

It's one thing to say you're pious—it's quite another to live out your piety in practical ways by providing assistance to parents. Paul instructed children and grandchildren to "make some return" to their parents by caring for them. Even if a person says he is a believer, Paul says that he is worse than an unbeliever and has denied the faith if he refuses to provide for his household. The family has the first obligation to care for its needy members. If the family is unable to do so, then the church must act. In cases of extreme hardship, such as that of Joy's mother with Alzheimer's, care for a parent may be assisted by the state.

ADVANCE CONSIDERATIONS FOR CAREGIVING   Every situation is unique and children must seek counsel and give prayerful consideration to their obligation to honor their parents. It is not always possible to take care of an extremely ill or demented parent; many facts must be considered before decisions are made. Once a decision is made, remember that it is not "set in stone." Just because you originally thought you would be able to care for your ailing parent doesn't mean you can't make other arrangements as circumstances change. Seek and accept godly counsel. Seek and accept medical counsel. Carrie's mother's physician told her to remove JoAnn from the convalescent home because she would get better care at home with her. Christians must consider every factor when making a decision. Just because society believes that government help is always advisable doesn't excuse believing children from their responsibilities. Jesus Himself referred to the customary practice of neglecting a parent's need as an example of Pharisaical hypocrisy (Matthew 15:1-9).

There are numerous trials intrinsic to caring for an ill parent. An ill parent's presence in the home will probably cause financial, emotional, and physical strain. For most people the care of an ill parent is piled on top of many other responsibilities. Running back and forth to the doctor or hospital, filling prescriptions, emptying bedpans, dispensing medication, and seeking to nurture a person who isn't used to being nurtured is difficult. Ill parents are frequently antagonistic or difficult to manage. A role-reversal can occur wherein the child is now having to cajole the parent into eating all his food or turning off the television.

Although a caretaker child who is in this position may feel discouraged or hopeless, she can be assured God will strengthen and encourage her as she learns to lean on Him continuously.

Here are some suggestions for personal study and homework for you or your counselee:

- Do an in-depth Bible study on God's concern for widows. What are God's promises to widows and those who care for them?
- Study the story of Ruth, a woman who chose to care for her widowed mother-in-law rather than live her own life of pleasure.
- Before your parents become ill, have a family meeting in which wills, finances, insurances, medical information, and desires of parents are discussed. If a parent suffers a stroke and is not able to communicate his or

her wishes to you, it will be more difficult for you to make decisions about his care if you haven't done so yet. What do your parents (and the rest of the family) think of organ donation? Do your parents want you to with-hold extreme measures of resuscitation? Do your parents want you to keep them on life support if they suffer some sort of brain damage and have no brain activity after a specified period of time? If there are several siblings, who will act as executor of the estate? Who will have power-of-attorney if decisions about finances must be made for an incapacitated parent? The answers to all these questions and others like them will enable you to make informed decisions with the least amount of stress during one of the most stressful times of your life.[39]

Some parents may not want to discuss these things. If this is the case, consider writing a loving letter to them, outlining your concerns and humbly asking them for help. Be sure to communicate to them that you want to honor them and their wishes and are not being morose.

• If it becomes apparent you will have custodianship of a parent with a particular disease, contact a support group for this disease immediately. These groups are run by people who know the pitfalls and progression of the disease and the problems inherent in caregiving. They will be able to help you in many practical ways. Contact your church and ask that one of the elders or leading women be given charge of watching over you, pray-ing for you, and contacting you during this time. Contact a close friend or another family member who would be bold enough to step in without being asked and give help. Don't refuse help. Tell the church to remember you in prayer. This is not the time to isolate yourself or move, if avoidable.

An Exciting New Time

The afternoon of life for a woman can be both challenging and difficult. It can also be a time when she is invited to look at life in new, more godly ways. It can be a time when challenges and opportunities abound. This doesn't have to be "the end" as Margie so wrongly thought. For the believer there is no end of life. There are changes in circumstance, but eternal life is assured to those who are God's children. Others have gone through these things; they have endured and overcome in faith. Your counselee can too as she learns from their lives and submits herself to the will of God.

Therefore, since we have so great a cloud of witnesses surrounding us, let us also lay aside every encumbrance, and the sin which so easily entangles us, and let us run with endurance the race that is set before us, fixing our eyes on Jesus, the author and perfecter of faith, who for the joy set before Him endured the cross, despising the shame, and has sat down at the right hand of the throne of God. For consider Him who has endured such hostility by sinners against Himself, so that you may not grow weary and lose heart (Hebrews 12:1-3, emphasis added).

Recommended Resources

Jay Adams, *Christian Living in the Home*, Grand Rapids: Baker Books, 1974.

William L. Coleman, *From Full House to Empty Nest*, Grand Rapids: Discovery House Publishers, 1994.

Barbara Deane, *Caring for Your Aging Parents*, Colorado Springs: NavPress, 1989.

Anne Marie Drew, *Empty Nest Full Life*, Nashville, TN: Dimensions for Living, 1995.

John Gillies, *Caregiving: When Someone You Love Grows Old*, Wheaton, IL: Harold Shaw Publishers, 1988.

Wayne Mack, *Strengthening Your Marriage*, Phillipsburg, NJ: Presbyterian & Reformed, 1977.

_____, *Your Family, God's Way*, Phillipsburg, NJ: Presbyterian & Reformed, 1991.

Robert Riekse and Henry Holstege, *The Christian Guide to Parent Care*, Wheaton, IL: Tyndale House, 1992.

Cliff Schimmels, *And Then There Were Two*, Wheaton, IL: Harold Shaw Publishers, 1989.

Charles Swindoll, *Strike the Original Match*, Wheaton, IL: Living Books, 1980.

CHAPTER 19

Counseling Women Facing Dying and Death

Carol W. Cornish, M.A. and Elyse Fitzpatrick, M.A.

The automatic doors opened and I (Carol) stepped from the stale warmth of the hospital lobby into the icy cold of a winter night. Up on the fourth floor, my grandmother lay dying. She was not aware of my visit that night because her illness had progressed to the point of semi-consciousness. She did not look peaceful. She looked like she was in pain and my heart was breaking for her.

Already I was thinking how terribly I would miss her when she was gone. I didn't want to let her go. I still wanted to be able to come home from college, throw my arms around her, and give her a big hug. I wanted to see the twinkle in her hazel eyes and feel the softness of her kiss on my cheek. I wanted to hear her gentle laughter and watch her at work in the kitchen.

It wasn't long after my hospital visit that my grandmother died. At that point, I learned to hate death. Death stole my grandmother from me. At the age of 19, I learned in an undeniable way how cruelly death is a part of life.

Until that point, I hadn't engaged in much serious thinking about my eternal destination. I was so engrossed in living day to day that I rarely stopped to think about it. Immersed in the ordinary events of everyday life, I gave little thought to the fact that I would one day die.

A Time to Die

Why People Die

As surely as we are all alive today, we will all someday die. This is an undisputed fact. Both the Scriptures and our own experience testify to this fact.

> *Just as man is destined to die once, and after that to face judgment, so Christ was sacrificed once to take away the sins of many people; and he will appear a second time, not to bear sin, but to bring salvation to those who are waiting for him (Hebrews 9:27-28 NIV).*

Why is this? God created Adam and Eve and placed them in a perfect environment. But they sinned and reaped a penalty—that penalty is death.

In response to the disobedience of man, God in His mercy provided a payment for sin so that, though sinners would die a physical death (the outer person), they need not die spiritually (the inner person). "For if by the transgression of the one, death reigned through the one, much more those who receive the abundance of grace and of the gift of righteousness will reign in life through the One, Jesus Christ" (Romans 5:17). While the penalty of sin has been removed from believers by Christ, believers, in union with Him, share the experiences of Christ. "They enter death with the assurance that its sting has been removed, 1 Corinthians 15:55, and that it is for them the gateway of heaven."[1]

While the immediate cause of someone's death might be a sickness or an injury that is not a direct result of any sin he or she has committed, the ultimate cause of all death is sin. Disease and trouble entered the world because of man's sin. All die because there is sin in the world and we are sinners. "How long, O LORD? Will you hide yourself forever? How long will your wrath burn like fire? Remember how fleeting is my life. For what futility you have created all men! What man can live and not see death, or save himself from the power of the grave?" (Psalm 89:46-48 NIV).

We will not escape death unless the Lord returns in our lifetime.

Keeping Eternity in View

Because of the inevitability of death, a wise Christian will live life within the perspective of the brevity of a human life span. Statistically speaking, the average American woman will live to be about 80 years of age. While that used to seem to me like a long time, it no longer does. And what is 80 years compared to eternity? The Bible calls our life span a mist, a vapor:

> *Come now, you who say, "Today or tomorrow, we shall go to such and such a city, and spend a year there and engage in business and make a profit." Yet you do not know what your life will be like tomorrow. You are just a vapor that appears for a little while and then vanishes away. Instead, you ought to say, "If the Lord wills, we shall live and also do this or that." But as it is, you boast in your arrogance; all such boasting is evil (James 4:13-16).*

Even though we do not know whether our death will be sooner or later, it is vital that we live our lives in the light of its eventuality. The verses in James show the arrogance of living as if we will not die—as if we had control over the length of our lives.

The apostle Paul describes the perspective we ought to have:

> *Therefore we do not lose heart, but though our outer man is decaying, yet our inner man is being renewed day by day. For momentary, light affliction is producing for us an eternal weight of glory far beyond all comparison, while we look not at the things which are seen, but at the things which are not seen; for the things which are seen are temporal, but the things which are not seen are eternal (2 Corinthians 4:16-18).*

Those of us who have seen many birthdays come and go certainly have ample proof that the outer man is decaying.

Are you keeping an eternal perspective on life, or has the seeming permanence of earthly things deluded and entrapped you? Are you preparing yourself to be a suitable helper to those who are dying? Are you preparing yourself to be a faithful servant to the end?

Our Greatest Comfort—The Sovereignty and Goodness of God

Close by the window so he could view the bird feeder in the tree outside, my (Carol) friend's father lay dying of pancreatic cancer. My friend is his only living child. Her mother died some years before of a heart attack during choir practice—a choir practice being led by her daughter, my friend.

For both my friend and her dying father, the sovereignty of God became the air they breathed during the several weeks he lay dying.

As I helped my friend during that time and afterward, she had many questions about dying and death. We searched God's Word together and found great comfort in its truths. We realized that when we seemed stuck on a question about death, our answer was usually to be found in the sovereignty of God over creation.

The sovereignty of God is comforting only to those who believe God is entirely good and completely in control of all things. Indeed this is what the Bible teaches about God: He is totally in control of the world and "causes all things to work together for good to those who love God, to those who are called according to His purpose" (Romans 8:28). He is perfectly holy, just, and righteous. After all, what real comfort is there in a God who is sovereign but cannot be trusted to *always* do good on our behalf? Or what help is there in a god who is entirely good but not able to always have power over people and events?

Of our Lord, the Scriptures say, "Behold, to the LORD your God belong heaven and the highest heavens, the earth and all that is in it" (Deuteronomy 10:14).

> *Thine, O LORD, is the greatness and the power and the glory and the victory and the majesty, indeed everything that is in the heavens and the earth; Thine is the dominion, O LORD, and Thou dost exalt Thyself as head over all. Both riches and honor come from Thee, and Thou dost rule over all, and in Thy hand is power and might; and it lies in Thy hand to make great, and to strengthen everyone (1 Chronicles 29:11-13).*

> *The God who made the world and all things in it, since He is Lord of heaven and earth, does not dwell in temples made with hands; neither is He served by human hands, as though He needed anything, since He Himself gives to all life and breath and all things (Acts 17:24-25).*

And Psalm 47 tells us that God is a great King over all the earth (verse 2) and that He reigns over the nations (verse 8). Our sovereign and good God is able and willing to help us in all things including our deepest distresses.

Some of you may be distressed that I (Carol) recently referred to Romans 8:28. Some Christians facing suffering today do not want to hear the words of this verse. Admittedly, it has been applied glibly, in an untimely manner, and without proper feeling by some who should have been more compassionate. But we are in danger of losing the truth and the consolation from this verse if we automatically label as unfeeling even those who use it properly.

In his discussion of Romans 8:28 and its comfort in trials, Martyn Lloyd-Jones says people think they need something other than theology to be soothed and eased. Lloyd-Jones is not talking about cold orthodoxy, he is talking about theology applied in its most helpful and wonderful fullness. He makes the case that in Romans 8:28 Paul "desires, therefore, to introduce [his readers] to the method which can be applied always, and everywhere, and in spite of all circumstances and conditions."[2] Paul was comforting them with the comfort he had received from Christ. He was showing them how he comforted himself with the truths of theology so that they could comfort themselves with it and not be dependent upon his presence with them.

The God Who Comforts

God has promised that He will comfort us:

> Blessed be the God and Father of our Lord Jesus Christ, the Father of mercies and God of all comfort; who comforts us in all our affliction *so that we may be able to comfort those who are in any affliction with the comfort with which we ourselves are comforted by God. For just as the sufferings of Christ are ours in abundance, so also* our comfort is abundant through Christ. . . . Indeed, we had the sentence of death within ourselves in order that we should not trust in ourselves, but in God who raises the dead (2 Corinthians 1:3-5,9, emphasis added).

In perhaps the best known of all the psalms, David said, "Even though I walk through the valley of the shadow of death, I fear no evil; for Thou art with me; Thy rod and Thy staff, they comfort me" (23:4). We know God demonstrates particular watchfulness when His children experience death: "Precious in the sight of the LORD is the death of His godly ones" (Psalm 116:15). Our longing for heaven is intensified as we are assured "He shall wipe away every tear from their eyes; and there shall no longer be any death; there shall no longer be any mourning, or crying, or pain; the first things have passed away" (Revelation 21:4). Our comfort is magnified as we marvel at these wonderful promises.

God cares about what is happening to the dying person and to the person's loved ones. He sees the sorrow and grief and He is there to comfort and guide. God can truly empathize with their feelings of grief and sadness. His only Son died. And God can give you hope because He raised His Son from the dead and He will also raise those who are in Christ.

> The Lord Himself will descend from heaven with a shout, with the voice of the archangel, and with the trumpet of God; and the dead in Christ shall rise first. Then we who are alive and remain shall be caught up together

with them in the clouds to meet the Lord in the air, and thus we shall always be with the Lord. Therefore comfort one another with these words *(1 Thessalonians 4:16-18, emphasis added).*

These verses imply we ought to receive comfort from the knowledge that we shall be raised to be with Him. Paul teaches that we do not have to "grieve, as do the rest who have no hope" (1 Thessalonians 4:13). Christians do not grieve as those who are not in Christ. We have the hope—that is, the confident expectation—that God is in control and will take the dying Christian to be with Him. We have the hope of the resurrection to comfort our hearts and assure us that our believing loved ones are not lost to us eternally. A friend whose daughter died in an accident told me (Elyse), "Now that she's in heaven I have a new perspective. I know that she'll be waiting there for me and we'll live together eternally. I can't wait for that day."

Ministering Comfort to the Dying and the Grieving

I was sitting, torn by grief. Someone came and talked to me of God's dealings, of why it happened, of hope beyond the grave. He talked constantly, he said things I knew were true.

I was unmoved, except to wish he'd go away. He finally did.

Another came and sat beside me. He didn't talk. He didn't ask leading questions. He just sat beside me for an hour or more, listened when I said something, answered briefly, prayed simply, left.

I was moved. I was comforted. I hated to see him go.[3]

These are the words of Joseph Bayly, who, along with his wife, lost three sons. Many people feel helpless and ill at ease when faced with the prospect of comforting grieving persons. Bayly points out the significant comfort that comes just from the presence of a friend. In the Old Testament book of Job, if the three friends who came to help Job had contented themselves with simply sitting with Job in silence, they would have rendered considerably more comfort to Job than when they started to counsel him.

Notice that Bayly said the second friend sat with him and spoke only when Bayly asked him a question. Even then, the friend answered briefly and when he prayed, he kept it short. What a wise friend!

What can we learn from this example? Grieving and dying persons are often so overwhelmed by their loss that it is difficult for them to concentrate or to try to track with lengthy explanations. Sit quietly with them. Perhaps an arm around the shoulder or a hand on the arm of a believing friend will communicate love and concern to them. It is not unusual for a person who is facing death, whether of a loved one or his own death, to repeatedly state his disbelief surrounding his situation. Do not point out to him the repetitious nature of his remarks. Let him verbalize his shock at his circumstances. Briefly communicate your love and concern. Be there through the process and don't neglect or abandon the person.

The Promise of Grace in Time of Need

Along with the sovereignty and goodness of God, the promise of grace in time of need is of utmost comfort to the dying Christian. In Hebrews 4:14-16 we are assured of the Lord's constant help:

> *Therefore, since we have a great high priest who has gone through the heavens, Jesus the Son of God, let us hold firmly to the faith we profess. For we do not have a high priest who is unable to sympathize with our weaknesses, but we have one who has been tempted in every way, just as we are—yet was without sin. Let us then approach the throne of grace with confidence, so that we may receive mercy and find grace to help us in our time of need (NIV).*

The process of dying can range from swift to slow, from peaceful to violent. In any case, we are assured that God will give needed grace for us to endure it with faithfulness. "God is our refuge and strength, a very present help in trouble. The LORD of hosts is with us; the God of Jacob is our fortress" (Psalm 46:1,7).

The Christian's Responsibility While Dying

Dying to the Glory of God

In Christian circles when death is discussed, it is usually talked about in terms of our being dead in sin and being made alive spiritually. But little discussion occurs concerning Christian responsibility during the dying process. Until very recently, dying in a manner that glorifies God has been a conspicuously absent topic since the days of the Puritan writers. While being sick to the point of death is traumatic and the most intense kind of difficulty, still, we Christians have the responsibility to glorify God to the very end.

Let me explain what I (Carol) mean by "dying to the glory of God." Being a Christian carries with it the responsibility to obey Christ's commands to love God and our neighbor (Mark 12:30-31). It is always our duty to love and serve. Even while dying, the Christian can, in whatever way possible, glorify God by loving and serving Him and by loving and serving others. For example, from her deathbed a grandmother might strive to speak lovingly to an unsaved grandchild about the gospel. She might gently challenge a wavering Christian to press on in faithfulness. She could glorify God by asking someone to read psalms to her or to sing hymns to her. These are actions that demonstrate love for God and faith in His care even in the face of death. They are also actions that demonstrate love and concern for others.

When I speak of dying to the glory of God, I do not mean to glamorize death in any way. Death is the result of sin. Death is the last enemy. It is right for Christians to hate what sin does. God hates it too. Louis Berkhof points out that "while death in itself remains a real natural evil for the children of God, something unnatural, which is dreaded by them as such,"[4] God still works it out for their spiritual advancement and best interests. "For He [Christ] must reign until He has put all His enemies under His feet. The last enemy that will be abolished is death" (1 Corinthians 15:25-26). " 'For I have no pleasure in the death of anyone who dies,' declares the Lord GOD" (Ezekiel 18:32).

You may be thinking this is a gruesome topic. Let me assure you that when you capture a sense of the Christian responsibility that is yours even while dying, it can be a source of great hope. To know that we can be of service to God and others even in the smallest ways in our weakest moments helps to give purpose to the afflictions associated with dying. Considering the nature of God and His attributes can bring us comfort and hope and help us die in such a manner as to glorify Him.

As long as we are in control of our faculties, we are responsible to bring glory to God by trusting in Him and His provision for us even as we lay dying. The dying often have periods of consciousness interspersed with periods of unconsciousness. During those times of consciousness, the dying person can serve God by glorifying Him through implicit trust and confidence in Him that He will see him through.

Setting Your Mind "Set your mind on the things above, not on the things that are on earth" (Colossians 3:2). This is especially necessary for the dying person. He is leaving this world and going on to the next. He needs to seriously consider this reality. For the Christian that next place is in heaven face-to-face with the Lord. If we train our minds while we are healthy to think on the things above, on the things that are true, noble, lovely, and so on as Paul says in Philippians 4:8-9, then we will be better able to think on heavenly things as we are dying. The habits of thinking that we have established in life will be evident as we die. We need to live this life as preparation for the life beyond this earthly one.

The Peace that Surpasses Comprehension God will help the dying Christian to be at peace. "You will keep in perfect peace him whose mind is steadfast, because he trusts in you. Trust in the LORD forever, for the LORD, the LORD, is the Rock eternal" (Isaiah 26:3-4 NIV).

> *Rejoice in the Lord always; again I will say, rejoice! Let your forbearing spirit be known to all men. The Lord is near. Be anxious for nothing, but in everything by prayer and supplication with thanksgiving let your requests be made known to God. And the* peace of God, *which surpasses all comprehension, shall guard your hearts and your minds in Christ Jesus (Philippians 4:4-7, emphasis added).*

> *"Do not fear, for I am with you; do not anxiously look about you, for I am your God. I will strengthen you, surely I will help you, surely I will uphold you with My righteous right hand." For I am the LORD your God, who upholds your right hand, Who says to you, "Do not fear, I will help you" (Isaiah 41:10,13, emphasis added).*

> Let not your heart be troubled; *believe in God, believe also in Me. In My Father's house are many dwelling places; if it were not so, I would have told you; for I go to prepare a place for you. And if I go and prepare a place for you, I will come again, and receive you to Myself; that where I am, there you may be also. And you know the way where I am going (John 14:1-4, emphasis added).*

Even while dying, the Christian has the responsibility to trust God and look to Him for peace—peace that comes in spite of the intense temptations that may be present to give in to panic and hopelessness. "For not one of us lives for himself, and not one dies for himself; for if we live, we live for the Lord, or if we die, we die for the Lord; therefore whether we live or die, we are the Lord's" (Romans 14:7-8). Christians are never alone, not even in death. We are always the Lord's and He is always with us.

Lessons from Scripture About Faithfulness While Dying

Our supreme example both in His living and His dying is the Lord Jesus Christ. The gospels describe how Jesus loved others and served others while He was dying.[5] Jesus was willing to submit to the Father's will no matter what the cost. He demonstrated tremendous distress and abhorrence in the garden of Gethsemane at the thought of being separated from His Father in order to be the sin-bearer.

While dying on the cross, Jesus honored and served His Father by 1) doing God's will and going to the cross to die for man's sin, 2) crying out to God in His distress at being separated from Him, 3) giving up His Spirit to Him, and 4) speaking words that fulfilled prophecy, thus honoring the Word of God.

Jesus loved others and served others by 1) being willing to endure the cross to provide a perfect sacrifice so God's mercy would be displayed and those who trust in that sacrifice for their sins could be saved from eternal damnation, 2) granting repentance and salvation to the thief who was crucified with Him, and 3) caring so much for His mother that He spoke to the apostle John from the cross and designated him to care for Mary.

Genesis chapters 49–50 and Hebrews 11 tell us about how Jacob conducted himself when he was dying. In these two accounts of his death, we see he was concerned for others and for the glory of God. His concern for others resulted in his blessing his grandchildren and giving specific directions to his children about what to do with his body after he died. Jacob glorified God by worshiping Him as he leaned on the top of his staff.

In Paul's second letter to Timothy, knowing that death was imminent, he told his young protégée, "I have fought the good fight, I have finished the course, I have kept the faith" (4:7). Even though he was alone in a dark prison cell, no negative foreboding was present in Paul's attitude or speech. Paul had lived well by keeping his eyes on heavenly treasure. Now he was dying well by looking forward to heaven and to receiving the crown of righteousness. Christ was everything to Paul while he was living (Philippians 1:21), and Christ remained everything to Paul as he was dying. In fact, we know from 2 Timothy 4:17 that despite Paul's dire circumstances, he seized opportunities to testify about Jesus Christ. He was still loving and serving Christ.

Other lives to study in the Scriptures are Moses (Deuteronomy 33–34), Joshua (Joshua 23–24), Stephen (Acts 7:54-60), and the saints in the "faith hall of fame" in Hebrews 11. These saints lived as aliens and strangers on this earth as they longed for a better country—the heavenly one.

What can we learn from these examples? We learn that even though a person is dying, he must still seek to minister to others and to bring glory to God. Being terminally ill does not excuse a person to be demanding and selfish. It is not a license to be self-absorbed, sullen, and unfaithful. We may be tempted to act in these ways as Satan will try to get a foothold in these last moments. If we conduct ourselves selfishly and sullenly, our lack of faithful servanthood must be confessed to God, His forgiveness received, and His cleansing a source of joy and contentment for us just as it has always been in our Christian walk.

Constant communion with Christ, growing in the grace and knowledge of God, results in living well and dying well. Be in love with the Lord. Be in daily communion with Him. If your relationship with Christ is vibrant, vital, and close, you will be greatly comforted by it in your own dying and in the deaths of your loved ones.

In a speech at the Texas Baptist Christian Life Commission's annual statewide conference, John Andersen, who is a hospice chaplain and a pastor said,

> *Churches should teach believers not only how to live, but also how to die as Christians. . . . We have a lot of books on how to care for the grieving. We have a lot of books on the dying process. But we talk very seldom about whether the dying person has any responsibility. The church can help the dying Christian teach others how to "die well" by recognizing his needs and the areas of ministry he can give and receive.[6]*

By speaking of a dying person's responsibilities, I am not saying she should pretend she is well when she is not or that she must not communicate ways that others can help her. For example, a terminally ill Christian who is in pain can certainly avail herself of pain-relieving medications and other palliative care. I am not advocating stoicism. But I am trying to point out that a dying Christian must make it her goal to serve God and others the best she can right up to the end of her earthly life.

Death with Dignity or Death with Faithfulness?

The Bible does not encourage dying people or their caretakers to pursue "death with dignity." Rather, the Bible talks about being faithful no matter what life brings. Therefore, rather than pursuing dignity, we ought to set our sights on being faithful to the end.

As in living from day to day, our dying days are ones that need to be marked by faithfulness "each according to his own ability" (Matthew 25:15). When we meet our Master face to face we want to hear Him say, "Well done, goodand faithful servant! You have been faithful with a few things; I will put you in charge of many things. Come and share your master's happiness!" (Matthew 25:23 NIV).

Dignity, like happiness, is a result of being faithful. It is not to be pursued in and of itself. When dignity is our goal, we become man-centered. But when faithfulness is our goal, we can be God-centered.

Jesus was not grasping at maintaining some form of dignity as He was dying. His death was dignified because He was obedient and faithful. Death with dignity is not something to strive for. Rather it is a by-product of trusting and obeying God to the very end.

Reluctance to Face the Issues

We realize some readers may be shocked by what we are saying about the conduct of a dying person. If so, we believe this shock may come from both our culture and our churches' reluctance to face these matters head on. Unless we are engaged in an occupation which confronts dying and death on a regular basis, we usually insulate ourselves from it. Only our own dying or that of someone close to us invades this fairy tale-like existence.

This modern state of mind is in sharp contrast with the way people have historically faced their lives. The old adage "live each day as if it were your last" sounds like wasteful folly to modern ears. The world, we think, has too much to offer us. In what is referred to as the parable of the rich fool, the rich man said to himself, "'You have plenty of good things laid up for many years. Take life easy; eat, drink and be merry'" (Luke 12:19 NIV). But God's response to this kind of thinking is that it reveals one to be foolish indeed. For we do not know when our souls will be demanded (verse 20).

If our affections are set on this world, we will be ill-prepared to die. We may find ourselves at the end of life struggling to hold onto our faith. If we do not grow in the grace and knowledge of God, we will not be prepared to die well. We must be like the people referred to in Hebrews 11, who lived as aliens and strangers in the world. They were not caught up with earthly things. Instead, they longed for a better country—a heavenly one!

Teaching Children About Death

Seventeen years ago, my (Carol) mother-in-law lay dying of breast and liver cancer. It was heartbreaking to watch this lovely, Christian woman slowly get weaker and thinner as she battled her disease. Chemotherapy left her without her thick hair. As the months passed, it became necessary for us to explain to our eight-year-old son what was happening to his beloved grandmother.

Children often more easily perceive our attitudes toward things than the facts of the matter. If your faith in God's sovereignty and goodness are firm, you can be immensely helpful to your child. Help children understand the difference between body and soul. It is best to keep your explanation simple and to the point. Be sure to give children ample opportunity to express their feelings about the dying person.

Listen carefully to the child's questions. Don't assume your questions are also your children's questions. They will be coming at this from a different perspective because of their lack of experience and their limited ability to think abstractly. Be sensitive and do not judge their questions and comments. Assure them that God is sad about death too, and someday He will bring an end to death.

Stages of Grieving Over Dying and Death

Everyone grieves differently and at their own pace when faced with serious loss. Do not expect a set series of stages to occur. There is no biblical evidence to suggest that grief occurs in stages as is proposed by writers such as Elizabeth Kubler-Ross.[7] Instead, grieving is more like the last weeks of winter in which you think the cold days are abating only to awaken the next morning to a layer of snow on the ground. Individual aspects of the experience of loss come and go and cycle back in on us again as we adjust to the ways our lives are changed by loss.

Sometimes grief never goes away completely. Depending upon the closeness of the relationship, the tremendous sadness may stay for a long time. If you have lost someone dear to you, the deep sadness will eventually lessen but it may never go away completely—and that is okay unless you have made an idol of this loved one and believe you can't live without him or her. But the good news is that the comfort of the presence of Christ with us and the immense joy He gives can exist side by side in our grief.

Elisabeth Elliot encourages those who are grieving to do something for someone else.

> *There is nothing like definite, overt action to overcome the inertia of grief. . . . Most of us have someone who needs us. If we haven't, we can find someone. Instead of praying only for the strength we ourselves need to survive, this day or this hour, how about praying for some to give away?*[8]

Pray for wisdom and for opportunity to minister to others even if you can only do it in very small ways.

What Do Dying People Need?

Dying people need loving, respectful, thoughtful help from those attending them. They need compassionate concern and the quiet presence of people who understand what it means to be a companion. Whether you are a doctor, nurse, technician, family member, friend, or co-worker, you must treat dying people as persons not objects. (For more specific ways to help the dying person and his or her caretakers, see the list of ministry opportunities at the end of this chapter.)

The more that you have faced your own dying the better able you will be to give compassionate help to a dying person. If you have learned from suffering in your own life, you will minister more effectively to the dying. If your trust in God's sovereignty and goodness has comforted and sustained you, you will be in a better position to comfort others (*see* 2 Corinthians 1).

Perhaps you don't have firsthand in-depth experience with the death of someone close to you. But, you need not have suffered through exactly the same thing in order to help a dying person. Be a good observer. Is she consumed with fear? Is she doubting God's love, concern, and involvement? Is she worried about those who will be left behind? Remind her briefly of God's promised help. Encourage her with His Word. Whatever losses you have experienced can be useful to you in helping someone who is dying if you will take a long look at your responses in those experiences and make yourself aware of what was comforting to you at the time.

If you are seeking to help people who have terminal illnesses or injuries, it will be important for you to know how they view their situations. What is their worldview? How do they make sense of life and death? Of course, there will be differences in how you help depending upon the condition of each person. Sadly, many people get to the end of life and regret that they did not make spiritual matters a priority. Thus, many people, even Christians, have serious questions, troubling doubts, and sometimes even immobilizing fears as they face dying and death. You can bring the truth and comfort as well as the challenge of God's Word to them in ways they may never have experienced.

Set Your House in Order

Good King Hezekiah was given a unique opportunity. During a severe illness, the Lord sent Isaiah the prophet to tell him, "Set your house in order, for you shall die and not live" (2 Kings 20:1). Hezekiah was given advance notice of his impending death, and God's counsel to him was, "Set your house in order." Upon receiving this news, Hezekiah prayed for healing and the Lord graciously granted him 15 more years. Although it seems Hezekiah was given a special privilege in knowing the exact time of his death, every Christian must be diligent to follow God's command to "set your house in order." As Peter Kreeft writes in his book *Love Is Stronger than Death,* "I am writing this book about death for an intensely personal reason. I have a terminal illness. You are invited to read it for the same reason. You too have a terminal illness. . . . Life is always fatal."[9] Indeed, for all of us, it has been decreed that at a certain time, unless the Lord's return is hastened, we will die (Ecclesiastes 3:2; 1 Thessalonians 4:17).

In every facet of our lives, God calls us to live faithfully, for His pleasure and glory, and to be wise stewards or managers over all He has given us (1 Corinthians 4:2). We must seek to advance the kingdom of God and fulfill His commands that our lives might glorify Him in death as in life. One of the primary ways we can do this is by "setting our house in order." We might seek to approach and plan for our death by asking this question, "In what way shall I set my house (what God has providentially provided for me) in order for His glory and the furtherance of His kingdom?"[10] God's providence[11] or care for His children extends to the time of our last breath and we must seek to faithfully manage all that He has so mercifully given us. Since God has providentially given you the time to read this, you should take the opportunity to use your time wisely by prayerful planning.

Talking with Family and Friends

Godly Examples   There may be no greater inheritance you can leave for your descendants than to talk with them about your life and death while you are able. In our culture, talking about death is considered morbid or macabre. "Death has become a taboo, an unnameable thing. . . . In the twentieth century, death has replaced sex as the principal prohibition."[12] We must be careful not to adopt the thinking of the world on this topic, but rather strive to live faithfully, honestly, and realistically for God's glory as demonstrated by former saints. Jacob was faithful to rehearse God's working in his life and give instructions to his children about his burial (Genesis 49:29-33). Before his death, Joseph made his kinsmen swear they would follow his wishes for his burial (Genesis 50:25). God told Moses of his impending death and Moses blessed the sons of Israel beforehand (Deuteronomy 32:48–33:29). On numerous occasions, Jesus spoke with His disciples about His death and sought to prepare them for its eventuality (Matthew 16:21; Mark 8:31–9:1). On the night of His death, He asked them to be with Him, to pray with Him (Matthew 26:36).

The apostle Paul made a special visit to the Ephesian elders because he knew they wouldn't see him again and he wanted to give them some final teaching (Acts 20). Consider the kinds of things he said to them: He reminded them of his teaching and his lifestyle (verses 18-21); he told them his life was not dear to himself—he was only interested in finishing the ministry the Lord had given him (verse 24). He made it clear they would never see him again in this life (verse 25), and that although others might come in to slander him (verses 29-30), he had lived honestly and righteously before them (verses 26-27,33-36). Finally, he commended them to "God and to the word of His grace" (verse 32), reminded them of his example (verse 31), and prayed with them. He was using the time the Lord had providentially given him to further the work of God. In the book of 2 Timothy we see Paul knew the time for his "departure" was fast approaching and asked Timothy to come to him. He requested that Mark be brought to him, possibly so that a reconciliation could be made (*see* Acts 15:36f), and also asked for his cloak and his Old Testament writings (*see* 2 Timothy 4:6-13). *Rather than being a taboo subject, the Bible is filled with illustrations of saints who sought to prepare, encourage, and instruct family and friends about impending death.*

Christians today should plan wisely for the eventualities we all must face. In addition to being prepared spiritually, we must also be prepared materially.

Adult children should lovingly seek to engage their parents in conversation about this topic. If they are unwilling or uncomfortable doing so, perhaps you could draft a letter explaining your love and concern that their wishes be understood and carried out. If, after prayerful patience, they continue to refuse to speak with you, perhaps you could bring in other respected members of the family or elders in the church who could calm any fears they might have. If all this fails, you can continue to love and pray for them and seek to prepare yourself in advance by study.

Time should be spent discussing a parent's assets and plans regarding long-term care and any eventual inheritances. In addition to financial and legal arrangements, there are a number of medical decisions that should be considered by family members including Advanced Medical Directives, home health care, hospice care, communication with physicians, and funeral arrangements.

Financial Planning This may be a very difficult topic to broach since some parents are very private about their money and some children may feel that talking about inheritances and dividing up property is mercenary. Rather than being mercenary or "nobody's business but our own," making financial arrangements before a time of crisis is very kind and loving. Heirs should be notified of the whereabouts of a personal record file that should contain information such as a will, the names and addresses of attorneys, insurance policies, legal documents (such as birth and marriage certificates, social security numbers), and other documents.[13] "A will is a legal document that specifies the details of how an individual wishes to dispose of his or her estate. . . . Unfortunately, about half of all Americans do not have wills."[14] A will should be drawn up and stored somewhere other than a safety deposit box, which is usually sealed immediately upon death. If the estate is more complicated, with real estate, stocks and bonds, or other holdings, difficulties in probate court and in some cases inheritance taxes can be avoided by having a living trust drawn up. "A living trust is a legal arrangement by which a person's property is held and administered by a trustee for the benefit of another."[15] Information on necessary documents can be obtained from your Area Agency on Aging or the American Association of Retired Persons.

Advanced Medical Directives

Technologically, we live in a time like no other. Extraordinary measures to prolong life are now available. Respirators can do what was impossible

50 years ago. People in cardiac arrest are oftentimes resuscitated. Persons who have injuries or illnesses that would have previously meant certain death are now able to be sustained and sometimes recover either partially or completely. Others are kept alive for years by artificial means. But the blessings accrued to us by modern medicine have also opened a Pandora's box of ethical dilemmas. In response to this new life sustaining technology has come new emphases on "death with dignity," "quality of life," and much discussion about euthanasia. Christians must think biblically and deeply about the decisions involved in dying faithfully. Since women make up 75 percent of all informal caregivers,[16] it is important that Christian women understand biblical teachings *before* an emergency situation occurs and life-and-death decisions are made. One of the fundamental areas of this decision-making process involves Advanced Medical Directives (AMD's).

"An Advance Medical Directive is a generic term for a form or document which expresses your preferences in the event you are physically and mentally unable to make medical care decisions for yourself."[17] Most people are familiar with one form of AMD, the "living will." There are, however, other forms of AMD's, including durable powers of attorney for health care and values inventories. To make things even more complex, the federal government passed the Patient Self-Determination Act on December 1, 1991. This law requires that "personnel at all hospitals, nursing homes, and hospices receiving Medicare and Medicaid reimbursement are to advise patients upon admission of their right to accept or refuse medical treatments and to execute an AMD."[18] Let's look more closely at two types of AMD's: the living will and Durable Power of Attorney for Health Care.

The Living Will A living will is a "specific kind of directive which is 'restricted to rejecting life-sustaining medical interventions, usually, although not exclusively, when a person is terminally ill.' "[19] At first glance it would seem as though this kind of document is a good idea, but it is generally thought that living wills are problematic for the following reasons. First, they are seen as one more step onto the slippery slope leading to devaluation of human life and euthanasia. "Living wills are the thin edge of a wedge to further unseat another facet of our moral-social structures. Will they not desensitize us to killing our old?"[20] For Christians who are concerned with pro-life issues this is certainly a major consideration. In addition, living wills may be so broad as to not be of any real help. Since none of us can look into the future and know what advances will be made nor what our condition might be ten years in the future, it is foolish to make blanket statements about what kind of care we may or may not want. "Living wills do not allow the kind of specificity that most patient's care will demand even in the terminal stage of their illness."[21] In addition to being not specific enough, living wills are vague in their terminology. "The language becomes even more vague . . . where the document talks about being kept alive with medications. What, in fact, is medication? What is natural and what is artificial? What are heroic measures? If a patient is placed on a respirator and recovers, is that a heroic measure?"[22] In order for a living will to be effective it would have to be drawn up by a team of lawyers seeking to cover every eventuality. This is simply impossible. Living wills also take life-and-death decisions out of the hands of the family and church, where they belong, and place them in the hands of the physicians. This may be very dangerous or costly depending on the physician's opinions in end-of-life issues. A preferable alternative to the living will is the Durable Power of Attorney for Health Care.

The Durable Power of Attorney for Health Care The Durable Power of Attorney for Health Care is a specific medical directive that "enables you to name a trusted relative or friend to make your medical decisions when you cannot do so for yourself. This includes your right to refuse treatment you would not want."[23] Remember that Durable Power of Attorney for Health Care is different from other durable powers of attorney. "The DPAHC has nothing to do with your finances or estate. It is limited to power over your medical care alone."[24] After a declaration of incompetency is made by a physician, this appointed person would then make all decisions regarding on-going health care. In deciding on someone to act in your place in medical decision-making, it would be wise to consider the following: Is this person a Christian who understands the sanctity of life as made in God's image, as well as the promise of eternal life and heaven for the believer? Does this person understand and agree with your values and perspectives, especially in the area of health care? Would this person be willing and able to stand against medical personnel who might have a differing agenda and who may have an authoritarian view of their profession? Does this person have the time to take on a burden that might become very time-intensive? Is this person a trusted and respected part of the family? Generally speaking, the husband has God-given authority over the wife (and vice versa if the husband is incapacitated—1 Corinthians 7:4) and the parents over the children (and vice versa if the parents are incapacitated and the children are adults). These and other considerations should be evaluated before choosing someone who will make decisions about your health care.

If no one in your family is available to fill this role, you should consider contacting someone in your church—an elder or trusted friend. Even after you have appointed a surrogate decision-maker, you should take time to talk with your closest associates and family, letting them know of your choice and the reasons for it. *Much heartache, confusion, and blame may be avoided in this difficult time if these things are discussed when people are not under the burden of a medical crisis.*

Life-and-Death Decisions

Because Christians believe strongly in the sanctity of life, care should be taken before any specific course of action is decided upon. This is a difficult and thorny topic, with questions about "pulling the plug," do not resuscitate orders, artificial hydration and nutrition, and organ donation adding to the confusion of an emotional and heart-wrenching time.[25] As a general rule, Christians may do nothing that will violate the sixth commandment, "Thou shalt not kill," by shortening life. We must take this restriction very seriously since we live in a time when the issues of "quality of life,"[26] "the 'right' to die,"[27] and "death with dignity,"[28] are all euphemistic code words employed by those who would favor laws permitting voluntary or assisted suicide. On the other hand, we must recognize that Christians are under no biblical obligation to needlessly prolong dying. Just because a certain medical procedure can be done, it doesn't necessarily follow that it must or should be done. In making these decisions, the Christian should ask, "How can I best use what God has provided?" At times, God's provision includes wonderful technology that has a good possibility of success. At other times, God's provision seems to point to a proper management of the time left and a conserving of resources that could be more properly used in God's kingdom. In addition, the Golden Rule, "Therefore, however you want people to treat you, so treat them, for this is the Law and the Prophets" (Matthew 7:12) may be helpful in determining a biblical course of action. Remember, however, there is a distinct and significant difference between letting a person die and killing him. Christians should not idolize life nor think this present life is all there is, nor should they fear death. In addition, unlike those who don't know God, Christians know suffering is meaningful and should resist pursuing actions that may violate God's commands simply to alleviate it. Each case is unique, and prayerful consideration, particularly with elders or other Christians who are familiar with bioethical issues and medicine, should be made.[29]

Relationships with Physicians If someone for whom you have responsibility becomes seriously ill, you should seek to communicate with his physician personally. If you have Durable Power of Attorney for Health Care or if you have already established a relationship with the physician through your loved one, most physicians will be glad to communicate with you. It is best to have a time when you and your loved one can speak to the physician about the patient's values and wishes before a life-threatening situation occurs. Unfortunately, in the case of a serious illness or trauma, your loved one may be in the care of more than one doctor. Perhaps he has a general practitioner, an internist, an oncologist, and a neurologist. Each of these physicians are concerned with a narrow area of care and each may be ordering differing treatments. Perhaps each one is placing only a small burden on your loved one, but the cumulative effect of all these small procedures can be overwhelming and may be needlessly prolonging dying in someone who has a very low likelihood for recovery. Since it is difficult to talk to every physician personally, it may be wise to call a patient care conference with all of the physicians involved as well as family members, the head nurse, pastor, and medical social workers. Specific questions about recovery rates and prognoses should be asked. Request that the answers be quantified, rather than just spoken of in generic terms. "Exactly what percentage of patients in this situation recover?" "What is the exact likelihood that these treatments will be successful?" These kinds of questions may help you (and the family) make wise and godly decisions.

Physicians are trained in the art of healing. They strongly desire to help and to do good. For many, death is viewed as a failure. This aversion to the realities of treating the dying is exacerbated by the lack of training in this area. "According to the American Medical Association's report on medical education, only 5 of 126 medical schools in the United States require a separate course in the care of the dying. Of 7048 residency programs, only 26 percent offer a course on the medical and legal aspects of care at the end of life as a regular part of the curriculum."[30] Because of this aversion to and unfamiliarity with death, many physicians will recommend procedures that may or may not be of any lasting benefit simply to avoid facing defeat. In addition, the legal profession and malpractice lawsuits have forced doctors into a defensive position. They feel they must do everything that can be done, both for the patient's sake and also to protect themselves from litigation.

On the other hand, once a decision has been made to withhold treatment and to opt instead for palliative care (care that has as its goal the alleviation of pain and seeks to comfort without the goal of curing), many physicians feel their job is over. They may believe they have failed and proceed to ignore or pass off the patient to the chaplain or pastor. This can be very disconcerting for a seriously ill patient who has come to trust his physician, as well as for the family, which feels abandoned.

When all else has failed, the physician can play a very real part in the strengthening and encouraging of his patient and his family by offering comfort. "In addition to adjusting patients' pain medication, 'sometimes just being there, holding their hand, reassures them and it makes the family feel better.' "[31] This is undoubtedly a difficult situation for most physicians. Donald Townsend, M.D., speaks honestly of this discomfort:

> We are summoned to communicate in a certain manner, to act a certain way, to have a certain attitude, and to touch in certain ways. Touching does something for me and for patients. It makes contact. It says that I still consider them to be alive. We intrinsically have an aversion to touch things that are dead. If I walk into a room and avoid physical contact, the patient and any others in that room are cut off from me.... Let's admit our discomfort. I get nervous in almost every patient's room.[32]

Physicians are not God. They cannot cure in the ultimate sense, they are not omniscient, inerrant, or omnipotent. Although it may be wise to take their counsel, we are not under any biblical obligation to obey them—especially when to do so may violate the commands of God or the desire to serve as a faithful steward.

Telling Terminally-Ill Patients the Truth   In *The Death of Ivan Ilyich,* Leo Tolstoy poignantly and forcefully describes the terrible experience Ilyich experiences upon his deathbed:

> What tormented Ivan Ilyich most was pretense, the lie, which for some reason they all kept up, that he was merely ill and not dying, and that he only need stay quiet and carry out doctor's orders, and then some great change for the better would result. . . . The pretense made him wretched: it tormented him that they refused to admit what they knew and he knew to be a fact, but persisted in lying to him concerning his terrible condition, and wanted him and forced him to be party to the lie.[33]

In the past, it was the prevailing practice to hide the truth about the seriousness of one's condition from him so that the "quality" of the life he had left would not be jeopardized. Fortunately, this practice is waning as people become more interested in having a say about their health care. For the Christian, a decision about whether to tell a dying loved one the truth or to keep the truth from him is obvious. We must never lie. Lying to a dying person is not only sinful but also stymies possible good. Examples of this good can include final communications with family members, testimony of God's faithfulness, reconciliations with estranged loved ones, arrangements for burial, and even repentance from sin. Some people who put off serving the Lord during their lifetimes come to Him on their deathbeds. We know Jesus will receive those who truly repent, even if it is at the last hour, for we have the example of the thief on the cross (*see* Luke 23:43). For the Christian, time spent in prayer and praise together can enrich the whole family and encourage young ones to serve the Lord. It can serve as a time when all the family is reminded about the realities of death and the blessed wonder of heaven, where "He shall wipe away every tear from their eyes; and there shall no longer be any death; there shall no longer be any mourning, or crying, or pain" (Revelation 21:4).

Although care should be taken to break the news gently and wisely, there can be no question in the good of doing so. As Jay Adams writes, "Every man is entitled to know that he is likely to die soon. Why should everyone else but the dying one know? Who is the principal person involved in the illness? . . . If Jesus needed to prepare for His death and to discuss it with God and others, so too do we."[34]

Decisions About Long-Term Care

Another sphere of concern may be that of arranging for long-term care. Usually, long-term care takes place in the home. It may also occur in a skilled nursing facility, or as in the case of the terminally ill, in a hospice situation. Long-term care does not usually occur in hospitals, since hospitals are primarily for acute care, rather than chronic or long-term terminal cases. Decisions about where to care for a loved one should be made with the counsel of everyone involved, including the patient, the family, the physician, the pastor, and the medical social worker (if any).

Home Health Care In some cases, a loved one may become unable to care for himself or may become chronically or terminally ill. Frequently, those who are either chronically or terminally ill can be cared for at home. The decision to place a parent, adult child, or other loved one in your home for care is difficult and agonizing for everyone involved. The parent or adult child may resent having to give up his independence and may worry about becoming a burden to the family. In addition, ill relatives don't usually move into a situation where a vacuum of activity exists. They frequently move in with a family that already has schedules and demands on its time, and is stretched to the maximum. Adding an aging or ill loved one to this mix may be trying for everyone involved. Grandma can't hear well, so she turns the television up too loud. Perhaps she feels cold all the time and the children complain because the house feels like an oven. Every part of the family's life will change because a new member has been added. Now, in addition to ball games, PTA meetings, and ballet lessons, mom may have to drive grandpa to the doctor once or twice a week. Difficult situations may arise when care for an ailing parent includes bathing and diaper changing. Prayerful thought and godly counsel is necessary before the decision to care for an ill or aging loved one is made. It is apparent that children are biblically responsible to care for their parents, but where that care takes place must be an individual, case-by-case decision (1 Timothy 5:8).

Presently, there are "seven million individuals who require [home health care] services because of acute illness, long-term health conditions, permanent disability or terminal illness."[35] Some of these individuals live with family and friends, others are able to live alone. There are more than 18,500 home care organizations which include home health agencies, home care aide organizations and hospices. These organizations provide services such as "skilled nursing and therapy of a curative or restorative nature."[36] Many of these organizations are certified by Medicare and are eligible to receive payment for services. This kind of health care is cost-efficient and much less expensive than either skilled nursing facilities or hospitals. The number of visits per week of home health care professionals will vary depending on the age of the client and whether he needs help with normal activities of daily living. Usually, a home health care agency can be recommended by a physician or you may locate one through your local Area Agency on Aging.

Skilled Nursing Facilities It may eventually become necessary to move your loved one from your home to a skilled nursing facility. "Skilled care facilities provide round-the-clock nursing services. A physician must certify that a patient is sick enough to need these services, and bills are covered by Medicaid for those who meet the income restrictions."[37] One of the main problems with skilled care facilities is their cost. Private care facilities cost from $1,800 to $2,500 and up monthly. Private care facilities are not usually covered by

Medicare, although some are mandated to. If your loved one does not have adequate insurance or a large cash reserve, you may have to confine your search for a suitable facility to those who accept Medicaid payments. This may be difficult and the quantity and quality of the homes may make your search troublesome. Care should be taken when choosing a facility. Specific questions about the training, morale, working conditions, and background of the staff are important. What precautions are taken to ensure patient security? In the case of dementia units, what is the ratio of staff to patient? How many nurses are on staff? Is this ratio the same at night as during the day? Will your loved one's physician be able to visit him there? Barbara Deane, co-founder of Christian Caregivers, encourages an unexpected visit at different times of the day to see how your loved one is being cared for. Horror stories about abuses in nursing homes abound. This does not mean you won't be able to find a good place for your loved one. It just means you will have to be cautious and alert. However, it may become apparent, in the course of time, that hospice care is the next step.

Hospice Care "Hospice is a coordinated interdisciplinary program of supportive services and pain and symptom control for terminally-ill people and their families. Hospice is primarily a concept of care, not a specific place of care."[38]

The American hospice movement began in the 1960s primarily through the influence of Dame Cicely M.S. Saunders. In 1994 approximately 222,000 persons received hospice services for an average of 59 days.[39] "These services included nursing care; services of a medical social worker, physician, counselor, and home care aide and homemaker; short-term in-patient care; medical appliances and supplies, physical and occupational therapies; and speech-language pathology services. Bereavement service for the family is provided for up to 13 months following the patient's death."[40]

Rather than thinking of hospice care as a place, it is better thought of as a philosophy of care during terminal illness. The first part of that philosophy is that the family is the unit of care. "Nothing that we do should serve to separate someone who is dying from his family."[41] A team of professionals is assigned to care for a terminally ill patient and his family. The family is encouraged to participate fully in caring for the patient in the final stage of life. Rather than isolating the patient in a hospital, away from home and loved ones, the patient may remain in familiar surroundings and have interaction with others who care for him and his family. Although it is difficult for the family to see a loved one in physical distress and be unable to do anything about it, they are encouraged to not withdraw from the dying patient. Death itself is an intensely isolating experience. "In death we are alone. Only in death are we completely alone. Death is the only completely individual event in our lives."[42] The Christian has the wonderful knowledge that even though no earthly person can accompany him on his journey, he has the Lord's assurance of His presence. Although none of us can experience the death of another in the most personal sense, family and the hospice team can make this intensely isolating time much less solitary. The hospice team offers help and support to the patient and family on a 24-hour-a-day, seven-days-a-week basis. "For patients and their loved ones, help is just a phone call away."[43] This care may be provided in the home, or in a hospice care facility that may be part of a skilled nursing facility or hospital.

Another facet of hospice care is the control of physical distress since care is focused on pain management and symptom control rather than cure. Contrary to the popular view that many persons suffer from uncontrollable pain (a perspective perpetuated by the euthanasia movement), studies have shown that "ninety-six percent of terminally ill patients can be free of pain; the remaining four percent can be made more comfortable."[44] Physicians can help many terminally ill persons manage their pain without having to be overly sedated, and can use the remaining months of their lives interacting with loved ones. Unfortunately, some physician's discomfort with the dying patient may thwart a concerted endeavor at relieving pain. This is evidenced by the fact that "seventy percent of cancer patients die with their pain untreated. . . ."[45]

The hospice focus is on palliative care rather than cure. "Hospice neither hastens nor postpones death: It affirms life."[46] Rather than ignoring or isolating the dying, hospice encourages interaction and care for them. As Dame Saunders writes, "Anything which says to the very ill or the very old that there is no longer anything that matters in their life would be a deep impoverishment to the whole of society."[47]

Physicians who consider that their patient has six months or less to live can recommend a hospice program. Medicare or private insurance usually reimburse the hospice service, although much of hospice is on a volunteer basis.

From a Christian perspective, hospice care has much to recommend it, particularly the emphasis on interaction with the family and the effort to sustain life as comfortably as possible. Although there is much to recommend hospice, care should be taken that the dying person's pastor or elders visit regularly and continue biblical counseling and care rather than rely on the social workers or chaplains, who may be very liberal in their views.

Final Arrangements When faced with the death of a loved one, many decisions are made in a short and traumatic time. The American Institute for Cancer Research publishes a very helpful pamphlet, *When a Loved One Dies: The Next Steps,* which may be obtained from your funeral director.

Notifying Others The first step to take after the death of a loved one is to notify your pastor or elder. This is not the time to isolate yourself from the help of the church. In fact, many churches have programs in place for just such an occasion and will be able to organize meals and household help for you, if needed. If you know a mortuary that you want to use, you should contact the funeral director and make an appointment. In the meantime, your pastor or elder may come over and help you in contacting other family members, friends, neighbors, and business associates. If you have a close friend or family member upon whose judgment you can rely, ask them to accompany you to a mortuary to make arrangements.

If a loved one dies at home and is not under the care of a physician who had seen him during the last 20 days, you will need to contact the police, who will then arrange for transportation to the coroner's office for autopsy. If the death occurred at home while under a physician's care, an autopsy is usually not needed, although you may request one. In either case, the funeral director will arrange to have the body moved from the coroner's office, your home, nursing care facility, or hospital to the mortuary.

Funeral Arrangements Numerous decisions must be made by family members upon the death of a loved one. These decisions can seem confusing and can be very expensive. Having a trusted family member or friend with you when making these decisions will stop you from making unwise arrangements in the midst of emotional turmoil. The following is a brief outline of some of these decisions and the approximate costs involved.[48]

Your funeral director will help you make plans for your loved one's service and burial or cremation. The first decision you will be asked to make is whether you want the body embalmed or not. Embalming, a process for preserving the body, costs around $250 and is usually required if you plan to have an "open casket" service. If you do not plan to have this type of viewing, the body does not usually have to be embalmed. Next, you will need to decide whether you want to bury your loved one in a casket or cremate him. Burial in a casket will necessitate your purchasing a casket (ranging in price from around $550 to $9,150). If you choose an "open casket," you will need to provide the clothing you want your loved one buried in and you will need to furnish the mortician with a photograph so that he can arrange your loved one in the most natural pose possible. In addition, you will need to decide upon a cemetery for burial in the ground or a mausoleum (for internment in a crypt). This does not necessarily need to be done immediately, but you will need to visit one (either public or private) in the first few days. At the cemetery you will have to choose the location of the plot and whether you want any markers placed on the grave. A marker can be very expensive but can also serve as a beautiful memorial that will last throughout the years.

If, on the other hand, you choose cremation, you will have other decisions to make. Cremation caskets and alternative containers range in price from $45 to $2,950. There is usually a crematory fee (approximately $200), and a fee if you want to have your loved one's ashes scattered over a designated area. You can also arrange to have the cremains buried at a cemetery or placed in a urn or container. Biblically speaking, there does not appear to be any prohibition against cremation, and some people may view it as better stewardship of God's provision. The only cautions that might need to be considered are how the rest of the family will respond and whether cremation is being ordered because of unbelief in the resurrection.

The funeral director will then help you decide if you want to have a public or private service. Certainly for Christians who have been active in a church, public services would allow friends and family to share sorrow and show respect for the deceased. You will need to designate a time for family visitation and viewing at the mortuary, as well as public visitation. A prayer service and/or a memorial service may also be held at the mortuary or in your church building. You will need to decide whether you want to have a public or private grave-side service and whether you want this grave-side service to immediately follow the church service. If it is to immediately follow the church or memorial service, you will need to make decisions about transporting the deceased to the cemetery. Other decisions on things such as officiants, musicians, pall-bearers, musical selections, registry book, memorial folders, prayer cards, and acknowledgment cards will have to be made. You will need to decide whether you want the newspaper to run an obituary and whether you want to have flowers sent to the mortuary or to have donations made to a specific ministry or non-profit organization. Your funeral director will help you decide the number of death certificates you will need in order to take care of all legalities.

As you can see, there are many decisions to be made regarding funeral arrangements. In addition, these arrangements can be very expensive. The average funeral costs around $5,000, although this figure may fluctuate quite a bit. Once again, you must ask yourself questions regarding wise stewardship. This is a good time to allow your trusted friend or family member to advise and counsel you. Try to avoid being overly influenced by funeral directors and prayerfully consider the lasting benefits or liabilities of your decisions.

As you can see, the most loving thing we can do for our family and friends is to make these arrangements in advance. Arrangements for every facet of this process can be made in advance with a mortuary and the money for the services can be placed in a trust. Many mortuaries also offer Forethought Policies that guarantee price stability no matter how much time has gone by since the original arrangements were made. What a blessing it would be to relieve your family of these decisions and expenses during what may be the most trying time of their lives.

Financial Matters   Immediate funds, such as death benefits, are not usually available automatically and must be applied for. The funeral director will probably help you apply for these benefits and may make you aware of other benefits. "The deceased's employer can also tell you if payments are due from unpaid wages, pay for unused vacation, illness benefits, group life insurance, disability income benefits, hospital benefits or worker's compensation payments."[49]

Insurance death claims may be filed by contacting the insurance company's local office or your insurance agent. You will have to present a certified copy of the death certificate. Care should be taken not to surrender a life insurance policy to any agent of the insurance company without receiving an authorized receipt. Automobile insurance companies should be notified if death resulted from an automobile accident.

Social Security and veterans benefits are frequently available. Social Security may also have a death payment to assist in meeting funeral expenses and survivor benefits. The Veterans Administration can assist you in ascertaining what payments are due from pensions, dependency and indemnity compensation, or death gratuities.

Creditors should be notified to make arrangements for payments or filings for extensions on bills due until the estate is settled. It is usually necessary to consult with your attorney regarding the transfer of property that is held jointly. Frequently, jointly-held property can be transferred to the survivor without probate action. Stocks and bonds that are held jointly can be transferred to the beneficiary by presenting required documents, such as certified copies of the death certificate, to the stock transfer agent.

Faithfully Planning for Death

As you can see, there are many decisions that must be made and much you can do to provide for and witness to your family even in your death. While these choices may be easy for you to determine now, it will be more difficult for your loved ones to choose during the crisis surrounding your death. Faithful living includes planning and providing.

Thorny Questions

In this section, I want to pose some questions which are frequently raised in situations surrounding dying and death. Many questions about this subject have no answer on this side of heaven. In those cases, we must simply be content with the answer, "God knows." The answers given below are simple and to the point. Much more could be said about all of them, and indeed, on some issues volumes have been written.

Q: If my prayer for my loved one isn't answered the way I want it answered, am I justified in concluding that God failed me? **A:** No. Such a conclusion would place one in the realm of putting self above God and judging the actions and motives of God.

Q: Is there such a thing as "soul sleep," meaning that people don't go immediately to heaven or hell when they die? **A:** "Everything Scripture says about the death of believers indicates they are immediately ushered consciously into the Lord's presence."[50] *See* 2 Corinthians 5:8 and Philippians 1:23.

Q: At the funeral of a person who never gave you cause to think he was a believer, how do you respond to people who say things that assume the person is in heaven such as, "Isn't it good that he's in heaven now?" **A:** Don't argue with them or attack their statements, but don't keep silent or nod your head in agreement since that would be tacit approval of their conclusions. Instead, state biblical truth in simple words such as, "All who demonstrate faith in Christ go to heaven." A response such as this avoids emotionalism and is objective. It gets the truth out without being unnecessarily offensive or insensitive to the occasion.

Q: Why doesn't God help my dying loved one who is in terrible pain? **A:** We don't know why some people suffer more pain than others as they are dying. We must be careful about what we conclude about God in such situations. To say God is not helping puts us in the position of judging God. It is better for us to acknowledge that we don't know why this is happening.

Q: If I am visiting a dying person who, as best I know, is not a Christian, am I obligated to query him about his spiritual state? **A:** Yes. Be sensitive, but do not miss the opportunity to perhaps be an instrument used to save his soul from hell. Be wise in what you say, be gentle, but tell him the truth.

Q: Is it okay to be angry that my loved one died? Is it okay to be angry at God because my loved one died? **A:** At sin, yes, at God, no. It is not unusual upon hearing a diagnosis of terminal illness for the dying person to be angry. If this anger is directed at sin and its effects, that anger is righteous. But be aware that anger at God is always sinful even in the face of death. In his book, *How Long, O Lord?*, D. A. Carson says,

> *Rage directed against God, as if he were unfair for passing the sentence that our sin deserved, is inherently foolish, as foolish as criticizing a judge for passing a just sentence on a bank robber. Our rage is better directed at the ugliness of death, the wretchedness of sin, our sense of betrayal and self-betrayal.*[51]

(Carson is speaking here of sin in a general sense, sin as the origin of all death.)

Q: Do people who are not saved when they die get a chance after death to surrender their lives to Christ and go to heaven? **A:** No. The decision made in this life is final. There is no second chance beyond the grave to be saved. Upon death, the person goes immediately to heaven or to hell without opportunity to reconsider. *See* Luke 16:19-31 and Hebrews 9:27.

Q: Doesn't everybody go to heaven? **A:** No. The Bible teaches that not all men go to heaven, but only those who have put their trust in Christ and believed on Him for the saving of their souls. *See* Matthew 7:13-23; 13:1-30; 25:1-46; Luke 13:23-28; John 5:24-29; Romans 2:5-16; Hebrews 9:27; 10:26-27; 2 Peter 3:7; Revelation 20:11-15.

Q: Do all infants and young children who die go to heaven? **A:** The eternal destination of infants and young children is known only to God. We can rest in this knowledge since God is always fair, just, and right.

The Rich Welcome

The faithful Christian who takes seriously his need to live his earthly life in preparation for eternal life will have a warm homecoming in heaven:

Therefore, my brothers and sisters, be all the more eager to confirm your call and election, for if you do this, you will never stumble. For in this way, entry into the eternal kingdom of our Lord and Savior Jesus Christ will be richly provided for you (2 Peter 1:10-11 NRSV).

Do you remember in the parable of the lost son how the father rejoiced at the sight of his son coming home again? The father said to his servants, "Let's have a feast and celebrate" (Luke 15:23 NIV). The death of a Christian is the passageway that takes him to the heavenly celebration: "You have come to Mount Zion, to the heavenly Jerusalem, the city of the living God. You have come to thousands upon thousands of angels in joyful assembly, to the church of the firstborn, whose names are written in heaven" (Hebrews 12:22-23 NIV).

Live your life with that celebration uppermost in your mind!

PRACTICAL WAYS TO SHOW YOU CARE
Shari Hofstetter, M.A.R.

Ten Ways to Care for a Loved One in the Hospital

Here are ten ways to help make a hospital stay easier

1. Remember that it is the patient who employs the hospital to provide appropriate care. Expect your desires and wishes to be respected. Let your doctor and the appropriate department heads know about good care and problems *as* they occur. It is important to develop a positive working relationship with the medical staff. If you communicate your expectations firmly, politely, and with respect, they will be more than ready to work with you to provide the best care possible. Remember to communicate the positive as well as the negative.

2. Get the facts. Information is the best medicine when facing uncertainty. Work with the medical staff to get the answers you need to make informed decisions. This may mean asking the same questions over and over, asking for medical terms to be translated into clear English, or asking for a second or third opinion.

3. Make sure the wishes of the patient are clearly understood by both family and the medical staff. If possible, draw up a *durable power of attorney* before hospitalization. The person designated by this document needs to know the specific desires of the patient and be capable of carrying them out if and when

it is necessary. Place a copy of all legal documents (DNR, Living Will, Donor Card, and so on) in the patient's chart. A notary public, legal forms, and advice can be provided by the hospital.

4. Talk through the prognosis of the illness and treatment options with loved ones as soon as possible. Make as many significant decisions as you can before entering the hospital but understand that viewpoints can change as treatment progresses. Reassess the big picture at regular intervals. This will help avoid misunderstandings and reduce stress.

5. Patient and family members may have difficulty expressing their fears and concerns. Allow ample opportunity for open communication in a safe environment throughout the duration of treatment. Do not hesitate to discuss issues as they arise with the medical staff. Honesty and concrete facts will go a long way to help alleviate fear, uncertainties and misconceptions.

6. Be involved in patient care plans as they are developed. Make sure that they clearly and realistically reflect the patient's goals for treatment. These goals will be reassessed at regular intervals; the patient's input is a valuable piece of the patient care process. Spiritual care is an important part of the patient care plan and prayer an important part of healing for many. Support your loved one in the expression of his/her religious beliefs and include their church as a significant part of their healing process.

7. Assist the medical staff in knowing their patient better. It is helpful for those involved in the treatment plan to be aware of the specific desires and preferences of the patient. Remember that they are only seeing one small part of your loved one's life. Help them understand a more balanced picture of who their patient is. Build on their desire to help restore your loved one to health.

8. Take care of each other and pace yourselves for the duration of the illness. Delegate responsibility for a variety of needs to more than a few individuals. Designate one or two people to interact with the medical team. Ensure that the information from both sides is communicated accurately and that all concerns are taken seriously and are appropriately addressed. This will cut down on the repetition of information as well as facilitate the relationship between patient and medical staff. Take turns spending time with the patient, include friends of the patient and members of his/her church as part of the support system. Respect the patient's personal desires about who visits when and for how long.

9. Hospitalization is an isolating experience for both patient and family. The normal routine of life is interrupted and privacy is a rare commodity. Bring in copies of favorite photos, a favorite pillow, special music, anything from home that will help the patient feel more comfortable (but won't be tragically missed

if they are lost). Arrange for family time in a location that provides more privacy than a double hospital room.

10. Make arrangements for the patient's discharge and home care as soon as possible. Include the specific wishes of the patient and take steps to ensure that he/she is involved in the decision-making process. Be careful not to burden a few with the total responsibility for supporting the patient at home. Hospital social services can be very helpful in making these decisions.

Ten Ways to Make a Hospital Visit Better

Suggestions to consider when visiting someone in the hospital

1. A hospital stay can be isolating and dehumanizing. Privacy and modesty are important considerations which need to be respected at all times. Remember that for the duration of the hospitalization the patient's room is his or her bedroom. This space should be treated with the same respect as their own home. Don't hesitate to ask if you are not sure what is appropriate or what may be upsetting to the patient. Don't sit on the bed unless invited to do so. And even then be careful not to interfere with any treatments, isolation requirements. Remember that an infection which you may not even notice may be deadly to the patient who is immune-suppressed.

2. Be polite to the hospital staff and respectful of the patient's daily schedule.

3. Allow your visit to support the patient in a way that is most meaningful to him/her at the time. Ask for suggestions if you are unsure. The simple willingness to share time with someone who is hospitalized is a precious gift. Make the length of your visit appropriate for the patient's situation. Do not stay too long. Several short visits can be less tiring for someone who is very ill. Longer visits help pass the time for more active patients confined to a bed or room for a lengthy hospitalization.

4. Ask the patient/family when the best time for a visit would be. You may be able to keep the patient company at a time when family members cannot be there. Thus you are ministering to both the patient and their caregivers.

5. Silent presence and quiet listening are powerful ways to support someone who is ill. Try to watch for signs of fatigue or uncomfortableness.

6. Activities can be wonderful diversions. A picnic or birthday party in the lounge can be a real morale booster. Whether it is a private time shared with family or an open invitation to the entire floor, make sure that you clear all

preparations with the patient's medical personnel. Careful plans may have to be made for the patient's diet or energy level. Usually a little creativity can go a long way to make a very special memory for everyone involved.

7. It is important for those who are hospitalized to stay in contact with family and friends. But when you are sick and in pain it is difficult to do even the simplest task—no matter how much you desire to do it. Help the patient write, address, and mail thank you notes.

8. If possible take the patient outside for a visit. Sunshine and fresh air can be very therapeutic. It will help long-term patients keep in touch with the seasons and the world outside the hospital.

9. Make arrangements for the paper to be delivered daily to the patient. If necessary, read it for him daily. Take care to note news items that may be of particular interest to the patient or something they may want to keep up with. Take the time to discuss points of interest to the patient. You are giving him a chance to interact with the world outside of his hospital bed. And you are reinforcing his individuality and purpose; both are easily lost during a lengthy hospitalization.

10. Help someone in the hospital vote. Absentee ballots are easy to obtain from the patient's hometown.

Gifts Other than Cards, Flowers, and Balloons

Thoughtfulness and creativity can make gifts appropriate for the recipient

1. Stamps, stationery, thank-you cards, blank cards, and the offer to assist with writing, addressing, and mailing correspondence for the patient. A re-sealable box for stationery and stamps provides convenient and safe storage.

2. Prepaid calling cards.

3. The offer of temporary housing or the use of a car to out-of-town relatives of the family to use when visiting.

4. A gift certificate to a favorite department store or leisure activity for when the patient gets well.

5. A journal for the patient/family to express thoughts and favorite memories.

6. Provide special music, tape player and batteries for the patient. Bring new/different music in periodically to provide variety.

7. A favorite book (large print books or audiotapes when appropriate). A series of books or a variety of books can be given over the course of a long illness.

8. Take the caregiver out for a meal other than hospital food. Arrange for people to provide meals at home for the family of the patient. By taking care of family members you are caring for the patient as well.

9. Enlarge the print of favorite scripture passages for the loved one to read easier. Add blank lines between the verses for those needing practice writing in rehab therapy.

10. A special, cheery bathrobe. This is especially nice for repeated visits to the hospital.

11. Make up a picnic basket and take it to the hospital for the patient and his or her family to enjoy.

12. Make arrangements for the patient to have animal visitors.

13. A special pillow for the hospital visit. Cover it with a colorful pillow-case. Don't forget to clearly mark the patient's name on the pillow.

14. Give the patient a "hospital makeover." Spend extra time for grooming needs not covered in basic patient care: hair cut, trimmed, or curled. Provide special powders, soaps or light perfume.

15. Blooming plants in a special container or basket will last longer than fresh flowers and the container can be used later for other things.

16. Give small knitting or needlework projects which the patient enjoys. Take the time to work on a project with them. Special memories can be made in hospital rooms as well as at home.

17. A scrapbook to keep cards and letters of encouragement. They can be read again in the future. It can also be a way to record special messages from medical staff who have worked with the patient over a long illness.

18. Bring in one of the patient's favorite games and play it with him or her. Time passes slowly in the hospital. You can help mark the days with special memories.

19. Make up a photo album with copies of the patient's favorite pictures. This gives the staff an opportunity to get to know their patient better and lets the patient show off his/her family.

20. A large and easy-to-read clock. Keeping track of time is difficult in the hospital.

21. A colorful calendar for long hospital visits helps the patient keep track of days and weeks.

22. A bouquet of colorful leaves in the fall, a handful of snow in the winter, a bunch of spring flowers, and sand from the seashore in the summer can all help to orient the long-term patient to the seasons that he or she is missing.

Ten Ways to Care for the Caregiver

Here are ten simple ways you can support someone who is caring for a loved one with a long-term illness

1. Instead of saying "call me if you need anything," ask to do specific helpful things like taking clothes to the dry cleaners, the dog to the vet, the car for a tune-up, doing food shopping or washing dishes. The caregiver may be too busy or too tired to stop and think of what you could do to help, let alone find the energy to ask for your help. Also, remember that asking for help may be difficult or even impossible for some people.

2. Life goes on despite a loved one's illness. Make arrangements for the caregiver to take time off at regular intervals to simply give them a break. Not only will you provide the opportunity for them to take care of themselves, you will also allow them to step out of the caregiving role and be in a "normal" relationship with their loved one. They will be better caregivers if their own needs are met. You can help them do this.

3. Offer to do errands with the caregiver or to spend time doing the caregiving with them. These are precious links into their world and an important way to provide companionship, support, and to validate their work. One of the best ways to love a person who is ill is to take care of their caregiver(s).

4. Tape religious services, concerts, baseball games, or favorite programs so that they can be enjoyed at a convenient time. Videotape special events that the caregiver or the sick individual cannot attend and watch it with him or her. Illness is an isolator. It cuts off the sick and their loved ones from daily routines. Sickness can consume so much energy that even the simplest event requires too much effort. Do what you can to help the family keep as many of their "normal" routines as possible.

5. Organize and maintain a phone chain that can inform individuals of the loved one's condition, prayer requests, and family needs. It can also be used to provide meals and volunteers. A phone chain will alleviate the repetition of medical details and requests for help and will more quickly pass on information to those who are waiting, concerned, and ready to help. Remember to be specific in asking for prayer requests and that requests for prayer can change by the day or even by the hour. If you can't visit in person, pray over the phone. Volunteer to be that special someone who is available even in the middle of the night to listen and to pray for immediate concerns.

6. Collect donations to help offset medical and other expenses not covered by insurance. Funds can also be donated to pay for a special item for the family

or to take care of something which was cut from the budget because of medical expenses.

7. Provide a favorite meal for the caregiver and his or her family. Be careful to include the loved one who is ill and any special needs he or she may have. Have a meal delivered from a favorite restaurant or give a gift certificate for a good take-out restaurant. Eat a meal with family members in the hospital cafeteria or provide the opportunity for the caregiver(s) to get away for a meal on a regular basis. Add movie or theater tickets to a gift certificate for a favorite restaurant. Do not forget to include arrangements for the care of the loved one who is ill.

8. Make it a point to remember holidays, family birthdays, and special occasions. The caregiver may not have time or energy to keep track of dates or make special holiday preparations. Illness in a family will change the way special events are celebrated. You can help the family keep important traditions alive and provide the opportunity for special memories that otherwise may be overlooked or lost.

9. Sincerely ask how the caregiver is doing when you ask about their loved one. Remember that gifts are as encouraging to caregivers as they are to the one who is sick. Be creative and remember the specific interests and tastes of the recipient. Prayer requests of the caregiver are just as important as those for the one who is ill. Remember to acknowledge the effort and sacrifice the caregiver continues to make in order to care for their loved one.

10. Continue to remember to express your love and concern for the family member who is ill and to support the caregiver(s) throughout the duration of the illness. As time passes and the immediate or first crisis is over there is often a drop in the expression of concern and involvement in the support of the family. Offer your help, and ask about the loved one who is ill and the welfare of those caring for him/her. Do not assume that if nothing is said that everything is all right. Silence may be a signal that things are wrong.

One of the best ways to love a caregiver is to love the one they are caring for.

Recommended Resources

John Bunyan, *The Pilgrim's Progress,* Uhrichsville, OH: Barbour & Co., 1995.

D. A. Carson, *How Long, O Lord?: Reflections on Suffering and Evil,* Grand Rapids: Baker Books, 1990.

Margaret Clarkson, *Destined For Glory,* New York: Walker & Co., 1987.

Barbara Deane, *Caring for Your Aging Parents: When Love Is Not Enough,* Colorado Springs: NavPress, 1989.

Sinclair B. Ferguson, *The Christian Life: A Doctrinal Introduction*, Carlisle, PA: Banner of Truth, 1989.

Paul Helm, *The Last Things: Death, Judgment, Heaven and Hell*, Carlisle, PA: Banner of Truth, 1989.

John Howie, *The Scots Worthies*, Carlisle, PA: Banner of Truth, 1995.

Peter Kreeft, *Love is Stronger than Death*, San Francisco: Ignatius Press, 1979.

Richard D. Land and Louis A. Moore, eds., *Life at Risk: The Crises in Medical Ethics*, Nashville, TN: Broadman & Holman, 1995.

John MacArthur, Jr., *The Glory of Heaven: The Truth About Heaven, Angels and Eternal Life*, Wheaton, IL: Crossway Books, 1996.

Franklin E. Payne, Jr., M.D., *Biblical Healing for Modern Medicine, Making Biblical Decisions, Biblical/Medical Ethics*, Escondido, CA: Hosanna House, 1989.

Joni Eareckson Tada, *Heaven Your Real Home*, Grand Rapids: Zondervan, 1995.

CHAPTER 20

Medical Questions Women Ask

Shirley V. Galucki, M.D.

Some years ago, one of my nieces, who has three brothers, was visiting her female cousins. All the girls were under the age of five. When it was time for their baths, the three girls went into the tub together. Suddenly my niece jumped out and ran to her mother. "Mom, I'm not the only one! They're just like me on the outside!"

Women are physically different from men! Early in life we discover certain obvious physical differences between ourselves and males, and other distinctives become apparent as we go through adolescence and beyond. Also, not all medical conditions affect women the same way as they affect men, and certain conditions affect only women. Some medical problems and life-stage changes are unique to the female body.

Understanding basic information about the female body and the physical changes women pass through during their lives will help you better understand women. This is especially true for those women whose main concerns may be physical or whose spiritual problems are aggravated by their physical condition. Therefore, basic medical knowledge will be helpful.

Scripture states that we are "fearfully and wonderfully made" (Psalm 139:14). The Bible does not say, "We were made to fear what our bodies may do!" When God crafted the female body, He did not make a mistake. We can rejoice that God has made us women! Appreciating how our bodies function normally and understanding diseases that specifically affect women will enhance our ability to effectively counsel women.

In this chapter I'm going to take you on a whirlwind tour of the phases of a woman's physical life. Then I'll address some of the specific medical issues you or the women you counsel may experience while passing through these phases. Pregnancy loss, premenstrual syndrome, infertility, perimenopause/menopause, sexual dysfunction, and postpartum depression are topics women regularly bring up in my office. I invite you to learn from the experiences of these women, which can help provide hope for the many who do not understand the workings of their body.

Basic Anatomy

Throughout our lives our bodies go through some wonderful changes. Therefore, it is helpful to start out with a basic understanding of our anatomy. The basic body parts that are unique in the woman are the breasts, vulva, vagina, uterus, ovaries and fallopian tubes. (A quality book of medical information such as the one mentioned at the end of this chapter can provide you with additional details about female anatomy and physiology which we do not have space for here.)

How am I put together?

The breasts are composed primarily of fatty tissue and glandular cells. Their development heralds the onset of puberty. Puberty is the transition a young woman's body goes through physically and biologically after which reproduction is possible. The vulva is the area surrounding the opening to the vagina and the opening to the urethra. The uterus is what holds a developing baby when a woman becomes pregnant. Each month during the reproductive years it is prepared for a fertilized egg. If a fertilized egg does not arrive in the uterus, the prepared lining sheds in what we call the menstrual period.

The vagina is the tubular opening between the vulva and the cervix. It is not an open area unless something is in it. Usually the side walls collapse against each other.

The cervix is the opening to the uterus. It is located at the top of the vagina. It has a small opening in the center through which the menstrual flow is passed to the vagina. It is also through this channel that the sperm must travel to get to the egg. When a pregnant woman is in labor, the opening in the cervix expands to allow the baby to leave the uterus.

Eggs are produced in the ovaries. When a girl is born, her ovaries have about two million eggs. This number decreases to 200,000-300,000 by the time she reaches puberty, and then down to around 25,000 by age 37 or 38. The menopause occurs when the ovaries are almost completely depleted of their eggs. The ovaries produce the hormones that regulate the menstrual cycle. In between the ovary and the uterus is the fallopian tube, which gathers the released egg each month and transports it to the uterus. If an egg is going to be fertilized, the fallopian tube is the place where this will occur. During a woman's life, many of her organs change in size, shape, and position in response to the hormone levels in her body.

What are estrogen and progesterone?

During a woman's development, the hormone that is most responsible for the changes that occur in her body is estrogen. A *hormone* is produced in one part of the body and affects other target organs. Estrogen is a hormone that mainly targets the breast, uterus, bone, and fat cells. The other major hormone in women is progesterone, which balances out the effects of estrogen. Estrogen aids in development of the breasts, causes the lining of the uterus to thicken each month in preparation for a possible pregnancy, maintains the vaginal and urethral tissue, and aids in cardiovascular health and bone maintenance.

What physical changes occur in a woman's life?

A woman's concentration of estrogen begins to increase at *puberty*. As the estrogen level increases, the reproductive organs mature. A visible change in the shape and contour of the body becomes evident as breasts develop and hips begin rounding out with increased fat stores. Next is the development of axillary and pubic hair. The onset of menses (periods) occurs later during puberty. Initially the ovary does not always produce an egg each month. Production of estrogen and progesterone may vary because of this, and so menstrual cycles may be irregular.

By the time a woman enters her twenties, her menstrual cycles tend to become more regular. In Figure 1 you will see the variations in hormones during

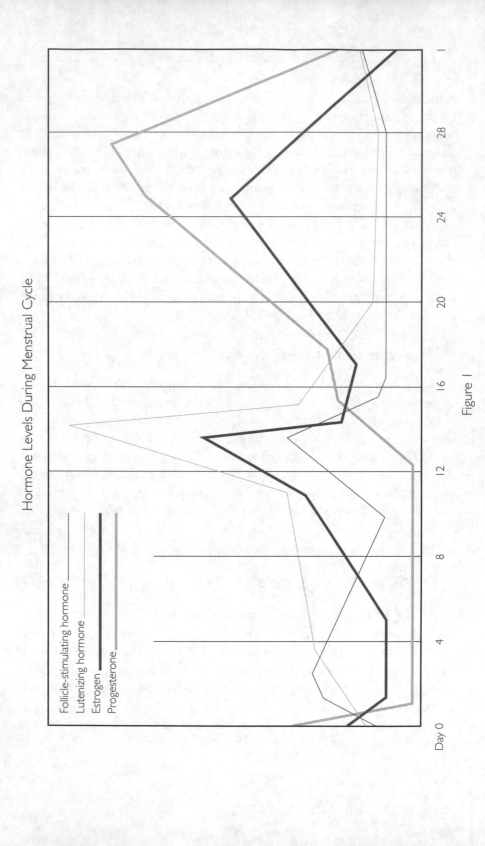

Hormone Levels During Menstrual Cycle

Follicle-stimulating hormone
Lutenizing hormone
Estrogen
Progesterone

Day 0   4   8   12   16   20   24   28   1

Figure 1

the menstrual cycle. The average menstrual cycle is 28 days, but the normal range is from 21-35 days. During the first half of the menstrual cycle estrogen increases and peaks with ovulation, at which time an egg is released. After ovulation, progesterone increases and if pregnancy does not occur during that cycle, it will drop and the next menstrual period will start.

A woman reaches peak bone mass in her mid-thirties. Then bone loss begins. In many women, premenstrual symptoms worsen during the late twenties and early thirties. This may be due to fluctuating hormone levels. The menstrual cycles are usually regular but some women may notice a shortening in the length of their cycle.

As women enter their forties, the perimenopausal period gets closer. *Perimenopause* is defined as the time period from one to seven years before the menopause all the way through one year after the menopause. It is characterized by a waxing and waning of the hormone levels. Many women will experience irregular menses during this time. The number of viable eggs in the ovary is rapidly decreasing, so estrogen and progesterone production may become more erratic. Because the hormone levels are fluctuating, many women develop hot flashes, vaginal dryness, and mood fluctuations. When ovulation does not occur, progesterone is not produced, and the menstrual period will not appear.

Generally, women go through menopause in their fifties. The last menstrual period occurs at about age 51, but the normal age range is anywhere from age 45 to 55. After menopause, the organs sensitive to estrogen (the breasts, the uterus, and the lining of the vaginal wall and urethra) decrease in size. Other changes also occur. Some of these are in the cardiovascular system, the skeletal system, and there are even changes in brain function.

After menopause, a woman's hormonal status does not change significantly, but the decreased estrogen levels continue to have an effect on the body. Gradually the risk of osteoporosis and cardiovascular disease rises. Vaginal atrophy and bladder changes also develop with the aging process.

Basic Issues

Let's look now at some issues that affect women at different stages of their lifetime and learn what we can about counseling women who are facing these issues.

Infertility

Karen and Jim had been married for three years. Since they were in their late twenties, they had hoped to start a family right after getting married. But after numerous different medical procedures and countless doctor visits, they were still childless. They knew God was in control and they were trusting Him. Personal privacy was important to them, so only a few of their closest friends knew the struggles and heartaches they were going through. One day someone bluntly asked them, "When are you two going to stop being so selfish, keeping all your money to yourself, and start a family?"

Infertility can be a difficult and lonely battle (for more on this, see chapter 10, "Counseling Women Considering Adoption"). Unfortunately, insensitive people, including Christians, can make the struggle harder. When counseling women with infertility, we must realize that for many this issue strikes at what has been their lifetime goal and what they had viewed would be the ultimate expression of being a woman. Seeking to ease the strain of unfulfilled dreams and yet not dash hope for the future realization of those dreams is the role of the supportive counselor.

Infertility can be the first major crisis with which a couple deals. Therefore, issues of communication and sensitivity to each other's needs are also being tested. Infertility evaluation and treatments often require that couples participate in sexual intercourse at exact times. This often puts a strain on a part of marriage that is supposed to be spontaneous and enjoyable.

How many couples suffer from infertility?

One out of every six couples is infertile at some point during their reproductive years. In recent years, this number has risen because of the many women who wait until their late thirties to bear children.

After what length of time would a couple (who are trying to get pregnant) be considered infertile?

It can take a normal couple a year of unprotected intercourse to get pregnant, so we do not label a couple as infertile until they have been trying for at least one year.

What are the causes of infertility?

Approximately 10-15 percent of infertility is caused by eggs not being released (this is called *anovulation*), 30-40 percent by abnormalities of sperm production, 30-40 percent as a result of pelvic disease, 10-15 percent by abnormalities of the sperm going through the cervical canal, and 5 percent to other causes. In a low percentage of patients, the cause cannot be found even after a thorough evaluation. Men and women each account for about 35 percent of infertility cases, and about 25 percent of the time it is a combination of both.

What does the evaluation of infertility involve?

The basic evaluation is tailored around the major causes of infertility. Both partners are involved in the work-up. The initial work-up includes a semen analysis, proof ovulation has occurred, evaluation to see how the sperm react to the cervical mucus, and checking to make sure that the path from the egg through the fallopian tube is not blocked. Depending on the results of the initial evaluation, further studies may need to be done.

A few of the studies done and an explanation of what they involve are listed here:

Semen analysis: Man produces a semen sample and it is evaluated for a variety of characteristics, including the number of viable sperm.

Basal Body Temperature Chart: Woman monitors her temperature daily with a special thermometer looking for variations that imply ovulation has occurred.

Post-coital test: Office evaluation around the time of ovulation several hours after a couple has had intercourse to see how the sperm react to the woman's cervical mucus.

Hysteroscopy: Test done in a radiology department where dye is injected into the cervix and then X-rays are taken to see if the dye flows out the fallopian tubes. Possible obstructions of the fallopian tubes are evaluated by this test.

Blood tests: Blood tests may be ordered by the health care provider depending on the couple's history.

Laparoscopy: Surgery where the pelvic organs are visualized through a small incision in the umbilicus (belly button).

What is involved in the treatment of infertility?

A wide range of options are available for treatment of infertility—from educating patients about the fertile time of the menstrual cycle to in vitro fertilization. Couples undergoing an infertility evaluation should be encouraged! Many times the application of a simple therapy will help them to conceive. Couples should be advised to ask questions of their health providers so that they understand exactly what is being recommended.

Great advancements have been made in treatments for infertility. However, each couple needs to decide how much they are willing to go through while attempting to have a child. Along with the great advancements, new areas of ethical concerns have emerged. In order to make wise decisions about infertility treatment, couples would be well-advised to consult the health care provider and a biblical counselor as well as devote time in prayer to seek guidance from God. The decisions related to infertility treatment are often difficult to make.

Premenstrual Syndrome

"Why am I feeling this way?" "I wonder if I could have PMS?" "I bet I have PMS." "I know I have PMS!" "I'm not myself today." "My period is due again this week. How am I going to cope this time?" Whenever I speak at women's gatherings, much interest in premenstrual syndrome (PMS) is evident, and many interesting comments are made about it.

The following two examples show the extremes of symptoms attributed to PMS. Maryann is a 22-year-old graduate student. She is engaged to be married to the man of her dreams; however, recently they began to have monthly fights. She would discuss returning his ring and write up lists of his faults. During these altercations, nothing he said seemed to make sense to her. Shortly afterward, Maryann would apologize and things would go more smoothly. After several episodes, Jim, her fiancee, made an observation. The arguments were always exactly one month apart. He wondered about any correlation between their occurrence and her menstrual cycle. Maryann's exam schedule in grad school was on a one-month cycle, and that cycle corresponded exactly with her menstrual cycle. The combination of previously mild premenstrual awareness along with the stress of exams made for one grouchy woman! This awareness, along with the end of the semester and the exam schedule, led to an easy solution to the conflict.

Greta is a 32-year-old mother of three. She made her own diagnosis of PMS initially when she began to notice wide swings in her moods. She charted daily how she felt and noted that she always had her symptoms after ovulation. They stopped when her menstrual period began. She stated that premenstrually she had no emotional control, felt like another person, was depressed, cried frequently because she felt so miserable, and ill-treated those around her.

When Greta was pregnant with her third child, her symptoms vanished. She continued to do well while she nursed her new daughter, but after she stopped nursing, her periods returned and so did her symptoms. Greta read all she could about PMS. She exercised regularly, watched her diet, and took several recommended vitamins. She consulted several health professionals who pre-scribed tranquilizers and birth-control pills, yet nothing seemed to help.

Then Greta was started on a different medication and referred for counsel-ing. She was very encouraged at her follow-up visit. She reported that she still had symptoms during the premenstrual period, but since she had started the new medication and the counseling, her symptoms were not as much of a problem. Greta felt her life had become more normal again.

What is PMS?

PMS is comprised of behavioral and physical symptoms that occur in the sec-ond half of the menstrual cycle and vanish after the menstrual period begins. This involves changes that take place between the time that the ovary releases an egg to the time the menstrual period starts.

How many women have these symptoms?

Estimates range from 5-95 percent of women! This huge variation obviously reflects differences in criteria for making the diagnosis. Most will agree that 2-3 percent of women are affected severely. This brings up an important distinc-tion: Many women are only mildly affected by some of the symptoms we are going to discuss. These mild changes are the body's natural response to hor-monal fluctuations. Some health providers refer to these symptoms as *premen-strual awareness.*

These variations in how a woman feels can be likened to the weather. Many of us would love to always have warm sunny days, but continuous warm sunny weather would leave us with a dry desert. Just as we adjust to changes in the weather by making modifications in our clothing or plans, when we are af-fected by premenstrual symptoms, we may have to learn to adapt so we can continue being productive.

Women should be careful not to use PMS as an excuse for inappropriate be-havior. We build homes and heat them so that changes in the weather do not make as much of an impact on our lives. In the same way, many women can learn ways to control and minimize their premenstrual symptoms.

Now, for some women, the premenstrual time is more like a blizzard. These women fall into the category of *premenstrual syndrome* rather than premen-strual awareness. They may need to declare "states of emergency" and call in extra help!

What are the symptoms attributed to PMS?

Amazingly, there are over 150 symptoms that people attribute to PMS! Some of the most common are depression, irritability, headache, difficulty concentrating, anxiety, bloating, tension, breast tenderness, food cravings, weight gain, and a sense of being overwhelmed emotionally.

What causes PMS?

Many theories have been espoused for the cause of PMS, but the bottom line is we really do not understand exactly what causes it. Hormone-level measurements have not consistently shown any difference between women with and without PMS.

How can you tell if a woman has PMS?

If a woman has symptoms consistent with PMS, you definitely need to advise her to see her physician, who will be able to make a definite diagnosis. A woman should chart her symptoms for three months to document whether there is any kind of pattern. This will enable the physician to make a correct diagnosis (*see* Figure 2).

You can suspect PMS if her symptoms occur during all three cycles, are present premenstrually but do not start before ovulation, and are absent for a minimum of seven days each cycle.

It is important to distinguish PMS from depression. Women with depression may have their symptoms exacerbated premenstrually, but their symptoms are present all month long.

If a woman does not have PMS, she may still have some premenstrual awareness that necessitates wise planning so she can function more effectively in her daily life.

How can I help others manage PMS or at least premenstrual awareness?

Most treatments for PMS require work. It is like shoveling snow after a snowstorm. Those who get out and shovel can go to work or take their children to school; those who don't make the effort keep themselves and their family hostage.

The first step is education. Women who experience mild agitation, anxiety, and irritation can often control their symptoms simply by keeping track of their cycles, understanding the changes in their bodies, and asking God to help them bridle their tongues during that part of the month. Self-control through

Premenstrual Symptoms Calendar

Cycle Day	1	2	3	4	5	6	7	8	9	10	11	12	13	14	15	16	17	18	19	20	21	22	23	24	25	26	27	28	29	30
Menses																														
Calendar Day																														

Symptom

Cycle Day 1 = first day of menstrual period.

For horizontal column "Menses," put a ✔ on days of menstrual flow.

Pick several of your most prominent symptoms.

Write each one in the left-hand spaces under "Symptom."

Daily, chart the presence or absence of these symptoms.

Leave blank if no symptom

1 = mild but tolerable

2 = moderate but annoying

3 = intolerable and severe

Figure 2

the power of the Holy Spirit is real; a woman doesn't have to be controlled by her symptoms.

Second, several studies have documented that women who exercise regularly experience less premenstrual anxiety than non-athletic women. Exercise decreases stress, appetite, and body fat, and increases energy levels, improves weight maintenance, and improves overall physical well-being. Some women may groan when you suggest that they exercise, but when we know that exercise can make a difference, we must encourage women to start up an exercise routine!

Third, women who are instructed in how to control their response to stress experience a decrease in their PMS symptoms. Remember Maryann? Her pre-menstrual symptoms affected her only when she was under a lot of stress. Many women note that they do not experience the usual symptoms when they are on vacation. You can encourage women not to schedule extra responsibilities during that time of the month. Then their families do not suffer from the extra stress, nor do they. You can teach your counselee how to depend on God in the midst of life's pressures (*see* Philippians 4:4-9; 1 Peter 5:7)

Advertisements for PMS vitamins can be seen in any health food store. Others promote PMS diets. Studies have not confirmed that women truly benefit from these regimens, but many individual women who suffer from specific symptoms note a response.

The best PMS prevention diets emphasize fresh food, small regular meals, and avoidance of simple carbohydrates (sweets). Caffeine can increase agitation, tension, sleeplessness, and according to some, increase breast tenderness. Drinking plenty of water helps to rid the body of extra fluid and acts as a natural diuretic.

For the patient with severe symptoms, there are several medical treatments available. There are some medications such as serotonin-uptake inhibitors (these are a specific type of antidepressant—please note that most antidepressants are *not* helpful with PMS), which have been shown to help control severe PMS symptoms. Only after women have explored all the non-medication alternatives should they consult with their physician about medications. [*Editors' note:* Among biblical counselors there is not unanimity on the use of antidepressant medication to treat such things as premenstrual syndrome and postpartum depression. Some biblical counselors see the short-term use of anti-depressant medications to relieve severe symptoms as compassionate and helpful. Thus relieved, the counselee is better able to participate in the counseling process. Other biblical counselors see the use of these medications as unproved, expedient, and detrimental to the spiritual progress of the counselee. They consider the use of antidepressant medication for these conditions as a yielding to pragmatism.]

There is hope! With the varied approaches available now, you can assure women that they can—with God's help—learn to control their symptoms so they are not controlled by PMS.

Pregnancy Loss (Miscarriage)

Mary is a 33-year-old Christian schoolteacher. Her husband is also involved full time in Christian ministry. They have a four-year-old son, who was conceived after extensive infertility evaluation and treatment. Two years after his birth they saw infertility specialists again and after two years conceived their second child.

Mary's first pregnancy had been uneventful and the second one was going just as well. She had looked forward to her 18-week checkup, during which the doctor said she would hear the baby's heartbeat. However, unlike her last visit, the doctor heard no heartbeat. An ultrasound was ordered to determine if all was well. It wasn't; the baby had died.

For Mary and her husband, gnawing questions surfaced. Why did this happen? Did we do something to cause our baby to die? Would this happen again? How do we tell our four year old?

The loss of a child during pregnancy is devastating to a couple. Most couples never consider that it could happen to them. They are wrapped up in the wonder of pregnancy and do not realize that one of every five to six pregnancies ends in miscarriage. A stillborn baby is rare, occurring at a rate of eight babies per 1,000 deliveries, but a stillbirth is an even more traumatic event because the mother has been bonding with her baby for nine months.

Rebecca and Jim had been married for about two years. Jim was going to seminary part time and working as a youth minister. Life was very busy. Rebecca was always optimistic and had an enthusiasm for serving the Lord that was contagious. Both eagerly awaited having children and were thrilled when Rebecca found out she was pregnant.

On a youth retreat during her eleventh week of pregnancy, Rebecca began spotting and subsequently miscarried. The loss was very difficult, but Rebecca was confident God was in control. Although she was saddened, she quickly went back to her optimistic self, certain that God had allowed this to happen to them so they could more effectively minister to other couples in the same situation.

After a few months, Rebecca again conceived. She and Jim were much more aware that this pregnancy could end in miscarriage, but everything went well up to 29 weeks. At that time she visited her doctor for a routine checkup. There was no heartbeat. An ultrasound done in the office quickly confirmed her worst fear. The lifeless body of a beautiful baby girl was delivered the next day. The grieving couple knew God had His purpose, but this time Rebecca was having a very difficult time returning to her cheerful self. Why did this happen so far into the pregnancy? Will we ever have a child? Why is it taking so long to feel normal again? Am I not trusting God enough?

What causes miscarriages?

The two major groups of causes of miscarriages are fetal and environmental. *Fetal* causes are genetic reasons that the pregnancy could not continue. Most commonly they involve chromosomal abnormalities, but they can also be caused by other genetic problems that are not evident in the chromosomes. Genetic abnormalities account for 50-60 percent of all miscarriages.

Environmental causes include uterine, hormonal, and immunologic abnormalities and infections. Uterine causes can be secondary to structural abnormalities in the uterus or cervix. In some women, the cervix cannot support a pregnancy. Once an incompetent cervix is identified it can be corrected surgically during the next pregnancy so that the subsequent baby is not lost. Hormonal changes can involve the thyroid hormones or the amount of progesterone the body produces during the second half of the menstrual cycle. Both of these areas can be evaluated by specific tests and corrected. Immunologic abnormalities are still very much under study and may provide answers for couples who previously did not have explanations for their miscarriages. Infections are suspected to account for some pregnancy losses, but definite proof is lacking.

When do miscarriages occur and how often do they happen?

Eighty percent of miscarriages occur during the first 12 weeks after the last menstrual period. About 15 percent of all pregnancies between 4 and 20 weeks of gestation will have a known miscarriage.[1] The incidence increases with age. In women over the age of 40, the risk is around 25 percent. The actual rate of pregnancy loss is greater than this because many losses occur before women realize that they are pregnant.

My counselee thinks that she caused her miscarriage when she took a hard fall the day before. Could that be true?

Most babies die a couple weeks before the miscarriage. The majority of experts agree that work, physical exercise, and sexual intercourse do not increase the risk of miscarriage. We do know that alcohol consumption and smoking can increase the risk of miscarriage, as can using some illegal drugs like cocaine.

Since most miscarriages are due to genetic abnormalities, can I encourage the woman I am counseling by telling her it was "probably for the best"?

While that could be true, you do not need to tell a woman that it was a good thing she miscarried when she is hurting over the loss of her hopes for a child. Although you have good intentions, such statements often come across as calloused and unfeeling. Another statement you'll want to avoid is, "You are young; you still have time to try for another child." Yet even if other children do come later, the couple is dealing *now* with the loss of a child. One patient who conceived after trying for several years and then miscarried told how hurtful it was when a friend tried to console her by telling her to "try again."

What causes stillbirths?

Around 25 percent of stillbirths have no known cause. Thirty percent are secondary to asphyxia (lack of oxygen getting to the baby, for various reasons). Twenty-five percent of stillbirths are due to complications that the mother has, such as high blood pressure, preeclampsia (a toxic condition developing in late pregnancy), or separation of the placenta from the uterus (abruption). Twenty percent are due to congenital abnormalities of the infant, and 5 percent are caused by infection.[2] Statistics like these vary from source to source, but at least these figures give some idea of the major reasons for stillbirth.

Postpartum Depression

The birth of a child is met with strong emotions. As Christians, we often quote the verse that says, "Children are a gift of the LORD" (Psalm 127:3). Because a child's birth is usually accompanied by joy, some people have a hard time understanding why someone would become depressed after the birth of a child—including the mother who just had the child and doesn't understand why she feels depressed.

Sandy is 29 years old and has just had her fourth child. Her husband is a busy professional and, although supportive, he is very busy with his work. After her other children were born, Sandy had bounced right back to normal health. But this pregnancy was different. Due to complications, Sandy's baby had to be delivered by cesarean section, and her recovery was not progressing as quickly as before.

Sandy is delighted with this new addition to her family, but she is overwhelmed, sore, and tired, for she must also pay attention to three other young children. In addition, Sandy is having difficulty sleeping even when the baby sleeps. Oftentimes Sandy wakes up crying for seemingly no reason, and she finds herself snapping at her children for trivial things. She is beginning to find it hard to enjoy life, and finds it difficult to sit and hold the baby except during feedings.

During her postpartum exam, Sandy tells her physician that everything is fine and that she is adjusting well. Her husband, however, called the day before, explained the situation, and asked the physician for help. After some additional, direct questions, Sandy breaks down and explains the difficult time she's having. The physician reassures her that help is available and that her problem doesn't suggest that she is an awful mother. A month later, after some counseling and with some extra support, Sandy says she is still tired (aren't all mothers of four!), but now she is enjoying her family and she no longer feels depressed.

Is postpartum depression the same as postpartum blues?

No. Postpartum blues is very common and usually occurs during the first week to ten days after the mother gives birth. Up to 70 percent of women experience postpartum blues to one degree or another. The symptoms can include weepiness, anxiety, ambivalent feelings about the baby, and confusion. These symptoms usually diminish on their own by the tenth day, but occasionally there can be brief relapses. Often it's sufficient to educate and encourage a counselee about the blues, for these feelings usually go away quickly. Encouraging women not to set high expectations for all they will accomplish in the immediate postpartum period and setting up good support services will help minimize the severity of the postpartum blues.

What is different about postpartum depression?

In postpartum depression, the symptoms are more severe and prolonged. Estimates vary on the incidence of postpartum depression, but approximately 10 to 15 percent of women experience depression during the postpartum period.

The symptoms are the same as those for the non-postpartum woman. Frequently it is hard to differentiate postpartum depression from the blues because many new mothers experience fatigue and weight loss.

Who gets postpartum depression?

Postpartum depression has no social, racial, or chronological boundaries. Studies have shown that if a woman lacks support and love from her husband (or boyfriend), or does not want to have the baby, she is at much greater risk for postpartum depression. Women with the highest risk for postpartum depression are those who had it after a prior pregnancy and those who have experienced bouts of depression that aren't associated with pregnancy. There are rare instances of postpartum depression in women with no predisposing signs, but most affected woman have either a history of depressive episodes or have life factors other than the pregnancy that would predispose them to depression.

How are these women treated?

The mainstays for the woman with postpartum depression are supportive care and reassurance. There is a range of severity, and those severely affected will benefit from antidepressants for six to twelve months while they are undergoing counseling. (*See* editors' note on page 530 of this chapter.) While on antidepressants it is generally recommended that breastfeeding be stopped because not enough is known about the impact these medications can have on babies.

What is the role of the counselor?

As I mentioned, reassurance and support are of prime importance. Equally valuable is enlisting the family's support. A mother's endeavor to meet the many demands of a newborn along with the care of her family can add to the frustration and sense of hopelessness that she feels. Those at home also need to encourage her and mobilize local support services that can help the entire family during this stressful time.

If you are counseling a woman who had severe depression after her last child, encourage her to discuss this with her physician during her next pregnancy. In women at very high risk, preventative medications can be initiated immediately postpartum. Biblical counseling during the woman's pregnancy can help her better prepare for the postpartum period. Enlisting support ahead of time from the woman's church will also be helpful.

What if a woman threatens suicide or seems to be having delusions postpartum?

Postpartum suicide attempts and/or delusions require the immediate help of the woman's physician. The physician can determine what sort of specialized help the woman's condition requires. This serious condition is rare, occurring at a frequency of 1-2.4 women per 1,000 deliveries. The duration is thought to be approximately two to three months.

Perimenopause/Menopause

As the baby boomer women approach menopause, more and more attention is being paid to the menopausal and perimenopausal years. Women are asking, "What is happening to my body?" "Do I have to live with these hot flashes?" "Am I going to hunch over like my mother did?" "Can I still keep up my level of activity?" And, "What is the deal with estrogen?"

Many advances in the medical field are helping to provide answers to the women who are asking questions, and many studies are currently going on to help answer the still unanswerable questions.

As women view menopause, they frequently are concerned because of the aging it represents. As we approach inevitable aging changes a scriptural perspective is invaluable. (*See* chapter 18, "Counseling Women in the Afternoon of Life," for further discussion of these issues.) Our goal in dealing with menopause is not to reinforce the worldview that idolizes youth, but rather to deal with the aging changes in our bodies in a way that glorifies God. Let's consider another case study as we look at practical counsel that can be offered to a menopausal woman.

Jenny is a 43-year-old pastor's wife with four children. Life is very busy for her. She is involved in her husband's work, her children's school, and her own career. Jenny loves her full life with its many demands. However, she is not sleeping well. At first, she can't tell why, but then she realizes that she is waking up during the night feeling hot. Her moods are fluctuating, and she is no longer her usual self. She talks with the Lord about her lack of patience and irritability, but despite her close walk with God, she finds herself struggling. Her menstrual periods have not been regular in the past, but now she has not had a menstrual period for almost a year. Her husband suggests that she see a doctor, and she knows it is time to get a professional evaluation.

Her physician does a complete exam along with a blood checkup and quickly confirms that Jenny is menopausal. Yes, it is early, but she has met all the criteria. Her physician discusses some lifestyle changes that will help her minimize some of the negative symptoms of menopause. After also discussing the risks and benefits of hormone replacement therapy, Jenny begins the treatment. Within a few weeks the hot flashes are gone, she is sleeping much better, and she feels like her old self again.

Menopause represents the end of a woman's menstrual periods. Usually it is diagnosed in the absence of menstrual periods for 12 consecutive months. As I stated earlier, the average age for menopause is 51 (in the United States), and most women usually become menopausal between ages 45 and 55, but menopause can occur as early as 30 or as late as 60. The majority of women pass through menopause uneventfully. However, it is helpful to understand what is happening to a woman's body during menopause because many of the symptoms can be effectively treated.

Above all, keep in mind that menopause is not a disease. It is a normal physiologic change. As we learn about menopause we will understand the changes that occur in women's bodies after menopause, and also some ways to help decrease the negative effects of menopause.

What are the symptoms associated with menopause?

A wide variety of symptoms are associated with menopause. Some of the most common are:

hot flashes	decreased sexual desire
irritability	crying spells
lethargy/fatigue	anxiety
depression	loss of urinary control
sleep disturbance	joint pain/backaches
vaginal dryness	headaches
weight gain	forgetfulness

What should I do if I think I might be going through menopause?

As in any time of transition, change often makes us remember things that we should be doing anyway. The best way to be prepared for menopause is to first be *educated* about the subject. Knowing what to expect can relieve a lot of excess stress which a woman could unnecessarily put on herself if she began noticing many of these symptoms but didn't know what to do.

Exercise can help minimize many of the symptoms and also decrease some of the negative responses a woman's body has to the decrease of estrogen in her system. Exercise helps to improve the body's well-being so it is more resistant to stress in relation to menopausal symptoms. Increased risks of osteoporosis and heart disease have frequently been linked with menopause; regular exercise (weight-bearing for osteoporosis) helps to decrease the risks of both of these concerns. Regular weight-bearing exercise and weight training in the postmenopausal woman, when accompanied by adequate calcium intake, can decrease the amount of bone loss a woman has after menopause. Exercise, such as walking, both increases the strength of the heart and helps to improve the balance of the types of cholesterol in the body.

Eating a low-fat, low-cholesterol diet is something that many women are probably tired of hearing about. Yet a healthy diet is another way a woman can help ease her transition through menopause. As a woman ages, her risk for heart disease continues to rise. Although a woman's risk of heart disease is lower than a man's, both men and women are more susceptible to heart disease as they age. Every 1 percent that a person lowers his or her cholesterol is associated with a 2-3 percent decrease in the risk of heart disease.

Caffeine intake not only can trigger hot flashes, but there is also evidence that caffeine helps to remove calcium from bones. Hot or spicy foods, hot drinks, and alcohol can also trigger hot flashes.

A diet rich in calcium is also necessary at the menopause because with decreased estrogen levels, women begin to lose bone matter at a more rapid rate. It is recommended that the perimenopausal woman consume 1000-1200 milligrams of calcium per day, and the menopausal woman consume 1500 milligrams of calcium per day.

If a woman is over 40, she should get *annual exams* by her health care provider. As a woman enters the menopausal years, a health care provider can help explain the normal and abnormal changes she can expect during this time period. Preventative screenings (mammogram, pap smear) can also be done at the annual visit. During the visit, a woman can talk about her symptoms, and her provider can discuss non-medical and medical approaches to menopause.

Lastly, a woman entering menopause does not need to panic. Women have been going through menopause for a long time. We are blessed to live in a time when more and more is being understood about menopause, and women are encouraged to discuss with doctors or health care providers the symptoms they're experiencing. Menopause is no longer a topic about which to be embarrassed.

What about hormone replacement?

After menopause the body's production of estrogen greatly decreases, with the greatest decreases in the few years immediately after menopause. The body's production of progesterone and testosterone also decreases.

There are three main reasons women consider hormone replacement therapy (HRT): relief of symptoms associated with menopause (hot flashes, vaginal dryness, mood fluctuations), prevention of osteoporosis, and prevention of cardiac disease.

Women should discuss their individual risks and benefits of HRT with their gynecologist. Statistics concerning the risks and benefits of HRT are continually being modified as new studies are completed. The decision for or against therapy is not an easy one. Those who opt for HRT should not be surprised if their therapy is modified over the years as more information becomes available.

Generally, women who have a uterus are placed on both estrogen and progesterone. There are several different regimens available, which can be modified if the patient has vaginal bleeding. Estrogen alone does increase the risk of uterine cancer, but when progesterone is added the risk is removed. Women without a uterus are usually placed on estrogen alone. Long-term therapy is beneficial for prevention of osteoporosis and cardiovascular disease as well as relief of symptoms such as vaginal dryness and hot flashes. Some women will choose to use HRT for a short time (one to two years) to help them with their hot flashes. Keep in mind that all medications, including HRT, have the potential to produce unwanted side effects. A woman considering HRT will need to decide whether the benefits outweigh the risks and side effects.

As a counselor, why would I be seeing a woman going through menopause?

The most common reasons a perimenopausal woman might seek counsel would be for depression or to deal with the multiple life stresses faced by her age group. Many perimenopausal women are dealing with the needs of their own children (often teens and young adults) and also beginning to have to deal with the needs of their aging parents. These situations increase a woman's susceptibility to the effects of stress.

Although some studies indicate that menopause itself does not *cause* depression, we know that many of the symptoms of menopause can *contribute* to depression. Some evidence indicates that estrogen may be a protective factor for depression. In addition, if a woman is having hot flashes at night and waking up two to four times a night, she is not getting adequate rest. Many women, after waking, have a difficult time getting back to sleep. The next day they have to cope with their usual stresses, but they have not had the benefit of a good night's sleep. In this case, hot flashes not only account for the symptoms of insomnia, but also daytime irritability and fatigue!

Encouraging a menopausal woman to be evaluated by her gynecologist will be helpful in several ways. First, she can be evaluated to make sure that she is making the transition normally. Some abnormalities in bleeding patterns are actually warning signs of more serious conditions, and her gynecologist can evaluate this with her. Second, individual concerns about menopause can be addressed. And finally, her provider can discuss the woman's individual benefits and risks for HRT. HRT will not treat the other stresses she has in her life, but it may help by treating some of her symptoms so that she has more energy to deal with the other issues.

Sexual Dysfunction

God gives to married couples the wonderful gift of the sexual relationship. It reflects the very essence of marriage and the oneness for which we were created. Difficulty in the sexual relationship, then, often puts a great strain on the marriage. As you counsel women with sexual difficulties, the marriage relationship should be discussed, but it is important to realize that sexual difficulties are not always associated with unhappy marriages.

Sexual dysfunction can have a number of causes. However, due to the limits of space, we will deal only with causes related to pain during intercourse (dysparunia). Pain can be secondary to any of the following: vaginal infections, vulvovestibulitis, low estrogen levels, abnormalities in the pelvis (endometriosis, pelvic infections, ovarian cysts, scar tissue), and vaginismus.

When a woman has a vaginal infection, the infection irritates the vagina and tenderness can result. The infection itself also can decrease the amount of lubrication produced during intercourse, causing intercourse to be painful. Vaginal infections can be diagnosed by a physician and are usually treated successfully with medications.

Vulvovestibulitis is an inflammation around the opening of the vagina. It can cause external pain as a couple is trying to have intercourse. Many times this resolves spontaneously. If necessary, treatments are available. Women can discuss these with their physicians.

Deep pain is often caused by abnormalities deeper in the pelvis. Endometriosis is a condition in which cells like those lining the inside of the uterus are found along the lining of the abdominal wall, or on the ovaries, uterus, or fallopian tubes. Some women with endometriosis do not experience any pain, others have pelvic pain all month long or just around the time of their menstrual period, and still others experience pain only during intercourse.

Depending on the situation, endometriosis is sometimes treated with medications, and other times with surgery. Ovarian cysts, pelvic infections, and scar tissue can also be diagnosed by pelvic exam, further tests or surgery.

As we learned earlier, a woman's body produces less estrogen as she ages. Thus there may be less lubrication in the vagina, which usually contributes to pain during intercouse. Pregnancy, breast-feeding, and post menopause are all times in a woman's life when her estrogen level is low. For the pregnant or breast-feeding woman, the addition of water soluble lubricants can help ease some of the discomfort. For the postpartum patient who is breast-feeding, other factors may cause pain—soreness from the delivery and from vaginal tears or from an incision made to widen the vaginal opening during birth (episeotomy).

The woman who has been postmenopausal for several years not only has decreased lubrication because of low estrogen levels, but her vaginal walls also begins to shrink (atrophy) and get thinner. This also makes intercourse more painful. Lubricants can help ease the discomfort as can regular intercourse. In addition, her physician may prescribe estrogen. This will enhance lubrication and, over time, help thicken the vaginal walls.

Vaginismus is marked by involuntary spasms of the perineal muscles (muscles around the vagina), which causes pain with or prevents intercourse. When counseling a couple, it is important to point out that these are involuntary spasms. They may result from a physical cause (lack of estrogen, vaginal infection), or as a result of shame, guilt, conflict, fear of children, or a history of abuse. That is, an emotional problem may be the cause of the physical symptom.

When the cause is not physical, it is important to investigate what past or present factors may have precipitated these spasms. The marriage relationship should also be considered. Even if the cause of the problem is not difficulty in the marriage itself, difficulties in the sexual relationship can put strain on the marriage relationship.

It is encouraging to know that vaginismus is highly reversible. Even if the root emotional cause is not dealt with, education and certain exercises that a trained professional can teach a patient will usually allow a couple to resume a very satisfying sexual relationship.

Counseling couples with sexual problems can be difficult. But if the cause is pain with intercourse, proper evaluation and treatment can usually lead to full resolution of the problem, or at least to a decrease in the amount of pain experienced by the woman.

Making Wise Medical Decisions

We who are counselors will frequently be faced with women who will ask questions about medical care or guidance in decisions they are making about medical care. They'll ask questions like those that we've examined in this chapter, or they may have other questions related to physical needs that are influencing their spiritual growth.

Below are some principles that you can use as guidelines for resolving medical questions.

1. *Pray for wisdom.* The God who formed us in the inward parts has *promised* to grant us wisdom when we ask (*see* James 1:5).

2. *Look to Scripture.* All medical writings fall short when compared with the knowledge we can gain from God's Word. Treatments change. Drugs go in and out of vogue. But God's Word never changes. Some medical issues may become more clear when viewed in the light of the knowledge God has given us in His Word. For example, the woman who is pregnant and having financial problems may go to her physician and be told that abortion is a medically safe procedure. If we are given the privilege to counsel this woman, we do not have to spend time reviewing medical journals to see if abortion is indeed safe. Rather, we can gently guide her to solid scriptural principles to assist her in the right decision.

God's precious Word also gives comfort to the believer facing medical problems or decisions that are not as clear in Scripture. God promises He will not give us more than we can handle, and He is an ever-present comfort in our afflictions.

3. *Seek medical advice.* If a woman asks questions or has problems that may be related to her physical health, you'll want to encourage her to see a physician or health provider. Any concerns a woman has about a decision or treatment plan should be discussed. Sometimes women forget some of their questions when they arrive at the doctor's office; you may want to suggest that your counselee write her questions ahead of time or bring a family member who understands the situation to the appointment. Also, the first treatment option presented by the physician is not always the only available one, so do encourage women to ask if there are any other options.

4. *Get a second opinion,* if necessary. Getting a second opinion does not mean you don't trust the first opinion. Legitimate differences of opinion will exist in the medical community; this does not necessarily mean that one person is right and the other is wrong. A second opinion (or option) may be better for the individual you are counseling, or the second opinion may help clarify the need to follow through on the first opinion.

5. *Read and learn.* The woman who is actively learning about her medical issues can participate in her own health care. The typical visit with a physician can in no way cover all the issues about any of the topics we have covered. Many women find great encouragement and help in the lay literature. Ask your health providers if they have any suggested reading on the topic of concern. Some offices even have libraries with books available for loan.

Glorifying God with Our Health

This chapter has been designed to touch on some of the medical issues a woman faces. Of course, there are many issues we haven't covered. In addition, the medical community is rapidly changing and becoming more complex. As a counselor you can derive comfort from the fact that even physicians have a difficult time keeping up with all the changes in medicine (maybe that is not so comforting!).

Ultimately, as we consider the influence that our physical health has on our life, we need to keep focused and remember that the body in which we dwell is not our end goal. Rather, our purpose is summarized by the old catechism reply that says, "Man's chief end is to glorify God and to enjoy Him forever!" God is powerful and not limited by the frailties we see in our bodies. It is common for us to limit God and think that He cannot help us handle a particular problem.

Many women never have an unusual symptom related to their femaleness, and that is wonderful. However, as members of the body of Christ and as counselors, it is helpful to learn about the physical problems women can face so that we are equipped to encourage them and help direct them to receive proper assistance.

Some women may rationalize physical problems by saying, "This is just the way it is," or "Before my period I'm short-tempered, and my husband and family will just have to deal with it," or "I will never be able to serve in ministry after losing my stillborn baby," or "God will never forgive me for my formerly promiscuous life." Sadly, these women have a small god. Scripture gives us solid guidelines we can turn to, such as: be kind one to another (Ephesians 4:32— note it does not say, "except if you are experiencing PMS"!); let your speech be always with grace seasoned with salt (Colossians 3:16—no exception is made for women who are perimenopausal); if we confess our sins God is faithful and just to forgive us (1 John 1:9—no sin is too big for God to forgive). Indeed, God is the God of all comfort!

Praise God we do not have to rely on ourselves (*see* 2 Corinthians 1). God promises to work with and through us. Faith does require action, and with some medical problems there may be steps a woman needs to take to find a solution. But she can rejoice in knowing that our God promises to take those steps with her!

Recommended Resource

Joe S. McIlhaney, Jr., *1250 Health Care Questions Women Ask,* Grand Rapids: Baker Books, 1992.

Chapter 1—The Philosophy of Biblical Counseling

1. A. W. Tozer, *The Root of the Righteous* (Camp Hill, PA: Christian Publications, 1955), p. 38.
2. *The Concise Oxford Dictionary of Current English* Sixth Edition (Oxford: University Press, 1976).
3. Matthew 7:3-5.
4. Jay E. Adams, *The Christian Counselor's Commentary—I Timothy, II Timothy, Titus* (Hackettstown, SC: Timeless Texts, 1994) p. 78.
5. First Corinthians 10:1-13 states that the events recorded in the Old Testament are specifically for our example. We are to learn what pleases God (verse 5). We are not to crave evil things (verse 6), worship idols (verse 7), act immorally (verse 8), try the Lord (verse 9), nor grumble (verse 10). Verse 11 makes this point clear: "These things happened to them as an example, and they were written for our instruction."
6. John MacArthur, Jr., *Our Sufficiency in Christ* (Dallas: Word Publishing, 1991), p. 64.
7. Ed Bulkley, *Why Christians Can't Trust Psychology* (Eugene, OR: Harvest House Publishers, 1993), pp. 50-51.
8. Hilton Terrell, as cited in Mark Horne, "The Battle for the Babble," *World Magazine*, July 3, 1993, p. 11.
9. Richard Ganz, *Psychobabble: The Failure of Modern Psychology and the Biblical Alternative*, (Wheaton, IL: Crossway Books, 1993), p. 47.
10. Paul Gray, "The Assault on Freud," *Time*, November 29, 1993, pp. 46-51.
11. Ibid., p. 49.
12. Ibid., p. 51.
13. Ibid., p. 51.
14. Thomas Szasz, *Insanity: The Idea and Its Consequences* (New York, NY: John Wiley & Sons, 1987), p. 5.
15. Ganz, *Psychobabble*, p. 30.
16. Raymond J. Corsini, *Current Psychotherapies*, 3rd ed. (Itasca: F.E. Peacock Publishers, Inc. 1984), preface.
17. Norman L. Geisler and Paul D. Feinberg, *Introduction to Philosophy: A Christian Perspective* (Grand Rapids, MI: Baker Book House, 1980), p. 13.

18. Charles Sykes, *A Nation of Victims: The Decay of the American Character* (New York, NY: St. Martin's Press, 1992), p. 50.

19. Ganz, *Psychobabble*, p. 39.

20. MacArthur, *Our Sufficiency in Christ*, p. 151.

21. Mark Horne, "The Battle for the Babble," p. 11.

22. You can use the following checklist as a guide when attempting to choose a counselor or discern whether a counseling book is biblical:

  • Does the author/counselor have sound theological training or only secular training?

  • Does the author/counselor have an expressed view of Scripture? Does he or she believe that it is sufficient, inerrant, and relevant?

  • How does the author/counselor use Scripture? Does he or she pull verses out of the context of the passage to prove a point or does he or she explain verses in their context and let the Bible speak for itself?

  • Does the author/counselor strive to appraise the world biblically?

  • Does the author/counselor believe that God or man is central?

  • Does the author/counselor encourage obedience to the great commandment?

  • Is Christ at the center of the counsel or is merely alleviating pain the goal?

  • Is sin called sin and taken seriously?

  • Is the author/counselor encouraging biblical self-examination or morbid introspection?

  • Is the author/counselor enthralled with the person of Christ?

  • Does the author/counselor encourage testing his or her beliefs and practices by the Scripture?

  • Check an author's endnotes and bibliography to see if he or she gleans more from biblical sources or from psychology.

23. Tozer, *The Roots of the Righteous*, pp. 17-18.

24. David Powlison, "Do You See?", *The Journal of Biblical Counseling*, vol. XI, no. 3, Spring 1993, p. 3.

25. David Powlison, "Integration or Inundation?" in Michael S. Horton, ed., *Power Religion: The Selling Out of the Evangelical Church?* (Chicago, IL: Moody Press, 1992), p. 206.

26. David Wells, "The Theologian's Craft" in John D. Woodbridge and Thomas Edward McComiskey, eds., *Doing Theology in Today's World* (Grand Rapids, MI: Zondervan Publishing House, 1991), p. 172.

27. David Wells, "The Theologian's Craft," p. 191.

28. David Wells, *No Place for Truth: Or Whatever Happened to Evangelical Theology* (Grand Rapids, MI: Eerdmans Publishing Company, 1993), p. 9.

29. David Wells, "The Theologian's Craft," p. 191.

30. John Howie, *The Scots Worthies* (Edinburgh: The Banner of Truth Trust, 1870), pp. 29-30.

31. Sykes, *A Nation of Victims*, p. 39, quoting Bernie Zilbergeld, *The Shrinking of America: Myths of Psychological Change* (Boston, MA: Little, Brown & Company, 1983), p. 83.

32. David Wells, *No Place for Truth*, p. 183.

33. Mark Horne, "The Battle for Babble," p. 11.

34. David Wells, *No Place for Truth*, p. 179.

35. In *No Place for Truth*, David Wells objects to the "self" movement, stating that the biblical gospel "asserts the very reverse—namely, that the self is twisted, that it is maladjusted in

its relationship to both God and others, that it is full of deceit and rationalizations, that it is lawless, that it is in rebellion, and indeed that one must die to self in order to live" (p. 179). Even secular psychologists question the validity of the self-esteem movement. For a brief discussion of these questions from a secular point of view, refer to *Newsweek* magazine, "The Curse of Self-Esteem: What's Wrong with the Feel-Good Movement," February 17, 1992.

36. David Powlison, "Do You See?", p. 4.
37. *Webster's Dictionary*, internet definition.
38. David Wells, *No Place for Truth*, p. 183.
39. A.W. Tozer, *I Call It Heresy* (Camp Hill, PA: Christian Publications, 1973), p. 9-10.
40. David Wells, *No Place for Truth*, p. 175.
41. Jeffery L. Sheler, "Spiritual America," *U. S. News and World Report*, April 4, 1994: 48-59.

Chapter 2—Methods of Biblical Counseling

1. Jay E. Adams, *Competent to Counsel: Introduction to Nouthetic Counseling* (Grand Rapids: Zondervan Publishing House, 1970), p. 50.
2. For a biblical understanding of the problems inherent with the term "unconditional love," see David Powlison, "Queries and Controversies" in *The Journal of Biblical Counseling*, vol. XII, no. 3, Spring 1994, p. 45.
3. Briefly, data must be gathered extensively in the following general areas of life: church/spiritual life, work, home, finances, education, physical health, history, core concepts. If while gathering data in any of these areas you discover that a person has obvious needs in that area, take the time to gather more intensive data there.
4. We do not recommend that counselors do marital counseling alone when both the husband and the wife are present. It is better for women counselors to work as a male-female team with male counselors when both spouses are willing (see chapter 4 for a discussion about cross-gender long-term counseling). There are many women, however, whose husbands are unwilling to get counsel. Counseling them individually (same gender) is appropriate as long as the discussion involves the wife's own responsibilities and growth and does not degenerate into a husband-bashing session.
5. This form is available in the Biblical Counseling Foundation's *Self-Confrontation Manual*, in John MacArthur, Jr. and Wayne Mack's *Introduction to Biblical Counseling*, and in Jay Adams's *The Christian Counselor's Manual*.
6. John C. Broger, *Self-Confrontation: A Manual for In-Depth Discipleship* (Nashville, TN: Thomas Nelson, 1994).
7. Wayne Mack, *A Homework Manual for Biblical Living*, vol. 1 (Phillipsburg, NJ: Presbyterian and Reformed, 1979) and *A Homework Manual for Biblical Counseling*, vol. 2 (Phillipsburg, NJ: Presbyterian and Reformed, 1980).
8. William T. Kirwan, *Biblical Concepts for Christian Counseling: A Case for Integrating Psychology and Theology* (Grand Rapids: Baker Book House, 1984), p. 20: ". . . I know a pastoral counselor who looks at all emotional disturbances as spiritual problems. He believes that all depression and despair result from violating certain scriptural principles. . . . [this] outlook now seems to be to be simplistic and incompatible with both psychological and biblical data." Although Kirwan states that this position is incompatible with "biblical data," he proceeds to cite his own experience, including personal therapy, as his criterion rather than the Scriptures.

9. In several places in Scripture, God is said to be jealous (Exodus 34:14) and angry (Exodus 4:14; Psalm 78:49-50). Jesus exhibited zealous anger in cleansing the Temple (Matthew 21:12-13; John 2:13-16). He displayed sorrow in response to His friends' grief over Lazarus's death (John 11:33-36), and the Jewish people's unbelief and the desolation thatwould soon come upon Jerusalem (Luke 19:41).

10. *See* Exodus 16:20; Leviticus 10:16-20; 1 Samuel 11:6; 20:34; 2 Kings 13:19; Nehemiah 5:6.

11. *See* Genesis 4:5-8; 49:5-7; 2 Chronicles 26:16-23; Jonah 4:1-11.

12. Proverbs 14:29; 17:14; 19:11; 25:28; 29:11. Proverbs teaches that anger is a learned behavior: "Do not associate with a man given to anger; or go with a hot-tempered man, lest you learn his ways, and find a snare for yourself " (22:24-25).

13. A.W. Tozer, *The Root of the Righteous* (Camp Hill, PA: Christian Publications, 1955, 1986), p. 15.

14. Gerald B. Smith, ed., A.W. Tozer, *I Call It Heresy* (Camp Hill, PA: Christian Publications, 1991), p. 49.

15. Mack, *Introduction to Biblical Counseling,* p. 217.

16. For a more comprehensive discussion on this topic, see Chapter Four by Carol Cornish, "The Essential Foundation: A Biblical View of Women."

17. Ephesians 1:15-18, Colossians 1:3-5, and 1 Thessalonians 1:2-3 all teach that hope is part of the character of a believer.

18. Second Corinthians 4:16 identifies the decaying of the outer man as an occasion when a person might lose heart or become discouraged.

19. For instance, many of the false doctrines in the Faith movement have caused Christians to lose hope. Taught that they should expect to be able to speak their desires into existence, and that God wants them to be rich, they find their experience conflicting with their expectation. Heresy always produces hopelessness, and true hope is sustained only in the truth of God.

20. Proverbs 13:12 (NIV) states, "Hope deferred makes the heart sick, but a *longing fulfilled* is a tree of life" (emphasis added).

21. James 1:25 promises that the effectual doer is blessed as he acts upon God's Word.

22. Psalms 18:35; 31:15; 37:24; 63:8; 73:23. God promises us comfort and deliverance in our trials—2 Corinthians 1:3-11.

23. Second Corinthians 4:17.

24. First Thessalonians 4:3 states that it is God's will for believers to be sanctified.

25. Ronald F. Youngblood, gen. ed., *New Illustrated Bible Dictionary* (Nashville, TN: Thomas Nelson Publishers, 1995).

26. Acts 20:32; 1 Corinthians 1:2, 30; 6:11.

27. First Thessalonians 4:7.

28. Leviticus 11:44; Matthew 5:48; Romans 6:19; 1 Thessalonians 4:3-5; 1 Peter 1:15-16.

29. There seems to be much confusion on this topic. I've heard people teach that all we have to do is "let go and let God." I think I know what they mean; they're saying that we should stop striving to establish our own self-righteousness. Sometimes, however, "letting go and letting God" gets misconstrued and people think it means "do nothing." On the other hand, I've talked with people who think that their entire perseverance in salvation rests upon their own shoulders. This perspective is contrary to Scripture as well.

30. Ecclesiastes 5:12.

31. Do not overlook the importance of restitution. It is commanded in both the Old and New Testaments as a demonstration of true repentance (*see* Exodus 22:1; Leviticus 5:16). Jesus commends Zacchaeus's repentance and offer to repay fourfold as a sign of his salvation—Luke 19:8.

32. The "thank list" is a wonderful tool for you to use in counseling. Have the counselee write out 10 or 15 things for which she is thankful. She should carry this list with her at all times. When she is tempted in some area, she can use it to turn her heart away from her sin and toward God's goodness.

33. 1 Peter 5:6-7 is a wonderful passage for worriers to memorize.

34. Jay E. Adams, *The Christian Counselor's Commentary: Romans, Philippians, 1 Thessalonians, 2 Thessalonians* (Hackettstown, SC: Timeless Texts, 1995), p. 180.

35. Kay Arthur, *Lord, Only You Can Change Me* (Sisters, OR: Multnomah Books, 1995).

36. Arthur, p. 141.

37. Second Corinthians 6:4-10.

38. A.W. Tozer, p. 12.

39. A.W. Tozer, p. 16.

40. Psalm 119:160: "The sum of Thy word is truth, and every one of Thy righteous ordinances is everlasting."

41. Psalm 119:142: "Thy righteousness is an everlasting righteousness, and Thy law is truth."

42. Romans 1:18-23.

43. A.W. Tozer, p. 14.

44. Second Corinthians 4:17-18.

Chapter 3—The Essential Foundation: A Biblical View of Women

1. Sinclair B. Ferguson, "The Fear of the Lord," *Discipleship Journal* (July/August 1989): 41-44.

2. D. Martyn Lloyd-Jones, *The Heart of the Gospel* (Wheaton, IL: Crossway Books, 1991), p. 124.

3. Eugene Peterson, *The Message: New Testament with Psalms and Proverbs* (Colorado Springs: NavPress, 1993), p. 389.

4. Louis Berkhof, *Summary of Christian Doctrine* (Grand Rapids: Wm. B. Eerdmans, 1938), p. 42.

5. J.I. Packer, *Knowing God*, 20th anniversary ed., (Downer's Grove, IL: InterVarsity Press, 1993), p. 20.

6. For a biblical discussion of codependency, see Edward Welch's "Codependency and the Cult of Self" in Michael Scott Horton, ed., *Power Religion: The Selling Out of the Evangelical Church?* (Chicago: Moody Press, 1992), pp. 219-43.

7. Sinclair B. Ferguson, *A Heart for God* (Colorado Springs: NavPress, 1985), p. 17.

8. Quoted in Warren and Ruth Myers, *Praise: A Door to God's Presence* (Colorado Springs: NavPress, 1987), p. 19.

9. *See* Deuteronomy 4:29; 1 Chronicles 16:11; 22:19; 2 Chronicles 12:14; 15:12-13; Psalm 63; 105:4; Isaiah 31:1; 55:6; Jeremiah 10:21; Amos 5:6; Matthew 4:19; 8:22; 9:9; 16:24; 19:21; John 10:27; 12:26; 17:3; Acts 17:27; 2 Thessalonians 1:8-9; Hebrews 11:6.

10. Jay E. Adams, *The Christian Counselor's New Testament,* rev. ed., (Hackettstown, NJ: Timeless Texts, 1994) , 337.

11. R.C. Sproul, *Before the Face of God: a Daily Guide for Living from the Book of Romans* (Grand Rapids: Baker Book House, 1992), p. 37.

12. Imaging God in no way suggests, contrary to New Age teaching, that man is God or a god. Man is a creature, God is the Creator. Man is not, was not, nor ever will be God.

13. *See* Psalm 139; Jeremiah 23:23-24; and Acts 17:24-31.

14. *See* Colossians 1.

15. John 14,17; Colossians 2:10.

16. Read and meditate on Luke 15:20; John 15:9-17; 17:20-26; Romans 8:35-39; 1 John 3:16; 4:7-21.

17. D. Martyn Lloyd-Jones, *The Unsearchable Riches of Christ: An Exposition of Ephesians 3:1-21* (Grand Rapids: Baker Book House, 1979), p. 253.

18. For more on this see Lloyd-Jones, *Unsearchable Riches,* pp. 274-76.

19. J.I. Packer, *Knowing God,* 20th anniversary ed. (Downers Grove, IL: InterVarsity Press, 1993), 62.

20. *See* Romans 8:6-7; 2 Corinthians 10:5; and Philippians 4:4-9.

21. D. Martyn Lloyd-Jones, *Spiritual Depression: Its Causes and Its Cure* (Grand Rapids: Wm. B. Eerdmans, 1965), p. 269.

22. You can learn more about this through a tape series by John MacArthur, Jr., entitled *Seven Steps to Spiritual Stability.* The tapes can be ordered from Grace to You, P.O. Box 4000, Panorama City, CA 91412, or by calling 1-800-55-GRACE.

23. I often find myself in disagreement with both "camps" on the issues of women's roles in church and home. It seems to me that the egalitarians (who believe that no gender-based role distinctions are taught in Scripture) make the Scriptures say less than they really do (mostly through irresponsible hermeneutics), and that the complementarians (who believe that the Scriptures do teach gender-based role distinctions) make the Scriptures say more than they do (mostly by clinging to tradition). For a good overview of this debate, I encourage you to listen to Mark Futato's tapes on the subject. These are listed at the end of the chapter. You will be encouraged by Dr. Futato's refreshing remarks that we hear too few sermons on the equality of man and woman before God.

24. Read with particular discernment any author who insists that masculinity and femininity are categories in which we ought to think about human beings. The Bible should be the source of all our categories for thinking about human beings and gender issues. The Bible never exhorts men to be masculine or women to be feminine. These words have come into the church from secular psychology and anthropology. Rather than bringing clarity to questions about men and women, they have significantly muddied the waters.

25. *See* Susan Foh, *Women and the Word of God* (Phillipsburg, NJ: Presbyterian and Re-formed, 1979), p. 127.

26. *See* Susan Hunt, *Spiritual Mothering: The Titus 2 Model for Women Mentoring Women* (Wheaton, IL: Crossway Books, 1992).

Chapter 4—Why Women Should Counsel Women

1. An earlier version of this chapter appeared under the title "Are You Really Your Sister's and Brother's Keeper?," *Journal of Pastoral Practice* 11 (Fall 1992) : 27-44.

2. In this chapter the term *biblical counselor* refers to pastors, counselors, disciplers, and other Christian workers who have gifts of encouragement and teaching which they use to minister to members of the body of Christ either in a local church, a counseling center, or other ministry.

3. Sinclair B. Ferguson, *Kingdom Life in a Fallen World* (Colorado Springs: NavPress, 1986), pp. 120, 121, 122.

4. Short-term counseling usually consists of a couple of sessions. More than two or three sessions would constitute long-term counseling.

5. Elyse Fitzpatrick, "Why Women Should Counsel Women," from the Christian Counseling and Educational Foundation in San Diego: Summer Institute on Biblical Counseling, 1994, tape #421-12.

6. Merrill Tenney, *New Testament Survey,* rev. ed. (Grand Rapids: Wm. B. Eerdmans Publishing Company, 1985), p. 337.

7. William Hendriksen, *New Testament Commentary: Exposition of the Pastoral Epistles* (Grand Rapids: Baker Book House, 1957), p. 365.

8. *The NIV Study Bible* (Grand Rapids: Zondervan Publishing House, 1985), p. 990.

9. Jay Adams, *A Theology of Christian Counseling* (Grand Rapids: Zondervan Publishing House, 1979), p. 276.

10. By saying this I am not suggesting that men and women are so different that they cannot understand one another.

11. Naomi Taylor Wright with Dick Bohrer, "Let's Let Women Counsel Women," *Moody* (November 1980), pp. 41-42.

12. At a later time, the counselee shared this journal entry with me.

13. Lois Mowday, *The Snare: Avoiding Emotional and Sexual Entanglements* (Colorado Springs: NavPress, 1988), p. 99.

14. Ibid., p.100.

15. Charles Stanley, *Temptation* (Nashville, TN: Oliver-Nelson Books, 1988), pp. 154-155.

16. Steve Levicoff, *Christian Counseling and the Law* (Chicago: Moody Press, 1991), pp. 84–85.

17. Marie M. Fortune, *Is Nothing Sacred? When Sex Invades the Pastoral Relationship* (San Francisco: Harper and Row, 1989), p. 107.

18. Jeffrey A. Kottler, *On Being a Therapist* (San Francisco: Jossey-Bass Publishers, 1990), p. 49.

19. Lois Mowday, *The Snare,* p. 83.

20. Peter Rutter, "Interview with Dr. Peter Rutter, Author of Sex in the Forbidden Zone, July 27, 1990," interview by Lewis Rambo, *Pastoral Psychology* (May 1991), pp. 326-27.

21. Ibid.

22. Jack Balswick and John Thoburn, "How Ministers Deal with Sexual Temptation," *Pastoral Psychology* (May 1991), p. 279.

23. Jerry Jenkins, *Hedges: Loving Your Marriage Enough to Protect It* (Brentwood, TN: Wolgemuth & Hyatt Publishers, Inc., 1989), p. 70.

24. Ibid., p. 83.

25. Tony Campolo, "Living with Your Spouse," *I Have Decided to Live Like a Believer,* #2 BE of series, American Video, n.d.

26. John H. Armstrong, *Can Fallen Pastors Be Restored? The Church's Response to Sexual Misconduct* (Chicago: Moody Press, 1995), pp. 190-91.

27. Andre Bustanoby, "Counseling the Seductive Female," *Leadership* (November 1988), p. 51.

28. David Powlison, "What If Your Father Didn't Love You?," *The Biblical Counselor,* Publication of the National Association of Nouthetic Counselors (May 1991), pp. 1-4.

29. Fitzpatrick tape.

30. Randy Alcorn, "Strategies to Keep from Falling," *Leadership* (November 1988), p. 45.

31. R. Kent Hughes and John Armstrong, "Why Adulterous Pastors Should Not Be Restored," *Christianity Today* (April 3, 1995), p. 34.

32. Dennis Rainey, *Lonely Husbands, Lonely Wives* (Dallas: Word Publishing, 1989), p. 81.

33. Peter Rutter, "Interview with Dr. Peter Rutter," p. 332.

34. Section 2 of the "Policy on Pastoral Counseling" (adopted November 1990), First Baptist Church, Doylestown, PA.

35. Sinclair B. Ferguson, *Kingdom Life in a Fallen World,* p. 119.

36. See chapter 17, "Counseling Women for Sexual Sins," by Diane Tyson.

37. R. Kent Hughes and John Armstrong, "Why Adulterous Pastors Should Not Be Restored," p. 34.

38. Elyse Fitzpatrick tape.

Chapter 5—Counseling Single Teen Mothers

1. Stanley Henshaw, "U.S. Teenage Pregnancy Statistics," The Alan Guttmacher Institute, August 5, 1993.

2. Carol D. Foster, Suzanne B. Szuyres, Nancy P. Jacobs, eds., "Women's Changing Role," Information Plus, 1996, p. 51.

3. Forrest and Singh, "The Sexual and Reproductive Behavior of American Women, 1982–1988," Family Planning Perspectives, vol. 22, no. 5, September/October 1990.

4. Carol D. Foster, p. 59.

5. Carol D. Foster, p. 59.

6. Carol D. Foster, p. 59.

7. Carol D. Foster, p. 55.

8. Kristin A. Moore and Nancy Snyder, "Facts At A Glance," *Child Tends, Inc.,* January, 1996.

9. Carol D. Foster, p. 61.

10. Carol D. Foster, p. 61.

11. Carol D. Foster, p. 61.

12. Rebecca A. Maynard, ed., "Kids Having Kids: A Robin Hood Foundation Special Report on the Costs of Adolescent Childbearing," June, 1996.

13. "Premarital Sexual Experience Among Adolescent Women—U. S. 1970-1988," *Morbidity and Mortality Weekly Report,* vol. 39, nos. 51-52, January 1991.

14. *Sex and America's Teenagers,* New York: Alan Guttmacher Institute, 1994.
15. Although God is the author of life, He is not responsible for Stacy's sin (James 1:13f).

Chapter 6—Counseling Women Discontent in Their Singleness

1. Sinclair B. Ferguson, *Deserted by God?* (Grand Rapids: Baker Book House, 1993), p. 166.
2. John Holzmann, *Dating with Integrity: Honoring Christ in Your Relationships with the Opposite Sex,* (Dallas: Word Books, 1990), p. 166.

Chapter 7—Counseling the Post-Abortion Woman

1. *Before Making A "Choice": Be Informed!* A pamphlet produced by the California Nurses for Ethical Standards, 5560 Centennial Avenue, Los Angeles, CA 90066. For copies, you can write, or call (310) 574-1031.
2. Paul E. Rockwell, M.D., as quoted by Dr. and Mrs. J.C. Wilke, *Why Can't We Love Them Both* (Cincinnati, OH: Hays Publishing, 1997), pp. 78-80.
3. *Is a Preborn Baby a Part of His Mother's Body?* A pamphlet produced by California Right to Life, (510) 944-5351. This pamphlet lists 13 reasons why a preborn baby is not to be considered a mere appendage to his mother.
4. Linda Cochrane, R.N., *Women in Ramah, A Post-Abortion Bible Study,* Christian Action Council, 101 W. Broad Street, Falls Church, VA 22046; and *In His Image: A Post-Abortion Bible Study,* Open Arms, Columbia, MO 65205, (314) 449-7672.
5. *See* chapter 2 on the methods of biblical counseling.
6. However, if the counselee is a lesbian, then a husband/wife team might be best. See chapter 3 on why women should counsel women.
7. By *church,* I am taking into consideration those who believe in the Bible's inerrancy and sufficiency. It is not recommended to send a counselee for help to a church—even if she has gone to it for many years—if it does not teach and practice the basic doctrines of Scripture, such as the depravity of man, the deity of Christ, the substitutionary atonement, and His resurrection and anticipated second coming.
8. Bill and Sue Banks, *Ministering to Abortion's Aftermath* (Kirkwood, MO: Impact Books, 1982); Teri Reisser, M.S. and Paul Reisser, M.D., *Identifying and Overcoming Postabortion Syndrome* (Colorado Springs: Focus on the Family); D.C. Reardon, *Aborted Women: Silent No More* (Westchester, IL: Crossway Books, 1987); Terry Selby, *The Mourning After: Help for Postabortion Syndrome* (Grand Rapids: Baker Books, 1990); Anne Speckard, *The Psycho-Social Aspects of Stress Following an Abortion* (Kansas City, MO: Sheed and Ward, 1987).
9. John H. Sammis, Daniel B. Towner, *Trust and Obey* (1887).
10. My own personal belief is that when any parent of a child comes to trust in Christ alone, then their children (even the aborted one[s]) are part of the kingdom of God. First Corinthians 7:14 says, "For the unbelieving husband has been sanctified through his wife, and the unbelieving wife has been sanctified through her believing husband. Otherwise your children would be unclean, but as it is, they are holy." This is an indication that the children of believers are set apart unto holiness. This doesn't guarantee their salvation, but it certainly is a comfort of some sort.

Chapter 8—Counseling Women in Problem Christian Marriages

1. For a more detailed description of these processes, see chapter 2 on the method of biblical counseling. Two excellent biblical counseling books are *The Christian Counselor's Manual* by Jay Adams (Grand Rapids: Zondervan Publishing House, 1973) and *Introduction to Biblical Counseling* by John MacArthur and Wayne Mack (Dallas: Word Books, 1994).

2. Martha Peace's *The Excellent Wife* (Bemidji, MN: Focus Publishing, 1995) and *The Excellent Wife Study Guide and Teacher's Guide* are available from Bible Data Services, 100 Colt Way, Peachtree City, GA 30269; or you can call (770) 486-0011.

3. John MacArthur, Jr., *God: Coming Face to Face with His Majesty* (Wheaton: IL: Victor Books, 1993).

4. Lou Priolo's tapes may be obtained from the Atlanta Biblical Counseling Center located at Glenwood Hills Baptist Church, 3001 Old Salem Road, Conyers, GA 30208; or you can call (770) 860-9010.

5. These resources are adapted for use in this chapter and used with permission from Lou Priolo of the Atlanta Biblical Counseling Center. For further information on these resources, you may obtain Lou Priolo's tape, "Biblical Resources to Protect a Wife," or, you can read chapter 14 of Martha Peace's book *The Excellent Wife*. There, I list eight resources for the wife's protection, which are:
   1. Learn to communicate biblically.
   2. Learn to overcome evil with good.
   3. Learn to make a biblical appeal.
   4. Learn to give a biblical reproof.
   5. Learn to biblically respond to foolish demands.
   6. Learn to seek godly counsel.
   7. Learn to biblically follow the steps of church discipline.
   8. Learn to biblically involve the governing authorities.

6. Martha Peace, chapter 14, see endnote #2.

7. Jay Adams, *The Handbook of Church Discipline* (Grand Rapids: Zondervan Publishing House, 1986).

8. With reservation we recommend Kay Marshall Strom, *Helping Women in Crisis* (Grand Rapids: Zondervan Publishing House, 1986), pp. 143-57.

9. Peace, pp. 94-96.

10. This section on loneliness was adapted from *The Excellent Wife*, pages 227-235.

Chapter 9—Counseling Women Married to Unbelievers

1. Jay E. Adams, *The Christian Counselor's Commentary: I Corinthians, II Corinthians* (Hackettstown, NJ: Timeless Texts, 1994), p. 50.

2. *Webster's Seventh New Collegiate Dictionary* (Springfield, MA: G. & C. Merriam Co., 1963), p. 630.

3. *Ibid.,* p. 65.

4. Jay Adams, *Solving Marriage Problems: Biblical Solutions for Christian Counselors* (Phillipsburg, NJ: Presbyterian & Reformed, 1983), pp. 110-11.

5. *Solving Marriage Problems*, p. 118.

6. Meditation is a lost art among Christians. *See* J.I. Packer, *Knowing God* (Downer's Grove, IL; InterVarsity Press), p. 23 to find out how to meditate.

Chapter 10—Counseling Women Considering Adoption

1. Transcribed videotape on adoption presented on "Straight Talk fom the Family Research Council" broadcast aired Wednesday, March 13, 1996. Information on the Family Research Council may be obtained by contacting FRC at their internet site: http://www. frc.org or by writing Family Research Council, 700 Thirteenth Street NW, Suite 500, Washington, DC, 20005, or by calling (800) 225-4008. Publications by the FRC are available upon request.

2. Family Research Council videotape on adoption.

3. ". . . of the 2.3 million U.S. couples who are infertile, 15 to 30 percent are infertile or unable to conceive as a result of an STD [sexually transmitted disease]. Furthermore, while the rate of infertility remained about the same from 1967 to 1982 at 2.4 million couples, infertility among couples aged 20-24 *increased* from 4 percent in 1965 to 11 percent in 1982. It is likely that a good portion of this increase in early-age infertility is directly attributable to sexually-transmitted diseases." Family Research Council, *In Focus*, "Many Couples Still Waiting to Adopt Children," December 19, 1995.

4. Family Research Council, "Many Couples Still Waiting to Adopt Children."

5. "Causes of infertility include a wide range of physical as well as emotional factors. Approximately 30 to 40 percent of all infertility is due to a 'male' factor . . . A 'female' factor is responsible for 40 to 50 percent. . . . The remaining 10 to 30 percent may be caused by contributing factors by both partners, or no cause can be adequately identified." Applied Medical Informatics, Inc., 1996.

6. Family Research Council, "Many Couples Still Waiting to Adopt Children."

7. Family Research Council, "Many Couples Still Waiting to Adopt Children."

8. Lisa O'Rourke and Ruth Hubbell, "Adopting Resources," internet article on international adoption, July 1988.

9. Transcribed videotape, *Straight Talk.*

10. Transcribed videotape, *Straight Talk.*

11. Transcribed videotape, *Straight Talk.*

12. William J. Bennett, *The Index of Leading Cultural Indicators* (published jointly by The Heritage Foundation and Empower America, 1993), p. 10.

13. See chapter 5 about developing a Mentor Mom program in your church to help teen moms.

14. See chapter 20 for a more detailed discussion of infertility.

15. Review the story of Rachel in Genesis 30.

16. OncoLink, "Infertility," article on the internet.

17. Gail Sheehy, *New Passages: Mapping Your Life Across Time* (New York: Ballantine Books, 1995), p. 111.

18. The harvesting of embryos is often used in these procedures. Therefore, fertilized eggs and embryos are destroyed, thus destroying human life.

19. Ronald F. Youngblood, ed., *Nelson's New Illustrated Bible Dictionary* (Nashville, TN: Thomas Nelson Publishers, 1995), p. 2.

20. The following is a summary of "Encouraging Adoption" by Gracie Hsu, an article that appeared in the Family Research Council newsletter *Insight* (internet article).

21. William J. Bennett, *The Index of Leading Cultural Indicators,* p. 16.

22. For a more biblical understanding of demons, see David Powlison's book *Power Encounters* (Grand Rapids: Baker Books, 1995).

23. *See* Gary Steven Shogren, "Recovering God in the Age of Therapy," *The Journal of Biblical Counseling* (Fall 1993): 14-19. He shows that "healing" in the Bible is always a spiritual matter of covenant relationship with God.

24. Amy Carmichael, *Toward Jerusalem* (Fort Washington, PA: Christian Literature Crusade, 1936).

25. Elisabeth Elliot, *A Chance to Die: The Life and Legacy of Amy Carmichael* (Grand Rapids: Fleming H. Revell, 1987).

26. Amy Carmichael, *Toward Jerusalem,* p. 94. Used by permission.

27. Family Research Council: (800) 225-4008.

28. National Adoption Information Clearinghouse, 5640 Nicholson Lane, Suite 300, Rockville, MD 20852.

29. Internet article written by Debra G. Smith of the National Adoption Information Clearinghouse: "It takes some soul searching on your part to decide whether the foster parenting option is one you want to choose. If you can stand some uncertainty, it is a viable option, especially if you have your heart set on a young child and you do not have the funds for a private agency or independent adoption. You must be able to maturely face the prospect of a child being reunited with birth parents, feel sincerely that unification is indeed in the best interest of the child at the time, and be able to handle your own grief that would accompany such a loss."

Chapter 11—Counseling Mothers of Children with Learning Difficulties

1. Rob Goldman/FPG, "The Eyes Have It," *Essence,* May 1996, p. 146.

2. Goldman, "The Eyes Have It," p. 146.

3. Joyce Tweedie, *Children's Hearing Problems: Their Significance, Detection, Management* (Bristol, England: IOP Publishing Limited, Techno House, 1987), p. 28.

4. Larry J. Brown and Ernesto Pollitt, "Malnutrition, Poverty and Intellectual Development," *Scientific American,* February 1996, p. 38.

5. Review chapter 16 on overeating and bulimia.

6. Larry J. Brown and Ernesto Pollitt, "Malnutrition," p. 42.

7. Julie Walsh, R.D., "How Caffeine Affects Kids," *Parents,* March 1996, p. 44.

8. From the Morbidity and Mortality Weekly Report, "Asthma Mortality and Hospitalization Among Children and Young Adults—United States, 1980-1993," *JAMA,* May 22/29, 1996, vol. 275, no. 20, p. 1535.

9. Beatrice Trum Hunter, "Allergic Reactions in Children," *Consumers' Research,* April 1996, vol. 79, no. 4, p. 8.

10. Jeremy Scholsberg, "Way Past Bedtime," *Better Homes and Gardens,* April 1996, p. 80.

11. Louis Paul Priolo, *How to Help Angry Kids* (Alabama City, AL: S.E.L.F. Publications, 1996) p. 46.

12. Tedd Tripp, *Shepherding a Child's Heart* (Wapwallopen, PA: Shepherd Press, 1995), p. 75.

13. Grades K-3 are the only ones considered because retaining older children is extremely rare. It is usually done only in cases of severe illness or injury. However, junior high and high school students may have to repeat certain subject areas.

14. Criteria for retention and promotion should always be used in a dynamic and flexible way, taking into account the beliefs and attitudes of the parents and the child. Rigid adherence to standards in this regard is usually harmful to the child because it fails to take into account his individuality.

15. For a more detailed discussion of the topic of self-esteem, see chapter 1, pages 25-31.

16. Barbara Novick, *Fundamentals of Clinical Child Neurophysiology* (Philadelphia: Grune & Stratton, 1988), p. 73.

17. Barbara Novick, *Fundamentals*, p. 43.

18. Barbara Novick, *Fundamentals*, p. 43.

19. Alan J. Watson, "The Teacher as Encourager," *Journal of Christian Education*, April 1994, vol. 37, no. 1, p. 5.

20. Jay E. Adams, "Why Is Biblical Counseling So Concerned About the Label Used to Describe People's Problems?", *The Journal of Biblical Counseling*, 1996, vol. 14, no. 2, p. 51.

21. Edward T. Welch, "What You Should Know About Attention Deficit Disorder (ADD)," *The Journal of Biblical Counseling*, Winter 1996, vol. 14, no. 2, p. 6.

22. A more precise description of the criteria for an ADD/ADHD diagnosis is found in the Diagnostic and Statistical Manual (DSM IV). We are using these criteria solely for the purpose of demonstrating how such a "diagnosis" is typically arrived upon.

23. Edward T. Welch, "What You Should Know About ADD," p. 28.

24. Edward T. Welch, "What You Should Know About ADD," p. 30.

25. Lawrence H. Diller, "The Run on Ritalin: Attention Deficit Disorder and Stimulant Treatment in the 1990s," *Hastings Center Report*, March-April 1996, p. 12.

26. Methylphenidate, marketed as Ritalin, is said to be "prescribed for 3 to 5 percent of all U.S. schoolchildren, and most of those taking the drug are boys." (No author listed), "Agency Survey Reports Overuse of Ritalin Among U.S. Children," *Mental Health Weekly*, March 4, 1996, vol. 6, issue 10, p. 6.

27. Edward T. Welch, "What You Should Know About ADD," p. 30.

28. Lawrence H. Diller, "The Run on Ritalin," p. 13.

29. Among biblical couselors there are marked differences of opinion about the prudence of the use of drugs such as Ritalin. Some biblical counselors always stand against it; others think it might be helpful in a limited number of cases over a very limited period of time. Almost all agree that is it over-prescribed and warn about the dangers inherent in thinking about ADD/ADHD as a physical "disease" requiring medication. This kind of medication does not cure ADD/ADHD in the same way that penicillin cures strep throat. In fact, no one seems to know why Ritalin helps to calm these kinds of children. Medicine does not change the heart or "heal" behavior. It might possibly help a child as he learns to manage his behavior in more godly ways, but it does not permanently change the way that his mind functions. Just remember this: A child that is ADD/ADHD has no disease that must be treated with medication. Because the author of this chapter is not a medical professional, absolute pronouncement about the benefits or detriments of any prescription drugs will be withheld.

30. Edward T. Welch, "What You Should Know About ADD," p. 35.

31. George C. Scipione, "Who Owns the Children of Divorce?" *The Journal of Pastoral Practice*, vol. VIII, no. 3, p. 46.

32. Edward T. Welch, "What You Should Know About ADD," p. 30.

33. Jim and Barbara Dycus, *Children of Divorce* (Elgin, IL: David C. Cook Publishing Company, 1987), p. 19.

34. Marie Winn, *Children Without Childhood* (Harrisonburg, VA: R.R. Donnelley and Sons Company, 1981), p. 127.

35. Carole Sanderson Streeter, *Finding Your Place After Divorce* (Wheaton, IL: Harold Shaw Publishers, 1992), p. 78.

36. Marie Winn, *Children Without Childhood,* pp. 134, 142.

37. George C. Scipione, "Who Owns the Children of Divorce?" p. 46.

38. For a more complete discussion about the responsibilities of parents whose children respond in ungodly ways, see chapter 12.

Chapter 12—Counseling Mothers of Rebellious Teens

1. *Webster's Encyclopedic Dictionary* (New York, N.Y.: Lexicon Publications, Inc. 1989).

2. In some cases, however, a child's death may be the result of a parent's sin. For instance, a drunken father may kill his whole family in a car accident.

3. Personal correspondence with Iain Duguid, Associate Professor of Old Testament at Westminster Theological Seminary in California, 1996.

4. Ezekiel 18 speaks at length about the possibility of a righteous father having an unrighteous son and vice versa (*see* verses 1-10, 14.)

5. Doris Van Stone, *Dorie, The Girl Nobody Loved* (Chicago: Moody Press, 1979); and *No Place to Cry — The Hurt and Healing of Sexual Abuse* (Chicago: Moody Press, 1990).

6. See chapter 4, "Essential Foundations," to learn how to gain eternal perspective on problems.

7. See J.I. Packer, *Knowing God* (Downers Grove, IL: InterVarsity Press, 1973), pp. 18-19 for a definition of Christian meditation.

8. For a fuller treatment of this topic, see chapter 9 "Counseling Women Married to Unbelievers."

9. See chapter 13, "Counseling Divorced Women and Single Moms," for an explanation of the difference between righteous and unrighteous divorce.

10. Terrye Coelho, "Father, I Adore You" (Maranatha! Music, 1973).

Chapter 13—Counseling Divorced Women and Single Moms

1. Jay E. Adams, *Marriage, Divorce, and Remarriage in the Bible* (Grand Rapids: Zondervan, 1980), p. 18.

2. I heartily recommend *The Peacemaker: A Biblical Guide to Resolving Personal Conflict* by Ken Sande (Grand Rapids: Baker Books, 1990). This practical and biblical resource provides help in addressing all sorts of conflict situations. Addressing conflict biblically will teach you to be more humble and lovingly honest with the people who are dear to you.

3. However, if you are being physically abused, you must take steps to protect yourself and your child(ren). See chapter 8, "Counseling Women in Problem Christian Marriages," and chapter 9, "Counseling Women Married to Unbelievers,"

4. Jay E. Adams, *Marriage, Divorce, and Remarriage,* p. 93.

5. "Living in peace" is a general principle found in Romans 12:18, and appears to be foundational to the requirements for believers married to unbelievers. They must remain in the marriage if the unbeliever is willing (except as noted previously), and they must consent to the divorce if that is the unbeliever's desire.

6. Jay E. Adams, *Marriage, Divorce, and Remarriage,* pp. 86-87. Adams also notes "that Scriptures record no threat of stoning for remarriage while one's spouse is alive. Yet if it were always adultery to do so, one would expect to discover at least a hint of it." He continues, "Christ's words about divorce in the Gospels . . . refer in part to Deuteronomy 24:1-4. The wife, in that discussion, would be 'defiled' because her husband would cause her to commit adultery by divorcing her for a cause lesser than sexual sin. . . . Yet neither the woman nor the second man who married her was stoned for the act. . . . Presumably, at least in such cases, we could say that Moses didn't require stoning for adultery."

7. Jay E. Adams, *Marriage, Divorce, and Remarriage,* p. 86.

8. *The Sermon on the Mount* by Sinclair B. Ferguson (Carlisle, PA: Banner of Truth, 1987) is an excellent resource for acquiring God's perspective on happiness.

9. See chapter 4, "The Essential Foundation," for a full discussion of the meaning and importance of our self-identity before God.

10. Ruth Myers, *31 Days of Praise* (Sisters, OR: Multnomah Books, 1994).

11. J.I. Packer, *Knowing God* study guide (Downers Grove, IL: InterVarsity Press, 1975), p. 6.

12. Eugene H. Peterson, *The Message* (Colorado Springs: NavPress, 1995), p. 559.

13. Romans 12:9-21.

Chapter 14—Counseling Women Abused as Children

1. U.S. Department of Health and Human Services, National Child Abuse and Neglect Data System, Working Paper 2, 1991; Summary Data Component, May 1993; Child Maltreatment 1992, May 1994; and Child Maltreatment 1993, April 1995.

2. *See* Psalm 72:12; 109:16,22,31; 113:7; Proverbs 15:15; 31:5; Isaiah 10:1-2; 32:7; 51:22-23; 54:14; Ezekiel 22:29; Zechariah 10:2.

3. *See also* 1 Thessalonians 5:14.

4. C.S. Lewis, *The Problem of Pain* (New York: Macmillan Publishing Company, 1962), p. 93.

5. Kay Arthur, *Lord, Only You Can Change Me* (Sisters, OR: Multnomah Books, 1995), p. 83.

6. False Memory Syndrome (FMS) may be defined as the creation by a therapist of false memories in a client through continuous suggestion. As Ed Bulkley states in *Only God Can Heal the Wounded Heart* ([Eugene, Oregon: Harvest House Publishers, 1995], p. 56), "The current theory among memory-recovery therapists is that if a person has some form of dysfunction (and with virtually every human problem being labeled as a dysfunction, nearly everyone qualifies), sexual abuse is probably a root cause— *especially* if the victim can't recall the abuse." Numbers of women have been coerced into believing they were victims of some forgotten abuse and have subsequently made charges against family members. This terrible tragedy is made all the more grievous

because Christian therapists are promoting it. It is important for you to ascertain whether the memory of abuse was discovered during therapy. Although the mantra, "If you think you may have been abused, you probably were," is the common belief among recovered memory therapists, it is wise to question all allegations of abuse. Not all therapists agree that wondering about abuse is a sure indicator of its presence. More importantly, it is not biblically sound to teach that truth is found by unquestioningly believing everything that may be found in the imagination of a sinful man. Sin has affected every part of our being, including our thought processes and imagination. Just because we can imagine something is no criteria for judging its accuracy. Imaginations may be particularly influenced by the specter of abuse, the opportunity to find a "reason" for besetting sins, and as an occasion to please a trusted therapist. The question of whether memories can be subconsciously repressed is open to debate. The processes by which memories are "recovered" is questionable enough that a discerning biblical counselor will abstain from them. True help can be given without wandering into the slough of hazy memories, vague dreams, and enhanced imagination.

7. There are numerous articles questioning the reliability of memories recalled during therapy, including the following: Leon Jaroff, "Lies of the Mind: Repressed-memory therapy is harming patients, devastating families and intensifying a backlash against mental-health practitioners," *Time* Magazine, November 29, 1993, p. 52; Paul R. McHugh, "Multiple Personality Disorder," *The Harvard Mental Health Letter*, vol. 10, no. 3; September 1993; Richard J. Ofshe, "Inadvertent Hypnosis During Interrogation: False Confession Due to Dissociative State; Misidentified Multiple Personality and the Santanic Cult Hypothesis," *The International Journal of Clinical and Experimental Hypnosis*, vol. XL, no. 3, 1992, 125-156; Elizabeth F. Loftus, "Repressed Memories of Childhood Trauma: Are They Genuine?" *The Harvard Mental Health Review;* Norbert Cunningham, "No Thanks for the Memories: 'Recovery Movement:' A Modern-Day Frankenstein Story?" *The Times-Transcript* (Moncton, NB, Canada), a five-part series beginning June 21, 1993; Bill Scanlon, "Skeptics Question Memories of Incest: Incompetent therapists turn patients' fantasies into repressed reality, some experts are saying," *Rocky Mountain News,* a three-part series beginning September 13, 1992; Amy Kuebeleck, "Repressed Memory of Abuse Questioned: Therapy blamed for recall of incidents that never happened," *The San Diego Union-Tribune,* December 20, 1993; "Child Sexual Abuse, Assault, and Molest Issues, Report No. 8," a report by the 1991-1992 San Diego County Grand Jury, June 29, 1992.

8. Paul Gray, "The Assualt on Freud," *Time* magazine, November 29, 1993, p. 49.

9. *See* Proverbs 14:23.

10. Let me refer you to the section about building hope in chapter 2, "The Methods of Biblical Counseling."

11. Michael Horton, *Where in the World is the Church?* (Chicago: Moody Press, 1995), p. 18.

12. Kay Arthur, *Lord, Only You Can Change Me,* p. 82.

13. Doris Van Stone and Erwin W. Lutzer, *No Place to Cry* (Chicago: Moody Press, 1990), p. 118.

14. Doris Stone and Erwin Lutzer, *No Place to Cry,* p. 27.

15. *See* Romans 15:4.

16. Ed Welch, "Exalting Pain? Ignoring Pain? What do we do with Suffering?" *The Journal of Biblical Counseling,* vol. XII, no. 3, Spring 1994, p. 4.
17. James 1:2-4.
18. Ed Welch, "Exalting Pain?" p. 15.
19. Ed Welch, "Exalting Pain?" p. 8, used with permission.
20. Ed Welch, "Exalting Pain?" p. 8.
21. Ed Welch, "Exalting Pain?" p. 8.
22. *See* Romans 3:10-18.
23. Ezekiel 18:20.
24. Ed Welch, "Exalting Pain?" p. 6.
25. Jay E. Adams, *From Forgiven to Forgiving* (Amityville, NY: Calvary Press, 1994).
26. *See* 1 John 1:9.
27. Hebrews 12:15-16.
28. Hebrews 13:5-6. *See also* Luke 12:4-5 where Jesus teaches that fear of man is to be shunned and fear of God is to be put in its place.
29. Galatians 6:2.

Chapter 15—Counseling Women with Addictions
1. *Webster's Ninth New Collegiate Dictionary* (Springfield, MA: Merriam-Webster Inc., 1983), p. 55.
2. Craig Nakken, *The Addictive Personality* (San Francisco: Hazelden, 1988), p. 10.
3. John Calvin, *Commentary on the Book of the Prophet Isaiah* (Grand Rapids: Eerdmans, 1956), p. 372.
4. John Calvin, *Isaiah,* p. 374.
5. Charles Spurgeon, "The Law Written on the Heart," *Journal of Biblical Counseling* (Winter 1994), pp. 25-32.
6. Sinclair B. Ferguson, *Kingdom Life in a Fallen World* (Colorado Springs: NavPress, 1986), p. 51.
7. Calvin, *Isaiah,* p. 381.
8. I highly recommend the reader to Margaret Clarkson's *Destined for Glory: The Meaning of Suffering* (Grand Rapids: Eerdmans, 1983) for an in-depth yet practical look at the issue of suffering from God's perspective as revealed in the Scriptures.

Chapter 16—Counseling Women for Overeating and Bulimia
1. Of course, some people weigh more than the tables for "average" weight recommend and are not over-fat. For instance, a football player may weigh 260 pounds, but not be over-fat because his weight comes from muscle mass. The best way to determine if a person's weight is a health risk is to have body fat measurements done by a health professional. For women, the ideal percentage of body fat is about 20 to 25 percent. Everyone requires some stored body fat for fueling energy—if the body has too little fat, it will begin to break down muscle tissue for energy requirements.

2. Nanci Hellmich, "Aging Boomers Fight the Battle of the Bulge," *USA Today*, January 4, 1996, internet article.

3. Department of Housing and Health Services (DHHS) publication no. (FDA) 92-1189, "The Facts About Weight Loss Products and Programs," presented as a public service by Federal Trade Commission, Food and Drug Administration, National Association of Attorneys General, internet article.

4. Weight Watchers of Philadelphia, Inc., corporate background, internet article.

5. DHHS publication no. (FDA) 92-1189.

6. "According to the U.S. Agriculture Department, the nation produces enough food for every man, woman, and child to consume 3,700 calories each day. However, the average woman needs only about 1,800 per day." (Lisa Page and Taku Sugimoto, Passport Educational Publishing, 1103 West Clark Street, Champaign, IL 61821. 1995).

7. C.S. Lewis, *The Screwtape Letters* (New York: Macmillan Publishing Company, 1961), pp. 76–77.

8. Vickie Borgia and Stacy Marple, "Body Image and 'Eating Disorders.'" *The Barnard/Columbia Women's Handbook*, 1992, internet article; author unknown, "You Can Never Be Too Rich or Too Thin," internet article.

9. See my reference to worry and the biblical methods for change in chapter 2 on the methods of biblical counseling.

10. There are several books you may use as a resource in learning the put-off/put-on dynamic. See the reference section at the end of chapter 2.

11. Passport Educational Publishing, 1995.

12. See chapter 20, "Medical Questions." Most physicians also recommend calcium supplements to help prevent the osteoporosis that almost always accompanies menopause.

13. Carol L. Otis, M.D. and Roger Goldingay, "Exercise Abuse—Have You Gone Too Far?" *Shape* magazine, October 1991, pp. 90-93. They recommend the following questions be asked to determine whether one is exercising too much:
    Do you feel guilty if a day goes by when you don't work out?
    Are you depressed if you are unable to exercise?
    Do you feel tired and lethargic, yet still have trouble sleeping?
    Do you have injuries that don't seem to heal?
    Are you reluctant to take time off to heal injuries?
    Are you ignoring aspects of your work, social life or family life in order to exercise?
    Do you feel compelled to work-out even if you are tired?
    Do you increase or decrease your exercise, based on your weight or what you have eaten?
    Do you suffer from insomnia, undesired weight loss, fatigue, lethargy, irritability, loss of menstrual periods, multiple chronic injuries, or stress fractures?
    If you answered "yes" to several of the above questions, you are probably exercising too much.

14. The U.S. Department of Agriculture suggests a diet of 6 to 11 servings of grain products (breads, cereals, pasta, and rice); 3 to 5 servings of various vegetables; 2 to 4 servings of various fruits; 2 to 3 servings of meat; and 2 to 3 servings of milk per day for a well-balanced diet. Fats, oils, and sweets are to be used sparingly.

15. The following is excerpted from "Weight Loss vs. Exercise: Trimming the Fat Wins," *U.S.A. Today,* December 26, 1995:

    The best exercise for your heart is pushing yourself away from the table, a new study suggests. Losing weight by itself works better than aerobic exercise by itself in reducing the risk of heart disease, a study of fat men found. The message, though, is to do both, researchers say. The findings were published in Wednesday's *Journal of the American Medical Association.*

16. Dixie Farley, "Eating Disorders: When Thinness Becomes an Obsession," *FDA Consumer,* (a publication of the U.S. Food and Drug Administration), May 1986.

17. Dixie Farley, "Eating Disorders."

18. Dixie Farley, "Eating Disorders."

19. Dixie Farley, "Eating Disorders."

20. Dixie Farley, "Eating Disorders."

21. Dixie Farley, "Eating Disorders."

22. Many women report an alteration in their cravings and eating during times of premenstrual syndrome (PMS). For instance, many women crave chocolate for comfort. It will be important for you to help your counselee monitor her eating especially right before and during her menstrual periods. She should avoid foods that aggravate the symptoms of PMS and menstrual cramps. These foods include caffeine, dairy products, hot dogs, sugar, alcohol, additional salt, white flour, pizza, and red meat. She can help relieve PMS by eating fruits (especially oranges, papaya, pineapple), vegetables, brown rice, oatmeal, corn, poultry, and fish. (Jackie Gross, Ithaca College, W.I.S.H.E.S. Information Provider, internet article.)

23. See also Numbers 11:6,13-24,31-34.

24. Notice also Luke 21:34: "Be on guard, that your hearts may not be weighted down with dissipation and drunkenness and the worries of life."

25. Remember our previous discussion of 1 John 2:15-16. Note the connection in this passage between lusts, pride, and loving the world. The standard of the world, "I must look good in order to be accepted and respected (worshiped and obeyed)," is in direct opposition to the Word of God, which commands that a woman's beauty be "not merely external." (See chapter 18, page 14 for a discussion on beauty.)

26. See Ed Welch, "Is Biblical Counseling Legalistic?" in *The Journal of Pastoral Practice,* XI:1, Fall 1992, pp. 4–21, for a discussion on the way people construct their own legalistic systems.

27. You can also use Psalm 103:3,12-13; Isaiah 30:15; Joel 2:12-13; Hebrews 10:17; 1 John 1:8-9.

28. *See* Philippians 2:13.

29. *See* chapter 2, "The Methods of Biblical Counseling."

Chapter 17—Counseling Women Involved in Sexual Sin

1. Millard J. Erickson, *The Concise Dictionary of Christian Theology* (Grand Rapids: Baker Book House, 1986), p. 59.

2. Elisabeth Elliot, *Discipline: The Glad Surrender* (Old Tappan, NJ: Fleming H. Revell Co., 1982), p. 54.

3. *See* John H. Armstrong, *Can Fallen Pastors Be Restored? The Church's Response to Sexual Misconduct* (Chicago: Moody Press, 1995).

4. If physical abuse or severe emotional abuse is occurring, a woman needs to take action to at least temporarily remove herself from the situation. *See* Chapters 8 ("Counseling Women in Problem Christian Marriages") and 9 ("Counseling Women Married to Unbelievers") for further guidance.

5. *See also* James 1 and 2 Peter 1.

6. *See* Lori Rentzel, *Emotional Dependency* (Downer's Grove, IL: InterVarsity Press, 1990) for an excellent description of this problem. Be aware, however, that this booklet contains unbiblical teaching about self-esteem. Also, the books recommended as resources come mostly from a psychological point of view, not a biblical one.

7. *See* Ezekiel 14:1-11.

8. *See* Titus 3:5-7.

9. To understand this better, see 2 Corinthians 3:18; Philippians 1:6; 1 Thessalonians 5:23; and 2 Peter 1:5-11.

10. *See* Isaiah 44:22 and Jeremiah 3:11,22.

11. *See* Mark S. Dorn, "Accountability: Checklist or Relationship?" *Discipleship Journal,* July/ August 1996, p. 80.

Chapter 18—Counseling Women in the Afternoon of Life

1. See chapter 20 for a discussion of this term.

2. There are many more than 10 percent of Americans who claim to be Christians, but as George Gallup found, "most actually know little or nothing of Christian beliefs, and act no differently than non-Christians." (*Signs of the Times,* 1991, p. 6).

3. Gail Sheehy, *New Passages: Mapping Your Life Across Time* (New York: Ballantine Books, 1995).

4. Gail Sheehy, *New Passages,* p. 107.

5. U.S. Census Bureau, "Fertility Indicators for Women 15 to 44 Years Old, by Age and Hispanic Origin," June 1994. Among non-Hispanic women aged 40 to 44, 17.9 percent are childless.

6. In 1994 there were 45 million unmarried women of all ages and races. Of these, 24 million have never married, 11 million are widowed, and 10 million are divorced.

7. U.S. Census Bureau, "Household Type and Presence and Age of Children," 1990.

8. Gail Sheehy, *New Passages,* p. 103.

9. Gail Sheehy, *New Passages,* p. 103.

10. Gail Sheehy, *New Passages,* p. 111.

11. Gail Sheehy, *New Passages,* p. 209.

12. See chapter 16, "Counseling Women for Overeating and Bulimia."

13. Cliff Schimmels, *And Then There Were Two: Empty Nesting After Your Kids Fly the Coop* (Wheaton, IL: Harold Shaw Publishers, 1989), p. *ix.* Used with permission.

14. There are also strains on men in marriages at this time of life. Of course, men experience certain physiological changes and notice, like their wives, they aren't young any longer. In addition, many men are facing the "down-sizing" crunch. After having devoted more than 30 years to education and building a career, many find themselves

in an unemployment line for the first time. Believing men and women must choose to define their lives in terms of the Word rather than the world.

15. William L. Coleman, *From Full House to Empty Nest: Learning to Enjoy Life Again Now That Your Children Are Grown* (Grand Rapids: Discovery House Publishers, 1994), p. 132.

16. Gail Sheehy, *New Passages,* p. 129.

17. Administration on Aging, "A Profile of Older Americans," 1995.

18. A "Family Caregiver Alliance Fact Sheet" on Alzheimer's says,

> Alzheimer's disease (AD) is an incurable neurological disease in which changes in the nerve cells of the brain result in the death of a large number of cells. This destruction of brain cells eventually leads to serious mental deterioration, dementia, and death. According to the U.S. Congress Office of Technology Assessment, there are an estimated 4 million to 6.8 million persons nationwide with dementia. Up to 500,000 Alzheimer's patients may reside in California. AD most commonly strikes individuals who are over 65. . . . About 11 percent of all Americans over 65 and 25-50 percent of those over 85 are believed to have the disease. . . . Alzheimer's patients fill more than half the beds in skilled nursing homes. The mid-range medical and social service costs for one Alzheimer's patient are estimated to be more than $47,500 over the course of the disease . . . the average annual direct and indirect costs for all Alzheimer's patients in the U.S. [updated in 1994] were a striking $82.7 billion.

Since large majorities of our congregations will deal with this problem either with a parent or spouse in the foreseeable future, it would serve the church to prepare now with support groups and outreach to caregiving families.

19. Statistics quoted from the Administration on Aging, "A Profile of Older Americans," 1995. The figures for the year 2020 are 53.3 million and for 2030 an astonishing 70.2 million! People in this age group will represent 13 percent of the population in 2000 and 20 percent by 2030!

20. For a fuller treatment of this topic and Titus 2:3-5, see chapter 4, "Why Women Should Counsel Women."

21. Ronald F. Youngblood, ed., *Nelson's New Illustrated Bible Dictionary* (Nashville, TN: Thomas Nelson Publishers, 1995), p. 1316.

22. God restores the years the locust ate (*see* Joel 2:25-26).

23. A.W. Tozer, *The Root of the Righteous* (Camp Hill, PA: Christian Publications, 1955), p. 137.

24. *See* Ezekiel 16 for a description of the correlation between idolatry and trust in one's beauty (especially verse 15).

25. This is the principle demonstrated in Matthew 6, especially verse 33. If you seek after the Lord and His kingship in your life, you will find God will provide everything you need.

26. W.E. Vine, *A Comprehensive Dictionary of the Original Greek Words and their Precise Meanings for English Readers* (McLean, VA: MacDonald Publishing Company), p. 737.

27. Quoted in A.W. Tozer, *Root of the Righteous,* p. 64.

28. *See* chapter 16, "Counseling Women for Overeating and Bulimia," for a biblical perspective on proper eating habits and exercise.

29. Gail Sheehy, *New Passages,* p. 49.

30. Investigate how biblical love functions by reviewing 1 Corinthians 13. Ask yourself: Do I treat my husband and children with patience and kindness? Am I jealous of them? The biblical perspective of love is a far cry from the lust and romantic sappiness portrayed in our culture.

31. *See* chapter 3, "The Essential Foundation," for a fuller treatment of this topic.

32. *See* chapter 5, "Single Teen Moms."

33. Anne Marie Drew, *Empty Nest, Full Life* (Nashville, TN: Dimensions for Living, 1995), p. 46.

34. A.W. Tozer, *Root of the Righteous,* p. 125.

35. If you put together Genesis 2:18, Genesis 2:24, Proverbs 2:17, and Malachi 2:14, you will see marriage is a covenant in which both spouses seek to provide companionship and fellowship to one another for life.

36. For examples, see Luke 4:26; 7:12; 18:3-5; and 21:2-3.

37. *See* Acts 6:1.

38. W.E. Vine, *Comprehensive Dictionary of Greek,* p. 571.

39. *See* chapter 19 for an in-depth discussion of these topics.

Chapter 19—Counseling Women Facing Dying and Death

1. Louis Berkhof, *Systematic Theology* (Grand Rapids: Eerdmans, 1939), p. 671.

2. Martyn Lloyd-Jones, *Why Does God Allow Suffering?* (Wheaton, IL: Crossway Books, 1994), p. 111.

3. Joseph Bayly, *The Last Thing We Talk About* (Elgin, IL: David C. Cook Publishing, 1969), pp. 55–56.

4. Louis Berkhof, *Systematic Theology,* p. 670.

5. Matthew 27; Mark 15; Luke 23; and John 19.

6. John Andersen, as quoted in Ken Camp, "Church Has Key Role to Play at Life's End," Baptist Press, February 21, 1997.

7. Elisabeth Kubler-Ross, *On Death and Dying* (New York: The Macmillan Company, 1969).

8. Elisabeth Elliot, *Facing the Death of Someone You Love* (Wheaton, IL: Good News Publishers, 1982), pp. 10-11.

9. Peter Kreeft, *Love Is Stronger than Death* (San Francisco: Ignatius Press, 1979), p. xi.

10. *See* David W. Hall, "Providence in the End of Life Ethics vs. The Pharisaic Fallacy," *Journal of Biblical Ethics in Medicine,* vol. 5, no. 1, Winter 1991.

11. Louis Berkhof defines providence as, "that continued exercise of the divine energy whereby the Creator preserves all His creatures, is operative in all that comes to pass in the world, and directs all things to their appointed end." Louis Berkhof, *Systematic Theology,* p. 166.

12. Philippe Aries, "The Reversal of Death: Changes in Attitudes Towards Death in Western Societies," in *Death in America,* ed. Philippe Aries, *et. al* (Philadelphia: University of Pennsylvania, 1975), p. 140. Quoted from Bryce J. Christensen, "Critically Ill: The Family and Health Care," *Journal of Biblical Ethics in Medicine,* vol. 6, no. 3, Summer 1992, p. 63.

13. Barbara Deane, *Caring for Your Aging Parents* (Colorado Springs: NavPress, 1989). This book gives names and addresses of agencies that can be very helpful in planning and caring for parents. Deane includes a list of items to keep in the personal record file from the Northern California Cancer Program.

14. Lawrence J. Gitman and Michael D. Joehnk, *Personal Financial Planning*, 7th ed. (Fort Worth, TX: The Dryden Press, Harcourt Brace College Publishers, 1996), p. 612.

15. Barbara Deane, *Caring for Your Aging Parents*, p. 124.

16. "Basic Statistics About Home Care 1996," National Association for Home Care, p. 9, internet article.

17. C. Ben Mitchell and Michael K. Whitehead, *A Time to Live, A Time to Die: Advance Directives and Living Wills* (Nashville, TN: The Christian Life Commission of the Southern Baptist Convention), p. 1.

18. C. Ben Mitchell and Michael K. Whitehead, *A Time to Live*, p. 2.

19. C. Ben Mitchell and Michael K. Whitehead, *A Time to Live*, p. 2.

20. James F. Kurfees, M.D., M.Th., "On Living Wills," *Journal of Biblical Ethics in Medicine*, vol. 2, no. 1, January 1988, p. 7.

21. C. Ben Mitchell and Michael K. Whitehead, *A Time to Live*, p. 8.

22. James F. Kurfees, M.D., M.Th., *On Living Wills*, p. 5.

23. C. Ben Mitchell and Michael K. Whitehead, *A Time to Live*, p. 11.

24. C. Ben Mitchell and Michael K. Whitehead, *A Time to Live*, p. 15.

25. These questions cannot be answered in this chapter. The decisions that appertain to the presence or absence of life are the most problematic. In the past, heart or lung failure would usually bring a pronouncement of death. Due to advances in technology, however, both heart and lung function can be sustained or prolonged artificially. A third category, "Brain death," has recently been added to the criteria when discerning whether death has occurred or not.

26. "Quality of life" arguments are nothing new. Indeed, the Nazis employed this line of reasoning to give them license to exterminate mentally retarded, deformed, or mentally ill Germans years before the Jewish Holocaust began. Allowing the medical community or the state to decide what "life is not worthy of life" is extremely dangerous. The questions that must always be asked in this discussion are, "Who decides whose life is not worthy?" "Who decides what life is of sufficient quality to continue?" "What is quality?" Christians must resist the euthanasia movement while there is still time.

27. "No one needs a right to die because death is inevitable. What is needed is maximum discernment of the time when all help for recovery is lost with the cautious attitude that allows for the particulars of each case. . . . When this phrase is applied to the terminally ill, it is easily broadened to justify anyone who desires to commit suicide. Facetiously asked, why shouldn't any depressed or anxious person be given the 'right to die' and escape their distress?" Franklin E. Payne, Jr., M.D., *Biblical/Medical Ethics: The Christian and the Practice of Medicine* (Milford, MI: Mott Media, Inc., 1985), p. 202.

28. "This phrase entails significant problems which should not be overlooked. On a Christian basis, death is never dignified. Death is inseparably related to sin. Death is a symbol and result of rebellion against God; death is the 'last enemy' (1 Corinthians 15:26). . . . An earlier use of this phrase appeared in a book published in Germany in

1920 as a motto for a movement to legalize the killing of those who had 'the right to the complete relief of an unbearable life.'" Franklin E. Payne, Jr., p. 201.

29. The Christian Life Commission of the Southern Baptist Convention, the *Journal of Biblical Ethics in Medicine,* and the following books may be helpful in making these decisions: Richard D. Land and Louis A. Moore, *Life at Risk: The Crises in Medical Ethics* (Nashville, TN: Broadman and Holman Publishers, 1995); Franklin E. Payne, Jr., M.D., *Making Biblical Decisions* (Escondido, CA: Hosanna House, 1989); *Biblical Healing for Modern Medicine* (Augusta, GA: Covenant Books, 1993); *Biblical/Medical Ethics* (Milford, MI: Mott Media, 1985).

30. Kathleen M. Foley, M.D., Memorial Sloan-Kettering Cancer Center, "Competent Care for the Dying Instead of Physician-Assisted Suicide," *The New England Journal of Medicine,* January 2, 1997, vol. 336, no. 1, pp. 55-58.

31. Christine Wiebe, "What Skills Do You Need to Care for Dying Patients?" American College of Physicians, *ACP Observer,* October 1996, p. 2, internet article.

32. Donald Townsend, M.D., "Physical and Spiritual Care of the Terminally Ill," *Journal of Biblical Ethics in Medicine,* vol. II, no. 1, January 1988, p. 19.

33. Leo Tolstoy, *The Death of Ivan Ilyich, The Cossacks, Happy Ever After* (New York: Penguin Books), p. 142.

34. Jay E. Adams, "Questions Concerning Pastoral Visitation of the Dying," *Westminster Theological Journal,* vol. XXXVI, no. 2, Winter 1974, p. 210.

35. National Association for Home Care, "Basic Statistics About Home Care 1996," internet article.

36. "Basic Statistics About Home Care 1996."

37. Barbara Deane, *Caring for Your Aging Parents,* p. 209.

38. *Frequently Asked Questions,* California State Hospice Association, internet article.

39. *Hospice Facts and Statistics 1996,* The Hospice Association of America, internet article.

40. *Hospice Facts and Statistics 1996.*

41. Cicely M.S. Saunders, "The Care of the Dying Patient and His Family," in *Ethics for Medicine,* Stanley Reiser, Arthur Dyck, William Curran, eds. (The Massachusetts Institute of Technology, 1977), p. 511.

42. Peter Kreeft, *Love Is Stronger,* pp. 24-25.

43. *A Word About Hospice and the California State Hospice Association,* internet article.

44. Barbara Deane, *Caring for Your Aging Parents,* p. 237.

45. Christine Wiebe, *What Skills Do You Need?,* p. 4.

46. *A Word About Hospice and the California State Hospice Association,* internet article.

47. Cicely M.S. Saunders, *Care of the Dying,* p. 513.

48. These approximate costs reflect Southern California. The actual cost in your area may be very different.

49. *When a Loved One Dies: The Next Steps,* The American Institute for Cancer Research, p. 30.

50. John MacArthur, Jr., *The Glory of Heaven: The Truth About Heaven, Angels and Eternal Life* (Wheaton, IL: Crossway Books, 1996), p. 71.

51. D.A. Carson, *How Long, O Lord?: Reflections on Suffering and Evil* (Grand Rapids: Baker Books, 1990), p. 112.

Chapter 20—Medical Questions Women Ask

1. Leon Speroff, Robert H. Glass, and Nathan G. Kase, *Clinical Gynecologic Endocrinology and Infertility,* 5th ed. (Baltimore, MD: Williams and Wilkins, 1994), p. 841.

2. Steven G. Gabbe, MD, Jennifer R. Niebyl, M.D., and Joe Leigh Simpson, eds., *Obstetrics: Normal and Problem Pregnancies,* 2nd ed. (New York: Churchill Livingstone, 1991), p. 378.

INDEX

About the Editors and Contributors

Carol Almy, M.D. has a private practice in dermatology and is on the faculty of Northwestern University Medical School in Chicago, Illinois. She and her husband, Gary, are adoptive parents.

Kaleen M. Chase holds an M.A.R. in Clinical Counseling from Westminster Theological Seminary (Philadelphia) and a B.A. in Elementary Education from Arizona State University. She is an educator in the state of Arizona, and has been since 1985.

Carol Cornish is a graduate of Biblical Theological Seminary with an M.A. in Biblical Studies with counseling concentration. She is a staff counselor and Bible study teacher at her church and is a frequent speaker at women's seminars and retreats sponsored by other churches. Carol is married and the mother of a grown son.

Elyse Fitzpatrick has been counseling women since 1989 and is presently a counselor at her home church in the north county area of San Diego. She holds a certificate in biblical counseling from The Institute for Biblical Counseling & Discipleship and an M.A. in Biblical Counseling from Trinity Theological Seminary, and is a member of the National Association of Nouthetic Counselors. A frequent speaker at women's conferences, she has been married for 23 years and has three adult children.

Shirley V. Galucki, M.D. is on the medical staff of Lahey Hitchcock Clinic (Manchester, New Hampshire) in the Department of Obstetrics and Gynecology. She has also served as a clinical instructor in Obstetrics and Gynecology at Temple University in Philadelphia. Shirley's husband, Lee, is a pastor, and they have three children.

Shari Hofstetter holds an M.A.R. from Westminster Theological Seminary and currently works as both a hospital and hospice chaplain. In addition to writing, she is an occasional lecturer and conference speaker. She and her husband, a pastor and professor, currently live in Philadelphia. Their family is soon to be increased by an adoptive infant daughter from China.

Penny Orr is a graduate of Biblical Theological Seminary with an M.A. in Biblical Studies with counseling concentration. She is on the women's ministry team at her church and is a staff counselor there. She speaks frequently at seminars and women's Bible studies.

Martha Peace is a registered nurse and a biblical counselor certified by the National Association of Nouthetic Counselors. She previously worked at the Atlanta Biblical Counseling Center and as an instructor at Carver Bible College. She is the author of *The Excellent Wife* and *Becoming a Titus 2 Woman*. She and her husband, Sanford, have been married for 30 years, and have two children and four grandchildren.

Eileen Scipione founded a pro-life center in San Diego, where she counseled post-abortion women and women in crisis pregnancy centers for 10 years. She holds a B.S. degree in Elementary and Special Education, and has home-schooled her five children. She is the wife of Dr. George Scipione, director of the Institute for Biblical Counseling & Discipleship in San Diego.

Lorrie Skowronski is a full-time counselor with the Christian Counseling Center in Dublin, Pennsylvania. She has an M.A. degree in Biblical Studies with counseling concentration from Biblical Theological Seminary. She also holds a certificate in Biblical Counseling from the Christian Counseling and Educational Foundation. Lorrie speaks at various women's conferences and oversees an internship program at the counseling center where she works. Because of her great interest in missions, Lorrie does missionary candidate assessment and missionary counseling for a local missions agency.

Mary Somerville has been a pastor's wife for over 26 years and in that role has discipled many women. She holds an M.A. degree in Pastoral Counseling from Trinity Evangelical Divinity School. For four years she counseled teen moms on her own. This eventually led her to begin a program that she has directed in Visilia, California, for the past five years. She wrote *Mentor Moms: A Handbook for Mentoring Teen Mothers* to help others begin similar evangelistic and discipleship programs in their churches and communities. Mary is the mother of two college-age children.

Diane Tyson is the director and one of the founders of Anchor Ministries, a counseling ministry for women and their families. She received her B.S. degree in Bible from Lancaster Bible College, and has an M.A. in Biblical Studies with counseling concentration from Biblical Theological Seminary. Diane has been active in local church ministries for over 35 years, has over ten years of counseling experience, and is a commissioned missionary of Heritage Bible Church. She has two sons and three grandchildren.